palgrave macmillan law masters

constitutional and administrative law

palgrave macmillan law masters

Series editor: Marise Cremona

Business Law Stephen Judge
Company Law Janet Dine and Marios Koutsias
Constitutional and Administrative Law John Alder
Contract Law Ewan McKendrick
Criminal Law Jonathan Herring
Economic and Social Law of the European Union Jo Shaw, Jo Hunt and Chloe Wallace
Employment Law Deborah J. Lockton
Evidence Raymond Emson
Family Law Kate Standley
Intellectual Property Law Tina Hart, Linda Fazzani and Simon Clark
Land Law Joe Cursley and Mark Davys
Landlord and Tenant Law Margaret Wilkie, Peter Luxton, Jill Morgan and Godfrey Cole
Legal Method Ian McLeod
Legal Theory Ian McLeod
Medical Law Jo Samanta and Ash Samanta
Sports Law Mark James
Torts Alastair Mullis and Ken Oliphant
Trusts Law Charlie Webb and Tim Akkouh

If you would like to comment on this book, or on the series generally, please write to lawfeedback@palgrave.com.

palgrave macmillan law masters

constitutional and administrative law

john alder

Emeritus Professor of Law, Newcastle University

Visiting Professor of Law, Bangor University

Eighth edition

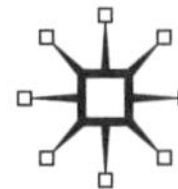

This edition first published 2011 by PALGRAVE MACMILLAN

Palgrave Macmillan in the UK is an imprint of Macmillan Publishers Limited, registered in England, company number 785998, of Houndmills, Basingstoke, Hampshire RG21 6XS.

Palgrave Macmillan in the US is a division of St Martin's Press LLC, 175 Fifth Avenue, New York, NY 10010.

Palgrave Macmillan is the global academic imprint of the above companies and has companies and representatives throughout the world.

Palgrave® and Macmillan® are registered trademarks in the United States, the United Kingdom, Europe and other countries.

ISBN: 978–0–230–28570–5 paperback

This book is printed on paper suitable for recycling and made from fully managed and sustained forest sources. Logging, pulping and manufacturing processes are expected to conform to the environmental regulations of the country of origin.

A catalogue record for this book is available from the British Library.

10 9 8 7 6 5 4 3 2 1
20 19 18 17 16 15 14 13 12 11

Printed and bound in the UK by Thomson Litho, East Kilbride.

Contents

Preface xiii
Table of cases xv
Table of legislation xxxi
Acknowledgements xxxv
References xxxvi

Part I The framework of the constitution 1

1 Introduction: constitutional themes and structures 3
1.1 What is a constitution? 3
1.2 Written and unwritten constitutions 7
1.3 The legal and the political constitution 13
1.4 Types of constitution 15
1.5 Public and private law 18
1.6 Resolving disagreement: uncertainty and incommensurability 20
Summary 22
Exercises 23
Further reading 23

2 Underlying political values: liberalism and republicanism 24
2.1 Introduction 24
2.2 Liberalism 24
2.3 Varieties of liberalism in constitutional thought 26
2.4 Freedom 35
2.5 Republicanism 38
2.6 Equality 40
2.7 Democracy 41
Summary 46
Exercises 47
Further reading 48

3 The sources of the constitution 49
3.1 Introduction 49
3.2 Statute law 50
3.3 The common law 51
3.4 Constitutional conventions 54
3.5 Constitutional silence and abeyance 66
Summary 67
Exercises 67
Further reading 68

4 Historical outline 69
4.1 Introduction 69

4.2 Saxon period 70
4.3 The medieval period: the beginning of parliamentary government 70
4.4 The Tudor period: the creation of the state 72
4.5 The seventeenth-century revolution 73
4.6 The eighteenth and early nineteenth centuries: the parliamentary system 75
4.7 The nineteenth and twentieth centuries: democracy and the central state 77
Summary 80
Exercises 80
Further reading 80

5 An overview of the main institutions of the UK constitution 81
5.1 Introduction: the dignified and efficient constitution: deceiving the people? 81
5.2 Legislature and executive 82
5.3 Non-departmental public bodies: quangos 92
5.4 The judicial branch 96
5.5 Local government 104
5.6 The police and the prosecution system 105
5.7 The Privy Council 107
5.8 The Church of England 108
5.9 Bodies monitoring government standards of behaviour 109
Summary 111
Exercises 112
Further reading 113

Part II Fundamental principles 115

6 The rule of law 117
6.1 Introduction 117
6.2 Historical background 120
6.3 Different versions of the rule of law 122
6.4 The core rule of law 123
6.5 The 'amplified' rule of law 129
6.6 The extended (liberal) rule of law: 'the principle of legality' 131
6.7 The international rule of law 133
Summary 134
Exercises 135
Further reading 135

7 The separation of powers 137
7.1 Introduction: Montesquieu's doctrine of the separation of powers 137
7.2 The mixed constitution 139
7.3 Other kinds of separation of powers 140
7.4 Judicial independence 140
7.5 The separation of powers in the UK 142
7.6 Separation of functions 143

7.7 Separation of personnel 147
7.8 Checks and balances 150
Summary 157
Exercises 157
Further reading 158

8 Parliamentary supremacy 160
8.1 Introduction 160
8.2 The meaning of 'Act of Parliament' 162
8.3 The three facets of parliamentary supremacy 163
8.4 Challenging parliamentary supremacy 165
8.5 Parliamentary supremacy and the rule of law 174
Summary 176
Exercises 177
Further reading 177

Part III International aspects of the constitution 179

9 The state and the outside world – *sic transit gloria mundi* 181
9.1 Introduction: the idea of the state 181
9.2 The UK as a state 182
9.3 Citizenship 184
9.4 Federalism 188
9.5 The Channel Islands and the Isle of Man 189
9.6 British overseas territories 190
9.7 International affairs 194
Summary 204
Exercises 205
Further reading 206

10 The European Union 207
10.1 Introduction: the nature of the European Union 207
10.2 Institutions 212
10.3 Community law and national law 217
10.4 Democracy and the European Union 221
10.5 Federalism and the European Union: subsidiarity 224
Summary 225
Exercises 226
Further reading 227

Part IV Government institutions 229

11 Parliament: constitutional position 231
11.1 Introduction 231
11.2 The House of Lords 233
11.3 The meeting of Parliament 234
11.4 The functions of the House of Commons 236
11.5 The functions of the House of Lords 237
11.6 Parliamentary privilege 239

11.7 Standards in the Commons 247
11.8 The courts and Parliament 251
Summary 253
Exercises 253
Further reading 255

12 The composition of Parliament and parliamentary elections 256
12.1 Introduction 256
12.2 The House of Lords 256
12.3 Reform of the House of Lords 259
12.4 Membership of the House of Commons 262
12.5 The electoral system 263
12.6 Eligibility to vote 267
12.7 The voting system 269
12.8 The constituencies 272
12.9 Voting procedures 273
12.10 Election campaigns 274
Summary 278
Exercises 279
Further reading 280

13 Parliamentary procedure 281
13.1 Introduction 281
13.2 The Speaker of the Commons 283
13.3 Legislative procedure 284
13.4 Financial procedure 287
13.5 Supervision of the executive 290
13.6 Redress of grievances 297
13.7 House of Lords procedure 298
Summary 299
Exercises 300
Further reading 300

14 The Crown 301
14.1 Introduction: the nature of the Crown 301
14.2 Succession to the monarchy 304
14.3 Financing the monarchy 305
14.4 The personal powers of the monarch 305
14.5 Crown immunities 307
14.6 The royal prerogative 309
Summary 317
Exercises 318
Further reading 318

15 Ministers and departments 319
15.1 Introduction 319
15.2 Appointment of the Prime Minister 319
15.3 The powers of the Prime Minister 322
15.4 The Cabinet 323
15.5 Ministers 325
15.6 Government departments 326

15.7 Ministerial responsibility 330
15.8 The civil service 337
Summary 343
Exercises 344
Further reading 345

16 Devolution 346
16.1 The general nature of devolution in the UK 346
16.2 Scotland 348
16.3 Northern Ireland 356
16.4 Wales 359
16.5 England 362
Summary 363
Exercises 363
Further reading 365

Part V Administrative law 367

17 The grounds of judicial review, I: illegality and *ultra vires* 369
17.1 Introduction: the constitutional basis of judicial review 369
17.2 Appeal and review 372
17.3 Nullity: void and voidable decisions 373
17.4 Classification of the grounds of review 374
17.5 Illegality: 'narrow' *ultra vires* 375
17.6 Errors of law and fact 377
17.7 'Wide' *ultra vires*: improper purposes and relevance 382
17.8 Fettering discretion 387
17.9 Legitimate expectations 388
Summary 393
Exercises 394
Further reading 395

18 The grounds of judicial review, II: beyond *ultra vires* 397
18.1 Irrationality/unreasonableness 397
18.2 Procedural impropriety: statutory procedural requirements 401
18.3 Procedural impropriety: the right to a fair hearing 403
18.4 Procedural impropriety: bias 406
18.5 Procedural impropriety: reasons for decisions 410
18.6 The European Convention on Human Rights 411
Summary 412
Exercises 413
Further reading 414

19 Judicial review remedies 415
19.1 Introduction 415
19.2 The range of remedies 416
19.3 The judicial review procedure: public interest safeguards 418
19.4 Standing (*locus standi*) 421
19.5 Choice of procedure: public and private law 423
19.6 Exclusivity 425

19.7 The exclusion and limitation of judicial review 427
Summary 433
Exercises 433
Further reading 434

Part VI Fundamental rights 437

20 Human rights and civil liberties 439
20.1 Introduction: the nature of human rights 439
20.2 The common law 442
20.3 The European Convention on Human Rights 443
20.4 The main Convention rights 444
Summary 457
Exercises 457
Further reading 458

21 The Human Rights Act 1998 459
21.1 The scope of the Act 459
21.2 Extraterritorial application 461
21.3 The Human Rights Act and Parliament 462
21.4 The executive and judiciary: remedies 466
21.5 Overriding protected rights 471
Summary 478
Exercises 479
Further reading 480

22 Freedoms of expression and assembly 482
22.1 Introduction: justifications for freedom of expression 482
22.2 The legal status of freedom of expression 484
22.3 Press freedom and censorship 486
22.4 The free flow of information 490
22.5 Press freedom and reputation: defamation 491
22.6 Press freedom and privacy 496
22.7 'Hate Speech' 499
22.8 Demonstrations and meetings 503
Summary 511
Exercises 512
Further reading 513

23 Exceptional powers: security, state secrecy and emergencies 514
23.1 Introduction: security and the courts 514
23.2 State secrecy: access to information 517
23.3 Disclosure of government information 522
23.4 The security and intelligence services 530
23.5 Surveillance 531
23.6 Emergency powers 535
23.7 Anti-terrorism measures 536
Summary 545
Exercises 546
Further reading 548

Postscript 549

24 Constitutional reform 551
24.1 Introduction 551
24.2 The nature of constitutional reform 553
24.3 Future directions 556
Summary 557
Exercises 558
Further reading 558

Index 559

Preface

As in previous editions my aims are firstly to explain the main principles of United Kingdom constitutional law in the context of the political and legal values that influence their development and secondly to draw attention to the main controversies. I hope that the book will provide a self-contained text for those new to the subject and at least a starting point for more advanced students.

In this edition in order to reflect the increasing importance of external pressures on the constitution I have introduced a new chapter on international affairs. I have also added a final chapter on constitutional reform. Thanks to the generosity of the publishers I have been able to provide more detailed treatment of some key areas, including judicial review, human rights and the range of semi-accountable public bodies. I have expanded the discussion of cases and have tried to signpost the text in various ways, including clearer headings, boxes and cross-referencing to make it easier to follow particular issues through the book.

I have updated the book to keep abreast of the shifts in the importance of different aspects of the constitution, most notably in this edition parliamentary privilege and judicial review for errors of law and fact, both issues having recently revived after a dormant period. Some important constitutional reforms are currently in progress, notably the possibility of changes in the voting system and restrictions on the power of the Prime Minster to dissolve Parliament. In keeping with the spasmodic and pragmatic nature of constitutional change in the UK other reforms since the previous edition have been relatively trivial. Probably the most notable is the long-awaited enactment, albeit in vague terms, of the existing general principles governing the civil service. It remains unclear what a civil servant is. Further reform of the House of Lords is promised but as yet no details are available. The Supreme Court has now been functioning for over a year. It is more accessible than its predecessor, the House of Lords, but there is no reason to expect any dramatic changes in the nature of its constitutional jurisprudence. It seems however that to a greater extent than has traditionally been the case, the courts are talking in terms of grand general principles, perhaps derived from Oxbridge high tables, related to the liberal version of the rule of law.

There are three themes underlying the book. First there is that of executive domination of Parliament, lubricated by patronage and insider networks and lacking strong accountability mechanisms. Although to some extent mitigated by recent reforms, this remains the outstanding political feature of the constitution. The second, more legally oriented theme is the tension between parliamentary supremacy and the rule of law as applied by the courts. This centres on judicial review and the Human Rights Act 1998. A few judges and several commentators have expressed views challenging the traditional doctrine of parliamentary supremacy but the outcome of the cases still conforms to tradition. The adjustments required to accommodate for example the pressures of devolution and international relations have taken place in the political arena rather than the courts.

The third theme is the importance in a free society of keeping alive different points of view and not attempting to impose any particular orthodoxy on the people. This requires a stronger separation of powers than we have today. However it shows itself in the accommodations between courts, Parliament and the executive that are required by the Human Rights Act 1998 and in the preservation of parliamentary supremacy so that anything can be changed.

Part I concerns general principles. These include basic constitutional concepts and issues (Chapter 1), a broad account of the moral and political ideals that have influenced the constitution (Chapter 2) and the sources of the constitution (Chapter 3). Chapters 4 offers a brief overview of the history the constitution, emphasising significant periods. Chapter 5 provides an overview the main institutions of government, and the most important aspects are expanded in later chapters. Pervasive legal values and doctrines are considered in Chapters 6, 7 and 8.

Part II concerns international relationships. Chapter 9 explains the various ways in which international requirements are filtered into our domestic constitution, while Chapter 10 discusses the most important international influence, namely the EU, which is firmly anchored into domestic law.

Part III is concerned with the powers of the central government institutions and the relationship between them. Parts IV and V deal with the rights of the individual against government: in Part IV judicial review of government action, the core of administrative law, and in Part V human rights both generally and in relation to topics that particularly relate to the political freedoms that underpin democracy and the rule of law. These include freedom of expression and assembly, secrecy and national security.

I am grateful particularly to Rob Gibson at Palgrave Macmillan for his excellent advice and support. I am also grateful for the comments of anonymous reviewers of the previous editions. I have updated this edition on the basis of material available to me on 31 January 2010. Further updates can be found on the companion website: www.palgrave.com/law/alder8e

John Alder
March 2011

Table of cases

A v B (Investigatory Powers Tribunal Jurisdiction) [2010] 1 All ER 1167, 432, 460, 467, 534
A v Head Teacher and Governors of Lord Grey School [2004] 4 All ER 587, 450, 468
A v Secretary of State for the Home Dept [2005] 2 AC 68, 41, 181, 185, 428, 459, 474, 477, 516, 517, 541
A v Secretary of State for the Home Dept (No 2) [2005] 3 WLR 1249, 447
A v UK (2009) ECHR 301, 530
A v UK (2003) 36 EHRR 917, 239
A v UK (1998) 27 EHRR 611, 448, 471
Adan v Newham LBC [2002] 1 All ER 931, 380
Adegbenro v Akintola [1963] AC 614, 307
A-G v Blake [1998] 1 All ER 833, 525
A-G v BBC [1981] AC 303, 99
A-G v Crayford Urban DC [1962] Ch 575, 377
A-G v De Keyser's Royal Hotel Ltd [1920] AC 508, 311, 314, 315, 316, 535
A-G v English [1983] 1 AC 116, 486
A-G v Fulham Corporation [1921] 1 Ch 440, 78, 375
A-G v Guardian Newspapers Ltd [1987] 1 WLR 1248, 525
A-G v Guardian Newspapers Ltd (No 2) [1998] 3 All ER 535, 443, 496
A-G v Jonathan Cape Ltd [1975] 3 All ER 489, 61, 525
A-G v Observer Ltd [1988] 1 All ER 385, 488
A-G v Punch [2003] 1 All ER 296, 486, 489
A-G v Times Newspapers Ltd [1991] 2 All ER 398, 488
A-G v Wilts United Dairies (1921) 37 TLR 884, 310
A-G for Canada v Cain [1906] AC 542, 311
A-G for Hong Kong v Ng Yuen Shiu [1983] 2 AC 629, 391, 404
A-G for New South Wales v Trethowan [1932] AC 526, 169
A-G for Northern Ireland's Reference (No 1 of 1975) [1977] AC 105, 535
A-G of Trinidad and Tobago v Lennox Phillips [1995] 1 All ER 93, 429
Agricultural, Horticultural and Forestry Training Board v Aylesbury Mushrooms [1972] 1 WLR 190, 374
A-G's Reference (No 4 of 2002) [2005] 1 AC 264, 539
A-G's Reference (No 3 of 2003) [2004] EWCA 868, 249
A-G's Reference (No 3 of 2009) [2010] 1 All ER 235, 130, 249, 498
Ahmed v Governing Body of Oxford University [2003] 1 All ER 917, 406
AIG Capital Parties Inc v Republic of Kazakhstan [2006] 1 All ER 284, 198
Air Canada v Secretary of State for Trade (No 2) [1983] 2 AC 394, 527
Aksoy v Turkey (1996) 23 EHRR 553, 517
Akumah v Hackney LBC [2005] 2 All ER 148, 376
Al Adsani v UK (2001) 34 EHRR 273, 198
Albert v Belgium (1983) 5 EHRR 533, 381
Albert v Lavin [1982] AC 546, 507
Ali v Birmingham Corporation [2010] 2 All ER 175, 381
Al Rawi v Security Service [2009] EWHC 2959, 529
AMEC Ltd v Whitefriars City Estates [2005] 1 All ER 723, 406, 408
Amman v Switzerland (2000) ECHR App no 27798/95, 532
Amphitrite v The King [1921] 3 KB 500, 308
Anderson v Gorrie [1895] 1 QB 668, 141
Anderson v UK (1997) 25 EHRR 172, 503
Anisminic Ltd v Foreign Compensation Commission [1969] 2 AC 147, 127, 174, 373, 376, 378–79, 431, 553
Anufrijeva v Southwark LBC [2004] 1 All ER 833, 417, 452
Appelby v UK [2003] NLJ 998, 487, 505
Arrowsmith v Jenkins [1963] 2 QB 561, 509
Arthur JS Hall v Simons [2000] 3 All ER 673, 142
Ashbridge Investments v Minister of Housing and Local Government [1965] 1 WLR 1320, 380
Ashby v Minister of Immigration [1981] NZLR 222, 385

Ashby v White (1703) 2 Ld Raym 938, 11, 252
Ashworth Hospital v MGN Ltd [2001] 1 All ER 991, 491
Associated Provincial Picture Houses Ltd v Wednesbury Corporation [1948] 1 KB 223, 397–98
Aston Cantlow and Wilmcote with Billesley Parochial Church Council v Wallbank [2003] 3 All ER 1213, 108, 455, 467, 469
Auckland Harbour Board v R [1924] AC 318, 288
Austin v Metropolitan Police Comr [2008 1 All ER 564, 445, 446, 508
Autronic AG v Switzerland (1990) 1 EHRR 485, 451, 488
AWG Group Ltd v Morrison [2006] 1 All ER 967, 407
Ayr Harbour Trustees v Oswald (1883) 8 App Case 623, 388

Bagg's Case (1615) 11 Co Rep 936, 371, 403
Barnard v National Dock Labour Board [1953] 2 QB 18, 402
Barrett v Enfield BC [1999] 3 All ER 193, 221
Bates Case (1606) 2 St Tr 371, 309
BBC v Johns (Inspector of Taxes) [1965] Ch 32, 310
BBC v Sugar (2010) 1 All ER 782, 519
BBC v Sugar [2007] 4 All ER 518, 379
Beatty v Gillbanks (1882) 9 QBD 308, 509, 510
Beckett v Midland Electricity plc [2001] 1 WLR 281, 156
Belgian Linguistics Case (1968) 1 EHRR 252, 456
Belize Alliance of Conservation NGOs v Dept of the Environment [2003] UKPC 63, 411, 419
Bellinger v Bellinger [2003] 2 All ER 593, 465
Benjamin v UK (2002) 13 BHRC 287, 146
Bentham v Netherlands (1986) 8 EHRR 1, 381, 411
Berkeley v Secretary of State for the Environment [2000] 3 All ER 897, 45, 218, 402
Bilston Corporation v Wolverhampton Corporation [1942] Ch 391, 241
Binyam Mohammed v Secretary of State for the Foreign and Commonwealth Office [2009] EWHC 152, 486
Blackburn v A-G [1971] 2 All ER 1380, 165, 171, 196
BM v Secretary of State for the Home Dept [2010] 1 All ER 847, 530
Board of Education v Rice [1911] AC 179, 403
Boddington v British Transport Police [1998] 2 WLR 639, 372, 373, 374, 426
Bonnard v Perryman [1891] 2 Ch 269, 420
Bowles v The Bank of England [1913] 1 Ch 57, 162, 243, 289
Bowman v Secular Society Ltd [1917] AC 406, 108, 501
Bowman v UK (1998) 26 EHRR 1, 44, 275, 483
Bradlaugh v Gossett (1884) 12 QBD 271, 241, 242
Brannigan and McBride v UK (1993) 17 EHRR 539, 516
Bribery Comr v Ranasinghe [1965] AC 172 133, 169, 190
Brind v Secretary of State for the Home Dept [1991] 1 AC 696, 197, 398, 400, 443
British Chiropractic Association v Singh [2010] EWCA Civ 350, 492
British Coal Corporation v R [1935] AC 500, 165
British Oxygen Co Ltd v Minister of Technology [1971] AC 610, 387
British Steel v Customs and Excise Comrs [1997] 2 All ER 366, 426
Brogan v UK (1989) 11 EHRR 117, 517, 540
Bromley LBC v Greater London Council [1983] 1 AC 768, 44, 375, 384, 388
Brown v Stott (Procurator Fiscal Dunfermline) [2001] 2 All ER 97, 119, 411, 449, 472, 473
Brunner v The European Union Treaty [1994] 1 CMLR 57, 224
Brutus v Cozens [1973] AC 854, 379, 510
Buchanan v Jennings [2005] 2 All ER 273, 243, 245, 246
Buckley v UK (1997) 23 EHRR 101, 475
Buckley v Valeo (1976) 424 US 1, 46, 274
Bugdaycay v Secretary of State for the Home Dept [1987], 380, 399
Bugg v DPP [1993] QB 473, 373
Bulmer Ltd v Bollinger SA [1974] 2 All ER 1226, 207
Burmah Oil Co Ltd v Lord Advocate [1965] AC 75, 120, 163, 311, 316
Burmah Oil Co Ltd v Bank of England [1980] AC 1090, 518, 527
Buron v Denman (1848) 2 Ex 167, 201
Bushell v Secretary of State for the Environment [1981] AC 75, 45, 103, 340, 404, 406
Bushell's Case (1670) 6 St Tr 999, 147

Cachia v Faluyi [2002] 1 All ER 192, 465
Calverley v Chief Constable of Merseyside Police [1989] 1 AC 1228, 418
Calvin v Carr [1980] AC 574, 405
Calvin's Case (1608) 7 Co Rep 1a, 302
Cambridge Water Company v English Counties Leather [1994] 2 AC 264, 53
Campbell v Hall (1774) 1 Cowp 204, 191
Campbell v MGN Ltd [2004] 2 All ER 995, 36, 452, 471, 475, 484, 485, 496, 497, 532
Campbell and Cozens v UK (1982) 4 EHRR 293, 501
Carltona Ltd v Comr for Works [1943] 2 All ER 560, 61, 89, 326, 340, 342, 402
Carl Zeiss Stiftung v Rayner & Keeler Ltd (No 2) [1967] 1 AC 853, 200, 202
Case of Proclamations (1611) 12 Co Rep 74, 54, 73, 191, 301, 309
Castells v Spain (1992) 14 EHRR 445, 483, 486, 490, 493, 502
Caswell v Dairy Produce Quota Tribunal for England and Wales [1990] 2 All ER 434, 420
Chahal v UK (1996) 23 EHRR 413, 202, 448, 456, 515, 541
Chandler v DPP [1964] AC 763, 182, 310, 314, 535
Chapman v Orion Publishing Group Ltd [2008] 1 All ER 750, 492, 496
Chapman v UK (2001) 33 EHRR 399, 451, 452
Charge to the Bristol Grand Jury (1832) 5 C & P, 535
Chatterton v Secretary of State for India in Council (1895) 2 QB 189, 492
Cheall v Association of Professional, Executive, Clerical and Computer Staff [1983] 1 All ER 1130, 405
Cheney v Conn (Inspector of Taxes) [1968] 1 All ER 779, 163
Chief Constable of North Wales Police v Evans[1982] 3 All ER 141, 420
China Navigation Co Ltd v A-G [1932] 2 KB 197, 187
Choudhury v UK [1991] App No 17439/90 12 HRLJ 172, 501
Christie v Leachinsky [1947] AC 573, 119
Church of Scientology of California v Johnson-Smith [1972] 1 QB 522, 244, 246
CILFIT Srl v Ministro della Sanità [1983] 1 CMLR 472, 217
Cinnamond v British Airports Authority [1980] 2 All ER 368, 405
Clark (Procurator Fiscal Kirkcaldy) v Kelly [2003] 1 All ER 1106, 147
Clark v University of Lincolnshire and Humberside [2000] 3 All ER 752, 426
Clarke v Bradlaugh [1881] 7 QBD 38, 241
CND v Prime Minister of the United Kingdom (2006) EWHC 2777, 182, 201, 428
Cocks v Thanet DC [1983] 2 AC 286, 426
Commission for Racial Equality v Dutton [1989] QB 783, 500
Commission v UK [1981] ECR 203, 210
Comrs of Crown Lands v Page [1960] 2 QB 274, 308
Coney v Choyce [1975] 1 All ER 979, 402, 420
Congreve v Home Office [1976] QB 629, 310, 376
Connor v Surrey CC [2010] 3 All ER 905, 417
Connors v UK (2004) 40 EHRR 189, 382, 453
Conway v Rimmer [1968] AC 910, 79, 526, 527
Cook v Alexander [1974] QB, 247
Cook v Sprigg [1899] AC 572, 201
Cooper v Hawkins [1904] 2 KB 164, 308
Cooper v Wandsworth Board of Works [1863] 14 CB (NS), 175, 371, 403
Copsey v WBB Devon Clays Ltd [2005] EWCA Civ 932, 38, 430, 454
Corporate Officer of the House of Commons v Information Comr [2009] 3 All ER 403, 243, 520
Costa v ENEL [1964] CMLR 425, 171
Costello-Roberts v UK (1993) 19 EHRR 112, 447
Council of Civil Service Unions (CCSU) v Minister for the Civil Service [1985] AC 374, 312, 370, 374, 389, 405, 429, 517
Cream Holdings v Banerjee [2004] 4 All ER 618, 489
Credit Suisse v Allerdale BC [1996] 4 All ER 129, 372, 373, 420
Cullen v Chief Constable of the RUC [2004] 2 All ER 237, 11, 130, 417, 426, 467
Culnane v Morris [2006] 2 All ER 149, 44, 132, 156, 245, 246, 277
Curiston v Times Newspapers [2007] 4 All ER 486, 247
Customs and Excise Comrs v ApS Samex [1983] 1 All ER 1042, 217

D v East Berkshire Community Health NHS Trust [2005] 2 AC 373, 126, 418
D v Home Office [2006] 1 All ER 183, 126, 426
D v NSPCC [1978] AC 171, 182, 527
D v UK (1997) 2 BHRC 273, 448

De Freitas v Ministry of Agriculture, Fisheries, Lands and Housing [1999] 1 AC 69, 400
De Jager v A-G of Natal [1907] AC 326, 188
Defrenne v SABENA (No 2) [1976] ECR 455, 219
Demicola v Malta (1992) 14 EHRR 47, 240
Derbyshire CC v Times Newspapers Ltd [1993] 1 All ER 1011, 493
Dimes v Grand Junction Canal Co (1852) 3 HLC 759, 407
Director General of Fair Trading v Proprietary Association of Great Britain [2001] The Times, 4 October, 467
Doughty v Rolls-Royce plc [1992] IRC 538, 219
Douglas and Zeta-Jones v Hello! Ltd [2001] 2 All ER 289, 489
Douglas and Zeta-Jones v Hello! Ltd (No 3) [2005] 4 All ER 128, 499
DPP v Clarke and Others [1992] Crim LR 60, 510
DPP v Collins [2006] 1 WLR 223, 487
DPP v Fidler [1992] 1 WLR 91, 511
DPP v Head [1959] AC 83, 373
DPP v Jones [1999] 2 All ER 257, 504, 509, 512
Dr Bonham's Case (1610) 8 Co Rep 114a, 1763, 371, 403
Duchy of Lancaster Case (1567) 1 Plow 325, 73, 302, 325
Duncan v Jones [1936] 1 KB 218, 507
Dunlop Rubber Co Ltd v Dunlop [1921] 1 AC 637, 491
Dunlop v Woollahra Municipal Council [1982] AC 158, 308, 418
Dunn v R [1896] 1 QB 116, 339
Duport Steels Ltd v Sirs [1980] 1 All ER 529, 142, 155
Dyson v A-G [1911] 1 KB 410, 370, 403

Edinburgh & Dalkeith Railway Co v Wauchope (1842) 8 CL and F 710, 162
Edwards v Bairstow [1956] AC 14, 379
Edwards and Lewis v UK (2003) 15 BHRC 189, 528
Ellen Street Estates Ltd v Minister of Health [1934] 1 KB 590, 164
Elmbridge BC v Secretary of State for the Environment, Transport and the Regions [2002] Envir LR 1, 406
Enderby Town Football Club v Football Association [1971] Ch 591, 406
Engelke v Musmann [1928] AC 433, 202
Entick v Carrington (1765) 19 St Tr 1029, 28, 77, 127, 183, 309, 372–73,
Equal Opportunities Commission v Secretary of State for Employment [1994] 1 All ER 910, 172
Ex parte Anderson (1861) 3 E & E 487, 189
Ex parte Brown (1864) 33 LJ QB 193, 189
Ex parte Canon Selwyn (1872) 36 JP 54, 166, 356
Ezelin v France (1991) 14 EHRR 362, 508, 509

Faccini Dori v Recreb [1995] 1 CMLR 665, 219
Feldbrugge v the Netherlands (1986) 8 EHRR 425, 381
Financial Times v UK [2009] Times Dec 16, 491
Findlay v Secretary of State for the Home Dept [1985] 1 AC 318, 390, 404
Findlay v UK (1997) 24 EHRR 221, 84
Fisher v R (1901) 26 Victoria LR 781 (approved by Privy Council in R v Fisher [1903] AC 158), 290
Fitt v UK (2000) 30 EHRR 480, 528
Foster v British Gas plc [1990] 3 All ER 897, 219
Fox v Stirk [1970] 2 QB 463, 268
Francis v Secretary of State for Work and Pensions [2006] 1 All ER 748, 455
Francombe v Mirror Group Newspapers [1984] 2 All ER 408, 526
Francovich v Italy [1993] 2 CMLR 66, 219, 220
Franklin v Minister of Town and Country Planning [1948] AC 87, 404
Fredin v Sweden [1991] ECHR Series A 192 1B-69, 455
Fressoz v France (1999) 5 BHRC 654, 487
Funke v France (1993) ECHR Series A 256-A, 443
Furnell v Whangarie High Schools Board [1973] AC 660, 404

Galloway v Telegraph Group [2006] EWCA Civ 17, 492
Garland v British Rail Engineering Ltd [1983] 2 AC 751, 171, 198
Gaskin v UK (1990) 12 EHRR 36, 474, 518
General Medical Council v BBC [1998] 1 WLR 1573, 99, 182
Ghaidan v Mendoza [2004] 3 All ER 411, 11, 120, 132, 220, 455, 463, 464, 471, 472, 477, 479
Gibson v East Riding of Yorkshire DC [2000] ICR 890, 220
Gibson v Lord Advocate [1975] SLT 134, 166

Gillan and Quinton v UK [2010] ECHR App no 158/05, 130, 447, 461, 473, 508, 540
Gillick v West Yorkshire CC [1986] AC 162, 370
Gillies v Secretary of State for Work and Pensions [2006] 1 All ER 967, 408
Godden v Hales (1686) 11 St Tr 1165, 74, 309
Goldsmith v Bhoyrul [1997] The Times, 20 June, 493
Goodridge v Chief Constable of Hampshire Constabulary [1999] 1 All ER 896, 527
Goodwin v UK (1996) 22 EHRR 123, 491
Gough v Chief Constable of the Derbyshire Constabulary [2001] 4 All ER 289, 472, 476
Gouriet v Union of Post Office Workers [1978] AC 435, 329, 427
Grand Duchy of Luxembourg v Parliament [1983] 2 CMLR 726, 215
Grau Gromis, Criminal Proceedings, Case Against [1995] All ER (EC) 688, 216
Grobbelaar v News Group Newspapers Ltd [2001] 2 All ER 437, 492
Guerra v Italy (1998) 26 EHRR 357, 451, 518
Gunn-Russo v Nugent Care Housing Society [2001] EWHC Admin 566, 518

Halford v UK [1997] IRLR 471, 532
Hall & Co Ltd v Shoreham-By-Sea Urban DC [1964] 1 All ER 1, 3698
Hamilton v Al Fayed [1999] 3 All ER 317, 173, 244, 245, 252
Hammersmith and Fulham LBC v Secretary of State for the Environment [1990] 3 All ER 14, 399, 404, 428
Hampshire CC v Beer [2003] EWCA Civ 1056, 423, 424
Handyside v UK [1976] 1 EHRR 77, 443, 473, 475
Harper v Secretary of State for the Home Dept [1955] Ch 238, 273
Harris v Minister of the Interior [1952] (2) SA 428, 169
Harris v Sheffield United Football Club Ltd [1988] QB 77, 507
Harrison v Duke of Rutland [1893] 1 QB 142, 504
Harrow LBC v Qazi [2004] 1 AC 983, 127, 452, 463, 475
Hatton v UK (2003) 37 EHRR 28, 451
Hazell v Hammersmith and Fulham LBC [1992] 2 AC 1, 377
Hector v A-G of Antigua and Bermuda [1990] 2 All ER 103, 483
Helle v Finland (1998) 26 EHRR 159, 412
Hellewell v Chief Constable of Derbyshire [1995] 4 All ER 473, 525
Helow v Secretary of State [2009] 2 All ER 1031, 409
Hickman v Maisey [1900] 1 QB 752, 504
Hirst v UK (No 2) [2004] App no 74025/01, NLJ 9 April 2004, 12, 268, 450, 477
Hirst and Agu v West Yorkshire Chief Constable (1986) 85 Crim App Rep 143, 509
HJ (Iran) v Secretary of State for the Home Dept [2010] 3 WLR 386, 448
HM Advocate v Murtogh [2010] 3 WLR 814, 451, 453
HM v Switzerland [2002] ECHR 39187/98, 37, 447
HM Treasury v Ahmed [2010] UKSC 2, 132, 544
Hoffman-La Roche & Co v Secretary of State for Trade and Industry [1974] 2 All ER 1128, 243
Homer v Cadman (1886) 16 Cox CC 51, 509
Home Secretary v AF [2009] UKHL 20, 530
Hone v Maze Prison Board of Visitors [1988] 1 All ER 321, 400, 406
HRH Prince of Wales v Associated Newspapers Ltd [2007] 2 All ER 139, 498
Huang v Secretary of State [2007] 4 All ER 15, 431
Hubbard v Pitt [1976] QB 142, 504

Informationsverein Lentia v Austria (1993) 17 93, 486
International Transport Roth GmbH v Secretary of State for the Home Dept [2003] 3 WLR 444, 476
Internationale Handelsgesellschaft mbH v Emfunhr-und vorratsstelle fur Getreide- und Futtermittel [1970] ECR 1125, 222
Invercargill City Council v Hamlin [1996] AC 624, 123
IRC v National Federation of Self-Employed and Small Business Ltd [1982] AC 617, 421

Jameel v Wall Street Journal Europe [2006] 4 All ER 1279, 496
Jasper v UK (2000) 30 EHRR 441, 528
Jeewan Mohit v DPP of Mauritius [2006] UKPC 20, 427
Jeffs v New Zealand Dairy Production and Marketing Board [1967] 1 AC 551, 403
Jersild v Denmark (1994) 19 EHRR 1, 486, 490, 500
JH Ltd v UK [2001] The Times, 19 October, 532

JH Rayner (Mincing Lane) Ltd v Dept of Trade and Industry [1990] 2 AC 418, 196, 197
John v Express Newspapers Ltd [2000] 3 All ER 257, 491
John v Mirror Group Newspapers Ltd [1996] 3 WLR 593, 494
John v Rees [1969] 2 All ER 274, 405
Johnston v Chief Constable of Royal Ulster Constabulary [1986] ECR 1651, 221
Johnstone v Pedlar [1921] 2 AC 262, 201, 202
Jones v Ministry of the Interior of Saudi Arabia [2006] UKHL 26, 37, 198
Jones v University of Warwick [2003] 1 WLR 954, 531
Jordan v Burgoyne [1963] 2 QB 744, 510
Joyce v DPP [1946] AC 347, 188
JT's Corporation v Commission [2000] The Times, 18 October, 224

Kay v Lambeth BC [2006] UKHL 10, 425, 445, 471, 475
Kay v Metropolitan Police Comr [2007] 4 All ER 31, 505
Kaye v Robertson [1991] FSR 62, 496
Keighly Case (1609) 10 Co Rep 139, 369
Keighley v Bell [1866] 4 F and F 763, 535
Khan v UK [2001] 31 EHRR 1016, 532
Khawaja v Secretary of State for the Home Dept [1983] 1 All ER 765, 380
Kirklees MBC v Wickes Building Supplies Ltd [1992] 3 All ER 717, 221
Klass v Federal Republic of Germany [1979–80] 2 EHRR 214, 119, 467, 473, 517
Kodeeswaran v A-G for Ceylon [1970] AC 1111, 339
Kokkinakis v Greece (1993) 17 EHRR 397, 473
Kostovski v Netherlands [1989] ECHR Series A no 166, 528
Kroon v Netherlands (1995) 19 EHRR 263, 471
Kuwait Airways v Iraqi Airways (No 1) [1995] 3 All ER 694, 197, 198, 200
Kuwait Airways v Iraqi Airways (Nos 4 and 5) [2002] 2 AC 883, 200, 201

Laker Airways Ltd v Dept of Trade [1977] QB 643, 309, 315, 316
Lambeth LBC v Kay [2006] 4 All ER 128, 461, 467
Lange v Atkinson and Consolidated Press NZ Ltd [1998] 3 NZLR 424, 495
Lavender & Son Ltd v Minister of Housing and Local Government [1970] 3 All ER 871, 388
Lawal v Northern Spirit Ltd [2004] 1 All ER 187, 397, 409
Lawless v Ireland (No 3) (1961) 1 EHRR 15, 516, 517
Leach v Money [1765] St Tr 1001, 77
Leander v Sweden [1987] ECHR Series A 116, 443, 518
Leech v Parkhurst Prison Deputy Governor [1988] 1 All ER 485, 404
Liberal Party v UK [1982] 4 EHRR 106, 264
Lindsey v UK [1979] 3 CMLR 166, 264
Lingens v Austria (1986) 8 EHRR 407, 486, 490, 493
Lion Laboratories Ltd v Evans [1985] 1 QB 526, 526
Liversidge v Anderson [1942] AC 206, 515, 517
Lloyd v McMahon [1987] 1 All ER 1118, 405, 406
Local Government Board v Arlidge [1915] AC 120, 403
Locobail (UK) Ltd v Bayfield Properties Ltd [2000] QB 451, 407, 408
London and Clydeside Estates Ltd v Aberdeen DC and Another [1979] 3 All ER 876, 402
Lonrho plc v Fayed (No 4) [1994] 1 All ER 870, 486
Lonrho plc v Secretary of State for Trade and Industry [1989] 2 All ER 609, 410
Lord Advocate v Dumbarton DC [1990] 2 AC 580, 308
Lord Advocate v The Scotsman Publications Ltd [1990] 1 AC 812, 525
Lord Luke of Pavenham v Minister of Housing and Local Government [1968] 1 QB 172, 379

M v Home Office [1993] 3 All ER 537, 61, 119, 126, 129, 137, 142, 143, 184, 218, 303, 308, 417
M v Secretary of State for the Home Dept [2004] 2 All ER 863, 129, 529, 543
M v Secretary of State for Work and Pensions [2006] 4 All ER 929, 451, 455
McC v Mullan and Others [1984] 3 All ER 908, 141
McCann v UK (1995) 21 EHRR 97, 535
McCartan-Turkington Breen v Times Newspapers Ltd [2001] 2 AC 277, 482, 485
Macarthy & Stone (Developments) Ltd v Richmond upon Thames LBC [1991] 4 All ER 897, 272, 310, 376
MacCormick v Lord Advocate [1953] SC 369, 166
MacFarlane v Tayside Health Board [2000] 2 AC 59, 123

McGonnell v UK (2000) 30 EHRR 289, 141, 148, 149
McIlkenny v Chief Constable of West Midlands Police [1980]2 All ER 227, 31, 82
McInnes v Onslow-Fane [1978] 3 All ER 211, 371, 404, 410
McLaren v Home Office [1990] IRLR 338, 424
McLeod v UK (1998) 27 EHRR 493, 125, 507, 508
McVeigh v UK (1983) 5 EHRR 71, 474
Mahon v Air New Zealand Ltd [1984] 3 All ER 201, 406
Malone v Metropolitan Police Comr [1979] Ch 344, 127, 531
Malone v UK (1984) 7 EHRR 14, 496, 517, 532
Mandla v Dowell-Lee [1983] 1 All ER 1062, 500
Manuel v A-G [1982] 3 All ER 822, 163, 165, 169
Marais v General Officer Commanding [1902] AC 109, 535
Marbury v Madison (1803 1 Cranch, 6
Marcic v Thames Water Utilities Ltd [2004] 1 All ER 135, 95, 417, 418, 451
Marckx v Belgium (1979–80) 2 EHRR 330, 454, 474
Marleasing SA v La Comercial Internacional de Alimentacion SA [1992] 1 CMLR 305, 220
Marper v UK [2008] ECHR 1581, 443, 451, 452, 455, 460
Marshall v Southampton and South West Hampshire Area HA (No 1) [1986] 2 All ER 584, 220
Marshall v Southampton and South West Hampshire Area HA (No 2) [1993] 4 All ER 586, 219
Matthews v Ministry of Defence [2003] 1 AC 1163, 308, 449, 477
Matthieu-Mohun v Belgium (1988) 10 EHRR 1, 257, 264
Maxwell v Dept of Trade and Industry and Others [1974] 2 All ER 122, 405
Mayne v Ministry of Agriculture, Fisheries and Food [2001] EHLR 5, 218
Mellacher v Austria [1989] ECHR Series A 169 315B, 455
Mercury Communications Ltd v Director General of Telecommunications [1996] 1 All ER 575, 426
Millar v Dickson [2002] 3 All ER 1041, 141
Minister of State for Immigration and Ethnic affairs ex parte Teoh (1995) 183 CLR 273, 390
Miss Behavin v Belfast City Council [2007] 3 All ER 1007, 485
Monson v Tussauds Ltd [1894] 1 QB 671, 493
Mortensen v Peters (1906) 14 SLT 227, 163
Moss v McLachlan [1985] IRLR 76, 508
Mutasa v A-G [1980] 1 QB 114, 187

N v Secretary of State for the Home Dept [2005] 2 AC 296, 448, 452
N v UK [2008] 47 EHRR 865, 447
National Farmers Union v Secretary of State for the Environment, Food and Rural Affairs [2003] EWHC 444, 315
Nakkuda Ali v Jayaratne [1951] AC 66, 400
Nissan v A-G [1970] AC 179, 201
NML Capital Ltd v Republic of Argentina [2010] 3 WLR 874, 198
Norris v USA [2010] 2 All ER 268, 452
Norwest Holst v Trade Secretary [1978] Ch 201, 404
Norwich Pharmaceuticals v Customs and Excise Comrs [1974] AC 133, 527
Nottinghamshire CC v Secretary of State for the Environment [1986] AC 240, 295, 399

Oberschlick v Austria (1995) 19 EHRR 389, 493
Observer and Guardian Newspapers v UK (1992) 14 EHRR 153, 487, 488, 525
Odelola v Secretary of State for the Home Dept [2009] 3 All ER 1061, 389
Oladehinde v Secretary of State for the Home Dept [1990] 3 All ER 393, 340
Olsson v Sweden, (1988) ECHR Series A vol 130, 451
O'Moran v Director of Public Prosecutions [1975] 1 All ER 473, 511
Open Door and Dublin Well Woman v Ireland (1992) 15 EHRR 244, 467, 475, 487
O'Reilly v Mackman [1982] 3 All ER 1124, 378, 391, 425, 426, 433
Oscar v Chief Constable of the RUC [1992] NI 290, 539
Otto Preminger Institut v Austria (1994) 19 EHRR 34, 453, 485, 499, 501, 512

Padfield v Minister of Agriculture, Fisheries and Food [1968] AC 997, 79, 382, 410
Page v Hull University Visitor [1993] 1 All ER 97, 372, 378, 379, 428
Paty's Case [1704] 2 Lord Raymond 1105, 252
Pearlman v Governors and Keepers of Harrow School [1979] QB 56, 379

Peck v UK (2003) 36 EHRR 719, 532
Pelling v Bruce-Williams [2004] 3 All ER 875, 486
Pepper (Inspector of Taxes) v Hart [1993] 1 All ER 42, 155, 156, 244, 515
Phillips v UK App no 41087/98 (ECHR) [2001] NLJ 1282, 449
Pickin v British Railways Board [1974] AC 765, 145, 160, 163, 241, 286
Pickwell v Camden LBC [1983] QB 962, 384
Plattform 'Arzte fur das Leben' v Austria (1988) 13 EHRR 204 A139, 507
Poplar Housing and Regeneration Community Association Ltd v Donoghue [2001] 4 All ER 604, 423, 465, 476
Porter and Another v Magill [2002] 1 All ER 465, 385, 407, 408–09
Prescott v Birmingham Corporation [1955] Ch 210, 376, 384
Preston v IRC [1985] 2 All ER 327, 389
Prince of Wales v Associated Newspapers [2006] EWHC 522, 497, 498
Prince's Case (1606) 8 Co Rep 1, 162
Prohibitions del Roy (1607) 12 Co Rep 64, 12, 52, 73, 121, 142, 302
Provident Mutual Life Assurance Association v Derby City Council [1981] 1 WLR 173, 403
Pubblico Ministero v Ratti [1979] ECR 1–1629, 219
Pulhoffer v Hillingdon BC [1986] AC 484, 379

R (A) v Croydon LBC [2009] 1 WLR 2577, 380, 381
R (A) v Secretary of State for Health [2010] 1 All ER 87, 185
R (A) v Secretary of State for the Home Dept [2006] EWHC 526, 390, 391
R (AB) v Secretary of State for Justice [2010] 2 All ER 151, 398, 451, 474
R (AM) v Secretary of State for the Home Dept [2009] EWCA Civ 219, 445
R (Abassi) v Secretary of State for the Foreign and Commonwealth Office [2002] EWCA Civ 159, 314, 389
R (Alconbury Developments Ltd) v Secretary of State for the Environment, Transport and the Regions [2001] 2 All ER 929, 43, 103, 146, 340, 369, 381, 401, 402, 412, 430, 441, 449, 459
R (Al-Hasan) v Secretary of State for the Home Dept [2005] 1 All ER 927, 408
R (Al Jedda) v Secretary of State for Defence [2008 1 AC 332, 197, 445, 460
R (Al Rawi) v Secretary of State for the Foreign and Commonwealth Office [2007] 2 WLR 1219, 386, 428
R (Al Saadoon) v Secretary of State for Defence, [2010] 1 All ER 271, 195, 462
R (Al-Skeini) v Secretary of State for Defence [2007] 3 All ER685, 270, 443, 460, 462
R (Amin) v Secretary of State for the Home Dept [2002] 4 All ER 336, 441
R (Anderson) v Secretary of State for the Home Dept [2002] 4 All ER 1089, 119, 123, 137, 142, 144, 146, 464
R (Animal Defenders International) v Culture Secretary [2008] 1 AC 1312, 460, 476
R (Anufrijeva) v Secretary of State for the Home Dept [2003] 3 All ER 827, 130
R (Association of British Civilian Internees; Far East Region) v Secretary of State for the Foreign and Commonwealth Office [2003] QB 1397, 401
R (B) v Secretary of State for the Foreign and Commonwealth Office [2005] 2 WLR 618, 462
R (Baiai) v Secretary of State for the Home Dept [2007] 4 All ER 199, 449
R (Bancoult) v Secretary of State for the Foreign and Commonwealth Office [2001] 1 QB 1067, 51, 131, 132, 192, 193
R (Bancoult) v Secretary of State for the Foreign and Commonwealth Office (No 2) [2008] 4 All ER 1055, 61, 133, 143, 191, 194, 303, 314, 389, 390, 429
R (Begum) v Head Teacher and Governors of Denbigh High School [2007] AC 100, 20, 40, 453, 460, 472, 474, 477
R (Bermingham) v Serious Fraud Office [2007] QB 727, 474
R (Bernard) v Enfield LBC [2002] EWCA 2282, 452
R (Bibi) v Newnham LBC [2002] 1 WLR 237, 390
R (Black) v Secretary of State for Justice [2009] UKHL 1, 146
R (Boggis) v Natural England [2010] 1 All ER 159, 419
R (Boyejo) v Barnet LBC [2009] EWHC 3261, 402
R (British American Tobacco UK Ltd) v Secretary of State for Health [2004] EWHC 2493, 485

R (Bulger) v Secretary of State for the Home Dept [2001] 3 All ER 449, 383, 422
R (Carson) v Secretary of State for Work and Pensions [2006] 1 AC 173, 455
R (Cart) v Upper Tribunal [2010] 1 All ER 908 DC, 97, 100, 118, 132, 369, 379, 427, 428, 432
R (Chaytor) v A-G [2010] UKSC 52 (SC), [2010] EWCA Crim 1910 (CA), 66, 126, 132, 239, 242, 250, 252
R (Chief Constable of the West Midlands Police) v Birmingham City Justices [2002] EWHC 1087 (Admin), 402, 403
R (Child Poverty Action Group) v Secretary of State for Work and Pensions, Times 22 Oct 2009, 126
R (Clift) v Secretary of State for the Home Dept [2007] 2 All ER 1, 455, 460
R (Conville) v Richmond on Thames LBC [2006] EWCA Civ 718, 387
R (Confederation of Passenger Transport (UK) Ltd) v Humber Bridge Board [2004] 4 All ER 533, 416
R (Corner House Research) v Director of the Serious Fraud Office (No 2) [2008] 4 All ER 927, 117, 124, 197, 429
R (Countryside Alliance) v A-G [2008] 2 All ER 95, 117, 124, 197, 429
R (D) v Secretary of State for the Home Dept [2006] 3 All ER 946, 445
R (DPP) v Havering Magistrates Court [2001] 3 All ER 997, 449
R (Douglas) v North Tyneside DC [2004] 1 All ER 709, 428, 450
R (Dudson) v Secretary of State for the Home Dept [2006] 1 All ER 421, 406
R (Edwards) v Environment Agency [2004] 3 All ER 21, 422
R (Electoral Commission) v City of Westminster Magistrates Court [2010] 1 All ER 1167, 277
R (Farrakhan) v Secretary of State for the Home Dept [2002] QB 1391, 428, 431
R (Feakins) v Secretary of State for Environment, Food and Rural Affairs [2004] 1 WLR1761, 422
R (Fuller) v Chief Constable of Dorset [2002] 3 All ER 57, 504
R (G) v Barnet LBC [2004] 1 All ER 97, 386
R (G) v Governors of X School [2010] 2 All ER 555, 381, 406, 411
R (C) v Immigration Appeal Tribunal [2004] 3 All ER 286, 420, 430, 432
R(G) v Metropolitan Police Comr [2010] 1 All ER 113,
R (Gentle) v Prime Minister [2008] 1 AC 1356, 196, 411, 427, 428, 446, 460, 476
R (Gillan) v Metropolitan Police Comr [2006] 4 All ER 1041, 516, 540
R (Green) v Police Complaints Authority [2004] 2 All ER 209, 107
R (H) v London North and East Region Mental Health Review Tribunal [2001] EWCA Civ 415, 464
R (H) v Secretary of State for Health [2006] 1 AC 441, 466
R (Hammond) v Secretary of State for the Home Dept [2006] 1 All ER 219, 141, 381
R (Heather) v Leonard Cheshire Foundation [2002] 2 All ER 936, 424
R (Hemmings) v Prime Minister [2006] EWHC Admin 293, 319
R (Hurst) v North London District Coroner [2007] 2 All ER 1025, 445, 461, 464
R (Jackson) v A-G [2005] 4 All ER 1253, 145, 151, 156, 160, 161, 163, 166, 169, 173, 174, 238
R (JL) v Secretary of State for the Home Dept [2009] 2 All ER 521, 445
R (JS) v Secretary of State for the Home Dept [2010] 3 All ER 881, 197, 198
R (Khatum) v Newham London BC [2004] Independent, 4 March, 385
R (Kurdistan Workers' Party) v Secretary of State for the Home Dept [2002] EWHC 644, 538
R (Laporte) v Chief Constable of Gloucestershire [2007] 2 AC 105, 473, 487, 507, 508
R (Limbuela) v Secretary of State for Social Security [2007] 1 All ER 951, 447
R (M) v Gateshead Council [2007] 1 All ER 1262, 386
R (M) v Secretary of State for Constitutional Affairs [2004] 2 All ER 531, 411
R (M) v Secretary of State for Work and Pensions [2006] EWHC 176, 451
R (Mahmood) v Secretary of State for the Home Dept [2001] 1 WLR 840, 475
R (McLellan) v Bracknell Forest BC [2002] 1 All ER 899, 471
R (Middleton) v West Somerset Coroner [2004] 2 All ER 465, 130, 411, 445
R (Mohamad) v Secretary of State for Foreign and Commonwealth Affairs [2010] 3 WLR 554, 130, 142, 430, 448, 490, 516, 527, 528

R (Morris) v Westminster City Council [2005] 1 All ER 351, 455
R (Pretty) v DPP [2002] 1 All ER 1, 123, 444, 446, 460, 474, 476
R (Pro-Life Alliance) v BBC [2003] 2 All ER 977, 142, 277
R (Purdy) v DPP [2009] UKHL 45, 451, 460, 473
R (Quintavalle) v Human Embryology and Fertilisation Authority [2005] 2 AC 561, 422
R (Quintavalle) v Secretary of State for Health [2003] 2 All ER 113, 218, 422
R (Rashid) v Secretary of State for the Home Dept [2005] EWCA Civ 744, 390, 393
R (Razgar) v Secretary of State for the Home Dept [2004] 3 All ER 821, 448
R (Reynolds) v IPPC [2009] 3All ER 237, 445
R (RK(Nepal)) v Secretary of State for the Home Dept [2009] EWCA Civ 359, 420
R (Roberts) v Parole Board [2006] 1 All ER 39, 530
R (Rogers) v Swindon Primary Health Care Trust [2006] EWCA Civ 392, 383, 398
R (S) v Chief Constable of South Yorkshire Police [2004] 4 All ER 193, 452, 455, 460, 472, 475, 476
R (Sinclair Gardens Investments) v Lands Tribunal [2005] EWCA Civ 1305, 428
R (Sivasubramaniam) v Wandworth BC [2003] 1 WLR 575, 420
R (Smith) v Parole Board [2005] 1 All ER 755, 406
R (Smith) v Secretary of State for Defence [2010] 3 All ER 1067, 428, 460, 462
R (Smith) v Secretary of State for the Home Dept [2006] 1 All ER 407, 147
R (Southall) v Secretary of State for Foreign and Commonwealth Affairs [2003] EWCA Civ 1002, 10
R (Szluk) v Governor of Full Sutton Prison [2004] EWCA 1426, 474
R (Theophilus) v Lewisham BC [2002] 3 All ER 851, 391
R (Ullah) v Special Adjudicator [2004] 3 All ER 785, 131, 444, 448, 460
R (Uttley) v Secretary of State for the Home Dept [2004] 4 All ER 1, 130
R (Weaver) v London and Quadrant Housing Trust [2008] EWCA 1377, 20
R (West) v Lloyds of London [2004] 3 All ER 251, 423
R (Weatherspoon) v Guildford BC [2007] 1 All ER 400, 420
R (Wellington) v Secretary of State for the Home Dept [2008] UKHL 72, 448
R (Wheeler) v Office of the Prime Minister [2008] EWCA 936, 393
R (Williamson) v Secretary of State for Education and Employment [2005] 2 All ER 1, 24, 35, 450, 471, 473, 501
R (Wright) v Secretary of State for Health [2009] 2 All ER 129, 381, 382, 411, 448, 451
R v A [2001] 3 All ER 1, 463, 464, 466, 477
R v Advertising Standards Authority (1990) 2 Admin LR 77, 425
R v Army Board of the Defence Council ex parte Anderson [1992] QB 169, 405
R v Abdrocar [2005] 4 All ER 869, 408
R v Barnsley Metropolitan BC ex parte Hook [1976] 3 All ER 452, 401
R v Barnsley Licencing Justices [1960] 2 QB 167, 409
R v Bottrill ex parte Kuechenmeister [1947] KB 41, 200, 202
R v Boundary Commission for England ex parte Foot [1983] 1 All ER 1099, 264, 273, 417, 420
R v Bow Street Metropolitan Stipendiary Magistrate ex parte Pinochet Ugarte (No 3) [1999] 2 All ER 97, 134, 196, 199, 407
R v Bow Street Stipendiary Magistrate ex parte Pinochet Ugarte (No 2) [1999] 1 All ER 577, 134, 407
R v Brent HA ex parte Francis [1985] 1 All ER 74, 522
R v Broadcasting Complaints Commission ex parte Owen [1985] QB 1153, 277
R v Broadcasting Standards Commission ex parte BBC [2001] QB 885, 487
R v Brown [1993] 2 All ER 75, 329, 526
R v Burah [1878] 3 App Cas 889, 190
R v Burns [1886] 16 Cox CC 355, 502
R v Camborne Justices ex parte Pearce [1955] 1 QB 41, 407
R v Cambridge HA ex parte B [1995] 2 All ER 129 (CA), 428, 430
R v Casement [1917] 1 KB 98, 188
R v Central Criminal Court ex parte Bright, Alton, Rusbridger [2001] 2 All ER 244, 490
R v Central Independent Television plc [1994] 3 All ER 641, 484
R v Chief Constable of Devon and Cornwall Constabulary ex parte Central Electricity Generating Board [1981] 3 All ER 826, 507

R v Chief Constable of Sussex ex parte International Traders Ferry Ltd [1999] 1 All ER 129, 217, 398, 507
R v Chief Constable of the Merseyside Police ex parte Calverley [1986] QB 424, 420
R v Chief Rabbi ex parte Wachmann [1993] 2 All ER 249, 425
R v City of Westminster Housing Benefit Review Board ex parte Mehanne [2001] 2 All ER 690, 386
R v Civil Service Appeals Board ex parte Bruce [1988] 3 All ER 686, 339
R v Civil Service Appeals Board ex parte Cunningham [1991] 4 All ER 310, 339, 410
R v Clarke and McDaid [2008] 1 WLR 338, 402
R v Commission for Racial Equality ex parte Cottrell and Rothon [1980], 405
R v Cornwall CC ex parte Huntingdon [1994] 1 All ER 694, 431
R v Coventry City Council ex parte Phoenix Aviation [1995] 3 All ER 37, 507
R v Criminal Injuries Compensation Board ex parte Lain [1967] 2 QB 864, 312
R v Criminal Injuries Compensation Board ex parte A [1999] 2 AC 330, 380
R v Criminal Injuries Compensation Board ex parte P [1995] 1 All ER 870, 315
R v Criminal Injuries Compensation Board ex parte Moore [1999] 2 All ER 90, 410
R v Crown Court at Sheffield ex parte Brownlow [1980] 2 All ER 444, 147
R v Devon CC ex parte Baker [1995] 1 All ER 73, 405
R v Disciplinary Committee of the Jockey Club ex parte the Aga Khan [1993] 2 All ER 853, 424
R v DPP ex parte Kebeline [1999] 2 AC 326, 389, 411, 459, 475, 528
R v DPP ex parte Manning [2000] 3 WLR 463, 410
R v East Berkshire HA ex parte Walsh [1985] QB 152, 424
R v East Sussex CC ex parte Tandy [1998] 2 All ER 769, 387
R v Felixstowe Justices ex parte Leigh [1987] QB 582, 422
R v Football Association ex parte Football League [1993] 2 All ER 833, 424
R v Foster [1965] QB 117, 311
R v Frankland Prison Board of Visitors ex parte Lewis [1986] 1 All ER 272, 409
R v Gaming Board ex parte Benaim and Khaida [1970] 2 QB 417, 404
R v Gloucestershire CC ex parte Barry [1997] 2 All ER 1, 104, 387
R v Goldsmith [1983] 1 WLR 151, 400
R v Goldstein [2006] 2 All ER 257, 130, 473
R v Gough [1993] AC 646, 407, 408
R v Governor of Brixton Prison ex parte Armah [1968] AC 192, 377
R v Grahame-Campbell ex parte Herbert [1935] 1 KB 594, 242
R v Grant [2005] 3 WLR 437, 130, 532
R v Greater London Council ex parte Blackburn [1976] 3 All ER 184, 388
R v Greenaway [1998] PL 357, 243, 249
R v H and C [2004] Times 6 February, 528
R v Hammersmith and Fulham LBC ex parte Beddowes [1987] 1 ALL ER 369, 388
R v Hampden (1637) 3 St Tr 825, 73, 309, 314
R v Hendon Rural DC ex parte Chorley [1933] 2 KB 696, 407
R v Higher Education Funding Council ex parte Institute of Dental Surgery [1994] 1 All ER 651, 410
R v HM Treasury ex parte Smedley [1985] QB 657, 54, 142, 327, 422
R v Horncastle [2010] 2 WLR 47, 460
R v Horseferry Road Magistrates Court ex parte Bennett [1994] 1 All ER 289, 130, 510
R v Horseferry Road Metropolitan Stipendiary Magistrate ex parte Siadatan [1991] 1 QB 260, 510
R v Howell [1982] QB 415, 507
R v Hull Prison Visitors ex parte St Germain [1979] QB 425, 404
R v Hull Prison Visitors ex parte St Germain (No 2) [1979] 1 WLR 1401, 405
R v Immigration Appeal Tribunal ex parte Jeyeanthan [1999] 3 All ER 231, 402
R v Inner London Education Authority ex parte Westminster City, 276, 385
R v Inspectorate of Pollution ex parte Greenpeace (No 2) [1994] 4 All ER 329, 422
R v International Stock Exchange of the United Kingdom and the Republic of Ireland Ltd ex parte Else (1982) Ltd [1993] 1 All ER 420, 217
R v IRC ex parte MFK Underwriting Agents Ltd [1990] 1 WLR 1545, 389
R v IRC ex parte Rossminster Ltd [1980] 1 All ER 80, 127

R v Jockey Club ex parte RAM Racecourses Ltd [1993] 2 All ER 225, 390
R v Jones [1999] 2 Crim App Rep 253, 274
R v Jones (Margaret) [2006] 2 WLR 272, 184, 195, 427, 428
R v Jordan [1967] Crim LR 483, 163
R v Khan (Sultan) [1996] 3 All ER 289, 531, 533
R v Lambert [2001] 3 All ER 577, 459, 464
R v Lancashire CC ex parte Huddleston [1986] 2 All ER 941, 30, 411, 420
R v Legal Aid Board ex parte Bateman [1992] 1 WLR 711, 422
R v Lewisham LBC ex parte Shell UK Ltd [1988] 1 All ER 938, 383, 385
R v Liverpool City Council ex parte Liverpool Taxi Fleet Operators Association [1975] 1 All ER 379, 391
R v Local Comr for Administration ex parte Bradford City Council [1979] QB 287, 101
R v Local Comr for Administration ex parte Liverpool City Council [2001] 1 All ER 462, 101, 415
R v Lord Chancellor's Dept ex parte Nangle [1992] 1 All ER 897, 339
R v Lord Chancellor's Dept ex parte Witham [1997] 2 All ER 779, 130, 132, 173, 376
R v Lord Saville of Newdigate [1999] 4 All ER 860, 399
R v Lords Comrs of the Treasury [1872] LR 7 QB 387, 290
R v Medical Appeal Tribunal ex parte Gilmore [1957] 1 QB 574, 431
R v Metropolitan Police Comr ex parte Blackburn [1968] 2 QB 118, 106
R v Minister of Agriculture, Fisheries and Food ex parte Hamble Fisheries Ltd [1995], 340, 390, 392
R v Minister of Agriculture, Fisheries and Food ex parte Monsanto plc [1998] 4 All ER 321, 417
R v Ministry of Defence ex parte Murray [1998] The Times, 17 December, 410
R v Ministry of Defence ex parte Smith [1996] QB 517, 315, 398, 399, 430
R v Ministry of Defence ex parte Walker [2000] 1 WLR 806, 390
R v Monopolies and Mergers Commission ex parte South Yorkshire Transport [1993] 1 All ER 289, 379
R v Nat Bell Liquors Ltd [1922] 2 AC 128, 377
R v Newham LBC ex parte Begum [2000] 2 All ER 72, 387
R v North and East Devon HA ex parte Coughlan [2000] 2 WLR 622, 391, 392
R v North Somerset DC ex parte Dixon [1998] Envir LR 91, 422
R v Northumberland Compensation Appeal Tribunal ex parte Shaw [1952] 1 KB 338, 378
R v Officer in Charge of Police Office Castlereagh Belfast ex parte Lynch [1980] HI 126, 539
R v Panel on Takeovers and Mergers ex parte Datafin plc [1987] QB 815, 371, 420, 423
R v Parliamentary Comr for Administration ex parte Balchin [1997] JPL 917, 101
R v Parliamentary Comr for Administration ex parte Dyer [1994] 1 All ER 375, 101
R v Parliamentary Comr for Standards [1998] 1 WLR 669, 249
R v Port of London Authority Ltd ex parte Kynoch [1919] 1 KB 176, 387
R v Port Talbot BC ex parte Jones [1988] 2 All ER 207, 403
R v Preston [1993] 4 All ER 638, 182
R v Radio Authority ex parte Bull [1997] 2 All ER 561, 277, 379, 398
R v Registrar of Companies ex parte Central Bank of India [1985] 2 All ER 79, 432
R v Rimmington [2005] UKHL 63, 119
R v Sang [1979] 2 All ER 222, 531
R v Sargent [2003] 1 AC 347, 533
R v Secretary of State for Education ex parte Begbie [2000], 389, 390, 393
R v Secretary of State for Employment ex parte Equal Opportunities Commission [1992] 1 All ER 545, 241
R v Secretary of State for the Environment ex parte Kirkstall Valley Campaign Ltd [1996] 3 All ER 304, 409
R v Secretary of State for the Environment ex parte Rose Theatre Trust [1990] 1 QB 504, 422
R v Secretary of State for the Environment, Transport and the Regions ex parte Spath Holme Ltd [2000] 1 All ER 884, 383
R v Secretary of State for Foreign and Commonwealth Affairs ex parte Everett [1989] 1 All ER 655, 429
R v Secretary of State for Foreign and Commonwealth Affairs ex parte Quark Fishing Ltd [2006] 1 AC, 3, 192, 193, 419, 460, 462
R v Secretary of State for Foreign and Commonwealth Affairs ex parte Rees-Mogg [1994] 1 All ER 457, 196, 422

R v Secretary of State for Foreign and Commonwealth Affairs ex parte World Development Movement Ltd [1995] 1 All ER 611, 290, 295, 384, 422
R v Secretary of State for the Foreign and Commonwealth Office ex parte Indian Association of Alberta [1982] QB 892, 192
R v Secretary of State for Health ex parte C [2000] FLR 471, 312
R v Secretary of State for Health ex parte US Tobacco International Inc [1992] 1 All ER 212, 391
R v Secretary of State for the Home Dept ex parte Adams [1995] All ER (EC)177, 448
R v Secretary of State for the Home Dept ex parte Bentley [1993] 4 All ER 442, 429
R v Secretary of State for the Home Dept ex parte Benwell [1985] QB 554, 424
R v Secretary of State for the Home Dept ex parte Cheblak [1991] 2 All ER 319, 418
R v Secretary of State for the Home Dept ex parte Daly [2001] 3 All ER 433, 398, 401
R v Secretary of State for the Home Dept ex parte Doody [1993] 3 All ER 92, 410
R v Secretary of State for the Home Dept ex parte Fayed [1997] 1 All ER 228, 404
R v Secretary of State for the Home Dept ex parte Fire Brigades Union [1995] 2 All ER 244, 144, 154–55, 175, 286, 290, 316, 369, 370, 399, 429
R v Secretary of State for the Home Dept ex parte Hargreaves [1997] 1 All ER 397, 392
R v Secretary of State for the Home Dept ex parte Hindley [2001] 1 AC, 387
R v Secretary of State for the Home Dept ex parte Khan [1985] 1 All ER 40, 390, 391, 392, 404
R v Secretary of State for the Home Dept ex parte McQuillan [1995] 4 All ER 400, 447
R v Secretary of State for the Home Dept ex parte Northumbria Police Authority [1988] QB 26, 310, 316
R v Secretary of State for the Home Dept ex parte Olahinde [1991] 1 AC 254, 402
R v Secretary of State for the Home Dept ex parte Phansopkar [1976] QB 606, 51
R v Secretary of State for the Home Dept ex parte Pierson [1998] AC 539, 131, 376
R v Secretary of State for the Home Dept ex parte Ruddock [1987] 2 All ER 518, 315
R v Secretary of State for the Home Dept ex parte Simms [1999] 2 AC 115, 11, 119, 132, 174, 376, 384, 443, 459, 482, 485
R v Secretary of State for the Home Dept ex parte Swati [1986] 1 All ER 717, 420
R v Secretary of State for the Home Dept ex parte Venables [1997] 3 All ER 97, 146, 383
R v Secretary of State for Social Services ex parte Association of Metropolitan Authorities [1986] 1 WLR 1, 420
R v Secretary of State for Social Services ex parte Joint Council for the Welfare of Immigrants [1996] 4 All ER 385, 130
R v Secretary of State for Social Services ex parte Sherwin [1996] 32 BMLR 1, 342, 343
R v Secretary of State for Social Services ex parte Wellcome Foundation Ltd [1987] 2 All ER 1025, 385
R v Secretary of State for Trade ex parte Anderson Strathclyde plc [1983] 2 All ER 233, 244
R v Secretary of State for Trade and Industry ex parte Greenpeace [1998] Envir LR 415, 422
R v Secretary of State for Transport ex parte Factortame [1990] 2 AC 85, 172
R v Secretary of State for Transport ex parte Factortame (No 2) [1991] 1 AC 603, 172, 221, 308, 553
R v Secretary of State for Transport ex parte Factortame (No 4) [1996] QB 404, 221
R v Secretary of State for Transport ex parte Factortame (No 5) [2000] 1 AC 524, 221
R v Secretary of State for Transport ex parte Pegasus Holidays (London) Ltd [1989] 2 All ER 481, 405
R v Secretary of State for Transport ex parte Richmond upon Thames LBC (No 4) [1996] 4 All ER 903, 410
R v Sefton Metropolitan BC ex parte Help the Aged [1997] 4 All ER 532, 387
R v Shaylor [2002] 2 All ER 477, 319, 340, 474, 484, 523
R v Sheer Metalcraft Ltd [1954] 1 All ER 542, 145, 297
R v Shoreditch Assessment Committee ex parte Morgan [1910] 2 KB 859, 377
R v Somerset CC ex parte Fewings [1995] 1 All ER 513, 29, 84, 105, 125, 369, 376, 383, 385
R v Somerset CC ex parte Garnett [1998] JEL 161, 422
R v Sussex Justices ex parte McCarthy [1924] 1 KB 256, 406
R v Waltham Forest LBC ex parte Baxter [1988] QB 419, 387

R v West Midlands Chief Constable ex parte Wiley [1994] 1 All ER 702, 527
R v Wicks [1998] AC 92, 374
Racz v Home Office [1994] 1 All ER 97, 418
Rantzen v Mirror Group Newspapers Ltd [1994] QB 670, 125, 494
Raymond v Honey [1983] 1 AC 1, 376
Re Clifford and O'Sullivan [1921] 2 AC 570, 535
Re GA (a child) [2001] 1 ECR 43, 471
Re G (Adoption) (Unmarried Couple) [2009] 1 AC 175, 460
Re Golden Chemical Products Ltd [1976] Ch 300, 340, 402
Re Guardian News and Media Ltd [2010] 2 All ER 799, 498
Re HK (an infant) [1967] 2 QB 617, 404
Re Lonrho plc [1990] 2 AC 154, 486
Re McKerr [2004] 1 WLR 807, 53, 196
Re Medicaments and Related Classes of Goods (No 2) [2001] 1 WLR 700, 408
Re Officer L [2007] 4 All ER 965, 411, 446
Re Parliamentary Privileges Act 1770 [1958] AC 331, 244
Re Racal Communications Ltd [1981] AC 374, 378
Re S (a child) [2004] 4 All ER 683, 487, 498
Re Webster (A Child) No 1 (2006) EWHC 2733, 486
Rees v UK (1986) 9 EHRR 56, 444, 451, 476
Reference re Amendment of the Constitution of Canada (1982) 105 DLR [3d] 1, 58, 60
Reilly v R [1934] AC 176, 339
Reynolds v Times Newspapers Ltd [2001] 2 AC 127, 491, 494
Ridge v Baldwin [1964] AC 40, 79, 373, 404, 405
Riordan v War Office [1959] 3 All ER 552, 339
Rivlin v Bilankin [1953] 1 QB 485, 242
RJR Macdonald Inc v Canada (A-G) [1995] 127 DLRI, 474
Roberts v Hopwood [1925] AC 578, 376, 384
Roberts v Parole Board [2006] 2 All ER 39, 24, 124, 131, 405, 530
Robinson v Secretary of State for Northern Ireland [2002] UKHL 32, 12, 51, 156, 348, 357
Rogers v Secretary of State for the Home Dept [1973] AC 388, 527
Rost v Edwards [1990] 2 All ER 641, 243, 245, 249, 251
Rowe and Davies v UK [2000] 30 EHRR 1, 528
Rowland v Environment Agency [2004] 3 WLR 249, 389
Roy v Kensington, Chelsea and Westminster Family Practitioner Committee [1992] 1 AC 624, 426
Runa Begum v Tower Hamlets London BC [2003] 1 All ER 731, 381, 382, 426

S v UK [2008] 25 BHRC 537, 451
S (children) (care plan) [2002] 2 All ER 192, 465
Salamander AG v European Parliament [2000] All ER (EC) 754, 216
Salesi v Italy (1993) 26 EHRR 187, 381
Saltpetre Case (1607) 12 Rep 12, 381
Schenk v Switzerland [1988] ECHR App no 10862/84 Series A no 140, 531
Schmidt v Secretary of State for Home Affairs [1969] 2 Ch 149, 388, 404
Science Research Council v Nasse [1980] AC 1028, 527
Scott v National Trust [1998] 2 All ER 705, 423
Seal v Chief Constable of South Wales Police [2007] 4 All ER 177, 374
Secretary of State for Education and Science v Tameside Metropolitan BC [1977] AC 1014, 105, 380, 388, 400
Secretary of State for the Home Dept v AF and Others [2008] Times 29th October 134, 129, 529
Secretary of State for the Home Dept v E [2008] 1 All ER 699, 447, 542, 544
Secretary of State for the Home Dept v JJ [2008] 1 All ER 613, 373, 374, 441, 446, 447, 473, 543
Secretary of State for the Home Dept v MB [2008] 1All ER 657, 129, 411, 447, 463, 516, 529, 544
Secretary of State for the Home Dept v Nasseri [2009] 2 WLR 1190, 466
Secretary of State for the Home Dept v Rehman [2002] 1 All ER 122, 447
Secretary of State for Justice v Jones [2009] UKHL 22, 421
Selisto v Finland (2006) 42 EHRR 144 Shah v Barnet London BC [1983] 2 AC 309, 487
Sharma v Browne-Antoine [2007] 1WLR 780, 126
Sheriff of Middlesex Case (1840) 11 Ad & El 273, 252
Shrewsbury and Atcham BC v Secretary of State for Communities and Local

Government [2008] EWCA Civ 148, 312, 315, 374
Sigurjónnson v Iceland (1993) 16 EHRR 462, 468
Sim v Stretch [1936] 2 All ER 1237, 491
Sivasubramaniam v Wandsworth County Court [2003] 1 WLR 475, 420
Skinner v Railway Labor Executives' Association 489 US 602, 514
Slim v Daily Telegraph Ltd [1968] 2 QB 157, 492
Smith v East Elloe RDC [1956] AC 736, 374
Smith v Kvaener Cement Foundations Ltd [2006] 3 All ER 593, 407
Smith and Grady v UK (2000) 29 EHRR 493, 401
Somersett's Case (1772) 68, St Tr 80, 77
Somerville v Scottish Ministers [2007] 1 WLR 2734, 351
South Bucks DC v Porter [2004] 4 All ER 775, 411
South East Asia Fire Brick Sdn Bhd v Non-Metallic Mineral Products Manufacturing Employees Union [1981] AC 363, 379
Southwark LBC v Tanner [2001] 1 AC 1, 386, 417, 452
Sporrong and Lonnroth v Sweden (1982) 5 EHRR 35, 445
State of Mauritius v Khoyratty [2006] 2 WLR 1330, 44
Stefan v General Medical Council [1999] 1 WLR 1293, 410
Stockdale v Hansard (1839) 9 Ad & E 1, 162, 243, 252
Stourton v Stourton (1963) P, 302, 239
Strauss Case (1956/7) HC 305 225, 246
Stretch v UK (2004) 38 EHRR 12, 389
Stringer v Minister of Housing and Local Government [1971] 1 All ER 65, 388
Sunday Times v UK (1979–80) 2 EHRR 245, 473, 488, 493
Sunday Times (No 2) v UK (1992) 14 EHRR 229, 525

Taylor v Chief Constable of the Thames Valley Police [2004] 3 All ER 503, 119
Taylor v Lawrence [2002] 3 All ER 353, 409
Tesco Stores v Secretary of State for the Environment [1995], 382, 384, 400
Thoburn v Sunderland City Council [2002] 4 All ER 156, 11, 51, 164–65, 172
Thomas v Luxembourg (2003) 36 EHRR 359, 487
Thomas v Sawkins [1935] 2 KB 249, 507
Thomas v Sorrell (1674) Vaughan 330, 74
Thompson and Venables v News Group Newspapers Ltd [2001] 1 All ER 908, 445, 490
Three Rivers DC v Bank of England (No 3) [2003] 2 AC 1, 418
Tolstoy Miloslavsky v UK (1995) 20 EHRR 442, 494
Tomlinson v Congleton DC [2003] 3 All ER 1122, 37
Toussaint v AG of St Vincent and the Grenadines [2008] 1 All ER 1, 244
Town Investments Ltd v Dept of the Environment [1977] 1 All ER 813, 303, 326
Trapp v Mackie [1979] 1 All ER 489, 142
Tre Tractorer Aktebolag v Sweden (1989) 13 EHRR 309, 381
Trustees of the Dennis Rye Pension Fund v Sheffield City Council [1997] 4 All ER 747, 426
Tsfayo v UK (2009) 48 EHRR 18, 382
Tweed v Parade Commission for Northern Ireland [2007] 2 All ER 273, 419
Tyrer v UK [1978] 2 EHRR 1, 445

V v UK (1999) 30 EHRR 121, 146
Van Colle v Chief Constable of Hertfordshire Police [2006] 3 All ER 963, 445
Van de Hurk v Netherlands (1984) 18 EHRR 481, 412
Van der Val v Netherlands [2000] The Times, 22 February, 224
Van Duyn v The Home Office [1974] 3 All ER 178, 217, 219
Vauxhall Estates Ltd v Liverpool Corporation [1932] 1 KB 733, 164
VGT v Switzerland (2002) 34 EHRR 159, 487
Virdi v Law Society [2010] 3 All ER 653, 408, 409
Von Hannover v Germany [2004] 40 EHRR 1, 452, 483, 497, 498

Wainwright v Home Office [2003] 4 All ER 969, 66
Walker v Baird [1892] AC 491, 201
Walker v UK [2006] ECHR App no 37212/02, 456
Wandsworth LBC v Michalak [2002] 4 All ER 1136, 455, 475
Wandsworth LBC v Winder [1985] AC, 426
Wang v Comrs of Inland Revenue [1995] 1 All ER 367, 402

Ward v Police Service of Northern Ireland [2008] 1 All ER 517, 540
Wason v Walter [1868] 4 QB 73, 247
Watkins v Secretary of State for the Home Dept [2006] 2 All ER 353, 11, 418
Weaver v London and Quadrant Housing Trust (2009) EWCA Civ 507(Admin), 423, 424, 469
Webb v EMO Cargo (UK) Ltd [1992] 4 All ER 929, 220
Webb v Minister of Housing and Local Government [1965] 2 All ER 193, 220
West Rand Central Gold Mining Co v R [1905] 2 KB 391, 299, 201
Western Fish Products Ltd v Penwith DC and Another [1981] 2 All ER 204, 388
Westminster Corporation v London and North Western Railway [1905] AC 426, 385
Wheeler v Leicester City Council [1985] 2 All ER 1106, 374, 400
White and Collins v Minister of Health [1939] 2 KB 838, 377
WH Smith Do It All Ltd v Peterborough City Council [1991] 4 All ER 193, 145
Wilkinson v Kitzinger [2006] The Times, 9 August, 449
Williams v Home Office (No 2) [1981] 1 All ER 1151, 342, 527
Wilson v First County Trust [2003] 4 All ER 97, 142, 156, 389, 459, 463, 466, 471, 475
Wingrove v UK (1997) 24 EHRR 1, 501
Winterwerp v Netherlands (1979) ECHR Series A vol 33, 381
Wolfe Tone's Case (1798) 27 St Tr 614, 77
Woolgar v Chief Constable of the Sussex Police [1999] 3 All ER 604, 525
World Wildlife Fund for Nature UK v Commission [1997] All ER (EC) 300, 224
Wychavon DC v Secretary of State [1994] The Times, 7 January, 219

X v Bedfordshire CC [1995] 2 AC 633, 95, 417
X v UK (1982] 4 EHRR 188, 190
X and Y v Netherlands (1985) 8 EHRR 235, 471
X Ltd v Morgan Grampian Publishers Ltd [1991] 1 AC 1, 53, 173, 491

YL v Birmingham City Council [2007] 3 All ER 957, 20, 423, 424, 452, 469, 470
Young, James and Webster v UK (1982) 4 EHRR 38, 119
Youssoupoff v Metro-Goldwyn-Mayer Pictures Ltd [1934] 50 TLR 581, 491

Z v UK [2002] 34 EHRR 3, 449, 467, 471, 473
Zamora The [1916] 2 AC 77, 429

Table of legislation

Access to Justice Act 1999, 150
Access to Personal Files Act 1987, 522
Act of Settlement 1700, 9, 50, 74, 108, 153, 262, 263, 304, 305, 324, 554
Act of Union with England 1706, 348
Act of Union with Ireland 1800, 77, 166
Act of Union with Scotland 1706, 108, 348
Act of the Union of Wales 1536, 359
Aliens Restrictions (Amendment) Act 1917, 502
Anti-Social Behaviour Act 2003, 506
Anti-Terrorism, Crime and Security Act 2001, 432, 456, 502, 533, 537, 541, 544
Appellate Jurisdiction Act 1876, 153
Armed Forces Act 2006, 84, 308
Australia Act 1986, 190

Bank of England Act 1998, 303, 328, 551
Bill of Rights 1688, 9, 50, 51, 54, 74, 75, 84, 234, 243, 244, 245, 246, 249, 251, 288, 301, 310, 377, 383, 389, 485
British Nationality Act 1981, 185–86
British Nationality (Falkland Islands) Act 1983, 186
British Nationality (Hong Kong) Act 1997, 186
British Overseas Territories Act 2002, 186, 190
Broadcasting Act 1990, 247, 488

Canada Act 1982, 165, 169, 190
Charities Act 2006, 501
Children Act 1989, 386, 465, 486
Church of England Assembly (Powers) Act 1919, 108
Church of Scotland Act 1921, 348
Civil Contingencies Act 2004, 236, 535
Civil List Acts 1952–75, 305
Civil Service (Management Functions) Act 1992, 326
Colonial Laws Validity Act 1865, 190
Communications Act 2003, 92, 277, 484, 488
Constitutional Reform Act 2005, 6, 50, 63, 97, 98, 99, 100, 102, 117, 141, 148, 149, 150, 151, 152, 153, 154, 157, 158, 326, 551, 555, 556
Constitutional Reform and Governance Act 2010, 50, 54, 88, 89, 96, 110, 182, 250, 257, 262, 263, 266, 296, 311, 313, 319, 337, 521, 551, 555
Contempt of Court Act 1981, 144, 147, 486, 489, 490
Corresponding Societies Act 1799, 121
Counter Terrorism Act 2008, 503, 537, 538, 541, 542, 544, 545
County Courts Act 1984, 97, 154
Courts Act 1971, 97, 154
Courts Act 2003, 97, 141, 147, 151, 153, 154
Courts and Legal Services Act 1990, 97, 494
Crime and Disorder Act 1998, 500, 503
Criminal Justice Act 2003, 146, 421
Criminal Justice and Court Services Act 2000, 146
Criminal Justice and Immigration Act 2008, 501, 502
Criminal Justice and Police Act 2001, 106, 511
Criminal Justice and Public Order Act 1994, 503, 504, 506, 510, 511, 532
Criminal Law Act 1967, 535
Criminal Procedure and Investigations Act 1996, 526, 527
Crown and Parliament Recognition Act 1689, 74
Crown Proceedings Act 1947, 308, 326, 417
Crown Proceedings (Armed Forces) Act 1987, 308

Data Protection Act 1998, 324, 520, 522
Defamation Act 1952, 156, 247, 485
Defamation Act 1996, 244, 247
Deregulation and Contracting Out Act 1994, 326, 403
Diplomatic Privileges Act 1964, 199
Disqualifications Act 2000, 263

Education (No 2) Act 1986, 485
Electoral Administration Act 2006, 262, 263, 265, 267, 268, 274, 276, 277, 278
Employment Act 1988, 339
Employment Rights Act 1996, 339, 526
Environmental Protection Act 1990, 485
European Communities Act 1972, 50, 51, 79, 144, 164, 171, 207, 217, 218, 289, 358

European Parliamentary Elections Act 1978, 222
European Parliamentary Elections Act 1999, 238
European Parliamentary Elections Act 2002, 215
European Union (Amendment) Act 2008, 196, 222
Exchequer and Audit Departments Acts 1866–957, 288, 295, 328
Extradition Act 2003, 203, 340

Football (Offences and Disorder) Act 1999, 503
Football (Disorder) Act 2000, 503
Forfeiture Act 1870, 257, 262
Fox's Libel Act 1792, 492, 502
Freedom of Information Act 2000, 51, 57, 60, 82, 88, 92, 183, 292, 294, 330, 335, 341, 361, 518–21, 551, 555, 556

Gender Recognition Act 2004, 50, 465
Government of Ireland Acts 1914, 1920, 238, 356
Government Resources and Accounts Act 2000, 183, 327
Government Trading Act 1990, 290
Government of Wales Act 1998, 346, 360
Government of Wales Act 2006, 63, 270, 346, 360
Greater London Authority Act 1999, 106, 270, 271, 362

Health Service Commissioners Act 1983, 324
Highways Act 1980, 509
His Majesty's Declaration of Abdication Act 1936, 304
Honours (Prevention of Corruption) Act 1925, 109, 259
House of Commons (Administration) Act 1978, 282
House of Commons (Disqualification) Act 1975, 84, 148, 262, 263
House of Commons (Disqualification) Act 1978, 340
Housing Corporation Act 2006, 130, 402
House of Lords Act 1999, 50, 233, 257, 258, 260, 556
Human Rights Act 1998, 8, 19, 26, 40, 50, 66, 95, 96, 99, 122, 124, 131, 134, 142, 145, 148, 164, 183, 185, 193, 197, 199, 201, 202, 220, 240, 245, 252, 304, 316, 350, 351, 355, 358, 360, 370, 376, 380, 384, 400, 401, 412, 418, 419, 423, 432, 439, 442, 443, 445, 450, 453, 459–77, 485, 489, 491, 496, 501, 502, 505, 507, 511, 515, 516, 525, 528, 532, 534, 536, 539, 551, 555, 556
Hunting Act 2004, 169, 238, 452

Identity Cards Act 2006, 531
Immigration Act 1971, 187, 316, 340
Immigration Act 1988, 187
Immigration, Asylum and Nationality Act 2006, 186, 187
Incitement to Disaffection Act 1934, 502
Income and Corporation Taxes Act 1988, 289
Inquiries Act 2005, 103, 147, 249
Insolvency Act 1986, 257, 262
Intelligence Services Act 1994, 322, 530, 531, 534
Interception of Communications Act 1985, 532
International Criminal Courts Act 2001, 202
Ireland Act 1949, 357
Irish Church Act 1879, 356
Irish Free State (Constitution) Act 1922, 356
Isle of Man Purchase Act 1765, 190

Judges' Remuneration Act 1965, 154
Judicial Committee Act 1833, 108, 263
Judicial Pensions and Retirement Act 1993, 153
Justice (Northern Ireland) Act 2002, 358, 359

Life Peerages Act 1958, 50, 258
Local Government Act 1972, 104, 376, 403
Local Government Act 1974, 102, 104
Local Government (Access to Information) Act 1985, 522
Lord Chancellor's Pension Act 1832, 149

Meeting of Parliament Act 1694, 74, 83, 234
Meeting of Parliament Act 1870, 236
Ministerial and Other Salaries Acts 1975, 1997, 54, 148, 263
Ministers of the Crown Act 1975, 54, 325, 326
Misuse of Drugs Act 1971, 464

National Audit Act 1983, 295, 296, 322
National Loans Fund Act 1968, 295, 296, 322
National Minimum Wages Act 1998, 322
Nationality, Immigration and Asylum Act 2002, 186, 187
Northern Ireland Act 1998, 63, 166, 271, 346, 348, 357
Northern Ireland (Emergency Provisions) Act 1978, 515, 537

Northern Ireland (Temporary Provisions) Act 1974, 537

Obscene Publications Act 1959, 486, 499
Official Secrets Act 1989, 518, 522–25, 526
Official Secrets Act 1911, 522

Parliament Acts 1911, 1949, 50, 64, 75, 78, 83, 151, 162, 167, 169, 170, 233, 234, 237, 238, 239, 259, 260, 353, 356, 554
Parliament (Elections and Meetings) Act 1943, 235
Parliamentary Commissioner Act 1967, 88, 101, 245, 324
Parliamentary Commissioner Act 1994, 101
Parliamentary Constituencies Act 1986, 263, 272
Parliamentary Elections and Political Parties Act 2009
Parliamentary and Health Services Commissioners Act 1987, 101
Parliamentary Papers Act 1840, 247, 252
Parliamentary Standards Act 2009, 250, 551
Peerage Act 1963, 258
Planning Act 1990, 382
Planning and Compulsory Purchase Act 2004, 105
Police Act 1996, 106, 502, 507
Police Act 1997, 106, 322, 534
Police and Criminal Evidence Act 1984, 509, 531, 540, 541
Police Reform Act 2002, 106, 107
Political Parties, Elections and Referendums Act 2000, 45, 49, 263, 265, 266, 267, 268, 274, 275, 276, 277, 293, 551
Pollution Prevention and Control Act 1999, 144
Prevention of Corruption Act 1916, 249
Prevention of Terrorism Act 2005, 94, 432, 456, 529, 537, 541
Prevention of Terrorism (Temporary Provisions) Act 1974, 537
Prevention of Terrorism (Temporary Provisions) Act 1984, 537
Prosecution of Offences Act 1985, 107, 302
Protection from Harassment Act 1997, 503, 511
Provisional Collection of Taxes Act 1968, 289
Public Audit (Wales) Act 2004, 183
Public Bodies (Admission to Meetings) Act 1960, 522
Public Bodies (Corrupt Practices) Act 1889, 109, 249
Public Interest Disclosure Act 1998, 526
Public Order Act 1936, 503, 510
Public Order Act 1986, 500, 501, 503, 505, 506, 509
Public Records Acts 1958, 1967, 1975, 521
Public Services Ombudsman (Wales) Act 2005, 102, 361

Racial and Religious Hatred Act 2006, 501
Railways Act 2005, 92, 94
Reform Act 1832, 259
Regency Acts 1937–53, 305
Regional Assemblies (Preparations) Act 2003, 362
Regional Development Agencies Act 1998, 362
Regulation of Investigatory Powers Act 2000, 340, 432, 532, 534
Rehabilitation of Offenders Act 1974, 492
Representation of the People Act 1948, 78, 264
Representation of the People Act 1981, 262
Representation of the People Act 1983, 83, 266, 267, 275, 277, 278
Representation of the People Act 1985, 235, 263, 268
Representation of the People Act 2000, 187, 263, 267, 268, 273, 274
Royal Assent Act 1967, 162, 286
Royal Marriages Act 1772, 304
Royal Titles Act 1953, 304

Scotland Act 1998, 49, 153, 166, 239, 270, 346, 347, 348–49, 350, 351, 352, 353
Scottish Parliament (Constituencies) Act 2004, 349
Security Services Act 1989, 432, 524, 530, 531
Security Services Act 1996, 531
Seditious Meetings Act 1817, 505
Septennial Act 1715, 234
Serious Organised Crime and Police Act 2005, 503, 505, 506, 511
Sexual Offences (Amendment) Act 2000, 238
State Immunity Act 1978, 126, 198, 199, 200
Statute of Wales 1084, 359
Statute of Westminster 1931, 169
Statutory Instruments Act 1946, 79, 122, 144, 296
Succession to the Crown Act 1707, 263
Supreme Court (Senior Courts) Act 1981, 97, 153, 409, 415, 417, 419, 420, 421

Terrorism Act 2000, 187, 442, 502, 503, 537, 540
Terrorism Act 2006, 503, 537, 540

Terrorist Asset Freezing (Temporary Provisions) Act 2010, 544
Town and Country Planning Act 1990, 382
Transport and Works Act 1992, 286
Tribunals and Inquiries Acts 1958, 1971, 1992, 79, 99, 103, 154, 372, 378, 410
Tribunals, Courts and Enforcement Act 2007, 97, 98, 370, 415, 417, 420

Utilities Act 2000, 92

Video Recordings Act 1984, 488

War Crimes Act 1991, 238
War Damage Act 1965, 163, 311, 535
Welsh Church Act 1914, 238

Acknowledgements

The author and the publisher are grateful to the following rights holders for permission to include copyright material: Taylor & Francis Group and University of Chicago Press for Hayek, *Law, Legislation and Liberty: The Mirage of Social Justice* (1978) vol 1, 128; John Murray Publishers for Sampson, *Who Runs This Place?* (2004); The Orion Publishing Group Limited for Berlin, *The Hedgehog and the Fox* (Weidenfeld & Nicolson 1953); and Independent Print Limited and Guardian News & Media Ltd for the small quotes taken from the *Independent*, the *Guardian* and the *Observer*.

Every effort has been made to trace copyright holders, but if any have been inadvertently overlooked the publisher would be pleased to make the necessary arrangements at the first opportunity.

References

Specific references to books and articles in the text are to writings that expand on the point in question. The Further Reading at the end of each chapter discusses fundamental and controversial general issues for those who require greater depth or more ideas and points of view. Short references in the text are to the Further Reading. Unless otherwise stated, the main classical works cited throughout are as follows:

Bagehot, *The English Constitution* (2nd edn, Kegan Paul 1902)

Dicey, *An Introduction to the Study of the Law of the Constitution* (8th edn, Macmillan 1915; 10th edn, Macmillan 1958)

Hobbes, *Leviathan*, ed Minogue (Dent 1973)

Locke, *Two Treatises of Government*, ed Laslett (Cambridge University Press 1960)

Mill, *Utilitarianism, On Liberty and Considerations of Representative Government*, ed Acton (Dent 1972)

Montesquieu 'L'Esprit des Lois', extracted in Stirk and Weigall (eds), *An Introduction to Political Ideas* (Pinter 1995)

Paine, *The Thomas Paine Reader*, ed Foot and Kramnick (Penguin 1987)

Part I

The framework of the constitution

Chapter 1

Introduction: constitutional themes and structures

The effective limitation of power is the most important problem of social order. Government is indispensable for the formation of such an order only to protect against coercion and violence from others. But as soon as to achieve this, government successfully claims the monopoly of coercion and violence it becomes a threat to individual freedom. To limit this power was the great aim of the founders of constitutional government. (Hayek, *Law, Legislation and Liberty* (1978) vol 1, 128)

1.1 What is a constitution?

In this chapter I shall introduce some basic concepts and themes relating to the nature of a constitution. The general idea of a constitution is relatively simple. A constitution provides the fundamental principles that create the structure and purposes of a human organisation. This has two purposes: firstly to run the organisation efficiently in the light of its goals; secondly to prevent those in charge of the organisation from abusing their powers. Conflict between these purposes is at the heart of the law.

Any organisation might have a constitution; for example most golf clubs do so. Similar basics apply to the constitution of a state such as the UK. Thus Lord Bingham, a leading judge, suggests that 'any constitution, whether of a state, a trade union, a college, a club or other institution seeks to lay down and define ... the main offices in which authority is vested and the powers which may be exercised (or not exercised) by the holders of those offices' (*R v Secretary of State for Foreign and Commonwealth Affairs, ex p Quark Fishing Ltd* [2006] at [12]).

In almost all countries the constitution comprises a special document or set of documents distinct from and superior to the ordinary law. The constitution in this sense usually has a status superior to the rest of the law, in the sense that it can be altered only by a special procedure such as a public referendum. The term 'constitution' is sometimes used as if it means only this but, as we shall see below, the UK has no written constitution in this sense. We have a constitution in the wider sense set out above of a group of principles and mechanisms dealing with the structure, powers and accountability of government and serving the interests of those in power. Our constitution consists of numerous pieces of ordinary legislation on particular topics of constitutional importance that have attracted the lawmakers' concern over the years, together with decisions of courts arising out of disputes generated by individuals, and a mass of informal political practices and understandings between officials known as conventions (see Section 3.4).

Insofar as the constitution has a special status, in the UK this is based on no more than the respect and reverence that politicians, officials and courts show for principles that they regard as 'constitutional'. There is a perpetual debate as to whether we should sacrifice the flexibility and benefit to the powerful of our untidy, pragmatic and secretive constitution in favour of the relative openness and certainty of a fully written constitution.

'Administrative law', which forms part of this book, deals with the detailed operations of government, especially with the rights of the individual against government. There is no hard and fast line between constitutional law and administrative law, which could be regarded as an application of constitutional law at a detailed level. Administrative law might deal with particular government functions such as immigration or taxation or the work of the numerous special tribunals and inquiries that decide disputes involving the decisions of government agencies. This book does not attempt to cover administrative law comprehensively since the subject has its own separate texts. Chapters 17, 18 and 19 on judicial review of administrative action deal with the core of administrative law. Other matters concerned with administrative law such as special tribunals, public inquiries and ombudsmen are discussed in their context where they raise general constitutional issues.

1.1.1 Concerns of the constitution

Constitutional law deals primarily with the following:

- the choosing and removing of rulers;
- the relationship between the different branches of government;
- the dividing up of powers geographically, for example the relationship between the central government and the devolved governments of Scotland, Wales and Northern Ireland;
- the relationship between the state and external bodies;
- the accountability of government;
- the rights of the citizen in relation to government.

This is reflected in the structure of this book. From the legal perspective there is an emphasis on methods of settling disputes, so the courts play a more prominent role than would be the case when studying the constitution from a political point of view.

Newer issues have placed the traditional model of the constitution under strain. In particular, state constitutions are challenged by globalisation, which in this context means the relative ease with which resources can be moved around the world, the international nature of problems such as environmental protection and the fact that individual countries are increasingly dependent on others for resources and security. State laws are sometimes ineffective for example in dealing with terrorism, environmental problems, human trafficking and financial corruption. Matters concerning international affairs have traditionally depended on the consent of each country. The constitution provides filter mechanisms which to a certain extent recognise and control the influences of international actions and relationships on our own law and vice versa (see Chapter 9), but otherwise the law has not adapted to globalisation. In most countries, particularly the UK, constitutional law is still based on seventeenth-century ideas of self-contained sovereign states.

1.1.2 The foundations of a constitution

In the UK the current regime claims to be democratic, meaning in our case that the people choose and remove the government according to rules made by the government. A constitution can of course adopt any form of government. A constitution is valid or 'legitimate' if enough of the people whom it concerns, both officials and members of the public, recognise it as worthy of obedience so that it is broadly viable. UK law takes this pragmatic view in the context for example of recognising the legality of a rebellion (see *Madzimbamuto v Lardner-Burke* (1969): takeover of a British colony by a group of white settlers held not valid because they were not yet fully in control).

Possible reasons for the acceptance of a system of government such as ideology, fear, self-interest, moral fervour and so on are irrelevant to its legal validity. The herd instinct of human beings, coupled with the desire of some individuals to impose themselves on others, may well be a sufficient explanation. On the other hand, a general sense among the people that the constitution is morally good, or at least that it is in their interests, might help the rulers stay in power. John Locke, the seventeenth-century philosopher who is often said to be the father of liberalism, thought the people had a right to rebel against an unjust constitution, thus justifying the seventeenth-century English revolution against the Crown.

The UK constitution has held together since the end of the seventeenth century by a combination of flexibility in supporting the accumulation of wealth by interests, today mainly professional and business, who have privileged access to governmental officials, and a predominant culture of deference to authority among the general population. In England patronage in the sense of giving access to power in return for favours has at least since mediaeval times been an important driving force in the conduct of government and the evolution of its institutions.

'Legitimacy' might also refer to an external standard that can be used to assess the constitution. The problem here of course is to identify what this is, if it is to be more than our personal preferences. Lawyers for example might refer to 'the rule of law', meaning widely accepted vague community values such as justice as identified by themselves. Thus legitimacy depends partly upon what Ward has called 'the popular imagination' (*A State of Mind? The English Constitution and the Popular Imagination* (Sutton 2000)). This is not confined to formal legal texts and the pronouncements of officials but includes art, drama, literature such as novels and poetry, and the press.

The symbolic device of the 'social contract' is often used with the aim of giving the constitution a plausibly objective foundation (see eg Section 2.3.5). The social contract is an attempt to explain why free and equal individuals should subject themselves to government. It claims that the people agree to obey the constitution, pay taxes and follow other policies in return for the government providing public services, comprising at least security and keeping order. It also provides a basis for those who claim that 'rights' such as welfare benefits are conditional upon obligations of good behaviour. However the social contract theory is somewhat implausible in that nobody has actually entered into any such contract and it does not explain why lawbreakers should not validly claim that they do not recognise the constitution. The social contract is therefore an example of the political ideology chosen by those who successfully claim power, in this case a 'liberal' ideology (Chapter 2).

1.1.3 The most basic constitutional concepts

Two closely related ideas have influenced democratic constitutions of the kind found in countries influenced by European cultures. They are 'the rule of law' and 'the separation of powers'. The rule of law is highly ambivalent. Its primary meaning is that it is a good thing to have rules made by a formal public process and known in advance. This helps the organisation to run effectively by keeping order and producing certainty. However it ignores the content of the rules, whether they are morally good or bad, and the question of who makes them. For example a concentration camp might be subject to the rule of law in this sense. A wider version of the rule of law invokes certain moral and political ideas which are claimed to be especially associated with law in the sense of government by rules. These include justice and fairness, openness, equality and freedom policed by independent courts.

The second concept, the separation of powers, requires that government be divided up into different branches of equal status and importance. This is intended to prevent one person or group holding dominant power. Each branch can restrain the others since any major decision would require the cooperation of all branches. The branches concerned are usually threefold, namely the legislature that makes the law, the executive that administers the country day-to-day and the judiciary – the courts that adjudicate on disputes concerning the law. In the UK, although we do have the three branches, they are not clearly separate according to any systematic plan. There is a relatively strong separation between the judicial branch and the other branches but there is a large overlap between the executive and the legislature in that all ministers must also be members of the legislature (Parliament). Moreover it is the executive that usually proposes the laws to be made by the legislature. This overlap partly explains why the legislative branch is widely regarded as weak and ineffectual as a means of controlling the executive and making laws.

The separation of powers is not of course foolproof. Firstly in order to avoid stalemate someone must have the last word. In particular there is a long-running and unresolved argument as to whether the elected lawmaking branch, Parliament, should do so or the unelected but independent courts. Different countries have reached different conclusions. For example in the US the Supreme Court has the last word subject only to an elaborate process for changing the constitution (*Marbury v Madison* [1803]). In the UK the predominant belief is that Parliament should have the last word but there are those who would give it to the judges (see Section 8.5). Secondly much hangs on who appoints the leading members of each branch since whoever does so could pack each branch with cronies or sycophants. This is a particularly murky area since most senior appointments are made by the Prime Minister, the party leader who heads the executive branch. However by virtue of the Constitutional Reform Act 2005 there is a relatively independent mechanism for appointing judges (see Section 7.8.2).

Some constitutions make grandiose and broad claims to shared ideals and purposes. For example the Constitution of Ireland refers to 'seeking to promote the common good with due observance of Prudence, Justice and Charity so that the dignity and freedom of the individual may be assured, true social order attained, the unity of our country restored and concord established with other nations'. The French Constitution famously refers to 'the Rights of Man' and the 'equality and solidity of the peoples who compose [the Republic]' (Art 1). The UK constitution makes no such claims, at least explicitly.

Many constitutions contain a list of basic rights of the citizen. These vary from state to state, reflecting the political culture of the ruling group in question. Constitutions also vary in the extent to which the courts may police other branches of government in respect of these rights. In the family of liberal democratic states to which the UK belongs these rights are primarily 'negative' rights in the sense of rights not to be interfered with by the state. They include the right to life, the right to personal freedom, the right to a fair trial, the right to privacy and family life, the right to freedom of expression, the right to assembly and association, the right to freedom of religion and the right to protection for property. 'Positive rights', such as the right to a decent standard of living, the right to a good environment and the right to medical care, might be regarded as equally important, but because these require hard political choices between priorities and large-scale public expenditure they are often regarded as a matter for the ordinary political process rather than as fully fledged legal rights enshrined in a constitution. Enforcement by a court would be practically impossible. Nevertheless some positive rights appear in many constitutions, for example those of Germany, Poland and Portugal. Some constitutions, for example that of Switzerland, also impose duties on citizens such as military service and voting.

1.1.4 Definitions of a constitution

It is probably not worth attempting to find a precise definition of a constitution, which is more a general idea than a precise legal concept. Like many vague concepts the term is best defined by how it is used in practice. Definitions vary according to the concerns of the particular definer. Many writers have tried to capture the essence of a constitution, each emphasising different aspects. The examples below are intended to illustrate the variety of approaches.

- Dicey (1915, 22), whose writings had a profound influence on how lawyers imagine the UK constitution, gives a wide definition: 'all rules which directly or indirectly affect the distribution and exercise of the sovereign power in the state'.
- King (2001) also offers a wide definition: 'the set of the most important rules that regulate the relations amongst the different parts of the government of a given country and also the relations between the different parts of the government and the people of the country'.
- Laws ('The Constitution, Morals and Rights' [1996] PL 622), a senior judge, described a constitution as: 'that set of legal rules which govern the relationship in a state between the ruler and the ruled'.
- Friedrich (*Limited Government: A Comparison* (Prentice Hall 1974) 21) exemplifies a romantic approach that stresses the (assumed) consent of the community: 'a constitution is the ordering and dividing of the exercise of political power by that group in an existent community who are able to secure the consent of the community and who thereby make manifest the power of the community itself'.
- Tully ('The Unfreedom of the Moderns' (2002) 65 MLR 204) offers a legally oriented definition capturing the notion that the constitution has a special status: 'the cluster of "supreme" or "essential" principles, rules and procedures to which other laws, institutions and governing authorities within the association are subject'.
- Marshall (2003, 31) adds 'a list of statutes or instruments that have an entrenched status and can be amended or repealed only by a special procedure'. As the chaotic nature of constitutional reform shows (see Section 24.1) we have no constitution of this kind.

1.2 Written and unwritten constitutions

As we have seen, most constitutions are set out in a single document or related group of documents which have the force of law, usually being superior to all other kinds of law in that laws which conflict with the constitution can be struck down by the courts. They also usually contain 'entrenched' provisions which protect the constitution from being changed by the government of the day, for example a referendum of the people or a two-thirds majority of the lawmaking assembly.

The UK has no written constitution in this sense. Its legal principles and rules, if written at all, are to be found in the same documents as the sources of any law, namely:

- Acts of Parliament (statutes) usually dealing with particular issues such as reforms to the court system;
- cases decided by the courts which establish precedents on particular issues often relating to individual rights.

Rules from these two sources can be changed in the same way as any other law. In this sense they are constitutional only because of the matters they deal with.

There are also many rules, practices and customs which are not law in that they cannot be directly enforced by the courts. They get their force only because they are consistently obeyed. The most important of these are known as 'constitutional conventions' (see Section 3.4). It is a prominent feature of the UK constitution that many of our most fundamental constitutional arrangements rely on conventions; for example the existence of and most of the powers of the Prime Minister have no legal force. Some conventions are recorded in writing, although this does not in itself give them greater validity. Others are informal and haphazard, passed on by word of mouth.

Our unwritten constitution might also include important international treaties such as the European Union treaties and the European Convention on Human Rights (ECHR). Treaties do not have the force of law unless enacted in domestic law as Acts of Parliament. For this reason our constitution is a *dualist* constitution. (The treaties mentioned above have in fact been enacted as statutes in the UK, although in the case of the ECHR only partly so (Human Rights Act 1998).)

A written constitution will not of course include all the rules needed for governing the country but will select what are considered to be the most basic rules. This varies considerably between different states. For example the methods of voting are important by any standards but do not feature in many constitutions. Some constitutions, such as that of the US, are relatively short and expressed in general terms. Others, like that of Portugal, run to hundreds of detailed pages. In his Hamlyn Lectures (2001), King distinguished in this context between what he called 'Capital C' constitutions, that is written ones, and 'small c' constitutions. Most countries have a mixture of both. The UK has only a small c constitution. We may have an incomplete and partly corrupt constitution but the term 'constitution', although originally meaning a government enactment, was used in Britain to describe our basic governmental principles at least by the seventeenth century.

Ridley (1988) by contrast claims that the UK has no constitution at all since he believes that constitutions must be superior to the government of the day and not changeable by it. Without a written constitution the UK seems to fail this test. However things may not be as they seem. There are arguments and devices within UK law for limiting the ability of governments to make constitutional changes (see eg Sections 8.4.2, 8.4.3). Moreover a written constitution does not in itself guarantee that the government of the day cannot alter it. A written constitution can say anything. The matter depends upon the precise terms of the constitution and the political power of the ruling group. Perhaps students might consider Ridley's challenge at the end of their course.

Whether or not we have a constitution in a strict sense, the term 'constitutionalism' applies to the UK. Constitutionalism is the belief that a state should have arrangements that limit the powers of the rulers and give the ruling regime its moral authority (legitimacy). Constitutionalism includes both legal and political limits on government.

It requires government officials to be accountable for their actions to an independent body, although not necessarily a court. It requires checks and balances between different governmental organs (see Section 7.8) and proper controls within each governmental organ. In a democracy it requires frequent elections open to all and subject to rules which prevent any candidate from having an unfair advantage (see Section 12.10).

The idea of a written constitution is a legacy of the revolutionary period in eighteenth- and nineteenth-century Europe, when, with mixed success, widespread uprisings challenged traditional aristocratic, colonial and religious regimes. Since the start of the French Revolution in 1789 almost every other nation has adopted a written constitution, sometimes as a reaction against a hated previous regime and sometimes to mark a new event such as independence from colonial status. Israel, New Zealand and Saudi Arabia are often said to be without written constitutions. But Israel has a 'basic law' which covers some of the content of a constitution, and a project to create a constitution is in progress. In Saudi Arabia parts of the Koran are regarded as higher law serving the function of a constitution. New Zealand has a Constitution Act 1986 but as in the UK this is an ordinary Act of Parliament and the constitution comprises a mixture of ordinary laws, political practices and international treaties.

The UK constitution has developed pragmatically, usually out of accommodations struck between different sectional interests. Those who benefit from the arrangements, notably the larger political parties and the legal profession, value the appearance of continuity and tradition as a means of social cohesion (or social control).The main reason why the UK has no written constitution seems to be cultural since the British people seem in the main to defer to domineering personalities rather than to rely on legal rules.

A written constitution in the form of 'articles of government' was introduced in England by the revolutionary regime of Oliver Cromwell in 1653 but after a year was superseded by a military dictatorship. The restoration of Charles II in 1660 was then promoted as a return to ancient values which previous monarchs were supposed to have subverted. In 1688 Charles' successor, James II, was deposed by a coalition of business and property-owning interests centred on Parliament, the main lawmaking body. The settlement drew on existing traditions but modified them by legislation designed to subordinate the monarchy to Parliament (Bill of Rights 1688, Act of Settlement 1700). Thus the revolution sought to assert traditional practices against, on the one hand, radical claims to absolute rule by the king and, on the other, democratic claims by relatively small factions among the ordinary people. A wholesale redesign of the constitution was not therefore politically expedient. During the following centuries the aristocracy gradually conceded power to professional and commercial groups. Attempts at popular uprisings were successfully suppressed by a combination of force, buying off leaders and moderate concessions.

During the eighteenth century the unwritten constitution was widely admired as a source of stability and justice, and the idea of the 'rule of law' was associated with it. The judge-made common law in particular was regarded as embedded in community values. By contrast, written constitutions were associated with tyrannous regimes imposed by force. On the other hand British governments could act through laws which the system enabled them to change easily. Unless these were mediated by ideas of justice administered by independent courts they could also be an instrument of tyranny. Historians disagree as to how impartial the rule of law was in practice. Eighteenth- and early nineteenth-century politics is sometimes characterised as aristocratic oligarchy oiled by patronage and bribery with a ruthless enforcement of public order and property rights against the lower orders (eg Porter, *England in the Eighteenth Century* (Penguin 1990)). Latterly the UK constitution, with its absence of a constitution outside the control of the government of the day, its restricted voting system and its concentration of power in the hands of large political parties controlling the executive, has become less admired and is sometimes regarded as the least democratic constitution in Western Europe.

1.2.1 The merits of a written constitution

There is no agreement as to whether it is preferable to have a written constitution (see also Section 24.3). The main advantages of a written constitution are said to be its certainty in clarifying and limiting the powers of the government and its status as embodying fundamental values which are likely to have the consent of the people. If it can be changed only by a special procedure (entrenchment) a written constitution provides some assurance that important rules have the consent of the people outside the control of temporary ruling regimes or the limited perspectives of judges. In the UK context in *R (Southall) v Foreign Secretary* [2003] it was held that there is no principle that fundamental constitutional change requires the approval of the electorate.

However there is no reason why the people should have any part in making a written constitution, which is likely to be drawn up by the ruling elite at the time. Thus an unwritten constitution invites those in power to invent or manipulate 'customs' or 'conventions' to suit their own interests. The claim that the informal constitution can easily adjust to changing politics exemplifies this. Thus Burke's adversary, the democratic activist Thomas Paine (1737–1809), labelled the British government as 'power without right'. In *The Rights of Man*, Paine asserted that without a written constitution authorised directly by the people there was no valid constitution (1987, 220–21, 285–96).

In the case of an unwritten constitution, changes and reforms can come from many sources (see Section 24.1), which could be regarded as a means of limiting the power of an elite. Dicey for example considered that our constitution is strengthened by the fact the rule of law depends on decisions by the courts (see Section 6.4.2).

Another possible advantage is that a written constitution encourages a rationalistic process of constitutional design which ideally creates a constitution as a logical scheme which governments must work within and which is independent of the whims of particular governments. By contrast an unwritten constitution tends to develop pragmatically in response to short-term factors. For example, even though they have been in force only since 2000, the provisions giving devolved powers to Wales have been constantly tinkered with (see Section 16.4). It been suggested that (along with a temperate climate) the organic, slow and evolutionary development of 'the mess that is Britain's constitution' encourages values such as freedom and democracy to develop and mature (see Kellner, *Democracy: 1000 Years in Pursuit of British Liberty* (Mainstream 2009) 28–29).

One might revere a written constitution, as is the case in the US, but the same applies to any symbol. For example Walter Bagehot (1826–77) thought that mystical reverence for royalty was essential to the authority of the UK constitution (or, as he considered it, the 'English' constitution).

The UK's unwritten constitution is often defended as enabling its people, guided by tradition, to adjust flexibly and peacefully to changing circumstances. It is also suggested that the complexity and subtlety of the UK's arrangements make it impractical and divisive to reduce the constitution to writing, an argument convenient to those enjoying power. For example Dicey (1915), the eminent constitutional lawyer, pointed out that a written constitution can be torn up, whereas the unwritten constitution of the UK is embedded in the structure and traditions of the law as a whole and so part of the 'rule of law' (see Section 6.4.2).

The absence of a written constitution has possible disadvantages. Firstly, there is no agreement as to what rules or principles are truly 'constitutional'. There is no doubt that rules concerning the circumstances in which a government should lose office are constitutional, but what of local government which exists to provide relatively limited services for local communities? The debate would turn on the political issue of whether Britain should be a highly centralised or a dispersed democracy. Thus the emphasis of constitutional law courses and textbooks varies according to the beliefs of individual teachers and writers.

Parliament and the judges give special weight to rights, principles or laws that they consider to be 'constitutional'. For example proposed legislation that Parliament regards as 'of first-class constitutional importance' is examined by a committee of the whole House rather than by the normal 'standing committee' (see Section 13.3.1). As an aspect of the 'rule of law' the courts require the lawmaker to use very clear language in order to exclude fundamental rights of the individual such as freedom of speech (see Sections 6.6, 8.4.5).

However there is disagreement whether in an unwritten constitution it is worth labelling some rights as 'constitutional rights' in order for example to stress their importance in connection with supporting democracy. Lord Steyn has remarked that to classify a right as constitutional strengthens its value in that the court is virtually always required to protect it (quoted by Cooke, in Andenas and Fairgrieve (2009, 691)). In *R v Secretary of State for the Home Dept, ex p Simms* [1999] at 412: right of a prisoner of access to the press, Lord Hoffmann stated that we apply 'principles of constitutionality little different from those which exist in countries where the power of the legislature is expressly limited by a constitutional document' (see also Laws LJ in *Thoburn v Sunderland City Council* [2002]: 'constitutional statutes'). There is authority that compensation can be awarded against a public official who violates a 'constitutional right' even where no loss or damage has occurred (*Ashby v White* [1703]: right to vote).

On the other hand in *Watkins v Secretary of State for the Home Dept* (2006): prisoner's access to a lawyer, the House of Lords rejected this argument on the ground that without a written constitution the notion of a constitutional right is too vague. Similarly in *Cullen v Chief Constable of the RUC* [2004] at 46, Lord Hutton said that a written constitution has a special significance. He referred to a right which a democratic assembly representing the people has enshrined in a written constitution. In the latter case a person who has suffered harm can recover damages, the written constitution being 'clear testimony that an added value is attached to the protection of that right'. Similarly in *Ghaidan v Mendosa* [2004] at 178, Lord Millet said that a written constitution would give the court greater legitimacy in reviewing legislation under the Human Rights Act 1998.

Secondly, it is sometimes said that a written constitution encourages the use of abstract, linguistic, legalistic techniques at the expense of the underlying political realities and human interests. However courts have often emphasised the need for a broad and flexible approach to constitutional interpretation that stresses the underlying moral and political context (eg *Robinson v Secretary of State for Northern Ireland* [2002]). Indeed the language of a written constitution may be very vague, leaving plenty of room for disagreement. For example the US constitution has been interpreted at different times as both justifying and outlawing slavery.

It can be argued that in a matter as large and open to disagreement as a constitution, human beings are not capable of sensible grand designs and that the flexible trial and error approach favoured in the UK is preferable. Edmund Burke (1729–97), a prominent parliamentarian and conservative thinker, claimed that the constitution has special status by virtue of its being rooted in long-standing custom and tradition. Burke regarded attempts to engineer constitutions on the basis of abstract reason as ultimately leading to tyranny. This is because he believed that humans, with their limited understanding and knowledge, are inevitably at the mercy of unforeseen events and that reasoning based on abstract general principles, by trying to squeeze us into rigid templates, is a potential instrument of oppression:

> the age of chivalry is gone ... That of sophisters, economists and calculators has succeeded; and the glory of Europe is extinguished for ever. (Burke, *Reflections on the Revolution in France* (1790))

Some people claim to identify massive underlying abstract forces which guide constitutional change generated by the inbuilt human desire to order experience by copying others. For example the 'Whig interpretation of history' postulates a gradual evolution towards ever greater democracy and respect for individual rights interrupted by the pretensions of absolute monarchy arising from the Norman conquest but triumphantly restored in 1688 by the revolution which placed Parliament in charge (see Kellner, *Democracy* (Mainstream 2009)).

Certainly the structural features of the UK constitution have historically evolved in the direction of removing powers from monarchs in favour of other groups and institutions, the balance of power constantly shifting between these. Superficially at least our constitution does have a coherent structure as a parliamentary or representative democracy which could be enshrined in a written text and indeed has been copied in many written constitutions.

Some claim that as a 'common law constitution' guided by principles laid down by the courts the UK constitution is guided by rational and coherent principles based on public reasoning by experts supported by the wisdom stored in thousands of decided cases (*Prohibitions del Roy* [1607]). This of course resists radical change and is difficult to reconcile with a constitution based on democracy in which the basic principles are decided by elected representatives of the people and anything can be changed. Indeed the European Court of Human Rights has emphasised the need to justify restrictions on individual rights on the basis of 'considered debate' rather than on 'unquestioning and passive obedience to a historic tradition' (*Hirst v UK* [2004]; Chapter 12).

The normal method of reconciling this apparent contradiction is to suggest that the courts act as a safety valve protecting the fundamental and permanent liberal values needed for democracy, such as freedom of speech, against the possibility that elected politicians might be irrationally swayed by mob sentiment in favour of giving up democracy, for example in response to fear of terrorism. However judges often disagree and choices between basic constitutional values may not be fully susceptible to reason. For example in human rights cases courts are often confronted by choices between competing values such as freedom of speech and security which can be made only by a subjective judgement which a judge is no better equipped to make than a politician or a civil servant.

Thirdly our unwritten constitution provides no controls or guiding legal principles concerning political innovations and reforms (see Section 24.1). These may sometimes be created without a legal basis or public debate and have no clear status even though they may have wide constitutional implications. For example many government functions have been devolved from ministers to 'executive agencies' and 'quangos' outside the main channels of government accountability to Parliament (see Sections 5.2.7, 5.3). A significant body created by government but without a formal legal basis is the Committee on Standards in Public Life. This monitors the full range of government activity from an ethical perspective with a view to making general recommendations. The 'Nolan' principles based on the committee's first report (Cm 2850, 1995) are widely recognised and incorporated into the processes of most public bodies. They are in themselves uncontroversial. They are 'selflessness, integrity, objectivity, accountability, openness, honesty and leadership'.

Daintith and Page (*The Executive in the Constitution* (Oxford University Press 1999) ch 1) classify those who attempt to understand our unwritten constitution as 'foxes', 'hedgehogs', 'rude little boys' and 'Humpty Dumpties'. A fox regards the constitution as no more than a collection of working practices developed by those who join the government enterprise. A hedgehog looks for a single grand overarching principle such as parliamentary supremacy. It is unlikely that in a matter as complex as government any such principle is credible. A rude little boy therefore asserts that the emperor has no clothes, the constitution being a fiction disguising a power struggle between control freaks. Humpty Dumpties, who probably include most academic commentators, seek to explain the constitution on the basis of vague theories of their own such as liberalism, fairness, social welfare and so on, sometimes claiming that these ideals are inherent in the rules. We shall meet examples of each approach throughout this book.

1.3 The legal and the political constitution

For the purposes of studying constitutional law, it is useful to distinguish as a working matter between law and politics. Unfortunately there is no agreed definition of 'law'. For the moment it is enough to say that 'law' means rules, principles and standards that (a) are recognised as coming from defined authorities (in the UK's case the courts and Parliament, the lawmaking assembly) and (b) are backed by the force of the state. 'Politics' comprise all other rules, values, practices and behaviour concerning the exercise of governmental power and disputes between different interests which call for collective action. They may or may not be translated into legal mechanisms but they are part of the constitution in its broad sense. Law therefore cannot rigidly be separated from politics but is a particular kind of application of politics (cf Loughlin, 2005).

Law can be distinguished from other aspects of politics in at least the following respects. It relies on impersonal and usually written sources of authority in the form of binding general rules. It emphasises the desirability of certainty, coherence and impartial public procedures for settling disputes. Most fundamentally, law authorises violence against individuals in the name of the community. Politics is concerned primarily with outcomes, for which law is only one among several instruments, and is more willing

..w to use emotions, personal relationships, rewards and compromises in order to ..eve those outcomes.

Griffith famously distinguished between the 'legal' constitution and the 'political constitution'. He remarked that 'the constitution of the United Kingdom lives on, changing from day to day for the constitution is no more and no less than what happens. Everything that happens is constitutional. And if nothing happened that would be constitutional also' (1979, 19). On one reading this suggests that there is nothing at all behind the idea of a constitution. However Griffith may merely be pointing out that the constitution is a mixture of competing forces, of which law in the shape of courts is only one. The relationship between them is determined by political events and is constantly changing (see Gee, 2008; Loughlin, 'John Griffin: An Appreciation' [2010] PL 643, 649).

The term 'political constitution' is confusing and has different meanings, sometimes conflicting and sometimes overlapping. These different meanings may influence how one might resolve basic constitutional problems, most notably whether the courts or the elected lawmaker should have the last word.

1. The belief that all constitutional actors, including of course judges, are influenced by political bias favouring certain interests (see Griffith, 1979). According to this view vague concepts which we will study later such as the 'rule of law' or human rights, although presented as objective principles, are masks for political prejudice, usually in favour of the status quo.
2. Much of the UK constitution comprises rules and principles that are not law in the sense that they are not enforceable in the courts but rely on political pressures and voluntary consent (Chapter 3).
3. Political activity and institutions operate within a framework designated by law (Hickman, 2005). Unlike (1), this suggests that there are objective principles around which we can unite. This gives the courts a starring role.
4. Fundamental *political* principles such as democracy underpin all aspects of the constitution and pervade the law (Gee and Webber, 2010). Unlike (3) these provide the framework within which law operates. The court's role is therefore subordinate.
5. A preference for political solutions reached by democratic methods rather than solutions imposed by unelected judges. Griffith thought that constitutional decisions should be made by political bodies rather than by courts because he thought that judges are likely to be biased in favour of established authority (1979, 335–36). It is also often argued that because there is perpetual disagreement as to the meaning and proper extent of fundamental values such as freedom and democracy, elected bodies representing the public as a whole should decide questions relating to their scope and limits rather than solutions being imposed from above by unaccountable judges under the guise of 'objective' principles.

The legal and the political constitution are interrelated in various ways. For example:

- Politics provides the purposes and values that underpin the constitution and give the law its content.
- Law operates as a delivery mechanism for particular political policies written into legislation.
- Conversely, values especially concerned with the legal process in the courts, which can be summarised as fairness and justice, feed into the political process.

For example, how far should anti-terrorist policies be subject to the right to a fair trial (see Section 23.7.2)?

- Within the law itself there is room for political activity arising out of disagreement between different judges and groups of lawyers. Because the limits of language mean that rules can never be entirely clear, judges may be influenced by their political beliefs in deciding between competing arguments. Endless disagreement underlies both law and politics. This is one reason why a diverse judiciary may be desirable (see Etherton, 2010).
- Politics determines the actual power relationship between the different branches of government: lawmaker, executive, judges, military and so on. For example, even if in law Parliament the lawmaker is supreme, if the culture of members of Parliament is weak, self-seeking and subservient the executive is likely to be dominant.

1.4 Types of constitution

There are several traditional ways of classifying constitutions. It must be emphasised that these are ideals or models and there is no reason to assume that real constitutions neatly fit into any single category. The types are:

- *Federal and unitary.* In a federal state (such as the US) the various powers of government are divided between different geographical units and a central government. Each level is protected against intervention by the others. The UK is a unitary state. In a unitary state there may be subordinate units such as the devolved governments of Scotland, Northern Ireland and Wales but ultimate power is held by the centre, which can override or repeal laws made by the subordinate units. The UK has a strong unitary constitution since Parliament is usually thought to have unlimited lawmaking power not subject to any higher authority: the doctrine of 'parliamentary supremacy' (Chapter 8). On the other hand the claim that EU law is superior to Parliament (see Section 8.4.4) and the political strength of devolution, particularly in Scotland, mean that at least at a political level there may be a tendency towards federalism.
- *Rigid and flexible.* This concerns whether it is easy for those in power to change the constitution to suit their own interests. In legal terms some constitutions are rigid in that a special process such as a referendum of the people may be required to change them. This is known as 'entrenchment'. In the UK no special process is required. However the courts may resist interpreting laws so as to undermine what they regard as constitutionally important matters. Whether a constitution is easy to change depends more on politics than on law. Any constitution can be ignored or overthrown.
- *Parliamentary and presidential.* The influential nineteenth-century commentator Walter Bagehot remarked:

  > The practical choice of first rate nations is between the Presidential government and the Parliamentary: no state can be first rate that has not had a government by discussion, and those are the only two existing species of that government. (1902, Introduction)

  The UK has an extreme parliamentary system. In a parliamentary system such as that of many western European countries the people choose representatives who form the legislature, Parliament. The head of government is the Prime Minister (the Chancellor in Austria and Germany), chosen by the Parliament. The Prime

Minister chooses and removes ministers, who comprise the executive government. Sometimes, as in the UK, these must also be members of the legislature. Parliament scrutinises government activities, consents to laws and provides the government with finance. It can ultimately dismiss the executive by withdrawing its support. Parliamentary government therefore looks strong and accountable. However in practice the executive is likely to be dominant, if only because of the human tendency to defer to leaders.

In a parliamentary system there is usually a separate head of state who formally represents the state and is the source of its authority but has little political power, except perhaps as a safety mechanism in the event of a serious political breakdown. In some states, including the UK, the head of state is a hereditary monarchy and thus relatively independent of political pressures. In republican states the head of state is elected either by Parliament or by the people.

In a presidential system such as that of the US, the leader of the executive, the President, is elected independently of the legislature and holds office for a fixed period, subject in some countries to dismissal by the legislature. Members of the executive need not and sometimes cannot be members of the legislature. The President is usually also the head of state. Presidential government gives the voter a greater choice. On the other hand accountability might be confused, and when the legislature and President represent different political parties government might be weak.

The device of a separate head of state in the parliamentary system has the advantages of separating the authority of the state, in the head of state, from its functional powers. In a parliamentary system the Prime Minister and other members of the executive are merely government employees who cannot identify themselves with the state as such and so claim reflected glory and immunity from criticism. The head of state has a symbolic role and also ensures continuity in the constitution. If the governmental system were to collapse, for example if no leader emerged from the political process, it would be the responsibility of the head of state to ensure that government continued. Conversely apart from this exceptional situation the Queen has little personal political power (see Section 14.4), so that any respect due to her as representing the state does not carry the risk of tyranny.

- *Unicameral or bicameral.* A unicameral constitution has a single lawmaking assembly. A bicameral constitution has two assemblies, each of which operates as a check on the other, the balance between them depending on the circumstances of the particular country. In the US for example the Senate, the upper house, represents the states which comprise the federal system, with the legislature of each state, irrespective of its size, choosing two members, whereas Congress, the lower and larger house, is elected by the people generally, each state being represented according to the size of its population. Some European constitutions, such as those of Denmark, Sweden and Greece, are unicameral, and in most European constitutions the upper house cannot override the lower house. It is questionable whether an upper house serves a useful purpose other than in a federal system on the US model, where each house can check the other from importantly different perspectives.

The UK constitution is bicameral. The lower house, the House of Commons, with about 646 members, is elected from the UK as a whole. The upper house, the House of Lords, with 733 members, is mainly appointed by the Prime Minister, in contrast to other European countries, where the upper houses are mainly elected. The House of Lords cannot normally override the Commons but serves as a revising chamber to scrutinise and amend legislation proposed by the lower house, thus providing an opportunity for second thoughts. There have been long-standing debates as to whether the House of Lords should be abolished or replaced by a wholly or partly elected chamber but no consensus has been reached. An elected upper house has been said either to pointlessly duplicate the lower house or to muddle the lines of accountability.

- *Monarchy, aristocracy and democracy*. In a tradition dating back at least to Aristotle, there are three fundamental types of government: monarchy, or rule by one person; aristocracy, literally rule by a group of the 'best' people; and democracy, rule by the many or the people as a whole. According to Aristotle, each form of constitution has its virtues but also corresponding vices or deviations. The virtues exist when the ruler rules for the benefit of others; the vices when the ruler rules for the benefit of him or herself. Modern constitutions draw on these elements but disagree as to the best combination of them. In those European countries where monarchy remains, the powers of the monarch are invariably limited, in some cases being purely ceremonial. The UK constitution is sometimes called a 'constitutional monarchy', meaning that the powers of the monarch are limited by law and in our case by convention. The UK retains an aristocratic element in the form of the House of Lords, one of the two parts of Parliament. However the House of Commons, the members of which are elected as representatives of the people, is the more powerful part of Parliament.

  Monarchy is usually inherited within a family, so that the holder's power is not dependent on temporary political forces. According to Aristotle, the main merit of monarchy is its authority and independence since monarchs have a quasi-godlike status. The corresponding defect is despotism. The merit of aristocracy is wisdom; its defect is oligarchy (rule by a selfish group). The merit of democracy is consent of the community; its defect is instability leading to mob tyranny. Aristotle postulated a vicious cycle in which a monarch becomes a despot, is deposed by an aristocracy, which turns into an oligarchy and is overthrown by a popular rebellion. The ensuing democracy degenerates into chaos, resolved by the emergence of a dictator, who takes on the characteristics of a monarch, and so on. Aristotle therefore favoured what he called 'polity', a 'mixed government' combining all three (but loaded in favour of the middle classes) and with checks and balances between different branches of government. This strategy remains at the heart of modern constitutional design. However a cynical view, 'the iron law of oligarchy', claims that whatever form the constitution takes power will inevitably accumulate in the hands of a group of selfish cronies – a king by whatever name and his courtiers. In contemporary conditions this might well be a political party: 'who says organisation says oligarchy ... the oligarchical structure of the building suffocates the basic democratic principle' (Michels, quoted in Lipset, *Political Parties* (Free Press 1966)).

- *Accountable: liberal and republican*. These are not constitutional principles as such but underlying ideas that strongly influence the content of European constitutions, including our own. A liberal constitution is based on the notion of individual freedom and that the role of government is limited by law and is to serve the individual, primarily by protecting individual freedom. This raises many difficulties (see Section 2.3). A republican constitution is more than just a constitution, such as those of France or Ireland, which have no monarchy. The idea of republicanism places less stress on individual freedom than liberals but emphasises political equality and that the government of the state should be self-government by citizens, with the executive being accountable to the citizens (see Section 2.5). It is regarded as an affront to human dignity to rely on the good will of our rulers however benevolent they are in practice (kindly slave owners). Rulers whose powers are exercised only on behalf of citizens must be constrained by law to ensure that the rulers are carrying out the instructions of the people. The UK does not have a republican constitution in the full sense, although there are republican elements such as government being accountable to an elected Parliament and a general assumption that all citizens have equal rights to participate in government. The contrast between liberal and republican ideals of government is reflected in disputes about the underlying purpose of judicial review of government (Section 17.1).

The UK constitution could baldly be summarised as:

- *lacking grand ideals*: but influenced by liberal notions of individual freedom and by the republican ideal that government should be accountable to citizens;
- *unwritten;*
- *with an incomplete separation of powers*: the judiciary being independent but the executive and legislature partly combined;
- *based on the rule of law and accountable government;*
- *unitary;*
- *flexible;*
- *a constitutional monarchy;*
- *parliamentary;*
- *a representative democracy with an aristocratic element;*
- *bicameral;*
- *dualist.*

1.5 Public and private law

Constitutional law is the most basic aspect of 'public law'. It is controversial as to whether there is a useful distinction between public law and 'private law'. Broadly, public law governs the relationship between the government and individuals and that between different governmental agencies. Private law concerns the relationship between individuals and also deals with private organisations such as companies. For reasons connected with a peculiarly English notion of the rule of law (see Section 6.4.1) the distinction between public law and private law is less firmly embedded here than in the continental legal systems that inherited the distinction from Roman law. It was believed by the likes of Dicey that the liberties of the individual are best secured if the same law, broadly private law, governs officials and individuals alike so that officials have no special powers or status.

Attractive though this may be, it is arguably unrealistic given the huge powers that must be vested in the state to meet public demand for large-scale public services and government controls over daily life and the movement of the population.

Some writers have rejected the distinction between public and private law, at least on the level of fundamental principle, arguing that the same basic values and concepts pervade all law and that any given function could be carried out by the state or a private body (Section 19.5). This is particularly important today, when it is politically fashionable to entrust public services to profit-making private bodies. Moreover there are numerous bodies not directly connected with the government which exercise large powers over individuals, such as sporting and professional disciplinary bodies, trade unions and churches. Outside the core functions of keeping order and defence, there is no agreement in the UK as to what is the proper sphere of the state and which bodies are subject to public law.

Conversely the Crown has the same legal powers as a private person, so government makes extensive use of private law in the contexts for example of contracts for the procurement of goods and equipment, employment and property. In this context the government's economic power is so great and its activities so wide ranging that it might be argued that these powers should be treated as having a distinctive public law character. At a very general level the rejection of the distinction between public and private law may be defensible. It is difficult to deny that values such as fairness and openness are common to the private and public sectors, and organisations such as charities that carry out functions for the benefit of the public on a non-profit basis have elements both of the public and of the private. A typical example is social housing, which is currently provided by numerous charitable and other housing associations, but with powerful government agencies behind the scenes setting standards, dictating objectives and punishing defaulters.

There are however important distinctions between public law and private law. These include the following:

- The government represents the whole community and its officials have no self-interest of their own. By contrast a private company and an individual both have a legitimate self-interest, including the profit motive. It follows that government should be accountable to the community as a whole for its actions. In the case of a private body by contrast accountability might be regarded as an unacceptable intrusion on its freedom.
- Arguably private law is fundamentally different from public law in that private law concerns the voluntary interaction of individuals, calling for compromises, recognition of agreed solutions and concessions to vulnerability, whereas public law calls predominantly for general principles designed to structure and contain power. For example in private law a promise made is normally binding, whereas this is not so in public law (see Section 19.5).
- The government has the ultimate responsibility to protect the community against disruption and external threats. For this purpose it must be entrusted with wide powers to use force. As we shall see in Chapter 23, concerning emergencies, it may be difficult or impossible to reconcile this with our belief that all power should be curbed by law.
- The distinction between public and private law has particular implications in two main contexts. Firstly there is the question of the scope of judicial review of decisions made by powerful bodies. This is limited to 'functions of a public nature' (Section 19.5). Secondly the protection of the Human Rights Act 1998 applies mainly against public bodies and against bodies certain of whose functions are public functions

(Section 21.4.1). A similar approach is taken in both contexts, the matter depending upon the extent to which the body in question is linked to the central government. A pragmatic approach is taken based on all the circumstances, such as whether the body in question has special powers, whether it is controlled or financed by the government and the public importance of its functions (eg *R (Weaver) v London and Quadrant Housing Trust* [2008]; *YL v Birmingham City Council* [2007]).

1.6 Resolving disagreement: uncertainty and incommensurability

We have emphasised that the focus of constitutional law is that of resolving disagreements. There is no single 'correct' recipe for a good constitution or what rules it should contain. Constitution makers often aspire to grand general principles and rely on abstract reason of the kind favoured by lawyers. However a constitution is the result of historical events and personalities and is influenced by feelings as well as reason. The institutions and concepts that appear in this book have emerged as a result primarily of different interest groups competing with each other, thereby influencing people to make and accept particular arrangements – all of which are temporary and changeable.

Constitutional law is therefore concerned above all with attempts to resolve conflicts between groups with different beliefs about the aims, powers and values of the state. These differences may be impossible to resolve according to any shared set of values or reasons. The main context for this is when the human right to personal freedom clashes with important social goals such as national security. When can we lock someone up without trial or restrict freedom speech to lessen the risk of a terrorist attack? Different beliefs, each of which may be valid from its own point of view, are said to be 'incommensurable' when there is no available rational common measure against which they can be compared and choices made between them – just as we cannot compare whether going for a swim is 'better' than having a nap. Lawyers like to use the metaphor of 'balancing' competing interests but balancing is impossible without an agreed scale which we can use to measure a quality common to both so that we can compare them.

For example to what extent should religious beliefs entitle their holder to special treatment? One way of 'balancing competing interests' which underlies much legal reasoning is cost/benefit analysis. This uses the technique of assuming as a start that the competing interests are equal and then counting the various harms and benefits that are involved in a dispute, attaching a weight to each one and comparing the outcome. This may merely disguise subjective moral or political choices. The problems here are firstly to measure the 'weight' of different kinds of harm and secondly the validity of the starting point. For example the supporters of a given religion may hold that harm is irrelevant and that fidelity to faith is absolute. Thus we have no objective way of balancing the interests involved. In practice a common outcome is that a minority's belief about itself gives way to how the majority (or the court) evaluates that minority (eg *R (Begum) v Head Teacher and Governors of Denbigh High School* [2007]: the banning of extreme version of Muslim dress in a school held to be valid in the general interest of the school community; *Copsey v Devon Clays Ltd* [2005]: religious observance against work schedules, the latter prevailing on cost/benefit terms).

The constitution might therefore be regarded as managing perpetual disagreement while scholars and politicians continue an apparently fruitless search for objectivity. A constitution will always contain gaps and uncertainties and produce unstable compromises. In the interests of order, there must be some respected mechanism to settle disputes (with sometimes an acceptance that some matters may be better left unsettled; see Section 3.5). This mechanism might consist of an elected assembly representative of the community (ie Parliament) or an independent body of trusted experts (ie a court of law). In the UK we have an uneasy compromise between the two. Indeed some scholars claim that the ultimate foundation of the UK constitution is the abstract idea of the rule of law, thus tipping the balance towards courts and lawyers (see Section 8.5). However, as we shall see, much of the UK constitution has not been reduced to legal rules, so that the courts are not always involved. Many uncertainties are in fact settled by political leaders in ways convenient to themselves, often advised by informally chosen persons, for example businesspeople and academics, who wish to associate with important people.

The most fundamental incommensurability pervading our constitution concerns choosing between two competing political aims both of which are valid. These have been famously characterised by Harlow and Rawlings (*Law and Administration* (3rd edn, Cambridge University Press 2009)) as 'red light' and 'green light' perspectives.

According to the red light perspective, which is derived from liberalism, a constitution seeks to control those in power since it is widely acknowledged that people with power over others can easily abuse their power, albeit sometimes accidentally or for good motives. Thus political thinkers over the centuries have worried about the corruptibility of those in power:

> now it is a universally observed fact, that the two evil dispositions in question, the disposition to prefer a man's selfish interests to those he shares with other people, and his immediate and direct interests to those which are indirect and remote, are characterised most especially called forth and fostered by the possession of power ... this is the meaning of the universal tradition, grounded on universal experience, of men's being corrupted by power. (Mill, 1972, 242)

Similarly, John Adams, one of the founders of the US Constitution, asserted that:

> despotism, or unlimited sovereignty or absolute power, is the same in a majority of a popular assembly, an aristocratic council, an oligarchical junta, and a single emperor.

By contrast the green light perspective, which is republican in origin, views government as a desirable cooperative enterprise. According to the green light perspective, a constitution should create a framework of rules which enable those who run the government to cooperate efficiently in providing public services and enable democratic participation in government. In the absence of such rules any cooperative enterprise is doomed to stalemate or chaos. The green light perspective therefore encourages the use of power but attempts to make it as open as possible.

An extreme example of the competition that can arise between red light and green light perspectives concerns the topic of anti-terrorist and other 'emergency' laws to deal with exceptional threats to security (Chapter 23). A red light perspective would worry about the possibility of officials abusing any wide powers that they are given, for example by using them against peaceful political protesters, and would favour control by the courts. A green light perspective would emphasise the need to trust officials with wide powers to deal with unexpected events and serious public dangers, but subject to democratic processes. Politicians and scholars endlessly search for the 'right balance' but of course both sides are right from their own standpoint and there is no objective balance. Any solution can lie only in public opinion. Other examples of incommensurability will be met throughout this book, most notably in the context of judicial review and human rights (see eg Sections 19.7 and 22.5).

Summary

- Having read this chapter, you should have a general idea of some basic constitutional concepts and how they relate to the UK. Constitutions deal with the fundamental framework of government and its powers, reflecting the political interests of those who design and operate them and providing mechanisms for the control of government. The constitution does not adequately address the international dimension of modern government.
- The ultimate aim of a constitution is to manage disagreement in circumstances where collective action on behalf of the whole community is required. Disagreement is inherent in political disputes and may not be resolvable by rational means. In this context we discussed the concept of incommensurability. There is an underlying dispute as to how far constitutional disputes should be settled by courts or by elected bodies.
- There is a tendency in any form of government for powers to gravitate towards a single group so that a primary concern of constitutional law is to provide checks and balances between different branches of government. We introduced the basic concepts of the rule of law, separation of powers and fundamental rights as underlying constitutional structures. These are discussed in detail in later chapters.
- Political and legal aspects of a constitution should be distinguished, although the boundary between them is leaky. The legal aspects of the constitution are a distinctive part of the wider political context, each influencing the other. There are also important constitutional principles in the form of conventions and practices operating without a formal legal basis.
- The distinction between written and unwritten constitutions is of some but not fundamental importance. We compared the main advantages and disadvantages of written and unwritten constitutions without committing ourselves to one or the other since the matter is one for political choice. The UK constitution is an untidy mixture of different kinds of law practices and customs and has a substantial informal element, lending itself to domination by personal networks.
- We introduced various formal definitions of a constitution without suggesting they were helpful. Different definitions tend to emphasise particular political or legal biases.
- We outlined the main classifications of constitutions, emphasising that these are models and that actual constitutions need not closely correspond to any pure model. The UK constitution is strongly parliamentary but weakly monarchical, with perhaps a tendency towards federalism.
- The distinction between public law and private law is important, particularly in the context of the Human Rights Act 1998 and of judicial review of powerful bodies. The courts have adopted a pragmatic approach.

Exercises

1.1 You are discussing constitutional law with an American who claims that the UK has no constitution. What does she mean and how would you respond?

1.2 Which of the definitions of a constitution contained in this chapter best fits the UK constitution?

1.3 To what extent does the UK have a 'political constitution'?

1.4 How well does the UK constitution fit the various methods of classifying constitutions mentioned in this chapter?

1.5 'It is both a strength and a potential weakness of the British constitution, that almost uniquely for an advanced democracy it is not all set down in writing' (Royal Commission on the Reform of the House of Lords, *Wakeham Report* (Cm 4534, 2000)). Discuss.

1.6 Should the courts have the power to overturn legislation?

1.7 Compare the merits of the parliamentary and presidential systems of government.

Further reading

Note: The Further Reading for this chapter marked * might usefully be revisited towards the end of the student's course, when fuller knowledge of the subject will have been gained.

Andenas and Fairgrieve (eds), *Tom Bingham and the Transformation of the Law* (Oxford University Press 2009)
*Bamforth and Leyland (eds), *Public Law in a Multi-Layered Constitution* (Hart 2003) ch 1
Barker, 'Against a Written Constitution' [2008] PL 11
Bellamy, *Political Constitutionalism* (Cambridge University Press 2007) ch 1
Etherton, 'Liberty, the Archetype, and Diversity' [2010] PL 727
*Ewing, 'The Politics of the British Constitution' [2000] PL 405
Feldman, 'None, One or Several? Perspectives on the UK's Constitution' (2005) 64 CLJ 329
Finer, Bogdanor and Rudden, *Comparing Constitutions* (Oxford University Press 1995) ch 1
*Gee, 'The Political Constitutionalism of JAG Griffith' (2008) 28 LS 20
*Gee and Webber, 'What Is a Political Constitution?' (2010) 30 OJLS 273
Griffith, 'The Political Constitution' (1979) 42 MLR 1
*Harvey, 'Playing with Law and Politics' (2001) 51 U Toronto LJ 171
Hennessy, *The Hidden Wiring: Unearthing the British Constitution* (Gollancz 1995) prologue, ch 1
*Hickman, 'In Defence of the Legal Constitution' (2005) 55 U Toronto LJ 981
King, *Does the United Kingdom Still Have a Constitution?* (Sweet and Maxwell 2001)
Loughlin, 'Constitutional Theory: A 25th Anniversary Essay' (2005) 25 OJLS 183
Loughlin, *Sword and Scales* (Hart 2005)
Loveland, 'A Critique of the Political Constitution' (2006) 122 LQR 340
Marshall, 'The Constitution: Its Theory and Interpretation' in Bogdanor (ed), *The British Constitution in the Twentieth Century* (Oxford University Press 2003) 29–35
Mc Cormick, *Institutions of Law* (Oxford University Press 2007) chs 1–4, 10
McIlwain, *Constitutionalism Ancient and Modern* (Cornell University Press 1947) ch 1
Munro, *Studies in Constitutional Law* (2nd edn Butterworths 1999) ch 1
Poole, 'Tilting at Windmills? Truth and Illusion in the Political Constitution' (2007) 70 MLR 250
Ridley, 'There Is No British Constitution: A Dangerous Case of the Emperor's Clothes' (1988) 41 Parliament Aff 340
Ward, *The English Constitution: Myths and Realities* (Hart 2004)

Chapter 2

Underlying political values: liberalism and republicanism

A free society is premised on the fact that people are different from one another. A free society respects individual differences. (Lady Hale in *R (Williamson) v Secretary of State for Education and Employment* [2005])

2.1 Introduction

Western European constitutions have been influenced by three broad and overlapping political perspectives. They are loosely termed 'liberalism', 'republicanism' and 'communitarianism'. Each emphasises a different aspect of human nature. Liberalism concentrates on our individuality, focusing on rights and freedom. Republicanism emphasises our social nature as what Aristotle called 'political animals' and concentrates on political involvement as equal citizens in governing ourselves. Communitarianism emphasises our nature as interdependent herd animals who live by copying each other. It emphasises the customs and traditions in which different communities are embedded. (Communitarianism has so far had little, if any, influence on UK law and will not be discussed separately.) Liberalism is the dominant belief system underpinning the UK constitution and is sometimes invoked by the courts. For example according to Lord Steyn in *Roberts v Parole Board* [2006]: 'in our system the working assumption is that Parliament legislates for a European liberal democracy which respects fundamental rights'. Republican ideas also play a part, surfacing in particular contexts such as voting rights and the political accountability of ministers.

We would not expect a particular constitution to fit into any single set of values but would expect to find values associated with both liberalism and republicanism scattered throughout the constitution, with some more prominent than others depending on the circumstances at any given time. Moreover each set of values has varying shades, so that in many contexts liberals and republicans reach the same practical conclusions.

2.2 Liberalism

Broadly speaking, liberals place a high value on individual freedom. It is difficult to identify concrete principles on which all liberals agree. However the following might be the main principles of liberalism:

- Liberalism emphasises the interests of the individual rather than the collective interests of the community. The state exists only to protect the interests of the individual.
- The interests of all individuals except those who harm others are worthy of equal concern and respect. This of course begs the question as to what counts as 'harm'.
- Individuals should be free to follow their own chosen way of life ('autonomy'). Liberalism attempts to place constraints on government in the interests of individual

freedom and to give the individual an area of private life that is out of bounds for the state. Liberal laws are therefore tolerant of minorities and dissenters.

- The state should not favour one way of life over another. This is particularly problematic since the state might have to choose between conflicting interests. For example, given that the state has to fund itself from taxation, unless it were to tax everyone equally, it has to make choices as to whom to tax, thus encouraging or discouraging particular projects.
- Liberalism claims to be rational. It seeks a constitution that free and equal people would rationally support. It recognises that there is likely to be irreducible disagreement even among people of good will and so favours caution about state intervention.
- Liberalism is international and favours cooperation between nations. Thus liberals broadly support organisations, such as the EU, that attempt to override national interests. An extreme version of liberalism, neo-liberalism, would use force to impose 'freedom' on other nations, thus exemplifying the paradox that, according to opponents of liberalism, undermines liberalism. Neo-liberalism lay behind the invasion of Iraq carried out by the UK in 2002.

Liberalism is not universally admired, sometimes being condemned as selfish and uncaring and favouring the individual over the group. A modest defence of liberalism is that at least it tries to make room for other beliefs, recognising the 'lurking doubt' in all human affairs and the desire to avoid conflicts. Liberal societies have been relatively stable and peaceful. Even if there is some objective truth as to how to live, it has so far eluded the human race. Indeed the desire for peace was the historical origin of liberalism as a response to the religious conflicts that disrupted Europe during the sixteenth and seventeenth centuries. Once the bond supplied by a dominant religion had been dissolved, it became impossible to govern people of widely different beliefs without either conferring a large amount of individual freedom or resorting to oppression, which would ultimately destroy the community.

2.2.1 Liberal beliefs in constitutional law

Liberalism is not wedded to any particular form of government. It is not necessarily democratic, although most liberals would regard democracy as the form of government most likely to support liberalism. Many liberals place faith in independent courts of law, thus linking liberalism with the 'rule of law' (Chapter 6). Some European states empower the courts or a specialised body to override legislation, for example Germany, Spain, Italy and France (Constitutional Council, but only prior to enactment). The UK does not do so, preferring informal and political mechanisms. Liberalism also favours democracy as the most likely form of government to secure individual freedom but unlike republicanism does not value democracy as an end in itself, having no objection in principle to securing individual rights through the undemocratic means of a court. Moreover, in contrast to republicanism, liberalism is not especially interested in whether citizens directly participate in governmental decision making but accepts government by an elite accountable to citizens.

Liberalism would emphasise in particular the following:

1. Decision makers must be open and accountable. It must be borne in mind that mechanisms for making a decision maker accountable are not the same for each kind of decision maker. For example it is arguably wrong to elect judges, however

democratic this seems, since election risks compromising the independence of a court to apply the law. Conversely the arguments for elected lawmakers are strong since they can be removed if they make laws to which the people object. In both cases it is normally important that the decision-making process be open and public, but sometimes confidentiality may be a competing concern, for example in cases involving the methods of the secret security services (see Section 23.3).

2. Government power must be limited and no single institution should have the last word so as irrevocably to close off debate. For example the lawmaker must not be able to bind future lawmakers (Chapter 9), and court decisions should allow dissenting judgments. The courts have an important role in protecting individuals against abuse of power and safeguarding fundamental rights but there must be checks and balances between the courts and the lawmaker. (The Human Rights Act 1998 to some extent provides machinery for this kind of accommodation.)
3. Individual rights are respected but are not necessarily absolute. There is considerable disagreement within liberalism as to when such rights can be overridden.
4. Departures from treating everyone equally must be justified. There must in particular be equal access to courts of law, and public office must be open to anyone with suitable qualifications.

2.3 Varieties of liberalism in constitutional thought

There are many varieties of liberalism, each applying the basic ingredients of freedom and equality in different ways. The following classical writers have influenced the development of constitutional thought in the UK and exemplify particular points on the map.

2.3.1 Thomas Hobbes (1588–1679): the impersonal state and individualism

A fundamental change in political thinking emerged in the sixteenth century when the church and the state became separated. The idea of the state as an impersonal organisation intended to serve everyone was revived from classical antiquity by republican thinkers such as Machiavelli. Hobbes was one of the earliest English exponents of this approach and, although not a liberal, generated ideas that are basic to liberalism.

Hobbes published his most influential work, *Leviathan*, in 1651 (1973) following a time of widespread political unrest when England was in the grip of religious turmoil and civil war between an authoritarian king and an equally authoritarian Parliament dominated by religious interests. (Of his other works, *The Elements of Law* is of particular interest.) He tried to explain the rationale of legal authority without drawing upon religion. Hobbes doubted whether it was possible to discover objective truth about anything. He had a strongly individualistic approach and, in common with modern liberals, believed that human affairs involve endless disagreement and therefore that a constitution has solid foundations only in the minimum on which it is possible rationally to agree. As with many liberal thinkers Hobbes' idea of government was based on an imaginary 'social contract' according to which free and equal people would choose to give up their natural freedom in exchange for the benefits of government. The controversial question is what form of government they would agree to, and to this question different liberals have different answers. Thus the social contract seems to be in essence a device for trying to reason out what kind of constitution would maximise well-being, a question that has never been answered to general acceptance.

According to Hobbes, the need for someone to settle disputes and keep order is the basic purpose of government. There must therefore be a single ultimate ruler, a sovereign, 'Leviathan', who has unlimited power and ultimately rules by force, to whom the people consent to surrender their natural freedom. Under that ultimate sovereign there can be many different detailed government arrangements.

Hobbes did not believe that humans are inherently wicked but thought that we are self-seeking and that our different ideas of good inevitably set us in conflict with each other – a war of 'all against all' – so that without government we would destroy each other. According to Hobbes, outside the private sphere of family and personal relationships we are motivated by three impulses: competition, fear and the desire for power over others. We constantly strive to fulfil new desires in a never-ending and ultimately doomed search for what he called 'felicity'. Hobbes therefore argued that any government is better than none and that 'the concord of many cannot be maintained without power to keep them all in awe' (*Elements of Law* XIX, 4).

Hobbes' most famous passage encapsulates both his basic principle and the beauty of his language:

> Hereby it is manifest, that during the time men live without a common Power to keep them all in awe, they are in that condition which is called Warre; and such a warre, as is of every man against every man ... In such condition, there is no place for Industry: because the fruit thereof is uncertain; and consequently no Culture of the Earth, no Navigation, nor use of the commodities that may be imported by Sea; no commodious Building; no Instruments of moving and removing such things as require much force; no knowledge of the face of the Earth; no account of Time; no Arts; no Letters; no Society; and which is worst of all, continuall feare, and danger of violent death; And the life of man, solitary, poore, nasty, brutish and short. (1973, 65)

Hobbes provided an early example of the 'social contract' device. This symbolises that government depends on the consent of the governed, hence Hobbes' relevance to contemporary democratic ideas. Hobbes' hypothetical contract is made between the people, who agree with each other to surrender their natural freedom to the sovereign. The sovereign is not itself a party to the social contract. This produces a 'covenant', a one-sided promise, to obey Leviathan. In order to minimise disagreement the sovereign must be a single unitary body, an 'artificial man'. This could be either a monarch or an assembly. Hobbes' sovereign has no special qualifications for ruling but is merely the representative of the community. The obligation of the sovereign derives from its gratitude to the people for the free gift of power.

Hobbes believed that humans have certain 'natural' rights based on keeping promises, respect for individual freedom and equality: 'Do not that to another, which thou wouldest not have done to thyself' (1973, 14, 15). He also believed, anticipating modern liberalism, that people are equal and that the ruler has a duty to leave the people as much liberty as possible without hurt to the public (*Elements of Law* XXVIII). However according to Hobbes, natural rights are no more than the rational hopes or expectations and have no binding force unless the lawmaker chooses to protect them. Hobbes believed that because the sovereign itself needs security the interests of the sovereign and the people naturally coincide. The sovereign therefore needs to keep the people happy. This echoes in contemporary debate about 'the rule of law', namely about whether the institution of law is a good in itself or whether it is only 'good laws' that produce good. It may be that modern technology, with its surveillance devices and weapons, makes a lawmaker less dependent on the happiness of the people than was the case in Hobbes' time.

Hobbes' government has two crucial features. Firstly, because of the uncertainty of human affairs, Leviathan must have unlimited power since otherwise there would be the very disagreement that the sovereign exists to resolve. Hobbes thought that, although some forms of government may be better than others, by definition the sovereign can never act unjustly to a subject because the subject has agreed to accept every decision of the sovereign. Secondly the sovereign exists for a single purpose, the welfare of his subjects, and has no authority to act for any other purpose. Thus the sovereign should act 'so that the giver shall have no just occasion to repent him of his gift' and 'all the duties of the rulers are contained in this one sentence, the safety of the people is the supreme law'. (By 'safety' Hobbes meant not just the preservation of life but general justice and well-being; see *Elements of Law* XXVIII, 1.) However Hobbes was clear that it is for the ruler alone to decide whether it needs to exercise its powers, and he provided no legal remedy against a ruler that exceeded its power, regarding the matter as one for divine retribution.

Hobbes' ideas have an important influence on the modern constitution in that they identify recurring themes and claims. They include the following:

- Government depends on the consent of the people and is the representative of the people.
- A single sovereign source of absolute power to protect the people, particularly in emergencies. This is among the most fundamental problems of constitutional law. In our case the doctrine of parliamentary supremacy reflects Hobbes' idea, as does the belief that in an emergency the executive should be entrusted with very wide powers (see Section 23.1). Indeed the German political theorist Carl Schmidt (a Nazi supporter) argued that, in view of the possibility of 'the exception' (ie an emergency), a sovereign must have absolute power always available. Repressive or corrupt governments may use Hobbesian arguments to justify restricting individual freedom, for example by claiming that unity is necessary because there is a threat to security. The contemporary question, contrary to Hobbes, is whether there should be any individual rights that are sacrosanct.
- All citizens are equal. No one should have powers or rights or be subject to special obligations based on factors such as birth, custom, social status or religion.
- Freedom is the natural state of affairs as opposed to a gift bestowed by authority. According to Hobbes, 'right is that liberty which the law leaves us' (*Elements of Law* XXIX, 5). It is true that the sovereign can make any law but unless it positively does so the individual is free to do what he or she likes: 'freedom lies in the silence of the laws' (*Entick v Carrington* [1765]). This is a primary sentiment behind the idea of the rule of law (Chapter 6). Conversely however there cannot be any guaranteed rights without law.
- The separation of politics from religion, church from state.
- The distinction between the public and the private spheres. In relation to areas of life not controlled by the state, namely those where public order and safety are not at risk, what I do is not the state's business.
- Laws concern external behaviour not matters of personal belief or conscience. For example under Article 9 of the European Convention on Human Rights (ECHR), freedom of religious belief is absolute but the 'manifestation of religion' can be restricted on certain public interest grounds (see Section 20.4.3).

- Laws should consist primarily of written rules made by the sovereign. Hobbes disliked the common law because it is made by courts. In a long-running dispute with Coke, the Lord Chief Justice, Hobbes attacked the view of the judges that law is 'artificial reason' that resides in the learning of an elite group (themselves) as a childish fiction (see Postema, *Bentham and the Common Law Tradition* (Clarendon Press 1986) 40–48). Hobbes recognised a place for rules derived from natural reason which must be applied where there are gaps in the written rules but thought that these depend on the tacit consent of the sovereign (*Elements of Law* XXIX, 10). This is echoed in the modern controversy about the basis of judicial review of government action, where one school of thought claims that the principles applied by the courts represent the assumed wishes of Parliament (see Section 17.1.1).

Hobbes was not concerned with republican issues of participation in government. Nor did he tackle the problem of how to make government accountable. He believed that by a 'natural law' the sovereign must respect the trust placed in him by the people. He did not deal with the problem that in all but the simplest societies, power must in practice be divided up and rulers must rely on advisers, thereby creating potential disagreements. Hobbes recognised however that some methods of government might be better than others and in the later part of his work *The Dialogues* (ed Cropsey (University of Chicago Press 1971)) made many suggestions, such as that the sovereign should act through general laws and should consult Parliament.

2.3.2 John Locke (1632–1704): individual rights and majority government

Locke is widely regarded as a founder of modern liberalism. Locke's writings (*Second Treatise of Government*, 1690) supported the 1688 revolution, which founded our present constitution against the claims of absolute monarchy. His approach was grounded in the Protestant religion, which stressed individual conscience and self-improvement by hard work. Locke believed that individuals had certain natural rights identified by reasoning about human nature and existing, as he saw it, to serve God. These are life, health, freedom and property. For him, the purpose of government is to protect these rights in the exceptional cases where conflicts arise. To this extent Locke's government serves the same function as that of Hobbes. However Locke's government has limited powers.

According to Locke, the people first hypothetically contract with each other unanimously to establish a government and then choose an actual government by majority vote. The government as such does not enter into a contract but takes on a trust, a one-sided promise, whereby it undertakes to perform its functions of protecting natural rights and advancing well-being. Thus, and opposite to Hobbes, government has duties but no rights of its own, an idea applied by contemporary judges (see LAWS J in *R v Somerset CC, ex p Fewings* [1995]).

Locke's basic principles can be found in modern liberal constitutions. Firstly there is the idea (shared with Hobbes) that government depends on the consent of the people. According to Locke, government should be appointed and dismissed periodically by a majority vote representing those with a stake in the community. However a majority to Locke meant only non-Catholic property owners since he thought that only these people have an incentive to loyalty to the community, the loyalty of Catholics being to the Pope. Locke justified majority voting on the basis that the majority commands most force but recognised that there is no logical reason why a majority should be 'right' in relation to any particular issue.

Secondly Locke was concerned to limit the power of government in order to protect the rights and freedoms of the individual. This is perhaps the most distinctive feature of liberalism, although liberals do not agree how this should be done, for example whether by courts or democratic mechanisms (Chapter 19). Locke himself did not favour detailed legal constraints on government, regarding the contribution of lawyers as 'the Phansies and intricate contrivances of men, following contrary and hidden interests put into words' (1960, para 12). He relied on dividing up government power so that no one branch can be dominant: the separation of powers (Chapter 7). He also insisted that governments should periodically be held to account by means of elections and upheld as a last resort the right to rebel against a government that broke its trust.

Thirdly Locke promoted 'toleration' of different ways of life provided they did not upset the basic political framework. For example he did not favour toleration of Catholics, whom he regarded as subversive. This apparent double standard is one of the alleged contradictions of liberalism. Thus liberalism downgrades some interests in order to protect itself, this being a justification often used today to defend illiberal laws aimed at terrorism but in their language of wider scope (Chapter 22).

A modern version of Lockean liberalism is reflected in the work of the American legal philosopher Ronald Dworkin. Dworkin regards the function of the law in the shape of the courts as being to apply principles of 'political morality' focusing on individual rights. The policies of government made in the general public interest should not be imposed at the expense of the basic rights of the individual. Dworkin writes from the perspective of the US Constitution, according to which the Supreme Court can override legislation it holds to be unconstitutional (see Dworkin, 1996, 1998). This is not currently the case in the UK, where the view might be taken that conflict between rights and the public interest is not always susceptible to the rationalist processes of a court (see Section 21.5).

2.3.3 David Hume (1711–76), Jeremy Bentham (1748–1832), John Stuart Mill (1806–73): utilitarianism and welfare liberalism

Welfare liberalism favours democratic mechanisms rather than the courts. From this perspective, the law is only one among several levers of government, others being persuasion and payment. The courts might be presented as in 'partnership' with government to secure good administration (see *R v Lancashire CC, ex p Huddleston* [1986] at 945, and the 'ill tempered outburst' by former Home Secretary David Blunkett asserting that the courts' role was to help the government deliver its policies [2003] PL 397).

The most influential version of welfare liberalism is utilitarianism. Utilitarianism is an example of an 'instrumental' moral perspective that evaluates conduct in terms of the results it produces. This of course begs the question of what counts as a good result. In the context of a constitution, this might be anything designated by the lawmaker. In the case of utilitarianism, it is the satisfaction of the preferences of as many people as possible. The case of *Copsey* (Section 2.4) is an example. David Hume was a founder of utilitarianism. He thought that government is a matter of practical compromise. He rejected the social contract as a fiction and regarded ideals of abstract justice as myths useful for persuading people to conform. Hume advocated a pragmatic society based on coordinating individual interests. He believed that our limited knowledge, strength and altruism provided the moral basis for a legal system. He thought that self-interest and our natural feelings for others would generate basic principles of cooperation, including respect for private property, voluntary dealings and keeping promises. Hume favoured the common law as a vehicle for this, which he described as a happy combination of circumstances, according to which the law is developed pragmatically in the light of changing social practices and values.

Jeremy Bentham is the most celebrated utilitarian. He gave intellectual respectability to the idea of an all-powerful central government making general laws and accountable to a majority of the people. Using the slogan 'the greatest happiness of the greatest number', Bentham measured utility by counting people's actual demands, giving each equal weight ('each counts for one and none for more than one') and refusing to treat any preference as better than any other: 'pushpin is as good as poetry'. Although utilitarianism could mean authoritarian government by experts, Bentham's version involves strong democratic controls to ensure that the law represents public opinion (see generally Craig, 'Bentham, Public Law and Democracy' [1989] PL 407). Bentham regarded law and courts as subordinate to utilitarian considerations. In particular he regarded legal certainty and judicial independence, what we call the 'rule of law', as a sham. He thought that the idea of natural rights was 'nonsense on stilts', claiming that rights were simply legal mechanisms, that law is merely a tool of government and public opinion is the ultimate authority.

Although as a crude instrument of policy utilitarianism is much favoured by officials, it is replete with problems, particularly in relation to justice and fairness. For example utilitarianism is consistent with slavery in that the standard of living of a majority might be held to outweigh the loss of freedom of a minority. A utilitarian could reasonably think that innocent people could be shot in order to disperse a public meeting or kept in jail even if wrongly convicted in order to preserve public confidence in the police (see Lord Denning in *McIlkenny v Chief Constable of the West Midlands Police* [1980] at 239–40). Utilitarianism also finds difficulty with the notion of rights and obligations. Why should I pay you what I have promised if I now discover a better use for the money, for example by giving it to a disaster fund? Can utilitarianism really give equal weight to all preferences without some non-utilitarian filter to exclude 'irrational' or 'immoral' preferences such as those of paedophiles? These and other problems have been widely discussed without a conclusion.

John Stuart Mill tried to reconcile utilitarianism with liberal individualism by claiming that maximising individual freedom is the best way to advance general welfare since it encourages the virtues of creativity. He believed that happiness could best be achieved by experimenting with different ways of life. This led to Mill's emphasis on freedom of expression and his influential 'harm' principle, namely that the only ground on which the state should interfere with freedom is to prevent harm to others. The state should not normally interfere paternalistically to protect a person for his or her own good. However this begs the question of what counts as 'harm' since harm can be defined as anything we dislike. For example does harm include 'offence' if someone makes fun of my religious beliefs (Chapter 20)?

Mill did not apply his harm principle to those who were unable fully to make rational judgements, such as children, a principle that, uncomfortably, Mill seemed to extend to colonised peoples. Moreover distortions creep in. For example Mill was less egalitarian than Bentham, since for Mill preferences were not equal. Mill favoured the 'higher' and more intellectual and artistic capacities of the human mind. He was also a romantic, reminding us that ideas such as justice may not be purely rational, in the sense of being possible to pin down as legal rules, but have an emotional and spiritual dimension (see Ward, 'The Echo of a Sentimental Jurisprudence' (2002) 15 L & Critique 107).

Mill preferred political to legal mechanisms, in his case a strong system of checks and balances between different branches of government and a belief in democracy. However he was not a wholehearted democrat. His utilitarian strain led him to favour decision making by experts and he favoured slewing voting rights in favour of the wealthy and educated. Mill's utilitarianism also prevented him valuing individual freedom as an end in itself but only as subordinate to the general good. For example it would be consistent with Mill to suggest that it is better for a minority of elite students at Oxbridge to have creative freedom in order to rule the country at the expense of a majority of students trained at 'inferior' universities to perform menial tasks. Moreover, although Mill emphasised that the individual is the best judge of how he or she should live, some ways of life, notably those of the artist or intellectual, are objectively better than others and can be favoured by the state.

2.3.4 Fredrich Hayek (1899–1992): market liberalism

Closely related to individualism, economic or market liberalism is concerned with harnessing what it regards as the primary human impulse of self-interest, in pursuit of the common good. It does so by encouraging competition between free individuals. According to market liberals, the state has neither the knowledge nor the competence to plan people's lives, and efficient solutions are best found through free interchange in the market, the price mechanism acting as a store of knowledge of supply and demand. There is no necessary connection between market liberalism and a liberal belief in individual freedom in moral and social matters. A market liberal such as the former British Prime Minister Margaret Thatcher might claim to harness valuable human impulses in the economic sphere while suppressing what he or she regards as harmful human impulses elsewhere. Market liberalism is therefore akin to utilitarianism in that it does not value freedom for its own sake but only as a means to an end, this end being wealth maximisation. Moreover market freedom may conflict with personal freedom since the rich may exploit the poor.

Hayek seems to assume, contrary to Hobbes, that within a society which maximises individual freedom, shared understandings will emerge on which enough people agree for life to be harmonious, what he called the 'spontaneous order'. Hayek thought that central government planning was doomed to fail because officials were not capable of acquiring sufficient knowledge of the millions of people going about their individual business to make effective decisions. However he relied strongly on the notion of the rule of law as a framework of certain general rules within which we can be 'free' to plan our lives (Chapter 6). Hayek's approach favours the common law since decisions made by judges could be justified as a step-by-step pragmatic response to problems thrown up by individuals.

Liberals do not usually regard particular economic policies or public service provisions as constitutional matters to be treated as part of the overriding framework of government but treat them as subjects of democratic choice. This recognises that there is a legitimate liberal disagreement as to how to maximise welfare. However, like the other liberalisms, market liberalism influences the underlying values of the constitution, in particular those of accountability and individual freedom. According to 'public choice' theory, politicians and public officials in common with others are driven by self-interest. Thus, if left alone, they will try to maximise their incomes, expand their territories and minimise their workloads. Market liberalism attempts to harness self-interest by creating competition in the provision of public services. Examples are the contemporary practices of privatisation, such as that of the railways and utility companies, and the splitting up of many civil service operations into semi-autonomous 'executive agencies' run on the model of private business. Where goods and services cannot actually be competed for, mechanisms are created to simulate competitive price mechanisms, for example by setting targets and standards with accompanying rewards and penalties.

For example social housing is sometimes allocated on the basis of 'choice-based lettings' whereby applicants bid for housing using 'currency' such as housing need, time spent on the waiting list and so on, as determined by officials. In terms of accountability, market liberalism favours legal rather than political regulation, hence the creation in recent years of statutory independent regulators for public utilities.

2.3.5 John Rawls (1921–2000): liberal justice, welfare and equality

An influential modern version of the social contract is that of John Rawls:

> Our exercise of political power is proper and hence justifiable only when it is exercised in accordance with a constitution the essentials of which all citizens may be reasonably expected to endorse in the light of principles and ideas acceptable to them as reasonable and rational. This is the liberal principle of legitimacy. (*Political Liberalism* (Columbia University Press 1993) 217)

One problem with this is its reliance on the word 'reasonably', since we may disagree as to what is reasonable. Who decides what is 'reasonably expected' in a society made up of people with many different beliefs? To answer this question Rawls proposed an 'original position' in which a representative group of people ignorant of their own circumstances, including sex, race or wealth, decide what would be a just constitution (*A Theory of Justice* (Oxford University Press 1972)). The purpose of this 'veil of ignorance' is to ensure equality and the removal of self-interested influences. However it also reduces the parties to clones, thinking as one and therefore not making an agreement at all in any real sense. Rawls was of course aware of this and later introduced the watered-down notion of an 'overlapping consensus'. This is a settlement that people from a wide variety of backgrounds might be prepared to acknowledge as reasonable. However underlying all this is the liberal assumption that people want to agree and might be willing to compromise. It is by no means obvious that this is the case. Rawls acknowledges this, claiming that his arguments are political rather than philosophical and apply only in a community that is broadly sympathetic to liberal values ('Justice as Fairness: Political Not Metaphysical' in Freeman (ed), *Collected Papers* (Harvard University Press 1999)).

Rawls' social contract comprises two fundamental 'principles of justice'. The first is that 'each person is to have an equal right to the most extensive basic liberty compatible with a similar liberty for others'. These liberties operate in the constitutional sphere. They include political freedoms, freedom of speech, personal liberty and the right to hold private property, matters dealt with in charters of rights such as the ECHR (Chapter 20). This has priority over the second principle, the 'difference principle', which is concerned with allocating the resources of society: 'Social and economic inequalities are to be arranged so that they are both (a) reasonably expected to be to everyone's advantage, and (b) attached to positions and offices open to all.' The difference principle involves wide questions of politics and economics outside the scope of this book. However one implication seems to be that fundamental freedoms cannot be overridden in the interests of some other social goal. As we shall see (Chapter 21), this is not the case in the UK.

2.3.6 Robert Nozick (1938–2002): 'libertarian' liberalism

To different degrees liberal individualists treat respect for the equality and freedom of the individual as an end in itself. Thus individual freedom is not regarded as a component of the general welfare, as with the utilitarians, but requires barriers between the individual and the state. Nozick provides an extreme example. Driven by the idea of minimising state power, Nozick relies on the notion of the natural rights of the individual, deriving these from a view of basic human nature similar to that of Locke, but without the religious element. Rather than inventing a social contract that he regards as redundant, Nozick works out what is the minimum amount of government needed to secure basic rights. He argues that rights of personal freedom and property are sacrosanct and the state should not use force against anyone without their consent (*Anarchy, State and Utopia* (Blackwell 1974)). Moreover the role of the state should be limited to providing services that could not be provided voluntarily by private persons. This leads to the minimum, or 'nightwatchman', state, the function of which is limited to protecting individuals against force, theft and fraud and enforcing contracts. The state can raise money for these purposes but taxation, particularly for redistributing from rich to poor, can be equated with theft or forced labour (cf Rawls above). Nozick therefore provides a model of a hypothetical minimum state that to some extent relates to contemporary ideas of privatisation.

2.3.7 Liberal pluralism: group liberalism

Liberal pluralism, sometimes called 'identity politics' or 'the politics of recognition', is related to communitarianism and not always regarded as a kind of liberalism (see Anderson, *Constitutional Rights after Globalism* (Hart 2005); Cover, 1983; Galston, 2005). It requires the state to respect the identities and way of life of different groups such as national, religious, ethnic or sexual minorities, as well as political associations, trade unions, vocational groups and the like. It may therefore conflict with other liberal ideas of equality. The groups protected by pluralism might be disadvantaged because of the stereotype of the 'normal' person represented by the ruling group, in our case the white, able-bodied, heterosexual, culturally Christian male.

Liberal pluralism requires active steps to ensure that all such groups have the leverage to participate fully in the life of the community and to express their own identity against that of the dominant group, for example by being represented in public institutions, using their own language and giving effect to their own law and courts, as in the case of Islamic and Jewish law. It is not enough merely to tolerate or attempt to integrate such groups into the mainstream, as is the dominant approach of UK law, since this implies only limited acceptance. The danger of identity politics is that it might encourage hostility between different groups, since its extreme 'identity' implies rejecting outsiders.

Liberal pluralism might therefore conflict with other kinds of liberalism, particularly where the values of the group conflict with more individualistic values; for example a religious sect might claim that corporal punishment is part of its religion (see *R (Williamson) v Secretary of State for Education and Employment* [2005]: claim overridden by interests of child; Chapter 20). A group might also claim that its way of life should be supported by the state, for example religious schools, or should have special treatment to compensate for past injustices. Liberal pluralism would put less stress on equality and rationality than would other forms of liberalism. Thus there is the problem of a group whose values are authoritarian: the famous liberal dilemma of 'tolerating intolerance'. According to Lord Walker in *Williamson*, 'in matters of human rights the courts should not show liberal tolerance only to tolerant liberals' (at [60]). For example a common liberal claim is that liberalism contains universal truths derived from reason, so that a liberal law should not permit a religious group to prevent its members leaving it (ECHR, Art 9). However such freedom might be unacceptable to a religion which teaches, along the lines of positive freedom (Section 2.4), that compulsion is in a person's best interests. Some liberals suggest the proper approach is that the members of any group must accept that the state, in order to protect itself, can override their interests provided the decision process used is fair to all interests. However there may not be agreement as to what a fair process means (see Raz, 'Multiculturalism' (1998) 11 Ratio Juris 193).

In terms of constitutional arrangements, we would expect liberal pluralists to emphasise open and dispersed government, local government and the equal representation of minority groups in public institutions such as the judiciary. The different devolved arrangements in Scotland, Northern Ireland and Wales (Chapter 16) could be presented as embodying this. It is often suggested that one part of the legislature, the House of Lords, might comprise representatives of important interest groups. At present the only such groups represented in Parliament are Church of England bishops (Chapter 11). Liberal pluralism would also favour voluntary mechanisms to enable individuals to participate in society, for example tax breaks for charities and other voluntary bodies ('civil society').

Liberal pluralism might not be sympathetic to the idea of an overarching state law and might be required to respect different interpretations of the law according to the culture and traditions of different religious or ethnic groups and to allow particular groups to use their own form of dispute resolution machinery, including courts. In the UK voluntary methods of arbitration are permitted in respect of commercial disputes, and a variety of forms of marriage are recognised. However these are subject to overriding requirements of the general law.

2.4 Freedom

The idea of freedom is therefore central to liberalism. Some regard freedom as an end in itself: 'he who desires in liberty anything other than itself is born to be a servant' (De Tocqueville, *L'Ancien Regime*, 1856). However it is difficult to regard freedom as an end in itself, let alone the highest end. Do we for example regard Hitler's freedom to pursue his interests as something good in itself, although offset by the harm he did? Moreover freedom may conflict with 'equality' since the strong are free to exploit the weak.

Freedom has different, vague and sometimes conflicting meanings. At the most basic level liberalism contains a conflict between two ideas of freedom. This affects the extent to which different political groups regard state intervention as a good or bad thing.

1. *Traditional or negative freedom* is what most of us understand by freedom: 'By Liberty, is understood... the absence of external impediments' (Hobbes, 1973, ch 14, para 1). For example negative freedom concentrates on the individual as 'author of his own life', that is freeing the individual from interference by the state. Social liberalism stresses individual rights and legal protection against abuse of government power. Economic liberalism relies on the idea of the free market and the belief that competing individuals pursuing their own self-interests are more likely to produce generally good outcomes than the state. The role of the state is a limited one of ensuring that the free market operates smoothly: a government with as few powers as possible beyond the basic functions of defence and keeping order. These two aspects of negative freedom do not necessarily go together politically and do not lead to any particular conclusion as to how freedom should be protected, whether primarily by a court or by democratic means. Arguably economic liberalism depends on a certain degree of social conformity in order to ensure that enough people buy the goods on offer and to control those who lose out from the adverse consequences of competition.

   A fundamental problem with negative freedom is that some freedoms are more important than others. Thus the relative importance of competing freedoms, such as freedom of the press against privacy (eg *Campbell v MGN Ltd* [2004]), may be controversial. There seems to be no common measure or litmus test to enable us to rank or compare different freedoms (eg *Copsey* below). Thus when the law restricts freedom in order to protect the freedom of others as liberalism recommends, for example by restricting demonstrators in order to protect those going to work, it is not maximising freedom as is sometimes suggested but only redistributing freedom among different people according to the lawmakers' preference as to which freedom is more attractive. This leads to the second kind of freedom.
2. *Positive freedom*, an older idea, is freedom not to do what we want as such, but to control our lives by doing what is good for us. Freedom in this sense means exercising the power of reason to make choices that enhance the possibilities of our lives, thus 'liberating' our higher nature from our animal instincts and allowing us to control our own destinies (autonomy). For example a drunk may have negative freedom but, having lost self-control, has no positive freedom. Plato (*c*428–*c*348 BC), who recommended authoritarian rule, insisted: you are not free when you are slave to your desires. Freedom is mastery by the rational self, mastery by knowledge of what is really good. (Gorman, *Rights and Reason* (Acumen 2003) 33). But the worm within positive freedom is the issue of who decides what is good (below).

The two kinds of freedom sometimes support each other since negative freedom enables us to exercise choices. However positive freedom is in one sense wider since it includes restrictions on freedom caused not just by interference by the state but also by social and economic conditions such as poverty or a bad environment. It requires government action to limit negative freedom, such as distributing resources such as education, wealth and health care to enable people to make genuine choices and so take control of their lives. This version of liberalism is similar to that favoured by the shifting centre-ground parties in the UK, where elections are won or lost.

In another sense positive freedom is narrower in that it concentrates only on freedom to do good things. Positive freedom also allows us to claim paradoxically that obeying the law is 'freedom', in that law gives us a degree of rational choice by providing stability, which enables us to plan our lives.

Attitudes of negative and positive freedom towards law therefore differ. Negative freedom regards law as a restriction and concentrates on limiting state power, thus reflecting the red light perspective mentioned in Chapter 1. Positive freedom (green light) is open to greater government control since it is consistent with the state designating what are valuable choices. Thus it could well be positive freedom in the minds of judges when they are required to decide which of two rights should prevail or whether some other public interest should outweigh the freedom of the individual. The distinction between positive and negative freedom sometimes underlies disagreements in the courts. For example in *Tomlinson v Congleton DC* [2003], the claimant had, despite warning notices, jumped into a pool owned by a local authority and broken his neck. The question was whether a local authority was obliged to do more to protect against this risk. Lord Hoffmann remarked from the negative freedom perspective that our liberal individualistic system meant that the nanny state should not be encouraged and that, given there was a clear warning notice, the claimant should be responsible for his own safety. By contrast Sedley LJ in the Court of Appeal had taken the view, characteristic of positive freedom, that the local authority should have taken precautions to guard people against their own irrationality.

According to Isaiah Berlin (1907–97), positive freedom has a sinister aspect. Who decides what is good and rational? As we saw in Chapter 1 human affairs are prone to disagreement and there are different ideas of what is rational. How does one compare and choose between different freedoms which are 'incommensurable', meaning that there is no objective way of measuring their importance? For example should one condone torture in the interests of good international relations (see *Jones v Ministry of Interior of Saudi Arabia* [2006] (Section 9.7.2)) or torture one person in order to save the lives, possibly, of many? Positive freedom might justify the state claiming that a particular way of life, for example one based on a religious cult, an economic theory or belonging to the European Union, is 'rationally' better than others and is therefore what the people would 'really' want if they could think properly, just as we say that someone who is drunk is not 'himself'. This justifies coercion in a person's 'own interests':

> Once I take this view I am in a position to ignore the actual wishes of men or societies, to bully, oppress, torture them in the name, and on behalf, of their real selves, in the secure knowledge that whatever is the true goal of man (happiness, performance of duty, wisdom, a just society, self-fulfillment) must be identical with his freedom – the free choice of his 'true', albeit often submerged and inarticulate self. (Berlin, 2002, 180)

For example a person detained in a hospital for 'his own good' could be claimed to be not 'detained' at all but freely submitting. Thus in *HM v Switzerland* [2002] the European Court of Human Rights held that placing a child in a foster home was not a 'deprivation of liberty' since it was a responsible measure in the child's own interests.

Berlin of course recognises that the state might sometimes have good reason for interfering with freedom. For example in *HM v Switzerland* Berlin's analysis would probably be that there was a deprivation of liberty, but one outweighed by a greater good. His point is that by lumping together freedom and other goods we are disguising hard choices between incommensurables. Thus Berlin is concerned that decision makers openly confront difficult choices. The best we can expect is a compromise that is widely acceptable.

Copsey v WBB Devon Clays Ltd [2005] illustrates the kind of compromise that has to be made. Neuberger LJ referred to 'enlightened capitalism and liberal democracy' in deciding that an employer could require a Christian employee to work on a Sunday. It was held that Article 9 of the ECHR, freedom to manifest religion, requires a balance to be struck between the reasonable needs of the employer and those of the employee, since Article 9 rights can be overridden on several grounds, including the 'rights and freedoms of others'. Perhaps a widely acceptable compromise was reached. The employer had seriously tried to accommodate the employee's Christian beliefs about Sunday working but in the circumstances this proved impossible and would cause unfairness to other workers. Thus the decision was based upon a subjective evaluation of the relative importance of the interests concerned. There is some indication in the case, although the judges were not fully agreed on this point, that freedom of contract is to be ranked especially highly, so that an employee is free to get another job. Mummery LJ went further in a liberal direction, holding that an employer was entitled to adopt a secular regime. The secular approach means that religious interests must not be given special weight or perhaps even feature in public life at all so as to ensure equality, but this conflicts with another cherished liberal belief, that of respecting an individual's choice of lifestyle.

2.5 Republicanism

Republicanism and liberalism overlap, but republicanism stresses cooperation rather than freedom, and also equality, in the sense of equal access to the processes of government. Originating in ancient Greece, revived in the Renaissance and developed in the seventeenth and eighteenth centuries (Machiavelli, 1469–1527; Harrington, 1611–77; Montesquieu, 1689–1755), republicanism builds on the idea of positive freedom (above). It stresses that the state exists for the benefit of all members of the community as free and equal citizens. Thus rulers have no rights of their own (other than as citizens) but only duties to the community. Its key concepts are limited and balanced government under law, citizenship and political equality. Republican ideas were widely canvassed during the revolutionary period of the seventeenth century but have not significantly influenced the structure of the UK constitution. However there has been a recent revival of interest in republican ideas, stimulated by evidence of widespread apathy among voters and disenchantment with political processes remote from popular experience (see eg Bellamy, 2007; Tomkins, 2005). Thus while liberalism separates the state from the community, drawing a line around state powers, republicanism incorporates the community into the state. Republicanism is concerned to ensure that no single person or group within the community can dominate others. This applies to private vested interests and democratic majorities as much as to government bodies. In this respect the devolved government arrangements especially for Northern Ireland (see Section 16.3) tend towards republicanism. Apart from concern with a separation of powers between different branches of government and with protecting political freedoms, republicanism involves such questions as whether individuals should be able to buy access to political offices or influence.

Republicanism stresses the right and the duty of citizens to participate in government. Positive freedom (above) links with this republican idea of democracy since we can rationally control our own lives if we participate in collective decision making, what Constant (1767–1830) called 'the freedom of the ancients'. Thus positive freedom might favour compulsory voting. Rousseau (1712–78) for example famously wrote that we should be 'forced' to be free, meaning that true freedom lies in collective participation by voting in public affairs. He assumed that each person would vote rationally in accordance with the public interest (the 'general will' rather than his or her selfish interests, the will of all) and that the minority who disagree with the outcome must therefore be 'wrong' (see Rousseau, *The Social Contract*, trans Cole (The Constitution Society 1762) book 2). Republicans do not necessarily exclude courts from resolving political disputes but favour democratic methods. Of particular importance, republicanism stresses that it is not enough that rulers in fact rule wisely and benevolently. In the interests of dignity, equality and freedom, all limits on the rulers must be secured by law so that the ruler cannot abuse his or her power. Anything less relies only on hoping that the slavemaster will be kind. This is perhaps where the UK's informal constitution is particularly vulnerable, relying as it does on informal arrangements between networks of individuals. Parliament sometimes enacts laws of draconian severity with little discussion, relying on assurances from the government that in practice the laws will be applied only in special and limited circumstances (such as anti-terrorism legislation; see Chapter 23). There is no reason to think that this is so. Many people advocate direct citizen participation in government along the lines supposed by Rousseau.

The separation of powers is consistent with the republican principle that power should not be concentrated in any single person or group. However republicans differ as to the best form of constitution to achieve the goal of free and democratic citizenship. Drawing on classical virtues, some republicans favour the notion of deliberative democracy, where disputes are settled by ensuring that citizens have the opportunity to participate directly in decision making. This seems to paint an idealised picture of groups of leisured and well-informed people with enough in common and sufficient good will to reach agreement. Others regard this as unrealistic in a complex society that depends on specialists and prefer a version of the representative system where ultimate power is vested in an assembly chosen by the people in free and fair elections to which the executive government is accountable (see Bellamy, 2007). The UK has provision for direct participation only exceptionally (see Section 2.7.2).

The UK constitution has a claim to be at least partly republican in the representative sense, although the House of Lords, which is part of Parliament, is appointed not elected. Those who support republicanism usually reject the notion that the courts should have the last word and regard the constitution as being safer in political hands. For example Tomkins (2005) places stress on the political doctrine that ministers are responsible to Parliament, regarding this as the golden principle of the constitution, while Bellamy (2007) stresses the importance of equal voting rights. Allan (2001) by contrast regards the courts as guardians of republican ideals and would permit them to disapply legislation that violated fundamental democratic values. This runs counter to the view that it is offensive to submit to unelected authority on fundamental matters and that participation is 'the right of rights' (see Waldron, 2001, 11, 12, 13).

In terms of the political values that underpin the constitution, human rights are strongly favoured by liberals. Human rights are favoured by many liberal lawyers because they raise the political importance of courts and lawyers substituting authoritative pronouncements by judges within the framework of rational argument that lawyers are good at for the wider-ranging discussions and compromises of the political forum. It must be stressed that these are only general tendencies. Some liberals may favour political solutions because of fears of judicial bias; some republicans may favour courts because of fear of political parties.

Republicans are more ambivalent about human rights. They recognise human rights, but in a more grudging way than liberals. A moderate republican would accept the idea of human rights, but as part of the general interest, and would therefore recognise more easily than a liberal that a right should give way to a social goal. A more extreme version of republicanism would regard possession of a right as conditional upon good behaviour in the sense of conforming to the dominant values of the group. (To a communitarian human rights may be regarded as divisive, selfish and frustrating community values.)

> The two republican approaches can be illustrated by the reasoning of the majority and minority in *R (Begum) v Head Teacher and Governors of Denbigh High School* [2006]. The House of Lords held that a ban on the wearing of a strict form of Muslim dress at a school was not an unlawful interference with the right of freedom of religion. Two lines of reasoning were used. The majority held that the right to religious freedom was not infringed at all. The child concerned could have attended other, more flexible schools, and the style of dress chosen was not required by mainstream Islamic doctrine. This is consistent with an extreme republicanism. Lord Nicholls and Baroness Hale held that a right had been infringed but was overridden by the important social purpose of fostering a sense of community by means of a dress code. This is a more moderate republicanism because it recognises both the importance of the individual claim and that there is a dilemma. By contrast, to the majority the right disappeared within the wider public good, so that the problem of balancing the two competing claims was avoided. A liberal approach would overlap with that of the minority but an extreme liberal might be reluctant to regard the social goal as important enough to override the right.
>
> The more extreme republican approach therefore reduces the problem faced squarely by liberals in deciding when, if at all, a right should give way to a social goal. The usual method of dealing with this problem is to draw upon the idea of 'proportionality', meaning that the right must be interfered with as little as is consistent with achieving the social goal. However social goals, such as security against terrorism, can be achieved to a greater or lesser extent. Therefore proportionality does not provide an objective solution. Thus we are faced with incommensurable subjective choices (see Section 1.6). The republican approach would tend to place these choices in the hands of the people through their representatives in Parliament, whereas liberals who tend to assume the existence of objective solutions may favour courts.

It is sometimes suggested that the Human Rights Act 1998 embodies a moderate republican approach. Not only does it recognise that a social goal often overrides a right but it also leaves the final choice to Parliament rather than the court. We shall discuss the Act in Chapter 21.

2.6 Equality

Liberalism and republicanism presuppose that all people are equal. However 'equality' has no clear meaning. Equality is merely a measure, the real question being 'equality of what?' For example liberalism emphasises equality between individual freedoms, whereas republicanism is concerned with equality in the political process.

We can distinguish broadly between 'formal' equality and 'substantive' equality. This is reflected in different versions of the 'rule of law' (Section 6.3). Formal equality is about procedures and appearances. It requires that everyone's rights be treated the same in terms of the application of the law, for example the right to a fair trial. It does not mean that the contents of the rights are the same. That is a matter of substantive equality. For example a landlord has greater rights over a house than a tenant and can often afford to go to court and get legal advice more easily than a tenant, but the two sets of rights will be given equal consideration by a court. Unless we adopt the difficult position that everyone should be treated identically (which conflicts with freedom), substantive equality means only that we should not treat people differently without a good reason. Thus John Stuart Mill, widely regarded as a founder of British liberalism, said that:

> all persons are deemed to have a right to equality of treatment except when some recognised social expediency requires otherwise. (1972, ch 5)

We may disagree about what counts as a good reason. This creates further conflicting concepts of equality. For example, while there is widespread consensus that we should not discriminate on grounds of personal characteristics such as race or gender, it is controversial whether there should be equality in respect of the distribution of wealth or public services (equality of outcome). Should resource allocation be based on need (equality of opportunity) or on merit (equality of desert)? Why should people who happen to be born with talents that suit the interests of the community be better off for that reason than those less fortunate? This raises political questions largely outside the scope of the law. Nevertheless equality is of primary importance in combating governmental action that arbitrarily targets certain groups.

For example in *A v Secretary of State for the Home Dept* [2005] legislation authorised the government to imprison foreign terrorist suspects without trial unless they voluntarily left the country. The rationale was that the terrorist threat was an emergency and the action was necessary to protect the public since under the ECHR it would have been unlawful to deport the people concerned, who would face torture in their home countries. Nine Law Lords heard the case and by a majority of eight decided that the detention was contrary to the human rights of those concerned. An underlying theme was that of equality. By targeting foreign terrorist suspects in this way, the government had not addressed the equal threat posed by British terrorists, who likewise could no be expelled. Conversely its measures included people who were not necessarily a threat to the UK.

2.7 Democracy

Liberalism and republicanism share ideals of democracy in a general sense, but there are different versions of democracy. Karl Marx famously said that democracy is the 'solved riddle of all constitutions. Here ... the constitution is brought back to its actual basis ... and established as the people's own work' (see Marks, *The Riddle of All Constitutions* (Oxford University Press 2000) 149). Similarly (perhaps) democracy has been defined as 'the people of a country deciding for themselves the contents of the laws that organise and regulate their political association'. (Michaelman, 'Brennan and Democracy' (1998) 86 California LR 399–400).

According to this definition there is unlikely to be much democracy in the world and yet most states label themselves democracies. Michaelman's aspiration is the republican one of citizen self-government by active participation, sometimes called 'deliberative democracy'. This might be practicable in a village where everyone knows everyone else, but it is unrealistic in contemporary nation states comprising millions of strangers with conflicting goals and interests and where the complexity of society requires decisions to be made by experts.

In the UK's liberal culture, democracy means government with the 'consent' of the people, a more slippery notion. The people cannot consent to anything until there are rules determining who counts as 'the people' and how they express their wishes. For example different voting formulae fixed by those currently in power produce very different outcomes (see Section 12.7). In England an element of consent to taxation, albeit only that of important landowners and clerics, was introduced during the mediaeval period (eg Magna Carta 1215, Art 14), and in this limited sense the seeds of democracy were planted. However the transition from a limited monarchy to governments elected by most of the adult population was a slow and reluctant one (see Section 4.5).

From the earliest times democracy has meant decisions made by a majority. The proposed European Constitution, quoting Thucydides (*c*460–400 BC), claims that:

> our constitution is called a democracy because power is in the hands not of a minority but of the greatest number.

The justification for majoritarianism is not that a majority is likely to be 'right', since this is clearly untrue, but that majority voting is fair since it treats everyone equally. However majoritarianism has well-known problems. Firstly, unless there is a simple choice between only two options, the mathematics of majority voting will not necessarily produce a majority preference. Secondly a majority may oppress unpopular minorities or introduce repressive laws as a panic response to an emergency or become the passive tool of a selfish ruling group. Thus John Adams, one of the founders of the US Constitution, feared 'elective despotism', and De Tocqueville (1805–59), commenting on the newly formed US Constitution, referring to the 'tyranny of the majority', said:

> I am trying to imagine under what novel features despotism may appear in the world. In the first place, I see an innumerable multitude of men, alike and equal, constantly circling around in pursuit of the petty and banal pleasures with which they glut their souls... Over this kind of men stands an immense, protective power which is alone responsible for securing their enjoyment and watching over their fate. (*Democracy in America,* trans Lawrence (Fontana 1968) vol 2, 898)

There is therefore a tension between constitutionalism, the rule of law and individual freedom on the one hand, and democracy on the other. This underlies important issues in constitutional law, in particular whether the courts should be empowered to overturn Acts of Parliament on constitutional grounds. Liberals are ambivalent about this. On the one hand judges could be regarded as undemocratic. On the other hand liberalism is not tied to democracy. A standard argument in this context is that there are certain fundamental requirements of democracy, such as freedom of expression, that should be protected by independent courts in case a democratic majority is seduced or panicked into overriding them. A republican answer is that it is those who are affected by the laws in question who should have an equal say in deciding what those laws should be, it being offensive to human dignity not to trust a democratic body (see Waldron, 2001; Bellamy, 2007).

2.7.1 Representative democracy

The characteristic form of modern democracy is 'representative democracy'. The ideal is that of government which the people can choose, call to account and remove. The people choose representatives directly, who appoint others to assist them subject to a clear chain of responsibility. As we shall see this chain is sometimes lacking in the UK. The representatives must explain their actions and must regularly submit themselves for re-election. A famous early statement is that of Fortescue (*On the Governance of the Kingdom of England*, 1537), who distinguished between *dominium regale*, the rule of the king alone, necessary in certain cases, for example to deal with an emergency, and *dominium politicum et regale*, the rule of the king with the assent of representatives of the community after discussion collectively in Parliament. More recently, in *R (Alconbury Developments) v Secretary of State for the Environment, Transport and the Regions* [2001], Lord Hoffmann informed us that in the UK:

> decisions as to what the general interest requires are made by democratically elected bodies or by persons accountable to them. (at 980)

Representative democracy favours the more individualistic versions of liberalism, since the citizen's only power is to vote as a private solitary act without any requirement for discussion. Representative democracy relies upon a passive population, provided that enough people vote to give those chosen some legitimacy. Republicans and communitarians who favour the active participation of citizens are less comfortable with representative democracy. Mill favoured a greater level of democracy at local level, not because it produced efficient government but in order to develop the abilities of local people to develop themselves by participating in public life. This does not apply to the contemporary UK constitution, where local government is substantially constrained by central government, so that local elected politicians have little significant power.

Typically the people choose a lawmaking assembly as the highest branch of government. In a presidential system the people also vote for the head of state (below). Bentham and his utilitarian followers recommended that even judges be removable by the people since the people are the final court, but this is not the case in the UK. Mill especially favoured representative democracy since it combines popular consent with a utilitarian reliance on experts. However, like many contemporary public officials, Mill distrusted 'the people'. He recommended slewing the voting system so that the highly educated had greater voting power. He also suggested that Parliament should include a quota of people with a 'national reputation' and that people on welfare benefits should be disqualified from voting on the ground they might be biased. Fear of democracy remains a significant theme of the constitutional debate in the UK. For example proposals to reform the House of Lords, which is currently wholly appointed, have foundered largely because of resistance to the idea of a wholly elected legislature (Chapter 12).

The term 'representative' is ambiguous. A representative assembly could be a 'portrait' or microcosm of those it represents, for example being representative in terms of the political balance of opinion or ethnic and racial groupings. Alternatively it could be an agent of the people, not having any specified composition but made up of people chosen for their personal qualities or party membership. The practical significance of this concerns different types of voting system designed to produce different outcomes (Chapter 12). The UK Parliament operates the agency model but the devolved regimes in Scotland, Wales and Northern Ireland combine both models.

Another basic issue is whether representatives in either model are bound by the views of those who voted for them or should vote according to their own consciences. The UK constitution has traditionally taken the attitude that representatives must not be bound by any outside commitments. For example elected local authorities must not bind themselves in law to carry out any political mandate on which they are elected (eg *Bromley LBC v GLC* [1983]). However within Parliament the Whip system encourages MPs to vote blindly for their party. Proceedings in Parliament cannot be challenged in the courts.

Representative democracy provides mechanisms for ensuring that the government is accountable to the electorate. However the existing rulers decide who is entitled to vote. It was only after a struggle lasting over 100 years that the principle of general adult suffrage was accepted, and even now, despite an adverse ruling of the European Court of Human Rights, convicted prisoners have no right to vote in UK elections (*Hurst v UK (No 2)* [2004] (although proposals are belatedly under discussion)).

Accountability is an ambiguous idea but basically means that decisions must be explained and justified. The main accountability devices required by representative democracies are as follows:

- right to question the executive (Chapters 13, 15);
- policing financial limits on government spending (Chapter 13);
- internal control mechanisms within government (Chapter 15);
- judicial review (Chapters 17, 18, 19);
- public consultation and access to information (Chapters 22, 23).

Each of these depends on a separation of powers between different functions of government (Chapter 7) and on safeguarding basic freedoms, including the freedom to form political parties and the freedom of the press to criticise government. The European Court and the UK courts have stressed the special importance of political freedom of speech in connection with the democratic process (eg *Culnane v Morris* [2006]; *Bowman v UK* [1998]; *State of Mauritius v Khoyratty* [2006]).

2.7.2 Participatory democracy

Sometimes called 'deliberative democracy', participatory democracy promotes direct participation by individuals and groups in decisions which affect them. Its supporters claim that it can harness 'reason' from a wide range of perspectives. However participants are voiceless without rules and leaders who stage-manage their involvement. Such rules may privilege some groups over others, notably the more articulate and those who benefit the rule makers. It is not clear how deliberative democracy can be organised. Notions such as town meetings have been proposed, although it is unclear what matters might be appropriate to their remit. Recognising that in a complex society full participation might be impracticable, many have argued (such as Hannah Ahrendt, 1906–75, from a republican perspective) that participation should apply to the smaller units that contribute to the political system such as local government, charities and the workplace (civil society). Habermas suggests a form of deliberative democracy that he regards as appropriate to contemporary circumstances in which the state is merely one among numerous community organisations, each comprising activists 'deliberating' on equal terms. The role of the law is to coordinate these units and to ensure that the discussions are open, fair and equal ('Three Normative

Models of Democracy' in *The Inclusion of the Other* (MIT Press 1996)). Liberals, notably Mill, have objected that deliberative democracy is likely to attract busybodies, the self-promoting, the corrupt, the ignorant and cranks. However representative democracy is not immune from these.

UK law provides for deliberative democracy only in a limited and piecemeal way:

- The jury system for serious criminal trials and in certain civil cases is the only example regarded as important enough to have constitutional status (Juries Act 1974). Indeed the jury system is sometimes promoted as an example of deliberative democracy since a randomly chosen panel of citizens makes a binding decision. It has been suggested that citizens juries should be enlisted to make decisions in constitutional cases as a response to the problem that many see in fundamental rights being determined by unelected judges (see Ghosh, 2010).
- The devolved regimes of Wales and Northern Ireland contain some provision for public involvement.
- Statute provides for referendums (Political Parties, Elections and Referendums Act 2000). However these are rarely held and are triggered by the government. Referendums were held in 1976 concerning continued membership of what is now the European Union, in 1997 concerning devolution and in 2004 concerning a proposal for a regional assembly in northeast England. There are referendum provisions relating to devolution in Northern Ireland and Wales (see Sections 16.3, 16.4). A referendum has been promised in respect of proposed changes to the voting system (Chapter 24). However it is often argued that the use of referendums would threaten the equality protected by representative democracy since a referendum is liable to be manipulated by vested interests.
- There are statutory public inquiries into many decisions relating to land development but the outcome is not normally binding on the government.
- There is also some participation in the provision for 'parish meetings' at local government level in small rural villages. However these have little power other than in relation to local amenities such as playgrounds.

In recent years the courts seem to have adopted a more sympathetic approach to direct participation, at least in cases where machinery has been provided by statute. (Compare *Berkeley v Secretary of State for the Environment* [2000]: participation a right for its own sake, with *Bushell v Secretary of State for the Environment* [1981]: participation does not entitle full information.) Participatory democracy shares with representative democracy a concern with freedom of expression, particularly freedom of the press and with public access to information. Thus Lord Bingham pointed out in *McCartan Turkington-Breen v Times Newspapers* [2000] at 922 that a 'free, active, professional and enquiring press' was all the more important to support a participatory democracy since the majority of people can participate only indirectly.

2.7.3 Political parties: market democracy

In practice democratic constitutions are dominated by political parties. Political parties publicise and coordinate different opinions and, as Burke somewhat idealistically asserted, make it possible to achieve by discussion a notion of the common good (*On the Present Discontents* (1770) vol II). Without them an elected assembly would be a rabble. However when Burke was writing, MPs were usually of independent means as opposed to the paid functionaries of the present day, and party structures were relatively loose. A modern political party can usually exclude independently minded people as candidates for election and ensure that MPs vote in accordance with the party line.

Liberalism regards political parties as self-governing voluntary bodies even though they are central to government. In the interests of freedom therefore there is resistance to legal controls over political parties, for example in respect of how they raise funds. On the other hand fair elections require certain controls – a tension characteristic of liberal democracy. For example in the US case of *Buckley v Valeo* [1976], restrictions on expenses for election advertising designed to ensure equal competition were held to violate the right to freedom of expression. A different view has been taken in the UK (Chapter 12).

'Market democracy', which is related to market liberalism (above), recognises the role of parties and argues that in contemporary circumstances elections provide only a limited choice. According to Weber (1864–1920) and Schumpeter (1883–1950), the voter's only power is to choose between products offered by competing party leaders who present themselves for election every few years. The vote provides the price mechanism.

Market democracy has significant implications for the constitution. No longer is the state the neutral umpire of Hobbes and Locke; it is a player in the game offering inducements for votes. In particular there is the danger that government will be captured by the vested interests of those who fund the parties. In the UK business interests bankroll the main parties. However supporters of market democracy argue that competition will ensure that one party is unlikely to stay in control permanently, provided that the electoral system properly reflects the range of opinion – a matter which is questionable in the UK (Chapter 12).

It could be argued that contemporary society is too fragmented and diverse to fit into the mould of large-scale contesting parties and is represented more accurately by single issue or special interest pressure groups. Modern governments may therefore be chosen not on the basis of broad ideological or class differences but on the basis of the personalities of the individuals standing for election. Moreover market democracy encourages government policies to be expressed in terms of outcomes, targets and 'value for money' rather than in terms of fairness and justice. The emphasis on outputs also blurs the divide between the public and private sectors since the means by which outputs are delivered ceases to matter.

Summary

- Having read this chapter you should have some general ideas and perspectives which you can use to assess the UK constitution.
- Constitutions are underpinned by an assortment of sometimes conflicting political values. Of these liberalism has strong contemporary influence. Liberalism separates the individual from the state and emphasises limitations on state power in the interests of individual freedom. Liberalism overlaps with republicanism; however the latter stresses equal participation as citizens and emphasises duties rather than individual rights. Both favour limited government.
- Liberalism also treats individuals as equal, the two ideas being capable of conflicting. Formal equality relating to fair procedures is a prime concern of the law. Substantive equality relating to the distribution of resources is primarily a matter of pre-legal political choices.

Summary cont'd

- A review of significant writers who have influenced liberal ideas reveals different and sometimes conflicting forms of liberalism, depending on the importance and meaning given to individual freedom as opposed to the general public interest. These include liberal individualism, market liberalism, welfare liberalism and liberal pluralism.
- The distinction between positive and negative freedom illustrates the kinds of disagreements that arise within liberalism. Positive freedom emphasises our ability to choose reason to exercise choice and links with republican ideas of citizen participation in government. It may also lead to authoritarian attempts to impose rational solutions. Negative freedom is the freedom to be left alone. It may be seen as impractical and selfish.
- Republicanism can be contrasted with liberalism. Republicanism does not separate the individual from the state but favours the notion of the virtuous, politically active citizen. It is associated with positive freedom and treats freedom as the right to participate in government. It stresses limited government and (usually) democratic rather than judicial controls over government. There are some republican elements in the UK constitution.
- There are different kinds of democracy, including deliberative/participatory democracy, representative democracy and market democracy.
- There are differences between a parliamentary and a presidential democracy. The former concentrates legal power in the legislature and usually involves a separate head of state with limited power. However in practice the executive may come to dominate the legislature. The latter divides power between the executive and the legislature as equals but the President is both head of the executive and head of state.
- Democracy has several variations, the main ones being representative democracy, deliberative democracy and market democracy. Representative democracy is the basis of the UK constitution but market democracy is in practice pursued by the political parties. Democracy is underpinned by ideas of constitutionalism and the rule of law, and the courts give particular importance to freedom of speech and of the press in the context of democratic processes.

Exercises

2.1 How would (i) a liberal and (ii) a republican arrange for (a) the appointment of judges, (b) the method of lawmaking, (c) the settlement of a dispute as to whether a religious group should be permitted to have polygamous marriages?

2.2 What are the main principles of a republican form of constitution? Give examples of such principles in the UK constitution.

2.3 Sedley (*London Review of Books*, 15 November 2001) describes a case where a French court upheld a ban on local funfairs where revellers had been permitted to shoot a dwarf from a cannon. The decision was made in the name of public morals and human dignity even though the dwarfs made their living from the spectacle and were among the chief opponents of the ban. Discuss in relation to the views of Nozick, Mill and Bentham.

2.4 Discuss from the perspective of different forms of liberalism the following legislative proposals:
(i) a ban on any religion that prevents its members from leaving it;
(ii) provision for a free market in unwanted babies;
(iii) a right for any person to have paid leave from work in order to practise his or her religion;
(iv) a ban on any person convicted of a crime from voting;
(v) a ban on 'faith schools'.

Exercises cont'd

2.5 'A democratic constitution is in the end undemocratic if it gives all power to its elected government' (Sir John Laws, 'Law and Democracy' [1995] PL 73). Explain and discuss.

2.6 To what extent is the UK constitution liberal or republican (perhaps best answered at the end of your course).

Further reading

Allan, *Constitutional Justice: A Liberal Theory of the Rule of Law* (Oxford University Press 2001)
Bellamy, *Political Constitutionalism* (Cambridge University Press 2007) chs 1, 3–6
Berlin, 'Two Concepts of Liberty' in Hardy (ed), *Liberty* (Oxford University Press 2002)
Crick, *Democracy: A Very Short Introduction* (Oxford University Press 2002)
Cover, 'Nomos and Narrative' (1983) 97 Harvard LR 4
Dworkin, *Taking Rights Seriously* (Duckworth 1996)
Dworkin, *Law's Empire* (Hart 1998)
Dyzenhaus, 'How Hobbes Met the Hobbes Challenge' (2009) 72 MLR 488
Galston, *The Practice of Liberal Pluralism* (Cambridge University Press 2005)
Ghosh, 'Deliberative Democracy and the Countermajoritarian Difficulty: Considering Constitutional Juries' (2010) 30 OJLS 327
Hayek, 'Freedom and Coercion' in Miller (ed), *Liberty* (Oxford University Press 1991)
Kymlicka, 'Citizenship Theory' in *Contemporary Political Philosophy* (2nd edn, Oxford University Press 2002)
Laws, 'The Constitution: Morals and Right' [1996] PL 622
Loughlin, 'Towards a Republican Revival' (2006) 26 OJLS 425
Morison, 'Models of Democracy: From Representation to Participation' in Jowell and Oliver (eds), *The Changing Constitution* (6th edn, Oxford University Press 2007)
Pettit, *Republicanism: A Theory of Freedom and Government* (Oxford University Press 1997) chs 1–3, 5, 6
Skinner, 'The Paradoxes of Political Liberty' in Miller (ed), *Liberty* (Oxford University Press 1991)
Tierney, 'Constitutional Referendums: A Theoretical Inquiry' (2009) 72 MLR 360
Tomkins, *Our Republican Constitution* (Hart 2005)
Tully, 'The Unfreedom of the Moderns' (2002) 65 MLR 204
Waldron, *Law and Disagreement* (Oxford University Press 2001)
Wolheim, 'A Paradox in the Theory of Democracy' in Laslett and Runciman (eds), *Philosophy, Politics and Society* (2nd ser, Blackwell 1969)

Chapter 3

The sources of the constitution

The historian can tell you probably perfectly clearly what the constitutional practice was at any given period in the past, but it would be very difficult for a living writer to tell you at any given period in his lifetime what the constitution of this country is in all respects. (Stanley Baldwin, Prime Minister, 1923–29, 1935–37)

3.1 Introduction

As we saw in Chapter 1 the UK is unique among the major nations in not having a written constitution. The UK's unwritten constitution is constructed partly out of the general sources of law. These include Acts of Parliament, the common law in the form of decisions of the higher courts, and the 'laws and customs of Parliament' made by each House in order to control its affairs. The conventional view is that statute law is the highest form of law in our constitution, although there is an argument that statute is subject to the 'rule of law', which is in the hands of the courts (see Section 8.5).

We also saw that the constitution relies heavily upon unwritten rules, practices and traditions not directly enforceable in the courts, the most important of which are known as 'constitutional conventions'. A typical example is that the government must resign if defeated on a vote of confidence in the House of Commons. All constitutions have some rules of this kind even if they are not labelled as conventions but because our constitution is unwritten we rely more heavily on such rules than most countries. There is of course no intrinsic difference between the content of a convention and that of a law. Any convention can be enacted as a law. Indeed the main principles concerning the relationship between the devolved Scottish Parliament and the Scottish Executive contained in the Scotland Act 1998 are modelled on UK conventions, albeit with some important differences (see Section 6.2.1).

There are also 'practices' which are of constitutional significance even though they are not in any sense binding as rules. The most obvious of these is the existence of political parties through which contenders for power organise themselves. There is no legal or conventional requirement that there be political parties and strictly speaking a political party is a private voluntary organisation, albeit becoming increasingly regulated to prevent parties abusing the electoral process (Political Parties, Elections and Referendums Act 2000). In a complex society containing many different points of view, parties are an inevitable means of coordinating and organising competing claims and no one would doubt that political parties are a necessary feature of democracy. Because by convention the leader of the majority party in the House of Commons normally becomes the Prime Minister, the internal rules of each party for choosing its leader are of fundamental importance (see Section 5.2.4). Indeed it has been said that:

> parties have substituted for a constitution in Britain. They have filled all the vast empty spaces in the political system where a constitution should be and made the system in their own image. (Wright, quoted in Nolan and Sedley, 1997, 83)

Broad cultural values such as 'fairness', 'freedom' and 'equality' are sometimes claimed to be sources of the constitution. Whether these are worth calling sources as such is debatable since they influence most aspects of human life. As we saw in the previous chapter the meaning of these ideas is open to fundamental disagreement, which makes them little more than slogans which can be applied to a range of conflicting causes. On the other hand they have driven legal reforms, for example anti-discrimination laws such as the Gender Recognition Act 2004, which allows transsexuals to marry and have new birth certificates. The long-standing debate as to whether the monarchy should be limited as it presently is to white European Protestants is also driven by a belief that our constitution should reflect the value of equality.

The distinction between a written and an unwritten constitution is sometimes expressed as one between a 'formal' and a 'functional' constitution. The UK has no formal constitution but may have a functional constitution in the sense that its separate miscellaneous components may work together to produce a viable system that delivers the basic principles we would expect to find in a constitution. Indeed a formal constitution may not be functional in this sense since its provisions may not actually be applied.

3.2 Statute law

From the sixteenth century it became increasingly established that Parliament, in the sense of the monarch, the House of Lords and the House of Commons combining to enact statutes (Acts of Parliament), is the supreme lawmaker, although some argue even today that the courts can overturn laws made by Parliament (Chapter 8). In the absence of a written constitution there can be no permanent answer to this fundamental issue. The most radical constitutional changes have been made by statute.

Magna Carta 1215, of symbolic value rather than for its specific provisions, which recognised the principles that the monarch rules by consent (of the most powerful and wealthiest mebers of the community) and the right to a fair trial; the Habeas Corpus Act 1640, which enacted the right to challenge arbitrary imprisonment (but as an ordinary statute was suspended several times to deal with government opponents); the Bill of Rights 1688, which, following the 1688 revolution, subjected the Crown to Parliament; the Act of Settlement 1700, which regulated succession to the Crown and gave the senior judges security of tenure; the Acts of Union with Wales (1536), Scotland (1707) and Ireland (1800); the Parliament Acts 1911 and 1949, which made the House of Lords subordinate to the House of Commons; the European Communities Act 1972, which made European law part of UK law; the Human Rights Act 1998, which incorporated provisions taken from the European Convention on Human Rights into UK law; the Life Peerages Act 1958 and House of Lords Act 1999, which reformed the composition of the House of Lords; the Constitutional Reform Act 2005, which strengthened the independence of the judiciary; the Constitutional Reform and Governance Act 2010, which despite its grand title makes relatively minor changes. Many other statutes raise constitutional issues, such as those dealing with elections, complaints against government, controls over government finance, immigration, the media, police powers, the security services and freedom of information.

Two things might be noted about these statutes. Firstly they do not add up to a general constitutional code; they deal with specific issues and are usually responses to particular problems. Thus whether a statute is enacted depends mainly on the interests of the government of the day. For example there are no statutes (other than some dealing with incidental matters such as pensions and salaries) limiting the powers of the Prime Minister or regulating the relationship between the executive and Parliament (contrast the devolved regimes in Scotland, Wales and Northern Ireland).

Secondly some statutes might have a special status and influence as symbolic of great events and important principles. This is true particularly of the Bill of Rights 1688 and also of Magna Carta 1215 (enacted 1297). Extracted from King John by the leading landowners in order to rectify their grievances, most of Magna Carta is no longer strictly in force and much of it concerns the particular claims of different groups of medieval property owners. (Articles 1, 9 and 29 (originally 39) remain in force; Article 1 concerns the freedom of the Church and may be obsolete; Article 9 guarantees the liberties of the City of London and has been superseded by other legislation; Article 29 gives citizens protection against deprivation of right or expulsion except by law.)

Many of the general principles and sentiments behind Magna Carta are still invoked in constitutional debate and by the courts. It established that in principle the King is subject to the law, in the sense of the customs of the realm that protected the rights of the landowners and local communities. It also foreshadowed the modern concept of proportionality in relation to penalties. Magna Carta remains of great symbolic value as capturing the essence of the rule of law and accountable government; for example 'to none will we sell: to no one will we delay or deny justice' (see *R v Secretary of State, ex p Phansopkar* [1976]: claim to right to reside in UK, right to a court hearing prior to deportation) and 'no freeman shall be taken or imprisoned or be outlawed or exiled or in otherwise destroyed ... but by ... the law of the land' (see *R (Bancoult) v Secretary of State* [2001], below Section 9.6). Magna Carta also includes the principles of no taxation without representation and the right to a fair trial.

In *Thoburn v Sunderland City Council* [2002], Laws LJ, in the context of the European Communities Act 1972, spoke of a 'constitutional' statute, meaning a statute which the courts will not read as overridden by other statutes unless very clear language is used (Chapters 7, 9; see also *Robinson v Secretary of State for Northern Ireland* [2002]: devolution legislation). The problem here is that we may not agree as to what counts as a constitutional statute.

Statutory instruments might occasionally have constitutional importance. These are laws made by the executive under powers delegated by an Act of Parliament and are not subject to full democratic scrutiny. They usually concern very detailed and technical matters and are unlikely to raise general concerns. However ministers are sometimes given powers to alter Acts of Parliament themselves, for example by designating bodies subject to the Freedom of Information Act 2000. Moreover statutory instruments are used to create constitutions for some dependent territories (see Section 6.7).

3.3 The common law

The common law developed by judges on a case-by-case basis claims legitimacy as the embodiment of the values of the community mediated by reason and given order and certainty by precedent. Liberals and communitarians might both find the common law congenial, although republicans would have doubts about whether the common law meets the aspiration of citizen participation in government and might regret the emphasis of the law upon confrontation and rights rather than on compromise (Chapter 2). However from a republican angle it might be claimed that all citizens are on an equal footing in the courts (subject to the obvious objection that the wealthy are at a practical advantage in being able to afford high-level legal assistance).

Historically the common law predates Parliament as lawmaker since the common law emerged from customary laws that are sometimes claimed to go back to the ancient Britons. Indeed the idea of an ancient common law constitution, threatened by the pretensions of monarchs, is part of the rhetoric of English constitutional debate, designed to instil reverence for precedent. The common law was strengthened from the thirteenth century by the practice of the King's judges touring the country on his behalf as 'the fount of justice', with the main courts later gravitating to London. Although judges are in theory Crown servants, from the seventeenth century it was established that the King cannot act as a judge himself but is bound by the law as made by the judges (see *Prohibitions del Roy* [1607]).This is an important marker establishing a separation of powers of sorts.

There is a tension between the classical common law view of the constitution – advocated with varying degrees of emphasis in the seventeenth century by conservative judges such as Coke (1552–1634), Hale (1609–76) and Mansfield (1709–93) and commentators such as Blackstone (1723–80) – and the modern political notion of the constitution as the application of unlimited democratic power vested in Parliament. Coke claimed that common law was the supreme arbiter of the constitution – an argument still pursued today (Chapter 8). According to Coke, the common law is a matter of reason, but:

> the artificial perfection of reason...gotten by long study and experience...No man (out of his private reason) ought to be wiser than the law, which is the perfection of reason. (Institutes, 1(21))

Artificial reason is apparently the collective wisdom of the judges imposed through precedents. The classical view envisages the common law constitution as the product of the evolutionary development of community practices adapting the law to meet changing circumstances and, importantly, recognising that disagreement requires practical judgements rather than general principles. Hale's famous metaphor of the Argonauts' ship has often been used, where the same ship in the sense of design and purpose that had set sail returns but has been so often mended that no piece of the original remains (Hale, *A History of the Common Law* (1713) 40).

Hobbes (Chapter 2) roundly condemned Coke's claims. He denied that there is anything special about lawyers' reasoning and refused to accept that custom and tradition in themselves carry any legal authority. According to Hobbes, the rule of law derives from authority, subject to 'natural reason' which is available to everyone. He objected to the common law on the ground that disagreement between judges picking over conflicting precedents creates the very uncertainty that the law exists to prevent. Jeremy Bentham (Chapter 2) also objected to the common law on the ground that relying on precedent was irrational. We might also be cynical about the notion that the common law represents community values and may regard it as the creation of professional lawyers, filtering experience through their own self-interest, even if unintentionally.

The distinctive characteristics of the common law have substantial influence on the constitution.

- The common law has largely developed through private law notions of personal liability and property rights, underlying Dicey's claim that the same rule of law applies to public bodies and private citizens alike (see Section 6.4.2). Arguably this has frustrated the development of public law principles designed to hold government to account.
- The common law can claim to be embedded in community values. Notions such as the reasonable person, 'reasonable expectations' and right-thinking members of society surface in common law argument (eg Sections 21.5, 21.6).
- The common law can be a focus for open and public debate about competing versions of justice (see eg *White v South Yorkshire Police Authority* [1999]). It is contentious as to how far unelected judges through the prism of particular disputes should lay down wide general principles. It is arguable that the intellectual influences upon the senior judges lag behind the times.
- The common law recognises disagreement about basic values. Its driving force is dispute. Disagreement is kept open through the practices of separate opinions by individual judges and dissenting judgments. Judges can change their minds subject to the loose rules of binding precedent.
- Some liberals argue that the courts are the guardians of fundamental freedoms and in extreme cases should have the power to override an Act of Parliament (Chapter 8). A compromise position is a 'twin' or 'bipolar' sovereignty between Parliament and the courts, according to which Parliament makes legislation and the courts interpret it in the light of basic values of justice and respect for individual rights, each respecting the autonomy of the other in its own sphere (*X Ltd v Morgan Grampian Publishers Ltd* [1991] at 48). Such an accommodation gives the courts considerable scope but requires them to give way to a clear expression of democratic will. The conventional approach, characteristic of the UK's reliance on voluntary practices, is that there is an 'understanding' among the personal networks that make up the institutions of government as to their respective roles and limits.
- It is difficult to reconcile the judges' common law power to make law with either the separation of powers (see Section 7.6.2) or democracy. Supporters of the common law usually argue that the common law supports democracy by protecting its basic values such as freedom of speech against the danger that an elected government might pervert democracy by becoming tyrannical. Against this it can be argued that there is nothing to prevent judges from supporting tyrannical governments and that it is offensive to entrust an unelected elite with the protection of fundamental values, the proper remedy against tyranny being to strengthen democratic mechanisms (see Waldron, *Law and Disagreement* (Oxford University Press 1999) 11, 12, 13).
- The courts are careful to respect the separation of powers to the extent that they are reluctant to develop common law principles in areas where Parliament has shown willingness to intervene (see *Re McKerr* [2004]: investigation of deaths; *Cambridge Water Co v English Counties Leather* [1994]: environmental protection).

3.4 Constitutional conventions

3.4.1 The nature and validity of conventions

We have seen that much of our constitution comprises principles and rules which are not directly legally enforceable but are valid only in as much as they are generally respected. Conventions deal mainly with the relationship between the different branches of government: the Crown, the executive and Parliament, ministers and the civil service, the Prime Minister and the Cabinet. There are for example no legal rules requiring there to be either a Prime Minister or a Cabinet, and the Office of Prime Minister and most of the powers of the Prime Minister are conventional. It is sometimes argued that fundamental principles relating to the structure of the constitution such as parliamentary supremacy and the separation of powers are conventions (*R v HM Treasury, ex p Smedley* [1985]). Conventions therefore express the contemporary political morality of the constitution, and one argument for their existence is their achievement in continually modernising the constitution. They also raise the question of who decides what the constitution is and how it should be changed. Their existence is an important example of how the UK constitution must be pieced together without a blueprint other than tradition and the opinions of 'important' people. Conventions also show a reluctance to develop the constitution according to principles of abstract reason.

Conventions and law are intertwined with each other. For example the legal definition of a minister as 'an office holder under her Majesty' (Ministers of the Crown Act 1975, s 8 (1)) is unhelpful since there are many such office holders who are not ministers. The matter makes sense only by applying the conventions that a minister is a political member of the government responsible to Parliament and must be a member of Parliament. Thus law is adjusted by the use of conventions to modern political ideas. Similarly the Ministerial and Other Salaries Act 1975 presupposes a network of conventions about politicians. The Constitutional Reform and Governance Act 2010 confers powers on the Prime Minister in relation to special advisers (see Section 5.2.5). The law therefore assumes the existence of the office of Prime Minister but does not create it. Indeed convention and law have sometimes blurred in that royal prerogative powers, legally in the hands of the Queen, are validly exercised directly by ministers, not merely on their advice. Conventions can of course be turned into law by enacting them as statutes (eg the *Ponsonby Convention*; see Section 9.7.1).

Here is an important example of how conventions and law interact. A fundamental group of conventions which would certainly feature in a written constitution concerns the position of the Queen as head of state. In law all government power emanates from the Crown, although the Crown's lawmaking power is heavily constrained. The following is the strict legal position. Apart from some special cases known as the 'royal prerogative' the Queen can make law only on the advice of Parliament (Bill of Rights 1688, Case of Proclamations [1611]). Crucially she cannot raise taxation or raise a standing army without the consent of Parliament (Bill of Rights 1688). Moreover the rights of individuals can only be interfered with by law. The Queen can veto laws proposed to her by Parliament. She can dissolve Parliament, although her power to refuse to summon Parliament is restricted. The Queen appoints any other persons she wishes to form the executive, the leading figures being known as ministers of the Crown. Within the law she can run the executive as she wishes.

However when the conventions are added, it appears that the monarch has very limited power, existing mainly as a ceremonial figurehead. The conventions have the effect of making our arrangements look more democratic. The monarch must apparently assent to all bills (proposed laws) submitted to her by Parliament. She must appoint as Prime Minister (leader of the executive branch) the person with majority support in the elected House of Commons, the elected part of Parliament the lawmaker. The Prime Minister then advises the Queen what other ministers to appoint, all of whom must also be or become members of Parliament. In respect of this and indeed all her powers she must act on the advice of the Prime Minister. In normal circumstances these conventions make the Prime Minister very powerful. In law if the monarch ignored these conventions and appointed a friend as Prime Minister nothing could directly be done. Any solution would be political. Probably Parliament would refuse to support the Prime Minister in a vote of confidence and refuse to raise taxes to support the executive, thereby making government impossible and forcing the Queen to respond to Parliament's wishes. The Queen might be required to exercise her legal powers in a political crisis if for example no leader had the support of Parliament (Chapter 14).

Some conventions and other practices and understandings are written down by officials in an uncoordinated profusion of 'concordats', 'memoranda', 'codes of practice' and the like. For example the Ministerial Code (2010) issued by the Cabinet Office comprises a mixture of conventions, advice about practice and administrative matters designed to guide ministers in the conduct of their functions. The Cabinet Office is currently attempting to produce a comprehensive guide to constitutional practice. A problem with these attempts to reduce practices to writing is that unless the document is approved by Parliament its authorship is of doubtful legitimacy.

Other conventions are wholly unwritten, residing only in the collective knowledge of those consulted about them. Thus opinions can be sought from those likely to come up with the desired answer. For example when it appeared before the General Election in 2010 that a 'hung Parliament' without a clear majority to appoint a Prime Minister was a possibility, a self-selected group of civil servants, members of the Queen's entourage and hand-picked academics drafted a set of principles to deal with the issue. (See Blackburn, 'The 2010 General Election and the Formation of the Conservative-Liberal Democrat Coalition Government' [2011] PL 30.) There was no publicly endorsed mechanism available. (Contrast the position in the devolved governments of Scotland, Northern Ireland and Wales, where statute comprehensively covers the matter (Chapter 16).)

Any constitution or set of formal rules is likely to be overlaid by unwritten customs and practices. This is partly because no set of written rules can deal with every possible situation but also because all written documents fall to be interpreted in the light of the practices, assumptions and beliefs, moral and political, of the interpreter. In the case of a constitution there are numerous inputs of thousands of people over time so that the nuances of the constitution are in constant flux. Even so, the UK constitution has relied on convention and practice to an unusually large extent. This can be defended as allowing the constitution to evolve easily to meet changing circumstances. It can be criticised as creating uncertainty but, more importantly, there is no authoritative means such as an independent court for deciding whether a particular convention or practice exists or what it means. Thus those in power have the opportunity to manipulate the constitution in their own interests. One of the main points of a constitution is that it should be an independent set of rules constraining all those who hold power.

Many conventions relate to the exercise of the prerogative powers that survive as vestiges of the legal powers of the Crown. These powers, if exercised, could have profound political consequences. They are however required to be exercised according to conventions which subject the Queen to Parliament. For example conventions require that the Queen must assent to a bill passed by both Houses of Parliament, and that Parliament must meet annually; they regulate the appointment and dismissal of the Prime Minister and other ministers (above); they make ministers accountable to Parliament for the conduct of their office (arguably the political cornerstone of the constitution) and require the government to resign if it is defeated on a vote of confidence in the House of Commons. These conventions are the core of the fundamental shift of power from a monarchical to a parliamentary system.

Some writers argue that the dependence of the UK constitution upon conventions and practices makes it no more than the wishes of those in power albeit subject to the constraints of history. Thus Hennessy (1995, 15–30) describes the UK constitution as generated by an inner circle of guardians mainly comprising senior officials and their friends (see eg Blackburn, 'The 2010 General Election Outcome and Formation of the Conservative-Liberal Coalition Government' [2011] PL 10). Hennessy recounts the Victorian conceit that conventions embody 'the general agreement of public men' about 'the rules of the game' (1995, 36, 37), a proposition that remains significant today. Similarly Bogdanor described the UK constitution as 'a very peculiar constitution which no one intended whereby the government of the day decides what the constitution is' (ibid, 165). Horwitz has argued ('Why Is Anglo-American Jurisprudence Unhistorical?' [1997] OJLS 551) that conventions were developed as undemocratic devices to reassure the ruling class that constitutional fundamentals would continue to be developed within government largely beyond the influence of the rising middle classes following rapid extension of the franchise after the Reform Act 1867. This echoes Mill's utilitarianism in so far as he preferred to leave government to an elite of professionals.

Thus conventions are transmitted through a network of personal, professional and family relationships, and the relationship between elected politicians and appointed civil servants, other members of official bodies and miscellaneous 'advisers' is mainly outside legal constraint. For this reason considerable trust must be placed in the integrity, independence and ability of those who hold public office and those who appoint them. The majority of senior public office holders, including ministers, heads of public bodies, individuals appointed to hold inquiries and members of the House of Lords, are in practice appointed by the Prime Minister. Indeed the same persons are constantly recycled in various roles and given payments, awards and titles. In recent years governments have often been accused of ruling through groups of 'cronies' and bypassing established formal practices in favour of advice from party political advisers and self-interested business and media leaders who may have personal links with government members. Senior civil servants and ministers may on retirement from office be offered lucrative positions in private companies with which they were connected while in office. Our constitution has no method in place (other than advisory bodies comprising those selfsame actors; see Section 5.9) for ensuring that the actors are independent of each other (see Public Administration Committee, *Lobbying: Access and Influence in Whitehall* (HC 2008–09, 36).

Thus the absence of formal parliamentary debate, or indeed any public and systematic discussion, exposes an important concern about the democratic legitimacy of conventions. Who determines the timing and nature of reforms? Are the voices of persons selected as likely to conform to the wishes of those in power given particular weight (for instance academics anxious for recognition)? Why should not the fundamentals of the constitution such as responsible and accountable government be protected against those they are intended to police? For example the government initially refused to allow either Parliament or the public access to the text of the Attorney General's legal opinion concerning the legality of the invasion of Iraq in 2003. By convention such advice is normally confidential (although there are precedents for disclosing the advice) but the refusal to disclose was seen as screening government from uncomfortable questions regarding the legality of the use of force. Indeed a successful complaint under the Freedom of Information Act 2000 was upheld in 2006, recognising a public interest in having access to information on how the Attorney General arrived at his conclusions.

Related to this is the republican argument (Chapter 2) that it is insulting to human dignity to rely on the goodwill of those in power to conform to proper standards of conduct. Respect for the equality of citizens requires that government be constrained by independent rules made democratically and known to all.

3.4.2 Definitions and binding force

It is important to distinguish constitutional conventions from other forms of constitutional behaviour such as practices, traditions and legal principles. It is necessary in particular to distinguish between conventions and practices, because practices, however important, are not binding at all. The party system provides an example of a practice fundamental to the workings of the constitution which has no binding force. There is a logical gulf between practice (what is) and rule (what 'ought' to be), although it must be conceded that well-established practices carry at least a presumption that they ought to be continued. This seems to be a basic psychological fact about human motivation. Furthermore a practice ceases to exist if it is broken. If a convention is broken, it ceases to exist only if no criticism follows. To this extent conventions are at the mercy of raw politics.

At a practical level, there is inevitable uncertainty as to whether some practices really are conventions (and so become obligatory). There is no consensus as to which practices have constitutional status: for example doubt surrounds the role of the Cabinet. Sometimes conventions are contained in written documents, mixed up with other rules and pieces of ethical or political advice, for example the Ministerial Code (2010) issued by the Cabinet Office and the codes of public morality promulgated by the Committee on Standards in Public Life (Chapter 5). The mere fact that a principle has been put in writing does not in itself make it a convention but might be evidence of a convention.

Sir Kenneth Wheare defined conventions as 'a rule of behaviour accepted as obligatory by those concerned in the working of the constitution' (*Modern Constitutions* (Oxford University Press 1966) 102). This emphasises that the crucial matter is the belief of the politicians to whom a convention applies that there is an obligation to act in a particular manner. A convention exists if, as a matter of fact, the belief is present (presumably held by most of those it affects?). But it is arguable that a convention ought to engage what politicians are bound to do and not merely what they actually consider their obligations to be. On the other hand who is to say what this should be?

Dicey famously defined conventions negatively as anything which is not law (1959, 24). He stated that apart from laws:

> The other set of rules consist of conventions, understandings, habits, or practices which, though they may regulate the conduct of several members of the sovereign power, of the Ministry, or of other officials, are not in reality laws at all since they are not enforced by the courts.

A further issue concerns the extent to which a practice must be accepted as binding before it is recognised as a convention. Since neither conventions nor non-binding practices are enforced by the courts, Dicey's test does not identify that which is a convention as opposed to non-binding practice. In this connection Munro (1999, 81) argues that non-legal rules are best viewed as of one type provided we accept that conventions vary in stringency. Thus while conventions are obligatory, they do not all have the same degree of binding force. Some may have exceptions (such as the personal powers of the monarch; see Section 14.4); some may not be regarded as important. It may be difficult to decide whether a particular pattern of behaviour amounts to a convention. For example is the Cabinet merely a working practice?

Does any disagreement about the status of the practice prevent it from being a convention? This seems unsatisfactory because if unanimity (rather than consensus) is required it suggests that a person whose actions ought to be governed by a conventional obligation can apparently destroy that obligation by disputing its existence. As Jaconelli (2005) observes, this places conventions on a flimsy basis.

A consensus may be said to arise if there is substantial support for the proposed convention. Evidence might be found through the collective memory of senior officials or persons recognised as constitutional 'experts'. Reliance may be placed upon the views of important non-elected officials who represent the continuity of power, such as Peter Hennessy's 'golden triangle' of Cabinet Secretary, the Queen's advisers and the Prime Minister's Principal Private Secretary (PPS). Hennessy (1995, 45, 46) describes how private secretaries, the sovereign's advisers at Buckingham Palace and officials of the Cabinet Office monitor and record practice in a 'Precedent Book', which, characteristically of the UK constitution, is not open to public inspection. Officials and politicians refer to the records so contained and this may eventually lead to a consensus that the practice is obligatory.

Conventions change their meaning incrementally as they are applied – that being one of their alleged advantages. On the other hand there is often doubt about the status of certain practices. For instance since the late 1970s it has become apparent that a government need not resign merely because it suffers a major defeat. A formal Commons vote of no confidence is needed. This makes it very difficult to remove a government. There is uncertainty as to whether there is a convention embodying the 'mandate' doctrine – the idea that governments are bound to attempt to honour election promises. If this doctrine exists it would complete the 'democratic chain' between the monarch and the people. The status and functions of the Cabinet are also uncertain. Recent Prime Ministers have preferred to rely upon informal groups of advisers (Chapter 15).

Jennings offered three tests to identify a convention (*The Law and the Constitution* (London University Press 1959) 136). First, are there any precedents? Second, do those operating the constitution believe that they are bound by a rule? Third, is there a constitutional reason for the convention? This has been accepted by the Canadian courts, although it is not clear why a court should have any say in the matter (*Reference re Amendment of the Constitution of Canada (Nos 1, 2 and 3)* (1982) 105 DLR (3d) 1).

In the absence of an authoritative decision maker such as a court there are plainly difficulties with precedents because there may be many occasions on which politicians disagree about the precedents they are supposed to follow. This uncertainty clouds even established conventional rules, such as the choice of a Prime Minister. For example King George VI and Neville Chamberlain wanted Chamberlain to be succeeded as Prime Minister by the then Foreign Secretary, Lord Halifax (and not Winston Churchill), at a crucial moment for Britain in the conduct of the Second World War. This was notwithstanding the established convention that a Prime Minister should have a seat in the Commons. Sometimes precedent is unnecessary because a convention might be created by agreement, for example by the Cabinet, or even laid down unilaterally by the Prime Minister (for instance the Sewel Convention; see Section 3.4.4). The important principles contained in the Ministerial Code (Cabinet Office, 2010) may well furnish an example of conventions laid down by prime ministerial edict. It is arguable however that a convention which is laid down in this way becomes valid only after it has gained general acceptance (see McHarg, 2008). A convention created by an agreement, such as a concordat (see Section 3.4.4), may perhaps be immediately binding.

Jennings also suggested that a convention exists if those subject to it regard themselves as bound by the rule. This is subject to the difficulties discussed in connection with Wheare and Dicey. Fundamentally the notion that conventions are essentially self-policing offends at least republican versions of constitutionalism since it denies the notion of limited government.

Jenning's requirement of a reason for the convention is also problematic. Who decides whether such a reason exists, and if the rule is in fact obeyed why should the reason matter? In the absence of an independent judge, the reason for a practice might depend upon contested political views as to what the constitution should be like.

3.4.3 The differences between law and convention

As we have seen, for Dicey the distinction between legal and political rules depended on the absence of direct power to enforce conventions through the courts. Jennings, by contrast, argued that law and convention share common characteristics, each resting ultimately on public acquiescence. Certainly the content of a convention is no different from that of a law, and a convention can be turned into law by enacting it as a statute. But this does not explain the different attitude of the courts to conventions when compared with laws.

At one level it is possible to understand how laws and conventions differ. A law does not lapse if it becomes obsolete, yet a convention can disappear if it is not followed for a significant period, or if it is broken without objection. Munro (1999) points out that a breach of the law does not call into question its existence or validity. He adds that individual laws do not rest upon consent – an unpopular law or a widely disregarded law is nevertheless a valid law. But a convention is valid only if it is accepted as binding. Another difference is that laws emanate from definite sources – the courts and Parliament – with, crucially, an authoritative mechanism (the courts) for deciding what the rule means and how it applies. In the case of conventions there is no such authoritative source. Moreover, as Dicey indicated, there is no direct judicial remedy when a convention is breached but this is not so with laws.

Nevertheless Dicey's distinction between law and convention has been criticised as too rigid. Some laws are less binding than others. For example procedural requirements stipulated by statute are sometimes 'directory only'. This means that such requirements need not always be obeyed (Section 18.2). Nor can importance be a distinguishing factor. Both laws and conventions deal with fundamental matters, and conventions can be as important as laws; indeed some conventions may be more important than some laws. On the other hand importance is irrelevant to the existence of a law but perhaps not to the existence of a convention. Many conventions function in a close relationship with laws since they direct how discretionary power will be exercised or prevent the exercise of anachronistic prerogative powers. Conventions provide principles and values that form the context of the strict law; as Jennings famously said, 'flesh which clothes the dry bones of the law'. Conversely some laws presuppose the existence of a convention (see Section 3.4.1 above).

It is also said that conventions are different from laws because they lack certainty. Munro (1999) demonstrates that certainty is not the issue. He argues that some social rules, such as the rules of cricket, can be clearly stated but they are manifestly not laws. Moreover many laws are uncertain and while the courts certainly rely on precedent they are free to depart from precedents in many cases.

Perhaps the crucial distinction between convention and law concerns the attitude of the courts. The courts do not apply conventions directly. This means firstly that there is no remedy in the courts for breach of a convention as such, and secondly that the views of a court as to whether a particular convention exists and what it means are not binding. The existence and meaning of a convention are matters of fact that must be proved by evidence and not matters of law for the court. On the other hand the courts do not ignore conventions. In particular a convention may form the political background against which the law has to be interpreted (see box). Furthermore statute may draw upon a particular convention, making it indirectly enforceable. For example section 36 (2) of the Freedom of Information Act 2000 exempts government information from disclosure if it prejudices or is likely to prejudice the convention of the collective responsibility of ministers of the Crown.

The following cases may help to illustrate the relationship between law and convention in the courts:

- In *Reference re Amendment of the Constitution of Canada* [1982], the Canadian Supreme Court, relying partly on British authority, recognised but refused to apply a convention. Under Canadian law any amendment to the Canadian Constitution required an Act of the UK Parliament following a request from the federal government of Canada. The Canadian government wished to amend the Constitution so as to free itself from this legal link with Britain. The UK Parliament would automatically pass any legislation requested by Canada.

  However there were important Canadian conventions on the matter. These required that the governments of the Canadian provinces be consulted about, and give their consent to, any proposed changes in the Constitution that affected federal–provincial relations. Some claimed that this had not been done. The Supreme Court was divided as to whether the convention in question existed. A majority held that it did, and went on to explain in some detail what the convention meant. Some of the judges doubted whether the court should have gone even this far, but as long as we remember that the court's view about the meaning of a convention is not in itself binding, it seems acceptable. In any event a larger majority held that, whatever the convention meant, it could not affect the legal rule that empowered the federal government to request an alteration to the Constitution. Thus the convention could not be enforced by legal remedies. The judges also denied that a convention can ever crystallise into law, for example by becoming established over a period of years. This seems to be equally true of English law (see Munro, 1999, 72ff).

- In *A-G v Jonathan Cape Ltd* [1975] the government sought to prevent publication of the diaries of Richard Crossman, a former Labour Cabinet minister. This involves balancing the confidential nature of any material against any public interest in favour of its disclosure. The government based its case upon the convention of collective Cabinet responsibility, arguing that this necessarily required that Cabinet business remain confidential to Cabinet ministers. The court refused to apply the convention as such. It held that the convention was relevant only to the problem of deciding where the public interest lay. His Lordship held that the diaries could be published because they dealt only with matters of historical interest and did not concern the activities of Cabinet ministers still in office, which the convention was intended to protect. Thus the convention was a crucial strand in the argument but not the law itself (see further Jaconelli, 2005).
- In *Carltona Ltd v Comr for Works* [1943] the courts accepted the legitimacy of civil servants taking decisions that are in law the responsibility of the minister without reference to the minister personally. The reason for this was that, by convention, the minister is responsible to Parliament for the acts of civil servants in his department so that in law the civil servant can be deemed to be merely the instrument of the minister.
- In *R (Bancoult) v Secretary of State (No 2)* [2008] the government argued that an Order in Council made under the royal prerogative by the Crown was an exercise of sovereign power and could not be challenged in the courts. The House of Lords firmly rejected this argument as 'little more than a makeweight' (Lord Rodger at [106]) on the ground that in reality the order was made by a minister (see also *M v Home Office* [1993]).

In relation to the notion of 'soft law', meaning principles which generate the development of legal rules, the distinction between law and convention becomes particularly blurred (see McHarg, 2008). This is where a convention forms the underlying rationale for a legal rule. An example is the well-established legal principle that anything the Crown can do can be done directly by a minister. This derives from the convention that the Queen must act on the advice of ministers, although of course she is not usually personally involved at all. The correct legal analysis is that the minister draws his or her power from the Crown. It might be that the best modern analysis is to envisage the Crown as analogous to a company of which the ministers are the directors, who can automatically act on behalf of the company. However, unlike company law, none of this is set out anywhere and depends on the convention to be understood. (Of course as a matter of tradition the Queen as head of state carries out certain functions in person, such as dissolving Parliament and giving the royal assent to statutes, and in these cases she must act on advice.)

3.4.4 The purposes of conventions

At the most general level conventions are claimed to ensure that the constitution reflects contemporary political values and so to manage evolutionary constitutional change without the risk of generating political controversy by attempting to reform legislation (cf attempts to reform the House of Lords by law; see Section 12.3). More cynically conventions enable constitutional principles to remain under the informal control of those in power rather than be subject to more open judicial or democratic processes. Conventions can also offer advantages in a society in which constitutional reform often finds a low place in the public's (and thus the government's) view of political priorities.

Most conventions concern the relationship between different components of government. Examples of the evolutionary development of such conventions relate to the gradual curbing of the powers of the monarch.

Conventions relating to the monarch ensure that vestigial prerogative powers are normally exercised only in accordance with advice received from ministers, who are accountable to Parliament. Indeed most prerogative powers are exercised directly by ministers without the monarch being involved at all. As we have seen, it is also a convention that the sovereign should assent to bills passed by both Houses of Parliament. The royal assent would seem to be automatic. Related to the convention governing the royal assent is the sovereign's obligation in almost all matters to act on the advice of ministers (whether collective advice or that offered by an individual minister), although there are ill-defined circumstances in which such advice need not be followed. For example the sovereign might be able to refuse a Prime Minister's advice to dissolve Parliament if a general election would be harmful to the interests of the country, such as might be the case in a national emergency, and an alternative viable government could be formed (Chapter 14). There is considerable debate about the extent to which, and on whose advice, the monarch can exercise these personal powers. The chain of conventions embodied in the doctrine of ministerial responsibility to Parliament is of fundamental importance, being intended to ensure that the legal powers of the Crown are subject to democratic control. Dicey (1915) suggests that these conventions reconcile legal sovereignty and political sovereignty. Allan (*Law, Liberty and Justice* (Oxford University Press 1993) 253) concludes that conventions 'give effect to the principle of governmental accountability that constitutes the structure of responsible government'. However the supposed chain of accountability is not complete. Dicey anticipated neither the dominance of the executive in Parliament, effectively exercising monarchical power, nor the dispersal of executive power to miscellaneous bodies, including private companies, outside the central government structure. Moreover if ministerial accountability is to be effective it assumes that members of Parliament will act independently and not through party loyalty. Accountability to Parliament is often accountability to the minister's own party.

Other conventions concern the relationship between the two Houses of Parliament. For example the somewhat uncertain 'Salisbury Convention' (designed in circumstances which no longer apply, where hereditary peers had a built-in majority in the House of Lords) requires that the House of Lords should not oppose a measure sent to it by the Commons which was contained in the governing party's election manifesto except perhaps where the matter is the subject of deep public controversy (see Turpin and Tomkins, *British Government and the Constitution* (6th edn, Cambridge University Press 2007) 643–45, 652–53).

New conventions have been introduced to meet new challenges, for example to deal with the relationship between the central government and the devolved governments of Scotland, Wales and Northern Ireland. The Sewel Convention requires that legislatures of the devolved territories should consent to any legislation made by Parliament that affects devolved matters (*Memorandum of Understanding* (Cm 5420, 1999)). There may also be a right of the Prince of Wales as heir to the Crown to meet with ministers, to obtain information from them, to comment on their policies and to argue for alternative policies, although this competes with the convention that the monarchy should not be involved with political controversy (see Brazier, 'The Constitutional Position of the Prince of Wales' [1995] PL 401).

A fashionable recent device is the promulgation of 'concordats' agreed between participants and intended to govern the relationship between different organs of government or to set out practices. These may have the status of convention, at least if they are generally acted upon. There are many of these between government departments, agencies and the devolved institutions of Scotland and Wales which clarify the relationship between these bodies and express their mutual obligations. A concordat made in 2004 between the government and the Lord Chief Justice concerning links between the judiciary and the executive underpins the reforms introduced by the Constitutional Reform Act 2005 (Chapter 7). These could be regarded as expressing new conventions designed to secure the independence of the judiciary.

There is another type of 'concordat', an example of which is the 'Enforcement Concordat' dealing with the relationship between regulated commercial interests and enforcement bodies. This merely sets out broad policy goals, for example that enforcement bodies should adopt a helpful and constructive approach and that information should be published in plain language.

It is sometimes suggested that convention requires there to be a referendum before legislation is introduced making fundamental constitutional change. However there have been few precedents for this. Referendums were held in 1975 concerning continued membership of what is now the EU, in 1978 and 1997 in relation to devolution in Scotland, Wales and Northern Ireland and in 2004 concerning the proposed introduction of a regional assembly in the northeast of England. There is likely to be a referendum on proposed changes in the UK voting system. Section 103 of the Government of Wales Act 2006 and section 1 of the Northern Ireland Act 1998 contain provisions for referendums.

3.4.5 Why conventions are obeyed

The main reason why conventions are obeyed is the adverse political consequences that might result from their breach. This is unsurprising since conventions are traditionally regarded as a matter of political ethics. It also produces the circularity that if a convention is not obeyed it may lose its binding force. For example the supposed convention that a minister should resign if there has been a serious wrongdoing in his or her department is usually ignored unless a minister loses political support (Chapter 15). Indeed the adversarial nature of politics means that even political sanctions are far from inevitable. The pressure of political opponents and party, the strength of prime ministerial support and the reaction of the press all play a large part in determining the fate of a minister.

Dicey unsuccessfully tried to link breach of convention to breach of law. He stated (1959, 439ff) that conventions are not laws and so not enforced by the courts, but he argued that even the 'boldest political adventurer' would be restrained from breaching conventions because (at least in the case of some conventions) it would eventually lead to the offender coming into conflict with the courts and the law of the land (1959, 445–46). He gave as an example the consequences that might follow if Parliament did not meet at least once a year, or if a government did not resign after losing a vote of confidence. Dicey argued that the government would have the statutory authority neither for raising (some) taxes nor for spending money.

Not all conventions can be similarly treated. For example the appointment of a non-member of Parliament as a minister will not lead to a legal violation. The absence of adverse political repercussions may fortify ministers who give inaccurate parliamentary answers but this failure is unlikely to lead to a breach of the law (although such a statement might create a binding 'legitimate expectation'; see Section 17.9).

If some conventions were breached, Parliament might be compelled to intervene to prevent a recurrence. Most famously this occurred after the Lords refused to pass the Finance Bill 1909, thereby disregarding the conventional principle that the Lords should ultimately defer to the wishes of the elected Commons. The Parliament Act 1911 removed the veto power of the Lords in respect of most public bills. If the sovereign (without ministerial advice) were to refuse to grant royal assent to a bill passed by both Houses, the prerogative power to refuse would soon be removed by legislation.

It also seems that conventions are obeyed because they are part of a shared and respected system of values. This is evident in the commonly accepted definitions of conventions that emphasise the consent upon which they depend for their existence (eg Sir Kenneth Wheare's definition above, and see Munro, 1999, 61). Jaconelli (2005) goes further and ventures the possibility that many conventions prescribe behaviour that is implicitly reciprocal. The party in power for the time being accepts the constraints that conventions impose upon its behaviour in the expectation that the opposition parties will do likewise when they attain office, although Jaconelli concedes that this would not furnish an obligatory basis to all conventions, such as those of an inter-institutional rather than inter-party kind. An example of the inter-institutional type would be that obligation of the monarch to assent to bills passed by both Houses. According to Jaconelli, prudence explains why such conventions are observed.

Conventions may apparently be breached or qualified (depending on one's viewpoint) as a safety valve where there is a conflict between what is normally constitutionally expected and current political consensus or expediency. In 1975 the Prime Minister 'suspended' the principle of collective Cabinet unanimity to allow ministers to express their views openly in a referendum campaign concerning membership of the European Economic Community (EEC). Any referendum on the future of sterling as the British currency might result in a similar temporary modification to collective ministerial responsibility.

3.4.6 Codification of conventions

Codification has different meanings and the fact that a set of rules is codified does not in itself determine the nature of the rules. Firstly it means an authoritative written version of the conventions in question. Strictly speaking this means turning the convention into law in the form of an Act of Parliament, although promulgation as a Standing Order or Resolution of Parliament would give it legal effect within Parliament itself. Conventions might also be codified in a less authoritative sense and not legally binding, for example in the form of a report of a parliamentary committee, a ministerial announcement, a concordat or a Memorandum of Understanding (see *Report of Joint Committee on Conventions* (2005–06, HL 1212–1, HC 1212–1).

The case for codification thus involves two distinct positions. The first asserts that conventions should be both codified and given legal force; the second that conventions might be codified within an authoritative text but with no legal status and so remain as non-legal political practices, as at present. Even under this version however, which has been adopted in Australia in relation to 34 constitutional practices, it is likely that the courts may cite those conventions that the process codified (see Sampford, '"Recognize and Declare": An Australian Experience in Codifying Constitutional Conventions' [1987] OJLS 369). Such an approach would address the lack of precision in the scope of some conventions and would enable us to say with certainty which usages are and which are not conventional. Establishing the certainty of conventions could safeguard the neutrality of those who apply them. On the other hand this approach might create uncertainty, for example as to the status of any interpretation of a convention that a court might give if the matter arose in litigation.

The more adventurous position involving codification and enactment raises a number of concerns similar to those surrounding the arguments for a written constitution. The first is that such a model of codification would damage the flexibility of the constitution and inhibit its evolutionary role in maintaining the relationship between the constitution and contemporary political values. One of the purposes of conventions has been to annul anachronistic law. It would be undesirable if conventions were to become fossilised and so impede further constitutional change. This might even prevent the development of qualifications limiting the scope of some conventions (as in the case of the 'suspension' of collective Cabinet unanimity in 1975).

Moreover as conventions are enforced as a matter of political dynamic, some argue that political flexibility might also be curbed if the courts were invited to pronounce on the breach of a conventional obligation. There are strong arguments that the demands of political morality ought to be a matter of collective decision reached through the medium of politics, and so fall outside the proper scope of the judicial function. To take the example of ministerial responsibility, we may conclude that apportioning blame is a political matter not a legal one. This means that the question of whether a minister's conduct in office is such that he or she should resign would seem to be a non-justiciable question, depending as it does on party support, the timing of the discovery, the support of the Prime Minister and Cabinet, and the public repercussions. But the issue is not so clear if a minister were to deny an obligation to answer any questions in the House of Commons. What would prevent the court granting a declaration that such behaviour was unconstitutional? Would the arguments be equally as strong if a minister deliberately misled Parliament, where resignation should be automatic? (See Ministerial Code, para 1.5; Second Report of the Public Service Select Committee (HC 1995–96, 313) para 26.)

There might also be practical difficulties in systematic codification. It would be impossible to identify all usages that are currently conventional, and immediately after a code was established there would be nothing to prevent the evolution of new conventions.

The case for a systematic codification of conventions is not self-evidently of merit. One possible approach (but one which would not overcome all the difficulties mentioned above) might be to enact some of the most important and widely accepted conventions. This would place those selected outside the scope of the executive and locate more extensive power in Parliament. Constitutional development would then be a matter of statutory reform, which itself would follow from more open debate and discussion.

3.5 Constitutional silence and abeyance

The absence of a rule set out in a statute or case or embodied in a convention might also be a source of the constitution in that it may indicate a deliberate choice to leave a question unanswered. Silence might indicate that the constitution prefers to avoid a controversial issue or to leave an area free for the actors to do what they like, subject perhaps to ordinary private law. The absence of legal or conventional rules governing the organisation of the central executive provides an example, as does the absence of rules controlling government privatisation. Silence also acknowledges the problem of incommensurability by discouraging attempts to lay down grand general principles (see Section 1.6). Thus in *R (Chaytor) v A-G* [2010] at [46] the Court of Appeal said that ' it would be to the public disadvantage for the constitutional relationship between the courts and Parliament to be tested to destruction'.

Silence might also encourage the opposite inference that government should have no freedom, for example where a law sets out a list of rights to which it gives special treatment, as is the case with the Human Rights Act 1998 (Chapter 19). Do we assume that this is intended to be a comprehensive list or can other rights be recognised to which we can extend similar protection by analogy? More generally where Parliament has not legislated in a particular area, does this mean that the common law should also refuse to go there, taking its lead from the democratic branch, or is this an invitation for common law to fill the gap (see Section 3.3 above)? (Silence might also contribute to stability by confining decisions to matters essential to the issue in hand.)

Constitutional silences are therefore ambiguous. Their most important function might be to discourage us from looking too closely into controversial areas into which it might be wiser not to venture. In other words silence enables us to let sleeping dogs lie and invites disputing factions to take comfort in the belief that the constitution does not rule out their concerns. Examples include the question of whether European law prevails over domestic law, whether Parliament can override certain basic principles of Scottish law (see Section 9.4.2), the relationship between Parliament and the courts and the extent of the Queen's personal powers (see Section 14.4). A similar notion of silence is embodied in the concept of a non-justiciable issue that the court refuses to determine or in which it will interfere only exceptionally (see Section 19.6.1). Similarly there may be values in the constitution – personal privacy is an example – which cannot easily be embodied in clear rules so that they are best undefined as providing only a general sense of direction or an attitude (see Lord Hoffmann in *Wainwright v Home Office* [2003] at 979).

The risk of constitutional abeyance is that without established guidelines the pressure of disagreement might eventually erupt into open conflict, with the constitution powerless to resolve the dispute – the Hobbesian nightmare. This was the case in the English Civil War of the seventeenth century against a constitution that did not clearly define the powers of the monarch. However it is arguable that a constitution and indeed the law itself can work only within a broad consensus of beliefs and is irrelevant in situations of fundamental disagreement.

Summary

- The UK constitution is embodied in individual statutes and in the common law, which is claimed to derive from the values embedded in the community. Statutes and common law principles that are regarded as 'constitutional' are given special treatment but within a context of considerable uncertainty. The common law introduces an element of openness, independence and flexibility into the constitution, although it challenges the idea of democracy.
- The UK constitution is also embodied in customs and practices, the most important of which are conventions. Conventions are pragmatically intertwined with law but are not directly enforceable in the courts. There is therefore no authoritative mechanism for interpreting, identifying or enforcing conventions.
- Conventions are of fundamental importance in the UK constitution. In their best light they enable the constitution to evolve pragmatically in accordance with changing political values. In their worst light they allow the government of the day and its favourites to manipulate the constitution in their own interests, for example by recruiting sycophantic academics to endorse a particular interpretation of a convention.
- There is disagreement about the definition of conventions. Accordingly it is not always clear which forms of constitutional behaviour are conventions and which are mere practices. Conventions are binding rules of constitutional behaviour while mere practices are not.
- Conventions are distinct from law, firstly in that there are no authoritative formal tests for the validity of conventions and secondly because conventions are not directly enforced by the courts. However there is no inherent difference in the content of laws and conventions and the courts use conventions, as they do moral principles, to help interpret, develop and apply the law.
- Some commentators have argued that conventions could be incorporated into the law, but even if this is achieved how many such laws would be justiciable? Codification might offer certainty in respect of those conventions included in the code, but new conventions would be evolved after the code was introduced and some flexibility in adapting existing conventions might be lost. There may be scope for extending 'soft' forms of codification such as the Ministerial Code.
- Constitutional silences or 'abeyances' play a useful role mainly by avoiding confrontation in respect of issues that are inherently controversial.

Exercises

3.1 'The British constitution presumes, more boldly than any other, the good faith of those who work it' (Gladstone). 'The constitution is "what happens"' (Griffith). Explain and compare these two statements.

3.2 To what extent does the common law influence the character of the UK constitution?

3.3 How are conventions recognised and enforced? Can they be distinguished from 'practices'?

3.4 'Conventions are intended to enable the ruling elite to manipulate government in its own interest.' Discuss.

3.5 Are conventions a desirable method of bringing about constitutional change?

3.6 What is the relationship between law and convention? Does it serve a useful purpose to distinguish between law and convention?

3.7 Should conventions be enacted into law or codified?

3.8 To what extent is silence a valuable constitutional device?

Further reading

Allott, 'The Theory of the British Constitution', in Gross and Harrison (eds) *Jurisprudence: Cambridge Essays* (Cambridge University Press 1992)
Bagehot, *The English Constitution* (2nd edn, Kegan Paul 1902) ch 1
Barber, 'Law and Constitutional Conventions' (2009) 125 LQR 294
Bogdanor and Vogenauer, 'Enacting a British Constitution: Some Problems' [2008] PL 38
Foley, *The Silence of Constitutions* (Routledge 1989)
Jaconelli, 'Do Constitutional Conventions Bind?' (2005) 64 CLJ 149
McHarg, 'Reforming the United Kingdom Constitution: Law, Convention, Soft Law' (2008) 71 MLR 853
Marshall, 'The Constitution: Its Theory and Interpretation' in Bogdanor (ed), *The British Constitution in the Twentieth Century* (Oxford University Press 2003) 36
Munro, *Studies in Constitutional Law* (2nd edn, Butterworths 1999) ch 3
Nolan and Sedley (eds) *The Making and Remaking of the British Constitution* (Blackstone 1997) ch 2
Postema, *Bentham and the Common Law Tradition* (Clarendon Press 1986) chs 1, 2
Sedley, 'The Sound of Silence: Constitutional Law without a Constitution' (1994) 110 LQR 270
Ward, *A State of Mind? The English Constitution and the Public Imagination* (Sutton 2000)
Wilson, 'The Robustness of Conventions in a Time of Modernisation' [2004] PL 407

Chapter 4
Historical outline

Paternal government, which is monarchy, was instituted in the beginning from creation; and that other governments have proceeded from the dissolution thereof, ... and be but pieces of broken monarchies cemented by human wit. (Hobbes, *The Body Politic* XXIV, 3)

4.1 Introduction

The purpose of this historical outline is to highlight themes that have influenced the contemporary constitution. Apart from an abortive draft under Cromwell in the seventeenth century, there has been no attempt to design a comprehensive constitution for the UK. All constitutions reflect myths or stories of how the constitution takes its particular form and how it is justified. Traditionalists claim that the UK constitution is the happy and pragmatic outcome of an evolution towards freedom and democracy ordered by benevolent customs.

On the one hand it has been said that control of the British state has been dispersed at least since the middle of the twelfth century, thus nurturing freedom and democracy (see Kellner, 2009). This dispersal comprised local government bodies in the form of counties and boroughs (urban communities), local representatives of the Crown such as sheriffs responsible for law and order, local magistrates and local representatives in Parliament. All of these remain (the sheriff only in ceremonial form).

On the other hand there have been strong centralising forces hostile to democracy, reflected today in the large powers available to ministers of the Crown under the royal prerogative. These have been generated historically by the position of the monarchy at the head of a hierarchy, wielding power by distributing patronage, honours and favours – a process that is prominent today. Another centralising influence was the common law, which under royal auspices developed from the thirteenth century. There was therefore a strong central direction for which local administration acted as a cover. However, from the mid-nineteenth century, increasing dependence on central resources meant that local administration openly became no more than an agent of the centre. The present government proposes to disperse more power locally (see *Final Report of the Commission on 2020 Public Services* 2010).

A prominent story, 'the Whig View of History', runs that the monarchy, through the Norman Conquest of 1066, had usurped an earlier, democratic regime, 'the ancient constitution', in which lay the roots both of the common law and of representative government. The King gradually gave way to Parliament as representing those worthy to have a stake in the community. From the nineteenth century Parliament broadened its membership until eventually the people as a whole controlled it, with the courts protecting their rights. The collapse of the French Revolution at the end of the eighteenth century was regarded as an awful warning of the dangers of radical constitution building. According to the myth, abuses are unlikely because apart from the odd maverick we can trust our rulers with wide discretionary powers and conflicts of interest since they are persons of high ability and integrity who can vouch for each other. Our rulers are also subject to political pressures to please at least enough of the public to keep them in office.

Another view is that the history of the constitution is driven by competition between rival interest groups, usually resulting in compromise, against a background of a docile population with a cultural tendency towards hierarchy, patronage and bribery, and of chance circumstances and personalities in an endless power struggle. Controls over government fluctuate in response to particular problems and in accordance with changing political beliefs. There is no single driving force: 'everything that happens is constitutional' (Griffith, 'The Political Constitution' (1979) 42 MLR 19). In the case of the UK constitution one recurring theme is money – as in the need of the government to ensure the consent of the wealthier sections of the community and the desire of Parliament (as representing the community) to control government spending albeit with limited success.

4.2 Saxon period

The monarchy dates back to Anglo-Saxon times before the Norman Conquest in 1066. After the withdrawal of the Romans in the fifth century, by the end of the tenth century 'England' as a unity, headed by a king (Edgar (959–75) was probably the first monarch in the modern sense), had emerged from rival kingdoms ruled by warlords. Ireland and Scotland, although subject to invasion by England, were independent kingdoms. Wales was a collection of principalities subject to invasion by England, with local rule in 1066. Wales was absorbed or conquered by the English by the end of the thirteenth century. English local government and law were imposed on Wales by the (English) Act of Union 1536.

All legal power and control of the executive derived from the monarchy and in theory still does. From pre-Norman times the hierarchical and centralised character of English society was apparent. Laws were made in the Witan, the King's hand-picked council of influential people. By the end of the tenth century a complex system of local government existed within the structure of counties that lasted until 1974. It was controlled by royal representatives in the shape of aldermen and sheriffs. (These offices survive today in characteristic English fashion as ceremonial and social.) There were local bodies within the counties organised into 'hundreds' and 'tithings' which acted as law enforcers, courts and tax collectors. A unified currency was introduced. England was probably the most centralised country in Western Europe at the time. UK residents and citizens remain 'subjects' of the Crown as opposed to being citizens in the republican sense of equal participants in the state. However, according to the myth of the 'ancient constitution', the King ruled subject to the consent of a council representing those with a property stake in the community.

4.3 The medieval period: the beginning of parliamentary government

After the Norman Conquest (1066) the King claimed jurisdiction over the whole of England, parts of France and, after the thirteenth century, Wales. The power of the monarchy derived partly from the hierarchical feudal system of landowning, with the King at its apex and the chief landowners and Church dignitaries (the two often overlapping) as royal advisers. This gave the King large powers of patronage to reward his supporters, an important modern lever of power. Thus contemporary government advisers are recruited substantially from today's barons: large businesses, the media and financial institutions. The powers of the monarch also survive in the form of the royal prerogative, a group of powers inherent in the Crown, some of which derive from the monarch's duty to protect the realm; others from landowning (see Section 14.6.2). The army comprised private armies raised by the King and other landowners, each of which had a feudal obligation to provide the King with resources.

England had a centralised but flexible legal regime in the shape of the common law, a system of justice deriving its authority from the King and created by the courts. The *Assize of Clarendon* (1166) established the King's power to administer law through judges and juries throughout the land, and Magna Carta (1215) promoted the basic ingredients of a fair trial. The King had bases throughout the country, and the county sheriff, as the King's representative, had wide law enforcement powers. Justice was carried out in the King's name by travelling judges and by local Justices of the Peace. During the seventeenth century it was established that the King personally could not participate in the decisions of the courts but until the 1688 revolution (see Section 4.5) the King could dismiss the judges.

The principle that the powers of monarchy were limited by the law was established by the end of the thirteenth century. Thus the judge Sir John Fortesque (*The Difference between an Absolute and Limited Monarchy* (1471)) distinguished between *dominium regale*, as in France, where the King makes his own laws and *dominium politicum et regale*, where the people assent to laws made by the King. Of course there is plenty of room for disagreement as to who count as 'the people'.

Magna Carta, extracted from King John by the leading barons, is widely regarded as a constitutional landmark. Although it is no longer directly in force, its underlying principles have been invoked in modern cases and copied in other constitutions. It was the result of a list of grievances presented by leading landowners and clerics to the King. Many of them concerned local and feudal claims that are now obsolete. Others remain applicable, including the right to a fair trial, the protection of the rule of law and the principle of no taxation without consultation of those affected. Magna Carta was altered and dishonoured over the years but remains of great symbolic value in that it embodies the principle that the law is not the will of the King but is contained in the customs of the community. This is one of the foundations of the common law and was the setting for the conflicts between the King and Parliament in the seventeenth century. Magna Carta was also one of the sources of the US Constitution and of human rights charters.

During the thirteenth and fourteenth centuries, Parliament with its two separate Houses split off from the King and progressively challenged his power. The King originally governed through a Council, which by the end of the thirteenth century became subject to Parliament (see *Provisions of Oxford* [1258]).

Parliament originated as a meeting of influential persons summoned by the King at regular intervals to give advice and later to agree to taxation The House of Lords, which perhaps evolved from the Saxon Witan (see Section 4.2), was composed of the great magnates: the nobility and Church dignitaries whose wealth, offices and status were ultimately conferred by the Crown. The House of Commons, from the thirteenth century, sent representatives to the House of Lords but from the middle of the fourteenth century met separately. It consisted of representatives of the leading local dignitaries and became increasingly assertive.

The House of Lords was interested only in its own members and the two Houses made separate grants of money to the King. The Commons were summoned by the King to consent to requests for taxation in return for redressing the grievances of subjects and passing laws requested by the Commons. This remains the core of the modern Parliament's formal role. The King was in constant need of money. This was raised through feudal dues, foreign adventures, strategic marriages, loans, control of certain trading activities, the sale of titles and honours, and taxation.

Thus, depending on economic conditions, the balance of power between the monarch and Parliament waxed and waned over the years.

Parliament began to make laws originally on the basis that it was declaring the existing customs of the realm. Parliament also had the status of a High Court, able to give final rulings on the law and to 'impeach' public officials for misconduct. Impeachment, in which the House of Commons brings accusations before the House of Lords, remains possible but depends on a resolution of the House and is unlikely to be used today. Parliament is still summoned and dissolved by the monarch but the modern monarch has very little choice in the matter. The executive branch consisted of the King and his chosen councillors and holders of particular offices. Some mediaeval offices, notably that of the Lord Chancellor, survive today, albeit in diminished form.

4.4 The Tudor period: the creation of the state

The Tudor period, spanning the sixteenth century, saw the emergence in Europe of the modern concept of the nation state as a self-contained impersonal structure served by a bureaucracy and with absolute authority within its territory (see Section 9.1). This replaced the more complex medieval regime in which Church, state and various interest groups such as landowners and trade groups coexisted uneasily. Throughout Europe the monarchy claimed to embody this absolute notion of the state, although less so in England, where the common law and Parliament were established counterforces.

Parliament could make new laws and the King had to ask the House of Commons for money in the form of direct taxation. The monarch was entitled to raise indirect taxes, such as duties on imports, and could also confiscate and sell property and control franchises and monopolies, such as the right to pursue certain trades. The monarchy might also borrow money or raise it from investing in overseas adventures such as piracy or through marriages with overseas royalty and so, unlike today, could sometimes rule without help from Parliament.

The Tudor monarchs ruled with relatively little need to summon Parliament, partly by confiscating Church property following the Reformation (1532–36) and partly from the proceeds of naval adventures and levies on overseas trade. This period also saw the emergence of the modern type of executive, comprising ministers, the most important of whom were styled secretaries of state; committees, notably the Privy Council, comprising the monarch's favourites and exercising the formal powers of the Crown; and a bureaucratic structure of civil servants.

During the sixteenth and seventeenth centuries medieval ideas of limited monarchy within common law clashed with the newer ideas of absolute monarchy and the nation state. Classical republican ideas of equal citizenship also surfaced (eg Sir John Harrington, 1561–1612) although these have not significantly influenced constitutional development in the UK. In the law courts the clash between Crown and Parliament was foreshadowed by controversy about the late medieval notion of the Crown's 'two persons': one (*gubernaculum*) concerned with protecting the realm and which claimed to be above the law, the other (*jurisdictio*) an official whose day-to-day duties primarily concerned the enforcement of private rights which were subject to the law (see *Duchy of Lancaster Case* [1567]). However it was widely accepted that only in Parliament could the King exercise the fullest lawmaking power.

4.5 The seventeenth-century revolution

The seventeenth century was a crucible of ideas, including sovereignty, individual rights, representation and, to a limited extent, democracy. The century was dominated by religious and financial conflicts between the Crown and Parliament. These led to the revolution of 1688, the foundation of the present constitution. The Stuart monarchs ran out of money and were under military pressure from Scotland and Ireland. They claimed the right to exercise the royal prerogative to raise certain taxes without Parliament but respected the common law by subjecting their powers to scrutiny by the courts (see *Case of Proclamations* [1611]; *R v Hampden* [1637]). The judges were servants of the Crown but asserted their independence from the Crown in deciding cases (*Prohibitions del Roy* [1607]). Nevertheless their position remained ambivalent since they could be dismissed by the King and the outcome of cases was not conclusive. For example Coke CJ's stand against royal interference with the courts in *Prohibitions del Roy* [1607] was followed by his dismissal for taking a similar stand in 1616 in the *Commendum* case. In *Darnall's Case* [1627] it was accepted that the King could imprison a person without trial, a power that was later removed by statute (Habeas Corpus Act 1640) albeit revived from time to time in later statutes.

From 1629 Charles I attempted to rule without Parliament. However, when he attempted in 1639 to impose the Anglican prayer book on the Scots, the resulting uprising forced him to summon Parliament, the 'Long Parliament', which lasted from 1640 until 1660 albeit dormant or suspended for most of its life. A shortlived compromise was reached in 1641 when the Star Chamber and other special prerogative courts introduced by the Tudors to support an administrative state were abolished. These events left English legal culture with a suspicion of special jurisdictions over governmental matters and a preference for the ordinary courts, reflected in Dicey's idea of the rule of law (see Section 6.4.2). From the religious perspective, the Church of England, headed by the King, was confronted on the one hand by the Catholic Church and on the other by Protestant groups, who dominated Parliament. Civil war broke out in 1642, resulting in victory for Parliament in 1646.

There was a wide-ranging constitutional debate at Putney between the ruling conservative establishment of landowners and business interests, led by Oliver Cromwell, and the more radical army rank and file, represented by the Levellers, who proposed a written constitution. This 'Agreement of the People' was based on religious freedom, equality before the law and universal male suffrage (later qualified by excluding servants and beggars). However Cromwell invoked custom and tradition in favour of more limited reforms. The Levellers, with their wider ideas of democracy, were defeated by force in 1649.

In 1649 Charles I was executed on the authority of Parliament, which was packed with army supporters. The House of Lords was abolished and a republic declared. In 1653 the remnants of Parliament were expelled and a military dictatorship, dominated by Protestants and with Cromwell as 'Lord Protector', was introduced. However after

Cromwell's death in 1658 it seemed that chaos could best be avoided by restoring the traditional constitution. A self-appointed group of political leaders restored the Crown in 1660 in the form of Charles II, the heir of Charles I. The House of Lords was also restored.

Charles II (1660–85) and his brother, James II (1685–88), ruled on the basis that there had been no republic and the republican legislation was expunged from the statute book. Towards the end of Charles' reign, at a time when he was heavily subsidised by the French, anti-Catholic sentiment was revived. Catholicism was associated in the public mind with absolute monarchy, an association that still scars the constitution by preventing the monarch from being or marrying a Catholic. There was a substantial exodus abroad by Catholics and other religious minorities, thereby sowing the seeds of the American Revolution and adding to the problem of Ireland (Section 16.3). The Exclusion Crisis (1679–81), in which a parliamentary majority attempted to bar Charles' Catholic brother, James, from the succession to the throne, reactivated the conflict between the monarchy and Parliament. Charles used his prerogative power to close Parliament and refused to summon Parliament again after 1681.

James II ruled with the support of Parliament from 1685. However James alienated both the main parties by favouring Catholics and attempting to override Parliament by virtue of suspending and dispensing powers under the royal prerogative. This had some success, at least to meet emergencies (*Thomas v Sorrell* [1674]; *Godden v Hales* [1686]). James suspended the penal laws against Catholics in 1687 and 1688. He also displaced thousands of local parliamentary candidates who would not vote according to his wishes.

The foundations of the modern constitution were laid by the 1688 'Glorious' revolution when James dissolved Parliament and fled the country. A self-appointed 'Convention Parliament' combining landowning and commercial interests offered the Crown to the Protestant William of Orange and his wife, Mary (James' daughter), supported by the Dutch military. In political terms the 1688 revolution was relatively conservative, being a compromise designed to satisfy all influential interests. It was justified in two inconsistent ways. On a Hobbesian premise, James II had abdicated, leaving a power vacuum which, according to the common law doctrine of necessity, must be filled in order to avoid chaos. On the other premise, based on Locke, James had broken his contract by misruling, so entitling the people to rebel. In Scotland and Ireland, continuing support for the Stuart monarchs was crushed by force.

The Convention also promoted the Bill of Rights 1688 dealing with the grievances against the Stuart Kings. It prohibited the Crown from exercising key powers without the consent of Parliament, including the powers to make laws, to tax, to keep a standing army in peacetime and to override legislation. It also protected freedom of speech and elections in Parliament, secured frequent Parliaments, protected jury trial and banned excessive bail. William and Mary then summoned a Parliament which ratified the Acts of the Convention (Crown and Parliament Recognition Act 1689). The Act of Settlement 1700 provided for the succession to the Crown and gave superior court judges security of tenure and therefore independence from the Crown. The Act of Settlement also links Church and state by requiring the monarch to be a member of the Church of England and not to marry a Catholic, contains safeguards to prevent a monarch born 'out of this Kingdom' embroiling the country in a foreign war and prohibits non-citizens from being members of Parliament or the Privy Council (cf Chapter 12). The Meeting of Parliament Act 1694 (the Triennial Act) required Parliament to meet at least every three years (by convention it must meet annually) and limited the life of a Parliament to three years (now five years, Parliament Act 1911).

Thus the 1688 settlement put in place the main legal structures we have today. It was based neither on democracy nor on the fundamental rights of the individual. If anything, it confirmed the principle of aristocratic rule. The House of Lords was a powerful body and the House of Commons was largely made up of landowners and traders dependent on the patronage of the Lords. Thomas Paine, who fled the country in 1792 having been charged with sedition for denying that Britain had a constitution, said in *The Rights of Man* (1791–92):

> What is [the Bill of Rights 1688] but a bargain which the parts of the government made with each other to decide powers. You shall have so much and I will have the rest; and with respect to the nation, it said, for your share, you shall have the right of petitioning. This being the case the Bill of Rights is more properly a bill of wrongs and of insult. (Paine, 1987, 292)

The 1688 settlement also led to the creation of the Bank of England in 1694 as a semi-independent institution which guaranteed the currency and through which the government could borrow money. This was an important reason for the successful expansion of the British government and the economy during the following century since it gave the Crown a secure source of funds.

4.6 The eighteenth and early nineteenth centuries: the parliamentary system

This period, the Enlightenment, was one of great intellectual and social change. Reason was promoted as replacing revealed religion, custom and traditional hierarchy. During this period the basic political structure of the UK constitution began to develop, mainly through non-legally binding conventions creating the parliamentary system. As is still the case, in law the monarch remained the head of the government, with power to appoint members of the House of Lords, to assent to legislation, to appoint and dismiss all ministers and to summon and dissolve Parliament, but unable to raise taxes or make law without the cooperation of Parliament. For most of the eighteenth century the monarch claimed to run the executive personally although the Commons could dismiss a ministry of which it disapproved. The Crown ran what was in effect a political party known as the 'Court and Treasury Party', which it controlled by giving government jobs to its supporters and manipulating elections. The main parties, the Whigs and the Tories, alternated in forming governments, although during the first half of the eighteenth century the Whigs predominated. Coalition governments were common.

A significant difference from the modern Parliament was that the party system was looser and the very existence of parties was controversial (eg lack of independence against rallying support for great causes). About half the MPs were independent of party allegiance and others frequently changed parties. One reason for the relative independence of MPs was that unlike today most MPs had private means and did not depend on their party for career advancement. Indeed an Act of 1710 (9 Anne c 5) imposed a property requirement on membership of the House of Commons (except for the eldest sons of peers and knights and the representatives of Oxford and Cambridge universities).

On the other hand the dominant political culture was adversarial and oligarchical, assuming a permanent contest between two elites led by aristocratic families contending for power. The parliamentary system which we have inherited was designed to replace civil war with a regulated and peaceful contest. This adversarial culture has had important consequences for our contemporary constitution. In particular:

- the 'first past the post' voting system, which gives the prize to the largest party with nothing for the runners-up, favours two dominant parties at the expense of other parties;
- we have an officially recognised 'Opposition Party' which is always supposedly ready to form an alternative government;
- the internal procedures in Parliament, even the seating arrangements, reflect the same assumptions. These do not exist in such extreme forms in other European democracies.

It was established by the late eighteenth century that the King must act on the advice of ministers and must appoint as Prime Minister the person who commands a majority of the House of Commons. Government policy was made by the Cabinet, a body of senior ministers originally chosen by the King but now on the advice of the Prime Minister. It was also established that the government must resign if it loses the confidence of Parliament. If an alternative government cannot be formed the monarch must dissolve Parliament, leading to an election and the summoning of a new Parliament. The Prime Minister could request the monarch to dissolve Parliament at any time. However the House of Lords was still coequal with the Commons and could veto legislation although the Commons controlled the raising and spending of money by the Crown.

At a time when most European states were absolute monarchies, the British constitution was widely admired from outside as a stable and liberal regime embodying the rule of law and a balance between Parliament and the Crown. The notion of the 'mixed constitution' was promoted, in which monarch, Lords and Commons acted as checks on each other in a balanced clockwork-like machine. The leading legal commentator Blackstone (1723–80) announced that the royal assent to legislation meant that the King could not propose evil but could prevent it and went on to eulogise the mutual checks between nobility, King and people that Parliament embodied. Blackstone also emphasised the importance of the rule of law and the independence of the judges.

From inside Britain the picture was more blurred. The electoral system was not democratic and bore little relationship to the distribution of the population. Only about 4 per cent of the populution had the right to vote. Elections were largely controlled by aristocratic families with a power base both in the House of Lords and in local affairs by bribery or by selecting candidates. There was a property qualification to vote in the rural counties. In the boroughs (towns) the right to vote depended on local charters and customs. In many cases this was attached to particular property and could be bought. There were numerous 'rotten boroughs' that only had a handful of electors, sometimes in the gift of particular families. For example in 1830 Gatton (patron Sir John Wood) had two MPs and seven voters. At the other extreme the expanding cities had few, if any, representatives. General elections did not necessarily relate to changes in government as is the case today but governments formed and reformed under royal and aristocratic influence.

Judges were politically appointed and were often members of Parliament and the Cabinet. Until the reign of George III (1760–1820) they had to be reappointed on the death of a monarch. The record of the rule of law was mixed. It protected rights in the formal sense that everyone had access to the same courts and whatever rights a person had were usually adjudicated impartially. However Parliament passed harsh laws for the benefit of its supporters, which the courts were required to apply. These included anti-poaching laws, Combination Acts forbidding trade unions and the like, and a taxation system that put the burden upon consumption as opposed to property, thus penalising the poor (see Thompson, *Whigs and Hunters* (Allen Lane 1975)).

The courts protected property rights and personal security strongly (eg *Leach v Money* [1765]; *Entick v Carrington* [1765]; *Wolfe Tone's Case* [1798]). The common law rejected slavery within England albeit reluctantly (*Somersett's Case* [1772]). Freedom of expression was less clearly protected, other than that of MPs. There were ruthless measures against public disorder, blasphemy and political offences such as sedition. These measures included the intermittent suspension of habeas corpus (an ancient procedure for ensuring the release of those unlawfully imprisoned). The common law, with its reliance on custom, faced severe challenge by rationalists such as Bentham (Chapter 2) who preferred legislation. Leading legal commentators, notably Blackstone, attempted with mixed success to rationalise the common law but it proved impossible to reconcile it with the developing notion of absolute parliamentary supremacy, a tension that remains today (Chapter 8).

Politicians such as Edmund Burke, who entered Parliament in 1765, still influence contemporary debate. Burke favoured traditional ideas of monarchy, custom and the unwritten constitution as opposed to equality and abstract reason, which he feared would lead to chaos and tyranny. He grounded the constitution in the limited right to choose and remove a representative government (see Pocock (ed), *Reflections on the Revolution in France* (Hackett 1987)). Burke's rival Thomas Paine (see Section 4.5) favoured equality, broader ideas of democracy and the establishment of a code of fundamental rights.

Some contemporary themes are emerging. There is still tension between the House of Lords and the House of Commons and between the courts and Parliament. The Crown still possesses wide legal powers restricted by conventions, the scope of which is unclear. Patronage is exercised by the Prime Minister and political parties, who nominate candidates for election and recommend peerages and public appointments. Then, as now, the permanent civil service was caught between two stools. On the one hand, efficiency required it to be distant from day-to-day politics. On the other hand, ministers required loyal servants. Various 'Place Acts' attempted a compromise by barring many categories of public official from membership of Parliament. Today we tackle the problem by barring most public officials from sitting in Parliament and creating a category of 'special adviser' – a civil servant with party political affiliations (Chapter 5).

Scotland, which had previously been a separate state under the same monarch, was united with England as 'Great Britain' with one Parliament, based on the English Parliament (Acts of Union 1706). The Act of Union with Ireland 1800 temporarily united Great Britain and Ireland as the UK. However, by 1921 most of Ireland had become an independent state. Northern Ireland, which from Tudor times had been occupied by Protestant settlers from England and Scotland, remains part of the UK.

4.7 The nineteenth and twentieth centuries: democracy and the central state

During the nineteenth century the political and economic circumstances of Britain changed. Rural communities dominated by aristocratic landowners were rivalled by conurbations dependent upon industrial production and overseas trade. This led to a rapidly increasing urban population of wage earners, demands for democratic government and the provision of public services. Between the first Reform Act of 1832 and the Representation of the People Act 1948, which finally introduced equal voting rights for most adults, Parliament gradually and reluctantly extended the right to vote. Many more electoral constituencies were created corresponding to the distribution of the population. Secret ballots and a register of electors were introduced, reducing corruption and intimidation. The balance of power between Parliament and the executive moved in favour of the executive. MPs were becoming professional politicians dependent for their livelihood on party support. Elections became the mass campaigns with which we are familiar today. After the First World War (1914–18) the moderately radical Liberal Party collapsed and the conservative Tories were confronted by the newly emergent Labour Party, then representing working-class interests and broadly in favour of a state with wide discretionary power.

Utilitarianism and economics replaced law as the intellectual fashion. For much of the nineteenth century free market ideas were dominant but coupled with strong state activity to provide basic services and to remedy injustices. Local authorities were created to provide the roads, utilities and public health services necessary to support business interests but their powers were interpreted restrictively by the courts to prevent them providing more than basic welfare services (eg *A-G v Fulham Corp* [1921]). An important landmark was the Northcote-Trevelyan Report of 1854, which led to the creation of a permanent, professional and non-party political civil service appointed on merit – an ideal retained today albeit increasingly vulnerable.

The extension of democracy led to a debate about the place of common law. Traditionalists regarded the common law as a hedge against tyranny while reformers such as Bentham despised the common law as an enemy of progress, democracy and efficient management. During this period of developing democracy the courts explicitly endorsed the principle of parliamentary supremacy (Chapter 8). In relation to the common law it is arguable that the broad justice-based system that predominated during the eighteenth century was challenged by more formalistic rule-based conceptions of law that suited the development of trade in the nineteenth century.

During Queen Victoria's reign (1837–1901) the monarchy reshaped itself as a symbolic representative of the nation standing outside party politics. By the end of the nineteenth century it was becoming established that the Prime Minister and most senior ministers must be members of the House of Commons and, it was increasingly claimed, that the unelected House of Lords was subordinate to the House of Commons. Lord Salisbury was the last Prime Minister to sit in the House of Lords (1892).

During the early years of the twentieth century there was persistent hostility between the House of Lords, which had an inbuilt Conservative majority, and the Liberal government. This concerned in particular the question of Irish home rule and the reluctance of the Lords to approve high taxation for welfare purposes. After a long struggle culminating in a general election, followed by King George's reluctant agreement to create enough peers to steamroller the legislation through, the Lords backed down. The Parliament Act 1911 endorsed the supremacy of the Commons by removing most of the powers of the House of Lords to veto legislation. However the House of Lords retains significant influence. Its main function is now that of a revising and delaying mechanism. In view of its relative independence from party politics it could also be regarded as a guardian of constitutional values.

Impelled by the demands of a larger electorate the executive began to increase in size and range of discretionary powers as successive governments provided a wider range of welfare services. These could be delivered only through large bureaucratic organisations making numerous detailed decisions, guided by a plethora of rules and technical specialists. During the twentieth century it became widely accepted that the state could regulate any aspect of our lives and that whether it should do so was a matter not for the constitution but for the everyday political contest. The traditional sources of law, Acts of Parliament and the courts, were supplemented by an array of tools that enabled the executive to act relatively quickly and informally but without detailed parliamentary scrutiny. These included delegated legislation made by government departments under powers given to them by statute and wide discretionary powers conferred on ministers and local authorities. Thousands of administrative tribunals staffed by government appointees were created to deal with the disputes generated by the expansion of state activity. Other bodies outside the traditional umbrella of parliamentary accountability were created to run services or to give advice. Executive control over Parliament increased. Parliamentary processes were too amateurish and controlled by government supporters to enable executive action to be thoroughly scrutinised. Statutory provisions were introduced which attempted to exclude scrutiny of governmental decisions by the courts. It was therefore feared that the executive had outgrown the constraints both of the rule of law and political accountability to Parliament.

The constitution made only limited responses to these developments. In the interwar period both ends of the political spectrum were worried. Some believed that the executive had taken over; others that an individualistically minded judiciary would frustrate social reforms. The *Report of the Committee on Ministers' Powers* (Cmd 4060, 1932) concerning delegated legislation and the *Report of the Committee on Administrative Tribunals and Inquiries* (Cmnd 218, 1958, the Franks Committee) recommended marginal reforms. These improved publicity, strengthened the powers of the courts, supplemented parliamentary scrutiny of the executive and introduced a Council on Tribunals to monitor and advise on administrative tribunals and statutory inquiries (Statutory Instruments Act 1946; Tribunals and Inquiries Acts 1958 and 1992). From the 1960s various 'ombudsmen' were set up to investigate complaints by citizens against government, but without enforceable powers.

Recognising the inevitability of executive power and reluctant to appear to be challenging democracy, the courts usually deferred to political decisions. However from the 1960s the courts woke up from what Sir Stephen Sedley has called their long sleep (in Andenas and Fairgrieve, 2009) and began to interfere more actively with government decisions. Landmark cases during the 1960s form the basis of contemporary administrative law. These include *Ridge v Baldwin* [1964], *Anisminic v Foreign Compensation Commission* [1968], *Conway v Rimmer* [1968] and *Padfield v Minister of Agriculture* [1968]. Judicial activism was further encouraged by the creation of what is now the Administrative Court in 1977 (Chapter 19) and the enactment in 1998 of the Human Rights Act.

There were also concerns about democracy. In 1972 the UK became a member of what is now the European Union (European Communities Act 1972). Much European law has thereby become binding in UK law but is not made by an elected body and is subject only to limited democratic scrutiny (Chapter 10). Concerns were also raised that the electoral system puts minorities into power and enables the large political parties to control both the executive and Parliament. These complaints amounted to fears that the constitution had degenerated into an oligarchy that did little more than allow the people to choose periodically between groups of cronies. Indeed in the eighteenth century the French philosopher Rousseau asserted that the British were slaves except at election time.

Summary

- The historical development of the constitution was driven by the gradual wresting of power from the monarch in favour of other interest groups focused mainly on Parliament.
- The 1688 revolution created a settlement that still forms the legal basis of the constitution. It attempts to combine respect for continuity and a balance of forces with the principle of parliamentary supremacy and collective party government.
- Despite a tendency to corruption, democratic reforms were introduced during the nineteenth and early twentieth centuries but without there being a complete democratic basis for the constitution.
- The common law and independent courts were regarded as important checks on government. In recent years the courts have been more active than previously in challenging government action.
- Latterly there have been concerns about the increased power of the executive in relation to Parliament.

Exercises

4.1 To what extent was the 1688 settlement a constitutional revolution?

4.2 Does the history of the UK constitution reveal a march towards a greater democracy?

4.3 What historical factors have led to the powerful position held by the executive in the UK constitution?

4.4 'Herein consists the excellence of the English Government, that all parts of it form a mutual check on each other' (Blackstone, 1765). To what extent was this true in Blackstone's time and is it true today?

Further reading

Bogdanor (ed), *The British Constitution in the Twentieth Century* (Oxford University Press 2003) Introduction

Chrimes, *English Constitutional History* (4th edn, Oxford University Press 1967)

Kellner, *Democracy: 1,000 Years in Pursuit of British Liberty* (Mainstream 2009)

Lyons, *Constitutional History of the United Kingdom* (Cavendish 2003)

McIlwain, *Constitutionalism Ancient and Modern* (Cornell University Press 1947) ch 4

Porter, *England in the Eighteenth Century* (Penguin 1990) ch 3

Sedley, 'The Long Sleep' in Andenas and Fairgrieve (eds), *Tom Bingham and the Transformation of the Law* (Oxford University Press 2009)

Wicks, *Evolution of a Constitution* (Hart 2006)

Chapter 5

An overview of the main institutions of the UK constitution

> **Small clusters of self-enclosed, self-serving groups on the peaks, and the public on the plain below. (Anthony Sampson, *Who Runs This Place?* 2004)**

5.1 Introduction: the dignified and efficient constitution: deceiving the people?

This chapter offers an overview of the contemporary structure of the UK constitution as a framework for a more detailed discussion of key topics in later chapters. Particularly important issues are cross-referenced.

It is often said that the glue which holds the unwritten UK constitution together is the propensity of the British to subservience and deference to officialdom. Writing in the mid-nineteenth century, Walter Bagehot (1902) regarded social class deference and superstition as the 'magic' ingredients that animated the constitution. Bagehot took a jaundiced view of the political sophistication of ordinary people and thought that government could only work effectively if its authority is buttressed by traditional institutions which command people's imagination and make them deferential to the rulers.

Bagehot distinguished between what he called the 'dignified' and the 'efficient' parts of the constitution. The dignified parts give the constitution its authority and encourage people to obey it. They involve the trappings of power, notably the royal prerogative that underpins the central government (Section 14.6), and the mystique of ceremonial and ritual. The efficient part of the constitution, which Bagehot located primarily in the Cabinet and which depends on the political balance of forces at any given time, carries out the working exercise of power behind the scenes. From this perspective all government boils down to an oligarchy of like-minded people in the form of a 'king' and his courtiers.

What is dignified and what is efficient changes over time. For example the eighteenth-century Hanoverian kings lost public respect by becoming virtually party politicians. William IV in 1834 was the last monarch to dismiss a ministry that had the support of Parliament. Towards the end of her reign Queen Victoria 'redignified' the monarchy by distancing herself from political partisanship and introducing the kind of pomp and ceremony that characterises the UK monarchy in modern times. But it remains unclear whether the monarch retains a vestige of political power (Section 14.4).

The distinction between the dignified and the efficient performs a useful function in a democracy by preventing working politicians from claiming to embody the state, a technique adopted by tyrants throughout history. For example the monarch and Parliament have authority, the latter because it is elected, while the government has power without authority in its own right. It gets its political legitimacy only from Parliament.

On the other hand the dignified element can reinforce tyranny by hiding reality. Bagehot thought that it would be dangerous to shed the light of reality upon the constitution. The 'noble lie' postulated by Plato in his *Republic* is designed to keep people happy with their designated roles: when humans were formed in the earth the rulers had gold mixed with them, the military silver and the workers lead. Even Plato's pupils found this hard to swallow but they thought that it is sometimes right to lie in the interests of the state.

There is the same thinking in the contemporary constitution. In *McIlkenny v Chief Constable of the West Midlands Police* [1980] at 239–40, Lord Denning MR took the view that it was better for the 'Birmingham Six' to remain wrongly convicted than to face the 'appalling vista' of the police being found to be guilty of perjury, violence and threats. The Scott Report into the sale of arms to Iraq (*Report of the Inquiry into the Export of Defence Equipment and Dual Use Goods to Iraq and Related Prosecution* (HC 1995–96, 115)) revealed that ministers and civil servants regarded it as being in the public interest to mislead Parliament, if not actually to lie, over government involvement in arms sales to overseas regimes. The Constitutional Reform Act 2010 prevents disclosure under the Freedom of Information Act 2000 of all correspondence between the Prince of Wales and ministers on the ground that it would weaken public confidence in the monarchy if people knew that the heir to the throne attempted to influence government (see Section 23.2.1; see also *Guardian* 16 September 2010).

5.2 Legislature and executive

In examining the legislature and the executive we shall distinguish between strict law, conventions and important but not binding political practices with a view to revealing the clumsily constructed patchwork that makes up the constitution. The fabric of the constitution comprises the Queen as head of state and the three traditional branches of government:

1. Parliament is the supreme lawmaker, comprising the elected House of Commons and the appointed House of Lords.
2. The Crown is the executive branch, known generally as 'the government'. It is accountable to Parliament and its decisions are in the main reviewable by the courts; that is, they can be set aside if unlawful and in particular if they are outside the powers given by Parliament.
3. The independent judiciary is the third branch, comprising courts and tribunals. These settle civil disputes, review the legality of government action and decide criminal prosecutions. Tribunals adjudicate on specialised matters, usually between government and individuals.

These three branches of government are the basis of the traditional doctrine of the separation of powers. According to this doctrine in its strict form each branch exercises different functions and operates independently of the others so that no single branch is dominant and each checks the others. However the separation of powers is imperfect in the UK. Firstly Parliament is widely regarded as the highest branch and as having unlimited lawmaking power which cannot be restricted by the other branches of government. Secondly the executive and the legislature are not separate. The UK constitution is an extreme example of a parliamentary system in that ministers who head the executive branch are also members of Parliament and are in a position to control Parliament. Thirdly judges make law under the common law and it is sometimes suggested that they can in extreme cases override Parliament (see Sections 8.4.5, 8.5).

5.2.1 The legislature

At the most basic legal level established by the 1688 revolution, the lawmakers are the Queen in Parliament and, subject (probably) to Parliament, the judges under the common law. Thus a strict separation of powers does not apply.

- The Queen in Parliament makes primary law in the form of Acts of Parliament (statutes). Parliament also provides the government with money and is meant to hold the executive to account. By convention the Queen is obliged to give her assent to all bills submitted to her by Parliament.
- The Queen cannot raise taxes or make new laws unless authorised by Parliament.
- Parliament is 'bicameral', comprising an elected lower house, the House of Commons, and an upper house, the House of Lords, most members of which are appointed by the Queen for life.
- A Parliament lasts for five years (Parliament Act 1911), at the end of which there must be a general election for membership of the House of Commons (Representation of the People Act 1983).
- A new Parliament is summoned by the Queen under the royal prerogative. Parliament must meet at least every three years and so cannot be dispensed with (Meeting of Parliament Act 1694). By convention Parliament must meet annually.
- Within the five-year period the Queen can dissolve Parliament under the royal prerogative whenever she wishes, again leading to a general election. By convention Parliament must be dissolved on the advice of the Prime Minister, who again by convention must so advise if his or her government loses the confidence of the House of Commons and an alternative government cannot command the support of the House. (This group of conventions is subject to a reforming bill; see Section 11.3). By convention the Queen must not be personally involved in the choice of Prime Minister.
- The House of Commons is the dominant body. The House of Lords can delay the enactment of statutes, but subject to exceptions – most importantly a bill to prolong the life of Parliament itself – the House of Lords cannot veto laws proposed by the Commons (Parliament Acts 1911 and 1949).

5.2.2 The executive: strict law

- In many countries the 'state' is a legal entity but the UK has no legal concept of the state as such, only the Crown. The executive comprises the Queen/Crown and her servants together with separate bodies created by statute for particular purposes, known as non-departmental public bodies. The Crown as the permanent executive is always in being. It can be terminated only by an Act of Parliament. However the legal status of the Crown as such is obscure. It is not clear how far the Crown is a separate legal entity from the Queen personally.
- The Queen can appoint and dismiss anyone she wishes as servant or adviser. Crown servants comprise ministers who hold particular offices, civil servants who act in the name of ministers, and the armed forces. There are no legal rules either restricting the number of ministers or other officials that can be appointed or concerning the structure and organisation of government departments. These are therefore matters for the preferences of governments from time to time.

- Most legal powers are conferred by statute on individual ministers. There are also important executive powers vested in the Crown under common law. These are known as the 'royal prerogative' (Chapter 14). This is a residue of the powers of the medieval monarchs. Some prerogatives can be justified as being a necessary aspect of the sovereignty of any state, for example the power to deploy the armed forces and to enter into treaties with other states. Prerogative powers are advantageous to the executive in that they do not need the consent of Parliament.
- Griffiths succinctly identified the basic legal position as follows: 'Governments of the United Kingdom may take any action necessary for the proper government of the United Kingdom as they see it, subject to two limitations. The first limitation is that they may not infringe the legal rights of others unless expressly authorised to do so under statute or the prerogative. The second limitation is that if they wish to change the law, whether by adding to their existing power or otherwise, they must obtain the consent of Parliament' ('The Political Constitution' (1979) 42 MLR 15).
- Apart from implementing the law, controlling public services and handing out jobs, honours and money, the executive makes subordinate legislation under powers delegated to it by Parliament. Parliament can of course give executive power to anyone. It has kept historical continuity by preserving the Crown as the central 'executive', although specific executive powers are also given to many other bodies which have been established by statute, notably local authorities. These are not part of the Crown unless the statute provides otherwise.
- The civil service appointed by the Crown and subject to a mixture of statute, royal prerogative and convention (see Section 15.7) has the dual role of offering impartial advice to ministers and carrying out the instructions of ministers in running the day-to-day affairs of the government. Reflecting the separation of powers, civil servants cannot be members of Parliament (House of Commons (Disqualification) Act 1975).
- The armed forces are also Crown servants. Under the Bill of Rights 1688 the existence of a permanent peacetime army requires statutory approval. However control over the armed forces, for example deployment, choice of weapons and declaring war, is a royal prerogative power and so does not require parliamentary approval. Some aspects of the armed forces, including military discipline and courts martial, are directly regulated by statute. There are concerns as to whether military courts are sufficiently independent to satisfy contemporary human rights-based notions of a fair trial (see *Findlay v UK* [1997]; Armed Forces Act 2006).
- Because the Crown is a legal person, the Crown can do anything which an individual can do unless excluded by statute. These 'private law powers', for example to own property and make contracts, derived from our constitutional history are controversial, seeming to contradict the principle that in a democracy government should have only those powers conferred on it by an elected lawmaker. These powers give the government considerable leverage, for example in influencing property and business matters such as the sale and purchase of arms, energy, computers or medicines. Parliament can of course regulate or remove these powers and as Griffiths points out they cannot be used to interfere with the legal rights of others. The Crown is therefore sharply different from other public bodies which have executive function, such as local authorities. These can be created only by statute and have no powers other than those specifically given to them by statute (see *R v Somerset CC, ex p Fewings* [1995]).

- In the absence of special statutory or, in the case of the police, common law powers, members of the armed forces and police have no special privileges They are subject to the same general law that applies to ordinary citizens, namely that force used must be in self-defence or in the defence of others or of property and must be reasonable in the circumstances. This reflects a traditional aspect of the rule of law (Chapter 6). However the pressures of the moment, such as being forced to act quickly in a chaotic or dangerous situation, are of course part of the circumstances. It is not clear whether there is a defence of obedience to superior orders (Section 23.6).

5.2.3 The executive: conventions

- By convention the Queen must normally act on the advice of the Prime Minister or other ministers. Indeed convention and law have blurred in that, except for what are called the 'personal prerogatives'(certain high-level formal matters such as dissolving Parliament and appointing ministers), royal prerogative powers are validly exercised directly by ministers, not merely on their advice.
- All ministers must be members of Parliament and collectively they are 'the government'. The most important ministers must be members of the House of Commons. Government business such as proposals for laws has priority in the Commons.
- The Queen must appoint as Prime Minister the person supported by a majority of the House of Commons and she must appoint and dismiss other ministers on the recommendation of the Prime Minister.
- Ministers are responsible to Parliament for their actions, although it is controversial what this means (see Section 15.5).
- If the government loses the support of the House of Commons in a vote of confidence, then it must resign. Unless an alternative government has the support of the Commons this leads to a dissolution of Parliament and triggers a general election.
- The Cabinet, a committee of senior ministers chaired by the Prime Minister, is responsible for government policy, co-ordinating the work of government departments and major decisions. Members of the Cabinet are collectively responsible to Parliament and must loyally support government decisions once made. Cabinet discussions are confidential. In the nineteenth century Bagehot regarded the Cabinet as the 'buckle' that holds the constitution together. Latterly the Cabinet may have declined in importance, thus illustrating the tenuous nature of conventions. Its role has arguably been usurped by strong overlord departments such as the Treasury and the Prime Minister's office and by informal committees appointed by the Prime Minister (see Burch and Holiday, 'The Blair Government and the Core Executive' (2004) 39 Gov't & Oppos 1).

These conventions thus create a model of representative democratic government in which the government is responsible through Parliament to the 'people' or at least to those of them permitted to vote. Arrangements for elections are a matter for Parliament in the same way as any other law. Thus Parliament both sustains the government and polices it. This leads inevitably to conflict.

Under the royal prerogative the armed forces are subject to the principle which is both law and convention that prerogative powers are exercised by ministers. Thus the military arm of the state is subject to the political arm and ultimately to Parliament.

5.2.4 Political practice: executive domination of Parliament

The third level (in addition to law and convention) is that of political practice, reminding us of Griffiths' famous aphorism: the constitution is 'everything that happens' (Chapter 1). We have seen that in our extreme parliamentary system ministers are also MPs, and therefore they are in a position to dominate the procedure of the House. The main reason for this is the strength of the party system. There is no law or convention requiring political parties to exist. Nevertheless political parties are an inevitable ingredient of a democratic system since elections must be contested by organised groups capable of raising sufficient money to be able to communicate effectively.

In practice Parliament is weak through its own choice. Except on relatively rare occasions most MPs will vote as required by their party, perhaps without studying the proposals in question. There is no law or convention requiring them to do this other than the convention of collective ministerial responsibility, which requires those MPs who are government ministers to support the government. About 100 MPs out of a total of about 650 are ministers. For example a majority of the 'payroll' vote supported the Labour government's decision to invade Iraq in 2002 while a majority of backbench members of the party voted against. The vote was won only with the support of opposition parties.

Three main factors strengthen the power of the executive over Parliament. The first factor is that by the procedural rules of the Commons government business has priority. This leaves only limited time for backbenchers to raise and discuss issues. This is reinforced by a system of party discipline known as the Whip system under which the Whips persuade individual MPs to vote for government measures in the House of Commons. Recent reforms have to some extent increased the influence of backbench MPs (see Section 20.1) but this is insignificant in relation to the government's power to control the extent to which proposed laws are discussed. The House of Lords is not dominated by the government but its proposals can be rejected by the Commons.

Secondly there is the voting system for Parliament, known as 'first past the post' – technically the 'single relative majority' system. This awards a seat in Parliament to whichever candidate has the largest number of votes in a local area known as a constituency. Other candidates get nothing, whatever their share of the vote. First past the post is therefore unfair to smaller parties. This contrasts with systems of proportional representation (PR) used in many other countries (including Scotland, Wales and Northern Ireland), under which seats are distributed among the parties according to their share of the total vote (see Section 12.7.1). PR is likely to weaken the power of the larger parties, allowing members of Parliament greater independence. The present system has been justified on the basis that it produces a strong government. A related factor is that the geographical constituencies are designated by an independent Boundary Commission according to loose requirements which allow social matters such as travelling distance and cultural affinities to be taken into account (see Section 12.8). This is designed to ensure that to some extent MPs represent natural communities. Thus there are variations in the number of voters in different constituencies. Also inevitably some localities traditionally favour a particular party since politics is to some extent based on economic interests.

A bill currently before Parliament (see Section 24.3) proposes to hold a referendum on the introduction of the 'alternative vote' (AV) system (see Section 12.7.1). This is designed to ensure that the winner has the support of 50 per cent of the votes but is likely to have only a limited effect on party control. The bill also proposes to reduce the number of constituencies and so of MPs and to make all constituencies roughly equal in population. This is likely to increase the influence of the executive.

Thirdly there is party control over individual MPs. Strictly speaking the MP's main role is that of a representative of his or her local constituency but party loyalties tend to come first. A strong motivation both for sitting MPs and for candidates for election is to please the party leaders since these people are influential in selecting and reselecting candidates and rewarding them with jobs in government. The government's proposed reform of electoral constituencies to make them roughly equal in terms of the number of voters is likely to strengthen party control in that it will weaken the connection between the MP and the local community since constituency boundaries are likely to be artificial.

The party also chooses the Prime Minister. Unlike in a presidential system the people do not elect the Prime Minister as such, who is simply elected as an ordinary MP by his or her local constituency. In practice the Prime Minister is usually the leader of the political party with an overall majority in the Commons, or where there is no overall majority as now the leader of the largest party. Of course at a general election many voters are likely to be thinking of the party leaders rather than their local MP. However among 25 prime ministers since 1900 only 10 have taken office following a general election. For example in 2007 Gordon Brown was chosen as leader by the Labour Party without opposition following the resignation of Tony Blair under pressure from his party.

A party leader is chosen under internal party arrangements. The rules of each party for choosing its leader are therefore crucial and are summarised here. They have no special legal status, nor are they constitutional convention; they are essentially private agreements. They attempt to provide a balance between MPs and ordinary party members and should be assessed in terms of their contribution to democracy.

1. Conservative Party
   - The sitting leader can be removed by a vote of confidence among MPs trigged by 15 per cent.
   - Candidates must be nominated by two MPs.
   - If there is only one candidate then he or she is automatically elected.
   - If there are two candidates, election is by a ballot of all party members.
   - If there are more than two candidates, there is a ballot by MPs to reduce number to two and then election is by a ballot of party members.
   - See Alderman (1999) 52 Parl Aff 260.
2. Labour Party
   - The sitting leader can be removed by a vote of confidence of MPs triggered by 20 per cent plus a majority of members voting at a party conference.
   - A candidate must be supported by 12.5 per cent of MPs, or 20 per cent if challenging a sitting leader.

- Votes are split equally between MPs and MEPs, party members and affiliated trade unions and other organisations (individual members voting within each union) who have not opted out of paying a political levy. Thus an MP might have three votes or more!

3. Liberal Democratic Party
   - A sitting leader can be removed by a vote of no confidence by MPs or a requisition of 75 local parties.
   - Nominations must be supported by 10 per cent of MPs and 200 members from not less than 20 local parties.
   - Election is by a ballot of all members (AV method; see Section 12.7.1).

Apart from choosing the leader the rules for the two main parties give strong powers to the party leadership over ordinary members. However when it is in opposition the rules of the Labour Party require that the Shadow Cabinet be elected by the MPs (these rules are currently being reconsidered in order to strengthen the leadership).

Controlling the executive is also difficult because of the strong culture of secrecy that pervades the operations of government. Supported by the legal principle that the executive is part of the Crown rather than employed on behalf of the people there is a basic assumption that government documents are confidential and that the public have no right of access to them. There are substantial qualifications to this, such as the Freedom of Information Act 2000 (which has many exceptions) and common law arguments based on the public interest (see Section 23.3). An independently minded parliamentary committee might press to see government documents (unlikely given executive dominance of Parliament) but MPs as such have no rights in the matter beyond those of the general public. The Parliamentary Ombudsman (see Section 5.4.4) has an enforceable right to see government papers except Cabinet-level papers (Parliamentary Commissioner Act 1967, s 8), and some, but by no means all, official inquiries (see Section 5.4.3) have a power to compel witnesses and documents. However these exceptions place the onus on those seeking information to justify doing so and can be easily invaded, for example by denials that a document exists or claims that it cannot be found. Pressure may also be placed on officials not to disclose information that might embarrass important persons (see eg *Observer* 25 October 2010).

5.2.5 Civil servants

There is no legal definition of a civil servant. The Constitutional Reform and Governance Act 2010 provides a general legal framework for the appointment and conduct of civil servants (see Section 15.7) but provides only that the civil service means the civil service of the state (s 1(4)). A civil servant can be described in a negative sense as a Crown servant who is not a minister, does not hold judicial office and is not a member of the armed forces (see *Report of the Royal Commission on the Civil Service* (Cmd 3909, 1931, the Tomlin Commission); Sandberg, 'A Whitehall Farce? Defining and Conceptualising the British Civil Service' [2006] PL 653). A single civil service applies to England, Scotland and Wales, but with responsibility to the ministers of the separate governments, and there is a separate civil service for Northern Ireland.

Civil servants are controlled by a mixture of statute, royal prerogative and convention. There is a statutory Civil Service Code (Constitutional Reform and Governance Act 2010, s 7), concerned with the appointment and conduct of civil servants (see Section 15.7). By convention ministers are responsible to Parliament for the actions of civil servants within their departments and the individual civil servant has no direct accountability. This makes for clear lines of responsibility but is arguably unrealistic given that the vast majority of detailed government decisions are taken by civil servants (see Section 15.8.3).

Civil servants have two kinds of obligation. The first is that they must give impartial advice to ministers. This is the main function of the core of senior civil servants. To this end civil servants must carry out their duties objectively and impartially (Constitutional Reform and Governance Act 2010, s 7(4)). Civil servants are appointed by a process supervised by independent civil service commissioners in order to minimise political bias (Constitutional Reform and Governance Act 2010). This helps to stabilise the constitution in a system where the political part of government is constantly changing. Unlike in the US, except for special advisers (see Section 5.2.6), civil servants are not automatically replaced when a government changes.

The second obligation is that all civil servants must loyally carry out instructions from ministers. In this context a civil servant is regarded as no more than an extension of the minister. It is obvious that no minister can make every decision in person, and neither can she or he be aware of the thousands of decisions that must be taken within a government department each year. Nevertheless the convention mentioned above is reflected in the legal principle that a minister can act through any civil servant in her or his department (see *Carltona v Comr of Works* [1943]; Sections 15.5, 18.2). Thus the constitution is supposed to create a chain of accountability through ministers to Parliament, whoever actually makes a given decision.

5.2.6 Tensions within the executive: special advisers

Special advisers are party political advisers appointed directly by ministers and working closely with them. They were formally recognised by a government announcement in 1974 but have probably always existed. They are temporary civil servants appointed for the purpose of providing 'assistance' to ministers, a purpose which goes beyond advice (Constitutional Reform and Governance Act 2010, s 15). Unlike other civil servants they are not required to be impartial or objective and they need not be appointed on merit in fair and open competition.

Special advisers serve as a link between the political and the permanent parts of the government. There has been concern that their activities, particularly in relation to communication with the media, may threaten the reputation of the civil service for impartiality. There is also a concern that permanent civil servants may be denied access to ministers and their role will be reduced to carrying out orders from special advisers (see Public Administration Select Committee, *Special Advisers: Boon or Bane?* (HC 2000–01, 293); HL Deb 7 November 2005, cols 482–98; Committee on Standards in Public Life, *Reinforcing Standards* (Cm 4557, 2000) and *Defining the Boundaries within the Executive* (Cm 5775, 2003)).

The position of special adviser has been put on a statutory basis by section 15 of the Constitutional Reform and Governance Act 2010, which applies to the UK government and to the devolved governments of Scotland and Wales. The powers of special advisers have been constrained (see Section 15.7.1). However, accountability has not been increased other than by requiring an annual report to Parliament concerning the number and cost of special advisers (s 16). There is no legal limit on the number of special advisers. In June 2010 there were 68 posts attached to UK government ministers, 14 of them in the Prime Minister's office. Special advisers lose their posts when their minister does so or after a general election.

The interaction of law, convention and practice described above has arguably resulted in a constitution in which absolute monarchical power has transferred from the monarch to the leaders of political parties. However the nature of Parliament's legal supremacy and the role of courts must be added to the story (see Chapter 8).

5.2.7 Loosening of the executive: executive agencies and non-ministerial government departments

Since the 1980s, many government functions have been removed from the traditional civil service structure of a pyramid topped by ministers and either transferred to private bodies operating under contracts with the government or exercised by executive agencies (originally called 'Next Steps' agencies), sometimes competing for work with private bodies, for example to run prisons. The theory behind these developments is 'public choice' theory, according to which accountability and efficiency are best served by harnessing self-interest in the form of competition. An obvious danger is that, owing to the tribalism that usually develops within an organisation, the delivery function carried out by an agency may become too far divorced from the core policy-making function.

Executive agencies are part of the civil service and remain subject to control by ministers. Each agency has a sponsoring government department and departments may each have several agencies. Many agencies provide crucial government services. Examples include the Courts Service, Jobcentre Plus, the Border Agency, the Driver and Vehicle Licensing Agency, the Prison Service and the Met Office.

The principle underlying the respective functions of the agencies and their sponsoring departments is that responsibility for service delivery should reside with the agency, while policy matters should be reserved for the department acting under ministerial control. 'Framework agreements' made between the agency and the sponsoring department (sometimes with the Treasury as a party) constitute the relationship between the two. The framework agreement contains the corporate strategy and financial arrangements under which the agency will work. It sets out the objectives of the agency and the division of responsibility between the agency and the department.

Agencies are permitted to run themselves semi-independently from their sponsoring government department, recruiting their own staff and managing themselves by copying the practices of private businesses. They do not make policy but carry out the work of government on a detailed level by applying policy made by ministers. However ministers retain complete powers of control over them.

A chief executive for each agency is appointed by the minister, usually for a fixed period, to be responsible for the day-to-day management of the agency. The chief executive is responsible to the minister but as accounting officer also appears before select committees of Parliament to answer MPs' questions about the functioning of the agency. Controversially this suggests that a convention may have been emerging under which agency chief executives are directly responsible to Parliament in their own right (see Section 15.7). MPs have also been encouraged to approach chief executives directly on behalf of their constituents and chief executives answer written parliamentary questions. The answers are published in *Hansard* (the official record of parliamentary proceedings) in order to avoid the bypassing of Parliament which might occur if chief executives responded directly to individual MPs.

Agencies therefore raise problems for the doctrine of ministerial responsibility in that ministers may attempt to avoid accountability to Parliament for mistakes made within agencies in defiance of the traditional convention that a minister is responsible for everything within his department. It is not clear how far ministerial responsibility applies to day-to-day administration (see Sections 15.7).

Agencies are distinct from non-ministerial government departments. These have long existed. They are departments which carry out basic governmental functions but in the interests of stability and impartiality are not subject to direct political control. They are normally created by statute and have a separate legal identity. They are however servants of the Crown and their staff are civil servants. They have direct statutory powers and are funded by Parliament. They include HM Revenue and Customs, the Crown Prosecution Service, the Serious Fraud Office and the regulators of several industries and of the education service. The Crown Estates and the Forestry Commission, which own much government land (substantial land is also owned by the Ministry of Defence), are also non-ministerial departments. They are directly accountable to Parliament.

A minister is accountable for a non-ministerial government body only to the extent that the minister has powers concerning it. The extent of this depends on the particular statute. Normally a minister appoints the chair or board. Dismissal powers vary according to the extent of independence and security desired. Sometimes a minister has power to give non-binding 'guidance' or binding 'directions'.

An important species of non-ministerial department is the statutory regulator. This constitutional innovation was introduced during the 1980s in connection with a policy of privatisation, namely transferring the provision of certain basic services from state ownership to private companies, such as those supplying gas, electricity and water, telecommunications, broadcasting and public transport. The political and economic rationale was market liberalism (see Section 2.3.4) in the form of assumptions firstly that market forces produced greater efficiency than state control, and secondly that provided that there was an element of government regulation, ownership was not important in relation to public benefit. This is a good example of constitutional change driven by the ideology of the government in power without there being a clear constitutional structure (see Section 24.1). The Financial Services Authority regulates banks and other financial businesses, which have always been nominally private.

Each industry has its own legislation and while the provisions as regards appointment and dismissal of the regulators are similar to those of quangos (see Section 5.3), there appear to be no overarching constitutional principles relating to the accountability and powers of this new breed of regulator.

In practice there is limited room for competition in these industries, so the standard justification for private enterprise is missing. Regulators are therefore a substitute for competition and their roles are complex and sometimes conflicting. They provide a means of accountability to ensure that the businesses are run efficiently, they protect consumers, they ensure competition where appropriate, they impose public interest values on the industries concerned, for example protecting vulnerable groups in relation to electricity and gas supplies, and they act as a delivery method for government policy. As in the case of all quangos the accountability of the regulators is limited and there are neither general procedures nor duties to disclose information other than the limited duties imposed by the Freedom of Information Act 2000 (see Section 23.2.1). There is no direct accountability to Parliament. Judicial review is available on the same basis as with other public bodies and there are sometimes rights of appeal. There are sometimes special tribunals, sometimes an Ombudsman scheme and there may be a consultative body to represent customers. (See eg Utilities Act 2000; Communications Act 2003; Postal Services Act 2000; Railways Act 2005; for a useful overview see Prosser in Jowell and Oliver (eds) *The Changing Constitution* (6th edn, Oxford University Press 2007)).

5.3 Non-departmental public bodies: quangos

Particular functions are conferred, usually by statute but sometimes informally, on many miscellaneous specialised bodies outside the central government (see Cabinet Office, *Public Bodies* (2009)). These bodies, of which there are currently about 900, are often called 'quangos' (quasi-autonomous non-governmental agencies) but there is no legal significance in these labels. Tribunals (see Section 5.4.3) can also be classified as non-departmental public bodies but are perhaps better regarded as part of the judicial system.

Quangos are usually managed by boards appointed by ministers. They are not usually part of the Crown (the governing statute normally determines this), so their members and staff are not civil servants. Some include representatives of particular interests or local councillors. Those of particular constitutional importance will be discussed in context in later chapters.

Quangos can be distinguished from non-ministerial government departments (see Section 5.2.7) in that the latter are fully part of the Crown, their staff are civil servants and they are answerable directly to Parliament in respect of all their activities. Thus quangos have greater independence and flexibility. A non-ministerial department is often concerned with the traditional enforcement function of government, such as regulating private activity, whereas providing grants is more characteristic of a quango. For example the Charity Commission, the Revenue and Customs Department and the regulators of rail and energy companies are non-ministerial departments.

Thus quangos enable selected functions to be exercised outside the parliamentary constraints of central government, giving at least an appearance of impartiality and greater independence than in the case of a government department. This might be because the function is technical or is regarded as uncontroversial or as requiring particular stability and continuity, or is a problem that the minister prefers to dump on someone else. Quangos also provide a useful source of patronage whereby a minister can give posts on the boards of quangos to persons he or she wishes to favour (but see Section 5.9). The same people are often recycled between several quangos.

The main quangos can be divided into advisory bodies and executive bodies although many have both functions. Advisory bodies, such as various health, education, trade, scientific and agricultural authorities and committees, have no decision-making power but give independent advice to ministers, thus legitimising government policy. Advisory bodies can be created by ministers, or indeed anyone else, without statutory authorisation.

For example the Office of Budgetary Responsibility (OBR), created immediately after the general election of 2010, makes independent financial forecasts. It is appointed by ministers, its staff currently comprises civil servants seconded from the Treasury and its offices are based on the Treasury. It may well be independent but there is nothing to ensure its independence. At least to supporters of republican principles (see Section 2.5) the assumption that those in power can be trusted without constitutional safeguards is a failing in the constitution. However the government proposes to put the OBR onto a statutory basis.

Executive bodies require statutory powers. They include the Electoral Commission, the Higher Education Funding Council, the Arts Council, the Homes and Community Agency, the Tenant Services Authority and the Environment Agency. Their powers include granting permits, requiring registration, enforcing compliance with standards and procedures, giving grants and making loans. They might also carry out operations, such as the flood relief work carried out by the Environment Agency.

There are also 'public corporations' which run operational services. During the 1980s many public corporations were converted into private companies supervised by a new breed of regulators (see Section 5.2.7). The surviving public corporations are constituted either by statute or under company law on the model of private companies. These may be wholly or partly owned by the government in the form of shareholdings or under statute, for example the BBC and the Independent Broadcasting Authority, the Post Office and, as a result of the recent financial crisis, some banks. This kind of body may be subject to the commercial pressures of a private company, so that public accountability is even more blurred.

Two special cases

The Bank of England, created in the seventeenth century in order to encourage loans to the government, is a quango that is central to the constitution. Its activities are interrelated with those of the Treasury. Its independence is partly safeguarded by statute (although as usual informal networking between bank and Treasury officials cannot be prevented). It administers the government's bank account, it determines the basic interest rate and it regulates aspects of the banking industry (see Section 15.6.1). The appointment of its Governor and Deputy Governor is not within the jurisdiction of the Commissioner for Public Appointments. Its Governor appears before Parliament in his own right.

Network Rail, which controls the infrastructure and operations of the rail system, is an anomaly. Hastily created by the government after the collapse of a former private body and some serious rail accidents, it is constituted as a non-profit body responsible to members drawn from the industry and government and carefully selected (non-troublesome) members of the public. The government is a shareholder and provides subsidy. There is also an Office of Rail Regulation, which is a non-ministerial government department concerned with the economic relationship between Network Rail and various private and state-owned train operating companies. The central government directly regulates the train operating companies in detail (Railways Act 2005). The extent to which Network Rail should be regarded as a public body is controversial.

Decisions made by quangos are formally independent of government. Setting up a quango therefore enables a minister to avoid direct responsibility. However ministers are likely to have substantial powers of control, including sometimes power to give general directions for which they are accountable to Parliament. Board members are usually appointed by a minister and funding is mainly provided by ministers from funds voted by Parliament to the minister's department. In addition ministers may produce non-statutory 'advice', 'guidance' or 'concordats' regulating the relationship between the quango and government departments or informally exercise influence over compliant members of quango boards.

In theory quangos might provide a vehicle for diverse democracy where independent opinions can be publicly expressed since civil servants have a duty of confidentiality. This may however be more apparent than real. Independently minded persons are unlikely to be appointed to the boards of quangos. Members of quangos are usually appointed for fixed periods and quangos can be created or dissolved either by statute or by ministers at any time.

Quangos do not enjoy a distinct basis for constitutional legitimacy since their accountability and independence are unclear. Firstly there are no general principles as to how they are structured. Each depends on its own arrangements and agreements within relevant government departments. Secondly there are no clear lines of accountability. Ministers may be accountable for their own involvement, in relation to appointments, funding and general oversight and policy, but there is no mechanism for direct accountability of the quango itself other than through the courts. However some quangos closely related to government departments are subject to the Parliamentary Ombudsman (see Section 5.4.4). Moreover there is no legal distinction between a quango and an individual appointed by a minister to carry out a specific function. For example the government's reviewer of anti-terrorism legislation, although statutory, is subject only to a provision requiring the Secretary of State to appoint a 'person' to carry out such reviews, with no requirement of independence (Prevention of Terrorism Act 2005, s 14(2)).

Specific constitutional issues are firstly whether a body is part of the Crown so as to enjoy legal immunities (in the case of statutory bodies the statute will usually make this clear; see Section 14.5); secondly whether it has any democratic element, this being unlikely; thirdly the extent to which it is accountable to Parliament (see Section 13.5) and fourthly whether it is a public body for particular purposes such as the Human Rights Act 1998 (see Section 21.3). Bodies with powers conferred by statute may also be immune from liability for damages provided that they do not exceed their statutory powers (see eg *Marcic v Thames Water Utilities* [2004]; *X (Minors) v Bedfordshire CC* [1995]).

The appointment of members of quangos has been subject to concerns that members are chosen from a pool of persons linked by personal, professional or political relationships. The process for ministerial appointments of members of the main quangos and also of some non-ministerial government departments and public corporations is subject to general regulation, monitoring and audit by the independent Commissioner for Public Appointments, who is appointed by the Prime Minister under the royal prerogative (Public Appointments Orders in Council 1995, 2002). The Commissioner has advisory powers only and does not take part in individual appointments.

The Commissioner has issued a code of practice which includes a requirement to advertise vacancies and to ensure that the selection is on merit and that the process is open, transparent and fair and encourages diversity (see Committee on Standards in Public Life, *Getting the Balance Right* (Cm 6407, 2005)). The appointment principles include independent assessors and 'proportionality', which enables simplified procedures to be used in the case of less important appointments (see Public Administration Select Committee, *Government by Appointment* (HC 2002–03, 135); Committee on Standards in Public Life, *Getting the Balance Right* (Cm 6407, 2005)). However the code does not prevent reappointments or recycling and, without positive attempts to identify suitable candidates, no code can fully address the problem that the pool of applicants is likely to be dominated by insiders.

There is a National Health Services Appointments Commission with a similar role. The NHS is not itself a quango but comprises a complex network of bodies governed by statute under which they are controlled in detail by ministers. Some are directly part of the Crown, some are quangos, and others such as doctors are linked to government by contracts.

The bodies we have discussed here are usually regarded as public bodies proper. There are numerous voluntary bodies and private companies, for example charities such as the National Trust, housing associations and the Royal Society for the Prevention of Cruelty to Animals, that carry out functions for the public good, sometimes under contract on behalf of the government with state funding and occasionally subject to special statutory provisions (eg National Trust Act 1907). It must be established in each context whether the body itself or a particular function of the body is regarded as public or private (see Section 19.5). These bodies are not subject to direct political accountability but are accountable only to their own members.

Comparison between quangos, executive agencies and non-ministerial government departments (NMDs)

- Executive agencies are not separate legal entities but are part of the Crown. Their staff are therefore civil servants. Quangos are separate legal entities or committees of individuals. Their staff are not civil servants. NMDs are separate legal entities but part of the Crown.

- Ministers are responsible for the acts of executive agencies. Ministers are only responsible for the acts of quangos and NMDs in relation to the actual involvement of the minister.
- Executive agencies may exercise powers on behalf of ministers under statute or the royal prerogative. Quangos may freely give advice to anyone who will listen but have no legal powers unless conferred specifically by statute. NMDs have direct statutory powers.
- An executive agency is required to carry out instructions from ministers as to any of its activities. A quango is nominally independent of ministers except where the minister has statutory power to intervene. However this difference may be unreal given the desire of those chosen to be members of quangos to please their patrons. Ministers may have specific statutory powers in relation to NMDs.
- As Accounting Officer, the chief executive of an executive agency must appear before parliamentary select committees but on behalf of the minister. The leaders of quangos and NMDs appear in their own right (see Section 15.7).
- Executive agency appointments, in common with most civil service appointments, are subject to regulation by the statutory Civil Service Commission with a view to preventing political involvement (Constitutional Reform and Governance Act 2010, ss 11–14). Quangos and NMDs are subject to regulation by the non-statutory Commissioner for Public Appointments.

5.4 The judicial branch

The third branch of government is the judiciary, which has the distinctive function of resolving disputes impartially. The right to a fair trial before an independent court is a fundamental feature of common law and also of the European Convention on Human Rights (ECHR). The judiciary reviews the legality of government action. Under the Human Rights Act 1998 it can scrutinise government decisions and Acts of Parliament for conformity with 'human rights' derived from the European Convention on Human Rights. The 1998 Act does not empower the courts to overturn an Act of Parliament although this might be possible by virtue of the common law (see Chapter 9).

In our extreme parliamentary system the distinction between the legislature and the executive is blurred but it is vital that the judiciary be independent of the other branches of government. This section outlines the main constitutional features of the judiciary. Further and more detailed matters particularly affecting judicial independence are discussed in Chapter 7. The discussion is concerned primarily with England and Wales as Scotland and Northern Ireland have a separate court system, although appeals from Northern Ireland and appeals in civil cases in Scotland are dealt with by the Supreme Court.

5.4.1 The main courts

The courts have traditionally been classified into superior courts and inferior courts.

- Superior courts include the High Court, which deals with major civil cases; the Court of Appeal, which in two divisions deals with civil and criminal appeals; and the Supreme Court. The High Court has an open-ended power to decide its own jurisdiction and so can never act beyond its powers. All other courts are created by statute and their powers are determined by statute. No new court can be created except by statute. The Administrative Court is part of the High Court, dealing with judicial review of public law decisions (Supreme Court Act 1981). Various specialised bodies are designated as superior courts although the effect of this is unclear. A body designated as a superior court is not equivalent to the High Court (see *R (Cart) v Upper Tribunal* [2010]), and the term 'superior court' has been described as a concept of uncertain import (at [16]). Its main significance is probably in connection with the personal liability of the judge (see Section 7.4).

- Inferior courts include the Crown Court, which deals with major criminal cases, and in certain respects has superior court status (Courts Act 1971); county courts, which deal with smaller civil cases (County Courts Act 1984); and magistrates courts, which deal mainly with minor criminal cases (Magistrates Courts Act 1980). Professional judges in these courts are circuit judges, who hear criminal cases in the Crown Court and civil cases in the county courts, and district judges and deputy district judges, who hear minor county court cases (Courts and Legal Services Act 1990) and magistrates court cases (Courts Act 2003). There are also lay magistrates, sitting usually in panels of three supported by a professional justices' clerk who advises them and who can exercise certain judicial functions on their behalf (Courts Act 2003). There are part-time professional assistant recorders and recorders who hear criminal cases in the Crown Court. These are normally practising barristers, the post being a road to promotion to higher judicial office.
- The highest court is the Supreme Court. This replaced the Appellate Committee of the House of Lords (so reinforcing at least the appearance of the separation of powers) in October 2009 (Constitutional Reform Act 2005). The Supreme Court hears appeals from all the UK jurisdictions except Scottish criminal cases (Constitutional Reform Act 2005). The Supreme Court operates effectively as a constitutional court dealing with disputes about devolution matters relating to the powers of the governments of Scotland, Wales and Northern Ireland. The Supreme Court also has the last word on human rights matters and judicial review of government action. Occasionally the Court of Appeal is designated as the final appeal court, and in any case permission either from the court below or the Supreme Court is required to take an appeal to the Supreme Court. Compared with other courts the proceedings of the Supreme Court are relatively informal. It can sit in panels of judges ranging from 3 to its full membership of 12, depending on the importance of the case. Unlike for example the US Supreme Court it (probably) has no power to strike down primary legislation (see Section 8.4.5).

5.4.2 The appointment and dismissal of judges

Judges are appointed under particular statutes by the Queen on the recommendation of the Lord Chancellor, or in the case of some junior judges and lay magistrates by the Lord Chancellor alone. There is no input from elected bodies, for example along the lines of Senate hearings into the appointment of Supreme Court judges in the US. Other than lay magistrates and tribunal members, judges are appointed from the ranks of professional lawyers. Before the Tribunals, Courts and Enforcement Act 2007, judicial appointments were restricted to those who had rights of advocacy in the High Court for a prescribed period – usually ten or seven years. This contrasts with the position in other European countries where there is a separate judicial profession. The UK system has the advantage of drawing on talented people who are familiar with the workings of the court process. The disadvantage is that this might reinforce the perception of the legal system as a closed elite. The 2007 Act was intended to increase judicial diversity. It allows the Lord Chancellor to specify the 'relevant legal qualification and experience' required for judicial appointments, which allows a wider range of legal experience to be eligible, such as legal executives, perhaps academic lawyers and other professionals whose work has not focused on advocacy.

Under the Constitutional Reform Act 2005, except in the case of lay magistrates and some minor offices, a person recommended by an independent Judicial Appointments Commission must be appointed (see Section 7.8.2). This reinforces the separation of powers by replacing a much criticised informal regime in the hands of the Lord Chancellor and Prime Minister. Prior to the 2005 Act the Lord Chancellor occupied an anomalous constitutional position, being nominally head of the judiciary but also the government minister in charge of the court system and the presiding officer in the House of Lords. Under the Act the Lord Chancellor ceases to be the head of the judiciary, being replaced in that role by the Lord Chief Justice. The Lord Chancellor no longer presides over the House of Lords but remains a Cabinet minister in charge of the Ministry of Justice, which funds and administers the court system. The Lord Chancellor's limited role in judicial appointments therefore strikes a balance between judicial independence and political accountability.

Senior judges have security of tenure designed to protect their independence. They can be dismissed only for misbehaviour by a resolution of both Houses of Parliament (see Section 7.4). The bulk of the judiciary (about 97 per cent) comprises inferior court judges and lay magistrates. They do not have full security of tenure but hold office under various statutes which make different provisions for dismissal.

5.4.3 Tribunals

Numerous specialised tribunals decide matters allocated to them by particular statutes. These are most commonly disputes between individuals and government bodies. In some cases, such as employment tribunals, they decide disputes between private persons. In some areas, such as immigration, tribunals deal with important questions of individual rights and freedoms. They were originally called administrative tribunals, thus blurring the distinction between the judicial and executive branches and raising fears that they were not independent (see *Report of the Committee on Administrative Tribunals and Enquiries* (Cmnd 218, 1957), the Franks Report). Subsequent reforms, the most recent being the Tribunals, Courts and Enforcement Act 2007 have drawn the tribunal system more closely towards that of the ordinary courts.

Tribunals are claimed to have the advantages of economy, speed and expertise compared with the ordinary courts – the price to be paid for this being rougher justice (Franks Report). Tribunal procedures are less formal than those of ordinary courts and do not necessarily involve lawyers. They are meant to be accessible to poorer people, with whom a substantial part of their work is concerned. However they may deal with complex legal matters, and those before them are often without legal representation, so their accessibility is questionable (see Genn, 'Tribunals and Informal Justice' (1993)

56 MLR 393). They can also be used to distance decision-making from the government itself so as to secure independence or, more cynically, to avoid responsibility.

Until the recent reforms (discussed below) the tribunal system had developed haphazardly, numerous tribunals having been established over the years under separate legislation. Tribunals deal with a range of specialised and technical matters. These include education, employment, taxation, health, immigration and asylum, land valuation, title and use, state benefits, transport, trading matters and the security services (see Council on Tribunals, *Annual Report 2004/05* (HC 2004–05, 472)). There are some common features (Tribunals and Inquiries Act 1992). Tribunals are often presided over by a lawyer chairperson sitting with one or two lay members. They are not bound by strict rules of evidence. Most tribunals must give reasons in writing for their decisions. Tribunals are linked into the judicial system since there is usually a right of appeal from a tribunal to the ordinary court system, although again this is somewhat haphazard. The High Court can also review tribunal decisions in the same way as those of other public bodies (Chapters 15–17). Tribunals have limited safeguards for their independence.

Depending on the particular statute, tribunal judges are appointed by ministers or the Lord Chancellor, and in some cases the consent of the Lord Chancellor is required for dismissal. In the case of many tribunals the Lord Chancellor can appoint only a person selected by the Judicial Appointments Commission (see Constitutional Reform Act 2005, s 85, Sch 14).

There is no conceptual distinction between a tribunal and a court proper. A constitutionally important distinction is whether the body in question exercises 'judicial' functions in the sense of the resolution of a dispute affecting individual rights. This may attract the right to a fair trial by an independent tribunal under Article 6 of the ECHR as applied by the Human Rights Act 1998 (see Section 20.4). It might also be important to decide whether a body is a court for the purposes of the law of contempt of court, which affects freedom of speech (Chapter 19). In this context it is irrelevant whether the body is called a court or a tribunal (see *A-G v BBC* [1981]; *General Medical Council v BBC* [1998]). It is necessary to rely on any definition of a court in a particular statute for a particular purpose, thus illustrating the pragmatic character of the UK constitution. Confusingly some bodies have the status of a court (or 'court of record', meaning a relatively high-status court) conferred by statute but are called tribunals, for example the Employment Appeals Tribunal (Employment Tribunals Act 1996).

A Council on Tribunals, whose members are appointed by the Lord Chancellor and Scottish ministers, has until now supervised both the tribunal system and statutory public inquiries (Tribunals and Inquiries Act 1992). The Council is concerned to implement the basic principles of openness, fairness and impartiality and to protect the independence of tribunals from the executive. However, characteristically of the UK system, it has only consultative and advisory powers, mainly concerning the procedural rules for tribunals made by the Lord Chancellor.

The administration of the tribunal system has recently been overhauled. As a result of the Leggatt Report (*Tribunals for Users* (TSO 2001)), a Tribunals Service under the Ministry of Justice has been established to administer and coordinate the main tribunals (see White Paper, *Transforming the Public Services: Complaints, Redress and Tribunals* (Cm 6243, 2004); Carnwath, 2009). The basic concerns are to rationalise the tribunal system and to strengthen the independence of tribunals from ministers and other bodies whose decisions they scrutinise and to make the tribunal system simpler and more open and user friendly. In *R (Cart) v Upper Tribunal* [2010] Sedley LJ described the reforms as a landmark in the development of the UK's organic constitution (at [1]). The Tribunals Courts and Enforcement Act 2007 gives effect to the main Leggatt reforms.

The Act creates two all-purpose tribunals, which can be grouped into specialist 'chambers'. These are the First Tier Tribunal and the Upper Tribunal. The latter is mainly an appellate body and has the status of a superior court (s 3). Its members have judicial independence (s 1) (see Section 7.4). There is a further right of appeal from the Upper Tribunal to the ordinary courts on a point of law albeit this is restricted (s 13). Although it has the same powers, rights, privileges and authority as the High Court (s 25), the Upper Tribunal is subject to judicial review by the High Court, but only to a limited extent (*R (Cart) v Upper Tribunal* [2010]; see Section 17.6).

The Upper Tribunal can also exercise judicial review functions similar to those of the High Court (see Section 19.1).

The members of the First Tier Tribunal are appointed by the Lord Chancellor and also include *ex officio* (meaning by virtue of their office) members of certain other tribunals and courts (s 4). The Upper Tribunal also comprises persons appointed by the Lord Chancellor and includes *ex officio* other senior office holders (s 5). Judges of ordinary courts are *ex officio* members of both tiers (s 6). Lawyer members of these tribunals are known as tribunal judges. The Lord Chancellor is empowered to transfer the jurisdiction of most of the existing tribunals to the new tribunals, thus rationalising and simplifying the tribunal system, possibly at the cost of the diversity, flexibility and focus of tribunals. However the new tribunals can be organised into 'chambers' based on groups of related specialisms. Some tribunals, notably employment tribunals and asylum and immigration tribunals, will remain separate.

- The Lord Chancellor's duty to uphold the rule of law under the Constitutional Reform Act 2005 applies also to tribunals under his jurisdiction.
- There is a new office, that of Senior President of Tribunals, to oversee and lead the tribunal judiciary.
- There is a new Tribunal Procedure Committee to make rules for tribunals.
- The Council of Tribunals is replaced by the Administrative Justice and Tribunals Council. This remains an advisory body but its remit is extended to include the administrative justice system generally, which comprises ombudsmen and dispute resolution mechanisms within government departments and other public bodies.

5.4.4 Administrative justice

Outside the formal tribunal system there are various mechanisms for resolving disputes between citizen and government. These include ombudsmen and internal grievance processes. The most prominent of these, and serving as a model, is the Parliamentary Commissioner for Administration (PCA).

The PCA investigates, on behalf of Parliament, complaints by citizens against the central government and certain other bodies closely related to the central government (Parliamentary Commissioner Act 1967; Parliamentary and Health Services Commissioners Act 1987; Parliamentary Commissioner Act 1994). Popularly known as the 'Ombudsman', the PCA is appointed by the Crown (on the advice of the Prime Minister) and has security of tenure similar to that of a senior judge (see Section 5.4.2).

Complaints must be made to an MP, who can decide whether to take the matter to the PCA. This is not subject to judicial review by virtue of parliamentary privilege and is intended to preserve the constitutional principle that the executive is responsible to Parliament. There has been considerable criticism of this rule on the ground that MPs may be reluctant to refer to the PCA in order to claim credit for themselves. Conversely MPs may be unclear about the PCA's power and refer inappropriate cases or even pass the buck by referring cases indiscriminately. The PCA also has discretion whether or not to investigate any particular case.

The PCA has no power to enforce its findings. It must report to the MP who referred the case. If it has found injustice caused by maladministration and considers that it has not been remedied, it may also lay a report before Parliament. The absence of direct enforcement powers may be advantageous in encouraging greater frankness by those being investigated. The PCA can see documents and interview civil servants and other witnesses, and the normal plea of government confidentiality cannot be used (Parliamentary Commissioner Act 1967, s 8(3)). However Cabinet documents can be excluded (s 8(4)) and the PCA must not name individual civil servants. Investigations are private (s 7(2)).

The decisions of the PCA are subject to judicial review and are not protected by parliamentary privilege (see Section 11.6; *R v Parliamentary Comr, ex p Dyer* [1994]; *R v Parliamentary Comr for Administration, ex p Balchin* [1997]).

There are considerable limitations on the powers of the PCA:

- Important areas of central government activity are excluded from its jurisdiction. These include foreign affairs, state security (including passports), legal proceedings, criminal investigations, government contracts, commercial activities other than compulsory purchase of land (but statutory powers exercised by contractors under privatisation arrangements are within the Ombudsman's jurisdiction), civil service employment matters and the granting by the Crown of honours, awards and privileges.
- The PCA can investigate only allegations of 'injustice in consequence of maladministration' (s 5(1)). Maladministration is not defined but means broadly some defect in the *process* of decision-making as opposed to its outcome: 'bias, neglect, inattention, delay, incompetence, inaptitude, perversity, turpitude, arbitrariness and so on' (the 'Crossman Catalogue', HC Deb 18 October 1966, vol 734, col 51). The PCA cannot directly question government policy or the merits of the exercise of a discretion (s 12; see *R v Local Comr for Administration, ex p Bradford City Council* [1979]).
- Complaints must be made in writing within 12 months of the decision being complained about.
- The PCA should not investigate a matter that is appropriate to a court unless in all circumstances it would be unreasonable to expect the complainant to apply to the court. The Ombudsman can take into account the complainant's personal circumstances but not the likelihood of success (*R v Local Comr for Administration, ex p Liverpool City Council* [2001]).

The House of Commons Public Administration Select Committee monitors the PCA. Reflecting the convention of ministerial responsibility, it is for the minister concerned to decide whether to give effect to the recommendations, for example by compensating the victim of the injustice or improving departmental procedures. The executive sometimes refuses to accept the PCA's findings (see Kirkham, 'Challenging the Authority of the Ombudsman: The Parliamentary Commissioner's Special Report on Wartime Detainees' (2006) 69 MLR 792). In this situation the Ombudsman can lay a special report before Parliament (s 10 (3)).

Other ombudsmen include Commissioners for Local Administration, appointed by the Crown on the recommendation of the Secretary of State, who perform a similar function in respect of local government. However, where a councillor has failed to do so, individuals can complain directly to the commissioners (Local Government Act 1974). The Local Government Ombudsman also has powers to give publicity to its recommendations. Other ombudsmen operate in a similar manner in respect of particular government bodies, for example in respect of the devolved governments of Scotland, Wales (see Public Services Ombudsman (Wales) Act 2005) and Northern Ireland, the NHS, the European Parliament, the police, social housing, the legal profession and judicial appointments (Constitutional Reform Act 2005). Ombudsmen share the dominant ethos of UK government by having no power to enforce their decisions but only to report.

In addition to statutory ombudsmen there are miscellaneous non-statutory bodies exercising similar functions and making unenforceable recommendations (eg the Adjudicator's Office on tax matters, the Independent Complaints Reviewer for the Land Registry, the Charity Commission and the Banking Ombudsman). There are no formal methods of accountability relating to these bodies or controls over their appointment and dismissal. However they may count as public bodies subject to judicial review (see Section 19.5).

There are also internal complaints procedures offering alternative dispute resolution (ADR) such as mediation or arbitration within government departments and agencies. These are subject to the tendency of officials in the UK to prefer the informal and secretive and the absence of a cultural awareness of what independence requires. Thus the general issue arising here is whether such internal processes are sufficiently independent to provide a fair trial in relation to a citizen's civil rights and obligations under the European Convention on Human Rights (see Section 20.4.2).

5.4.5 Inquiries

Some government decisions, particularly in relation to planning and other land use matters, are taken in the name of ministers following an inquiry held by an independent inspector. In some cases, notably routine cases under town and country planning legislation, power to make the decision is delegated to the inspector. Unlike tribunal decisions that primarily concern factual or legal issues, the subject matter of such decisions may also concern controversial political issues, relating for example to airport building or rural development. The inquiry system is therefore intended to provide an independent element as part of a wider process and is not a self-contained judicial process along the lines of a court.

Inquiries are sometimes described as 'quasi-judicial'. They follow a procedure broadly similar to that of a court but are more flexible and less formal. Formal rules of evidence do not apply. People whose interests are affected by the decision in question have a right to appear and give evidence. Others can speak at the discretion of the inspector, who can also allow cross-examination. This discretion is usually exercised liberally.

The independence and openness of inquiry procedures is partly safeguarded by the Tribunals and Inquiries Act 1992. This requires in particular that evidence must be disclosed in advance, reasons must be given for decisions and where the minister overrules the inspector the parties must be given a chance to comment and, in the case of disagreement about facts, to reopen the inquiry (see eg Town and Country Planning (Hearings Procedure) (England) Rules 2000 (SI 2000/1624)).

Unlike tribunals, inquiries are primarily part of a larger administrative process and therefore not independent of political influence. Nevertheless provided that judicial review is available, this distinctively British process has been upheld as compliant with the right to a fair trial under the ECHR. This is because there is a substantial policy or political element involved which is appropriate for the injection of a democratic element as opposed to the impartiality expected from a court of law (see *R (Alconbury Developments) v Secretary of State for the Environment, Transport and the Regions* [2001]). Furthermore the involvement of ministers and civil servants, with their close, secretive relationship, means that policy advice may not be subject to independent scrutiny at the inquiry (see *Bushell v Secretary of State for the Environment* [1981]).

Special inquiries can be held to investigate events of public concern, for example serious incidents or allegations of misconduct by officials. Under the Inquiries Act 2005 a minister may establish such an inquiry, decide its terms of reference and appoint the person to hold it. Ministers have considerable control. For example a person with a direct interest in the subject of the inquiry or a close association with an interested party cannot be appointed unless the minister considers that impartiality would not reasonably be affected (s 9). Ministers also have powers in relation to public access to the inquiry and to publication of its report. The published parts of the inquiry report must be laid before Parliament (see also Chapter 8). A constitutional difficulty with this type of inquiry arises because senior judges are sometimes asked to hold them. This may appear to compromise the independence of the judiciary (see Beatson, 'Should Judges Conduct Public Inquiries?' (2005) 121 LQR 221). Under section 10 of the Inquiries Act 2005 the Lord Chief Justice or the Senior Law Lord must first be consulted when it is proposed to appoint a judge to hold an inquiry.

Another form of inquiry is a Royal Commission. Again this is established by ministers, in this case under the royal prerogative. The members of a Royal Commission are usually persons with previous links with government. The report of the commission is usually laid before Parliament. Royal Commissions have no power to compel attendance or disclosure of information. They are commonly employed to consider constitutional issues, for example the Royal Commission on the House of Lords (Section 12.3).

In practice, ministers often prefer to set up informal, non-statutory inquiries presided over by persons of their own choosing and with procedures and terms of reference set by themselves. These sometimes sit in public (eg the Chilcot Inquiry into the invasion of Iraq; yet to report) but have no legal powers to compel witnesses to attend, to examine documents or to take evidence on oath, under which lying would be a criminal offence. For example in January 2011 the Cabinet Secretary refused to permit the Chilcot Inquiry to make public letters sent by the then Prime Minister, Tony Blair, to George Bush, the US President, allegedly concerning the proposed invasion of Iraq. The Hutton Inquiry (2004) into the death of David Kelly, a senior civil servant, in circumstances relating to the invasion of Iraq was also established informally, albeit it was presided over by a senior judge. The government was exonerated from blame. There seem to be no constitutional safeguards to ensure that such inquiries are independent of the executive.

In the interests of public confidence in good government the courts have developed the following principle in dealing with statutory government decision-making procedures: whether in the view of a 'fair-minded and informed observer' taken as knowing all the circumstances there is a 'real possibility' or 'real danger' of bias (see Section 18.4). Does the appointment of inquiry chairs meet these standards, and should it? For example in 2010 a retired appeal court judge, Sir Peter Gibson, was appointed to hold an inquiry into allegations that members of the UK security services had been involved in torture. During part of the relevant time Sir Peter had been the statutory overseer of the security services and had previously investigated allegations of misconduct. He had issued reports describing the security services as 'trustworthy, conscientious and dependable'. The government has maintained that for non-statutory inquiries there is no duty to pass legally relevant tests of impartiality and independence (see *Guardian* 30 July 2010; www.reprieve.org.uk/2010_07_20_torture_inquiry_gibson_letter_text).

5.5 Local government

Local authorities exercise a range of functions within geographical areas based on urban conurbations, traditional counties (albeit substantially redefined since the Local Government Act 1974) and communities within those counties. Local authorities are elected and have tax-raising powers and might therefore be considered to have some constitutional significance. From both liberal and republican perspectives (see Section 2.5) local government could be regarded as providing a check and balance on central government in the sense of an alternative source of democratic power. Mill claimed that it is desirable in the interests of democracy and individual self-fulfilment for people to have closer contact with governmental bodies than is possible at central government level. In particular local democracy generates different political perspectives and healthy disagreement and debate. On the other hand, particularly where personal welfare services, health and education are concerned, it may be unfair for different levels of service to be provided in different, sometimes neighbouring, areas (see *R v Gloucestershire CC, ex p Barry* [1997] for judicial disagreement).

In the UK local authorities are entirely creatures of statute (Local Government Act 1972) and as such are subject to comprehensive central government control. This is often exercised in characteristic British manner not by using formal legal powers, although these exist in abundance, but through advisory circulars and letters and personal contacts or for example through conferences and meetings. Thus there is the appearance of local independence but without the substance. Local government is primarily funded by grants from the centre. All its powers derive from particular statutes, sometimes requiring the consent of ministers for their exercise.

Since they are elected, local authorities might be considered to have a certain independent constitutional status (see eg *Secretary of State for Education and Science v Tameside MBC* [1977]). However the courts may give little weight to local democracy, regarding local authorities as subordinate agents of Parliament (see *R v Somerset CC, ex p Fewings* [1995] per Laws J). Moreover local authorities, despite having some tax-raising powers, have little financial independence, more than two-thirds of their resources being provided by central government in the form of grants, some of which are earmarked for certain purposes. By contrast some constitutions specifically protect local government autonomy. For example the Italian constitution protects regional and local autonomy according to the 'subsidiarity' principle that decisions should be taken at the nearest possible level to those affected by them. (See also Carnwath, 'The Reasonable Limits of Local Authority Power' [1996] PL 244.)

Local authorities have executive powers and limited lawmaking powers to make bylaws for prescribed purposes such as keeping order in public places and traffic control. Their geographical boundaries are designated by central government. Their main functions are to provide local political and strategic influence and deliver at an operational level services designated by central government, usually subject to central government power to intervene by means of devices such as injections, 'default powers' to take over a function and appeals. Some functions, such as housing and education, have been substantially removed from local control in favour of separate private and semi-public bodies regulated from the centre.

From a liberal perspective, the weakness of local government threatens the checks and balances required to limit government. There is occasional provision for public consultation but such deliberative democracy (Chapter 2) is normally a matter for the discretion of the local authority (see eg Local Government Act 2000, ss 7, 27; Planning and Compulsory Purchase Act 2004, s 18).

The democratic structure of local authorities and the relationship between elected councillors and appointed officers are controlled by central government (Local Government Act 2000). The ethical conduct of local councillors is policed by the Standards Board for England, a body appointed by central government which has the power to suspend or disqualify local councillors (Local Government Act 2000). In its Tenth Report (*Getting the Balance Right* (Cm 6407, 2005)), the Committee on Standards in Public Life recommended that the Standards Board should operate on a more local basis and that its composition should be more independent than is currently the case. However the government elected in 2010 proposes to abolish the Standards Board.

5.6 The police and the prosecution system

The police have a claim to special constitutional status since they are authorised to use violence and are closely connected with the judicial process. It is therefore important that the police are seen to be independent of the executive. On the other hand the police service is funded by taxation so that democratic accountability is desirable. An accommodation must be struck between these concerns. This issue underlies the constitutional position of the police. Although they are officers of the Crown, in the sense that their common law powers derive from the Crown's duty to keep the peace, the police are not Crown employees. Control over the police has been split three ways, a complex and tension-ridden arrangement that can be justified as a liberal mechanism for controlling power.

Firstly there is the traditional status at common law of the 'constable' as an independent officer of the Crown with inherent powers of arrest, search and entry to premises, some common law and others statutory, and owing duties to the law itself to keep the peace (see Police Act 1996, s 10; *R v Metropolitan Police Comr, ex p Blackburn* [1968] at 136). All police officers and also prison officers are constables. Each police force is under the direction of its Chief Constable (in London the Metropolitan Police Commissioner) with regard to operational matters.

Secondly there is a tradition that the organisation of the police should be locally based and subject to democratic control so as to avoid the concentration of power associated with a 'police state'. Under the Police Act 1996 local police forces are organised on the basis of counties and amalgamations of county units. There are special arrangements in London comprising the Metropolitan Police and the City of London Police Force, limited to the square mile that technically comprises the City (Greater London Authority Act 1999). Each local force is answerable to a local police authority that comprises a mixture of local councillors, justices of the peace and persons appointed by the Home Secretary, with elected members a bare majority. The political balance of the elected members must reflect that of the council as a whole (Criminal Justice and Police Act 2001, s 105). The Chief Constable must have regard to the objects and targets set out in an annual plan made by the police authority (Police Act 1996, s 8). The police authority appoints and removes the Chief Constable and certain other senior officers.

Thirdly the central government has wide and increasing powers over police forces conferred by statute, usually upon the Home Secretary (Police Act 1996, Part II; Police Reform Act 2002). These are subject to no specific constitutional principles but seem to be generated by pragmatic considerations and the desire of particular governments to exercise control. In particular the Home Secretary's approval is needed for the appointment and removal of a Chief Constable and he or she can require a police authority to suspend or remove a Chief Constable. The Home Secretary can also provide funding, set performance targets and make regulations concerning discipline and resources, including requiring the use of specified equipment. The Home Secretary can also require the merger of local forces and draw up a national policing plan and a code of practice for chief officers. As usual the Home Office exercises informal influence through non-statutory 'advice', 'guidance' and personal networks.

Technical support for policing may be too expensive to provide locally and modern crime is no respecter of local boundaries. Therefore there are an increasing number of national bodies, including the National Police Data Bank, the Mutual Aid Coordinating Centre, the National Criminal Intelligence Service and the National Crime Squad (Police Act 1997) which carry out police operations, operating formally by agreement with local forces. They are regulated by central boards, the membership of which strikes a balance between a minority of independent persons appointed by the Secretary of State and nomination by chief officers and local police authorities from among their members. A Central Police Training and Development Authority has also been created (Criminal Justice and Police Act 2001), the objectives of which are decided by the Secretary of State, who can also give it detailed guidance and directions. There is therefore a considerable momentum towards a national police force.

The Police Reform and Social Responsibility Bill proposes to introduce a further element into the control of policing, namely an elected local Commissioner for each force, broadly similar to those existing in the US. The Commissioner would lay down general polices which the Chief Constable would be required to follow. There is a continuing debate as to whether this level of democracy is desirable since it would compromise the independence of the police. On the other hand it would be a counterforce against political interference by central government, which might be a greater threat to police independence.

Originally the police themselves conducted most prosecutions. However the Prosecution of Offences Act 1985 created a separate Crown Prosecution Service (CPS), which is under the control of the Director of Public Prosecutions (DPP). Crown prosecutors in local areas have powers to prosecute and conduct cases subject to discretion given by the DPP under the Act. The DPP is appointed by the Attorney General, who is answerable in Parliament for the CPS. In some cases the consent of the Attorney General is required for a prosecution, particularly where political or large commercial interests are involved. The Attorney General has conflicting roles. As well as being responsible for the prosecuting service, he is the government's chief legal adviser and a member of the government itself, appointed and dismissed by the Prime Minister. (He also brings legal actions on behalf of the public interest against public bodies; see Section 15.6.) This blurring of roles is characteristic of the culture of UK government and attracts public suspicions of lack of independence. For example there has been unease in respect of particular decisions not to prosecute policemen alleged to have killed members of the public (see eg *New Statesman* 22 July 2010).

The CPS has power to take over most criminal prosecutions (s 3) or to order any proceedings to be discontinued (s 23). Except where an offence can only be prosecuted by a person named in the relevant statute (eg the Attorney General or a specified public authority), any individual may bring a private prosecution, but the CPS can take over such a prosecution (s 6(2)). The Police Complaints Authority has an independent role in investigating complaints against the police (Police Reform Act 2002; see *R (Green) v Police Complaints Authority* [2004] for a useful general account of the process but a narrow approach to whether information should be disclosed).

5.7 The Privy Council

The Privy Council exercises both legislative and judicial powers. It is the descendant of the medieval 'inner council' of trusted advisers to the King. Over the centuries most functions of the Privy Council were transferred either to Parliament or to ministers. Members are appointed by the Queen on the advice of the Prime Minister, and any British citizen is eligible. There are currently over 400 Privy Counsellors, including Cabinet ministers, senior judges and miscellaneous worthies who have gained the approval of the Prime Minister. The Cabinet is sometimes said to be a committee of the Privy Council, although there is no legal basis for this assumption. However Cabinet ministers and leading opposition politicians are invariably appointed Privy Counsellors. One reason for such appointments is that Privy Counsellors swear an oath of secrecy, thus assisting government business to be kept out of the public domain.

Apart from its judicial functions (discussed below), the role of the Privy Council is largely formal. Its approval is needed for certain important exercises of the royal prerogative, known as Prerogative Orders in Council, including for example laws for overseas territories, and also for Statutory Orders in Council, where Parliament gives power to the executive to make laws in this form. Approval is usually given by a small deputation of counsellors attending the Queen. The Privy Council also confers state recognition and legal personality by granting charters to bodies such as universities and professional, scientific and cultural organisations. It can exercise some degree of supervision over such bodies.

The Judicial Committee of the Privy Council is the final court of appeal for those few former British territories that choose to retain its services, in which capacity it is familiar with broad constitutional reasoning. It also has jurisdiction in respect of ecclesiastical courts, peerage claims, election petitions and appeals from the Channel Islands and the Isle of Man. Its former appeals jurisdiction in relation to the medical profession is now exercised by the Administrative Court (Chapter 17). The Judicial Committee comprises the Law Lords together with judges of the country under whose laws the appeal is heard. Not being strictly a court, the Judicial Committee can give advisory opinions to the government (Judicial Committee Act 1833, s 4), although this is rare.

5.8 The Church of England

The relationship between Church and state is ambivalent. On the one hand neither Christianity nor any other religion is part of the law as such (*Bowman v Secular Society* [1917]). On the other hand we do not have a formal separation between Church and state such as exists in France or the US. The Church of England is the Established Church in England, and the Presbyterian Church of Scotland the Established Church in Scotland. The Church of England has certain links with the state, the result of the historical chance that Henry VIII was the founder of the Church of England. These links are sometimes justified even by supporters of other religions on the basis that the Church provides religious services open to all without discrimination and that it helps the state to curb the extremes of religious fanaticism.

There are several particular connections between the Church of England and the state:

- The monarch, as nominal head of the Church of England, must on succession be or become a member of the Church (Act of Settlement 1700, s 3) and must swear an oath to support the Established Churches of England and Scotland (Act of Union with Scotland 1706).
- Church laws (measures) are legally binding and must be approved by Parliament (Church of England Assembly (Powers) Act 1919).
- There are special ecclesiastical courts subject to control by the ordinary courts if they exceed their powers or act unfairly.
- The Queen, on the advice of the Prime Minister (which as usual is binding on her by convention), appoints bishops (see Ecclesiastical Jurisdiction Measure 1963).
- The 26 most senior bishops are members of the House of Lords until retirement.
- Finally everyone has certain rights in connection with baptisms, weddings and funerals.

A Church body is not a public body as such, at least for human rights purposes (see *Aston Cantlow and Wilmcote with Billesley PCC v Wallbank* [2003]; Section 21.4.1). However particular Church functions available to the public, such as weddings and funerals, might be public functions and as such subject to control by the courts. The

Anglican Church in Wales is not established (Welsh Churches Act 1914, a measure passed without the consent of the House of Lords).

5.9 Bodies monitoring government standards of behaviour

The informal nature of much of the UK constitution makes our arrangements heavily dependent on trusting those in power. A series of scandals from the 1980s onwards have exposed significant corruption, ambivalence and incompetence within central government and Parliament. They have included the 'Westland affair', where ministers and civil servants appeared to conspire against each other (see Treasury and Civil Service Committee, *Civil Servants and Ministers: Duties and Responsibilities* (HC 1985–86, 92-II)), and the 'Arms to Iraq' affair, which involved allegations that ministers had tried to cover up breaches of United Nations sanctions against Iraq (see the Scott Report; Section 15.7.2). There have recently been allegations of collusion during the 1970s between the government and the Catholic Church in relation to a priest suspected of involvement in terrorism in Northern Ireland (see *Guardian* 25 August 2010).

There have been allegations that MPs, peers, civil servants and ministers have given privileges to and have received favours from business interests (see *Guardian* 28 August 2010; Sections 11.7, 11.8), worries about donations to and manipulation of the voting system by political parties (see Section 12.10), concerns about appointments to quangos being influenced by personal networking (see Section 5.3), allegations of the sale of peerages, and conflicts concerning media management by government advisers. In one case a government adviser accused of leaking information to the press apparently killed himself. The ensuing Hutton Inquiry, held by a government-appointed former judge with terms of reference selected by the government, exonerated the government and blamed the BBC (*Report of the Inquiry into the Circumstances. Surrounding the Death of Dr David Kelly C.M.G.* (HC 2004, 247)). There is also the 'revolving door' through which former government officials and ministers obtain jobs with firms that do business with government. The exposure during 2009 of the extent to which MPs and peers had been abusing their expense allowances has led to criminal convictions and to the introduction, for the first time, of an independent statutory regulator for MPs (see Section 11.7.2).

There are statutory provisions aimed at preventing corruption by public officials. These include the Public Bodies (Corrupt Practices) Act 1889 and the Honours (Prevention of Corruption) Act 1925. The latter was enacted in response to the sale of peerages on behalf of the then Prime Minister, Lloyd George. It requires specific evidence of an offer or agreement to sell an honour. This is difficult to establish since such arrangements may be only implicit in informal conversations. After a long investigation during 2006–07 into allegations that peerages were being sold by the Blair government the CPS decided to bring no charges. There are provisions concerning misconduct in elections (see Section 12.10) and common law offences of abuse of public office and corruption. Public officials are also subject to the ordinary criminal law, but with some exemptions for MPs in relation to their core duties (see Section 11.6).

The Committee on Standards in Public Life covers the whole field of government. It was appointed in 1994 by the Prime Minister as a permanent advisory committee but has no statutory basis. Its terms of reference include the UK Parliament, UK members of the European Parliament, central and local government and other publicly funded bodies. The Committee reports to the Prime Minister, so there is no independent mechanism, but its reports are published. The Committee does not investigate complaints against individuals. It has become highly influential. Its recommendations are widely followed and sometimes incorporated into law.

In its first report (*Standards in Public Life* (Cm 2850, 1995)) the Committee, under the chairmanship of Lord Nolan, promulgated seven 'Principles of Public Life' that are widely regarded as representing the core values of public service. They are 'selflessness, integrity, objectivity, accountability, openness, honesty and leadership'. They are supported by what Nolan called 'common threads', these being mechanisms used to embed the principles into governmental institutions. These are codes of conduct, independent scrutiny and guidance and education.

The Nolan principles are enshrined in all governmental codes of conduct and in statutory provisions relating to government appointments. For example there is a Ministerial Code (2010), a Civil Service Code (2006), a Local Government Code and Codes of Conduct for MPs and the House of Lords. The codes are not usually enforceable by law and there is not always independent scrutiny. For example the Ministerial Code is enforced by the Prime Minister and the House of Lords Code by the House itself. The Code of Conduct for MPs is policed by the Parliamentary Standards Commissioner, who reports to the Standards and Privileges Committee of the Commons. The Civil Service Code, Special Advisor's Code and Diplomatic Service Code now have statutory backing but no specific enforcement mechanism (Constitutional Reform and Governance Act 2010).

The Standards Board, a relatively powerful body, has statutory powers to investigate complaints about the conduct of elected members of local government, including a power of suspension (Local Government Act 2000; see Section 5.5). This raises questions about democratic values and can be contrasted with the lack of enforcement powers available against members of the central government.

The main scrutiny bodies will be discussed in their contexts. The Nolan principles regarding public appointments are particularly important. Against the background of a tradition that gives ministers large powers of discretion in appointments and a culture of personal networking, it is regarded as improper for politicians to interfere with senior public appointments. The Nolan formula for public appointments – 'appointed on merit by fair and open competition' – has now become standard usage in legislation. The Committee on Standards has promulgated general principles of appointment according to open and published criteria that all public bodies should follow and which require independent representation on appointment bodies. Many such bodies are policed by a non-statutory Commissioner for Public Appointments (see Section 5.3). The Nolan Committee also recommended that ministers should not be able to choose between shortlisted candidates (Tenth Report, *Getting the Balance Right: Implementing Standards of Conduct in Public Life* (Cm 6407, 2005)). The government rejected this proposal.

There are both advantages and disadvantages in codes of conduct, which might be compared with conventions in this respect (Section 3.4). Firstly those investigated may be more prepared to cooperate with a non-enforceable code. On the other hand unless there is independent enforcement such codes may not command public confidence. Moreover complaints may be made for party political reasons (see Tenth Report above). The formality of a legal code might discourage this. The vagueness of many of the codes is also a mixed blessing. On the one hand the codes are flexible and could produce negotiated outcomes which are practical and acceptable to the persons concerned. On the other hand the flexibility of the codes risks attempts to manipulate them.

The work of the Committee on Standards provides a good illustration of the problems of an informal constitution when trust in government is lost. In its Tenth Report (above) the Committee warned that the codes might be undermined by appearing to be over-zealous or over-bureaucratic and attracting public cynicism. The Committee particularly emphasised the principle of 'proportionality', which concerns adjusting processes to the particular context, taking account of the importance of the activity and the risks and costs involved. It also emphasised the importance of the culture of the particular organisation.

Summary

This chapter has identified the main features of the mix of law, conventions and political practice that forms the constitution and points out important sources of conflict which will be followed up in later chapters.

- To be legitimate a government must be effectively in control. However some commentators suggest that the government must also be supported by a moral basis, although the meaning of this is obscure. A distinction can be drawn between the 'dignified' part of the constitution that gives the government its authority and the 'efficient' part that is the practical exercise of power.
- The Crown, which in law is the executive branch of government, must be distinguished from the Queen personally as head of state.
- The Queen in Parliament is legally the supreme lawmaker but by convention the Queen must assent to all Bills presented by Parliament.
- Parliament comprises an unelected upper House with limited powers (House of Lords) and an elected lower House (House of Commons). The upper House is currently undergoing reform but there is disagreement as to what form this should take.
- By convention the executive is accountable to Parliament. In practice however the influence of political parties and the power of the Prime Minister mean that Parliament tends to be subservient to the executive.
- The Queen must appoint the leader of the majority party in the Commons as Prime Minister and must accept the Prime Minister's advice in appointing all other ministers and also senior judges and other public functionaries.
- There are conventions to safeguard democracy against both legislature and executive. The executive must have the support of Parliament. Parliament must meet annually. By law Parliament cannot last for more than five years, and before then by convention Parliament can remove the executive by a vote of confidence. The Prime Minister can also dissolve Parliament. The dissolution of Parliament triggers the summoning of a new Parliament, preceded by a general election. These mechanisms are weakened by the executive domination of Parliament. They are currently being reviewed.
- The executive formally comprises ministers of the Crown. Statutory powers are normally given to individual ministers and the central government is therefore fragmented.
- The Cabinet as the central policy-making body may be in decline with the rise of informal networks and powerful overlord departments.
- Permanent civil servants are a source of impartial advice and act in the name of ministers. Special advisers are personal, political appointees of ministers. There are tensions between these groups, and the role of civil servants may be unstable.

Summary cont'd

- According to the doctrine of ministerial responsibility, ministers are responsible to Parliament for the conduct of their departments and for agencies sponsored by their departments. The civil service is responsible to ministers but not directly to Parliament. Ministerial responsibility is becoming weaker and its scope and effect unclear.
- In recent years executive powers have been distributed across a wide variety of public and private bodies outside the central executive, again obscuring the convention of ministerial responsibility.
- The judiciary is usually regarded as subordinate to Parliament. There is a tension between the judiciary and the executive arising out of the courts' powers of judicial review.
- Senior judges have strong security of tenure. The appointment of judges was previously made by the Lord Chancellor, and in the most senior cases the Prime Minister. Recent reforms have introduced the safeguard of an independent Judicial Appointments Committee to make binding recommendations.
- Tribunals adjudicate relatively small and specialised disputes between government and individual. They are relatively informal but subject to special safeguards to secure their independence and fairness. There are other methods of administrative justice but these suffer from the absence of enforcement powers and sometimes questionable independence.
- Public inquiries form part of the process for making some governmental decisions. They are presided over by independent inspectors who have an element of public participation and are subject to special safeguards. Ministers may set up inquiries into particular events or issues. These have limited independence.
- The police are regulated by an unstable combination of local and central government.
- The Church of England has particular constitutional links with the state but is not a state religion.
- Weaknesses in the traditional methods of accountability have led to attempts to formulate standards of ethical conduct for persons holding public office. These do not generally have legal status and are enforced within government itself.

Exercises

5.1 Is it possible to identify the three most fundamental principles of the constitution? If so, what are they?

5.2 What mechanisms enable the executive to dominate Parliament? Are there any counter-mechanisms?

5.3 What are the main constitutional differences (i) between the police and the armed forces and (ii) between executive agencies, non-ministerial government departments and quangos?

5.4 Assess the arguments for and against civil service impartiality.

5.5 Outline the constitutional problems raised by the following:
(i) special advisers;
(ii) inquiries;
(iii) quangos.

Exercises cont'd

5.6 You are a minister faced by a need to regulate the admission of students to university. What structure would you set up for this purpose and how would it be accountable, if at all?

5.7 Assess the arguments for and against the Church of England having special constitutional status.

5.8 'The UK constitution is comfortable with deceiving the public.' Do you agree?

Further reading

Bogdanor, *The New British Constitution* (Hart 2009) ch 1
Cabinet Office, *List of Ministerial Responsibilities* (2010)
Carnwath, 'Tribunal Justice: A New Start' [2009] PL 48
Commissioner for Public Appointments, *Annual Reports*
Committee on Non-Departmental Public Bodies, *Report on Non-Departmental Public Bodies* (Cmnd 7797, 1980)
Committee on Standards in Public Life, *Reports* <http://www.public-standards.gov.uk> (an excellent resource)
Finer, Bogdanor and Rudden, *Comparing Constitutions* (Clarendon Press 1995) ch 2
House of Commons, *Government by Appointment: Opening up the Patronage State* (HC 2002–03, 165-I, Cm 6056)
Leopold, 'Standards of Conduct in Public Life' in Jowell and Oliver (eds), *The Changing Constitution* (6th edn, Oxford University Press 2007)
Le Sueur, 'Courts, Tribunals, Ombudsmen, ADR: Administrative Justice, Constitutionalism and Informality' in Jowell and Oliver (eds), *The Changing Constitution* (6th edn, Oxford University Press 2007)
Oliver, 'Standards of Conduct in Public Life: What Standards?' [1995] PL 497
Power Commission, *Power to the People: An Independent Inquiry into Britain's Democracy* (Rowntree Trust 2006)
Sampson, *Who Runs This Place?* (John Murray 2004) chs 1–4, 7, 8
Van Gervan, 'Scandals, Political Accountability and the Rule of Law: Counting Heads?' in Andenas and Fairgrieve (eds), *Tom Bingham and the Transformation of the Law* (Oxford University Press 2009)
Woodhouse, 'Delivering Public Confidence: Codes of Conduct; A Step in the Right Direction' [2003] PL 511

Part II

Fundamental principles

Chapter 6

The rule of law

Every law is contrary to liberty. (Jeremy Bentham)

The rule of Law, the enemy alike of dictatorship and anarchy, the friend by whose good offices authority and liberty can alone be reconciled. (Lord Hailsham)

6.1 Introduction

The concept of the rule of law has two broad strands of meaning. In its most basic, 'core' sense the rule of law means that government should be subject to clear rules which bind everyone equally, including the government itself. In a wider sense it refers to moral and political values that underlie the law, of which the keystone is universal access to independent courts (see Bingham, 2009). It is widely believed that good government, wealth and individual happiness are dependent upon the rule of law as an underlying political ideal.

In its core sense the rule of law is said to have two advantages. Firstly it helps us to plan our affairs with certainty by knitting together and organising the diverse activities of government. Secondly it restrains those in power from imposing their personal whims on us. This is an aspect of the idea of 'constitutionalism' which means that the powers of government should be limited. The rule of law is one method of doing this (see *R (Corner House Research) v Director of the Serious Fraud Office* [2008] at [24], [25]).

The rule of law is often asserted as an ideal. For example, following Aristotle in the third century BC, the Massachusetts Constitution (1781) refers to 'a government of laws not men'. The preamble to the UN Universal Declaration of Human Rights refers to the rule of law as 'essential'. The principle is embodied in the European Convention on Human Rights in that where a state is permitted to interfere with a human right, its intervention must be 'prescribed by law' as well as being 'necessary' in a democratic society. The European Union claims to be based on the rule of law. Within UK law, as we shall see, the rule of law is frequently invoked by judges.

However the UK constitution is not wholly derived from the rule of law. The rule of law is not the same as the German concept of *Rechstaat*, which means that the state and the constitution as a whole should be embodied in legal rights, a republican idea (see Section 2.5). In view of our heavy reliance on conventions and the goodwill of our rulers the UK is hardly a *Rechstaat*. The rule of law as it is understood in UK concerns essentially the rights of individuals where there happen to be legal rules.

The Constitutional Reform Act 2005 assumes that the rule of law applies in the UK, asserting that:

> This Act does not adversely affect:
> (a) the existing constitutional principle of the rule of law, or
> (b) the Lord Chancellor's existing constitutional role in relation to that principle.

There can of course never be complete government by law since, whatever rules are made, there is always room for discretion and uncertainty, if only because language is imperfect and not all circumstances can be foreseen. Nevertheless the rule of law is a significant but not a foolproof means of preventing domination by malicious or capricious rulers.

The meaning and importance of the rule of law are much contested. This is evidenced by the varying amount of space devoted to the topic in textbooks. There is a huge literature on the subject. The main areas of debate are as follows:

- Is the idea of the rule of law any more than empty rhetoric?
- Does the rule of law cause harm? For example the wealthy can take advantage of laws more effectively than the poor since they can afford better lawyers. Thus the rule of law is said to encourage the rich and powerful to harass people who cannot fight back.
- Should the rule of law sometimes be overridden in favour of more important values? For example in an emergency should the government be free to act without constraint? Should rules sometimes give way to compassion or mercy?
- Does the rule of law necessarily include questions as to whether a law is morally good or bad? At one extreme the rule of law merely claims that rules are a good thing in themselves. In itself it tells us nothing about the content of those laws. From this perspective rules made by an evil tyrant, for example to kill all dissenters, comply with the rule of law.

Craig (1997) has distinguished between 'formal' and 'substantive' versions of the rule of law. The formal version centres on the shape and application of the law, whether it has been properly made, whether it is clear and fairly applied. The substantive version opens out to the content of the law, whether it is fair and just. The danger of a broad approach is of course that it could reduce the rule of law to a discussion of whether the particular commentator likes the law in question, making the rule of law empty rhetoric.

The notion of the rule of law also includes the process of making and applying law. Most importantly there should be independent courts to interpret and apply the law – independent both of the lawmaker and of the executive which enforces the law. Without independent courts the notion of rules becomes meaningless (see *R (Cart) v Upper Tribunal* [2010] at [34]–[37]). Thus the separation of powers and the rule of law are closely related. The venerable Victorian constitutional lawyer A. V. Dicey suggested that the rule of law favoured our unwritten constitution over the written constitutions of the rest of the world because it was made by the courts (see Section 6.4.2).

There is widespread disagreement as to what the rule of law entails and whether the concept is of any value. The following are a range of examples:

- Bellamy (2007) points out that the rule of law has been enlisted in the political debate from opposite perspectives. On the one hand lawyers have used it to assert the importance of the courts, meaning that access to the courts should not be impeded, that the courts should be independent of the executive, that the courts should be able to control those in power and that fundamental rights should be respected (eg *M v Home Office* [1993]; *R v Secretary of State for the Home Dept, ex p Simms* [1999]; *R (Anderson) v Secretary of State* [2002] at [27], [39]). On the other hand those favouring political solutions associate the rule of law with the importance of the democratic process as producing valid laws that should be obeyed precisely because they have been through that process. From this perspective the judges have the more limited role of interpreting and applying laws validly made by Parliament but not pronouncing on their wisdom or their conformity to a higher law. However it does not follow that law is the best or only way to achieve this. Bentham (see Section 2.3.3) was unhappy with what he called 'Judge and Co'. He thought it strange that courts should be bound by precedent since to him this merely reproduces errors. He also thought the common law, which he called 'dog law', was unjust in that we may be ignorant of the wrong until the case is decided (*Truth versus Ashhurst* (1823); see *R v Rimmington* [2005] at [33]). He thought that laws should be no more than guidelines and in the end should give way to his master principle of the greatest happiness of the greatest number.

- The rule of law is also invoked as meaning that there is a duty to obey the lawful government. Thus the rule of law is two-sided since it also requires that there should be protection against government. In *Brown v Stott* [2001] Lord Hope said:

  > The rule of law requires that every person be protected from invasion by the authorities of his rights and liberties. But the preservation of law and order on which the rule of law also depends, requires that those protections should not be framed in such a way as to make it impracticable to bring those who are accused of crime to justice. The benefits of the rule of law must be extended to the public at large and to the victims of crime also. (at 128)

  In *Brown v Stott* the House of Lords held that the normal right to remain silent was overridden by a requirement to disclose the name of the driver of a car in connection with a drink-driving charge. This was because of the social importance of road safety. However it was also emphasised that any specific unfairness should be compensated for by ensuring that the proceedings were fair overall.

- There are grandiose claims associating the rule of law with liberal beliefs such as dignity, freedom and democracy – for example in relation to the European Convention on Human Rights (see *Klass v Federal Republic of Germany* [1979]; Young, *James and Webster v UK* [1982]) and by the International Commission of Jurists, which equates the rule of law with 'the conditions which will uphold the dignity of man as an individual'. (See Raz, *The Authority of Law* (Clarendon Press 1979) 210–11). Thus behind the idea of the rule of law are beliefs about what is good law and that laws should be made in an acceptable way by the right kind of people. For example in *Taylor v Chief Constable of the Thames Valley Police* [2004] the Court of Appeal stressed the fundamental principle that a policeman must give clear reasons for arresting someone, Sedley LJ (at [58]) basing this on the value of human dignity (see also *Christie v Leachinsky* [1947]). However these liberal values are not exclusive to law and law may not be sufficient to protect them.

- The rule of law is connected with 'equality' in its formal sense ('formal' meaning shape or appearance). Thus everyone who falls within a given rule is treated the same under it. However this is procedural and has nothing to do with the substantive equality of a law. For example a statute which gives a landlord virtually an absolute right to evict a tenant is not contrary to the rule of law.
- As John Stuart Mill remarked:

> the justice of giving equal protection to the rights of all is maintained by those who support the most outrageous inequality in the rights themselves. (1972, ch 5)

- The rule of law is often claimed to be a necessary foundation of democracy in as much as both assume the equality of persons. For example by ensuring that officials keep within the powers given to them by the people and treat people equally, the rule of law is both the servant and policeman of democracy (see Lady Hale's speech in *Ghaidan v Mendoza* [2004] at [132]). However laws can protect other forms of government, and historically the idea of the rule of law long predated democracy. In one sense the rule of law seems to be at odds with democracy in that it usually depends on decisions being made by an elite of unelected judges. For example in *R (Countryside Alliance) v A-G* [2007] Lady Hale remarked that 'democracy is the will of the people but the people may not will to invade those rights which are fundamental to democracy itself' (at 114).

To its supporters the rule of law is a valuable achievement of the human mind as an upholder of equality and dignity: a defence not only against tyrants but also against well-meaning busybodies. To its detractors it represents empty formalism at the expense of deeper values of human sympathy.

6.2 Historical background

Aristotle in the third century BC encapsulated the idea of the rule of law: 'it is better for the law to rule than one of the citizens so even the guardians of the law are obeying the law' (see Bingham, 2009). In England the rule of law is claimed to go back to the Anglo-Saxon notion of a compact between ruler and ruled under which obedience to the King was conditional upon the King respecting customary law. The English version stresses government under law and also the common law as law made by independent courts. Magna Carta (1215) is said to have reinforced the principle that the state can act only through law. By endorsing Magna Carta, the King was forced to commit what were previously unwritten customs to formal writings. Although Magna Carta did not itself hold for long its symbolic effect was immense:

> no freeman shall be taken or imprisoned or be disseissed of his freehold, or liberties or free customs or be outlawed or exiled or in any wise destroyed ... but by ... the law of the land. (see Thompson, *Magna Carta: Its Role in the Making of the English Constitution* (Octagon1972))

The rule of law was famously invoked by the thirteenth-century jurist Bracton as 'a bridle on power':

> the King should be under no man but under God and the Law because the Law makes him King. (quoted in *Burmah Oil Co Ltd v Lord Advocate* [1965] at 147)

This was a conscious break from the Roman law tradition, which regarded law as the will of the ruler. Although Bracton accepted that in the sphere of government the King had some autocratic powers (the royal prerogative), he regarded the King as confined by law in respect of decisions concerning the rights of subjects.

The rule of law was asserted against the King in the seventeenth century. This time emphasis was placed on the connection between the common law and reason and on the independence of the judges from the King. According to Coke CJ, the rule of law protected both ruler and subject, the ruler against criticism, the subject against tyranny: 'The golden and straight metwand of the law and not the uncertain and eroded cord of discretion' (*Institutes* (*c*1669) Part 4, 37, 41 ; see also *Prohibitions del Roy* [1607]).

Later in the seventeenth century John Locke, an ally of Parliament against the King, equated law, reason and freedom, which as we saw in Chapter 2 has its dangers:

> Law in its true notion is not so much the limitation as the direction of a free and intelligent agent to his proper interest and prescribes no further than is for the general good of those under that law ... for all the power the Government hath being only for the good of the Society, as it ought not to be Arbitrary and at Pleasure, so it ought to be exercised by established and promulgated Laws: that both the People may know their duty, and be safe and secure within the limits of the law, and the Rulers too kept within their due bounds not to be tempted by the Power they have in their hands, to imploy it to such purposes, and by such measures, as they would not have known and own not willingly. (*Second Treatise on Government* (1690) VI, 57; IX, 137)

During the eighteenth and early nineteenth centuries the constitution was particularly influenced by the rhetoric of the rule of law. The constitution was regarded as a delicately balanced machine held in place by law; as George III put it, 'the most beautiful balance ever framed' (Briggs, *The Age of Improvement* (Longman 1959) 88). The rule of law protected individual rights imagined as being grounded in ancient common law tradition:

> The poorest man may in his cottage bid defiance to all the forces of the Crown. It may be frail, its roof may shake, the wind may blow through it, the storm may enter, the rain may enter, but the king of England cannot enter. (Lord Brougham, *Historical Sketches of Statesmen in the Time of George III* (1845); (Unless of course the King gets a law enacted, which he might readily do.)

It was widely asserted that the relative stability and economic prosperity enjoyed by Britain during that period was connected with a commitment to the rule of law. By contrast France with its

> demagoguary, revolt, beheadings and ... unruly mobs stood in English 'common sense' as a dreadful warning of all that can go wrong, a sort of conceptual opposite to England's altogether more sensible ways. (see Pugh, 'Lawyers and Political Liberalism in Eighteenth and Nineteenth Century England' Halliday and Karpick *Lawyers and the Rise of Western Political Liberalism: From the Eighteenth to the Twentieth Centuries* (Clarendon Press 1997) 168)

However the rule of law was consistent with harsh and repressive Acts of Parliament such as the notorious anti-poaching 'Black Acts' (see Thompson, *Whigs and Hunters* (Allen Lane 1975)), periodic suspension of *Habeas Corpus* and the Corresponding Societies Act 1799, which outlawed radical political and cultural organisations. Indeed because laws are often vague, those who looked at the consequences of the law, such as Bentham, thought its claims to objectivity and balance were spurious and that the constitution was held together by aristocratic power and influence (today professional networkers, perhaps). 'Talk of balance, ne'er will it do: leave that to Mother Goose and Mother Blackstone' (Bentham, *Works*, quoted by Loughlin, 'John Griffith: An Appreciation', [2010] PL 649).

With the expansion of democracy that took place from the mid-nineteenth century, influential lawyers such as Dicey attempted to reformulate and defend the idea of the rule of law against what they perceived as threats from both democratic ideas and the authoritarian influences of continental Europe. Dicey is often credited with coining the concept of the rule of law and his version of it (see Section 6.4.2) remains influential today. In 1928 Lord Chief Justice Lord Hewart published *The New Despotism*, in which he asserted that the rule of law was under threat from the executive. This led to the establishment of the Committee on Ministers' Powers, whose terms of reference were 'to report what safeguards were desirable or necessary to secure the constitutional principles of the sovereignty of Parliament and the supremacy of the law'. Described as having 'the dead hand of Dicey lying frozen on its neck', the Committee's report (Cmd 4060, 1932) gave the constitution a clean bill of health, albeit with a powerful dissent from the socialist Laski. The Committee recommended some strengthening of the powers of Parliament in relation to delegated legislation (Statutory Instruments Act 1946) and asserted the importance of control by the ordinary courts over the executive.

Subsequently the rule of law became associated with a belief that conservative and, in recent years, liberal-minded judges were determined to frustrate the more collectivist policies of left-wing governments (see Griffith, *The Politics of the Judiciary* (Fontana 1997)). More recently, with the introduction of the Human Rights Act 1998, there has been a revival of interest in the rule of law as a means of bringing together the ideas of law, liberalism and democracy.

6.3 Different versions of the rule of law

A broad distinction can be made between the rule of law as government *by* law (versions 1 and 2) and the rule of law as government *under* law (version 3). The three versions are as follows:

1. *The 'core' rule of law.* This means government by law in the form of general rules as opposed to the discretion of the ruler. This encourages certainty so that we can plan our lives and avoid problems. It also implies 'equality' in the sense that everyone who falls within a given rule must be treated the same in accordance with it. All it requires is that there be rules validly made. It does not specify their content. The core rule of law is therefore consistent with hideously repressive regimes. Moreover many rules of law are vague (eg what does 'deprivation of freedom' mean? see Section 20.4.1), leaving room for much disagreement.
2. *The 'amplified' rule of law.* Recognising that the core rule of law cannot stand alone, the amplified rule claims that certain principles relating to fairness and justice are essential to the notion of law as guiding conduct and that these at least moderate bad laws. It is not claimed that these principles cannot be overridden by other factors. It is primarily procedural, similar to Craig's 'formal' version of the rule of law (Section 6.1).
3. *The 'extended' rule of law.* This is the most ambitious version, similar to Craig's 'substantive' version. It claims that law encapsulates the overarching values of the community – assumed to be liberal, such as freedom of expression – in the care of impartial judges (see Allan, 2001). It claims also to link law with republican ideas of equal citizenship. In as much as this version relies upon vague and contestable concepts, it conflicts with the core rule of law. Thus an action can be lawful in the

core sense but still contrary to the rule of law in the extended sense (see *R (Anderson) v Secretary of State* [2002] at [39]).

6.4 The core rule of law

Hayek, the conservative political theorist (see Section 2.3.4), is probably the most enthusiastic champion of the core rule of law. Hayek (1960) asserted of the rule of law:

> stripped of all technicalities this means that government in all its actions is bound by rules fixed and announced beforehand – rules which make it possible to foresee with fair certainty how the authority will use its coercive powers in given circumstances, and to plan one's life accordingly.

It has been claimed that the core rule of law is a universal human good irrespective of the content of any particular law since it favours reason, certainty and equality, acts as a restraint to prevent rulers behaving capriciously or maliciously and prevents officials from picking on individuals. It has been argued that in order to be credible even a bad ruler might act through law thereby behaving better than he or she otherwise might have done. (See Thompson, *Whigs and Hunters* (Allen Lane 1975).)

The core rule of law could be regarded as mechanical and cruel, allowing officials to hide behind rules to avoid personal responsibility, and ignoring sentiments such as compassion, mercy and common sense in favour of ruthless logic (see eg Hutchinson and Monahan (eds), *The Rule of Law: Ideal or Ideology* (University of Toronto Press 1987)). A legalistic perspective is heavily rational, relying on linguistic reasoning turning on verbal definitions and categories, perhaps at the expense of the social or moral interests involved and makes compromise and cooperation difficult (eg *R (Pretty) v DPP* [2002]).

6.4.1 The core rule of law and discretion

The core rule of law can never fully be realised in practice. The meaning or scope of a rule is rarely clear enough or comprehensive enough to be applied to every case, so discretion (meaning a choice between alternative goals not guided by a rule) is unavoidable. To self-styled 'critical' legal scholars this inherent vagueness of law is a fundamental objection to the idea of the rule of law, which they regard as a mask for naked power. The standard liberal reply is that vagueness is a matter of degree and in some circumstances is to be welcomed (see Kutz, 'Just Disagreement: Indeterminacy and Rationality in the Rule of Law' (1994) 103 Yale LJ 997). Most laws in practice have a widely accepted meaning. And even where laws are vague, there are widely accepted standards of 'practical reasoning': consequences, moral values, analogy with precedents, appeals to widely shared feelings and so on. In order to be legitimate a judge's interpretation must not diverge far from public opinion. Even though there may be no objective 'right' answer it is possible to justify a solution which would be widely accepted. This is how the common law might be reconciled with the rule of law. It claims to conform to widely accepted community standards: 'ordinary notions of what is fit and proper' (*MacFarlane v Tayside Health Board* [2000] at 108; *Invercargill City Council v Hamlin* [1996] at 640–42).

Moreover discretion may be desirable in many contexts. The rule of law is not the supreme value. It is widely recognised that the provision of public services must involve the exercise of discretion in individual cases where the circumstances are too various, unpredictable or complex to be encapsulated in rules. For example the police do not have to prosecute everyone; the Inland Revenue may release a taxpayer from a tax burden. It would be difficult to lay down detailed rules in advance governing access to health or education. Resources are limited and hard choices have to be made between competing goals. Sometimes mercy and compassion may be better than strict justice according to law.

The courts do not claim that the rule of law is an absolute and recognise that it might be outweighed by important public interests, notably security. In *R (Corner House Research) v Director of the Serious Fraud Office* [2008] the House of Lords held that a prosecuting authority could discontinue a prosecution of alleged corruption involving members of the Saudi royal family on the ground that, had the investigation continued, the Saudi government would have withdrawn cooperation with the UK intelligence services, thereby increasing the risk of a terrorist attack (see also *Roberts v Parole Board* [2006]: release of prisoner on parole, reliance on undisclosed evidence; the House of Lords disagreed as to importance of the rule of law).

There must also be wide emergency powers to some extent outside both law and democracy to deal with unforeseen and exceptional threats. Even the European Convention on Human Rights can be derogated from to meet an emergency (Human Rights Act 1998, s 14). Even here however a limited supervision by a court may be sacrosanct (see Section 23.1).

Thus the rule of law may involve compromises. The law can prescribe broad guidelines within which decisions must be made and in particular lay down procedures policed by the courts that must be followed to ensure that government keeps within the rules it makes and acts fairly and reasonably (Chapters 16–18). Emergency powers can be hedged with legal safeguards, for example a requirement that they lapse after a set period (see Section 23.1).

A scene from Shakespeare's *Merchant of Venice* illustrates some of the above points. Shylock, a member of a disadvantaged minority, asked the court to enforce his bond against Antonio, a member of the ruling elite. The bond required a pound of Antonio's flesh if he defaulted on payment. Portia, posing as a judge, first made an appeal to mercy, which failed. Shylock pointed out that, if mercy were given, people would be less likely to obey the law and disadvantaged minorities would be particularly vulnerable. Portia then opportunistically invoked the rule of law in its strict narrow sense by interpreting the bond literally so as not to include the shedding of any blood, thus making it impossible to enforce. This crude approach ignores the widely held understanding that laws should be interpreted in their context and according to their purpose or spirit. From this perspective the shedding of blood was an integral part of the bond. It is a different question, outside the scope of the rule of law in its strictest sense, whether a law, based on a free market that enforces such a bond, is good or bad.

The core rule of law is a basic requirement of the European Convention on Human Rights (ECHR). Under many of its provisions the state can override a right only if it acts 'in accordance with the law' or its action is 'prescribed by law'. This means that the state can act only through definite rules, the application of which is predictable in advance (see Section 20.4.3). For example *R (Purdey) v DPP* [2008] concerned the DPP's discretion whether to prosecute for murder the claimant's husband for assisting her to travel to Switzerland to commit suicide in order to alleviate her suffering from a terminal illness. The House of Lords held that the right to respect for family life under the ECHR can be overridden by a law that is accessible and clear enough to ensure that individuals could foresee, if necessary with legal advice, the consequences of their conduct. The DPP must therefore publish guidelines as to how he would exercise his discretion (see also *McLeod v UK* [1998]; Section 22.8.1).

6.4.2 Dicey's version of the rule of law

Dicey proposed a version of the core rule of law similar to that of Hayek and also consistent with republican ideas of equality (see Section 2.5). Although dating from 1875, this has been of great influence among English lawyers. Dicey's version has only limited application to modern conditions. Nevertheless it contains some valuable ideas. Dicey formulated a threefold version of the rule of law, as follows:

1. The absolute supremacy or predominance of 'regular' law

> No man is punishable or can be lawfully made to suffer in body or goods except for a distinct breach of law established in the ordinary legal manner before the ordinary courts. (Dicey, 1915, 183)

This means firstly that no official can interfere with individual rights without the backing of a specific law. Officials have no special powers merely because they are agents of the state. In *R v Somerset CC, ex p Fewings* [1995], which concerned an unsuccessful claim by a local authority to ban hunting on its land, Laws J said (at 524) that the principles that govern the application of the rule of law to public bodies and private persons are 'wholly different' in the sense that:

> the freedoms of the private citizen are not conditional upon some distinct and affirmative justification for which he must burrow in the law books…But for public bodies the rule is opposite and so of another character altogether. It is that any action to be taken must be justified by positive law.

Laws J described this as one of the 'sinews' of the rule of law. However he was dealing in that case with a body created by statute. Statutory bodies cannot do anything that is not authorised by the statute (see Section 17.5). By contrast the Crown – that is the central government – can do anything that a private individual can do unless forbidden by statute, that is anything that does not violate the legal rights of others (see Section 5.2). Dicey's rule of law is therefore ill equipped to deal with the many ways in which modern governments might harm individuals without infringing their strict legal rights, for example by withdrawing funding.

Dicey also believed that government should not have wide discretionary powers. For example in *Rantzen v Mirror Group Newspapers* [1994] the Court of Appeal condemned the wide discretion given to juries to fix the amount of damages in libel cases as violating the rule of law. We have already suggested that it is impossible and undesirable to avoid discretion if we want government to run welfare services such as health, education and social security. Discretion may also be desirable to mitigate the harshness of applying rules strictly in all circumstances. However Dicey did not rule out all discretionary power but only 'wide arbitrary or discretionary power of constraint'. He insisted on limits to and controls over the exercise of discretion. These include guidelines based on the purposes for which the power is given and standards of reasonableness and fairness. This aspiration is to some extent met by the courts' powers of judicial review of government action.

2. Equality before the law

> Here every man, whatever his rank or condition, is subject to the ordinary law of the realm and amenable to the jurisdiction of the ordinary [courts]. (Dicey, 1915, 189)

Equality before the law is essential in the interests of public confidence (see *Sharma v Browne-Antoine* [2007] at [14]) and this aspect of Dicey has stood the test of time. Dicey was not concerned with equality in a general sense. He did not mean that no official has special powers – this would have been obviously untrue. Dicey had two specific ideas in mind. Firstly he meant that 'every official, from the Prime minister down..., is under the same responsibility for every act done without legal justification as any other citizen' (ibid). Officials as such enjoy no special protection from legal liability. For example officials and private persons alike are liable if they use excessive force in defending others against criminal acts. And in *M v Home Office* [1993] it was held that a minister cannot refuse to comply with a court order on the basis that he is a servant of the Crown (see also *D v Home Office* [2006]). Thus liability is personal to the individual official, who cannot shelter behind the notion of the state (see Section 6.1).

There are exceptions but these must be rigorously justified (see eg *R (Chaytor) v A-G* [2010]). Judges are immune from personal liability in respect of their actions in court (see Section 7.4), Parliament is immune in relation to its internal proceedings (see Section 11.6), and the Crown has certain immunities (see Section 14. 5). In many cases foreign governments and heads of state are immune from the jurisdiction of the UK courts, at least in civil actions (State Immunity Act 1978; see Section 9.7.2). Public bodies are sometimes protected against legal liability in the interests of efficiency, particularly in cases involving discretionary decisions (see eg *D v East Berkshire Community Health NHS Trust* [2005]: false accusation of child abuse against parents). Dicey's principle can therefore be overcome by showing some justification for an inequality.

Furthermore, modern statutes may provide a comprehensive framework so as to define the power of government and to restrict the use by government of the ordinary private law, thereby denying Dicey's assumption that the same 'regular' law applies to all (see eg *R (Child Poverty Action Group) v Secretary of State for Work and Pensions* [2009]: government could not rely on the general law in order to claw back benefits which it had paid out by mistake; it could reclaim only as authorised by statute, that is where there was a false statement or a failure to disclose relevant information).

Secondly Dicey meant that disputes between government and citizen are settled in the ordinary courts according to the ordinary law rather than in a special governmental court. In this respect Dicey compared English law favourably with French law, where there is a special system of law dealing with the powers of government (*droit administratif* enforced by the Conseil d'Etat). Dicey thought that special administrative courts would give the government special privileges and shield the individual wrongdoer behind the cloak of the state. However Dicey later came to believe that, in view of the increasing power of the executive, he might have been too optimistic about the ordinary courts' ability to protect the individual and began to cast around for other solutions (Dicey, 'Development of Administrative Law in England' [1915] LQR 31).

Nevertheless this aspect of Dicey's teaching has been influential. As recently as the 1970s, there was resistance to the idea of a distinction between public and private law.

Since 1977 however there has been a special procedure for challenging government decisions, albeit within the ordinary court system (Chapter 18). However in partial vindication of Dicey, attempts to distinguish between public law and private law have floundered (Sections 19.1, 21.5). There are also numerous special tribunals dealing with disputes between the individual and government. However they are usually subject to the supervision of the ordinary courts and the rule of law requires that attempts to exclude the ordinary courts be strongly resisted (eg *Anisminic v Foreign Compensation Commission* [1969]; Section 17.6).

Sometimes Dicean equality backfires. In *Malone v Metropolitan Police Comr* [1979] it was held that at common law the police are free to tap telephones since there was no legal prohibition against a private person doing so (a gap in the law subsequently closed by statute; see Section 22.5). In *Harrow LBC v Qazi* [2004] it was held that a local authority can rely on its private property rights as a landlord over the human rights of a tenant. It is therefore arguable that a principle of equality is not adequate to remedy abuses of the wide-ranging powers of modern government.

3. The constitution is the 'result' of the ordinary law

> [T]he general principles of the constitution are with us the result of judicial decisions determining the rights of private persons in particular cases brought before the courts. (Dicey, 1915, 191)

This derives from the common law tradition. Dicey believed that the UK constitution, not being imposed from above as a written constitution, was embedded in the very fabric of the law, dealing with concrete situations and backed by practical remedies in the hands of the courts. According to Dicey this strengthens the constitution since a written constitution may contain grand but vague abstractions and also can more easily be overturned. Moreover because the common law developed primarily through the medium of private disputes, it biases the constitution against governmental interests by treating private law, with its concentration on individual rights, as the basic perspective. Perhaps Dicey's version of the rule of law shows mainly that he trusted judges and feared democracy.

The seminal case of *Entick v Carrington* [1765] illustrates all three aspects of Dicey's rule of law. The Secretary of State ordered two King's messengers to search for Entick, accused of sedition, and to bring him with his books and papers before the Secretary of State. Entick sued the messengers. The court held firstly that the plea of 'state necessity' was unknown to common law because there was no statute or common law precedent from which it could be derived (aspect 3), secondly that the practice of issuing general warrants giving officials wide discretion was unlawful (aspect 1) and thirdly that the messengers had no specific statutory authority regarding the particular papers they seized and so could be sued in ordinary courts like other private citizens (aspect 2).

However Parliament can easily pass laws in defiance of Dicey's rule of law, so his third aspect at least has limited significance. For example in *R v IRC, ex p Rossminister Ltd* [1980] Parliament gave a general power to tax officials to enter and search private premises which the courts upheld, rejecting *Entick v Carrington* as irrelevant antiquarianism.

Students sometimes approach Dicey's version of the rule of law as if it were the only available version. It is true that Dicey's version has been influential in the UK but it is today of limited importance compared, for example, with procedural and substantive perspectives on the rule of law or international approaches to the rule of law. Dicey's version is dominated by his Victorian assumption that private law provides the basic legal framework and that governmental intervention is something exceptional and undesirable.

6.4.3 The core rule of law and freedom

It is sometimes asserted that the core rule of law is inherently supportive of freedom. Montesquieu and Locke thought that freedom means doing what the law allows. Since laws restrict freedom ultimately by force this seems paradoxical. It may be preferable to regard the rule of law, as Hobbes did, as the price to be paid for preventing the worst excesses of freedom rather than to attempt to reconcile these incommensurable goods. Of course my freedom is protected if a law stops you from entering my property, but what the law is doing is transferring freedom from you to me according to what the lawmaker happens to prefer. As Hobbes put it, 'freedom lies in the silence of the laws', and in *The Pilgrim's Progress*, Bunyan asks:

> he to whom thou was sent for ease, being by name legality, is the son of the Bond-woman ... how canst thou expect by them to be made free?

Some laws may indeed aim at protecting various kinds of freedom but does anything in the nature of law guarantee freedom? Hayek (see Section 2.3.4) claimed that in itself the rule of law guarantees freedom: 'When we obey laws, in the sense of general abstract rules laid down irrespective of their application to us, we are not subject to another's will and are therefore free' (1960, 153–54). By this he meant that we are free from the whims of an individual person. This relates to the republican meaning of freedom as non-domination (see Section 2.5). However kind or reasonable a ruler may be, we are nevertheless at his mercy unless he is bound by rules, and so in a sense we are slaves dependent on his goodwill. The ancient notion of positive freedom (Section 2.4) is also relevant in the sense that the people should be free to participate in the law-making process. Hayek might also have meant that we are free to plan our lives around laws and so avoid them, in the sense that outside any law there must be a zone of freedom. However some laws such as  taxation laws may be avoidable only by suicide. The debate therefore seems to be playing on meanings of freedom since we are hardly free if surrounded by restrictive laws.

However as with many legal concepts there is an underlying political agenda. Hayek indicated that the rule of law in his sense makes for a very limited kind of government, leaving market forces to prevail. Firstly Hayek suggested that a government which accepted the rule of law would not enact repressive laws since these would harm its own supporters. Secondly laws must be general and so not pick out individuals for special treatment and this in itself limits government interference. These requirements rule out large areas of state activity involving discretionary economic powers, such as giving aid to industry or much social welfare. Hayek recognised that his proposals were likely to lead to economic inequality and perhaps hardship but assumed that these were outweighed by the advantages of individual freedom.

In common with many economic liberals, Hayek believed that the certainty created by the rule of law would encourage wealth creation through a free market and that the poor would be better off than under alternative regimes. There is no historical evidence either way. However departing from the core idea of the rule of law as rules set out in advance, Hayek favoured the common law as a response to concrete practical problems rather than as being imposed in the abstract by governments that have neither the skills nor the knowledge to plan for the future.

In linking the rule of law to freedom, Hayek might have been thinking of 'positive freedom' in the sense of reason used to expand the possibilities of life (see Section 2.2.1). Indeed he referred to freedom as the absence of *arbitrary* restraint not all restraint. Reason in the form of applying rules does sometimes expand the possibilities of life by combating confusion and uncertainty. Locke endorses this:

> Law in its true notion is not so much the limitation as the direction of a free and intelligent agent to his proper interest and prescribes no further than is for the general good of those under that law. (*Second Treatise of Government* (1690) VI, 57)

In this sense, by obeying rational laws we are apparently exercising freedom since as rational creatures we are 'obeying laws that we have made ourselves' (Kant). On the other hand, as Berlin pointed out (see Section 2.2.1), this notion of freedom is trickery. There are different kinds of reason and unless a law has a freedom-loving content there is no guarantee that it will offer significant life possibilities to anyone except the friends of the lawmaker.

Thus although in a limited sense it is true that the rule of law is conducive to freedom, in practice the core rule of law needs to be supplemented by some idea of 'good law' to have any serious chance of protecting freedom. This leads us to the other versions of the rule of law.

6.5 The 'amplified' rule of law

According to supporters of this wider version of the rule of law, the notion of law as rules necessarily implies certain moral principles that are inherent in the idea of government by rules. They concern the idea that, in order to guide conduct and be acted on, rules must be clear, look to the future and be applied impartially and publicly. These constitute what is primarily a procedural or formal version of the rule of law in the sense that they have little to say about the content of a law as opposed to how it is made and applied. The fundamental idea is a requirement that there should be access to independent courts and a fair trial, particularly to challenge government action (see Lord Bingham in *A v Secretary of State for the Home Dept* [2005] at [42]; Lord Woolf in *M v Secretary of State for the Home Dept* [2004] at 873; see also *Secretary of State for the Home Dept v MB* [2008]: right to fair trial has core irreducible minimum, but see *Secretary of State v AF* [2008]).

The American legal theorist Lon L. Fuller (*The Morality of Law* (Yale University Press 1969)) includes the following moral principles as embodying the rule of law:

- generality: for example officials not exempt from the rules (*M v Home Office* [1993]);

- promulgation so that laws can be known in advance (eg *R (Anufrijeva) v Secretary of State for the Home Dept* [2003]: decision to refuse asylum-seeker status took effect from the date when the claimant was informed of it);
- non-retroactivity: no punishment without a law in force at the time the act was committed (see ECHR, Art 7(1)). However this is not applied generously. For example in *R (Uttley) v Secretary of State for the Home Dept* [2004] a rape committed in 1983 was prosecuted in 1995. The House of Lords held that a sentence heavier than the maximum available in 1983 could not be imposed but allowed a higher sentence than the equivalent in 1983. The requirements of the amplified rule of law are not absolute. For example retrospective law might occasionally be desirable to deal with a particularly serious social problem or an administrative blunder (eg Housing Corporation Act 2006);
- clarity: a law should be sufficiently clear and certain to enable a person to know what conduct was forbidden before he did it (*R v Goldstein* [2006] at [32]–[33]). This is especially important in the context of human rights (see Section 20.4.3; *Gillan v UK* [2010] at [76]);
- consistent application: for example *R v Horseferry Road Magistrates Court, ex p Bennett* [1994]: fair trial not given to person brought before the court by kidnapping even if court process itself is fair, but evidence can be used in court even if has been obtained unlawfully (see *Attorney General's Reference (No 3 of 2009)* [2010]);
- the practical possibility of compliance: for example *R v Secretary of State for Social Services, ex p Joint Council for the Welfare of Immigrants* [1996]: regulations which deprived asylum seekers of benefits unless they claimed asylum status at the port of entry would frustrate their right of appeal;
- constancy through time: frequent changes in the law might offend this. For example between 1997 and 2006 more than 60 Acts of Parliament were produced in response to media coverage of incidents in the criminal justice system (see *Independent* 16 June 2006);
- Raz (1977) adds a right to legal advice: *R v Lord Chancellor, ex p Witham* [1997]: increases in legal fees denied access to courts for low-income people (see also Lord Millett in *Cullen v Chief Constable of the RUC* [2004] at [67]; *R v Grant* [2005] at [52]: breach of lawyer–client confidentiality an affront to the rule of law);
- Raz also includes 'natural justice': in the sense of a right to a fair hearing in one's own defence (see Section 18.3);
- Raz also adds 'openness': for example *R (Middleton) v West Somerset Coroner* [2004]: victims of a misuse of state power in relation to the death of prisoners entitled to public inquiry (see Lord Bingham at [5]). The amplified rule of law includes the principle of open justice not only to protect the parties but also to support the democratic public interest in judicial accountability and the free flow of information through press reporting. In *R (Mohammed) v Secretary of State (No 1)* [2010] the Court of Appeal emphasised the rule of law in the context of a claim by the government that the content of certain documents from the US government should not be revealed in open court (at [38]–[41]). However the rule of law in this sense is not absolute and might be outweighed by other serious concerns such as national security (see Section 23.3.3).

The amplified rule of law might be criticised as narrow in that by concentrating on procedure rather than substance it favours those who can enlist the support of the legal profession, that is the well-to-do. It proponents might respond that the rule of law is not meant to address all social problems but is merely one aspect of good government (see Sunstein, 1996).

Related to the amplified rule of law is a political version of the rule of law derived from the republican tradition (see Bellamy, 2007; Chapter 2). From this perspective law is a collective enterprise made by numerous people with many different interests – majorities and minorities alike. Indeed any of us might sometimes be part of a majority and sometimes a minority. The focus is not therefore on courts alone but on ensuring that the laws are made by a regular democratic process in which the representatives of all interests in the community have a voice. English law has not seriously engaged with this idea.

6.6 The extended (liberal) rule of law: 'the principle of legality'

This version of the rule of law overlaps with but goes beyond the amplified rule of law. It claims somewhat extravagantly that law provides the overarching values of the community against which acts of government must be evaluated. Thus when Aristotle pronounced that it is better for the law to rule than for any of the citizens to rule (*Politics* III.16, 1087a), he was probably referring to understandings about justice among an elite group with common values and traditions designed to bring about their own collective good. The philosopher Ronald Dworkin has put forward an influential American version of this approach based on the idea that law as determined by apparently omnipotent courts should constitute a coherent set of principles, a 'fit' which imposes justice and fairness and gives effect to individual rights against the encroachment of the state (see Section 2.3.2).

The Dworkinian approach has been taken up on this side of the Atlantic. Often called 'the principle of legality', this version of the rule of law claims to restrain 'bad laws' by interpreting legislation and evaluating executive action in the light of common law values. Basic common law rights may be 'curtailed only by clear and express words and then only to the extent reasonably necessary to justify the curtailment' (per Lord Bingham in *R (Daly) v Secretary of State* [2001] at 537–38). In this way the rule of law claims to support liberal democracy. The principle of legality has been reinforced by the Human Rights Act 1998. It applies both to procedural matters, thus encompassing the amplified rule of law above, and to matters of substance such as freedom of speech and non-discrimination. In *R (Bancoult) v Secretary of State for the Foreign and Commonwealth Office* [2001], Laws LJ referred to 'thick' and 'thin' versions of the rule of law. He considered that the extended 'thick' version did not apply to dependent overseas territories (see Section 6.6).

Examples of the principle of legality include the following:

- personal freedom: *A v Secretary of State* [2005]; *R v Secretary of State, ex p Pierson* [1998]; *Roberts v Parole Board* [2006] at [93]; *R (Ullah) v Special Adjudicator* (2004) at [43];

- freedom of expression: *R v Secretary of State for the Home Dept, ex p Simms* [1999] at [131]; *Culnane v Morris* [2006];
- privacy (*R (Daly) v Secretary of State* [2001]);
- discrimination against gay couple: *Ghaidan v Mendosa* [2004] at [9];
- access to the courts: *R v Lord Chancellors Dept, ex p Witham* [1997]; *R (Chaytor) v A-G* [2010]; *R (Cart) v Upper Tribunal* [2010] (see also Section 19.7.2);
- asset freezing of terrorist suspects: *HM Treasury v Ahmed* [2010].

The suggested link between liberal values, the rule of law and common law seems to be twofold. Firstly, and echoing Dicey (see Section 6.4.2), the common law is not merely imposed from the top by a lawmaker but is generated by disputes freely brought before the courts by individuals and requires the exercise of power to be rationally justified. Secondly there is the idea that the law must be applied according to the understanding of those subject to it as equal citizens. In this respect common law's independence from government means that it can plausibly claim to represent the values of the community. According to Allan:

> The principle that laws will be faithfully applied, according to the tenor in which they would reasonably be understood by those affected, is the most basic tenet of the rule of law: it constitutes that minimal sense of reciprocity between citizen and state that inheres in any form of decent government, where law is a genuine barrier to arbitrary power. (2001, 62)

This brings in a republican dimension but, as we saw in Chapter 1, republican and liberal perspectives may conflict – republicanism stressing the desire for citizen participation as equals in decision making, liberalism stressing the citizen's right to be left alone. Sir John Laws, a leading contemporary judge, has tried to combine liberal and republican perspectives. He asserted that because the courts derive their powers from common law and have no electoral mandate to pursue any particular policy they must fall back on what he considered to be the only possible moral position, namely individual freedom: 'The true starting point in the quest for the good constitution consists in ... the autonomy of every person in his sovereignty' (Laws, 'The Constitution: Morals and Rights' [1996] PL 622, 623; see also 'Law and Democracy' [1995] PL 72). (However such philosophical assumptions are controversial, and concepts such as freedom and equality are inherently vague and applied differently by different groups. As we saw in Chapter 2, liberalism has several competing forms, so attempts to impose a liberal orthodoxy seem dogmatic. Moreover common law derives its legitimacy not from abstract philosophy but from community values, whatever they happen to be. The common law is therefore not necessarily liberal. Although confined by the accumulation of precedent, common law arguably tracks the opinions of the dominant group in the legal community at any given time.) While legal education and tradition secure a certain conformity, there is no reason to assume that the precedents are sufficiently clear or the values of the community sufficiently uniform and stable to form a credible basis for coherent liberal principles. The extended rule of law may therefore be no more than the temporary preferences of a fashionable group of lawyers.

Indeed in *R (Bancoult) v Secretary of State for the Foreign and Commonwealth Office* [2001], Laws LJ held that the extended version of the rule of law based on the underlying rights and values of domestic common law does not apply to British overseas territories.

These have to be content with what he called a 'thinner' rule of law, by which he meant something akin to the amplified rule of law in the sense of an obligation to conform to the rules fairly applied (but see Lord Bingham dissenting in *R (Bancoult) v Secretary of State for the Foreign and Commonwealth Office (No 2)* [2008]; see also Section 6.7).

The extended rule of law may conflict with the ideals behind the core rule of law of certainty and respect for general rules. This is because the nature of fundamental rights and the balance between fundamental rights and other aspects of public interest such as security are inherently uncertain and ultimately depend on a political preference.

The late Lord Bingham (2007), the former Senior Law Lord and probably the foremost judge of the past decade, proposed a version of the rule of law which combines elements of both the amplified and the extended rule of law. His core notion was that 'all persons and authorities within the state, whether public or private, should be bound by and entitled to the benefit of laws publicly and prospectively promulgated and publicly administered in the courts'. Particular elements are that laws should:

- be intelligible and precise enough to guide conduct;
- minimise discretion, recognising that discretion cannot be removed completely;
- apply equally to all unless differences are clearly justified;
- give adequate protection to fundamental human rights (Lord Bingham acknowledged the lack of agreement as to whether this is an appropriate rule of law matter as opposed to a matter of politics);
- include machinery for resolving disputes without excessive cost or inordinate delay;
- provide for judicial review requiring decision makers to act reasonably, in good faith, for the purposes for which powers are granted without exceeding the limits of those powers;
- embody fair adjudicative procedures;
- ensure that the state complies with international law (a controversial proposal; see Section 9.7). (See also Bingham, 2009.)

Lord Bingham's general approach probably represents a widely shared view as to what good law should be like in a liberal society. Whether the label 'rule of law' adds anything is questionable. It is sometimes suggested that the rule of law in its extended sense is the foundation of the constitution to the extent that the courts might refuse to apply a statute that conflicted with the rule of law (see Section 8.4).

6.7 The international rule of law

The idea of the rule of law comes under particular stress when there is a clash between different legal regimes, in particular between international and domestic law. International law as such is not automatically part of UK law but international principles can filter into our law by various means (see Section 9.7).

The idea of the rule of law is represented in international law by the notion of *ius cogens*, that is certain absolutes that all nations are expected to recognise, such as the prohibition against torture (see *R v Bow Street Stipendiary Magistrate, ex p Pinochet Ugarte (No 3)* [1999] at 198–99). Since the Second World War there have been several attempts to draw up internationally binding codes of basic human rights and to promote liberal values under the banner of the rule of law. However such concepts are vague and are applied in different ways in different cultures. Indeed in order to command support from as many nations as possible treaties are often written in cloudy language so as to avoid clear commitments, thus reflecting the notion of constitutional abeyance (see Section 3.5).

For example the Declaration of Delhi (1959), issued by the International Commission of Jurists, proclaimed that the rule of law is intended to establish 'social, economic, educational and cultural conditions under which [individuals'] legitimate aspirations and dignity may be realised'.

International instruments include the United Nations Universal Declaration of Human Rights (1948), the Refugee Convention (1951) and the Torture Convention (1984). There is an International Criminal Court to deal with war crimes, crimes against humanity and genocide, which has been incorporated into UK law (International Criminal Court Act 2001). Torture is an offence in the UK wherever and by whomever committed (Criminal Justice Act 1988). Of most direct concern to UK law is the European Convention on Human Rights. Individuals have a right to petition the European Court of Human Rights in respect of violations by states. Under the Human Rights Act 1998, most provisions of the Convention have belatedly been made binding in UK law, although they do not override Acts of Parliament.

Summary

- The rule of law is an umbrella for assorted ideas about the virtues of law mainly from a liberal perspective. They centre upon law as reason and law as a means of controlling aggressive government. They do not fit easily with ideas of democracy, or with government as a provider of welfare services, or with communitarian ideas.
- The rule of law in its core sense emphasises the importance of general rules as binding on government and citizen alike. The core sense of the rule of law is morally ambivalent since it can also be regarded as an efficient tool of tyranny.
- In an amplified sense, the rule of law requires the law to reflect certain basic values derived from the nature of rules as guides to conduct. These centre upon the law being clear and accessible and upon the right to a fair trial. However they are also consistent with repressive laws.
- In an extended sense the rule of law is claimed to be the guardian of the basic liberal values of the community, entrusted to the courts because of their role as guardians of impartial reason. It is claimed to be translated into rights such as non-discrimination, freedom of expression and access to government information. However there is no reason to believe that these values or reason itself are the prerogative of courts and they have to be accommodated against the social goals of elected governments. Why courts should do this is a theme to be pursued in later chapters.
- The rule of law as expounded by Dicey has significantly influenced the UK constitution. Dicey advocated that government discretion should be limited by definite rules of law, that the same law could in general apply to government and citizen alike, and that Britain does not need a written constitution because, in his view, the common law made by independent courts with

Summary cont'd

practical remedies provides a firmer foundation for individual rights. This has greatly influenced the thinking of the legal profession but may be unsuited to the control of modern government. It is also difficult to reconcile the rule of law in this sense with the principle that Parliament has unlimited power which can be harnessed by a strong executive.

- Other modern ideas of the rule of law include the increasing importance of international treaties which attempt to establish codes of fundamental rights and freedoms that governments should respect.

Exercises

6.1 Do you agree with Thompson that the rule of law is an 'unqualified human good'?

6.2 To what extent is Dicey's version of the rule of law of value today?

6.3 'The Rule of Law functions as a clear check on the flourishing of a rigorous democracy. Attempts to characterise the rule of law as the butler of democracy are false and misleading' (Hutchinson and Monahan). Critically discuss.

6.4 To what extent, if at all, is the rule of law conducive to (a) freedom and (b) equality?

6.5 Do the following violate the rule of law?
(i) the Queen being exempt from legal liability;
(ii) a statute banning press criticism of the Prime Minister;
(iii) a statute which states that an allegation relating to the conduct of the security services cannot be made in the ordinary courts;
(iv) a statute which gives a discretion to the Education Secretary to decide what courses will be taught in universities;
(v) a statute requiring that any law concerning the treatment of prisoners must be interpreted literally without any presumption in favour of human rights.

6.6 'The rule of law clearly forms an essential element of liberal democracy and plays its part in providing a theoretical basis for an independent judiciary but it forms only one side of a balanced constitution' (Carol Harlow). Explain and critically discuss.

Further reading

Allan, *Constitutional Justice: A Liberal Theory of the Rule of Law* (Oxford University Press 2001)
Allan, 'The Rule of Law as Liberal Justice' (2006) 56 U Toronto LR 41
Allan, 'Law, Justice and Integrity: The Paradox of Wicked Laws' (2009) 29 OJLS 705
Bellamy, *Political Constitutionalism* (Cambridge University Press 2007) ch 2
Bingham 'The Rule of Law' (2007) 66 CLJ 67
Bingham, *The Rule of Law* (Penguin 2009)
Craig, 'Formal and Substantive Concepts of the Rule of Law: An Analytical Framework' [1997] PL 467
Endicott, 'The Impossibility of the Rule of Law' (1999) 19 OJLS 1
Hayek, *The Constitution of Liberty* (Henry Regnery 1960) 133–61, 205–19
Horowitz, 'The Rule of Law: An Unqualified Human Good?' (1977) 86 Yale LJ 15
McCorquodale, 'The Rule of Law Internationally: Lord Bingham and the British Institute of International and Comparative Law' in Andenas and Fairgrieve (eds), *Tom Bingham and the Transformation of the Law* (Oxford University Press 2009)

Further reading cont'd

Marshall, 'The Constitution: Its Theory and Interpretation' in Bogdanor (ed), *The British Constitution in the Twentieth Century* (Oxford University Press 2003) 51

Michaelman, 'Political Truth and the Rule of Law' (1988) 8 Tel Aviv U Stud L 283

Poole, 'Dogmatic Liberalism? T.R.S. Allan and the Common Law Constitution' (2002) 65 MLR 65

Poole, 'Back to the Future: Unearthing the Theory of Common Law Constitutionalism' (2003) 66 OJLS 435

Poole, 'Questioning Common Law Constitutionalism' (2005) 25 LS 142

Raz, 'The Rule of Law and Its Virtue' [1977] LQR 93

Sadurski, 'Law's Legitimacy and "Democracy-Plus"' (2006) 26 OJLS 377

Sunstein, *Legal Reasoning and Political Conflict* (Oxford University Press 1996) ch 4

Tivey, 'Constitutionalism and the Political Arena' (1999) 70 Pol Q 175

Waldron, 'The Rule of Law in Contemporary Legal Theory' (1989) 2 Ratio Juris 79

Chapter 7

The separation of powers

Political liberty is nothing else but the diffusion of power. (Lord Hailsham)

7.1 Introduction: Montesquieu's doctrine of the separation of powers

The separation of powers, although by no means universal, is widely regarded as one of the pillars of a liberal constitutional democracy. Article 16 of the (French) Declaration of the Rights of Man (1789) states that 'a society where rights are not secured or the separation of powers established has no constitution'. It is widely believed that in all societies there is a tendency for power to gravitate towards a single leader who is likely to abuse his or her power. The separation of powers attempts to combat this by providing mechanisms to make it difficult for any single power group to dominate and to ensure that government action requires the cooperation of different groups, each of which helps to keep the others within bounds. The doctrine is therefore closely associated with the rule of law (see *R (Anderson) v Secretary of State* [2002] at [27]). It is also central to republicanism (see Section 2.5) as a means of preventing any one group from dominating.

A widely accepted division of power is based on the functions of government. With variations, it can be traced to Aristotle (384–322 BC). Its best-known version is that formulated by Montesquieu (1689–1755), who divided government into three branches: the legislature, the executive and the judiciary. The legislature makes the laws, the executive enforces and puts the law into effect, and the judiciary settles disputes and imposes sanctions for breaking the law. Thus:

> [i]n the government of this commonwealth, the legislative department shall never exercise the executive and judicial powers, or either of them: the executive shall never exercise the legislative and judicial powers, or either of them: the judicial shall never exercise the legislative and executive powers, or either of them: to the end it may be a government of laws and not of men. (Massachusetts Constitution 1780, Art XXX)

Montesquieu was no democrat and placed faith in aristocratic government subject to limits. His idea of limits on power was what he called 'dissonant harmony'. He believed that disagreement was a healthy feature of politics and that the need for different interests to cooperate would prevent any power being used excessively. As he famously stated, 'power must be checked by power'. He thought that if any two of the three functions fall into the same hands the outcome is likely to be tyranny. According to the doctrine of the separation of powers, each branch has different functions but each uses its power to police the limits of the others. Conversely, within the limits of its powers, each branch should be independent of the others. As Nolan J put it:

> The proper constitutional relationship between the executive and the court is that the courts will respect all acts of the executive within its lawful province, and that the executive will respect all decisions of the court as to what its lawful province is. (*M v Home Office* [1992])

A balance must therefore be struck between the three powers. Moreover there must be an understanding as to which of them should have the last word in the event of a stalemate since the separation of powers is capable of producing gridlock. The way this is done depends on the political fears and worries of the day. Montesquieu feared the legislature most. He vested the executive in the monarchy, believing that this gave the constitution stability and continuity. The executive and legislature would, according to Montesquieu, check each other. For instance the executive could not make laws or obtain finance without the support of the legislature but in Montesquieu's view the legislature should not be able to remove the executive. Montesquieu thought it appropriate that the executive should summon the legislature as and when needed but did not explain how an abuse of this power might be dealt with. However in the UK constitution the meeting of the legislature is protected by statute and convention and the legislature can remove the executive.

In the contemporary UK we regard the executive as the most dangerous branch as it commands the resources of the state, including the use of force, and is in a position to dominate the legislature. Indeed by the end of the nineteenth century Mill, influenced by de Toqueville's writing on the emerging American democracy, feared:

> the only despotism of which in the modern world there is real danger – the absolute rule of the head of the executive over a congregation of isolated individuals all equal and all slaves. (*Autobiography* (1873))

Recently the desirability of an independent judiciary has been emphasised as a check on both an increasingly powerful executive and the democratic legislature. Argument rages as to whether the judiciary or legislature should have the last word.

There is disagreement as to the importance of the doctrine of separation of powers. It has been argued both that the separation of powers in the UK is insignificant and that our constitution depends on the separation of powers. Jennings (*The Law and the Constitution* (University of London Press 1959)) argues that there is no important difference between the three functions, the executive and judicial being essentially a more detailed kind of lawmaking. Marshall (*Constitutional Theory* (Oxford University Press 1971)) argues that the separation of powers is an umbrella for a miscellaneous collection of principles, each of which can be justified on its own terms, for example judicial independence. On the other hand Barendt (1995) and Munro (1999) regard the doctrine as an important organising and critical principle.

However the commentators sometimes debate the separation of powers from extreme positions. The situation seems to be that the UK constitution embodies the separation of powers in pragmatic ways in particular contexts but that it applies strongly in relation to the judiciary, particularly in view of the recent creation of the Supreme Court (see Section 7.7.2).

However the debate may be confused where different protagonists are using the concept of the separation of powers in different senses. In particular separation of powers can mean:

1. separation of function between different units of government;
2. separation of personnel in the membership of different units of government;
3. checks and balances between different units of government.

The strictest version of the doctrine, such as that adopted in the US, would aim at all three, although of course practicalities mean that the reality is likely to fall short of the ideal. As with the rule of law, the separation of powers is no more than an underlying set of values.

7.2 The mixed constitution

Montesquieu also insisted on a different kind of separation of powers, namely one between class interests. This reflects the 'mixed constitution' based on Aristotle's three forms of government: monarchy, aristocracy and democracy (Chapter 1). Aristotle believed that any single form of government was unstable, leading to a permanent cycle of disasters. In particular democracy – in the sense of the rule of the majority – leads to anarchy, which is overcome only by the intervention of a dictator, who will eventually be overthrown by force in favour of either aristocracy or democracy, each of which in turn will collapse. He therefore favoured a blend of democracy and aristocracy: democracy to provide consent, aristocracy to provide stability and wise leadership. Aristocracy meant literally 'rule by the best', by which Aristotle meant an educated group wealthy enough to be independent.

The early Roman republic adopted similar ideas ('power in the people, authority in the Senate' – Cicero) but was later replaced by dictatorship ('what pleases the prince has the force of law'). For Montesquieu, all three elements of the mixed constitution should be represented in the legislature since this was the supreme body. Each element would check the others. The monarch could veto legislation but not initiate it: 'prevent wrong but not do wrong'. The aristocratic and the elected elements would have to agree to make changes in the law.

Montesquieu, an aristocrat himself, believed that an aristocracy based on inheritance produced an independent, educated and leisured class who would protect freedom and curb the democratic element ('liberty is the stepchild of privilege') while the other elements of the constitution could prevent the aristocracy from using their powers selfishly. This is reflected by contemporary advocates of the supremacy of the judiciary as a kind of aristocratic elite, albeit one not based directly on inheritance (Sections 19.5 and 21.5).

Blackstone (1723–80), an influential compiler of English law, also praised the mixed constitution:

> Herein indeed consists the true excellence of the English government that all the parts of it form a mutual check upon each other. In the legislature the people are a check on the nobility and the nobility a check upon the people...while the king is a check upon both which preserves the executive power from encroachments. And this very executive power is again checked and kept within due bounds by the two Houses...For the two Houses naturally drawing in two directions of opposite interest, and the prerogative in another still different from them both, they mutually keep each other from exceeding their proper limits...like three distinct powers in mechanics, they jointly compel the machine of government in a direction different from what either acting by itself would have done...a direction which constitutes the true line of the liberty and happiness of the country. (*Commentaries on the Laws of England* (Oxford University Press 1787) 154–55)

Montesquieu claimed to find both kinds of separation of powers in the British constitution, in that the executive power was centred upon the Crown and the legislature had two parts, one (the House of Lords) being aristocratic. However in Montesquieu's time the conventions that removed power from the Crown in favour of ministers, who were also members of the legislature, had not yet crystallised. Moreover Montesquieu may not have appreciated that the English constitution gave Parliament unlimited power over the Crown (cf Claus, 2005).

The mixed constitution remains a significant element of the formal legal structure in the form of the monarchy and the House of Lords. However, politically, the monarchy and the House of Lords are relatively impotent. It is worth remembering that originally aristocracy simply meant government by the 'best'. The hereditary principle which was the historical basis of the House of Lords was rationalised on the ground that inherited landholding gave a powerful interest in the government of the country through which the lower classes enjoyed 'virtual representation'.

Today the House of Lords is mainly an appointed aristocracy since an automatic link between inheritance and political influence is no longer acceptable, at least openly, although a rump of hereditary peers remain. There are currently proposals to remove the unelected element entirely from the House of Lords (see Section 12.3). However fear of democracy remains and many people are attracted by the idea of an appointed aristocracy (particularly if it includes themselves). This raises the difficulty of whom we can trust to identify the 'best' so as to avoid Aristotle's corruption of aristocracy into an oligarchy of cronies. Unfortunately it has not proved possible to agree.

7.3 Other kinds of separation of powers

There are other kinds of separation of powers which serve the same function of preventing the concentration of power. Examples are:

- Between elected politicians and appointed civil servants providing expert advice (Chapter 15). John Stuart Mill's approach is broadly the form of representative democracy practised in the UK. Mill (1972) thought that most governmental functions should be entrusted to experts, with democracy through elected representatives providing the elements of consent and control. Thus in the UK constitution the people's only legal power is to choose at intervals an individual as a representative for each locality in the House of Commons, out of which the executive is formed under conventions over which the people have no control.
- Between the 'dignified' and the 'efficient' parts of the constitution (see Section 5.1), for example the Queen and ministers.
- Between geographical areas, most effectively in a federal constitution. In the UK there is only the more limited separation of devolution (see Section 16.1). However even this can produce political constraints.

7.4 Judicial independence

Judicial independence is an aspect of the rule of law in its own right. It overlaps with but goes beyond the separation of powers. For example the common law principles of natural justice require that a judge should not be vulnerable to personal bias (see Section 18.4). Separation of powers concerns the independence of the judicial system as an institution. Judicial independence requires the independence of individual judges from any pressures that threaten not only actual impartiality but also the appearance of impartiality. Article 6 of the European Convention on Human Rights (ECHR) includes both elements by requiring 'a fair and public hearing... by an independent and impartial tribunal established by law'. For example in *Millar v Dickson* [2002] the Privy Council found a violation of Article 6 where the prosecuting authority, the Scottish Lord Advocate, was also responsible for renewing the appointment of a temporary judge even though there was no complaint about the actual impartiality of the judge in question. As Lord Hope stated:

> Central to the rule of law in a modern democratic society is the principle that the judiciary must be, and must be seen to be independent of the executive. (at [41])

Article 6 applies to all decisions that affect 'civil rights and obligations' (see Section 18.6). It does not require a formal separation of powers but requires that in the particular circumstances the court is not only independent but appears to be so (*McGonnell v UK* [2000]). Courts of a 'classic kind' must usually sit in public and be fully independent and impartial, and there must be a full opportunity to give evidence and challenge witnesses (see *R (Hammond) v Secretary of State for the Home Dept* [2006]). However sometimes these ideals might be compromised by competing considerations such as security and the desire to protect children.

Statute sometimes acknowledges judicial independence.

- Under the Courts Act 2003 the Lord Chancellor has a general duty to ensure an 'efficient and effective' court system (s 1).
- The Constitutional Reform Act 2005 imposes the following somewhat vague duties (s 3):
  1. The Lord Chancellor and other ministers of the Crown with responsibility for matters relating to the judiciary or otherwise to the administration of justice must uphold the continued independence of the judiciary.
  2. The Lord Chancellor and other ministers of the Crown must not seek to influence particular judicial decisions through any special access to the judiciary.
  3. The Lord Chancellor must have regard to:
     (i) the need to defend that independence;
     (ii) the need for the judiciary to have the support necessary to enable them to exercise their functions;
     (iii) the need for the public interest in regard to matters relating to the judiciary or otherwise to the administration of justice to be properly represented in decisions affecting those matters.

Judicial independence and the separation of powers overlap particularly in relation to the appointment and dismissal of judges since judges must be immune from interference by the executive. Beyond the separation of powers, judicial independence requires that judges should be protected against attacks on their conduct in court. They are immune from personal actions for damages in respect of acts within their powers or done in good faith (*McC v Mullan* [1984]; Courts Act 2003, ss 31–35). However superior court judges may enjoy complete immunity (*Anderson v Gorrie* [1895]). Under section 9.3 of the Human Rights Act 1998, where an action for damages is brought in respect of a judicial act, there is no liability in respect of an act in good faith except for an unlawful arrest or detention. Anything said in court by judges, advocates and witnesses is absolutely privileged against an action in libel and slander but advocates are not protected against liability for negligence (see *Trapp v Mackie* [1979]; *Arthur JS Hall v Simons* [2000]).

Judicial independence does not mean that judges should not be accountable. Accountability has different meanings. It means firstly that a decision maker must explain and justify his or her actions and secondly that a decision maker might be penalised if his or her actions fall short of required standards. Judges are to some extent accountable in the first sense. They normally sit in public, disclose all material before them and give reasons for their decisions. Judicial decisions are open to scrutiny by the media (see Chapter 22). Open justice in this sense is regarded as fundamental to the rule of law (see *R (Mohamad) v Secretary of State* [2010]; Section 23.3.3). A three-tier appeal system and review by the senior courts of decisions of lower courts and tribunals contribute to accountability, as does the Criminal Cases Review Commission, which deals with miscarriages of justice.

Traditionally judges have not participated in public debate (see McMurdo, 'Should Judges Speak Out?' Judicial Conference of Australia 2001; www.jca.asn.au). However in 1987 the Lord Chancellor relaxed the notorious 'Kilmuir' rules made in 1959 by the then Lord Chancellor which restricted such participation and the matter is now left to the discretion of the individual judge.

7.5 The separation of powers in the UK

The separation of powers in Montesquieu's sense has limited but important application in the unwritten UK constitution and has been endorsed by the judges. As Lord Steyn put it in *R (Anderson) v Secretary of State* [2002]: '[o]ur constitution has never embraced a rigid doctrine of separation of powers. The relationship between the legislature and executive is close. On the other hand, the separation of powers between the judiciary and the legislative and executive branches of government is a strong principle of our system of government' (at [39]).

In the same case Lord Bingham emphasised that '[t]he European Court was right to describe the complete functional separation of the judiciary from the executive as "fundamental" since the rule of law depends on it' (at [27]). (See also Lord Templeman in *M v Home Office* [1993] at 540; Lord Hoffmann in *R (Pro-Life Alliance) v BBC* [2003] at 997; Lords Nicholls and Hope in *Wilson v First County Trust* [2003] at 116, 130; Lord Diplock in *Duport Steels v Sirs* [1980] at 157; Sir John Donaldson in *R v HM Treasury, ex p Smedley* [1985] at 593.)

Most obviously there are indeed three branches of government, with broadly separate functions: the legislature (Parliament), the executive (the Crown) and the judiciary. All three historically originated with the Crown (Chapter 3) but gradually became substantially separate institutions.

There is a strong separation between the courts and the other branches. Although judges are in theory Crown servants, from the seventeenth century it was established that the King cannot act as a judge himself (see *Prohibitions del Roy* [1607]). One aspect of the 1688 revolution was to give what are now the senior judges security of tenure against removal by the executive (see Section 7.8.3).

M v Home Office [1993] concerned whether the court could treat the Home Secretary, a minister of the Crown, as being in contempt of court for disobeying a court order. The court rejected the argument that because the courts and ministers were both historically part of the Crown, the Crown would in effect be in contempt of itself. At first instance Simon Brown J ([1992] at 107), citing Montesquieu, pointed out that at least since the seventeenth century the courts had been recognised as an institution separate from the Crown itself and that the Queen had only a symbolic relationship with the three branches of government. Moreover a minister exercising powers conferred on him by law was not to be treated as part of the Crown since to do so, as Lord Templeman remarked (at 540), would undo the consequences of the Civil War. Similarly in *R (Bancoult) v Secretary of State for the Foreign and Commonwealth Office (No 2)* [2008] the House of Lords held that it had jurisdiction to review a Prerogative Order in Council since such an order was in reality made by ministers not the Crown itself.

There is a weaker separation between executive and legislature. The conventions governing the parliamentary system blur the separation between the legislature and the executive since by convention ministers must be members of Parliament. Depending on the political and personal forces of the day, either the executive is subordinate to Parliament or (more likely) the executive dominates Parliament. Bagehot (1902) claimed that the 'almost complete fusion' between the executive (by which he meant Cabinet ministers) and the legislature was the 'efficient secret' of the constitution. However, although Bagehot's writings have been highly influential, his analysis is widely regarded as oversimplified ('a television man before his time'). For example there are various devices which attempt to ensure that neither the executive nor Parliament can completely dominate the other. Moreover the functions and processes of the two branches are not fused. Ministers must publicly announce and defend their policies in Parliament whereas executive decisions are taken in secret by self-selected groups. Indeed Montesquieu (1995) himself recognised that there might be an overlap between the legislature and the executive, although emphasising that there should be some separation between them:

> But if there were no monarch, and the executive power should be committed to a certain number of persons selected from the legislative body, there would be an end then of liberty.

In this context, it is worth remembering that Montesquieu feared democracy. On the other hand the contemporary House of Commons chooses to be subservient to the executive.

We shall now outline the main concerns of the separation of powers in the UK. Some of these are developed in later chapters. We shall distinguish between separation of functions, separation of personnel, and checks and balances. Bear in mind that these three forms of separation of power overlap.

7.6 Separation of functions

The lawmaker makes general rules, the executive implements the law and makes government policy, and a judge acts as an independent referee by applying rules to a dispute. The judicial function is associated with courts. There is however no clear definition of a court other than the circular one of a body exercising a judicial function whatever its name (eg Contempt of Court Act 1981, s 19).

This assumes that the three functions of government can be conceptually distinguished, in the sense that the activities of lawmaking, judging and carrying out executive tasks are different in significant respects, irrespective of who carries them out. This is a controversial theoretical issue but constitutional thinkers have, since the time of Aristotle, agreed that there is at least a distinction between the making of general rules, which requires the participation of a wide range of people, the implementation of those rules, which requires professional expertise, and the resolution of disputes, which requires above all impartiality. This idea unites for example Locke, Rousseau and Mill despite their different ideas as to the purpose of government (Chapter 2).

The executive function is particularly difficult to define. It comprises anything that is neither judicial nor legislative. Whether a matter is executive may depend not on any natural quality it has but on the mechanism chosen to deal with it. For example imposing a penalty in connection with a court ruling is part of the judicial function (see Lord Steyn in *R (Anderson) v Secretary of State* [2002]) but arguably an 'administrative penalty' imposed mechanically, such as a parking ticket, is not. Nor arguably is a decision based on government policy such as granting planning permission for a new building. A grant of planning permission creates a new right, but a judicial function, strictly speaking, is meant only to determine existing rights under the law. Decisions which may have serious impacts but which do not strictly affect legal rights, such as placing a person on a register of wrongdoers, are also executive in nature. Unlike a minister or a traffic warden, a court exercising a judicial function cannot initiate action but must respond to disputes which others bring before it. Thus the judiciary is often claimed to be the 'least dangerous branch', having no weapons at its disposal and having no particular axe to grind.

7.6.1 Parliament and the executive: delegated legislation

There is overlap between the functions of Parliament and of the executive in that while Parliament has no executive functions (except in relation to its own internal affairs) the executive is involved in lawmaking. In practice most English legislation consists of delegated or secondary or subordinate legislation (the terms being synonymous) made by ministers and other bodies outside Parliament under powers conferred by Act of Parliament. It is commonplace for a statute to lay down a general principle and then to confer power upon a minister to make detailed rules fleshing out the principle.

Delegated lawmaking powers are sometimes very wide, and often permit the minister to alter Acts of Parliament past or future (the 'Henry VIII' clause; for example European Communities Act 1972, s 2(4); Pollution Prevention and Control Act 1999). A statute might also come into effect only when a minister triggers it. However the minister cannot decide not to bring the statute into effect (*R v Secretary of State, ex p Fire Brigades Union* [1995]).

Delegated legislation comes under many names, including regulations, orders, directions, rules and bylaws. Little hinges on the terminology used. However a compendium term, 'statutory instrument', applies to most delegated legislation made by ministers and to Statutory Orders in Council (Statutory Instruments Act 1946). Statutory instruments must be formally published, and, in accordance with the rule of law, it is a defence in criminal proceedings to show that an instrument has not been published and that it is not reasonable to expect the accused to be aware of it (s 4). However it seems that failure to publish does not affect validity for other purposes (see *R v Sheer Metalcraft* [1954]).

Delegated legislation has often been criticised as an infringement of the separation of powers. It can be made without the public and democratic processes represented, albeit imperfectly, by Parliament. However it is difficult to imagine a complex and highly regulated society that could function effectively if all laws had to be made by Parliament itself (see *Report of the Committee on Ministers' Powers* (Cmd 4060, 1932)). Most delegated legislation is subject to a limited amount of parliamentary scrutiny by means of being laid before the House, although this is usually nominal. There are also committees that scrutinise statutory instruments (see Section 13.5.5).

Unlike a statute the validity of delegated legislation, even if it has been approved by Parliament, can be challenged in the courts if it is outside the powers conferred by its parent Act, according to the grounds of judicial review applicable to all executive action. It can also be set aside by the courts if it violates the ECHR as applied by the Human Rights Act 1998.

Delegated legislation must be distinguished from what is often called 'quasi-legislation'. This comprises rules, standards, policies, guidance or advice issued for example in circulars by the government without statutory authority to make rules. Quasi-legislation is not strictly binding but must be taken into account and is in practice normally followed. Indeed, depending on its content, it may create a 'legitimate expectation' that the government will comply with it (see Section 17.9).

7.6.2 Parliament and the judiciary

Our common law system means that the judges are also lawmakers and their function is not confined to interpreting laws made by others. There are certain checks and balances, although these depend on the judges restraining themselves. One such check is the judges' duty to follow precedent so as to limit the possibility of making up new law according to a judge's personal preferences. Another is the fact that the judges must make their law only in the context of the particular case before them. Another is the supposed principle that a court must ultimately defer to Parliament (Chapter 8). In *WH Smith Do It All Ltd v Peterborough City Council* [1991], Mustill LJ remarked that:

> according to the doctrine of the separation of powers as understood in the UK, the legislative acts of the Queen in Parliament are impregnable. (at 196)

Parliament and the courts avoid interfering with each other. A court cannot usually investigate parliamentary proceedings or challenge statements made in Parliament (*Pickin v British Railways Board* [1974]). However the courts can decide whether statutory requirements have been complied with even where they relate to parliamentary processes (*R (Jackson) v A-G* [2005]; see Section 8.4.3). In relation to its own composition and internal affairs the House of Commons has exclusive power to decide disputes and punish offenders (see Section 11.6.2).

Cases in progress should not be discussed in Parliament except in relation to matters of national importance or the conduct of ministers (see May, *Treatise on the Law, Privilege, Proceedings and Usage of Parliament* (Butterworths 1997) 383–84, 542–43). Ministers do not answer questions on cases in progress. There should be no criticism of a judge's personal character, competence or motives except on a substantive motion for his dismissal, although backbenchers but not ministers may criticise individual judgments.

7.6.3 The executive and the judiciary

The executive sometimes makes judicial decisions when it decides for example whether a given person is entitled to a welfare payment or a school place. Indeed ministers are often required to decide appeals against government decisions, even those in which their own department has an interest. However the practice of ministers determining planning appeals does not violate the right to a fair trial under the ECHR, at least where the decision is one based on policy, provided that there is the safeguard of judicial review by the courts (*R (Alconbury Developments) v Secretary of State* [2001]). Moreover what the separation of powers importantly requires is that each body should have the last word in relation to its particular function. Thus Parliament can approve, veto or alter laws proposed to it and the judiciary can review executive action and has the last word as to what a law means.

Until recently the separation of powers was violated in that the Home Secretary played a prominent role in the sentencing process. In the case of prisoners serving life sentences he or she could decide the 'tariff' period that must be served before the prisoner became eligible for release on parole. He or she could also control the sentences of young persons imprisoned indefinitely 'at Her Majesty's pleasure'. There is also the royal prerogative of mercy to release or pardon convicted persons, exercisable on the advice of the Home Secretary. In the party political context of the UK, it is easy to believe that these powers are open to abuse (eg *R v Secretary of State for the Home Dept, ex p Venables* [1997]: use of opinion poll in the *Sun* newspaper).

In a series of cases the European Court has held that the involvement of the executive in the sentencing process is normally a violation of the right to a fair trial (ECHR, Art 6; see *R (Anderson) v Secretary of State for the Home Dept* [2002]; *Benjamin v UK* [2002]; *V v UK* [1999]). English law has accepted this by removing the Home Secretary's power in most contexts in favour of a judge or the independent Parole Board (eg in the Criminal Justice and Court Services Act 2000, s 60; Criminal Justice Act 2003, s 269).

However in *R (Black) v Justice Secretary* [2009] the House of Lords (Lord Phillips dissenting) upheld the power of the Home Secretary to override the Parole Board in the case of a 'determinate' sentence, meaning a sentence for a fixed period. The reason for distinguishing between determinate and indeterminate sentences is that, in the case of a determinate sentence, the sentence has already been decided by a judge. Any later intervention by the Home Secretary is not therefore part of the sentencing process but a matter of prisoner management. In the case of an indeterminate sentence the Home Secretary is directly imposing the sentence in defiance of the judicial function. (Should a matter affecting individual liberty depend on such an abstract legalistic distinction? Their Lordships suggested that the involvement of the Home Secretary although lawful was an undesirable anomaly.)

A distinction can also be drawn between fixing a sentence and the royal prerogative of mercy, which allows the executive to release a prisoner for example on compassionate grounds or where new evidence comes to light throwing doubt on the conviction. It is arguable that the politically accountable executive is the most appropriate body to exercise this kind of power. Thus the executive should periodically review an indefinite sentence, at least in the case of a young person, in order to refer it to the relevant body for possible reduction (*R (Smith) v Secretary of State for the Home Dept* [2006]). The prerogative of mercy remains with the Home Secretary, who can refer the matter to the independent Criminal Appeals Board, which can also directly refer doubtful convictions to the Court of Appeal (Criminal Appeals Act 1995).

Magistrates clerks are members of the civil service (Courts Act 2003) but have certain judicial functions in connection with criminal proceedings and also advise magistrates on the law, participating in their private deliberations. The Courts Act 2003 makes some concession to their independence by providing that when exercising judicial functions they are not subject to directions from the Lord Chancellor or any other person (s 29). It has been held that the activities of magistrates clerks do not violate judicial independence provided the clerk advises only on matters of law and procedure and not the actual decision, and any matters that the parties might wish to comment upon are raised in open court (*Clark (Procurator Fiscal Kirkcaldy) v Kelly* [2003]). It is difficult to see how these protections are safeguarded given that the deliberations are in private. In *Kelly* the Privy Council relied on the right of appeal, the 'well understood conventions' and the clerk's professional code as safeguards.

Another vital safeguard in the criminal process is that juries should not be vetted by the executive (*R v Crown Court at Sheffield, ex p Brownlow* [1980]) and cannot be required to give reasons for their verdicts or punished for giving or failing to give a verdict (*Bushell's Case* [1670]). It is an offence for anyone to publish information as to what was said in a jury room (Contempt of Court Act 1981, s 8(1)).

It is important for judicial independence that judges have no duty to advise the executive. However judges are sometimes appointed to carry out investigations or inquiries into allegations against government or significant incidents. This carries the risk of compromising the independence of the judiciary by making them appear to be involved in politics (eg the Scott Report into arms sales to Iraq (HC 1995–96, 115) and the Hutton Report into the death of a government adviser in the context of the decision to invade Iraq (HC 2004, 247)). In some countries, such as the US and Australia, the practice of judicial inquiries of this kind is unconstitutional (see Drewry, 'Judicial Inquiries and Public Reassurance' [1996] PL 368; Woodhouse, 2004, 140). As part of the 'concordance' between judges and Parliament entered into in relation to the constitutional reforms of 2005, a senior judge must be consulted on any proposal to appoint a judge of the rank of circuit judge or above to hold an inquiry under section 10(1) of the Inquiries Act 2005 (Section 7.6.3).

7.7 Separation of personnel

In view of the risk of bias or conflict of interest, the same individuals should not be members of more than one of the three branches or exercise more than one function. This principle has traditionally been applied pragmatically and not consistently. We have already seen that the UK constitution does not comply with this, most importantly by its requirement that ministers must also be members of Parliament. In theory this strengthens executive accountability to Parliament. In practice, owing to the subservience of MPs, it enables the executive to dominate Parliament. Ambivalence between the minister's two capacities is most notable in connection with the problems of ministerial responsibility to Parliament and more generally enables the executive to control parliamentary procedure (see Chapter 13; Sections 6.3, 15.7.2).

7.7.1 Parliament and the executive

There is however some separation of personnel between Parliament and the executive. No more than 95 ministers can sit and vote in the Commons (House of Commons (Disqualification) Act 1975, s 2(1)), thus preventing the government from packing the Commons with sycophants. Other ministers can be members of the House of Lords without apparent limit. However there are limits on the number of ministers who can be paid (Ministerial and Other Salaries Acts 1975, 1997). Nevertheless there seem to be no shortage of MPs willing to be unpaid junior ministers known as parliamentary private secretaries, who under the Ministerial Code must be loyal to the executive.

Certain officials for whom conflicts of role are especially likely (civil servants, police, regulators, members of the armed forces and so on) cannot be members of the Commons (House of Commons (Disqualification) Act 1975, s 1; see Section 12.4).

7.7.2 Parliament and the judiciary: the new Supreme Court

Separation between Parliament and the judiciary is especially important and has mainly been upheld in the UK. In particular judges cannot be members of elected bodies. The highest appellate court is the Supreme Court, which started work in October 2009 (Constitutional Reform Act 2005). It is wholly separate from Parliament. Before then appeals were heard by a panel of judges sitting as part of Parliament, the Appellate Committee of the House of Lords, a relic of the days when the monarch's chief advisers sat in judgement. These judges were full members of the House of Lords as a lawmaker. Despite this clear breach of the separation of powers, the impartiality of the Law Lords was not in doubt and conventions prevented them from participating directly in the political business of the House or speaking on matters that might arise in an appeal. There were also advantages in links between the two branches since these could provide a valuable exchange of information.

Nevertheless there was unease both because of the appearance of bias and because of the limited role the Law Lords could play in Parliament (see Bingham, 2002). The introduction of devolution for Scotland, Wales and Northern Ireland also exposed an anomaly if the judges who decided disputes between the devolved regimes and the UK were also members of the UK Parliament. The fair trial requirements of the ECHR were also a consideration, even though these relate to individual cases rather than to institutional structure as such (see *McGonnell v UK* [2000]).

The Supreme Court has the appeal functions formerly exercised by the House of Lords and in devolution cases of the Privy Council. It therefore has features of a constitutional court although it has only the same powers as its predecessors and its membership is similar. It has been suggested that its very existence could influence a gradual movement towards a US-style court that can override the legislature (see Webber, 2004). Devolution, the Human Rights Act 1998 and the impact of EU membership mean that the courts have greater political significance than was traditionally the case. However there is no evidence that the judges are either more or less willing to take on an interventionist political role than was previously the case. For many years senior judges have been participating actively in public debate on matters concerning the constitution through speeches and contributions to the media (see Sedley, 2009).

The Court comprises 12 judges, usually sitting in panels of 5, although there are larger panels in important constitutional cases. The Court has some administrative independence, being able to make its own procedural rules, and has its own budget. However the House of Lords had special protection against the executive by virtue of parliamentary privilege (see Section 11.6). The Constitutional Reform Act 2005 contains provisions which give some protection to all courts against political pressures (see Section 7.7.3).

One reason for creating the court was to enhance public understanding of and confidence in the judicial system. To this end its proceedings are filmed for the benefit of the media (who so far have shown limited interest), it has an excellent website and its premises are accessible to the public, including information and exhibitions.

7.7.3 The executive and the judiciary: the Lord Chancellor and the Attorney General

Before the Constitutional Reform Act 2005 came into force, the office of Lord Chancellor violated the separation of functions in respect of all three branches. Often described as a walking contradiction of the separation of powers, the office was created by Edward the Confessor (1042–66). As the King's secretary and the holder of ecclesiastical office ('the conscience of the King'), during the medieval period the Lord Chancellor became primarily concerned with legal processes, being both judge and administrator. He was the nominal head of the judiciary and was responsible for most judicial appointments (see Section 7.8.2). The Lord Chancellor also presided over the House of Lords but unlike the Speaker of the Commons had no power to control proceedings since the House regulates itself collectively (Chapter 13).

More importantly the Lord Chancellor, also known as the Secretary of State for Justice, is currently the minister responsible for the administration of the courts, legal aid, human rights, constitutional reform and the electoral system. The Lord Chancellor is in formal status superior to the Prime Minister and has a higher salary and pension than other ministers (Lord Chancellor's Pension Act 1832). However like other ministers the Lord Chancellor is appointed and dismissed by the Prime Minister and has no security of tenure.

Before the 2005 Act there was therefore a potential conflict of interest in the Lord Chancellor's functions (see *McGonnell v UK* [2000]: similar role in the Channel Isles). However it is arguable that the overlapping roles of the Lord Chancellor supported rather than infringed the separation of powers by acting as a buffer or lubricant between the three branches. As a member of the House of Lords and therefore unelected, he had a certain independence from party politics. As a spending minister, he could seek to ensure that the courts are properly resourced, and as a judge could defend the judiciary against executive interference.

On the other hand as a member of the government, the Lord Chancellor was bound by collective ministerial responsibility (see Section 15.7.1) and had no security of tenure to stand up to the Prime Minister. Unlike other judicial offices there were no qualifications for appointment. For example the Lord Chancellor between 2003 and 2007 was a barrister who was formerly a flatmate of the Prime Minister. It has also been argued that our constitution should evolve according to custom and tradition and not be engineered and that the antiquity of the office is evidence that it is good. This kind of argument succeeded in so far as the historic title and ceremonial trappings of the office have been retained.

The Constitutional Reform Act 2005 removes the Lord Chancellor as Speaker of the House of Lords, which now elects its own Speaker. He also ceases to be head of the judiciary, transferring this role to the Lord Chief Justice as President of the Courts of England and Wales (s 7). The Lord Chancellor is now primarily an ordinary minister, remaining in charge of the Ministry of Justice, which controls the administrative and financial aspects of the courts. The courts must bid for public money just like any other department so that for example legal aid (an essential element of access to justice) competes for resources with other government departments (Access to Justice Act 1999). This could distort the judicial process in favour of taking short cuts. The Lord Chancellor retains a role in connection with the appointment of judges (see Section 7.8.2).

The Lord Chancellor need not be a lawyer or a member of the House of Lords but must be qualified by experience as a minister or member of either House of Parliament, or practising or academic lawyer (Constitutional Reform Act 2005, s 2). The special access that judges had to Parliament through the Lord Chancellor is replaced by section 5(1), which empowers the Chief Justice of any part of the UK to lay before Parliament or the relevant devolved assembly written representations on matters relating to the judiciary or the administration of justice that appear to him to be of importance. On appointment the Lord Chancellor must swear an oath to protect the rule of law and judicial independence and 'to discharge my duty to ensure the provision of resources for the efficient and effective support of the courts for which I am responsible' (s 17).

The Attorney General also has conflicting roles, being a member of the government and of Parliament and the government's chief legal adviser. He plays a part in the judicial process, particularly in relation to decisions to prosecute and is responsible for bringing legal actions against public bodies on behalf of the public interest (see Section 15.6).

7.8 Checks and balances

Checks and balances involve each branch having some control over the others but also require each branch to be protected against interference by the others. The checks and balances concept may therefore conflict with other aspects of the separation of powers. In the UK, in keeping with the 'insider' tradition, but violating republican aspirations to equality and citizenship, many checks and balances, such as the various commissions and committees dealing with standards of government, are not legally enforceable (Chapter 5).

Readers should identify examples of checks and balances throughout the book. Some highlights will briefly be discussed here.

7.8.1 The executive and the legislature

- The Prime Minister can advise the Queen to dissolve Parliament but it must meet again within a year. It is proposed to limit this power (see Section 24.1).
- The Queen in an emergency could invoke her royal prerogative powers to dismiss the Prime Minister, dissolve Parliament or refuse to dissolve Parliament (Section 14.4).
- Individual ministers must appear before Parliament and explain the conduct of their departments.
- The executive must resign if it loses the support of the House of Commons, leading to a dissolution if an alternative government cannot command the support of Parliament.

- The House of Lords, the composition of which is not dominated by the executive, could be regarded a partial check over the executive. However under the Parliament Acts 1911 and 1949 the House of Lords cannot veto a bill introduced in the Commons, other than a bill to prolong the life of Parliament and certain other minor exceptions. In *R (Jackson) v A-G* [2005] the House of Lords disagreed but left open whether there might be exceptional cases – for example where the executive was attempting to subvert fundamental democratic principles or abolish judicial review – where the Parliament Acts could not be used (see [20], [41], [101], [102], [139], [176]–[178]).

7.8.2 The executive and the judiciary: judicial appointments

The executive has an input into judicial appointments on the basis that a democratically accountable element is desirable. A direct legislative input such as the hearings by Congress used in the US would create a risk that judicial appointments and behaviour would be politically partisan. On the other hand since judges make decisions with political consequences and have considerable scope to be influenced by political preferences it is arguable that their political views should be brought into the open.

There are checks and balances to safeguard judicial appointments. These were put in place by the Constitutional Reform Act 2005, replacing a much criticised informal regime for judicial appointments which was in the hands of the Lord Chancellor and, in the case of appointments to the Court of Appeal and House of Lords, the Prime Minister. However there will still be a limited political input by the Lord Chancellor.

The centrepiece of the new process is an independent Judicial Appointments Commission, which in substance will make most judicial appointments under the 2005 Act. Appointments are made either by the Queen on the recommendation of the Lord Chancellor or in the case of lay magistrates and certain other junior judges by the Lord Chancellor directly (Constitutional Reform Act 2005, s 14; Courts Act 2003, s 10). The Lord Chancellor can recommend or appoint only a person selected by the Judicial Appointments Commission or in the case of Supreme Court judges and certain senior judicial officers a special commission or panel.

There are elaborate arrangements to ensure the independence of the Commission. Its 15 members are appointed by the Queen on the recommendation of the Lord Chancellor. It must comprise a lay chair plus five judges, one of each level, one practising solicitor and barrister, one tribunal member, one lay magistrate and five lay members (Constitutional Reform Act 2005, Sch 12). The senior judicial element must be chosen by the Judges' Council, which is a representative body. The lay members must be selected by a panel of four persons. These comprise a lay chair (who must not be a lawyer, judge, MP or member of the Commission or its staff) selected by the Lord Chancellor with the agreement of the Lord Chief Justice, the Lord Chief Justice, a person nominated by the chair and the chair of the Commission. Civil servants are excluded from membership of the Commission. The Lord Chancellor, with the agreement of the Lord Chief Justice and subject to the approval of Parliament, can increase the number of members. Commissioners hold office for a fixed term that is renewable but cannot be more than ten years in total. They can be removed on the recommendation of the Lord Chancellor on the grounds of criminal conviction, bankruptcy, failure to perform duties, unfitness or inability.

The Supreme Court, which from 2009 replaced the House of Lords as the highest appeal tribunal, is subject to special provisions. Its first members were the present Law

Lords. Thereafter its members are to be appointed by the Queen on the recommendation of the Prime Minister, who must recommend the person notified to him by the Lord Chancellor, who in turn must recommend a person selected by a special Selection Commission (ss 26, 28). This Commission comprises the President and Deputy President of the Supreme Court, one non-legally qualified member of the Judicial Appointments Commission and their equivalents in Scotland and Northern Ireland, nominated by the Lord Chancellor on the recommendation of the appropriate body. The Commission must consult the senior judges, the Lord Chancellor and the leaders of the devolved governments.

A member of the Supreme Court must have held high judicial office for at least 2 years or satisfied the judicial eligibility condition (below) for at least 15 years or practised in the senior courts for at least 15 years (s 25). Thus persons without judicial experience could be appointed. Selection must be solely on 'merit' (undefined) and the judges between them must have knowledge or experience in practice of the law of each part of the UK, thus acknowledging the differences between English law and that of the devolved regimes (s 27).

Appointments of the Lord Chief Justice, Heads of Divisions and Lords Justices of Appeal are made by the Queen on the recommendation of the Lord Chancellor following selection by a panel of four comprising the chair of the Commission, a lay member of the Commission and two prescribed judges (ss 67, 71, 76, 80). Similar provision applies to the Senior President of Tribunals main tribunals (s 75(A–G)) Appointments to the High Court and the lower courts are made by the Queen or the Lord Chancellor, in both cases following a selection by the Commission (s 85).

Appointments must be made solely on merit (s 63), subject to the appointee being of 'good character' (undefined). Subject to this, 'diversity' must be encouraged. The Lord Chancellor may request an appointment to be made and issue procedural guidance to the Commission (s 65). Judges of the main courts and some tribunals have traditionally been appointed from a pool of experienced practising lawyers. Under sections 50 and 51 of the Tribunals Court and Enforcement Act 2007 this pool has been widened in the form of the 'judicial eligibility condition', which enables members of other designated professions such as legal executives and accountants to be eligible for judicial appointment. This contrasts with the position in other European countries where there is a separate judicial profession. The UK system has the advantage of drawing on talented people from outside government who are familiar with the workings of the court process. The disadvantage is that this might reinforce the perception of the legal system as a closed elite.

In relation to all levels of appointment the powers of the Lord Chancellor are similar (Constitutional Reform Act 2005, ss 29, 73, 82, 90). The commission or panel must submit one name to the Lord Chancellor, who cannot put forward any other name. He can reject a nomination or refer it back for reconsideration but in either case once only. He can reject only on the ground that the candidate is not 'suitable' and require reconsideration on the ground of inadequate evidence of suitability or evidence of unsuitability. He must give reasons. If the Lord Chancellor rejects a nomination, the same name cannot be put forward again for that vacancy. Where a selection has been referred for reconsideration and the same name is put forward the Lord Chancellor must accept it. If a different name is put forward he can reject this. However, where a selection has been referred for reconsideration and not chosen again, the Lord Chancellor can put forward the original name. In the case of the Supreme Court a reconsideration can also be required if the judges between them would not have knowledge or experience in practice of the law of each part of the UK.

These provisions are designed to make it difficult for any interest group to dominate the appointment process. However, given the vagueness of the appointment criteria and the fact that the government system in the UK is pervaded by informal personal networks, it is doubtful whether it is possible to ensure that the appointment process is fully independent or likely to widen the range of candidates.

These provisions do not apply to the appointments of lay magistrates or to tribunal appointments. Although magistrates deal with relatively minor matters they account for the majority of criminal cases. Magistrates are appointed by the Lord Chancellor (Courts Act 2003, s 10), who may seek advice from the Judicial Appointments Commission and must consult locally (Constitutional Reform Act 2005, s 106). Most tribunal members are appointed by the Lord Chancellor on the recommendation of the Commission, in some cases from a pool of specialists in the area of the tribunal's work.

The changes made by the Constitutional Reform Act can be criticised from three directions. Firstly some might regard them merely as cosmetic tinkering, ignoring wider questions of principle such as the independence and accountability of the judges, whether positive measures should be taken to widen the pool from which judges are selected, whether the Supreme Court should be confined to important constitutional issues and whether it should be able to overrule Acts of Parliament. Secondly traditionalists might regard the reforms as expensive, disruptive and unnecessary in the light of the (to them) successful accommodation achieved by the existing arrangements. Thirdly those with a utilitarian bent might consider the proposals a wasted opportunity for fine tuning of detailed matters such as the reorganisation of the mechanisms for appeals.

7.8.3 The removal of judges

Senior judges – that is judges of the High Court and above – have security of tenure designed to protect their independence. As a result of the 1688 revolution they hold office during 'good behaviour' (Act of Settlement 1700, provisions now repealed). In itself this is hardly conducive to independence since what matters is who decides whether they have misbehaved. Today they can be dismissed by the Crown following a resolution of both Houses of Parliament (an important constitutional role for the House of Lords) and probably then only for misbehaviour (Supreme Court Act 1981, s 11(3); Appellate Jurisdiction Act 1876, s 6). An alternative interpretation of these provisions is that the Crown can dismiss a judge for misbehaviour without an address from Parliament, but on an address a judge can be dismissed irrespective of misbehaviour. Section 33 of the Constitutional Reform Act 2005, which applies similar provisions to the new Supreme Court, continues the ambiguity. No judge has been subjected to these provisions since the nineteenth century, when a judge was dismissed for embezzling court funds.

In the case of judges of Northern Ireland and Scotland there is the additional safeguard of a Special Tribunal (Constitutional Reform Act 2005, ss 133, 135; Scotland Act 1998, s 95).

In exceptional circumstances judges can be removed by the Lord Chancellor on medical grounds (Supreme Court Act 1981, s 11(8)). The Lord Chancellor can also suspend a judge pending an address or on grounds of criminality (s 108). Senior judges must retire at 70 (Judicial Pensions and Retirement Act 1993).

Other judges do not have full security of tenure. They hold office under various statutes that make different provisions for dismissal.

- Circuit and district judges can be dismissed by the Lord Chancellor for incapacity or misbehaviour (Courts Act 1971, s 17; County Courts Act 1984, s 11; Courts Act 2003, s 22).
- Lay magistrates can be removed by the Lord Chancellor for incapacity or misbehaviour, persistent failure to meet standards of competence prescribed by the Lord Chancellor and declining or neglecting their duties (Courts Act 2003, s 11).
- Justices' clerks, who advise lay justices, are civil servants and have no security of tenure. They are appointed by the Lord Chancellor (Courts Act 2003, s 27), and can presumably be dismissed on the same basis as other civil servants.
- Part-time judges (recorders) who hear criminal cases are appointed for fixed periods renewable by the Lord Chancellor (Courts Act 1971).
- Tribunal members are usually appointed for fixed terms either by a minister or by the Lord Chancellor and in some cases can be dismissed only with the consent of the Lord Chancellor (Tribunals and Inquiries Act 1992). Most judicial salaries can be reduced only by Parliament (Judges' Remuneration Act 1965; Constitutional Reform Act 2005, s 14).

There is a Judicial Appointments and Conduct Ombudsman empowered to investigate complaints concerning appointments and disciplinary matters and to report to the Lord Chancellor (Constitutional Reform Act 2005, ss 62, 99–105, 110–13). The report is apparently not published.

7.8.4 Judicial review

The courts provide a check over the executive by means of judicial review in the Administrative Court, where they try to draw a line between the *legality* of government action, which they are entitled to police, and the *merits* of government action, meaning whether a government decision is good or bad, which is a matter for Parliament. However the limits of judicial review are vaguely defined. In some cases the courts will refuse to intervene or intervene only selectively. How this balance is struck is a controversial question (see Section 19.7.1).

In *R v Secretary of State, ex p Fire Brigades Union* [1995], Lord Mustill said:

> It is a feature of the peculiarly British conception of the separation of powers that Parliament, the executive and the courts each have their distinct and largely exclusive domain. Parliament has a legally unchallengeable right to make whatever laws it thinks right. The executive carries on the administration of the country in accordance with the powers conferred on it by law. The courts interpret the laws and see that they are obeyed. This requires the courts to step into the territory which belongs to the executive, not only to verify that the powers asserted accord with the substantive law created by Parliament, but also that the manner in which they are exercised conforms with the standards of fairness which Parliament must have intended. Concurrently with this judicial function Parliament has its own special means of ensuring that the executive in the exercise of delegated functions, performs in a way that Parliament finds appropriate. Ideally it is these latter methods which should be used to check executive errors and excesses; for it is the task of Parliament and the executive in tandem, not of the courts, to govern the country. In recent

> years however, the employment in practice of these specifically parliamentary remedies has on occasion been perceived as falling short and sometimes well short of what was needed to bring the performance of the executive in line with the law and with the minimum standards of fairness implicit in every parliamentary delegation of a decision making function. To avoid a vacuum in which the citizen would be left without protection against a misuse of executive powers the courts have had no option but to occupy the dead ground in a manner and in areas of public life, which could not have been foreseen 30 years ago. (at 267)

In this case Lord Mustill was in a dissenting minority that refused to intervene in a decision of the Home Secretary not to make an order bringing into force a new Act dealing with criminal injuries compensation, but to introduce another, less generous scheme under royal prerogative powers. He considered that this was a matter for Parliament itself. The majority however considered that the matter was appropriate for the court as a check on executive discretion. They held that although they could not require the Home Secretary to bring the Act into force, they could quash the prerogative scheme and ensure that he kept the matter under review. Thus different aspects of the separation of powers may conflict.

7.8.5 Parliament and the courts

According to traditional doctrine Parliament has unlimited lawmaking power and an Act of Parliament cannot be overturned in the courts. However the courts can decide whether a document is a genuine Act of Parliament, a proposition that raises important issues (see Section 8.4.3). The courts also check Parliament since they have power to interpret statutes independently and can do so in the light of the moral values associated with the rule of law (see Section 6.6). On the other hand the intentions of the democratic branch must be respected, so a compromise must be struck based on the limits of interpretation, although these are uncertain. In *Duport Steels Ltd v Sirs* [1980], Lord Scarman said:

> the constitution's separation of powers, or more accurately functions, must be observed if judicial independence is not to be put at risk ... confidence in the judicial system will be replaced by fear of it becoming uncertain and arbitrary in its application. Society will then be ready for Parliament to cut the power of the judges. (at 551)

He meant that the judges must observe the law by sticking to the language of legislation even at the expense of their own views of justice or policy.

The Humans Rights Act 1998 attempts to strike a balance between the three branches by requiring the courts to scrutinise acts of all three branches in the light of the main provisions of the ECHR and to interpret legislation if possible to comply with the ECHR. However Parliament can override Convention rights by using very clear language. The court cannot set aside such an Act but can make a non-binding declaration of incompatibility in respect of an Act that it considers to be incompatible with the ECHR (see Section 20.3.). However some judges have suggested that in extreme circumstances the courts might overturn an Act of Parliament (see Section 8.4.5).

In relation to statutory interpretation *Pepper v Hart* [1993] presents problems. The traditional approach based on the separation of powers has been that the courts should not look at what was said in Parliament as an aid to statutory interpretation. The intention of Parliament is assumed to be identified by the objective language of the statute. However the courts can always consider background material such as official reports as evidence of the policy behind a statute, a distinction that might be regarded as artificial.

In *Pepper v Hart* the House of Lords held that, where the language of an Act is ambiguous, the court can look in *Hansard* (the official record of the proceedings of the House) to discover what the promoters of the Act (usually ministers) intended on the basis of statements made in Parliament. Thus if applied liberally *Pepper v Hart* could threaten the separation of powers by putting the executive in a privileged position over both Parliament and the courts. A statute is the collective enterprise of Parliament, over which the executive should not have special control. There is also a rule of law issue in the sense that a statute should be read as understood by a member of the public (see Lord Hoffmann in *Robinson v Secretary of State for Northern Ireland* [2002] at [40]).

Later cases have taken a cautious approach to *Pepper v Hart*, emphasising that it is for the courts to decide what a statute means and that the statements of ministers, however explicit, cannot control the meaning. In *R (Jackson) v A-G* [2005] at [97] Lord Steyn suggested that trying to discover the intentions of government from ministerial statements made in Parliament is constitutionally objectionable. It has also been stressed that such statements have not generally proved helpful and that *Pepper v Hart* should be applied strictly according to its particular circumstances – namely where the legislation is obscure or ambiguous or would lead to absurd results, and then only if the statements to be used are clear (*R v Secretary of State for Environment, Transport and the Regions, ex p Spath Holme* [2000] at [211]; *Wilson v First County Trust* [2003] at [58], [59], [139], [140]; *R (Jackson) v A-G* [2005] at [40], [98], [172]).

In *Spath Holme* a distinction was made between the meaning of a specific provision and the general purpose of an Act. A minister's statement in *Hansard* cannot be used to determine the latter unless the executive attempts to enforce a statute in a way that contradicts a statement made by the minister when promoting the statute in Parliament. Here the executive might be prevented from contradicting what was said. Lords Nicholls and Cook dissenting found this distinction artificial.

In *Wilson* the House of Lords held that, apparently in all cases, *Hansard* can be used to discover factual and policy background to an Act, including its likely impact, but not to evaluate ministerial statements as to its rationale. For example in *Culnane v Morris* [2006] the court was aided by the parliamentary debates in concluding that section 10 of the Defamation Act 1952 was not aimed at altering the general law relating to privilege in defamation (see Section 22.5; see also *Beckett v Midlands Electricity plc* [2001]at [30], [34], [38]).

The courts cannot interfere with internal parliamentary proceedings, give orders to Parliament or penalise anyone in respect of things said in Parliament. However statements made in Parliament can be used as evidence in court (see Section 11.6). Conversely Parliament restrains itself from commenting on judicial cases in process, although there are no legal safeguards in this respect.

Summary

- The doctrine of the separation of powers means that government power should be divided into legislative, executive and judicial functions, each with its own distinctive personnel and processes, and that each branch of government should be checked so that no one body can dominate the others.
- In Montesquieu's version, the separation of powers is complemented by the idea of the mixed constitution in which different class interests check and balance each other, particularly in the legislature. There is a vestige of the mixed constitution in the institutions of monarchy and the House of Lords. However the idea of the mixed constitution shorn of its historical association with a hereditary aristocracy might still be valuable as providing a check over crude majoritarian democracy, linking with the idea of deliberative democracy.
- The question of judicial independence can be regarded as an aspect of the separation of powers but could be considered an issue in its own right irrespective of other aspects of the doctrine. Judicial independence is safeguarded by the right to a fair trial and public trial under the ECHR. This applies more stringently to ordinary courts than to administrative bodies. There is a tension between judicial independence and ensuring that judges are accountable.
- The separation of powers comprises separation of function, institutions and personnel and includes the notion of checks and balances. The particular blend in any given case depends on the preoccupations of the particular country. There is little agreement among writers as to whether the separation of powers is a valuable idea or in what sense it applies in the UK. Separation of powers ideas have influenced our constitutional arrangements but in a pragmatic and unsystematic way.
- In the UK there is no strict separation of personnel, particularly between the legislature and the executive. Concern about executive domination is the main driving force.
- The Constitutional Reform Act 2005 attempted to strengthen the separation of powers by creating a Supreme Court to replace the Appellate Committee of the House of Lords, injecting an independent element into judicial appointments and removing the Lord Chancellor's roles as head of the judiciary and Speaker of the House of Lords. It could be that aspects of these reforms, particularly in relation to the Lord Chancellor, strengthen institutional separation but weaken checks and balances.
- The power of the courts to review government action creates a tension between functional separation of powers and checks and balances.
- There are concerns about the relationship between the courts and Parliament, in particular in the context of the use of parliamentary proceedings in the interpretation of statutes.

Exercises

7.1 'The separation of powers is a misleading and irrelevant doctrine'. Discuss.

7.2 What safeguards are there for judicial independence in the UK constitution? Are they comprehensive?

7.3 'In the government of this commonwealth, the legislative department shall never exercise the executive and judicial powers, or either of them: the executive shall never exercise the legislative and judicial powers, or either of them: the judicial shall never exercise the legislative and executive powers, or either of them: to the end it may be a government of laws and not of men' (Massachusetts Constitution 1780, Art XXX). Does the UK constitution live up to this?

Exercises cont'd

7.4 It is sometimes said that the UK constitution embodies a 'fusion' between the legislature and the executive. Do you agree? Is it desirable that the composition of the executive and legislature be separate?

7.5 'In some quarters the *Pepper v Hart* principle is currently under something of a judicial cloud ... In part this seems ... to be due to continued misunderstanding of the limited role ministerial statements have in this field' (Lord Nicholls in *R (Jackson) v A–G*, (2005) [65]). Explain and critically discuss.

7.6 The replacement of the Appellate Committee of the House of Lords 'put[s] the relationship between the executive, the legislature and the judiciary on a modern footing, which takes account of people's expectations about the independence and transparency of the judicial system' (Department of Constitutional Affairs, 2003). Discuss in the light of the Constitutional Reform Act 2005.

7.7 Does the present role of the Lord Chancellor comply with the separation of powers?

7.8 Critically assess the roles of (i) the Home Secretary and (ii) the Attorney General in relation to the separation of powers.

7.9 Bill, a High Court judge, is alleged to have been sexually harassing the junior staff of the High Court Registry. Parliament is not sitting and the Lord Chancellor advises the Queen to make an example of Bill by dismissing him forthwith. Advise Bill. What would be the position if Bill was (i) a circuit judge or (ii) a lay justice?

Further reading

Barber, 'Prelude to the Separation of Powers' (2001) 61 CLJ 59

Barendt, 'Separation of Powers and Constitutional Government' [1995] PL 599

Barendt, *An Introduction to Constitutional Law* (Clarendon Press 1998) ch 7

Bingham, *A New Supreme Court for the United Kingdom* (Constitution Unit 2002)

Claus, 'Montesquieu's Mistakes and the True Meaning of Separation' (2005) 25 OJLS 419

Cooke, 'The Law Lords: An Endangered Heritage' (2003) 119 LQR 49

Department of Constitutional Affairs, *Constitutional Reform: A Supreme Court for the United Kingdom* (2003)

Department of Constitutional Affairs, *Judicial Diversity Strategy* (2006)

Ewing, 'The Unbalanced Constitution' in Campbell, Ewing and Tompkins (eds), *Sceptical Essays on Human Rights* (Oxford University Press 2001)

Hale, 'A Supreme Judicial Leader' in Andenas and Fairgrieve (eds), *Tom Bingham and the Transformation of the Law* (Oxford University Press 2009)

Kavanagh, '*Pepper v Hart* and Matters of Constitutional Principle' (2005) 121 LQR 98

Keene, 'The Independence of the Judge' in Andenas and Fairgrieve (eds), *Tom Bingham and the Transformation of the Law* (Oxford University Press 2009)

McHarg, 'What Is Delegated Legislation?' [2006] PL 539

Munro, *Studies in Constitutional Law* (2nd edn, Butterworths 1999) ch 9

Sedley, 'The Long Sleep' in Andenas and Fairgrieve (eds) *Tom Bingham and the Transformation of the Law* (Oxford University Press 2009)

Steyn, 'The Weakest and Least Dangerous Department of Government' [1997] PL 84

Further reading cont'd

Steyn, '*Pepper and Hart*: A Re-examination' (2001) 21 OJLS 59

Vogenauer, 'A Retreat from *Pepper v Hart*? A Reply to Lord Steyn' (2005) 25 OJLS 629 (see also Sales, 'A Footnote to Professor Vogenauer's Reply to Lord Steyn' (2006) 26 OJLS 585)

Webber, 'Supreme Courts, Independence and Democratic Agency' (2004) 24 LS 55

Woodhouse, 'The Constitutional and Political Implications of a United Kingdom Supreme Court' (2004) 24 LS 134 (see *Constitutional Innovation: The Creation of a Supreme Court for the United Kingdom; Domestic, Comparative and International Reflections* (2004) 24 LS Special Issue)

Chapter 8

Parliamentary supremacy

The classic account given by Dicey of the doctrine of the supremacy of Parliament, pure and absolute as it was, can now be seen to be out of place in the modern United Kingdom. (per Lord Steyn, *R (Jackson) v A-G* [2005] at [106])

8.1 Introduction

The doctrine of the separation of powers leaves open the question of who has the last word when there is stalemate between the three branches of government. The UK constitution has traditionally answered this by entrusting unlimited lawmaking power to Parliament. Thus the doctrine of parliamentary supremacy or sovereignty maintains that Parliament has unlimited legal power to enact any law without external restraint.

> The classical doctrine of parliamentary sovereignty was most famously stated by Dicey (1915, 37–38): 'Parliament means, in the mouth of a lawyer,... the [Queen], the House of Lords and the House of Commons; these three bodies acting together may be aptly described as the "[Queen] in Parliament, and constitute Parliament'. The principle of parliamentary sovereignty means neither more nor less than this, namely, that Parliament thus defined has, under the English constitution, the right to make or unmake any law whatever and further that no person or body is recognised by the law of England as having the right to override or set aside the legislation of Parliament.

Parliamentary supremacy is a legal principle, meaning that a law formally made by Parliament, in the above sense, must conclusively be accepted as valid by the courts (*Pickin v British Railways Board* [1974]). Dicey was careful to distinguish legal sovereignty from political sovereignty. He described legal sovereignty as 'the power of law making unrestricted by any legal limit' and contrasted this with political sovereignty, meaning the body 'the will of which is ultimately obeyed by the citizens of the state' (1915, 70). (There is however no reason there should be a single sovereign in this sense; citizens might obey different bodies in different contexts.)

Dicey recognised both 'internal' and 'external' political limits on the lawmaker. Internal limits are those inherent in the rules and practices of Parliament. Within Parliament a combination of the convention that requires the Queen to assent to all legislation and the law that subordinates the House of Lords to the House of Commons makes the House of Commons in practice the supreme body. The political and moral pressures imposed by constitutional conventions, patronage and party discipline are also internal limits.

The external limits consist of what those subject to the law are prepared to accept. Parliament cannot in practice pass any law it wishes. Moreover valid laws might be condemned as unconstitutional in a broad sense. Thus in *Madzimbamuto v Lardner-Burke* [1969], Lord Reid said, '[it] is often said that it would be unconstitutional for the UK Parliament to do certain things, meaning that the moral, political and other reasons against doing them are so strong that most people would regard it as highly improper if Parliament did these things. But that does not mean that it is beyond the powers of Parliament to do such things. If Parliament chose to do any of them the courts could not hold Parliament to account' (at 723).

Both internal and external limits would come into play for example if Parliament attempted to legislate to override the devolved powers of the Scottish Parliament (see Chapter 16). This would undoubtedly be lawful but the 'Sewell Convention' (see Section 16.1), which requires the consent of the Scottish Parliament to such legislation, and the likelihood of political objections act as severe constraints (see Elliott, 2002).

Dicey thought that political sovereignty lay in the electorate and that this would make democracy 'self-correcting' (see Craig, *Public Law and Democracy in the UK and the USA* (Oxford University Press 1991) ch 2). However later in life, particularly after the powers of the House of Lords were curbed in 1911, Dicey realised that the executive was increasingly dominating Parliament (1915, 'Introduction').

However we should not take an extreme legalistic position and claim that law and politics are entirely separate, since the fact that Parliament has enacted a law means that the community has indicated that it is politically important enough to justify the use of state force. Indeed judges have recognised that at this level, which is the foundational principle of the constitution, law and politics are inseparable (see *R (Jackson) v A-G* [2005] at [126]). Thus we might be concerned if the law is out of step with political reality.

Indeed Dicey's version of the doctrine of parliamentary supremacy is increasingly being questioned. In the absence of a written constitution, the foundations of the doctrine of parliamentary supremacy, resting as they do on no more than widespread acceptance, look frail.

Challenges to parliamentary supremacy include:

- External legal requirements, notably those of the EU.
- Pressures from within, such as Scottish devolution, mean that the legal doctrine is out of line with political reality.
- Parliament might be able to redefine or redesign itself, effectively limiting its own supremacy, for example by requiring a referendum for some legislation.
- The claim that the 'rule of law' is supreme, meaning that the supreme authority is the common law. In the absence of a written constitution it is said that the courts 'conferred' sovereignty on Parliament and can take it away again.

Even if it is true that political power tends to end up in the hands of a single leader, there is no logical reason why there should be a single legal sovereign with unlimited powers. For example in the US power is carefully divided so that no single entity has unlimited legal power. Even the last word, the power to change the constitution, is divided in complex ways between different groups who must agree to make the change. However as Hobbes argued (see Chapter 2), it may be necessary as a last resort to give absolute power to a single body to deal with an emergency, including the power to decide whether an emergency exists. (Even here safeguards can be put in place.)

8.2 The meaning of 'Act of Parliament'

Parliamentary sovereignty concerns only lawmaking power. Specifically it is concerned only with an Act of Parliament (a statute). An Act of Parliament, as the preamble to every Act reminds us, is an Act of the monarch with the consent of the House of Lords and the House of Commons: the Queen in Parliament. In certain circumstances however the consent of the House of Lords can be omitted under the Parliament Acts of 1911 and 1949. Even if we believe that the House of Commons is the political sovereign, a resolution of the House of Commons has in itself no legal force, except in relation to the internal proceedings of the House (*Bowles v Bank of England* [1913]; *Stockdale v Hansard* [1839]).

Dicey's legal sovereign is therefore divided, comprising three bodies: Queen, Lords and Commons. Only in combination can they exercise the power of Parliament. Thus Blackstone, who defended parliamentary supremacy in the eighteenth century, linked the doctrine with that of the mixed constitution (see Section 7.2). Indeed Dicey denied that there was a logical need for an ultimate sovereign (1915, 143), merely pointing out that the evidence suggested that we have in fact adopted the doctrine of parliamentary supremacy.

The courts therefore obey not Parliament as such but an Act of Parliament, a statute. Two questions arise from this. First, what rules create an Act of Parliament? Second, to what extent can the courts investigate whether these rules have been obeyed? There are complex procedural rules for producing statutes but not all of them affect the validity of a statute.

Three levels of rule can be distinguished:

1. The basic definition of a statute as a document that received the assent of the three institutions constituting the Queen in Parliament: Queen, Lords and Commons. The royal assent signed by the Queen is usually notified to each House separately as a formality but is sometimes pronounced by commissioners before both Houses assembled in the House of Lords (Royal Assent Act 1967). The preamble to a statute invariably recites that the required assents have been given. A court is not bound by a document that does not appear on its face to have received the necessary assents but conversely must accept the validity of a document that does so appear (*Prince's Case* [1606]). This is called the 'enrolled Act rule' and precludes the courts from investigating whether the proper internal procedures have in fact been complied with (*Edinburgh & Dalkeith Rly v Wauchope* [1842]). The official version of a statute was traditionally enrolled upon the Parliament Roll. Today there is no Parliament Roll as such, but two official copies of the Act are in the House of Lords' Library and the Public Record Office.
2. In some cases the basic requirements have been modified by statute. In principle the court can investigate whether statutory requirements have been complied with. In particular under the Parliament Acts 1911 and 1949, if the Commons so decides and subject to important exceptions, a bill can become law without the consent of the House of Lords after a delaying period (see Section 11.5). The Parliament Act 1911 partly excludes the courts by providing that a certificate given by the Speaker

to the effect that the requirements of the Act have been complied with is 'conclusive for all purposes and shall not be questioned in any court of law' (s 3). However this does not prevent the court from deciding the prior question of whether the bill falls within the 1911 Act at all (see *R (Jackson) v A-G* [2005] at [51]). Similarly the Regency Act 1937 provides that the royal assent can be given by a specified Regent, usually the next in line to the throne, if the monarch is under 18, absent abroad or ill and in certain other events. In this case the court may also be able to investigate whether the Act has been properly applied.

3. There is a complex network of rules concerning the composition and internal procedure of each House. These include the various stages of passage of a bill, voting procedures and the law governing qualifications for membership of either House. They comprise a mixture of statute, convention and the 'law and custom of Parliament' enforced by the House itself. It is settled that ordinary courts have no jurisdiction to enquire into any matters related to the internal affairs of the House. Quite apart from the enrolled Act rule (above), these are matters of parliamentary privilege and are exclusively within the jurisdiction of the House itself (see Section 11.7). This is true even if it is alleged that the bill has been introduced fraudulently (see *Pickin v British Railways Board* [1974]).

8.3 The three facets of parliamentary supremacy

Dicey's doctrine has three separate aspects:

1. Parliament has unlimited lawmaking power in the sense that it can make any kind of law.
2. The legal validity of laws made by Parliament cannot be questioned by any other body.
3. A Parliament cannot bind a future Parliament.

These do not stand or fall together and we shall discuss them separately.

8.3.1 Freedom to make any kind of law

Dicey claimed that Parliament can make any laws it wishes irrespective of fairness, justice and practicality. For example the UK courts are bound to obey a statute which concerns anywhere in the world. Whether or not the relevant overseas courts would recognise it is immaterial (eg *Manuel v A-G* [1982]: Canada). Parliament can also do the physically impossible. It has been said that Parliament cannot make a man a woman, or a woman a man, but this is misleading. The so-called laws of nature are not rules at all. They are simply recurrent facts. A statute which enacted that all men must be regarded as women and vice versa would be impractical but would be legally valid.

According to Dicey, Parliament can enact laws that are grossly immoral or unjust. Dicey relied on examples of valid statutory provisions that are arguably grossly unjust. However these do not prove that the courts would apply a statute that they considered even more unjust. Nevertheless modern cases support Dicey. They include retrospective legislation (*Burmah Oil Co Ltd v Lord Advocate* [1965]; War Damage Act 1965) and statutes conflicting with international law (see *Mortensen v Peters* [1906]; *Cheney v Conn* [1968]) or with fundamental civil liberties (*R v Jordan* [1967]). However there have been dissenting voices, some of them judicial (see Section 9.4.5).

8.3.2 Parliament cannot be overridden

Firstly, international bodies do not have the power in English law to declare an Act of Parliament invalid. Whether they have the power to do so within the terms of their own system is a different question. In this respect a constitution is like a game: the rules depend on which version of the game you are playing. Secondly, in the event of a conflict between a statute and some other kind of law, the statute must always prevail. However this leaves open the possibility that a statute itself might authorise some other lawmaking authority to override statutes. This was probably achieved by the European Communities Act 1972 (Section 8.4.4) but still leaves it open to Parliament to repeal the Act in question, thereby destroying the authority of the other body.

8.3.3 Parliament cannot bind its successors

In a sense this is a genuine limit on Parliament although it also means that Parliament cannot be restricted by a previous statute, so preserving parliamentary supremacy. This is a vital principle closely associated with democracy, that no generation should be able to tie the hands of the future. For example Edmund Burke argued that the 1688 revolution had permanently enshrined a constitution which included the House of Lords. Thomas Paine answered this as follows:

> Every age and generation must be as free to act for itself, in all cases, as the ages and generations which preceded it. The vanity and presumption of governing beyond the grave is the most ridiculous and insolent of all tyrannies. (1987, 204)

The English courts make it relatively easy to override earlier statutes. They usually apply the 'implied repeal' doctrine, according to which a later statute that on an ordinary reading is inconsistent with an earlier statute impliedly repeals the earlier statute to the extent of the inconsistency. The court is not required to attempt to reconcile the two and it is irrelevant that the earlier Act states that it cannot be repealed (see *Vauxhall Estates Ltd v Liverpool Corp* [1932]; *Ellen Street Estates Ltd v Minister of Health* [1934]). The content of the two statutes must be directly inconsistent. For example in *Thoburn v Sunderland City Council* [2002] (the 'Metric Martyrs' case) a 1985 statute which allowed goods to be sold in pounds and ounces did not impliedly repeal section 2(4) of the European Communities Act 1972, which empowered ministers to make regulations altering Acts of Parliament for the purpose of implementing EC law.

The implied repeal doctrine is sometimes regarded as an essential part of parliamentary supremacy. This is not so. The implied repeal doctrine, although consistent with parliamentary sovereignty, is merely a particular approach to statutory interpretation, albeit one attractive from a democratic point of view. Although Lord Maugham in *Ellen Street Estates* at 597 said that it would be impossible to enact that there shall be no implied repeal, there is nothing to prevent a statute from requiring the courts to interpret legislation as overriding another statute only if express or very clear language is used, thus putting a partial brake on change. For example section 3 of the Human Rights Act 1998 requires all other statutes to be interpreted in accordance with the rights protected by the Act 'if it is possible to do so' (see Section 20.2). Another example might be a provision in a statute stating that it shall be repealed only by an Act which expressly states that it is to do so. It has also been claimed that under common law some statutes and some legal rights are so important that they can be repealed only by express words or possibly by necessary implication. In *Thoburn v Sunderland City*

Council at [62]–[64], Laws LJ stated that a 'constitutional statute', in the sense of a statute 'which conditions the legal relationships between citizen and state in some general overarching manner, or enlarges or diminishes the scope of what are now regarded as fundamental rights', would be so protected.

8.4 Challenging parliamentary supremacy

There are various arguments that Parliament can after all be legally limited. Parliamentary supremacy was a historical response to political circumstances, namely as the focus for rebellion against the Stuart monarchs. It does not follow that the same response is appropriate today. The Victorian period, during which Dicey promoted the doctrine, was one of relative stability and prosperity. The people, or at least the majority, were benefiting from the spoils of empire, and the belief that Parliament, backed by democratic values, could deliver stability and prosperity was still plausible. Popular revolution as experienced elsewhere had been staved off by cautious reforms. Latterly, different forces, both domestic and international, have arisen which have made parliamentary sovereignty appear parochial, politically unreal and intellectually threadbare. These forces include the global economy, devolution, membership of the EU and other international obligations and the increasing powers of the executive over Parliament.

Thus there is no longer a political consensus that Parliament should be legally unlimited and no compelling legal reason why it should be. In the absence of a written constitution enshrining parliamentary supremacy the principle has no foundation other than its general acceptance, from the lawyer's point of view, by courts. Indeed this has led to a counter-argument that the real sovereign is the 'rule of law' as engineered by the courts. The public are of course treated as passive bystanders in the debate.

The main challenges to parliamentary supremacy are as follows.

8.4.1 Grants of independence

If Parliament were to pass an Act giving independence to a piece of territory currently under UK jurisdiction, such as Scotland, could a later Act revoke that independence? For example the Canada Act 1982 provides that 'no Act of the United Kingdom Parliament passed after the Constitution Act 1982 comes into force shall extend to Canada as part of its law' (s 2). Although as a matter of political reality the answer is no, unless the territory in question either consents or is conquered by force, the legal answer is yes as far as the UK courts are concerned (*British Coal Corp v R* [1935]; *Manuel v A-G* [1982]). Dicey therefore remains triumphant. There is however a dictum by Lord Denning in *Blackburn v A-G* [1971] that legal theory must give way to practical politics. All his Lordship seems to be saying is that it would be impossible in a practical sense for Parliament to reverse a grant of independence. On the other hand a legal principle that is so out of line with common sense might well be worth reconsidering.

8.4.2 Acts of Union: was Parliament born unfree?

This is a more substantial challenge. The UK Parliament is the result of two treaties. First the Treaty of Union with Scotland in 1706 created the Parliament of Great Britain out of the former Scottish and English Parliaments. The Treaty required among other things that no laws which concern private rights in Scotland shall be altered 'except for the evident utility of the subjects within Scotland'. There were also powers securing the separate Scottish courts and Presbyterian Church 'for all time coming'. The new Parliament was created by separate Acts of the then Scottish and English Parliaments, giving effect to the treaties. Some Scottish lawyers therefore argue that Parliament was 'born unfree', meaning that the modern Parliament cannot go beyond the terms of the Acts that created it. They suggest that the protected provisions of the Act of Union cannot be altered by Act of Parliament. In effect the Union created a new Parliament combining the qualities of both the old Parliaments. In relation to the protected Scottish provisions, this does not necessarily have the quality of supremacy inherent in the former English Parliament (see Munro, 1999, 137–42). A contrary argument is that parliamentary supremacy is an evolving doctrine that developed after the Acts of Union.

In the case of Northern Ireland, there was a Treaty of Union in 1798 which preserved certain basic rights in Ireland, including the continuance of the Protestant religion and the permanence of the Union itself. The Treaty was confirmed by the Act of Union with Ireland 1800, which created the present UK Parliament. The Act covered the whole of Ireland, but what is now the Republic of Ireland later left the Union. It might be argued that section 1 of the Northern Ireland Act 1998, which provides for the Union to be dissolved if a referendum so votes, would be invalid as contrary to the Act of Union. The 1998 Act makes no express reference to the Act of Union with Ireland, section 2 merely providing that the Act overrides 'previous enactments'. Political circumstances in Northern Ireland make this ambiguity understandable. Section 37 of the Scotland Act 1998 expressly states that the provisions of the Act are to take priority over the Act of Union. This leaves open the question whether an Act can do this at all.

The issue has surfaced in a few cases, in all of which an Act of Parliament was obeyed. In *Ex p Canon Selwyn* [1872] (Ireland) the court denied that it possessed the power to override a statute. In two Scottish cases, *MacCormick v Lord Advocate* [1953] and *Gibson v Lord Advocate* [1975], the Scottish courts were able to avoid the issue by holding that no conflict with the Acts of Union arose. However in both cases the argument in favour of the Acts of Union was regarded as tenable, particularly by Lord Cooper in *MacCormick*. However his Lordship, with the apparent agreement of Lords Keith and Gibson, suggested that the issue might be 'non-justiciable', that is, outside the jurisdiction of the courts and resolvable only by political means. On this view a statute that flouts the Acts of Union may be unconstitutional but not unlawful. In both cases the courts left open the question whether they could interfere if an Act purported to make drastic inroads into the Act of Union, for example by abolishing the whole of Scottish private law (see also *R (Jackson) v A-G* [2006] at [105]: Lord Hope acknowledging that the Acts of Union might not be repealable). Thus the courts carefully steered around a constitutional abeyance (see Section 3.5).

8.4.3 Redefinition theory

Suggested most prominently by Jennings (*The Law and the Constitution* (University of London Press 1959)), the redefinition theory attempts to circumvent the rule that Parliament cannot bind its successors. The argument has various labels, sometimes being called the 'new view', sometimes the 'entrenchment' argument, sometimes the 'manner and form' theory and sometimes the distinction between 'continuing' and 'self-embracing' sovereignty. The redefinition argument is essentially that if Parliament can do anything, it can 'redesign itself either in general or for particular purpose', as Baroness Hale put it in *Jackson* (at [160]). It can do this so as to make it difficult to change an Act that it 'entrenches'; for example an Act might provide that a referendum of the people is required to change certain laws. Whether in any particular case it has done so and what, if any, limits are imposed on the redefined Parliament is a matter of interpretation of the legislation in question. The redefined body can act only within the terms of the law that created it.

Suppose for example that a statute enacts a bill of rights and goes on to say that 'no law shall be passed that is inconsistent with the bill of rights nor shall this statute be repealed expressly or impliedly without a referendum of the people'. What Parliament has done in this example is to add to the existing requirement of Queen, Lords and Commons a further requirement of a referendum, thus redefining itself for the particular purpose of the bill of rights. An entrenched statute can still be repealed but not without following the special procedure. However as long as it does so within those terms, it may be able to change those terms themselves for the future (eg by holding a referendum as to whether in future the referendum requirement should be repealed).

Indeed the Acts of Union (see Section 8.4.2) could be regarded as examples of redefinition of three Parliaments.

The redefinition argument can be supported as follows:

1. There must be rules of law that tell us what counts as an Act of Parliament and these must be logically prior to Parliament, which can speak only through these rules: without them Parliament is merely a rabble of individuals. These rules therefore define Parliament. What these rules currently are is outlined above, namely that an Act of Parliament requires the consent of the Queen, the Lords and the Commons.
2. A document which purports to be an Act of Parliament but which has not been passed according to these basic rules has no legal force, so the courts must ignore it.
3. If Parliament can do anything it can change the rules which define what counts as an Act of Parliament.
4. Parliament arguably has already redefined itself for certain purposes in the Parliament Acts by dispensing with the requirement of House of Lords consent and also under the Regency Acts (above). In *Jackson* the House of Lords held that a law passed without the House of Lords under the Parliament Act procedure was indeed a full Act of Parliament of a kind created by the Parliament Act 1911 and modified by the Parliament Act 1949. The scope of an Act so created depends on the terms of the earlier Act that created it. A majority of their Lordships held that Acts made under the Parliament Acts can do anything that an ordinary Act could do, including probably altering the Parliament Acts themselves, for example to remove exceptions. However Lord Steyn in particular suggested that the court had an inherent power to override Acts that were grossly unconstitutional such as an Act to exclude the courts or to abolish democracy. This is of course a separate argument from the redefinition issue.

The redefinition argument can be attacked on three fronts:

1. If Parliament were to ignore the special procedure by passing a statute in the ordinary way, the courts would simply obey the most recent Act of Parliament and thus treat the special procedure as impliedly repealed. However this misses the point, since according to the redefinition argument a document that has not been produced

under the special procedure is not a valid statute and so must be ignored, just as an ordinary law would be ignored if it did not have the royal assent. Therefore there are no competing statutes for the implied repeal doctrine to engage with.

2. It can be argued that any Act which confers lawmaking power subject to a special procedure is in reality delegating power to a subordinate body since, by definition, subordinate legislation is legislation made under the authority of another body and is inherently restricted by the terms of reference given to it. If this is so, then the superior body can always legislate to override the subordinate. However it is equally possible logically to regard what is happening as a body redefining itself. In both cases the change in the law must be made in accordance with the lawmaking procedure in force at the time. This argument seems to have been rejected in *Jackson* on the basis that whether a law is primary or subordinate depends on the intention of the statute that creates the new lawmaking process.
3. Professor Wade (1955) argues that the meaning of 'Parliament' is 'fixed' by a rule which is 'above and beyond the reach of Parliament': a fundamental constitutional principle which he takes to be common law. Parliament cannot simply make itself supreme, so there must be some independent explanation of why it is so. Wade argues that the explanation lies in the 1688 revolution, which created the fundamental settlement of Queen, Lords and Commons, a rule that is unique in character, a political principle standing outside and above the ordinary legal system and giving it its validity. Wade argues that because this rule gave Parliament its power, it cannot be altered by Parliament at best producing delegated legislation.

Wade accepts that the doctrine of parliamentary supremacy could in political reality be abolished but would regard this as a revolution, that is the introduction of an entirely new basic principle. How will we know whether such a revolution has taken place? Wade would place the matter in the 'keeping of the courts', so that if the courts were to accept the redefinition theory, this would authoritatively signify the 'revolution'.

Wade's approach has several objections (see Gordon, 2009):

- Why should the court be the privileged guardian of the revolution? Surely it is for the courts under the separation of powers doctrine to apply the existing law not to declare what the basis of the constitution is. Wade seems arbitrarily to substitute judicial sovereignty for parliamentary sovereignty
- A change brought about in accordance with the existing law, which was the case with the Parliament Act 1911, is surely worth distinguishing from a revolution that is associated with extra-legal activity if not always violence. Indeed it seems a misuse of language not to do so.
- Even if we accept the idea of Wade's 'higher rule', this does not exclude the redefinition theory. Why should the higher rule, supposedly made by those in charge of the 1688 revolution, not authorise its creature – Parliament – to alter the rule itself?
- Wade has to assume that laws made by the Commons and Queen under the Parliament Acts are not true Acts of Parliament. This is inconsistent with *Jackson*.

There is judicial support for the redefinition theory from former UK territories (see *A-G for New South Wales v Trethowen* [1932]; *Harris v Minister of the Interior* [1952]: South Africa; *Bribery Comr v Ranasinghe* [1965]: Sri Lanka). *Trethowen* went so far as to suggest that the court could grant an injunction to prevent a bill being submitted for royal assent if it did not comply with the entrenched procedure. This seems unlikely to apply in England since the courts have consistently refused to interfere with the conduct of parliamentary proceedings. The issue would arise in the UK if a court were asked to obey a document that failed to comply with an entrenched provision.

However these cases are unreliable authority. They have been explained on the basis that the legislatures in these countries were not truly supreme in the same way as the UK Parliament, since a UK Act had established the powers of the legislatures in question. However in *Harris* the Statute of Westminster 1931 had given the South African Parliament unlimited lawmaking power. Moreover the court stressed that its reasoning did not assume that the legislature was subordinate. Indeed in both *Trethowen* and *Ranasinghe* there were dicta that the same arguments might apply to the UK Parliament. Thus it was said in *Ranasinghe* (at 198) that the legislature can alter the very instrument from which its powers derive.

In *Manuel v A-G* [1983] the Canada Act 1982 was claimed to be invalid in that it was enacted without relevant consents as required by section 4 of the Statute of Westminster 1931, which at the time applied to Canada as a former UK dominion. The purpose of the 1982 Act was to free Canada from its constitutional links with the UK. The Court of Appeal was prepared to recognise the possibility of redefinition. However, as a matter of interpretation, section 4 merely required that the Act had to state on its face that it had received the relevant consents. The 1982 Act did so state and the court could not investigate the internal proceedings of Parliament to see whether the statement was true. Obviously the matter depends on the precise terms of the redefinition in question (a point to watch in any exam question!).

The most important case is *R (Jackson) v A-G* [2005]. The Hunting Act 2004, which outlawed hunting with dogs, had been enacted under the Parliament Acts 1911 and 1949 against persistent opposition from the House of Lords. The Hunting Act was challenged on two main grounds:

- The first ground was that Parliament could not redefine itself, so that a law passed under the 1911 Act could at best be delegated legislation, power being delegated by Parliament in the 1911 Act to the Commons and Queen. Delegated legislation unlike statute can be challenged in the courts. The Hunting Act was passed under the Parliament Act 1949, which shortened the delaying powers of the House of Lords. The 1949 Act was enacted without House of Lords' consent under the 1911 Act's procedure. It was suggested, and assumed to be correct, that unless there is clear authority to do so from the parent Act, a delegate cannot enlarge its own powers. Therefore the 1949 Act was invalid, so that the Hunting Act fell with it.
- The second ground was that even if Parliament could redefine itself, it could not do so under the Parliament Act procedure but needed an ordinary Act of Parliament. It was argued that there are implied limits intended by the 1911 Act which prevent the Parliament Act procedure from being used to further reduce the powers of the Lords. This also made the 1949 Act invalid.

Nine Law Lords held that the 1949 Act and therefore the Hunting Act were lawful and that Acts passed under the Parliament Acts were not delegated legislation. Thus they endorsed the possibility of redefinition although without directly confronting Wade's argument (above). Moreover as regards the scope of the 'redefinition' there was nothing to prevent the Parliament Act 1949 from reducing further the powers of the House of Lords. The matter depended on the interpretation of the 1911 Act. Lord Steyn (at [81]–[86], [91]–[93]) treated the definition of Parliament as a dynamic matter that Parliament itself could change (see also Lord Bingham at [35]–[36], Baroness Hale at [160], Lord Carswell at [174], Lord Browne at [187]).

However caution is required. It was stressed that the 1911 Act did not transfer power to a body other than Parliament or limit the power of the democratic House of Commons. It merely constrained the House of Lords (at [25]). The courts might therefore draw back from accepting a more radical kind of redefinition. Baroness Hale in particular left 'for another day' the question whether Parliament could redefine itself 'upwards', for example by requiring a referendum for a particular measure in addition to the normal procedure (at [163]).

As to the second ground, it was held that since laws made under the Parliament Acts were full statutes, the Parliament Act 1911 was not subject to any implied limitation that would invalidate the 1949 Act. The Hunting Act was therefore valid.

However their Lordships disagreed as to whether the Parliament Acts applied to bills to alter the Parliament Acts themselves. The 1911 Act expressly does not apply to the following (s 2):

- a bill to prolong the life of Parliament beyond five years. This is a safeguard to prevent a government exploiting a Commons majority to avoid an election;
- a private bill, which is a bill concerning specific persons or places, and a bill to confirm a provisional order, a largely unused procedure for approving particular projects;
- a bill introduced in the House of Lords.

These limitations arguably set the boundaries of any redefinition. However they might be overcome in two stages. First, using the Parliament Acts the Commons might alter the 1911 Act itself so as to remove them since the 1911 Act does not expressly exclude this. It would then, using the altered Parliament Acts, pass a statute, for example extending Parliament's life to ten years. Lord Nicholls (at [59]), Lord Steyn (at [79]), Lord Hope at ([118], [122]) and Lord Carswell (at [175]) suggested that this would be unlawful as subverting the clear intention of the 1911 Act. Lord Rogers (at [139]) was sympathetic to this view. Lord Bingham (at [32]) and Baroness Hale (at [159]) took the contrary and more logical view, arguing that since Acts passed under the Parliament Acts were full statutes, the courts could not prevent this, however politically undesirable it might be. Lords Walker and Browne did not express a view.

A further issue was discussed. The Court of Appeal in *Jackson* had suggested that a bill which made fundamental constitutional changes such as abolishing the House of Lords altogether or violating basic democratic rights could not be passed under the Parliament Acts, which could be read as implicitly limiting such fundamental changes (Lord Woolf seemed to support Wade's argument above). Apart from the uncertainty of this notion, the 1911 Act was introduced for the very purpose of

enabling important changes to be made against the opposition of the Lords. Their Lordships in *Jackson* did not commit themselves on this point but suggested different views, albeit tentatively. Lord Bingham (at [32]), Lord Nicholls (at [61]), Lord Hope (at [127]) and Baroness Hale (at [159], [166]) thought that there would be no legally enforceable limitations provided implicitly by the 1911 Act, although Lord Bingham (at [41]) drew attention to the fact that the Parliament Acts weaken the checks and balances over a powerful executive. Lord Carswell (at [178]) and Lord Browne (at [194]) cautiously left open the possibility. Lord Steyn (at [102]) went furthest, taking the view that fundamental changes might be rejected by the courts – not merely those made under the Parliament Acts but also by the full Parliament (see Section 8.4.3).

8.4.4 European Community law

This challenge to parliamentary supremacy has attracted considerable support, being regarded as realistic in contemporary political circumstances. The EU and its powers were created by a series of treaties between the member states. Member states are obliged under the treaties to give effect to those community laws that are intended by community law to be binding within domestic law. However, as with all treaties, the law of the EU enters the legal systems of each member state in accordance with the laws of that state.

It is sometimes argued that by enacting the original EU Treaty the UK has therefore surrendered part of parliamentary supremacy (see *Blackburn*). If this is right then a democratic body has committed the sin of trying to bind the freedom of future generations. We shall discuss the EC law in more detail in Chapter 10 but will outline the position as regards parliamentary supremacy here.

The European Communities Act 1972 incorporated EU law into UK law. The Act states that 'any enactment, passed or to be passed ... shall be construed and have effect subject to the foregoing provisions of this section' (s 2(4)). The provisions referred to require among other things that the English courts must give effect to certain laws made by European bodies (s 2(1)). Section 3 of the Act also requires UK courts to follow the decisions of the European Court of Justice (ECJ), the court of the EU. The effect of the above provisions seems to be that a UK statute, even one passed after the relevant EC law, must give way to EC law. Not surprisingly the ECJ, which is part of the internal EC system, favours the supremacy of the EC (see *Costa v ENEL* [1964]). However this in itself is not enough since the matter depends on UK law.

Conflict between UK law and EC law may arise where a UK statute is inconsistent with an existing EC law. There are opposing arguments based on differing perspectives as to the effect of the 1972 Act.

On the one hand it might be argued along traditional lines that since a statute made EC law binding in the UK, a statute can reverse this. According to this argument it might be conceded that, given the importance of EC law and the clear intention in the Act that it should take priority, it should take very clear words in an Act to override an EC law, so that the ordinary implied repeal doctrine is excluded (Section 8.3.3). Thus the courts would try to interpret legislation so as to avoid a conflict with a binding rule of EC law. According to Lord Diplock in *Garland v British Rail Engineering Ltd* [1983] a statute that unambiguously states that it is to override European law will arguably prevail. Similarly in *Thoburn v Sunderland City Council* [2002] Laws LJ attempted to treat the matter as one of a strong presumption against repeal, regarding the 1972 Act as an example of a 'constitutional statute'. However the case of the EU is possibly even stronger in that nothing short of an express statement along the lines of 'this Act is to override EC law' would suffice.

On the other hand it could be argued that the 1972 Act had the effect of imposing a European perspective on the UK courts, thus requiring the courts to give priority to EC laws since European law does not recognise our version of parliamentary supremacy. In *Jackson* Lord Hope (at [105]) and Baroness Hale (at [159]) treated EC law as modifying parliamentary supremacy. Independently of both arguments it might be conceded that a UK statute could validly expressly repeal the 1972 Act, effectively taking us out of the European Union.

The UK courts have reached an ambivalent solution which is consistent with both the above perspectives, favouring the 'constitutional abeyance notion' (see Section 3.5). In *R v Secretary of State for Transport, ex p Factortame* [1990] there was a clash between EU law and the Merchant Shipping Act 1988. Lord Bridge said, 'By virtue of s.2(4) of the Act of 1972, Part II of the 1988 Act is to be construed and take effect subject to directly enforceable community rights...This has precisely the same effect as if a section were incorporated in...the 1988 Act...which enacted that the provisions were to be without prejudice to the directly enforceable community rights of nationals of any member state of the EC' (at 140). Thus his Lordship treated the matter as one of interpreting the Act in question so as to conform with the EC rule, not of overriding it. However the House of Lords refused to grant an injunction to prevent the Act being enforced, holding that it had no power to defy an Act of Parliament. The matter was referred to the ECJ, which held that the UK court should enforce the EC law. In *R v Secretary of State, ex p Factortame (No 2)* [1991] the House of Lords fell into line and 'disapplied' the UK statute. This could avoid a direct challenge to parliamentary supremacy on the basis that to 'disapply' merely means that the statute has no application to the particular case. On the other hand *Factortame* could be taken as supporting the second perspective, which modifies parliamentary supremacy, arguably signalling Wade's 'constitutional revolution' (see also *Equal Opportunities Commission v Secretary of State for Employment* [1994]).

8.4.5 The common law

This challenge is largely the creation of proponents of traditional, Lockean, liberalism (see Section 2.3.2). It is sometimes suggested that parliamentary supremacy may be conditional on compliance with fundamental values embodied in the rule of law and democracy, so that in extreme cases the court might refuse to apply a statute (see Allan, 2001; Section 8.5). Some judges have supported this. Some judges have suggested that parliamentary supremacy is no longer appropriate and that 'the rule of law' enforced by the courts is the true sovereign (see eg Lord Steyn in *R (Jackson) v AG* [2005] at [104] and Lord Hope *ibid* at [107], [120]: 'step by step parliamentary supremacy is being qualified'). The late Lord Cooke, following Wade's approach (see Section 8.4.4), suggested that an attempt by Parliament to override basic rights would be a 'revolution' on which the last word rests with the courts (in Andenas and Fairgrieve (2009) 689–91).

Early cases such as *Dr Bonham's Case* [1610] possibly suggested that a completely unreasonable statute may be overridden, but at least since Tudor times there has been no serious challenge to parliamentary supremacy. Nevertheless in the absence of a written constitution we cannot rule out judicial rejection of the doctrine. Indeed the courts themselves inevitably have to decide the limits of their own powers when a case comes before them. Thus it has been said:

> whoever hath an absolute authority to interpret any written or spoken laws, it is he who is truly the lawgiver and not the person who just spoke or wrote them. (Bishop Hoadley's sermon preached before King George I, 1717)

Contemporary judges in the main support ultimate parliamentary supremacy but are sometimes ambivalent. Emphasis has been placed on the courts' power to moderate Parliament by interpreting statutes in the light of common law principles. Compromise has been rationalised by claiming that Parliament implicitly recognises this. More strongly it has been suggested that there is 'dual sovereignty' between Parliament and the courts. In *X Ltd v Morgan Grampian Publishers Ltd* [1991], Lord Bridge referred to the 'twin foundations' of the rule of law, namely 'the sovereignty of the Queen in Parliament in making the law and the sovereignty of the Queen's courts in interpreting and applying the law' (at 13). In *Hamilton v Al Fayed* [1999], Lord Woolf MR referred to 'the wider constitutional principle of mutuality of respect between two constitutional sovereignties' (at 320).

However it is arguably fallacious to treat interpretation as a sovereign act. Interpretation requires attention to possible meanings of the text to be interpreted and is an inherently limited exercise, albeit sometimes with considerable latitude. It is true that there is no further appeal against the interpretation put on an Act by the highest court. But it still makes sense to suggest that the court's interpretation may be wrong in law just as a referee's decision in a sport may be wrong. A rule which says that a decision of a judge cannot be challenged is separate from the question of whether or not that decision is lawful.

The courts can put partial brakes on Parliament's freedom by means of the 'principle of legality' (see Lady Hale in *R (Jackson) v AG* [2005] at [159]; Section 6.6). This relates to the 'extended' rule of law (see Section 6.6). The courts do not interpret statutes mechanically but will apply them in the context of the rule of law, which embodies respect for fundamental values and individual rights. There are many presumptions of statutory interpretation, the overall effect of which is that Parliament must use very clear language if it wishes to override values of fairness and justice developed by the courts.

Thus in *R v Lord Chancellor's Dept, ex p Witham* [1997], Laws J asserted that:

> In the unwritten legal order of the British State, at a time when the common law continues to accord a legislative supremacy to Parliament, the notion of a constitutional right can in my judgement inhere only in this proposition that the right in question cannot be abrogated by the state save by specific provision in an Act of Parliament...General words will not suffice. And any such rights will be creatures of the common law, since their existence would not be the consequence of the democratic process but would be logically prior to it. (at 783)

The courts therefore act as a check and balance by ensuring that Parliament does not inadvertently or lightly override basic rights.

Thus in *R v Secretary of State for the Home Dept, ex p Simms* [1999] Lord Hoffmann said:

> The principle of legality means that Parliament must squarely confront what it is doing and accept the political cost. Fundamental rights cannot be overridden by general or ambiguous words. This is because there is too great a risk that the full implications of their unqualified meaning may have passed unnoticed in the democratic process. In the absence of express language or necessary implication to the contrary, the courts therefore presume that even the most general words were intended to be subject to the basic rights of the individual. (at 131)

Anisminic Ltd v Foreign Compensation Commission [1969] is sometimes regarded as a judicial attempt to subvert Parliament under the cloak of interpretation. The applicant challenged a ruling by the Commission refusing it compensation under a statutory scheme. The governing Act included an 'ouster clause' designed to protect the Commission against challenge in the courts. This stated that a 'determination' of the Commission 'under the Act' shall not be questioned in any court of law. Nevertheless the House of Lords, applying a presumption that the jurisdiction of the courts should not be excluded, allowed the challenge on the ground that a ruling which was flawed by an error of law was a nullity and so did not count as a 'determination under the Act'. However Parliament could have anticipated the line that the court might take and could have used tighter language if it wanted to exclude challenge, thereby making it explicit that it was overriding widely shared values (see Section 19.7.2).

8.5 Parliamentary supremacy and the rule of law

The common law arguments against parliamentary supremacy rely on the idea of the rule of law. As Dicey pointed out (1915, ch 13), in one sense parliamentary supremacy conforms to the rule of law in that Parliament's will can be expressed only through statutes and there are rules of law defining what a statute is. This relates only to the core rule of law. Parliamentary supremacy conflicts with the rule of law in its amplified and extended senses (see Sections 6.5, 6.6). For example Parliament sometimes enacts retrospective laws and often confers wide discretionary powers on the executive even to alter Acts of Parliament.

Dicey's view depended on the pivotal role which he thought that the House of Lords played in checking the excesses of the Commons and upon his assumption that the common law was the guardian of basic values. He also believed that public opinion was a modifying force. Today the House of Lords is subordinate to the Commons and, as we have seen, there is no longer widespread agreement, if there ever was, as to what the values of the constitution should be. In his later years Dicey realised that the power of political parties, an increasingly diverse electorate, external threats and the need for governments to provide expensive public services put the traditional place of Parliament as the centre of the constitution into question.

Lakin (2008) argues that the conventional basis of parliamentary supremacy, namely that the doctrine is a 'political fact' widely accepted by officials and acquiesced in by the public (see Lord Hope in *R (Jackson) v A-G* [2005] at [120]) is flawed. According to Lakin the doctrine is so uncertain that it is implausible to suppose that officials have accepted it. Lakin therefore argues that the doctrine of parliamentary sovereignty is a myth and that only the law itself can determine what is legally valid. Lakin sees no need for a concept of sovereignty as such but prefers a network of legal principles. Drawing upon Dworkin (see Section 2.3.2) Lakin regards the courts as enforcing fundamental rules of political morality. However Lakin's argument seems vulnerable to the same objection as he makes to the traditional doctrine, namely that political morality is uncertain and also depends ultimately upon widespread acceptance as a political fact. Moreover the Hobbesian principle that someone must have the last word seems inevitable (see also Craig, 2003).

Allan (2001) argues in republican fashion (see Section 2.5) that it is inconsistent with the political assumptions of a liberal society on which the rule of law is based that the legislature, or indeed any part of the government, should be all powerful. Allan claims that in the common law tradition the courts have the duty to protect the fundamental values of society. Relying on the fact that the court is concerned not with the statute generally but with its application to the individual case, Allan suggests that the court can legitimately hold that a statute which appears to be grossly unjust in the particular context does not apply to the particular case. This approach could be reconciled with parliamentary supremacy on the basis that Parliament cannot foresee every implication of the laws it makes and can be assumed to respect the rule of law. In *Cooper v Wandsworth Board of Works* [1863] Byles J put the matter more strongly when he said that 'the justice of the common law will supply the omission of the legislature'.

Those supporting the courts might argue in favour of the high standard of public reasoned argument practised in the courts and the relative objectivity and independence of judges. A much canvassed argument is that the representative democracy which gives Parliament its legitimacy is an imperfect democracy and does not necessarily reflect the views of a majority of voters. In particular Parliament has become dominated by the executive (see Lord Mustill in *R v Secretary of State, ex p Fire Brigades Union* [1995]; Section 7.8.4). Thus the usual defence of Parliament, that it can make laws which are informed by a wider range of opinions than are available to a court and which carry the consent of those subject to them, can be presented as hollow. On the other hand it seems bizarre to remedy a failure of democracy by suggesting an even more undemocratic mechanism.

Arguments in favour of Parliament are also republican, indeed more so than Allan's arguments (above). They point to the indignity of political decisions being made on their behalf by people we have not chosen and also to the fact that judges are not accountable. (The latter point is sometimes contested by pointing out that judges sit in public and give reasoned verdicts.) They might also deny that lawyers should have a privileged status, since Parliament comprises a larger cross-section of the community that can make a better-informed decision (see Bellamy, 2007). The liberal values that the rule of law embraces are widely accepted but they are not peculiar to law. Ideas such as freedom and equality are the source of much political disagreement which judges may be in no better position to resolve than anyone else (see Section 2.4).

Summary

- The doctrine of parliamentary supremacy provides the fundamental legal premise of the UK constitution. The doctrine means that an Act of Parliament must be obeyed by the courts, that later Acts prevail over earlier ones and that rules made by external bodies, for example under international law, cannot override Acts of Parliament. It does not follow that Parliament is supreme politically, although the line between legal and political supremacy is blurred.
- Parliamentary supremacy rests on frail foundations. Without a written constitution it is impossible to be sure as to its legal basis other than as an evolving practice which is usually said to depend on the 1688 revolution. It is possible to maintain that the common law is really supreme. The question of the ultimate source of power cannot be answered within the legal system alone but depends on public acceptance.
- Parliament is itself a creature of the law. The customary and statutory rules which have evolved since medieval times determine that, except in special cases, Parliament for this purpose means the Queen with the assent of the House of Lords and House of Commons. However this can be modified, as in the case of the Parliament Acts 1911 and 1949.
- The courts can determine whether any document is an Act of Parliament in this sense but cannot inquire into whether the correct procedure within each House has been followed.
- The doctrine has two separate aspects: first that the courts must obey Acts of Parliament in preference to any other kind of legal authority, and second that no body, including Parliament itself, can place legal limits upon the freedom of action of a future Parliament. The first of these principles is generally accepted but the second is open to dispute.
- The implied repeal doctrine is sometimes promoted as an aspect of parliamentary supremacy but is merely a presumption of interpretation. Some statutes can be repealed only by clear language.
- The doctrine of parliamentary supremacy is subject to considerable attack.
- Grants of independence to dependent territories can probably be revoked lawfully in the eyes of UK courts.
- The possibility that parts of the Acts of Union with Scotland and Ireland are unchangeable is probably outside the courts' jurisdiction.
- The 'redefinition' argument proposes that by altering the basic requirements for lawmaking, Parliament can redesign itself to impose restrictions on enacting legislation.
- Parliament limited the freedom of future Parliaments in relation to certain laws made by the European communities.
- The role of the common law as constituting 'dual sovereignty' through the courts' exclusive power to interpret Acts of Parliament leads to argument that parliamentary supremacy is conditional upon acceptance by the courts. This links with the extended version of the rule of law (Chapter 7).
- Dicey attempted to reconcile parliamentary supremacy with the rule of law by pointing out that Parliament is defined by law and can act only through the instrument of law, so that independent judges interpret its legislation. This relies on the separation of powers.

Exercises

8.1 Does the doctrine of parliamentary supremacy have a secure legal basis?

8.2 To what extent can the courts investigate whether an Act of Parliament has complied with the proper procedure?

8.3 'Every age and generation must be as free to act for itself, in all cases, as the ages and generations which preceded it. The vanity and presumption of governing beyond the grave is the most ridiculous and insolent of all tyrannies' (Thomas Paine). Discuss with reference (i) to the implied repeal doctrine and (ii) to the redefinition argument.

8.4 Marshal the arguments for and against the proposition that the UK Parliament cannot legislate inconsistently with EC law.

8.5 Consider the validity and effect of the following provisions contained in (fictitious) Acts of Parliament:

(i) 'There shall be a bill of rights in the UK and no Act to be enacted at any time in the future shall have effect, in as far as it is inconsistent with the bill of rights, unless it has been assented to by a two-thirds majority of both Houses of Parliament and no Act shall repeal this Act unless it has the same two-thirds majority.'

(ii) 'The Acts of Union with Scotland and Ireland are hereby repealed.'

(iii) 'This Act shall apply notwithstanding any contrary rule of European Community law.'

8.6 'The sovereignty of Parliament and the supremacy of the law of the land – the two principles which pervade the whole of the English constitution – may appear to stand in opposition to each other, or to be at best countervailing forces. But this appearance is delusive' (Dicey). Discuss.

8.7 'The classic account given by Dicey of the doctrine of the supremacy of Parliament, pure and absolute as it was, can now be seen as out of place in the modern United Kingdom' Lord Steyn in *R (Jackson) v AG* [2005] at [106]. 'The rule of law enforced by the courts is the ultimate controlling factor on which our constitution is based', Lord Hope *ibid* at [107]. Explain and critically discuss.

8.8 What, if any, limitations are there on the powers exercisable by Parliament under the Parliament Acts 1911 and 1949?

Further reading

Allan, *Constitutional Justice* (Oxford University Press 2001) ch 8

Allan, 'In Defence of the Common Law Constitution' (2009) LSE Working Papers 5/2009

Bellamy, *Political Constitutionalism* (Cambridge University Press 2007) chs 1, 3

Bradley, 'The Sovereignty of Parliament – Form or Substance?' in Jowell and Oliver (eds), *The Changing Constitution* (6th edn, Oxford University Press 2007)

Clark and Sorabji, 'The Rule of Law and Our Changing Constitution' in Andenas and Fairgrieve (eds), *Tom Bingham and the Transformation of the Law* (Oxford University Press 2009)

Craig, 'Constitutional Foundations, the Rule of Law and Supremacy' [2003] PL 92

Ekins, 'Judicial Supremacy and the Rule of Law' (2003) 119 LQR 127

Ekins, 'Acts of Parliament and the Parliament Acts' (2007) 123 LQR 91

Elliott, 'Parliamentary Sovereignty and the New Constitutional Order: Legislative Freedom, Political Reality and Convention' (2002) 22 LS 340

Further reading cont'd

Goldsworthy, *The Sovereignty of Parliament: History and Philosophy* (Oxford University Press 1999) chs 1, 2, 9, 10

Goldsworthy, 'Legislative Sovereignty and the Rule of Law' in Campbell, Ewing and Tompkins (eds), *Sceptical Essays on Human Rights* (Oxford University Press 2001)

Gordon, 'The Conceptual Foundations of Parliamentary Sovereignty: Reconsidering Jennings and Wade' [2009] PL 519

Jowell, 'Parliamentary Supremacy under the New Constitutional Hypothesis' [2006] PL 562

Lakin, 'Debunking the Idea of Parliamentary Sovereignty: The Controlling Factor of Legality in the British Constitution' (2008) 28 OJLS 709

MacCormick, 'Does the United Kingdom Have a Constitution? Reflections on *MacCormick v Lord Advocate*' (1978) 29 Northern Ireland LQ 1

Marshall, 'The Constitution: Its Theory and Interpretation' in Bogdanor (ed), *The British Constitution in the Twentieth Century* (Oxford University Press 2003) 42–51, 62–64

Munro, *Studies in Constitutional Law* (2nd edn, Butterworths 1999) chs 5, 6

Wade, 'The Basis of Legal Sovereignty' [1955] CLJ 172

Part III

International aspects of the constitution

Chapter 9

The state and the outside world – *sic transit gloria mundi*

9.1 Introduction: the idea of the state

The term 'state' derives from 'status' and originally meant a recognised function in the overall scheme of things. In ancient Greece and Rome and parts of medieval Europe the 'city state' was regarded as an independent, self-governing community existing primarily for military purposes. In Britain there was a looser connection of local rulers under a central monarchy.

The contemporary idea of the state is that of the 'nation state'. As defined in international law a state is a geographical area with a permanent population with an independent government in control (see McCormick, 2007). There is no necessary connection between the ideas of a nation and of a state, although sometimes the two terms are used interchangeably, for example the National Health Service. A nation is a cultural, political and historical idea but is not a legal concept. It signifies a relatively homogeneous community marked out by a common language, common ethnicity or shared cultural traditions. A state is defined by law and based on geographical boundaries drawn up by officials. However a nation may have a moral claim to be a state with its own laws and government (see Lord Hoffmann in *A v Secretary of State for the Home Dept* [2005]). As the history of Ireland, the Balkan states, Pakistan and many African states sadly reveals, the artificiality of state boundaries sometimes generates violence and even genocide. The term 'country' has no legal significance and is often used loosely to refer either to a nation or to a state

The nation state as a self-contained geographical area with complete control over its internal affairs has been the basic unit of political and legal organisation since the Treaty of Westphalia 1688 created the principle that states are equal and independent in relation to their internal affairs. It was a reaction against the loose, medieval political structure of rival warlords (to some extent held together by the Church) and also against the re-emergence in the fifteenth century of republican ideas of citizen self-rule. The association of the ideas of nation and state can be used by those in power as a means of inspiring loyalty (eg the Constitution of Ireland, Art 9).

Throughout mainland Europe the state was governed and represented by a monarch imposing law from above. It is commonly claimed that Britain throughout retained the tradition that the ruler requires the consent of the 'community', although there has been disagreement as to who is included in the 'community'. During the eighteenth century, generated by Enlightenment ideas of scientific reason, secularism and equality, the state developed as an impersonal command structure designed to advance the general welfare. This is broadly the position today. Under the influence of democracy, the state has become an all-purpose organisation with no limitations as to the functions it might have or any consensus as to the relationship between citizen and state other than the temporary accommodations produced by the balance of powers within the state.

Today the interdependence of states against shared evils such as terrorism and environmental damage, advances in communications and mobility labelled as 'globalisation' which enable people and money to move swiftly around the world, and also atrocities committed by governments against their own people have placed the Westphalian model in doubt. However state constitutions, including that of the UK, remain geared to seventeenth-century ideas in this respect.

9.2 The UK as a state

The UK is a state in international law but it is not a nation. The UK comprises England, Scotland, Wales and Northern Ireland. The Channel Islands and the Isle of Man are not part of the UK but belong to the Crown and there are various small 'British overseas territories' scattered around the world. Scotland, Wales and England might claim to be nations. Northern Ireland is a province of the UK within the nation of Ireland, part of which is a separate state: the Republic of Ireland. The Queen is the head of the Commonwealth, which is a loose association of former UK territories. The Commonwealth has no constitutional links with the UK.

'Britain', although identified for some purposes, such as relations with Northern Ireland, has no legal identity but means England, Wales and Scotland collectively. England was a nation state before the union with Scotland in 1707, but now has no legal status. English law applies in England and Wales and is the basis of the law in many former British territories, including the US. Scotland, Wales and Northern Ireland have devolved government (Chapter 16). Scotland and Northern Ireland have their own legal systems, which share much in common with English law, although Scotland has also been influenced by French civil law. In all jurisdictions, other than Scottish criminal cases, the highest appeal court is currently the UK Supreme Court.

English law has historically been dominated by the idea of monarchy. Unlike other European legal systems (see eg the Constitution of Ireland, Arts 4–6) it has no legal concept of the state, replacing it with the concept of the Crown. Thus in *R v Preston* [1993], Lord Mustill remarked: 'The Crown as the source of authority means that the UK has never found it necessary to create the notion of the "state" as a single legal entity' (at 663). In English law the concept of the state is used loosely to describe any governmental activity (such as state schools).

Where legislation refers to the 'state', its meaning depends on the particular context, for example the community as a whole (*Chandler v DPP* [1964]), the 'sovereign power' (*General Medical Council v BBC* [1998]) or the executive branch of government (*D v NSPCC* [1978]). The civil service is defined as the 'civil service of the state' (Constitutional Reform and Governance Act 2010, s 3). In context this seems to mean the Crown or the central government. Sometimes the 'state' refers to the whole system of government. For example foreign states have wide immunities from liability in the courts (see Section 9.7). In *CND v Prime Minister* [2006] there was an unsuccessful attempt to prosecute the Prime Minister for the international crime of aggression in relation to the invasion of Iraq. Lord Hoffmann gave as one reason the fact that the crime of aggression can be committed only by a state and not by individuals and it would be inappropriate for the court to judge the state of which it is a part.

The non-statist nature of English law has at least the following important consequences:

- The UK constitution regards government essentially as a loose collection of institutions and persons headed by the Crown. The various government institutions have gained their separate identity over time by hiving off from original roles as servants or advisers to the monarch. The concept of the Crown originally meant the monarch and perhaps still does. The Crown also means the central government collectively. However the notion that the Crown is an individual person in the form of the Queen means that the government has the same powers and rights as an ordinary individual to hold property, enter contracts and so on. Because the government has enormous financial resources this gives it considerable power in addition to special powers it has under statute and, again thanks to the history of the monarchy, the royal prerogative (see Section 14.1).

- There is a distinction in statist constitutions between 'public law', which regulates the state itself and its relationship with citizens, and 'private law', which the state uses to regulate the relationship between its citizens. The UK constitution has not historically recognised such a distinction. The individualised nature of our public bodies (above) means that officials are regarded as ordinary citizens embedded in the general private law except in as much as they are given particular powers. It has been regarded as a strength of our constitution that a single system of law applies to officials and individuals alike. Unless a particular law provides otherwise, officials have no special powers or status and are individually responsible for any legal wrongs they commit. Thus the doctrine of *raison d'état* as a general justification for government power is not recognised (*Entick v Carrington* [1765]). Public bodies have no special powers to interfere with the rights of individuals or corporate bodies unless conferred on them by an Act of Parliament or, in the case of the Crown, the royal prerogative.
- However the increasing powers given to governmental officials and the trend towards privatisation have led to attempts to distinguish between public and private law and between public and private bodies and functions, particularly in connection with judicial review of government action, European law, human rights and access to information. A successful definition of a public body or public function has yet to be produced and it cannot be assumed that these terms will be defined in the same way in each context.

For example the Freedom of Information Act 2000 (Chapter 21) provides a list of public bodies that can be altered by ministers. The Government Resources and Accounts Act 2000 (Chapter 13) refers unhelpfully to a 'government department or a body exercising public functions' (s 7(3)). The Public Audit (Wales) Act 2004 similarly refers to 'functions of a public nature' but also includes 'a body entirely or substantially funded from public money'. The Civil Procedure Rules 2000 (SI 2000/2092, 54.1(2)), which deals with judicial review, refers to 'a feature or combination of features which impose a public character or stamp' (see Section 19.5.1). The Human Rights Act 1998 does not provide a definition (see Section 21.3.1).

- One reason why we cannot clearly distinguish between the public and the private is that our non-statist tradition allows us to allocate governmental functions haphazardly between the central government proper (ministers) and other bodies specially created for the purpose and also to transfer functions to private bodies.

Similarly there are no legal principles governing the question of whether and on what terms the government can hand over assets to the private sector. Whether these are sold (and at what price) or given away (and to whom) depends on particular legislation or government practice. We regard the distinction between functions that should be carried out by the state and those appropriate to the private sector as a political matter outside the law. There are some advantages in the UK approach. Particular decision making bodies must be openly identified and cannot hide under the general state umbrella. There are also disadvantages in that there is no constitutional principle to prevent public powers being farmed out to bodies that are not democratically accountable.

- On a more technical level, unlike the governments of other European states, our government is fragmented between different bodies and there is no single entity which can hold property or enter into legal transactions on behalf of the state. Various devices have been devised to deal with this. Standardised statutory provisions deal with the transfer of assets and functions within government and to outside bodies (see Section 15.5). For most legal purposes the Attorney General represents the government. Government powers and property are vested by particular legislation or under the royal prerogative either in the Crown or in particular ministers or departments. There are no significant legal provisions restricting the arrangement of government departments other than the Treasury, which has important functions relating to Parliament (see Sections 13.5, 15.6.1). A minister can act through any civil servant in his or her department (see Section 15.8.5) but without statutory authority cannot transfer power to other ministers or to anyone else. However the royal prerogative powers of the Crown can be exercised directly by any minister.
- In a statist system the state is both a creation of the law and the producer of law. Judges are the authoritative interpreters of the law but not its creators. Judicial opinions are regarded as making more concrete the laws emanating from the state but do not traditionally have an independent lawmaking role. By contrast the historical basis of the common law gives the courts an independent basis of legitimacy. The authority of the common law lies in community values. In the common law system judges are regarded as individuals charged with doing justice. Judicial decisions are normally fully reasoned and dissents are commonplace. However in *R v Jones (Margaret)* [2006], which concerned an attempt to accuse the government of a war crime in invading Iraq, Lord Hoffmann expressed concern about the theoretical difficulty of the court taking action against the 'state' of which it is a part (at [65], but see *M v Home Office* [1993]: Crown courts and ministers must be separated).

9.3 Citizenship

In its general sense citizenship means full membership of a state. The legal concept of citizenship has some connection with citizenship in its wider, republican sense (see Section 2.5). In the republican sense citizenship is about having equal rights in the community, participating in government and shouldering community responsibilities. The republican idea of citizenship is sometimes used to suggest that human rights are dependent on good behaviour whereas 'liberal' citizenship primarily concerns the rights and entitlements of individuals against the state. However recent citizenship legislation has imposed requirements relating to assimilation into national culture (below) (see Bellamy, 'Constitutive Citizenship vs. Constitutional Rights: Republican Reflections on the EU Charter and the Human Rights Act' in Campbell, Ewing and Tomkins (eds), *Sceptical Essays on Human Rights* (Hart 2001)).

The notion of citizenship as it first emerged in ancient Greece presupposed a small community roughly equal in wealth and from similar social backgrounds. Indeed women, foreigners and slaves – making up most of the population – were excluded. In today's larger and more diverse communities it is difficult to suppose that common values can be applied uniformly to all. Cultural practices and loyalties, such as language and family customs, militate against detailed notions of the rights and obligations of citizenship and raise the problems of liberal pluralism (Section 2.3.7).

The unpleasant side of citizenship is that it entails 'exclusion', in the sense of an unwelcoming attitude to those regarded as non-citizens, who in UK law are labelled 'aliens'. Traditionally aliens have fewer rights than citizens. In particular the state has a wide discretion to expel aliens, although this is limited by human rights obligations to secure access to the courts and not to place a person at risk of torture or inhuman or degrading treatment (see Section 19.3). In *A v Secretary of State for the Home Dept* [2005] the House of Lords held that it was contrary to the Human Rights Act 1998 to discriminate between citizens and non-citizens in relation to anti-terrorism measures where there is a similar risk from both groups.

Although there is a status of 'British citizen' (below), those subject to the jurisdiction of English law are strictly speaking not citizens but 'subjects' of the Crown. A subject includes anyone within the territory of the UK since such a person can lay claim to the protection of the Crown. All who are physically present in the UK can claim the protection of the common law and can seek judicial review against the government. Despite the word commonly being associated with subservience, the notion of a 'subject' is sometimes said to give valuable protection in that it presupposes a relationship of mutual respect between ruler and ruled which is safeguarded by law. Thus in return for 'allegiance' (loyalty) the Crown is obliged under common law to protect the rights of the subject and keep the peace. Thus in his speech on the scaffold (1649) Charles I announced that:

> I must tell you, that [the people's] liberty and freedom consists in having the government of those laws, by which their life and their goods may be considered most their own; 'tis not for having a share in government that is nothing pertaining to 'em. A subject and a sovereign are clean different things.

Citizenship by contrast carries with it obligations to conform to the wishes of the majority. For example Rousseau proclaimed that a citizen must submit to the general will, whatever that might be, and it is sometimes claimed that human rights are conditional upon good behaviour.

In English law citizenship is mainly concerned with the right to reside, rights concerned with political participation and sometimes rights to access to public services and taxation (below). Other legal rights and duties depend on presence in the territory or sometimes, particularly in relation to health and welfare services, a more specific connection such as lawful residence (see eg *R (A) v Secretary of State* [2010]: access to health service denied to failed asylum seeker). In exceptional cases, notably the Channel Islands, non-citizens have restricted property rights.

UK citizenship law is complex due to the many changes that have been made in order to control immigration following the collapse of the British Empire and to assuage post-imperial guilt. It can only be sketched here. The British Nationality Act 1981 (BNA) as amended is the main legislation. There is no legal concept of citizenship of any other unit within the UK. There is a notion of citizenship of the EU. However this merely endorses certain rights within member states which under European law apply to citizens of other EU states.

The following have 'British' citizenship under the Act:

- Those born or adopted in the UK (s 50). However at least one parent must also be either a citizen or settled in the UK. If the parents are not married this must be the mother.
- Those descended from a British citizen (s 2). At the time of birth at least one parent must be a citizen other than by descent or be a citizen working abroad for the British government, having been recruited in the UK, or in certain cases working for the EU, having been recruited in a member state.
- Persons who were citizens or who by virtue of specified family connections (patrials) had a right of abode in the UK under the regime that existed before 1983 (s 11).

Citizenship can be acquired by registration or naturalisation:

- Registration is a right available to persons who were born in the UK or who fulfil certain requirements of residence or parentage and who satisfy the Home Secretary that they are of 'good character' (BNA, s 4; Immigration, Asylum and Nationality Act 2006, s 58).
- Naturalisation (BNA, s 6) is a matter for the discretion of the Secretary of State and is available to anyone, subject to requirements of residence or family connection, presence in the UK within a qualifying period of years, language, good character and 'knowledge of life in the UK' as determined in accordance with regulations made by the Home Secretary (Nationality, Immigration and Asylum Act 2002, s 4; Borders, Citizenship and Immigration Act 2009, ss 39, 40). Thus a communitarian and potentially illiberal element has been injected into the law.

Certain other categories, although largely obsolete relics of empire, attract special immigration privileges in specific contexts too specialised to be discussed here. Some require registration; most are subject to immigration control (below). These categories include British subjects, which covers members of previous British territories, Commonwealth citizens, citizens of the United Kingdom and colonies, British protected persons and British overseas citizens. Most persons connected with British dependencies, other than certain military bases in Cyprus (formerly 'British dependent territories citizens', now 'British overseas territories citizens'), have a right to be full citizens (British Overseas Territories Act 2002). In the case of the Falkland Islands (which Argentina claims), this is automatic (British Nationality (Falkland Islands) Act 1983). Some citizens of Hong Kong, which the UK surrendered to China in 1997, have certain rights to registration as British citizens (British Nationality (Hong Kong) Act 1997). Others (British nationals overseas) can acquire a British passport, although this in itself carries no legal rights, being essentially an identity document (BNA, s 12).

All other persons are 'aliens'. Unless statute requires otherwise, while present in the UK, aliens (other than those from countries with whom we are formally at war) have the same rights and duties in English law as citizens. However citizens of the EU and the broader European Economic Area (Norway, Iceland, Liechtenstein: Lisbon Agreement 2004) have substantial rights to reside in the UK.

Citizenship can be renounced by registration with the Secretary of State (BNA, s 12). However registration becomes ineffective unless the person in question acquires citizenship of another state within six months.

The Home Secretary can by order remove citizenship (a) on the grounds of public good unless deprivation of citizenship would make the person stateless or (b) where citizenship was acquired by fraud, false representation or concealment of a material fact (Nationality, Immigration and Asylum Act 2002, s 4; Immigration, Asylum and Nationality Act 2006, s 56). There is a right of appeal (below).

Citizenship is legally important mainly in the following respects:

- It confers a right to live in the UK under immigration law. However non-citizens who were ordinarily resident in the UK without restrictions on 1 January 1983 do not need leave to enter and remain (Immigration Act 1971, s 1(2)). The Home Secretary has discretionary powers to give other non-citizens leave to remain either for specific periods or indefinitely. These are guided by Immigration Rules. The Home Secretary can revoke indefinite leave on grounds of public good (Immigration, Asylum and Nationality Act 2006, s 57). Citizens of the European Economic Area and their families have freedom of movement within the UK (Immigration Act 1988, s 7). Citizens of the Republic of Ireland, the Channel Islands and the Isle of Man are not subject to immigration control although passport checks have recently been introduced (Immigration Act 1971, ss 1(3), (9)).
- A citizen cannot be expelled from the UK or its dependencies (Magna Carta, Art 29; *R v Bhagwhan* [1972]). However, as with all basic rights, this gives way to the clear wording of an Act of Parliament (or in the case of certain dependencies to law made under the royal prerogative; see section 9.6).
- British, Irish and Commonwealth citizens lawfully resident in the UK may vote in parliamentary and local elections (Representation of the People Act 2000) and elections for the devolved governments.
- Non-citizens (other than Commonwealth and Irish citizens) cannot be members of either House of Parliament (British Nationality Act 1981, Sch 7).
- Honours cannot be conferred upon non-citizens except Commonwealth citizens.
- British citizens have a right to call upon the protection of the Crown when abroad, although this is not enforceable in the courts. The main consequence of the Crown's duty to protect British citizens abroad is that the Crown cannot require payment for such protection unless the person concerned voluntarily exposes himself or herself to some special risk (see *China Navigation Co Ltd v A-G* [1932]; *Mutasa v A-G* [1980]).
- British citizens abroad are subject to special taxation laws.
- British citizens cannot generally be removed from the UK. There are two exceptions:
  (i) anyone can be extradited to another country to stand trial for a criminal offence or serve a sentence;
  (ii) under the Terrorism Act 2000 border controls can be exercised over travel between the UK and Northern Ireland.

- British citizens owe allegiance to the Crown wherever they are in the world (see *R v Casement* [1917]). Allegiance has two main consequences. Firstly the Crown probably cannot plead the defence of 'act of state' against a person who owes allegiance (Section 14.5). Secondly the offence of treason is committed against the duty of allegiance. Aliens resident and perhaps even present in the UK also owe allegiance (*de Jager v A-G of Natal* [1907]). A person who holds a British passport apparently owes allegiance even if he has never visited the UK and even if the passport has been fraudulently obtained (see *Joyce v DPP* [1946]). It seems that apart from renouncing citizenship, allegiance cannot be voluntarily surrendered (*R v Lynch* [1903]).

9.4 Federalism

The UK constitution is a 'unitary' constitution with an overriding supreme lawmaker which can devolve power to subordinate units but is free to take the power back. In a federal state such as the US, the constitution divides power between a central government and separate units in such a way that each unit is independent within its own sphere and neither can override the other except as specified by the constitution. Each has its own constitution, legislature and courts.

How powers are allocated varies according to the history and political concerns of the state in question. There may be demarcation problems to be resolved by the courts, so federal constitutions have a strong legalistic element. There is usually a single citizenship of the central state, the federal government being responsible for foreign affairs, defence and major economic matters, while private law issues are the responsibility of the states. Criminal offences, social regulation and public services may be allocated to either level.

Usually particular matters are given to the federal level, with the residue left with the states, but the converse sometimes applies (eg in Canada). Switzerland provides an extreme example of a constitution where both the powers of the federal government and its personnel are severely limited in favour of the autonomy of the cantons. The relative political power of each level depends on the circumstances of each country and cannot necessarily be discovered from the law itself.

Federalism is practicable where the component units have sufficient in common economically and culturally to enable them to cooperate, while at the same time each unit is sufficiently distinctive to constitute a community in its own right but not sufficiently powerful to aspire to a role on the international stage. Thus a delicate balance must be struck. The US and Australia are relatively successful federations, whereas Canada with its split between English-speaking and French-speaking regions is less stable. Yugoslavia with its many ethnic tensions was tragically unsuccessful once Soviet control was removed.

Federalism is more a matter of degree than of absolutes. The term 'federal' is not a legal definition but an abstract model. There is no reason why any particular constitution should correspond neatly to the model. It is probably best to regard terms such as 'federal' or 'unitary' not as precise definitions but as a political spectrum ranging from loose associations of countries for particular purposes to simple one-government states.

Federal and devolved governments both respond to the idea of group liberalism and particularly of national and local identities (Chapter 2). Federalism also gives effect to republican values of equality and division of power (Section 2.5). During the late nineteenth century there were some advocates of a federal UK as a way of avoiding home rule for Ireland. John Stuart Mill (1972, ch 13) argued in favour of devolved rather than federal government. He suggested that smaller devolved units encourage individuals to participate in public affairs and that the UK constitution did not require the protection of a federal framework since our culture was less obsessed with uniformity than the cultures of continental countries. This is a political debate relevant to the EU. On the other hand Mill would give the most important powers to the centre since there may not be enough serious issues at local level to justify the time of competent public officials or attract the interest of talented people. He also thought that local government was at risk of corruption by small business interests. Dicey (1915, 171), the influential Victorian constitutional lawyer, strongly opposed federalism, claiming that it tends towards conservatism, creates divided loyalties and elevates legalism to a primary value, making the courts the pivot on which the constitution turns and perhaps threatening their independence. Devolved government is therefore a pragmatic compromise (cf Olowofoyeku, 'Decentralising the United Kingdom: The Federal Argument' (1999) 3 Edinburgh LR 57).

The Royal Commission on the Constitution (Cmnd 5460, 1973) argued against a federal constitution for the UK on the following grounds:

- There would be a lack of balance since the units are widely different in economic terms, with England being dominant.
- A federal regime would be contrary to our constitutional traditions in that it would elevate the courts over political machinery.
- The UK was thought to require central and flexible economic management since its resources are unevenly distributed geographically, much of it comprising thinly populated hills.
- Apart from Northern Ireland, regional issues were not high on the agenda of the main parties, which suggested that there was little public desire for federalism.

9.5 The Channel Islands and the Isle of Man

The Channel Islands (Jersey, Guernsey and Sark) and the Isle of Man have special constitutional status, being neither part of the UK nor British overseas territories. They are subjects of the Crown, which makes laws for them in the form of Prerogative Orders in Council. They have their own legislatures, executive and judiciary and can make laws governing their internal affairs. Their status derives from feudal ownership by the Crown as successor to the Duke of Normandy. The common law does not apply in the Channel Islands and their internal law is local customary law. As Crown territories, the protection provided by the judicial review powers of the High Court applies (see *Ex p Brown* [1864]; *Ex p Anderson* [1861]). The European Convention on Human Rights (ECHR) applies to the Channel Islands. They are not members of the EU but there are special treaty arrangements. Channel Island citizens are British citizens (British Nationality Act 1981, ss 1, 11, 50(1)).

Parliamentary supremacy was extended to the Channel Islands by a Prerogative Order in Council of 1806. However there is a presumption of interpretation that an Act will not apply to the Channel Islands in the absence of express words or necessary implication.

Sark, with a population of 600, is subject to Guernsey law but retains a feudal structure (the only one in the western world) under which a hereditary ruler, the Seigneur (to whom the Crown granted the right by letters patent of 1565 and 1611), owns the land and appoints the main judicial and executive officers. However under pressure from the European Court of Human Rights a Constitution of 2008 introduced a democratic majority into the legislature, the Chief Pleas (see Reform (Sark Law) Order in Council 2008). The Seigneur can speak in the Chief Pleas but cannot vote. He has a temporary veto over legislation. 'Aliens' under UK law cannot stand for election (see *R (Barclay) v Secretary of State for Justice* [2009]). Contrary to the separation of powers the Chief Judge (the Seneschal) presides over the Parliament. However he can neither speak nor vote.

The position of the Isle of Man is broadly similar to that of the Channel Islands. The Crown's rights seem to derive from an ancient agreement with Norway, confirmed by statute (Isle of Man Purchase Act 1765 (repealed)). Legislation made by its elected legislature, the Tynewald, must be assented to by the Queen in Council. (See generally Royal Commission on the Constitution, 1973, Part XI and Minutes of Evidence VI, 7, 13, 227–34; *X v UK* [1982].)

9.6 British overseas territories

In the case of most of the former British Empire, all legal ties with the UK have been severed by Acts of Parliament (eg the Canada Act 1982; the Australia Act 1986). The Commonwealth remains as an informal grouping of former UK possessions but has no legal significance. The UK retains some dependent overseas territories. Previously called colonies, they are now 'British overseas territories' (British Overseas Territories Act 2002). They are mainly scattered islands. They include Anguilla, Bermuda, British Indian Ocean Territories (BIOT), British Virgin Islands, Cayman Islands, Falkland Islands, Gibraltar, Montserrat, the Pitcairn Islands, St Helena, South Georgia and South Sandwich Islands (SGSSI), and the Turks and Caicos Islands.

All overseas territories are subject to the overriding principle of parliamentary supremacy. However Acts of the UK Parliament do not apply to them unless they specifically so provide. Moreover under the Colonial Laws Validity Act 1865, legislatures in overseas territories have full power to make local laws, even if this is inconsistent with a UK statute of general effect or with the common law (s 5). This may extend to altering their own constitution but only in the 'manner and form' required by any UK law applying to the territory at the time (see *Bribery Comr v Ranasinghe* [1965]; *R v Burah* [1878]).

The application of the common law and the powers of the UK executive depend on historical factors, namely how the territory was acquired. There is an important distinction between 'settled' colonies and 'ceded and conquered' colonies (see *R (Bancoult) v Secretary of State for the Foreign and Commonwealth Office (No 2)* [2008]). A settled territory is one in which there were no developed political institutions when British settlers first arrived (such as SGSSI). A ceded territory previously had its own governmental institutions and was either ceded (given up) to Britain (often in a peace treaty following armed conflict) or conquered by force.

In the case of settled territories the powers of the executive are restricted; English common law as it stood at the time of settlement is deemed to have applied to the territory, which means that the limitations placed on the royal prerogative in England apply in that territory. In effect the settlers took English law with them. Most significant are the restrictions laid down in the *Case of Proclamations* [1611], after which the King could not introduce new laws without the consent of Parliament. In settled colonies therefore the Crown does not have the power to pass laws for the colony under the royal prerogative, just as it does not in England. The legislative function in the territory can only be exercised under the powers given by an Act of Parliament (see British Settlement Acts 1837 and 1945). Under the Acts statutory instruments made by ministers can create constitutions for each territory and delegate powers to local officials. Such powers are usually expressed as being for the 'peace, order and good government' of the territory but it is unclear whether this ritual phrase has any specific legal effect (below).

In the case of ceded territories the powers of the Crown are more extensive (*Campbell v Hall* [1774]). The reason for the distinction is of course that extended powers were needed to suppress the existing governments in conquered territories. English common law does not automatically extend to the territory, which means that the *Case of Proclamations* does not apply. Thus the Crown has full power to make law under the royal prerogative and to impose its own governmental arrangements and taxation including overriding fundamental rights (see *Bancoult (No 2)* at [96]–[101]). New laws can be framed for the territory either by a Prerogative Order in Council or by letters patent or royal proclamation. Also governors can be appointed ('commissioned') to make laws within the authority conferred on them by the Crown (in formal 'Royal Instructions' and in subsequent despatches).

Such powers are also usually expressed as being for the 'peace, order and good government of the territory'. However it seems that this requirement does not limit the width of the prerogative lawmaking power and the courts will not inquire into the matter (see *Bancoult (No 2)* at [31], [47]–[50], [109], [127]–[130]). However a similar requirement contained in a statutory instrument in respect of a *settled* territory might limit the executive's power since such power would be only subordinate.

The Crown can deprive itself of the prerogative lawmaking power. Lord Mansfield in *Campbell v Hall* [1774] decided that, where there is a local legislature, the power is transferred from the Crown to the colony in question and cannot be recovered.

In *Campbell* the Crown had issued a proclamation empowering a colonial governor to establish a local legislative assembly, although by the date of the action none had been created. Despite the formally announced intention to decentralise government, the Crown had subsequently attempted to impose a new tax directly on the colony and the court held that this was unlawful. Although the assembly had not actually been established it was held that by promising to create one the Crown had lost its power to pass laws under the prerogative for that colony. The reason for this was that the Crown had sought investment and invited settlers to the colony, who would have relied on the promise to create a local assembly. Their private interests would have been better served under this decentralised arrangement than under direct rule. The quandary for Whitehall was that taxes had to be levied if the colonies were not to be a burden on British taxpayers but, after *Campbell*, unless it continued with direct rule, the Crown had to rely on local assemblies to agree to the required taxation.

More generally, *Campbell* indicates that prerogative powers are not unlimited and in particular a formal promise governing the future exercise of prerogative powers can bind the Crown. It is unclear whether *Campbell* – the authority of which has never been doubted – is a decision that is now to be confined to its own facts or whether it establishes a wider principle of constitutional law, the boundaries of which remain unclear.

There is a further complication. Where a British overseas territory of either kind has its own government, even a rudimentary one, it may be that the Crown is 'divisible', meaning that the Crown in relation to the territory is a separate legal entity from the Crown of the UK (*R v Secretary of State for the Foreign and Commonwealth Office, ex p Indian Association of Alberta* [1982]; *R v Secretary of State for Foreign and Commonwealth Affairs, ex p Quark Fishing Ltd* [2006] at [9], [20], [76]). If this is correct the courts will assess the Crown's actions in relation to the interests of the territory in question and not those of the UK. Moreover, unless statute provides otherwise, the Crown should act on the advice only of the government of the territories concerned, not that of UK ministers (see Twomey, 'Responsible Government and the Divisibility of the Crown' [2008] PL 742).

In *Quark* Baroness Hale rejected the divided Crown doctrine as artificial (at [95]). In *Bancoult (No 2)* (see below), the House of Lords also rejected the divided Crown doctrine. Lord Hoffmann, following the eminent eighteenth-century jurist William Blackstone, stated that in relation to dependent territories there was a single undivided Crown (at [47]–[50]). The divided Crown doctrine is more plausible in relation to independent states, such as Australia, which have chosen to retain the UK monarch as their head of state.

The divided Crown doctrine is sometimes defended on the basis that it may be politically difficult to separate the interests of the UK government as such from its interests in the dependency and undesirable for a court to try to do so. A formal if artificial distinction is therefore useful (see *Quark*).

The judicial review powers of UK courts apply to overseas territories of both kinds – *Quark* (settled territory) and *R (Bancoult) v Secretary of State for the Foreign and Commonwealth Office (No 1)* [2001] (ceded territory). This means that the Crown's prerogative powers are limited by general notions of fairness and rationality which give way only to clear words in a statute (Chapter 18). However Laws LJ has suggested that common law presumptions that protect the individual in domestic law against interference from the state have limited application to overseas territories (*Bancoult (No 1)*; see Section 6.6). Moreover the Human Rights Act 1998 does not automatically apply to overseas territories (*Quark* (see below)).

The complexities discussed here are illustrated in the following cases.

R v Secretary of State for Foreign and Commonwealth Affairs, ex p Quark Fishing Ltd [2006] concerned a *settled* territory, South Georgia and South Sandwich Islands (SGSSI), comprising mainly a shifting population of scientists. It had a government, albeit one comprising only a part-time civil servant Commissioner. The Secretary of State on behalf of the Crown, acting under the constitution of SGSSI (a statutory instrument made under the British Settlements Act 1837), had ordered the Commissioner to refuse a fishing licence to the claimant. His reason for so doing concerned the UK's relationships with neighbouring countries. The Court of Appeal applied the divided Crown doctrine, holding that the decision was unlawful since it was not made for the benefit of SGSSI but for the purposes of the separate UK government.

The claimant also sought damages under the Human Rights Act 1998, which makes the main human rights under the European Convention on Human Rights binding in domestic law. A majority of the House of Lords (Lord Bingham especially applying the divided Crown doctrine) agreed that the decision was made by the Crown of SGSSI not that of the UK. Therefore the Human Rights Act 1998 did not apply since the Act applies only to the UK government. However Lord Nicholls and Lady Hale thought that the divided Crown doctrine (which Lady Hale at least thought questionable) was irrelevant. Their rationale was that, except in special cases, the Human Rights Act 1998 only applies within the UK itself (see Section 21.1.1). The Act might however apply to dependent territories if the ECHR has been extended to them, as the Convention so provides.

R (Bancoult) v Secretary of State for the Foreign and Commonwealth Office (No 1) [2001], involved a *ceded* territory, also with its own government. The Commissioner of the British Indian Ocean Territories (BIOT), which comprised a group of islands, was delegated power under the royal prerogative to make law for the territory. On the instructions of the UK government, he made an order (the Immigration Ordinance 1971) expelling the population of the territory from the islands, resettling them elsewhere. The population consisted mainly of plantation workers, some of whose families had lived there for several generations. It was UK government policy to use the territory as a military base jointly with the US and for this purpose it wished to remove the inhabitants, treating them as temporary workers so as to avoid problems with the United Nations. The Divisional Court held that the decision was unlawful since it bore no relationship to the interests of the inhabitants. Laws J also thought that the prerogative power could not be exercised so as to exile a permanent inhabitant from the territory in which he has a right to live.

Following this decision the Foreign Office announced that the islanders would be compensated and allowed to go home. However subsequently the Crown itself on the advice of UK ministers, under pressure apparently from the US, made an Order in Council under the royal prerogative which purported to change the Constitution of BIOT by denying the exiled inhabitants a right of abode in the territory.

In *R (Bancoult) v Secretary of State for the Foreign and Commonwealth Office (No 2)* [2008] the House of Lords held that it had jurisdiction to review a Prerogative Order in Council since such an Order was in reality made by ministers not the Crown itself (another example of convention shaping the law; see Section 3.4.2). Although an Order in Council was primary legislation it did not have the democratic credentials that made a statute unchallengeable. However this Order was valid. A majority held (Lord Bingham and Lord Mance dissenting) that the Order was not an abuse of power since the royal prerogative was not limited by any requirement that the law must be for the benefit of the inhabitants of the territory. There was a single Crown which, provided that the interests of the territory were considered, could prefer the larger interests of the UK as a whole. Any right could be removed by a Prerogative Order in Council since this was an exercise of full lawmaking powers. Moreover the ritual phrase 'peace, order and good government [of the territory]' did not limit the scope of the prerogative power and the court would not inquire whether the Order was in fact for the peace and good government of the inhabitants. This was a general matter of policy unsuitable for a court (at [109]). The majority also considered that the inhabitants' rights to their homeland, violated at the previous stage, had been compensated with their agreement and that any statement the government had made was not sufficiently clear and unambiguous to create an enforceable 'legitimate expectation' that they would be allowed to return (see Section 17.9). Lord Bingham (in his final case) strongly dissented. He applied the 'principle of legality' (see Section 6.6), holding that only clear words in a statute could take the fundamental right to a home. (The majority held, perhaps illogically given that they agreed that the Order in Council was reviewable, that the words of the Order itself were clear enough to override the right.)

Bancoult (No 2) and *Quark* are therefore in conflict in relation to the divided Crown doctrine, and Lord Hoffmann, who was a member of both panels, changed his mind (see *Bancoult (No.2)* at [48]). The fact that *Quark* concerned a settled territory does not seem material since the distinction between settled and ceded territories relates only to the source and scope of the powers, not to the identity of the governments. If anything the divided Crown doctrine is even less plausible in relation to a settled territory since the theory behind it seems to be that the settlers take English law with them. However in a settled territory there is no power to make law under the prerogative, so the ritual phrase 'peace, order and good government [of the territory]' if used, as was the case in *Quark*, in the statutory constitution of the territory may have some bite.

9.7 International affairs

It is often argued that the state is no longer appropriate as the basic constitutional unit. It is said that pressures from within towards devolution to areas of regional identity, and pressures from outside towards globalisation, have weakened the legitimacy of the state. It is pointed out that we live in a 'global' economy of interdependent countries supported by electronic communication and dominated by highly mobile organisations that can operate in many countries. Unelected international governmental bodies such as the United Nations, the World Trade Organization, the International Monetary Fund and the European Commission wield considerable influence over national governments. Influential businesses such as banks and media organisations are capable of putting pressure upon state governments (eg using the press to investigate politicians' private lives). They have assets and operations scattered globally which can readily be moved around. Thus while an international business is of course subject to state laws, enforcing these may be almost impossible. Contemporary problems require international cooperation and sometimes shared laws. These problems include the environment, terrorism, financial wrongdoing, computer fraud and hacking, refugees, human and drug trafficking, fugitive offenders, international trade and financial regulation.

Such developments can be rationalised by making the assumption that states have passively consented to them. International law contains few democratic mechanisms and involves the cooperation of peoples with different cultures and legal values. It has been suggested that democracy and the rule of law can flourish only at the margins where there is a large measure of stability and consensus. Moreover globalisation is a one-way street that involves the 'developed' liberal world imposing its ideas on the allegedly 'undeveloped' world – but rarely, if ever, the other way round. (See Harden, *Liberalism, Constitutionalism and Democracy* (Oxford University Press 1999); Marks, *The Riddle of All Constitutions* (Oxford University Press 2000)). The particular problem for constitutional law is to identify methods by which principles and rules made internationally can be filtered into domestic law and given effect without sacrificing fundamental constitutional principles, in other words trying to strike a balance between constitutionalism and international requirements.

Specific issues include the following:

- To what extent are international treaties and other forms of international law binding in UK law?
- To what extent are foreign states and their officials subject to UK law?
- What is the role of the law in relation to external matters such as sending forces abroad or dealing with extradition requests and with refugees?

9.7.1 Treaties and international law

Customary international law consists of principles generally accepted and evidenced by the practice of states. Customary international law has traditionally been part of the common law and so can be applied directly by the court. However this principle is not popular today, being highly undemocratic. International custom is difficult to establish and customary law gives way to other common law principles (*Chung Ch Chung v R* [1939] at 168; *R (Al Saadoon) v Secretary of State* [2010] at [58], [59]). In particular customary law cannot create new crimes in the UK since this should done only by the democratic process of Parliament (see *R v Jones (Margaret)* [2006]: campaigners who damaged military aircraft to prevent the international crime of aggression had no defence).

Related to custom are certain fundamental principles which are regarded as generally accepted by the international community. These include duties not to harm other states, for example by pollution or unfair use of common resources such as waterways, and international crimes such as torture, genocide and war crimes. In the case of pollution and resource issues enforcement largely depends on international arbitration but international crimes are increasingly enforced through treaties to which effect is given in domestic law.

Today the main method for imposing constitutional order on an unruly world is through international treaties. A treaty (sometimes called a 'convention' but nothing to do with constitutional conventions) is a binding agreement between states or international organisations such as the UN and states. After a treaty is agreed by representatives of each party it has to be ratified (confirmed) according to the law of each state involved. Ratification brings the treaty into force at international level. In the UK treaties are ratified by ministers under the royal prerogative subject to some scrutiny by Parliament (below).

A treaty is 'non-justiciable' (see Section 19.7.1). Thus a court cannot consider whether a treaty making power has been unlawfully exercised or review the content of a treaty or prevent a minister from ratifying it, although the court might feel able to comment on the implications for domestic law of the issues raised. (See *R v Secretary of State for Foreign and Commonwealth Affairs, ex p Rees-Mogg* [1994]; *Blackburn v A-G* [1971].) Similarly a domestic court cannot normally determine disputed questions of international law (*R (Gentle) v Prime Minister* [2008]). However the common law is an open system which can draw on principles from other jurisdictions and from international law as a means of evaluating and improving the law (see Lord Bingham in *Fairchild v Glenavon Funeral Services Ltd* [2003]).

In addition to ratification a treaty may have to be made enforceable in domestic law. In some states international law, including treaties, is automatically part of domestic law, often being made such by the constitution (a *monist* system, eg Constitution of Russian Federation 1993, Art 15(4)). In the UK, which has a *dualist* system, this is not so. Irrespective of ratification a treaty cannot directly alter rights and duties in domestic law unless it is first enacted by Parliament in a statute, either by adopting the language of the treaty or by setting out the treaty as a Schedule to the Act (see *JH Rayner (Mincing Lane) Ltd v Dept of Trade and Industry* [1990]). This is separate from any parliamentary scrutiny needed for ratification (below). Thus there is protection against lawmaking by the executive. Treaties which do not directly affect domestic law require only ratification.

It has been suggested that this dualist approach is too narrow and that general principles of international law embodied in treaties concerning fundamental rights such as freedom from torture and freedom of speech should automatically be part of the common law irrespective of their enactment in statute (see Lord Steyn in *Re McKerr* [2004], although his position has not received general support; see *R v Bow Street Metropolitan Stipendiary Magistrate, ex p Pinochet Ugarte (No 3)* [1999]).

In the UK treaties are made and ratified by ministers under the royal prerogative and are not subject to parliamentary approval before ratification, unless of course a particular statute requires this (eg European Union (Amendment) Act 2008, ss 5, 6: certain alterations to EU treaty).

Part 2 of the Constitutional Reform and Government Act 2010 places the ratification of treaties on a statutory basis by enacting a previous convention, the 'Ponsonby Convention', under which a treaty was subject to limited parliamentary scrutiny before ratification. Section 20 applies to all treaties (except certain EU treaties that require statutory approval, certain tax treaties and treaties made by UK dependencies and the Channel Islands and Isle of Man). The main provisions are as follows:

- A treaty must be laid before Parliament for 21 days and published in a way that the minister 'thinks appropriate'.

- If the House of Commons resolves that the treaty should not be ratified the minister can lay a statement before Parliament that it should be ratified anyway and explaining why.
- After another 21 days the treaty can be ratified unless the Commons passes a further resolution that it should not be ratified. This process can be repeated but given the strength of the executive and the lack of background information available to Parliament the executive is likely to prevail.
- If the House of Lords but not the Commons resolves not to ratify the treaty it can be ratified anyway.

In cases which in a minister's opinion are exceptional a treaty can be ratified without complying with the above. Before or as soon as possible after ratification the minister must lay a copy of the treaty before Parliament, publish it and lay a statement before Parliament explaining why the case is exceptional (s 22). Parliament has no power in this situation.

The UK courts have been divided as to the effect of a treaty that has not been incorporated into English law (see Higgins, 2009; Collins, 2009). On a strict traditional view a court can ignore a treaty that has not been incorporated into domestic law since otherwise it would be allowing the executive to make law (see *JH Rayner v Dept of Trade*; *Brind v Secretary of State* [1991] at 748). However if the parties raise the issue the court can interpret a treaty, although it is reluctant to interpret treaties from scratch (see *R (Corner House Research) v AG* [2008], where it was suggested by Lord Browne (at [65]) that the court should accept the interpretation of the executive provided that it was tenable.

It is not feasible to insulate domestic legal issues from international issues. In recent years important treaty obligations have been directly applied domestically irrespective of formal incorporation (eg *Kuwait Airways v Iraqi Airways (No 1)* [1995] and *(Nos 4 and 5)* [2002]: UN Resolutions; see Section 9.7.2). The UN Refugee Conventions (Cmd 9171, 1951; Cmnd 3906, 1967) are particularly important in this respect in that they require the UK to give asylum to those at risk of persecution in their own country (eg *R (JS) v Secretary of State for the Home Dept* [2010]).

Treaties and other forms of international law may be sucked into domestic law indirectly. For example under the Human Rights Act 1998 decisions of the European Court of Human Rights under the ECHR must be taken into account by UK courts even though the ECHR has not been incorporated into UK law. The European Court in turn sometimes applies other international instruments, all of which must therefore be considered by the UK court.

For example in *R (Al-Jedda) v Secretary of State* [2008] an Iraqi citizen was interned by the army acting under UK jurisdiction in a British army camp in Iraq. He alleged that his human right to freedom under Article 5 of the ECHR had been violated. The House of Lords held that the claimant's right had not been violated. This was because the European Court took the view that in some circumstances other international obligations, in this case to comply with a UN peacekeeping resolution, could override the protection of the ECHR. The House of Lords, faced with a hard choice, held that the claimant's rights could be overridden only to the extent that was necessary to comply with the UN resolution. This involved a careful examination of the resolution and related principles of international law.

There has also been controversy concerning whether a statute incorporating a treaty should be interpreted literally or flexibly in order to give effect to the intention of the treaty. The latter is the prevailing approach (see *Garland v British Rail Engineering Ltd* [1983] at 771). Indeed the courts should interpret and apply any treaty according to international law principles not domestic law (see *R (JS) v Secretary of State for the Home Dept*).

9.7.2 Acts of foreign governments: state immunity and acts of state

Traditionally the acts of foreign governments have been given substantial respect in UK courts. Much of this remains out of concern for international relations. However the increasing importance of international standards has led to inroads being made on this principle. The law is subject to continuing evolution. In the past there was general common law immunity for acts of foreign governments but as international transactions have increased this has become more relaxed (see UN Convention on Jurisdictional Immunities of States and Their Property (not yet ratified); *Jones v Ministry of Interior of Saudi Arabia* [2006] per Lord Bingham).

The current position depends primarily on the State Immunity Act 1978. The state itself has complete immunity from civil liability (claims for compensation etc) for the acts of its agents even if carried out outside instructions. This applies to the body exercising sovereign authority, meaning the 'executive organs of the central government', to the head of state and to ambassadors representing the state. The Act's protection for serving governments and their servants is a blanket one (see eg *NML Capital Ltd v Republic of Argentina* [2010]). It applies to unlawful acts and even to violations of fundamental international principles such as torture (*Jones v Ministry of Interior of Saudi Arabia*). In *Al Adsani v UK* [2001] the European Court of Human Rights held that this immunity is not a violation of the ECHR and can be justified on the ground of international relationships.

There are certain exceptions. The main ones concern commercial transactions (sales and loans), contracts to be performed within the UK, contracts of employment made in the UK or to be performed there, patents and trademarks, personal injury and property damage within the UK, the ownership, possession and use of property, commercial shipping matters and certain taxation matters. However the property of the state central bank or monetary authority cannot be enforced against (see *AIG Capital Parties Inc v Republic of Kazakhstan* [2006]).

The immunity is more limited in the case of individual officials and separate bodies acting as agents of the state ('separate entities'; State Immunity Act 1978, s 14) and also in the case of former heads of state. These might be personally liable. However the immunity of the state cannot be circumvented by suing the individual. The individual servant or separate entity is therefore only liable in respect of actions which are not carried out as 'governmental' functions. For example running an airline by a state-owned company was held not be a governmental function even though the aircraft in question had been confiscated by the government and handed over to its subsidiary company (*Kuwait Airways v Iraqi Airways (No 1)* [1995], see below). A governmental function therefore seems to mean the basic lawmaking, executive and judicial activities of government.

In *Jones v Minister of the Interior of Saudi Arabia* the House of Lords, citing a wide range of international authorities, held that torture carried out by individual officers under the orders of the Saudi government was a governmental function so that the officers were immune even though torture is prohibited by a fundamental principle of international law (see Torture Convention (Cm 1775, 1990)). The state itself had blanket immunity (above). Thus two incommensurable principles had to be 'balanced' (see Section 2.2.1). It was also held that state immunity complies with the Human Rights Act 1998. It is controversial whether international conventions on immunity should exclude human right abuses (see Fox, 2006).

Criminal proceedings are different. Criminal liability concerns punishment and is centred on the individual not the state as such. In *Jones v Minister of the Interior of Saudi Arabia* Lord Bingham emphasised the distinction between civil and criminal proceeding (at [19]). Immunity in criminal cases depends on the Diplomatic Privileges Act 1964 as applied to a head of state by section 20 of the State Immunity Act 1978.

Thus, under the international law of diplomatic immunity (see Vienna Convention 1961), serving heads of state, serving diplomats and their households other than UK nationals have complete immunity from criminal prosecution arrest and detention. However *former* heads of state are immune only in relation to the proper functions of the state. In *Pinochet* (below) it was held that the former President of Chile had no immunity since for criminal purposes torture should not be regarded as a proper function of the state. This is because all parties to the Torture Convention 1984 have agreed to make torture wherever committed a crime in their states. It is not clear whether the *Pinochet* principle applies to breaches of international law other than torture.

R v Bow Street Metropolitan Stipendiary Magistrate, ex p Pinochet Ugarte (No 3) [1999] illustrates the difficulties of applying international values. Pinochet was the former head of state of Chile making a private visit to the UK. The Spanish government requested that he be extradited to Spain to stand trial in respect of murders and torture that he was alleged to have organised in Chile during his term of office. The Torture Convention 1984 was put into English law by the Criminal Justice Act 1988. The Convention requires a state either to prosecute or extradite an alleged offender. Pinochet relied on state immunity. The House of Lords, unusually comprising seven judges, held that Pinochet was not entitled to immunity. However their Lordships took different routes to their conclusions.

Lords Browne-Wilkinson, Hutton, Saville and Phillips, forming the majority, held that state-sponsored torture violated fundamental principles of international law that Chile had accepted by signing the Convention. Torture was therefore not to be regarded as a proper state function for the purposes of criminal liability. They held however that Pinochet could only be extradited for offences that were alleged to have taken place after 29 September 1988, when the Act came into force, since treaties as such cannot alter rights in English law (above).

Lord Millett, supported partly by Lord Hope and Lord Hutton, was more radical. He argued that, irrespective of the 1988 Act, torture was an international offence under customary international law and was therefore unlawful at common law whenever and wherever committed. Lord Hutton said that 'certain crimes are so grave and so inhuman that the international community is under a duty to bring to justice a person who commits such crimes' (at 163).

Lord Goff, dissenting, held that the State Immunity Act 1978 should protect Pinochet because it does not specifically exclude torture as an official act. He emphasised legal certainty, pointing out the difficulty of drawing lines between different kinds of wrongdoing and the problems that might be faced by former heads of government who ventured into countries whose interests they had damaged while in office. (In the end the Home Secretary refused to extradite Pinochet on health grounds.)

The doctrine of 'act of state' also gives protection to foreign governments. The term has a range of meanings. In the present context it means two things (see also Section 9.7.2). Firstly it means that for reasons of mutual respect, UK courts will not normally question the acts of foreign governments within their own territories. This applies not only to actions against the state itself but in any litigation where the matter arises. However this is not an absolute rule and, although the court will exercise great caution, acts which violate clear principles of international law can be questioned (see *Kuwait Airways v Iraqi Airways (Nos 4 and 5)* [2002] (below)). The difficulties and risks of a court delving into foreign politics are obvious.

Secondly an act of state in a more technical sense is a claim that certain facts as declared by a sovereign government (meaning the highest government authority) cannot be challenged in any litigation. This applies both to foreign governments and to the UK government. An act of state in this sense includes claims to territory (eg *Buttes Gas v Hammer (No 3)* [1982]), conferring sovereign immunity (eg *Mighell v Sultan of Johore* [1894]), recognising a new government or state (eg *Carl-Zeiss-Stiftung v Raynor and Keeler (No 2)* [1967]) and declaring war (eg *R v Bottrill, ex p Kuchenmeister* [1947]).

A wider issue overlapping with but not to be confused with immunity and act of state is that of *justiciability*. Sometimes a policy act of government, such as a decision to use troops, will not be investigated by the court or will be subject only to limited investigation on the ground that the court does not consider that it has the expertise, tools or constitutional legitimacy to dig deeper. In *Buttes Gas v Hammer* the doctrine was justified at the international level as applying 'where there are no judicial or manageable standards ... or the court would be in a judicial no-man's land' (at 938). The doctrine of justiciability has wider application and will be discussed later (see Section 19.7.1)

Kuwait Airways v Iraqi Airways (No 1) [1995] concerned the Iraqi invasion of Kuwait in 1990, where Iraq claimed that Kuwait was Iraqi territory. Iraqi forces seized aircraft belonging to Kuwait and took them to Iraq. The Iraqi government later made a law transferring the aircraft to the state-owned Iraqi Airways, which used the aircraft for its business. The aircraft were later destroyed in a UN attack on Iraq and the Kuwaiti airline sued Iraqi Airways for compensation. The Kuwaiti case depended on the Kuwaiti airline still being in the eyes of the law the owners of the aircraft. Many difficult issues were raised, of which two concern us. Firstly the House of Lords held that the Iraq government itself was immune under the 1978 Act but that, after the law transferring ownership was issued, Iraqi Airways was not using the aircraft for governmental purposes. There was therefore no immunity. (Lords Mustill and Slynn dissented, holding that the law transferring ownership, which was certainly governmental, could not be separated from the activities which followed.)

However in *Kuwait Airways v Iraqi Airways (Nos 4 and 5)* [2002] Iraqi Airways raised the second argument that the confiscation and the law transferring ownership to Iraqi Airways were acts of state and non-justiciable. The House of Lords rejected this argument on the ground that the Iraq government had committed a flagrant breach of a fundamental principle of international law and this overrode any claim to act of state. Lord Hope stressed that the reach of the law should evolve in keeping with contemporary circumstances.

9.7.3 Control of external affairs

The courts are reluctant to investigate government policy decisions in relation to foreign affairs. They may regard them as non-justiciable (above), including for example decisions to go to war and other dispositions of the armed forces (see *CND v Prime Minister* [2006] at [30], [65]). Such decisions, which are usually taken under the royal prerogative and so subject to little if any parliamentary scrutiny, may have serious effects on individual rights. However rights protected by the Human Rights Act 1998 are justiciable, although the court may exercise restraint in the sense that the nature of the issue may influence the decision as to whether there is a protected right at stake (see *Gentle*: decision to invade Iraq; see also *Amin v Brown* [2005]).

Furthermore, the defence of 'act of state' (used in yet a difference sense to those discussed above) prevents the state being liable for injuries it causes to non-UK citizens overseas. This version of act of state dates from the days of imperial aggression. The Crown is not liable for injuries caused in connection with bona fide acts of government policy overseas, provided that the action is authorised or subsequently ratified by the Crown (eg *Nissan v A-G* [1970]: British troops billeted in Cyprus hotel: not an act of policy; *Buron v Denman* [1848]: British naval officer set fire to barracks in West Africa in order to liberate slaves: Crown subsequently confirmed the action).

The defence of act of state does not apply to acts done within the UK itself, except against 'enemy aliens', that is citizens of countries with which we are formally at war (*Johnstone v Pedlar* [1921]: US citizen imprisoned: Crown liable). This is because the Crown owes a duty to protect anyone who is even temporarily on British soil. Indeed for the same reason the defence may not be available against a British subject anywhere in the world. In *Nissan* the House of Lords expressed divided views (see also *Walker v Baird* [1892]). It seems unfair to favour people with no substantial link with the UK merely because they happen to hold British passports.

Some UK government actions may also be 'acts of state' in the two senses discussed in the previous section and not challengeable for that reason. In respect of acts of state of these kinds even British subjects may be deprived of rights. For example in *Cook v Sprigg* [1899] the Crown annexed Pondoland and refused to honour railway concessions granted to British subjects by the former government (see also *West Rand Central Gold Mining Co v R* [1905]). This kind of act of state may affect rights within the UK. It includes a declaration of war, which permits citizens of the enemy state in the UK to be detained (see *Johnstone v Pedlar; R v Bottrill, ex p Kuechenmeister*), the recognition of a foreign government (*Carl-Zeiss-Stiftung v Rayner & Keeler*) and conferring diplomatic immunity (*Engelke v Musmann* [1928]). Current practice seems to be to avoid formal declarations of war. For example the invasion of Iraq in 2002 was not a formal war.

9.7.4 International co-operation

This includes the sensitive areas of immigration, security and crime, which traditionally have been the core functions of the state. The topic is too large and various to be dealt with in this book and we will confine ourselves to sketching some key examples which affect domestic law. The UK has been jealous of its rights in relation to security and law enforcement and has opted out of many EU functions concerned with policing and justice matters. Moreover different political and cultural values embodied in legal practices have led to a cautious approach in relation to overseas legal systems. On the other hand humanitarian concerns and need for co-operation with other states (comity) have led to important treaties which have been implemented in domestic law. Examples are as follows.

- UK criminal law normally applies only within the territory, but some crimes such as torture and war crimes are regarded as so heinous that they can be prosecuted wherever committed (see Torture Convention 1984; Criminal Justice Act 1988). The International Criminal Courts Act 2001 gives effect to treaty obligations to ensure that alleged war criminals (genocide, war crimes, crimes against humanity but not the crime of 'aggression') can be arrested in the UK, prosecuted in the International Criminal Court in the Hague and serve sentence here.
- Although it basically applies only within the UK, in exceptional cases the Human Rights Act 1998 can apply to acts done by the UK government overseas, at least in territory where it can be said to be directly exercising some of the functions of government, for example within military prisons in Iraq (see Section 21.2). However the Act does not apparently apply to dependent territories unless perhaps the ECHR has been specifically extended to them (see Section 9.6).
- Certain UN Conventions, including the power to freeze assets belonging to suspected offenders, can be given effect by Order in Council under the United Nations Act 1947 (see Section 23.7.6).
- Under the UN Refugee Conventions 1951 and 1967 the UK must give refuge to asylum seekers.
- Under the Human Rights Act 1998, giving effect to requirements of the ECHR, a person cannot be deported or extradited (below) to a country where there is a risk that the state will interfere with or condone interference with his or her basic human rights (see *Chahal v UK* [1996]; Section 20.4.2).

9.7.4.1 Extradition

Extradition is a response to a request from another state to send a person to it either to be tried or sentenced for a criminal offence or because that person has escaped from custody. Extradition therefore raises a conflict between mutual co-operation and the question of whether the justice system in the other country is such that serious injustice is not being done. The law is highly complex and only the main considerations will be sketched here.

Under the Extradition Act 2003 requesting states are graded into two categories:

- Firstly there are the highly trusted *Category 1* countries, mainly other EU members but others can be added by Order in Council. A state which retains the death penalty cannot be a Category 1 state (s 1). Extraditable offences are offences committed in the requesting state and not the UK, contained on a list of offences specified in the *European Arrest Warrant Framework Decision* of the EU Council (2002/584/HA; Extradition Act 2003, Sch 2) and punishable with at least three years' imprisonment. International crimes such as genocide are also extraditable (s 64(6), (7)). Offences punishable by 12 months' or more imprisonment may also be extraditable even if partly committed in the UK but must be offences both in the UK and in the requesting country.
- Where the requesting country issues a warrant to a designated authority in the UK certified as such by the Secretary of State (these are the usual prosecuting agencies) naming the suspect and specifying the offence the offender must be arrested and brought before a senior district judge. A provisional arrest of a suspect in advance of a warrant is permissible. The court's function is limited to checking whether the accused is the right person and the offence is an extraditable offence. The question of guilt or innocence is not investigated and little discretion is involved. There is an appeal to the High Court and with permission to the Supreme Court, but only if the High Court certifies that a point of law of general public importance is involved.
- The accused must be extradited unless certain 'extraneous considerations' apply, in which case the accused cannot be extradited. These include double jeopardy (s 12), lapse of time where extradition would be unjust or oppressive (s 14), discrimination (s 13), age (below the age of criminal responsibility in the UK, which is 10 years), human rights (s 21) and 'Speciality', meaning the absence of an agreement between the UK and the requesting state that the suspect will be dealt with only in relation to the matters specified in the warrant. There are provisions relating to the offence of hostage taking under which a person cannot be extradited if his trial would be prejudiced because he cannot communicate with the authorities.
- In respect of Category 2 states, which include all other states, the main differences are as follows:

  (i) There must be an extradition treaty between the requesting state and the UK.
  (ii) The extradition request is made to the Home Secretary.
  (iii) The warrant is a UK warrant issued by a court.
  (iv) The offence must be an offence in the UK as well as in the requesting state.
  (v) The court must be satisfied that there is sufficient evidence to justify the extradition, namely a prima facie case. In the case of requests from the US the treaty negotiated by the government of Tony Blair dispenses with this safeguard.
  (vi) After rights of appeal have been exhausted the final decision is taken by the Home Secretary, who has a limited discretion (s 93). She can consider whether on the grounds of physical or mental condition extradition would be unjust or oppressive. She must also take into account whether the death penalty is involved and the Speciality issue (above). The Home Secretary is not involved with Category 1 cases.

The former exclusion for 'political offences' was abolished by the 2003 Act. However the UK can refuse to extradite a person who was acting as an agent for the UK government, on national security grounds, if the conduct in question was not criminal in the UK due to authority given by the Secretary of State (s 203; see Sections 23.4, 23.5).

Summary

- The UK constitution has no unified concept of the state. This leads to a fragmented system of government but may protect individual freedom.
- Citizenship entitles a person to reside in the UK and has certain other miscellaneous consequences. There is no legal concept of the citizen corresponding to the republican notion of equal and responsible membership of the community.
- The UK constitution does not distribute power geographically so as to limit the power of the state. The UK is therefore not a federal state. The UK has devolved governments subordinate to the centre (see Chapter 16).
- British overseas territories are subject to the jurisdiction of the UK courts but not generally to the Human Rights Act 1998. The lawmaking power of the UK government depends on whether the territory in question is a settled territory. The powers of the executive are wider in the case of a ceded territory.
- The traditional 'divided Crown' doctrine is questionable and the cases conflict.
- The Queen is head of the Commonwealth. This has no constitutional connection with the UK.
- International law does not automatically apply in domestic law but is filtered into UK law by Parliament and the courts. Customary international law is to a limited extent recognised by the common law. A treaty must be ratified by the Crown, normally with the consent of Parliament.
- The courts have recently become more liberal in their use of treaties in domestic law but a treaty cannot directly alter legal rights and duties unless incorporated into a statute. Treaties can be used to help the interpretation of statutes.
- Substantial immunity from control by the courts is given to foreign governments and heads of state by statute but this only applies to individual officials and separate public bodies in respect of government functions as such.
- Foreign governments, and sometimes the UK government exercising functions in relation to foreign affairs, are also protected by the overlapping concepts of 'act of state'. This has at least three different meanings: conclusive evidence of a state of affairs, an act of high policy that is non-justiciable and a defence to an action against the Crown for causing injury or damage abroad. However important international standards have made some inroads into this.
- There are arrangements for cooperation with other states in relation to criminal jurisdiction. Problems arise because of different legal cultures. Safeguards depend on the relationship with the other state.

Exercises

9.1 To what extent does UK law recognise the concept of the state? Is the concept of the Crown an adequate substitute? (See also Section 14.1.)

9.2 What is a federation? Outline the advantages and disadvantages of a federal structure compared with a devolved structure.

9.3 To what extent does the UK constitution provide satisfactory means of giving effect to international treaties?

9.4 Explain and illustrate the different meanings of 'act of state'.

9.5 The UK government decides to recognise Cornwall as an independent state. In order to help the new Cornish government to get established, the Prime Minister sends an army platoon to Cornwall as a peacekeeping force. Bill, a UK citizen, and Hilary, a US citizen, each own a hotel in Cornwall. Bill also runs a taxi business from his hotel. Hilary's hotel is damaged by British troops during a birthday party for their corporal. The Cornish head of state uses Bill's hotel as his office while a new palace is being built. He has not paid his bill for several weeks. Also, on the instructions of the Cornish government, Cornish soldiers commandeered Bill's fleet of taxis for use in military operations.

(i) Advise Bill and Hilary as to any remedies available to them in the English courts.

(ii) On a shopping trip to London the Cornish head of state is arrested and charged with an internationally recognised crime, namely kidnapping English holidaymakers in Cornwall. Advise him. What would be the position if he had resigned office immediately before his trip?

9.6 The (imaginary) island of Stark was settled by the UK in the seventeenth century. It has a population of 600. It is governed by a Commissioner employed by the Foreign Office, who is advised by an elected Council. The UK government makes an Order requiring all the inhabitants to leave the island. The reason it gives is that it fears the island will soon be devastated by a volcano. George, whose family has lived on Stark for many years, is told by an American friend that the government's real motive is to hand the island over to the US for a naval base. Advise George as to whether he can successfully challenge the Order in the English courts. Would it make any difference if Stark had originally been seized by Britain from France?

9.7 The Government of Carribia, an independent Commonwealth country, is overthrown by a rebel force, The People's Front. Cane, the displaced Prime Minister of Carribia, requests the aid of the British government. British troops are sent to Carribia and are authorised under an agreement between the British government and Cane to 'use all necessary measures to restore the lawful government of Carribia'. During the British troops' campaign on the island they requisition buildings owned by Ford, an American citizen, for use as a military depot, and destroy the home of Austin, a British citizen, in the belief that it is being used as a base by the rebels. Ford and Austin sue the British government for compensation. Discuss. Would your answer differ if Carribia was a British overseas territory?

9.8 Ruritania is an independent member of the Commonwealth. The Queen is also the Queen of Ruritania. Last week a military coup in Ruritania succeeded in capturing the palace occupied by the Governor General, who represented the Queen. The military commander requests the Queen to abdicate in favour of himself as King. The situation in Ruritania is currently uncertain and forces loyal to the Queen are attempting to secure control. The British government advises the Queen not to abdicate in the interests of trade between the UK and Ruritania. The Commonwealth Secretary-General advises her to abdicate. How would you advise the Queen?

9.9 Suppose that a new government recognised by the UK has been installed in Ruritania (above) and the former Governor General has fled to the UK. The Ruritanian government requests the UK to extradite the former Governor General on charges of fraud in relation to his private affairs. Advise the UK government.

Further reading

Brown, 'Moving from Cosmopolitan Legal Theory to Legal Practice: Models of Cosmopolitan Law' (2008) 28 LS 430

Collins, 'Aspects of Justiciability in International Law' in Andenas and Fairgrieve (eds), *Tom Bingham and the Transformation of the Law* (Oxford University Press 2009)

Dyson, *The State Tradition in Western Europe* (Martin Robertson 1980) chs 1, 4

Feldman, 'The Internationalization of Public Law and Its Impact on the United Kingdom' in Jowell and Oliver (eds), *The Changing Constitution* (6th edn, Oxford University Press 2007) ch 5

Fox, 'In Defence of State Immunity' (2006) 55 ICLQ 399

Higgins, 'National Courts and the International Court of Justice' in Andenas and Fairgrieve (eds), *Tom Bingham and the Transformation of the Law* (Oxford University Press 2009)

Lowe, 'Rules of International Law in English Courts' in Andenas and Fairgrieve (eds), *Tom Bingham and the Transformation of the Law* (Oxford University Press 2009)

Walker, 'The Idea of Constitutional Pluralism' (2002) 65 MLR 317

Chapter 10
The European Union

Europe has never existed. It is not the addition of national sovereignties in a conclave that creates an entity. One must genuinely create Europe. (Jean Monnet, 1888–1979)

In this chapter we shall discuss the main legal principles relating to the European Union as they affect the UK constitution. We shall not discuss the internal workings of the EU except from this perspective. Readers should also refer to Chapter 9, which discusses the impact of the EU on parliamentary supremacy.

10.1 Introduction: the nature of the European Union

The EU is a unique legal arrangement, being both international and embedded in the constitutional law of the UK. The legal basis of the EU comprises various treaties which are intended to be directly enforceable within the law of the member states as well as having enforcement provisions at the European level. Treaties as such cannot alter domestic law but EU law was made effective in the UK by the European Communities Act 1972. Many areas of domestic law – principally commercial, agricultural, employment, environmental and social welfare matters – are affected by EU law, which was famously described by Lord Denning as an 'incoming tide' (*Bulmer Ltd v Bollinger SA* [1974]).

What was originally called the Common Market was created after the Second World War (1939–45) as an aspiration to prevent further wars in Europe and to regenerate the European economies. The prototype was the European Coal and Steel Community created by the Treaty of Paris (1951). This is now abolished. Two other communities were created in 1957 by two Treaties of Rome. They were the European Community (EC) (formerly called the European Economic Community) and the European Atomic Energy Community (Euratom). The communities shared the same institutions.

The founder members of the EU were France, Germany, Italy, Luxembourg, Belgium and the Netherlands. Membership has steadily increased. The UK became a member in 1972 (European Communities Act 1972), membership being confirmed by a referendum in 1975. There are now 27 members, including former communist countries, thereby altering the original balance and introducing a wide range of economic, political, cultural and religious perspectives that challenge the old-fashioned blend of republicanism and liberalism of the founder members. Members who joined at later dates are Austria, Denmark, Finland, Greece, Ireland, Portugal, Spain and Sweden. The following joined in 2004 under the Nice Treaty (2003): Cyprus, the Czech Republic, Estonia, Hungary, Latvia, Lithuania, Malta, Poland, Slovakia and Slovenia. Bulgaria and Romania joined in 2007. Turkey, Serbia and Iceland have applied for membership.

The objectives of the communities were originally economic, primarily to encourage free movement of people, services, goods and capital between member states. However the organisation was heavily influenced by a desire to protect agricultural interests, espoused principally by France. This has left the EU with a substantial financial burden in that nearly half of its budget is still devoted to agricultural subsidies. The interests of the EU have steadily widened, partly by a process of interpreting the existing objectives liberally and partly by the member states formally agreeing to extend the areas of competence of the EC. For example the Single European Act 1987 made environmental protection a separate area of competence and the Lisbon Treaty (2009) has added space, policy, energy, tourism, civil protection and administrative cooperation. The EU has also developed substantial security, justice, policing and foreign policy objectives in an attempt to increase its influence on the world stage. However there is provision for states to take competencies back and indeed to leave the EU. This requires the agreement of the European Council and the Parliament (see Section 10.2).

A series of treaties broadened the scope of the EU but also introduced measures under which individual states could participate to different extents:

- *The Single European Act 1987* was intended to strengthen community institutions and widen the scope of community powers. It created the European Council of heads of state and strengthened the role of the European Parliament. It broadened the scope of EU law, in particular to include environmental protection. It also initiated a gradual process of reducing the power of individual states to veto community proposals.
- *The Maastricht Treaty* (1992) created the EU as an umbrella political organisation but at the time without its own legal identity. Maastricht also instigated progress towards monetary union, including the creation of an independent European Central Bank. There is now a single European currency, the euro, which is regulated by the European Central Bank. The UK does not participate in this. The possible effect of the single currency upon the independence of the UK Parliament is one reason why the decision whether or not to join the euro is widely regarded as raising important constitutional issues. There is also freedom of movement between the mainland EU states under the *Schengen Agreement*. The UK is not a party to this. Thus the Maastricht Treaty enabled participation in the EU at different levels.
- *The Amsterdam Treaty* (1997) introduced further safeguards and flexibility arrangements in favour of national governments, which can opt in or out of some provisions. Involvement in the European enterprise is therefore sometimes described as 'variable geometry'.
- *The Nice Treaty* (2003) made some reforms to cater for the larger membership of the community. These included the creation of the Court of First Instance and enlarging the membership of the European Parliament.
- *The Lisbon Treaty* (Cm 7294, 2009) is an attempt to rationalise and consolidate the European Union as a supranational organisation. It replaces the so-called Constitutional Treaty which was rejected in 2005 by referenda in France and Germany. Illustrating perhaps the political and symbolic sensitivity of the idea of a written constitution, the Lisbon Treaty reproduces the main provisions of the abortive constitution minus its constitutional rhetoric. Instead it is drafted as a complex amending treaty overlaying previous treaties. The Lisbon Treaty is intended to strengthen the European Union as an international organisation and to streamline

its decision-making processes in view of the large increase in its membership. The main changes made by the Lisbon Treaty will be discussed in their contexts (see also House of Lords Select Committee on the European Union, Tenth Report (HL 2007–08, 62)). There is also provision in the Lisbon Treaty for closer cooperation between member states in foreign affairs and defence matters, including sharing military resources, whereby it is intended to increase the international role of the EU – a role the EU has so far failed to achieve, having been preoccupied for many years with its own internal organisation and with 'harmonising' the laws of member states. These matters are outside the scope of this book.

- The main treaties as revised by the Lisbon Treaty are the *Treaty on European Union* (TEU) and the *EC Treaty*, now to be called *The Treaty on the Functioning of the European Union* (TFEU). The TEU deals with general political principles and the basic structure and functions of the institutions. The TFEU deals with the specific powers and functions of the EU, its legal machinery and the detailed composition, powers and processes of the institutions. It also deals with the Charter of Fundamental Rights. In 1991 the European Court of Justice (ECJ), which is charged not only with securing compliance with the law but also with advancing the aims of the communities, described the EC Treaty as a 'constitutional charter' based on the rule of law. It emphasised that individuals as well as states are the subjects of community law, although in fact individuals other than those employed by the EU have only limited rights to instigate proceedings in the Court (see *Opinion on the Draft Agreement on a European Economic Area* [1991] ECR I-6084).

The rule of law is a primary concern. All EU laws and decisions must fall within the powers conferred by the treaties and cannot go beyond what is necessary for achieving the objectives of the treaties. As with all treaties, an alteration to the EU treaties requires the consent and ratification of member states. To this end there is an elaborate procedure for consultation involving the EU institutions and national Parliaments and an intergovernmental conference (TEU, Art 48).

The following are the broad areas of competence of the EU (TFEU). They are ordered historically. They overlap, and some (notably the internal market) have a higher priority than others, acting as a general theme. The same is true to a lesser extent of the environment, which must be integrated into all policies. There are sometimes provisions for states to opt out or take individual measures.

- the internal market: free movement of goods within the EU;
- free movement of export and imports (customs union);
- agriculture and fisheries;
- free movement of persons, services and capital;
- establishment (setting up businesses etc);
- providing services within member states;
- movements of capital;
- freedom (mainly immigration), security (policing) and justice (cooperation between court systems); this is a sensitive area due to different legal cultures within the Union (the UK has opted out of much of this);

- transport;
- competition, taxation and 'approximation' (harmonisation) of national laws in order to achieve the single market;
- economic and monetary policy (the UK has opted out of the single currency, the euro);
- employment;
- social policies: living and working conditions, social security, high employment, labour relations;
- European Social Fund: employment in deprived areas (eg Cornwall);
- education, vocational training, youth and sport;
- culture;
- public health;
- 'trans-Europe networks': transport, telecommunications, energy infrastructure;
- industry (competitiveness);
- economic, social and territorial cohesion (reducing regional disparities);
- environment;
- energy;
- tourism;
- civil protection;
- administrative cooperation;
- external relationships.

Before the Lisbon Treaty the powers of the EU bodies were grouped into three main policy areas, or 'pillars': economic development, common foreign and security policy, and cooperation in justice and home affairs. Only the first pillar, which of course is very large, together with immigration, was regulated by law. The Lisbon Treaty enables all areas of EC concern in principle to be legally enforceable. The EU now has three kinds of power (TFEU, Arts 3–6):

- *Exclusive power* concerns customs, competition in relation to the internal market, the euro, the common fisheries policy and common commercial policy. In these cases, member states cannot legislate independently at all.
- In most other cases there is *shared power*. Here member states can legislate, at least until the EC has decided to intervene (see *Commission v UK* [1981]).
- *Supporting, co-ordinating or complementary functions* are primarily for the member states but the EU can exercise funding powers. This category includes health, industry, culture, tourism, education, vocational training, youth and sport, civil protection and administrative cooperation.

There is a tension between EU law and the independence of member states (see Section 10.5). This is reflected in the voting arrangements of the Council of Ministers, which, usually in conjunction with the Parliament, is the primary lawmaking body, comprising ministers from all the member states. There has been a steady movement away from a principle of unanimity, which preserves control by individual states, to 'qualified majority' voting, which is weighted in favour of the larger states. Unanimity is required for taxation, defence, foreign policy and social security, although under the so-called *Passerelle* [bridge] clause the Council can alter this (see Section 10.4).

The Lisbon Treaty extends the 'variable geometry' of the EU by introducing arrangements for 'enhanced cooperation' under which at least nine states may apply to the Council of Ministers to 'opt in' to exercise extra powers in relation to the 'non-exclusive' functions of the EU. This must be a last resort and must not undermine the internal market or economic, social or territorial cohesion (TEU, Art 20). Thus the aspiration towards universal abstract rules and ideals cutting across cultural differences is far from achieved (see Section 1.6).

The EU generates its values mainly from individualistic and economic liberalism (see Section 2.3). Its values are declared to be respect for human dignity, freedom, democracy, equality, the rule of law and human rights. In certain circumstances the Council of Ministers can suspend membership rights of states which are judged to have seriously violated these values (TEU, Art 7).

There is some republican element (see Section 2.5). For example it is made clear that every citizen has an equal right to participate in the democratic life of the Union (TEU, Arts 9, 10). However this is realised only by limited voting rights for political parties in the European Parliament (below) and various opportunities to make requests of officials. There is a concept of citizenship of the EU that is conferred automatically on citizens of the member states (TEU, Art 9; TFEU, Arts 20–22). This is additional to state citizenship and gives certain rights. These are free movement and residence within the EU, the right to stand or vote in local government and devolved government elections and in elections to the European Parliament on the same terms as nationals, and various rights of access to EU institutions (see Section 10.4).

Democracy has not been the highest value of either the original or the revised union. Democratic government is a requirement of membership and the EU claims to act on the principle of representative democracy. By this it means the right to vote for representatives in the European Parliament and the fact that the European Council and the Council of Ministers (below) are made up of representatives of the member states, albeit not necessarily elected ones (see TEU, Art 10). The EU is a paternalistic concept intended to impose a particular vision of the good life built around a combination of welfare and market liberalism. The various unelected European institutions therefore have a larger share of power than the elected European Parliament. However the democratic element in EU processes has been strengthened by the Lisbon Treaty, mainly by improving links with national Parliaments (see Section 10.4).

The historian Tony Judt doubted the democratic credentials of the EU. He characterised the EU as similar to the enlightened European despots of the eighteenth century with their 'ideal of efficient, universal administration, shorn of particularisms and driven by rational calculation and the rule of law' (*New York Review of Books* 1995, quoted by Wheatcroft, *Guardian*, 9 August 2010).

It is important to be clear that the European Convention on Human Rights (ECHR) is not a creation of the European Union but is under the auspices of the Council of Europe, which is a completely different organisation with its own court, the European Court of Human Rights. The main connection between the two organisations is that European law takes account of the ECHR, and all member states and the EU itself are parties to it.

The EU has its own Charter of Fundamental Rights, which has the same status as the treaties themselves and can in principle be legally enforced (TEU, Art 6). The Charter overlaps with but goes beyond the ECHR, including workers' rights such as the right to strike, data protection and bioethics, as well as the nebulous concepts of dignity, freedom, solidarity, citizenship and justice. However the UK has opted out of making the Charter enforceable in our domestic courts. Also the Lisbon Treaty guarantees that the Charter cannot be used by the European Court to alter UK labour laws and social rights. The UK has also opted out of the Charter in respect of asylum and immigration matters and can pick and choose which rights to accept in the areas of justice and home affairs.

There are also many provisions relating to discrimination in EU law. Most generally Article 19 of the TFEU requires that member states must control discrimination based on sex, racial or ethnic origin, religion or belief, disability, age or sexual orientation (see also TEU, Art 2). Discrimination on the ground of nationality is not included. Indeed the EU could be regarded as a highly nationalistic enterprise, a club of relatively wealthy nations.

10.2 Institutions

The EU has lawmaking, executive and judicial powers which are blended in a unique way that does not correspond to traditional notions of the separation of powers or liberal democracy. The primary concern is to provide a balance between the interests of the Community and those of the member states. There are no clear lines of accountability. Power is divided between institutions, some of which share the same functions. Such democratic accountability as there is takes the forms of (i) a limited degree of accountability to an elected European Parliament and (ii) arrangements made under the constitutions of the individual states. The balance between the different bodies, particularly in relation to the Parliament, varies according to the treaty provision under which a particular issue arises. It might be said that the primary distribution of power creates a tension between a centralising rationalist element represented by the Commission and the Court and a negotiating cooperative element represented by the Council and the Parliament.

The main institutions are as follows:

- Council of Ministers;
- European Council;
- European Commission;
- European Parliament;
- European Court of Justice.

Other important community institutions include the Court of Auditors and the Committee of Permanent Representatives (COREPER), comprising senior officials who prepare the Council's business and are very influential, and the European Central Bank. There are also advisory and consultative bodies, notably the Economic and Social Committee and the Committee of the Regions. These are outside the scope of this book.

10.2.1 The Council of Ministers

This is the primary lawmaking body, in conjunction in many cases with the Parliament. The Council's main function is to approve or amend laws proposed by the European Commission, although in some cases it can ask the Commission to make a proposal. It also decides the budget, adopts international treaties and is responsible for ensuring that the objectives of the Treaties are attained. The Council is made up of a minister representing each member state who must be authorised to commit the government. The membership fluctuates according to the business in hand. A President holds office for six months, each member state holding the office in turn.

The Council is biased towards national interests rather than towards an overall 'community view'. The community view is represented by the Commission (below), creating a distinct kind of separation of powers and a recipe for political tension.

The way in which Council decisions are made is therefore all important. When it considers draft legislation it must meet in public (TFEU, Art 15). Certain decisions (albeit a shrinking category) must be unanimous, thus permitting any state to impose a veto. An increasing number of decisions are made by a qualified majority, whereby votes are weighted according to the population of each state. From 2014 under the Lisbon Treaty a 'double weighting' will be applied. This will require a majority of 55 per cent of states (at least 15, and with a blocking minority of 4), together with 65 per cent of the population, thus reflecting the more varied membership of the EU (TEU, Art 16(4)). Sometimes a simple majority suffices.

10.2.2 The European Council

The European Council is a twice-yearly meeting of heads of state, together with the President of the Commission. It 'provide[s] the Union with the necessary impetus for its development and shall define the general political guidelines thereof' (Single European Act 1987). The Council as such has no lawmaking power but is the most important political influence on the European Union. It appoints the Commission (below). It is particularly important in relation to foreign and security policies. It seems to tip the balance of power away from the supranational elements of Commission and Parliament towards the intergovernmental element. It makes reports to the European Parliament after its meetings and also a yearly written report on the progress of the Union. The Lisbon Treaty has created the office of President of the Council, whom it elects for two-and-a-half years (TEU, Art 15(2)). The President is chair of the Council but has no executive powers. The President cannot hold any national elected office. The purpose of this office is apparently to strengthen the public profile of the EU.

Under the Lisbon Treaty there is also an office of High Representative for Foreign Affairs, appointed and dismissed by the European Council with the agreement of the President of the Commission and working with the Council to develop foreign policy and to represent the EU abroad (TEU, Art 18).

10.2.3 The European Commission

The Commission is the executive of the EU (TEU, Art 17). It represents the interests of the EU as such. It is required to be independent 'beyond doubt' of the member governments. It is responsible to the European Parliament.

The main functions of the Commission are:

- to propose laws or political initiatives for adoption by the Council. The Council or the Parliament can request the Commission to submit proposals;
- to make laws itself, either directly under powers conferred by the Treaty or under powers delegated to it by the Council;

- to enforce EC law against member states and the other EC institutions. The EC has no police or law enforcement agencies; it enforces the law by issuing a 'reasoned opinion', negotiating with the body concerned and if necessary initiating proceedings in the ECJ (Art 226);
- to administer the EU budget;
- to negotiate with international bodies and other countries.

Because membership of the Council of Ministers fluctuates, it is vulnerable to being dominated by the permanent officials of the Commission. The Commission is driven by an abstract rationalist ideology reflecting the rule of law in its narrow sense, as opposed to the politically driven negotiating character of the Council. The effective operation of the system depends on a threefold network of understandings between Commission, Council and Parliament.

The political legitimacy of the Commission is weak. The number of commissioners is determined by the European Council, which also fixes their salaries. The Commission currently comprises 27 members, one member from each state irrespective of its size. There is however provision to reduce the number of commissioners from 2014 to comprise two-thirds of the member states on a revolving basis (TEU, Art 17(5); TFEU, Art 244). Whether this can be achieved is controversial.

The President of the Commission is chosen by the European Council with the approval of the Parliament. The Vice President is the High Representative for Foreign Affairs (above). The European Council appoints the other commissioners with the agreement of the President, the candidates being nominated by the member states. Each commissioner is appointed for a renewable term of five years. The appointment of the Commission as a body must be approved by the Parliament. The appointment process takes place within six months of the elections to the Parliament, thereby strengthening democratic input. However the Parliament cannot veto individual candidates, so accountability is weak.

The whole Commission can be dismissed by the Parliament. The President can be dismissed by the European Council for serious misconduct. Individual commissioners have limited independence. The President assigns departmental responsibilities (directorates-general) to the other commissioners, who are required to conform to the political direction of the President. Members of the Commission cannot formally be dismissed during their terms of office but can be 'compulsorily retired' by the European Court on the ground of inability to perform their duties. Moreover individual commissioners must resign at the President's request. Individual commissioners can it seems also be withdrawn by their governments, thus placing doubt on the independence of the Commission.

10.2.4 The European Parliament

The European Parliament is the only elected institution. It does not initiate law and was originally created as an 'advisory and supervisory' body. However it increasingly participates in the lawmaking process. It has a maximum of 751 seats (temporarily raised by treaty amendment to 754). These are allocated in proportion to the population of each member state, ranging from 6 to 96. Elections are held every five years. Since 1979 members of the European Parliament (MEPs) have been directly elected by residents of the member states, the detailed electoral arrangements being left to each country.

Elections to the EU Parliament in Britain are on the basis of a 'closed party list' (European Parliamentary Elections Act 2002). There are 87 seats, divided into electoral regions (nine for England, one each for Scotland, Wales and Northern Ireland, with 71, 8, 5 and 3 members respectively). Each party lists its candidates in order of preference and votes can be cast for either a party or an individual standing separately. The seats are allocated in the order set out on the list by the parties in proportion to the share of the vote achieved by each party.

A Parliament lasts for five years and is required to meet at least once a year. It meets roughly once each month, alternating expensively between Strasbourg and Luxembourg. Its members vote in political groupings and not in national units. It meets in public. Freedom of speech and proceedings within the Parliament are protected but, unlike the UK Parliament, the European Parliament does not seem to enjoy privilege against interference from the courts, and the ECJ can review the legality of its activities (*Grand Duchy of Luxembourg v Parliament* [1983]).

The Parliament's main functions are as follows:

- New laws must normally be proposed by the Commission, although the Parliament can ask it to do so. As a result of a gradual extension of the Parliament's powers, culminating in the Lisbon Treaty, most areas of lawmaking require the consent both of the Council of Ministers and the Parliament (Ordinary Legislative Procedure). Under the Special Legislative Procedure in certain cases regarded as especially sensitive, such as competition law and exemptions from the internal market, the Parliament need only be consulted, while in other cases, including discrimination law and the admission and withdrawal of member states, the Parliament can veto a measure but cannot amend it. Some provisions concerning external trade are made by the Council alone.
- The Parliament approves the EU budget jointly with the European Council. It can veto only the whole budget – a sanction too extreme to be of practical use.
- It approves treaties, the appointment of the Commission and its President, the admission of new member states and certain other important matters. It must be consulted on the appointment of certain other senior officials.
- By a two-thirds majority that is also an absolute majority of all members, it can dismiss the entire Commission but not individual members of it. Again this sanction is too extreme to be of much use.
- It can question members of the Commission orally or in writing. Commissioners often appear before its committees, although it has no legal power to compel this.
- It can hold committees of inquiry into misconduct or maladministration by other EC bodies.
- It appoints an Ombudsman to investigate complaints by citizens, residents or companies based in member states against EC institutions (other than the ECJ).
- Any citizen, resident or company based in a member state can petition it on a matter that comes within the EC's field of competence and affects him, her or it directly. (Apart from the Parliament's limited powers, the fragmented nature of community decision making makes parliamentary accountability weak, a problem compounded by the fact that the implementation of EC laws and policies is carried out by national governments. The accountability of MEPs is itself weak since elections are in large constituencies and there is little relationship between an individual member and the voter. It is not surprising that the turnout for elections to the Parliament is usually low (around 25%).)

10.2.5 The European Court of Justice

The ECJ comprises judges appointed by agreement between the governments of the member states. Unlike national judges they have little security of tenure, being appointed for a renewable term of six years and dismissible by the unanimous opinion of the other judges and advocates-general (Statutes of the Court, Art 6). As well as the judges there are eight advocates-general, who provide the ECJ with an independent opinion on the issues in each case. The opinion of the advocates-general is not binding on the ECJ but is highly influential.

There is one judge from each member state. Appointments must be made from those eligible for the highest judicial office in each member state and also from 'jurisconsults of recognised competence'. This permits such persons as academic lawyers or social scientists to be appointed. The judges elect a President for a renewable period of three years. The ECJ sits as a Grand Chamber of 11. There is also a Court of First Instance, sitting in panels of three or five. This hears cases of kinds designated by the Council (unanimity is required). There are no specific qualifications for appointment to the Court of First Instance other than being a person 'whose independence is beyond doubt and who possesses the ability required for judicial office'. The Court of Justice hears appeals on a point of law from the Court of First Instance.

The ECJ's task is to ensure that 'in the interpretation and application of the EC treaty the law is observed'. The 'law' consists of the treaties themselves, the legislation adopted in their implementation, general principles developed by the Court, the *acquis communautaire*, which is the accumulated inheritance of community values, and general principles of law common to the member states, including the European Convention on Human Rights. There is also 'soft law', which is not binding but must be taken into account. Soft law includes 'declarations and resolutions adopted in the community framework; international agreements and agreements between member states connected with community activities'. It has been suggested that parts of the EU system are 'entrenched' in the sense that not even the Treaty itself could be altered in defiance of them. However in *Grau Gromis* [1995] the ECJ accepted that 'the Member States remain free to alter even the most fundamental parts of the Treaty'.

The main jurisdiction of the ECJ is as follows:

- enforcement action against member states who are accused of violating or refusing to implement European law. These proceedings are usually brought by the Commission but can be brought by other member states, subject to their having raised the matter before the Commission. The Commission first gives the member state a chance to state its case. The Court can award a lump sum or penalty payment against a member state which fails to comply with a judgment of the Court that the state concerned has failed to fulfil a treaty obligation. The EC has no enforcement agencies of its own. The Court therefore depends on national law to enforce its rulings;
- judicial review of the acts or the failure to act of community institutions. Such actions can be brought by other institutions and by member states. An individual or private body can bring an action only in special circumstances where the community act in question is directed to the individual in person or is of 'direct and individual concern to him or her' (eg *Salamander v European Parliament* [2000]). In contrast to its reluctance to permit individuals to sue the EC, the Court has been liberal in supporting individual rights against national governments;

- preliminary rulings on matters referred by national courts. This is the linchpin of the ECJ's role as a constitutional court. Any national court, where it considers that a decision on the question is necessary to enable it to give judgment, may request the ECJ to give a ruling on a question of community law. The role of the European Court is confined to ruling upon the question of law referred to it. It then sends the matter back to the national court for a decision on the facts in the light of the Court's ruling. A court against whose decision there is no judicial remedy in national law (ie the highest appeal court or any other court against which there is no right of appeal or review) must make such a request. UK courts are required to follow decisions of the ECJ (European Communities Act 1972, s 3(1)). The power to give preliminary rulings does not apply to the Court of First Instance.

It may be difficult to decide whether a reference can or should be made. The parties have no say in the matter (*Bulmer v Bollinger* [1974]). A court need not make a reference if it thinks the point is irrelevant or 'reasonably clear and free from doubt' (the *acte-claire* doctrine) or if 'substantially' the same point has already been decided by the ECJ (see *CILFIT Srl v Ministro della Sanita* [1983]). In *R v International Stock Exchange, ex p Else (1982) Ltd* [1993], Bingham LJ said that 'if community law is critical to the decision the court should refer it if it has any real doubt' (at 422). The court can take into account the convenience of the parties, the expense of the action and the workload of the European Court (ibid; *Van Duyn v Home Office* [1974]; *Customs and Excise Comrs v Aps Samex* [1983]).

It may also be difficult to decide whether the law is sufficiently clear to entitle the UK court to decide for itself. Much depends upon how English legal culture responds to the different reasoning methods of the ECJ, that is whether the UK court approaches the problem by way of our traditional 'literal' approach to questions of interpretation or takes a broader approach, focusing on the 'spirit' as opposed to the letter of the law, in the continental manner (below). The same applies to the question of whether a decision in the matter is 'necessary' for the resolution of the case. We may not know this until we know what the relevant community law means.

The ECJ's jurisdiction over criminal and security matters depends on the consent of the state concerned. It has no jurisdiction in respect of the operations of the police and other law enforcement agencies. However in other areas, for example policing demonstrations, the ECJ can require the police to give priority to EC aims such as freedom of trade (see *R v Chief Constable of Sussex, ex p International Traders Ferry* [1999]).

It is often said that the constitutional glue that holds together the communities and the member states in a constitutional framework is the rule of law represented by the ECJ. The Treaty itself is not explicit as to the relationship between the ECJ and the law of the member states, but the ECJ has developed principles that have enabled it to favour EC law. According to some commentators the ECJ has, in defiance of the normal values of judicial impartiality and democracy, taken upon itself the political agenda of promoting the European enterprise. It has attempted to enlist national courts by requiring them to defer to EC law and by conferring on individuals European law rights that are enforceable in national courts. On the other hand it has injected some democratic principles into EC law, albeit in a sporadic fashion.

10.3 Community law and national law

Sections 2 and 3 of the European Communities Act 1972 require UK courts to apply EC law in accordance with the decisions and general principles of the ECJ. We saw in

Section 8.4.4 that the doctrine of parliamentary supremacy has been modified by the 1972 Act to the extent that a binding EC law overrides an inconsistent UK statute unless perhaps the statute specifically states that it is to prevail.

There are different ways of approaching the relationship between EC law and national law. One is to regard EC law as a distinct system in which the UK courts must participate by applying European methods as if they were federal courts. On this basis the UK court dealing with an EC matter is effectively a European court. Another would be to regard EC law as 'processed' into English law under the authority of the European Communities Act 1972, to be approached in much the same way as other legislation in the light of the strict reasoning methods of English law. The choice between these two approaches influences the extent to which the courts are willing to subordinate UK law to EC ideas.

There seems to be no consistent practice among the English judges and examples of both approaches can be found. In *Mayne v Ministry of Agriculture, Fisheries and Food* [2001] it was held that UK regulations implementing an EC Directive do not apply to future amendments of the Directive unless they are clearly worded as doing so. However in *Berkeley v Secretary of State for the Environment* [2000] Lord Hoffmann emphasised the importance of giving effect to EC law's environmental purposes.

There is also a 'spillover effect' whereby rights initially established for European purposes are later extended to domestic contexts on the basis that it would be unjust for domestic law to be more restrictive than EC law (eg *M v Home Office* [1993]: interim relief against the Crown). More generally it has been said that involvement with Europe has accelerated the tendency to approach the interpretation of legislation from a broad purposive perspective as opposed to the narrow linguistic perspective traditionally favoured by the English courts (Lord Steyn in *R (Quintavalle) v Secretary of State for Health* [2003]).

Some EC measures take effect in domestic law 'without further enactment' (European Communities Act 1972, s 2(1)) and are automatically part of UK law. This is determined by EC law itself (below). In other cases there must be a conversion to UK law, usually in the form of a statutory instrument (s 2(2)). Certain measures, including taxation, the creation of new criminal offences and retrospective laws, can only be implemented by an Act of Parliament (Sch 2). The relationship between parliamentary supremacy and EC law was discussed in Chapter 9.

The main kinds of EC legal instrument are as follows (see TFEU, Art 288):

- *The Treaty.* Treaty provisions are sometimes directly enforceable in the UK courts (below).
- *Regulations.* These are general rules which apply to all member states and persons. All regulations are 'directly applicable' and as such are automatically binding on UK courts except where a particular regulation is of a character that is inherently unsuitable for judicial enforcement.
- *Directives.* A Directive as such is not automatically binding but is sometimes so (below). It is a requirement to achieve a given objective but leaves to the individual states the choice of forms and methods to implement the Directive. A Directive may be addressed to all states or particular states. A time limit is usually specified for implementing the Directive.
- *Decisions.* A Decision is 'binding in its entirety' but if it specifies those to whom it is addressed it is binding only on them.

- *Opinions and recommendations.* These do not have binding force. However the ECJ has power under Article 228(6) of the TFEU to give an opinion at an early stage of a matter, for example in relation to a proposed treaty.

10.3.1 Direct applicability and direct effect

'Direct effect' must be distinguished from 'direct applicability', which applies only to EC regulations. Regulations are always binding whereas 'direct effect' depends upon the quality of the particular EC instrument. Where the direct effect doctrine applies, the national court must give a remedy which as far as possible puts the plaintiff in the same position as if the Directive had been properly implemented. This might for example require national restrictions to be set aside, national taxes to be ignored or national rules that are stricter than a Directive covering the same ground to be set aside (eg *Defrenne v SABENA* [1976]: retirement restrictions; *Pubblico Ministero v Ratti* [1979]: excessive labelling requirements). It has been suggested that the ECJ developed the direct effect doctrine in order to make use of domestic law enforcement agencies as a means of compensating for the weak enforcement provision offered at EC level through the Commission (see Weatherill, 1995, 101ff).

Direct effect applies to the Treaty and Directives. A Treaty provision that has direct effect is enforceable against anyone upon whom its provisions impose an obligation. Directives however can be enforced only 'vertically', that is against a public authority or 'emanation of the state', and not 'horizontally' against a private person (see *Marshall v Southampton AHA (No 1)* [1986]; *Faccini Dori v Recreb* [1995]). The reason seems to be that the state, which as we saw above has the primary duty to implement a Directive, cannot rely on its failure to do so, an argument that it would be unfair to apply to a private body. It also follows that the state cannot rely on an unimplemented Directive against an individual (see *Wychavon DC v Secretary of State* [1994]).

For the purpose of direct effect, any public body seems to be regarded as an emanation of the state (*Marshall v Southampton AHA (No 1)*). However the meaning of 'public body' varies with the context. For this purpose a public body must (i) exercise functions in the public interest subject to the control of the state and (ii) have special legal powers not available to individuals or ordinary companies (see *Foster v British Gas* [1990]). All the activities of such a body, even those governed by private law, for example employment contracts, seem to be subject to direct effect. The privatised utilities of gas, electricity and water are probably emanations of the state but it is unlikely that the privatised railway companies would be since, although they are subject to state regulation and receive state subsidy, they have no statutory obligation to perform public duties or significant special powers (see *Doughty v Rolls-Royce* [1992]).

To have direct effect an instrument must be 'justiciable', meaning that it is of a kind that is capable of being interpreted and enforced by a court without trespassing outside its proper judicial role. In essence the legal obligation created by the instrument must be certain enough for a court to handle.

The tests usually applied are as follows (see *Van Duyn v Home Office* [1974]):

1. The instrument must be 'clear, precise and unconditional'. It must not give the member state substantial discretion as to how to give effect to it. For example in *Francovich v Italy* [1993] a Directive concerning the treatment of employees in an insolvency was not unconditional because it left it to member states to decide which

bodies should guarantee the payments required by the Directive (see also *Gibson v East Riding of Yorkshire DC* [2000]: Directive about paid leave did not make clear what counted as working time). However the fact that a Directive leaves it to the state to choose between alternative methods of enforcement does not prevent it from having direct effect if the substance of the right is clear from the Directive alone (*Marshall v Southampton AHA (No 2)* [1993]). The European Court interprets the precision test liberally, bearing in mind that apparent uncertainty could be cured by a reference to the Court.

2. The instrument must be intended to confer 'rights'. A problem arises here in respect of purely 'public' interests, for example some environmental concerns such as wildlife conservation. It is arguable that a body with a public law right sufficient to give standing in national law to challenge the government's action, such as a pressure group (see Section 19.4), could rely on the direct effect doctrine. In other words the 'rights' requirement is no more than an aspect of the general principle that the claimant must have a genuine interest.
3. The time limit prescribed by a Directive for its implementation must have expired.

10.3.2 Indirect effect

Even where a European law lacks direct effect, the courts must still take account of it. Member states are required to 'take all appropriate measures' to fulfil European obligations and the objectives of Directives must be given effect. In *Marleasing v La Comercial Internacional de Alimentacion* [1992] the ECJ held that all domestic law, whether passed before or after the relevant community law, must be interpreted 'so far as possible' in the light of the wording and purposes of the Directive in order to achieve the result pursued by the latter. However *Marleasing* involved a law (in the Spanish civil code) that could be interpreted in different ways. It is uncertain therefore whether clear, unambiguous domestic law must give way to a European rule. This raises the difference between the narrower traditional approach of English law and the more liberal European approach. In *Webb v EMO Cargo (UK) Ltd* [1992] Lord Keith said that *Marleasing* applies to laws passed at any time provided that their language is not distorted. In *Ghaidan v Mendoza* [2004], which concerned an analogous provision in the Human Rights Act 1998 (Chapter 19), Lord Steyn accepted that *Marleasing* created a strong obligation. Sympathetic interpretation of EC law may avoid confrontation between EC law and the domestic principle of parliamentary supremacy.

10.3.3 State liability

Even where a Directive does not have direct effect, an individual may be able to sue the government in a domestic court for damages for failing to implement it. This was established by the ECJ in *Francovich v Italy*, where the Directive was too vague to have direct effect. Nevertheless the Court held that damages could be awarded against the Italian government in an Italian court. The Court's reasoning was based upon the principle of giving full effect to EC rights. This is a powerful and far-reaching notion. In order to obtain damages:

1. The Directive must confer rights for the benefit of individuals.
2. The content of those rights must be determined from the provisions of the Directive (a degree of certainty is therefore needed).

3. There must be a causal link between breach of the Directive and the damage suffered (see also *R v Secretary of State for Transport, ex p Factortame (No 4)* [1996], *(No 5)* [2000]).

In domestic law damages cannot normally be obtained against the government for misusing its statutory powers and duties (see *Barrett v Enfield BC* [1999]). The *Francovich* principle, which was subsequently accepted by the House of Lords (*Kirklees MBC v Wickes Building Supplies* [1992]), is therefore of great significance. *Francovich* leaves the procedures for recovering damages to national courts but any conditions must not make recovery impossible or excessively difficult. There may also be a developing principle that legal remedies must be equally effective in each member state (below). The *Francovich* principle also avoids the 'vertical' enforcement rule (Section 10.3.1) since failure to implement a Directive against a private person would entitle the plaintiff to sue the government.

10.3.4 Effective remedies

There is a general obligation to give effective remedies to protect rights in EC law. The courts originally took the view that this obligation merely required that the remedies available in European cases should be no worse than those in equivalent domestic cases. However it now appears that the courts must sometimes provide better remedies in relation to European rights than would be available domestically. For example in *R v Secretary of State, ex p Factortame (No 2)* [1991] the House of Lords granted an injunction to prevent a statute being enforced in order to protect an EC right (see also *Johnston v Chief Constable of Royal Ulster Constabulary* [1986]).

It remains to be seen how much freedom a member state has in adjusting its remedies to its own circumstances. For example in *Factortame (No 2)* the court still had a discretion whether to issue the injunction based upon the justice and convenience of the circumstances. The English courts are very cautious about issuing interim injunctions and will do so only as a last resort. The governing principle is that the remedy must be adequate and effective, but member states can choose among different possible ways of achieving the object of a Directive.

10.4 Democracy and the European Union

A democratic government is a requirement of membership and the Union claims to function on the basis of representative democracy and respect for equality, freedom, the rule of law, democracy and human rights (TEU, Art 2; TFEU, Art 10), Nevertheless a fundamental constitutional problem of the EU is the 'democratic deficit'. As we have seen, powers are fragmented between the non-elected Council and Commission, with the latter as the driving force. The Commission is accountable to a limited extent to the Parliament. The Council of Ministers is representative of the member states, so its members are responsible to their own legislatures. The European Parliament has an increasingly significant role but cannot initiate or (sometimes) amend legislation. Some of the founders of the European communities, such as Jean Monnet (1888–1979), a businessman, were paternalistic idealists who had little interest in democratic processes, assuming perhaps that the 'European spirit' could gradually be infused into public opinion by example and propaganda. Not surprisingly the EU has failed to achieve a significant political role.

Indeed the treaties may not be wholly compatible with the premise that democracy is about governing with the consent of the people and cannot be tied to any particular substantive goals. For example Article 4(3) of the TEU provides that:

> member states shall take all appropriate measures, whether general or particular, to ensure fulfilment of the obligations arising out of this Treaty or resulting from actions taken by the institutions of the Community. They shall facilitate the achievement of the Community's tasks. They shall abstain from any measure that could jeopardise the attainment of the objectives of the Treaty.

This seems to impose an obligation to place EU goals above democracy (see *Internationale Handelsgesellschaft* [1970] at 1135). On the other hand the member states, acting collectively within procedures prescribed by Article 48 of the TEU, have the ultimate power to change the treaties.

The EU relies mainly on the democratic processes of the member states. In the UK proposed EC legislation is scrutinised by Parliament, although it may not have any power of veto or amendment. Council and Commission documents are made available to both Houses, ministerial statements are made after Council meetings, questions can be asked, and in addition to the ordinary departmental committees there are select committees in each House to monitor EU activity. The House of Lords Select Committee is particularly well regarded and its reports are a valuable resource. In addition to scrutinising new legislation it makes wide-ranging general reports on the EU. However Parliamentary scrutiny is patchy. This is due to the limited information available to Parliament from EU institutions and to time pressures.

The government must place proposals for changes in EU law before select committees of the Commons and the Lords, together with an explanatory memorandum. The committees report to their respective Houses. There may be a convention that no UK minister should consent in the Council to an EC legislative proposal before Parliament has considered the matter unless there are special reasons, which must be explained to the House as soon as possible. However this is not consistently followed. The volume of EC legislation is greater than the time available and much European business is conducted without MPs having the opportunity to consider it in advance.

There are four specific democratic constraints:

1. By virtue of the European Parliamentary Elections Act 1978, no treaty which provides for an increase in the powers of the European Parliament can be ratified by the UK without the approval of an Act of Parliament (s 6). It is perhaps ironic that this provides protection only against the elected element of the EC.
2. A treaty that alters the founding treaties of the European Union must be ratified by statute (European Union (Amendment) Act 2008, s 5).
3. A minister of the Crown may not support a decision in the Council of Ministers to alter its voting arrangements without the approval of Parliament (European Union (Amendment) Act 2008, s 6).
4. EU treaties, in common with other treaties, must normally be ratified by Parliament (see Section 9.7.1). The European Union Bill proposes that important Treaty amendments, in particular those increasing EU powers, removing vetoes or altering the number of Commissioners, will in some cases require a referendum, in others an Act of Parliament.

The Lisbon Treaty has increased the role of national Parliaments:

- National Parliaments have increased rights to information and draft legislation from EU bodies. Draft legislation must be submitted 8 weeks before the Council begins to consider it (TEU, Art 11; Protocol on the Role of National Parliaments in the EU [2004] OJ C310/204).
- A national Parliament can veto Council proposals to change voting arrangements by means of the so-called *Passerelle* principle (TEU, Art 48). The *Passerelle* principle applies to all EU policies except defence and enables the Council of Ministers by unanimous vote to alter requirements for unanimous voting to qualified majority voting and to change the Special Legislative Procedure in the Parliament to Ordinary Legislative Procedure.
- A national Parliament can veto proposals in the areas of 'freedom, justice and security' (which deal with immigration, courts and police matters). These matters are subject to enhanced scrutiny by Parliament and it can pick and choose which measures to accept (see House of Lords Select Committee on the European Union, Second Report (HL 2008–09, 25)).
- There are special provisions concerning 'subsidiarity' (see Section 10.5).

There is a somewhat bizarre provision in the Lisbon Treaty for a 'citizen's initiative'. One million citizens from at least one-third of member states with the signatories distributed in proportion to the size of the country can 'invite' the Commission to consider a proposal (TEU, Art 11(4); TFEU, Art 24). Detailed arrangements have not been prescribed and the Commission is not bound by the invitation.

As regards the executive, accountability is weak in that there is no minister specifically dealing with the EU. However the main departments have European sections and there are numerous committees liaising between UK and EU institutions. The Foreign Office acts as a co-ordinating body and a junior minister is responsible for 'Europe'. Thus there is a complex network of negotiating machinery involving the competing interests of the UK and the EU, the UK and other member states, and interdepartmental rivalries, with Parliament on the sidelines. In keeping with the ethos of UK government, the operation of EU matters relies on informal contacts between unelected officials.

The devolved governments of Scotland and Wales have some involvement at European level, although they are represented in the Council of Ministers by UK ministers. Within their allocated subject areas the devolved governments are responsible for implementing EC law. Although having no right to do so, Scottish and Welsh ministers have sometimes attended Council meetings on behalf of the UK government. Scottish and Welsh ministers have direct representation at lower levels, for example on the Committee of the Regions. Both devolved legislatures have European committees (see Mather, 'The Impact of European Integration', in O'Neill, 2004).

Democracy depends on open decision making and wide access to information about governmental activity. Openness is claimed to be a principle of the EU (TFEU, Art 15). Council proceedings on legislative matters must be in public and its decisions must be made public. There is a public right of access to the European Parliament. Council and Commission documents must be disclosed to any citizen of the EU and to any person residing in or having a registered office in a member state. This includes documents both drawn up by them and received. Citizens also have a right to communicate with

EU institutions and to a written reply in the same language. There are however many exceptions in particular contexts relating to most important community activities. (These include data protection for individuals (TFEU, Art 16), security, defence and military matters, international relations, financial, monetary or economic policy, privacy and the integrity of the individual. Commercial interests, legal matters, inspections, investigations and audits are also excepted, subject to a public interest test. Internal documents are excepted if disclosure would seriously undermine the decision-making process, again subject to a public interest test.) No specific enforcement measures are provided.

The Court has taken a more vigorous attitude to the right to information. In *World Wildlife Fund for Nature v Commission* [1997], which concerned information about Commission policy on environmental protection, the Court of First Instance held that, although at the time there was only a voluntary undertaking to disclose information, having adopted it the Commission is bound to respect it. The Court also held that exceptions should be interpreted restrictively so as not to inhibit the aim of transparency and that the Commission must give reasons for refusing to disclose information. The Court has also refused to accept blanket immunity for particular kinds of information and required the Commission to balance the public right to know against a clear public interest in secrecy in the particular case (see *JT's Corp v Commission* [2000]; *Van der Val v Netherlands* [2000]).

10.5 Federalism and the European Union: subsidiarity

The EU is difficult to fit into a coherent constitutional structure. In particular there is a conflict between the ideal of European integration and that of national identity. This tension suggests the possibility of a federal model since, as we saw in Chapter 6, federalism is intended to reconcile this kind of tension by marking out spheres of independence for each unit. While some idealists, notably Jean Monnet, pursued the agenda of a federal Europe, the thrust of the original initiative was towards the pragmatic integration of economic policy as the basis of evolution towards what the treaties call 'ever closer union' but with no agreed final destination. The Lisbon Treaty emphasises that the powers of the European Union are conferred on it 'upwards' by the member states. Indeed the German Supreme Court has held that ultimate power remains with the member states (see *Brunner v European Union Treaty* [1994]).

At present the EU has an important feature of federalism in that the powers of the EU are itemised and limited by the treaties, with the member states having residual independence (TEU, Arts 4, 5). The principle of 'proportionality' is stressed, namely that EU powers shall not exceed what is necessary to secure the objectives of the treaties. The 'conferral principle' (TEU, Art 5(2)) states that the powers of the EU are conferred on it by the member states. Thus fears that the EU is a 'superstate' are ill founded. Furthermore, major increases in the powers and competences of EU institutions require the consent of member states in the Council of Ministers and if treaty changes are involved, in the case of the UK, by Parliament. As we have seen there are also several ways in which individual states can opt into or opt out of particular EU powers (see Sections 10.1, 10.4).

On the other hand at a detailed level the powers of the EU include a wide range of commercial, environmental and economic matters, and one of the main preoccupations of the Commission is to 'harmonise' national laws, apparently as an end in itself, invoking narrow rule of law ideas.

The tension between the interests of member states and those of the EU is expressed through the concept of subsidiarity. Introduced by the Maastricht Treaty (1992), subsidiarity is a vague term with no agreed meaning. It can therefore be enlisted to serve different political interests. Historically it is an authoritarian doctrine used by the Catholic Church to legitimise a hierarchical power structure. Subsidiarity can also be regarded as a pluralist liberal principle that decisions should be made at a level as close as possible to those whom they affect. In the EU context subsidiarity concerns the distribution of powers between the Community and national governments. On the one hand it enables the EU to make decisions that cannot effectively be made by the member states, and on the other hand it enables the member states to act for themselves where this is more appropriate.

Subsidiarity was formally introduced into EU law by the Maastricht Treaty and, together with the principle of proportionality, is embodied in Article 5 of the TEU:

> In areas that do not fall within its exclusive competence, the Community shall take action, in accordance with the principle of subsidiarity, only if and insofar as the objectives of the proposed action cannot be sufficiently achieved by the Member States either at central level or at regional level but can rather, by reason of the scale or effects of the proposed action, be better achieved at Union level ... Any action by the Community shall not go beyond what is necessary to achieve the objects of this Treaty.

Article 10 announces that 'decisions shall be taken as openly and as closely as possible to the citizen', thereby giving a republican flavour to the EU.

These provisions are characteristically vague and are unlikely to be directly enforceable in law but may operate at a political level, thereby indirectly influencing the law.

The Lisbon Treaty gives an important role to national Parliaments in connection with subsidiarity. If one-third of member states raise an objection to a Commission proposal on subsidiarity grounds the Commission must reconsider it and must give reasons for continuing with it. If a majority do, the Council of Ministers by a 55 per cent majority or the Parliament must vote for it to proceed (see Protocol on the Role of National Parliaments in the EU).

On the whole the Lisbon Treaty has maintained a balance between national and EU institutions and is not the charter for EU supremacy that was sometimes feared. Unlike the usual form of federation the EU is dependent on its powers being channelled through the laws of the member states and has no enforcement mechanisms of its own. The EU is arguably more like a confederation or an intergovernmental body than a genuine supranational body but is perhaps best regarded as a unique legal order not reducible to other forms.

Summary

- The EU (EC) exists to integrate key economic and increasingly social and security policies of member states, with the primary aims of providing an internal market and creating a powerful European political unit. The constitution of the EU is an evolving one aimed at increasing integration between its member states. Some functions are exclusive to the EU while others are shared with member states. However there is substantial provision for individual states to opt out of certain European powers, although not the core areas of the single market. The UK has opted out of several areas of EU activity, and the EU Charter of Fundamental Rights (not to be confused with the ECHR) is not enforceable in UK courts.

Summary cont'd

- EC law has been incorporated into UK law by the European Communities Act 1972, which makes certain EC laws automatically binding in the UK, requires other laws to be enacted in UK law either by statute or by regulations made under the 1972 Act, and obliges UK courts to decide cases consistently with principles laid down by the European Court of Justice. In some cases questions of law must be referred to the ECJ. The ECJ has developed the role of constitutional court and is sometimes regarded as being a driving force for integrationist policies that enlist national courts in the project of giving primacy to European law.
- The main policy and lawmaking bodies are the Council of Ministers, which is the main lawmaking body; the European Council of heads of state, responsible for policy direction and making key appointments; the appointed European Commission, which is the executive of the EU; and the elected European Parliament, which participates in the lawmaking process and has powers to control the Commission and the EU budget. Taken together these bodies are meant to balance the interests of national governments and those of the EU as such, but not to follow strict separation of power ideas.
- There is only limited democratic input into the EC lawmaking process but the role of national Parliaments has recently been strengthened and there is provision, albeit limited, for direct input by 'citizens' initiative'.
- Lawmaking and policy-making power are divided between the Council and the Commission, with the Commission as the driving force but the Council having the ultimate control. Voting sometimes has to be unanimous but there is increasing use of qualified majorities, where voting is weighed in favour of the more populous states. The Parliament does not initiate laws but has certain powers of veto and can sometimes suggest amendments.
- Not all EC law is directly binding on member states. Regulations are binding. Other laws, including the Treaty itself, are binding if they satisfy the criteria of 'direct effect' created by the ECJ. Directives must also satisfy the criteria of direct effectiveness and can have direct effect against public bodies (vertical direct effect) but not against private bodies (horizontal direct effect). However the concept of 'indirect effect', which requires domestic law to be interpreted so as to conform to EC law, may alleviate this. The government may also be liable for damages if its failure properly to implement an EC law damages an individual in relation to rights created by the EC law in question.
- The doctrine of 'subsidiarity' is ambivalent. It seems to have little concrete legal content and can be applied in favour of giving greater power to the member states or reinforcing the power of central European Union bodies. National Parliaments may require proposed EU laws to be reconsidered on subsidiarity grounds.
- Membership of the EU may not have fundamentally altered the doctrine of parliamentary supremacy, but the UK courts have accepted that a statute which conflicts with a binding EC rule must be 'disapplied'. There is a general political principle – perhaps an emerging convention – in favour of the supremacy of EU law.

Exercises

10.1 Explain the constitutional structure of the European Union. To what extent is it federal? Does it conform to the separation of powers?

10.2 It is a requirement of membership of the EU that the member state have a democratic form of government, but it has often been remarked that the EU would not satisfy the conditions for membership of itself. Do you agree?

Exercises cont'd

10.3 What powers does the UK Parliament possess in relation to the EU?

10.4 To what extent can UK citizens participate in EU politics?

10.5 To what extent can the UK government influence the appointment of the European Commission?

10.6 Explain the relationship between UK courts and the European Court of Justice. To what extent is the ECJ a constitutional court?

10.7 (i) What is the purpose of the direct effect doctrine and what are its main limitations?
(ii) An EC Directive requires member states to ensure that compensation is paid to part-time workers who are made redundant. The compensation must be paid by the employer. The UK has not implemented the Directive. Jeff, a part-time employee of Dodgy Burgers plc, is made redundant. His employer refuses to pay him compensation. Advise Jeff as to his legal rights, if any.

10.8 To what extent is the EU a democratic body?

Further reading

Brazier (ed), *Parliament, Politics and Law Making* (Hansard Society 2004) ch 9

Budge, Crewe, McKay and Newton, *The New British Politics* (3rd edn, Pearson 2004) chs 8, 9

Craig, 'Directives: Direct Effect, Indirect Effect and the Construction of National Legislation' [1997] Europ L Rev 519

Craig, 'Britain in the European Union' in Jowell and Oliver (eds), *The Changing Constitution* (6th edn, Oxford University Press 2007)

Gallagher, Laver and Mair, *Representative Government in Modern Europe* (McGraw-Hill 2004) ch 5

Harden and McGlynn, 'Democracy and the European Union' [1996] Pol Q 32

Harlow, 'European Governance and Accountability' in Bamforth and Leyland (eds), *Public Law in a Multi-Layered Constitution* (Hart 2003)

Hartley, 'The European Court, Judicial Objectivity and the Constitution of the European Union' (1996) 112 LQR 411

Jones, Kavanagh, Moran and Norton, *Politics UK* (5th edn, Pearson 2004) ch 31

O'Neill (ed), *Devolution and British Politics* (Pearson 2004) ch 11

Rogers and Walters, *How Parliament Works* (6th edn, Pearson 2006) ch 12

Walter, 'European Constitutionalism and European Integration' [1995] PL 266

Ward, *A Critical Introduction to European Law* (2nd edn, Butterworths 2003) chs 1, 2

Weatherill, *Law and Integration in the European Union* (Oxford University Press 1995)

Part IV

Government institutions

Chapter 11

Parliament: constitutional position

The virtue, spirit and essence of a House of Commons consists in its being the express image of the feelings of the nation. It was not instituted to be a control on the people. It was designed as a control for the people. (Edmund Burke)

The minister, whoever he at any time may be, touches it as with an opium wand and it sleeps obedience. (Thomas Paine, *The Rights of Man*, Pt 2)

11.1 Introduction

Parliament comprises two Houses, the unelected House of Lords and the elected House of Commons. The supreme lawmaker is the Queen in Parliament. The word 'Parliament', which meant a parley or conference, entered into official language about the middle of the thirteenth century. It described a formal meeting summoned by the King between himself and the elite members of society for the purposes of advising him and legitimising his tax demands on the people.

A dominant feature of the contemporary UK constitution is its extreme parliamentary system. This is derived from conventions under which the leader of the government (the Prime Minister) is chosen by the House of Commons, the executive depends on the support of the Commons, and all ministers must be members of Parliament, although not necessarily in the elected House. The Crown can make law only in conjunction with Parliament and by convention cannot veto any law duly presented by Parliament. The House of Commons controls government finance, and the Bank of England, the state bank, is underpinned by Parliament.

The traditional function of Parliament has been to represent the people against the Crown. Its formal functions, as they have gradually emerged, are to enact legislation, sustain the government by choosing and removing it and providing it with money, scrutinise government action and redress the grievances of the people. This reflects Mill's ideal of representative democracy as government by experts subject to control by the people. These functions may well conflict, particularly as in our parliamentary system ministers who head the executive are also MPs. Parliament is also therefore a recruiting ground for ministers and a process for legitimating executive action. Most laws are proposed by the executive, so the activities of Parliament are reactive. Individual MPs can propose legislation but the time available for this is so limited that such attempts rarely succeed. Under the rules of procedure in the Commons, government business has priority (see Section 13.4).

Parliament acts as a mechanical way of translating the popular vote into the appointment of an executive, since by convention whoever commands a majority in the House of Commons is entitled to form a government. Owing to the distortions of the electoral system, a popular majority does not necessarily translate into a parliamentary majority (see Section 12.5).

Although the legal supremacy of Parliament probably remains in place, its political power and prestige have declined in recent years. This is the result of an accumulation of factors – some new, others long-standing – which together raise doubts as to whether Parliament is still the most important institution of the constitution. These factors include:

- the increasing influence of international lawmaking which in practice restricts national legislatures (eg the EU, NATO, the UN, and the ECHR);
- at the other end of the scale, the devolution of powers to the nations within the UK, albeit to differing extents;
- the increase in the power of the executive;
- powerful political parties funded by business interests;
- a more assertive and activist judiciary;
- recent scandals involving improper expenses claims by many MPs.

The UK version of the parliamentary system gives exceptionally strong powers to the executive, particularly the Prime Minister (see Section 15.2). The main reason for the dominance of the executive is the strong two-party adversarial system that has developed in UK politics since the early twentieth century. During the twentieth century the present practice of highly disciplined parties emerged, in which internal differences are suppressed, at least when it comes to supporting the leadership in a parliamentary vote. One reason for this is that most MPs are paid professional politicians dependent on party conformity. Another is the media-driven nature of modern politics, which favours charismatic leadership.

Thus Parliament is the setting of a party/market democracy (see Section 2.7.3). The party leaders can pressurise their supporters in the House of Commons partly because, like the eighteenth-century aristocracy, they can influence the choice of election candidates and partly because there are many opportunities of patronage through appointments as ministers or to influential committees. Control of parliamentary business and the timetable in the House of Commons is largely in the hands of the government party, although this has recently been slightly modified. Each party has a highly organised 'whip' system dedicated to enforcing party discipline and persuading members to vote in the required way. In some circumstances, usually where matters of personal conscience are at issue, there may be a 'free' vote.

Executive domination of Parliament must not however be overstated. Parliament is a separate institution with large powers of its own and it could overcome the executive were it so minded. Its current subservience is voluntary. Government proposals must be publicly explained in Parliament and ministers must justify their decisions in public if required to do so by Parliament. The independent Speaker, who chairs the sittings of the Commons, is responsible for ensuring fair and focused debate, for ensuring that ministers answer questions properly and for protecting the interests of minorities. The Opposition, the second largest party in the Commons, is a formal institution protected by the law of parliamentary procedure – a government and Prime Minister in waiting. It has a duty to oppose government policy, short of frustrating the governmental process, and forms a 'shadow Cabinet' ready to take office. There is funding designated by the House of Commons ('Short Money', named after the MP who proposed it) for the parliamentary work of opposition parties. This is determined by a formula based on the number of seats and votes the party received in the previous election. There is also funding for the Opposition leader's office. The funding of the House of Commons is also determined by the House as a separate charge on public funds and so is relatively independent of the executive. In practice however recent opposition parties have been extremely weak as a result of internal conflicts and failure to recover from damaging election defeats.

While there is no law to this effect, it is often claimed that an MP has a duty to exercise independent judgement on behalf of all his or her constituents and not merely those who voted for him or her. However in practice many MPs mechanically support the party that sponsors them, although there are a few independent voices. Occasionally an MP changes parties. Once elected, unless he or she becomes disqualified to sit in Parliament (see Section 12.4), an MP cannot be removed until the next election. However the main parties have proposed the introduction of 'recall' machinery which would enable a proportion of the electorate, so far unspecified, to trigger a special election to remove a sitting member.

11.2 The House of Lords

The purpose of the second chamber is to act as a check on the main chamber by providing an opportunity for second thoughts. In the UK the appointed House of Lords is subordinate to the elected House of Commons. This is secured by the Parliament Acts 1911 and 1949 and by conventions, notably the 'Salisbury Convention', which requires the Lords to accept proposals contained in the government's election manifesto. The House of Lords should also defer to the Commons on matters of government finance since this is a matter between the Crown, who asks for money, and the Commons, who supply it. The government has accepted the recommendation of the Parliamentary Joint Committee on Conventions (*Conventions of the UK Parliament* (Cm 6997, 2006)) that these conventions be codified but has not yet done so. In relation to reform there is a consensus that the powers of the upper house should remain broadly as they are now.

The House of Lords is unusual among second chambers in the following respects:

- Its members are not elected. Most of them are appointed by the Crown (by convention the Prime Minister). There are also 26 senior Church of England bishops.
- Members other than the bishops sit for life. Membership is a legal right on appointment as a peer and can be removed only by statute.
- Until the House of Lords Act 1999, the bulk of members were hereditary peers whose descendants enjoyed permanent seats. As the first stage of a reform programme, the 1999 Act removed all but 92 hereditary peers.
- The House is large, having about 740 members, compared with 650 in the Commons. However attendance is on average about 50 per cent.
- Members receive no payment other than expenses. As a result of allegations about misuse of expenses it is proposed that this should consist of a flat rate of £300 per day's actual attendance.
- Members have no constituencies and are accountable to no one. About 25 per cent of the members are independent of political parties.
- By long-standing practice, the proceedings of the House are regulated by the House itself without formal rules or disciplinary sanctions, members being treated as bound by 'personal honour'. This has not prevented some peers from abusing their position and there is a now a Code of Conduct (2009, amended 2010). This is policed by a Commissioner for Standards, who reports to the House through its Standards and Privileges Committee. In 2010 three peers were suspended for false expense claims.

Being undemocratic, the position of the House is controversial. It could be variously depicted as a constitutional abomination, a valuable ingredient of a mixed constitution or a historical survival that, from a pragmatic perspective, might nevertheless have some useful functions. The Parliament Act 1911 removed the power of the House of Lords to veto most legislation. Its preamble stated that this was a precursor to replacing it by a second chamber 'constituted on a popular basis' and 'limiting and defining' its powers. However there has been no agreement as to how that should be done. In 2000 the Wakeham Report (Royal Commission on the House of Lords, *A House for the Future* (Cm 4534, 2000)) endorsed the Conservative view that the House of Lords should remain subordinate to the Commons (thus ensuring the clear democratic accountability of the government), that it should provide constitutional checks and balances and that it should provide a parliamentary voice for the 'nations and regions of the United Kingdom'.

Despite numerous consultations, government papers and parliamentary debates and reports (see White Paper, *House of Lords Reform* (Cm 7027, 2007) for a useful history) no agreed proposals for further reform of the House of Lords have emerged – a pattern that has been repeated since 1911 (see Section 12.3).

11.3 The meeting of Parliament

Parliament is summoned and dissolved by the Crown under the royal prerogative, the alleged abuse of this power being a major contribution to the seventeenth-century revolution. The modern law is overlaid by statute and convention, its foundations being established by the 1688 revolution. The main principles give considerable power to the Prime Minister but also contain important checks over the executive. They are as follows:

- 'Parliament ought to be held frequently' (Bill of Rights 1688, Art 13) and must meet at least once every three years (Meeting of Parliament Act 1694). By convention Parliament meets annually, backed by administrative necessity, for example to authorise taxation and public spending.
- Parliament terminates automatically after five years from the date of its summons (Septennial Act 1715; Parliament Act 1911, s 7). This is the fulcrum of the constitution in that the government must submit to a general election and by convention must resign if it loses its majority. This period cannot be altered without the consent of the House of Lords, so to some extent it is entrenched against the executive (Parliament Act 1911, s 2(1)). It is arguable however that this safeguard can be removed in two stages by first using the Parliament Act procedure to repeal section 2(1) (see Section 11.5).

  The five-year period is intended to strike a balance between the desire for MPs to be independent of populist pressures and the need to ensure that they do not go native and forget their dependency on the voters.
- Within five years Parliament may be dissolved by the monarch (law) on the advice of the Prime Minister (convention). This is one of the main sources of prime ministerial power. A Parliament usually lasts for about four years, dissolution being timed for the political advantage of the Prime Minister. The current Prime Minister proposes not to exercise this power of early dissolution. It is also possible that in certain extreme cases the monarch can exercise personal choice whether or not to dissolve Parliament (see Section 14.4)

- A Prime Minister whose government is defeated on a vote of confidence in the House of Commons must resign. Unless an alternative leader can be supported by the House of Commons, which is most unlikely, the outgoing Prime Minister must ask for a dissolution of Parliament, which the monarch must normally grant. This also gives the Prime Minister power over Parliament, in that Parliament cannot dismiss the Prime Minister without dismissing itself.
- After a Parliament is dissolved or terminated by the five-year limit the Queen must summon a new Parliament. Subject to the above, there is no time limit for this. Usually the same proclamation dissolves Parliament and summons a new one within about a month. A general election must be held, according to a complex formula, within about three weeks from the date of the summons of the new Parliament (Representation of the People Act 1985, Sch 1). During the election period, the meeting of Parliament could be further postponed by the monarch by 'prorogation' under the royal prerogative (see Prorogation Act 1867). The effect of prorogation is to suspend Parliament until recalled by the monarch. This might be appropriate for example if the election does not produce a clear winner. (It turned out not to be necessary in 2010.) Sometimes Parliament is prorogued a few days before it is dissolved but there is no legal or constitutional reason for this.
- The Fixed Term Parliament Bill 2010 proposes to alter these long-standing arrangements. Under the Bill a Parliament will last for five years subject to a power of the Prime Minister to vary this by two months. Within the five years Parliament can be dissolved only in two cases. The first is where the government loses a vote of confidence and an alternative government cannot be formed within 14 working days. The second is where there is a vote of at least two-thirds of the Commons or a Motion without a division in favour of a dissolution. The Speaker's certificate on these matters is conclusive. The Bill thus moves the balance of power away from the Prime Minister. After a dissolution the monarch must summon a new Parliament by proclamation (above). The Bill therefore seems to remove any royal prerogative power in relation to dissolution. It does not affect prorogation.

It is arguable that the courts could have jurisdiction over this statutory arrangement. However this is questionable. Firstly the Bill seems to be concerned with internal proceedings in Parliament (see Section 11.6.2). Secondly a court might regard the matter as inherently non-justiciable (see Section 19.7.1).

- A Parliament is divided into 'sessions'. These are working periods of a year, usually running from November (about 170 sitting days). Sessions are ended by being prorogued by the monarch under the royal prerogative, thus being under the control of ministers (above). Each session is opened by the monarch, with an address from the throne which is written by the government and outlines its legislative proposals. A general debate on government policy takes place immediately afterwards.
- Within a session, each House can be adjourned at any time by resolution of the House. Adjournments apply to daily sittings and the breaks for holidays and over the summer. The rump of the session following the summer break by convention is used to finish outstanding business.
- The Speaker can suspend individual sittings of the Commons for disciplinary reasons.
- There is machinery for recalling each House by proclamation while it stands prorogued (Parliament (Elections and Meetings) Act 1943, s 34) and also under

emergency legislation (Civil Contingencies Act 2004). An adjourned Parliament can be summoned by proclamation (Meeting of Parliament Act 1870) and also by the Speakers of both Houses at the request of the Prime Minister or perhaps at the request of the leader of the Opposition. However it does not seem to be possible for ordinary MPs to recall Parliament in order to debate any crisis that may arise while Parliament is not sitting. This again illustrates the subservience of Parliament to the executive. Government has many powers under the royal prerogative, notably to deploy the armed forces and declare war, which it can exercise without reference to Parliament.

On the one hand these principles illustrate the constitutional checks and balances that attempt to prevent any single group from being dominant, an objective on which liberals and republicans unite. Parliament and the executive can each control the other but only at the cost of terminating itself and inviting the people to choose a successor. On the other hand their operation in practice illustrates the limitations of checks and balances when matched against political forces towards oligarchy. Montesquieu, writing in the eighteenth century (see Section 7.2), praised this system as a balance of equal constitutional forces. However Montesquieu relied on the existence of a powerful aristocracy in the House of Lords and did not have to confront the circumstances of modern political parties.

11.4 The functions of the House of Commons

The main functions of the Commons are as follows:

- choosing the government indirectly by virtue of the convention that the person who commands a majority of the Commons is entitled to form a government. The Commons has no veto over individual appointments nor can it dismiss individual members of the government (another prime ministerial power);
- sustaining the government by supplying it with funds and authorising taxation. The size and complexity of modern government means that parliamentary control over finance cannot be exercised directly. Parliamentary approval of the executive's budget and accounts is largely a formality. Detailed scrutiny and control over government spending takes place mainly within the government itself through the medium of the Treasury (Chapter 15). However a substantial parliamentary safeguard is provided by the National Audit Office, headed by the Comptroller and Auditor-General (see Section 13.5.4);
- legislating. Any member can propose a bill but in practice the parliamentary timetable is dominated by government business and legislation is usually presented to Parliament ready drafted by the executive. This is why Bagehot thought that the absence of a strict separation of powers made the UK constitution an effective machine for ensuring government by experts. There are certain opportunities for private members' bills but these rarely become law (see Section 13.3.1);
- supervising the executive. By convention ministers are accountable to Parliament and must appear in Parliament to participate in debates, answer questions and appear before committees (see Section 15.7). The House of Commons can require a government to resign by a vote of no confidence. These sanctions are rarely used since the resignation of the government is likely to result in a general election, putting the jobs of MPs at risk;

- redressing grievances raised by individual MPs on behalf of their constituents. There are certain opportunities to raise grievances in debates but they are usually pursued by correspondence with ministers or by the Parliamentary Ombudsman. By convention every constituent has a right of access to his or her MP, which can be exercised by visiting Parliament if necessary. Individuals may also petition Parliament (see Section 13.7);
- debating matters of public concern. Again there are limited procedural opportunities for such debates.

11.5 The functions of the House of Lords

A common justification for a second chamber is to represent the different units of a federal system, with the first chamber representing the popular vote as for example in the US. The conventional justification for the existence of a second chamber in the UK is that it acts as a revising chamber to scrutinise the detail of legislation proposed by the Commons and to allow time for second thoughts, thus acting as a constitutional safeguard against the possible excesses of majoritarianism and party politics. According to the Wakeham Report (above), the functions of the second chamber include, and should continue to include, the following:

- to provide advice on public policy, bringing a range of perspectives to bear that should be broadly representative of British society and in particular to provide a voice for the nations and regions of the UK and ethnic minorities and interest groups. The present composition of the Lords obviously does not reflect this aspiration;
- to act as a revising chamber, scrutinising the details of proposed legislation within the overall polices laid down by the Commons. By convention, supported by the Parliament Acts 1911 and 1949 (Chapter 13), the House of Lords does not discuss matters of government finance, this being a prerogative of the Commons;
- to provide a forum for general debate on matters of public concern without party political pressures;
- to introduce relatively uncontroversial legislation or private bills as a method of relieving the workload of the Commons. Any bill other than a financial measure can be introduced in the Lords;
- to provide ministers; thus unelected persons can be appointed as ministers. However by convention the Prime Minister and the Chancellor of the Exchequer must be members of the Commons;
- to provide committees on general topics, such as the European Communities Committee and the Science and Technology Committee. These are highly respected;
- to permit persons who have made a contribution to public life, other than party politicians, to participate in government. It is often claimed that the House of Lords is a valuable source of expertise in that outstanding persons from all walks of life can be appointed. However its expertise may be patchy, being skewed in favour of persons who have received government patronage in the past. The contemporary House of Lords is dominated by former officials, politicians and leading members of the elite professions and business interests. Moreover appointment to the Lords is likely to be at the end of a career, thus risking out-of-date expertise. There have been allegations that seats in the Lords can be bought (see Section 12.2);

- to act as a constitutional check by preventing a government from prolonging its own life, in respect of which the Lords has a veto (Parliament Act 1911). The consent of the Lords is also needed for the dismissal of senior judges (see Section 5.4.2);
- to act as a constitutional watchdog. It has no specific powers for this purpose but has a Constitutional Committee which examines the constitutional implications of bills brought before the House.

These functions can be pursued in the House of Lords partly because its procedure and culture differ significantly from those of the Commons. In particular, party discipline is less rigorous and the House of Lords is less partisan than the Commons. Members of the House of Lords other than bishops are removable only by statute and are therefore less susceptible to political pressures than MPs. The House as a whole controls its own procedure, making it relatively free from party constraints, and is subject to less time pressure than the Commons. Its members have a considerable accumulation of experience and knowledge. The House of Lords cannot therefore easily be manipulated by the government, is attractive to external lobbyists and can ventilate moral and social issues in an objective way. Occasionally members of the House of Lords will respond to their individual consciences, or to public opinion, and defeat government proposals.

11.5.1 The Parliament Acts

Under the Parliament Acts 1911 and 1949, subject to a delaying period, most statutes can be enacted without the consent of the House of Lords, thus ensuring that the democratic will prevails. There are exceptions (Parliament Act 1911, s 2(1)): private bills, bills to prolong the life of Parliament and bills introduced in the Lords itself. Introduced mainly to allow important constitutional measures to be passed, the Acts have recently been used to steamroll through government measures (see Lord Bingham in *R (Jackson) v A-G* [2005] at [41]). Before 1991, the 1911 Act was used only three times (Government of Ireland Act 1914; Welsh Church Act 1914; Parliament Act 1949). Since then it has been used four times for relatively minor purposes (War Crimes Act 1991; European Parliamentary Elections Act 1999; Sexual Offences (Amendment) Act 2000; Hunting Act 2004). The Parliament Acts do not apply to delegated legislation, which sometimes requires the approval of Parliament.

The conventional view is that subject to the limits specifically mentioned in the 1911 Act any statute can be enacted under the Parliament Acts. It is not clear whether this applies to an alteration to the Parliament Acts themselves to further reduce the powers of the Lords. If the Parliament Acts do apply to such bills then the limits currently contained in the 1911 Act could be removed in two stages, first by repealing that part of the Act, and then by legislating free of those limitations. On the other hand it could be argued that the 1911 Act should be read as not intending that its limitations should so easily be circumvented (see the disagreement in *Jackson*, discussed in Section 8.4.3). It seems clear however that the House of Lords could be abolished under the Parliament Acts.

The Parliament Act 1911 as amended by the Parliament Act 1949 gives the House of Lords an opportunity to delay legislation, thus giving the Commons an opportunity to reconsider (s 2). The Lords can reject a bill in two parliamentary sessions provided it is sent to them at least one month before the end of each session and no more than one year elapses between the second reading in the first session and the date the bill passes the Commons in the second session. After the second session the bill can receive the royal assent without the consent of the Lords. (However if the Commons amends a bill after it has come back from the Lords in the first session, then it may not count as the same bill unless the amendments were suggested by the Lords.) In the case of a 'money bill' the Lords can delay only for one month, provided the bill is sent to them at least one month before the end of a session (Parliament Act 1911, s 1). A money bill is a public bill that in the opinion of the Speaker deals exclusively either with central government taxation or central government spending, borrowing or accounts. This definition is narrow since few bills deal exclusively with these matters. The Speaker must certify that the Parliament Act's procedure has been followed and his certificate cannot be questioned in a court (Parliament Act 1911, ss 2(2), 3). However a court can decide whether a bill falls within the limits of the Parliament Act in the first place (*Jackson*).

11.6 Parliamentary privilege

In *R (Chaytor) v A-G* [2010] the Court of Appeal said that 'properly understood the privileges of Parliament are the privileges of the nation and the bedrock of our constitutional democracy' (at [5]–[7]). It is important that a legislature can control its own affairs and be protected against interference by outsiders. Interference by the Crown with parliamentary business was an ingredient of the seventeenth-century revolution, and at the beginning of every Parliament the Speaker symbolically asserts the 'ancient and undoubted privileges' of the House of Commons against the Crown. The House of Lords also has privileges, but does not have the power to punish. The Nicholls Report (Report of the Joint Committee on Parliamentary Privilege (1998–99, HL 43–1, HC 214–1)) recommended reforms but these have yet to be implemented. The devolved legislatures of Scotland, Wales and Northern Ireland do not have parliamentary privilege but are protected against liability for defamation (eg Scotland Act 1998, s 41).

Some parliamentary privileges are mainly of historical or symbolic interest. These include the collective right of access of the Commons to the monarch. Members of the Commons also enjoy immunity from civil, as opposed to criminal, arrest during a period from 40 days before to 40 days after every session. In the case of peers the immunity is permanent and seems to be based on their status as peers rather than membership of the House (*Stourton v Stourton* [1963]). Now that debtors are no longer imprisoned, civil arrest is virtually obsolete, being concerned mainly with disobedience to court orders. Members and officers of both Houses have automatic exemption from jury service (Juries Act 1974) and the House can exempt members from giving evidence in court.

The two most important privileges overlap. They are (i) the collective privilege of each House to control its own composition and procedure and (ii) freedom of speech. They prevent actions in the courts against MPs who fall within their scope. We shall discuss these below. We shall also discuss the conflicts that have arisen between Parliament and the courts over parliamentary privilege. At present there is an uneasy stalemate. Parliament has never unequivocally accepted that the courts have the power to determine the limits of its privileges. The ordinary courts accept that Parliament has the exclusive power to regulate its own internal affairs but claim the right to determine the limits of parliamentary privilege (see *Chaytor*). Parliamentary privilege in relation to the freedom of speech of an MP has been upheld by the European Court of Human Rights as a proportionate way of securing the independence of the legislature (*A v UK* [2003]).

11.6.1 Contempt of Parliament

Breach of a specific parliamentary privilege is one kind of 'contempt' of Parliament. A parliamentary privilege is a special right or immunity available either to the House collectively (eg to control its own composition and procedure) or to individual members (eg freedom of speech). Contempt is a general term embracing any conduct, whether by MPs or outsiders:

> which obstructs or impedes either House of Parliament in the performance of its functions or which obstructs or impedes any member or officer of the House in the execution of his duty or which has a tendency directly or indirectly to produce such results. (May, *Parliamentary Practice* (Butterworths 1997) 108)

This is very wide. It includes for example abuses by MPs of parliamentary procedure, breaching confidences, refusing to obey a committee, causing disruption in the House, improper or dishonest behaviour by MPs, and harassment of, or allegations against, MPs in newspapers. Contempt not only protects the 'efficiency' of the House but also its 'authority and dignity'.

Perhaps the most striking feature of contempt of Parliament is that Parliament accuses, tries and punishes offenders itself. This is an aspect of the wider principle that Parliament claims to look after its own affairs without outside interference. The ordinary courts have no jurisdiction over the internal affairs of Parliament (below) and there are no independent safeguards for the individual. On the one hand this is an assertion of a version of the separation of powers. On the other hand it seems to violate rule of law values and the European Convention on Human Rights (ECHR) concerning the right to be judged by an independent court (see *Demicola v Malta* [1992]). The immunity of Parliament from interference by the courts is reinforced by the Human Rights Act 1998, which provides that Parliament is not a public body for the purpose of the Act (s 6(3); see Section 21.3). This prevents an action being brought against Parliament under the Human Rights Act 1998.

The procedure for dealing with a contempt of Parliament, or a breach of privilege, is as follows (see Committee of Privileges, Third Report (HC 1976–77, 417):

1. Any member can give written notice of a complaint to the Speaker.
2. The Speaker decides whether to give priority over other business.
3. If the Speaker decides not to do so, the member may then use the ordinary procedure of the House to get the matter discussed. This would be difficult in practice.
4. If the Speaker decides to take up the matter, the complaining member can propose that the matter be referred to the Committee on Standards and Privileges or that some other action be taken, for example an immediate debate. A select committee can in certain cases refer a contempt against itself direct to the Committee (HC Deb 18 March 1986, vol 94, cols 763–64).
5. The Committee (currently 10 senior members chaired by an Opposition MP) investigates the complaint. The procedure is entirely up to the Committee. Witnesses are examined but there is no right to legal representation. The accused has no legal right to a hearing or to summon or cross-examine witnesses.

   The Nicholls Report (above), endorsed by the Sixth Report of the Committee on Standards in Public Life (*Reinforcing Standards* (Cm 4557, 2000)), had recommended that a panel containing independent persons be used and that there should be legal representation and a right of appeal (see also Eighth Report (*Standards of Conduct in the House of Commons* (Cm 5663, 2002)).

6. The Committee reports back to the House, which decides what action to take. This could range from a reprimand, through suspension or expulsion from the House, to imprisonment for the rest of the session, renewable indefinitely. The House of Lords can imprison for a fixed term and can also impose a fine. The Nicholls Report recommended that punishment of non-members should be a matter for the ordinary courts and limited to a fine.
7. The Speaker also has summary powers to deal with disruptive behaviour in the House or breaches of the rules of debate. He or she can exclude MPs and others from the Chamber until the end of the session (HC Standing Orders 24–26) and make rulings on matters of procedure. The Speaker of the House of Lords has no procedural or disciplinary powers.

The conduct of MPs and the justice and effectiveness of the internal disciplinary process came into the public spotlight during the 1990s when several MPs were accused of accepting payments to give favours to outside interests. Further problems arose during 2008–09 when it was revealed by the press that many MPs had been abusing their expense allowance claims, some grotesquely so, and that there was no effective way to police this. There was considerable public concern on the theme of distrust of government in general. Perhaps as an overreaction, machinery was introduced which for the first time brings an external element into policing the behaviour of MPs (below).

11.6.2 'Exclusive cognisance'

Parliament claims exclusive control over its own internal affairs – a hard-won right emerging from the seventeenth-century confrontations between Crown and Parliament (eg *Eliot's Case* [1629/1668]). In accordance with the separation of powers, no legal process is possible in respect of any matter before the House and no one can be prevented from placing a matter before Parliament (*Bilston Corp v Wolverhampton Corp* [1942]). For example, although the qualifications for being a member of Parliament are fixed by statute, each House has the exclusive right to decide who will actually sit, to regulate all internal proceedings and to expel members. The courts cannot order a minister to present a matter to Parliament even where a change in the law is required by European law (*R v Secretary of State for Employment, ex p Equal Opportunities Commission* [1992]). Nor can the courts decide whether the procedures under the internal rules of each House of Parliament for enacting legislation have been properly followed (*Pickin v British Railways Board* [1974]). Unlike the statutory privilege of freedom of speech (Section 11.6.3) this privilege can be waived by the House and does not belong to individual MPs.

In *Bradlaugh v Gossett* [1884] Charles Bradlaugh, a well-known freethinker, had been duly elected to the Commons. The House refused to let him take his seat because it deemed that as an atheist he had no statutory right to take the oath. In fact the courts had previously ruled in his favour (*Clarke v Bradlaugh* [1881]). Nevertheless the court held that it had no power to intervene since this was a matter exclusively to do with the internal procedure of the House.

What counts as an internal proceeding in Parliament? On one view anything that happens within the precincts of the Houses of Parliament (the Palace of Westminster) is protected. In *R v Grahame-Campbell, ex p Herbert* [1935] the Divisional Court held that the House of Commons bar was exempt from the liquor licensing laws and so could sell drinks without restriction. (However another explanation of this case is that the Palace of Westminster, a royal palace, enjoys Crown immunity from statute law; see Section 14.5). Protection within the precincts probably applies only to official arrangements within the House such as the salaries and expenses scheme for MPs (see below) and to the House's machinery for discipline and order. For example the Sergeant at Arms may control the entry of law enforcement officials into the Palace of Westminster. Thus in 2008 the police searched the parliamentary office of Damian Green, then a senior Opposition MP, in connection with an investigation into a leak of information from the Home Office. This may have been politically unwise but since the Speaker had apparently given permission it was not a contempt of the House. In 1986, in the *Zircon* affair, the Committee of Privileges ruled that the showing to MPs, within the precincts, of a film about a secret security project was not protected by privilege and could therefore be the subject of an injunction since this was not part of the business of the House (see Committee of Privileges, First Report (HC 1986–87, 365)).

Similarly, the immunity of an individual MP probably applies only to the official business of the House. Criminal offences and civil wrongs not committed for the purpose of the core functions of Parliament (of legislating and holding the executive to account and raising citizens' grievances) are not protected (*Bradlaugh v Gosset* at 278). If a wrong is committed for the purpose of parliamentary business it should not matter whether it is committed within the physical limits of the House (eg *Rivlin v Bilankin* [1953]: libellous letter about a private matter posted within the precincts not protected).

In *Eliot's Case* [1668], a constitutional landmark, after many years of controversy an MP was held to be immune from liability for sedition in respect of a speech in Parliament but not from liability for causing a riot.

Recently in *R (Chaytor) v A-G* [2010] the Supreme Court held that parliamentary privilege does not exempt an MP from ordinary criminal liability other than in relation to his duties regarding the core functions of Parliament such as debates and questions. The case involved a prosecution of several MPs for falsely claiming expenses. It was held that the court could not review expense scheme itself, being set up by Parliament internally. However this did not cover the application of the scheme to the fraudulent behaviour of MPs in respect of their own affairs, since they were not acting in pursuit of their parliamentary duties. (The phrase 'the walls of Parliament' used in some of the cases should be understood metaphorically not literally.) It was for the Court to determine the limit of parliamentary privilege. The Court was not bound by decisions made by parliamentary bodies, although it would treat them with respect. For example it may sometimes be more suitable or fairer for an MP to be dealt with by Parliament itself. The main general principle emerging from this case (which contains a useful review of a considerable range of authority) is that parliamentary privilege should be clearly related to its purpose, namely to protect the public interest in the independence of Parliament, and that it is subject to the rule of law.

(See also *Corporate Officer of the House of Commons v Information Comr* [2009]: expense claims are subject to Freedom of Information Act (Section 23.2.1); *R v Greenaway* [1992], unreported; *Chaytor* at [40]: MP taking a bribe not protected; *Rost v Edwards* [1990]: Register of Members' Interests not protected on the basis that not a core function; *A-G for Ceylon v de Livera* [1963]; *Buchanan v Jennings* [2005] at 124; *Prebble v Television New Zealand* [1995] at 340; see further Report of the Joint Committee on Parliamentary Privilege (1998–99, HL 43–1, HC 214–1).

The privilege only applies to the internal processes of the House. Resolutions of the House of Commons cannot alter the general law. This requires a statute (*Stockdale v Hansard* [1839]; *Bowles v Bank of England* [1913]). Similarly approval by the House of subordinate legislation or a government decision cannot make valid something unlawful under the general law (*Hoffman La Roche v Trade and Industry Secretary* [1974]). However in considering whether government action is unreasonable the court will be especially deferential to decisions that have been approved by Parliament (see Section 19.7.1).

The Ombudsman who investigates citizens' complaints against the executive and reports to Parliament is not protected by privilege because he deals with external matters (see Section 5.4.4). By contrast the Parliamentary Commissioner for Standards, who polices the conduct of MPs and so is concerned with matters internal to the House, is subject to privilege and so is not subject to review by the courts (see Section 11.7.1). (The position as regards the Independent Parliamentary Standards Authority (see Section 11.7.2) is unclear since IPSA has both external and internal aspects.)

11.6.3 Freedom of speech

Article 9 of the Bill of Rights 1688 (part of the revolution settlement for the purpose of protecting MPs against the Crown) states that:

> The Freedom of Speech or Debates or Proceedings in Parliament ought not to be impeached or questioned in any court or place out of Parliament.

Article 9 overlaps with the exclusive cognisance privilege discussed above (see *Re McGuinness* [1997]: Speaker's decisions not reviewable). However freedom of speech deserves attention in its own right. It is the central privilege of an individual MP, who must be at liberty to speak and write freely and frankly without pressure from outside bodies, whether participating in a debate, asking questions of ministers, acting in a committee or raising the problems of his or her constituents.

For example in October 2009 a 'super-injunction' was sought to prevent the press publishing the content of a parliamentary question concerning the business activities of a company. Super-injunctions prevent the publication not only of the information itself but even of the fact that the injunction has been granted. The application was withdrawn and the Lord Chief Justice expressed concern about the violation of a fundamental constitutional principle (see Judicial Communications Office Press Release 20 October 2009; Gay and Home, HC Research Note SN/PC/02024 (2009): a useful general summary; see also Geddis, 'What We Cannot Talk About We Must Pass Over in Silence: Judicial Orders and Reporting Parliamentary Speech' [2010] PL 443).

Article 9 prevents civil and criminal proceedings against an MP and also prevents parliamentary materials from being used as evidence against an MP in court proceedings (*Church of Scientology of California v Johnson-Smith* [1972]: MP sued for defamation for statement made on TV).

However Article 9 does not exclude the use of parliamentary material in court to establish what was said in Parliament for other purposes. For example, although evidence of something a minister said in Parliament cannot be used to determine whether he is acting honestly (*R v Secretary of State for Trade, ex p Anderson Strathclyde* [1983] at 238–39), it can be used as evidence of the reasons for executive action (*Toussaint v A-G of St Vincent and the Grenadines* [2008]) and under the *Pepper v Hart* rule as an aid to statutory interpretation (see Section 7.6.2). In *Pepper v Hart* [1993] the House of Lords took the view that the purpose of Article 9 was only to prevent MPs from being penalised for what they said in the House.

The immunity exists for the public benefit not that of the MP. Nevertheless the Defamation Act 1996 amended the Bill of Rights 1688 in order to accommodate Neil Hamilton, a Conservative MP who wished to sue a newspaper for defamation, relying upon parliamentary material for the purpose. Section 13 permits an MP to use things said in Parliament in evidence provided that the MP waives his or her own immunity; cf *Hamilton v Al Fayed* [1999]. This illustrates the frailty of constitutional principle against party political government. The Nicholls Committee (above) proposed that Article 9 should be waived only by itself. The current Defamation Bill proposes to give effect to this.

- *'Proceedings in Parliament'*. The meaning of 'in Parliament' has not been settled and is an example of a constitutional silence (see Section 3.5). In 1688 it was no doubt thought that the phrase was self-explanatory. It certainly includes speeches and written or oral questions by an MP in the House or in committee proceedings. However the work of a modern MP goes beyond this. Much of an MP's time is spent in writing letters and attending meetings in the UK and abroad with ministers, constituents, pressure groups, local authorities, business organisations, foreign officials and so on. MPs also appear on radio and television and increasingly communicate on the Internet.

  Anything said in the Chamber as part of the business of the House and in committees or reports related to the business of the House is certainly protected. Parliamentary committees often visit places around the country, and interference with their proceedings wherever they take place is a contempt of Parliament (eg a disturbance at Essex University in 1969 (HC 1968–69, 308)). On the other hand, even within the House itself, speech unrelated to parliamentary business probably enjoys no privilege (see *Re Parliamentary Privileges Act 1770*; *Chaytor*).

There are many borderline cases since the limits of an MP's duties are vague. However for reasons concerned with the rule of law the onus is on the MP to show that he falls within the immunity since this is an exception from the basic assumption of equality before the law (see *Chaytor* at [41], [42]; *Rost v Edwards*). It is clear that statements by an MP to the media are not covered by parliamentary privilege, although they may be covered by qualified privilege (below). Thus an MP could be liable if he or she repeats in the media or anywhere else anything said in Parliament (*Buchanan v Jennings*). Statements made in election campaigns (*Culnane v Morris* [2006]) or at public meetings are not protected by parliamentary privilege.

The main area of uncertainty concerns things said or written by MPs as part of their duties on behalf of their constituents, for example a letter complaining to the Secretary of State about an NHS hospital. In the case of *Strauss* [1956] the House of Commons by a tiny majority (218 to 213) rejected a recommendation by the Committee of Privileges that such letters should be protected by parliamentary privilege. *Strauss* concerned a complaint about the activities of the London Electricity Board. This was not a central government department, so the minister to whom Strauss wrote was not directly responsible to Parliament for its day-to-day activities. It is not clear what the reasons for the Commons resolutions were, and the vote may have been on party lines.

On the basis of *Strauss*, a letter from an MP is privileged only if it is to do with a matter currently being debated in the House or is the subject of an official parliamentary question. In 1967 a Select Committee on Parliamentary Privilege (HC 1967–68, 34) had recommended that privilege be widened to include all official communications by an MP, but the Nicholls Report (above) favoured the narrow view. In contemporary circumstances it is likely that any extension of privilege will be made by statute. For example a decision by an MP to refer a matter to the Parliamentary Ombudsman has absolute privilege (Parliamentary Commissioner Act 1967, s 10(5)).

- *'Impeached or questioned'*. Parliament has taken the view that it is contempt even to commence legal proceedings by serving a writ upon an MP in respect of a matter which Parliament considers to be privileged. This is a direct challenge to the courts since if this view is right then the courts have no power to decide the limits of parliamentary privilege. We shall discuss this below.
- *'Out of Parliament'*. Article 9 of the Bill of Rights 1688 is not restricted to legal proceedings but prevents interference with the freedom of speech of MPs by any outside body. This could include publishing MPs' home telephone numbers (*Daily Graphic Case* (HC 1956–57, 27)), accusing MPs of drunkenness (*Duffy's Case* (HC 1964–65, 129)) or making press allegations of conflict of interest by MPs. However Article 9 has not been used against media criticism of speeches by MPs. Nor does Article 9 prevent courts or other bodies from looking into matters which are also before Parliament, provided that the parliamentary processes or things said in them are not criticised (see *Hamilton v Al Fayed*). The Human Rights Act 1998 might also restrain an expansive interpretation of Article 9. Although an action could not be brought against Parliament itself, the court is required to interpret all legislation, including Article 9, 'if it is possible to do so', in a way that conforms to the rights set out in the Act, one of which is freedom of expression (s 3).

As with any liberty, the price to be paid is that an MP might abuse privilege to make untrue allegations against persons who cannot answer back or to violate privacy.

(See the *Child Z* case (HC 1995–96, vol 252, paras 9, 10), where a child was named in defiance of an order of the Court of Appeal.) Thus the limits of freedom of speech have to be defined. There are therefore limitations placed upon members' freedom of speech by Parliament itself, for example by rules of procedure or possibly by party discipline within the House. Indeed these restrictions are themselves immune from control by the courts because of the exclusive cognisance privilege (Section 11.6.2). The Speaker, who presides over the House of Commons, has a duty to control procedure impartially. Internal rules exist to prevent MPs misusing their privilege of freedom of speech, for example by attacking people who cannot answer back or by commenting upon pending legal proceedings. For example 'the invidious use of a person's name in a question should be resorted to only if to do so is strictly necessary to render the question intelligible and the protection of parliamentary privilege should be used only as a last resort' and 'in a way that does not damage the good name of the House' (see HC Deb 17 March 1986, vol 94, col 26).

11.6.3.1 Qualified privilege

Independently of the Bill of Rights 1688, an MP performing his official duties may be protected by 'qualified privilege'. Qualified privilege is not confined to MPs and is available to anyone who has a legal or moral duty to make the statement in question and where the recipient has a corresponding interest in hearing it (see Section 22.5). Qualified privilege is much narrower than parliamentary privilege. It does give complete immunity but covers only statements made in good faith and taking proper care. It applies only to defamation (the law relating to statements that damage reputation) whereas full or 'absolute' parliamentary privilege covers every kind of legal action. It is a defence to an action, so the MP must subject herself or himself to the burden of legal proceedings. Even if she or he eventually wins, the expense and uncertainty of litigation may discourage an MP from speaking freely.

Qualified privilege could apply to cases such as *Strauss* and to a media interview or press statement (*Church of Scientology v Johnson-Smith*) or to a statement made in an election campaign (*Culnane v Morris*: anti-BNP leaflets). Political freedom of expression is regarded as of the highest importance, and the scope of qualified privilege is correspondingly generous (*Culnane*). The public have a general interest in a democracy of receiving information and opinions from MPs. In *Buchanan v Jennings* the Privy Council held that an MP who in a television interview endorsed a defamatory statement he had made in the New Zealand Parliament could not claim full parliamentary privilege. In principle qualified privilege would be possible. However it is doubtful whether an MP repeating what he had said in the House could claim qualified privilege because the statement would already be accessible to the public. An MP who makes a defamatory statement which is not related to his parliamentary duties would not have qualified privilege.

In relation to the *Strauss* case an MP's letter to a minister is likely to have qualified privilege. In *R v Rule* [1973] it was held that a constituent's letter to an MP has qualified privilege.

11.6.3.2 Publication of parliamentary proceedings

A controversial aspect of contempt of Parliament concerns public access to parliamentary information, which arguably should be unrestricted except where the disclosure would harm the public interest. However parliamentary committees often sit in private and 'leaks' of reports of select committees have been prohibited since 1837, although action is only likely to be taken if the leak causes substantial interference with the function of a committee. The House of Commons has waived any more general right to restrain publication of its proceedings and has authorised the broadcasting of its proceedings, subject to a power to give directions. It has also undertaken generally to use its contempt powers sparingly (HC 1967–68, 34, para 15).

Each repetition of an unlawful statement is a new wrong. Thus even if a statement by an MP is protected, the media may be liable for repeating it. Therefore additional protection is required to safeguard the right of democratic access to information.

- Documents published by order of Parliament or correct copies, such as *Hansard*, have full parliamentary privilege (Parliamentary Papers Act 1840, ss 1, 2).
- The publication by the press of fair and accurate extracts or abstracts from authorised reports of parliamentary proceedings are protected if the publisher shows that they are published in good faith without malice (s 3), as are broadcasts of parliamentary proceedings (Defamation Act 1952, s 9; Broadcasting Act 1990, s 203(1)).
- Other press reports including parliamentary sketches and probably broadcasts and Internet reports are protected by the general law of qualified privilege provided that they are honest and fair (*Wason v Walter* [1868]; *Cook v Alexander* [1974]). Section 15 of the Defamation Act 1996 protects fair and accurate reports of legislative proceedings and other public meetings anywhere. Here it is for the claimant to show that the publication was not in good faith. Qualified privilege applies only to defamation (see Section 11.6.3.1)

Where a report is embellished with additional material which may flesh it out or comment on it, the privilege is lost unless the ordinary reader can clearly distinguish the reportage from the other material (see *Curiston v Times Newspapers* [2007]). The privilege does not in any case apply to the additional material, although this may be protected by the more general defence of 'responsible journalism' (see Section 22.5.3). As we have seen above, if an MP repeats in the media a statement he has made in Parliament probably neither he nor the broadcasters are protected even by qualified privilege.

11.7 Standards in the Commons

Following the recommendations of the First Report of the Committee on Standards in Public Life (Cm 2850, 1995) there is a Code of Conduct for MPs (2005). In keeping with parliamentary privilege, this is policed by the House itself.

The primary duty of an MP is to be an independent representative of his or her constituents. There are obstacles to the independence of MPs. First and foremost there are party loyalties. Secondly many MPs are sponsored by outside bodies, including trade unions and business interests, who may contribute towards their expenses. Some MPs accept employment as paid or unpaid 'consultants' to businesses and interest groups, such as the Police Federation, or hold company directorships. MPs are also frequently offered 'hospitality', or gifts, or invited on expenses-paid 'fact-finding' trips. There are also 'all-party' subject groups of MPs which involve relationships with outside bodies (see HC 1984–85, 408). Except in the case of a private bill, a member is free to vote on a matter in which she or he has a personal interest. There is therefore a risk that MPs are susceptible to lobbying by private interests.

It is often said that sponsorships and consultancies enable MPs to keep in touch with informed opinion outside Westminster and to develop specialised knowledge. They also enable MPs without private means to supplement their parliamentary salaries. The process of enacting legislation is also helped by consultation with interested parties. There is much 'lobbying' of civil servants and it is desirable that this should be counterbalanced by MPs having their own access to outside interests. On the other hand, apart from the risk of corruption, MPs might also spend time in company boardrooms that may generate little understanding of social problems and would be better spent helping their constituents. Compromises are therefore made.

In the *Brown* case [1947] an MP sponsored by a trade union was dismissed by the union for not advocating its interests in Parliament. The Committee of Privileges voted that a contract could not require an MP to support or represent his or her sponsor's interests in Parliament, nor could the sponsor punish the MP for not doing so. However it was not contempt to dismiss a consultant if for whatever reason the employer or sponsor was unhappy with his or her services. This somewhat evasive compromise does not seem to take the matter much further. It would be a contempt to threaten to dismiss an MP unless she or he took a certain line in Parliament but not, apparently, to dismiss her or him after the event. Arguably pressures from local constituency parties would also be contemptuous.

Since the seventeenth century, resolutions of the House have declared that certain kinds of external influences are in contempt of Parliament. The latest distinction seems to be between promoting a specific matter for gain, which is forbidden, and acting as a consultant generally, which is acceptable. There have been many resolutions attempting to capture this elusive matter.

For example a resolution of 1995 which amends a resolution of 1947 (HC 1994–95, 816 (see HC Deb 6 November 1995, cols 604, 661) states that:

> It is inconsistent with the dignity of the House, with the duty of a Member to his constituents, and with the maintenance of the privilege of freedom of speech for any Member of this House to enter into any contractual agreement with an outside body, controlling or limiting the Member's complete independence and freedom of action in Parliament or stipulating that he shall act in any way as the representative of such outside body in regard to any matter to be transacted in Parliament; the duty of a Member being to his constituents and to the country as a whole, rather than to any particular section thereof: and that in particular no Members of the House shall, in consideration of any remuneration, fee, payment or reward or benefit in kind, direct or indirect, which the Member or any member of his or her family has received, is receiving or expects to receive –
> (a) advocate or initiate any cause or matter on behalf of any outside body or individual, or
> (b) urge any other Member of either House of Parliament, including Ministers, to do so by means of any speech, Question, motion, introduction of a bill, or amendment to a Motion or a Bill.

A further resolution restricts the extent to which a member may participate in a delegation to ministers or public officials; see Code of Conduct for MPs (HC 2009–10, 735):

> A member should not initiate, participate in or attend any such delegation where the problem to be addressed affects only the body with which the member has a relevant paid interest except when that problem relates primarily to a constituency matter.

The MPs' Code of Conduct (2009) forbids paid advocacy, prohibits payment for promoting or opposing any matter in Parliament, requires openness and frankness and forbids the use for gain of information received in confidence for the purpose of parliamentary duties.

There are also criminal offences involving members of public bodies. Misuse of public office is a common law offence and there are also offences under the Public Bodies (Corrupt Practices) Act 1889 and the Prevention of Corruption Act 1916. These offences may include cases where MPs are offered bribes. However an MP might sometimes be protected by Article 9 of the Bill of Rights 1688. Nevertheless in *R v Greenaway* [1998] a Conservative MP had accepted a bribe to use his influence to help a person acquire UK citizenship. The court held that parliamentary privilege did not apply because the offence occurred when the bribe was received and therefore the court did not need to investigate what went on in Parliament. It is arguable that an MP is not a 'public servant' and does not hold a public office as such, so is outside these offences (see *A-G's Reference (No 3 of 2003)*).

MPs must enter information about their financial interests in a Register of Members' Interests (see Code of Conduct for MPs (2009)). The register itself has been held not to be protected by parliamentary privilege on the ground that it is a public document (*Rost v Edwards* [1990]). The categories of interest required by the register have been strengthened to include full details of an employment contract, the provision of services such as consultancy, company directorships, employment or offices, professions and trades, names of clients, financial sponsorships, overseas visits as an MP, payments received from abroad, land or property, shareholdings and 'any interest or benefit received which might reasonably be thought by others to influence the member's actions in Parliament'. However the precise value of such payments need not be entered. According to the register, only one in five MPs is without an external source of income.

11.7.1 The Parliamentary Commissioner for Standards

Following the First Report of the Committee on Standards in Public Life (Cm 2850, 1995) the House of Commons appointed a Parliamentary Commissioner for Standards empowered to investigate complaints of misuse of the Commons register and to report to the Standards and Privileges Committee of the House of Commons (HC Standing Orders (Public Business) (1995) No 150). The Commissioner can also investigate complaints by MPs and the public concerning the Code of Conduct and give advice to MPs. The decisions of the Commissioner are subject to parliamentary privilege and are not subject to judicial review (*R v Parliamentary Comr for Standards* [1998]).

Parliament can appoint and dismiss the Commissioner. In 2001 Elizabeth Filkin did not have her contract renewed. She had attracted a reputation as an assiduous investigator. In its Eighth Report (Cm 5663, 2002) the Committee on Standards in Public Life recommended that the independence of the Commissioner be strengthened. The Commissioner should be appointed for a non-renewable term of five to seven years, should have the power to call for witnesses and documents and should not be an employee of the House. This has not been implemented.

The Commissioner cannot investigate the interests of ministers acting as such, thus reflecting the separation of powers. There is no independent mechanism for this purpose. Compliance with the Ministerial Code is a matter for the Prime Minister. Independent inquiries in the form of a Royal Commission or under the Inquiries Act 2005 can be held into ministerial misconduct (Chapter 5). However these are set up by ministers. The Tribunals of Inquiry (Evidence) Act 1921, under which Parliament could order an inquiry, was repealed by the 2005 Act.

11.7.2 The Independent Parliamentary Standards Authority

IPSA is responsible for the salaries and expenses of MPs and has a role in the administration of MPs' pensions. Revelations in the press during 2008–09 that many MPs had been abusing their expenses claims caused considerable public concern. This led to legislation which for the first time introduced an element of outside policing into the affairs of Parliament. MPs' expenses had previously been dealt with relatively informally within the House (see Committee on Standards in Public Life, Twelfth Report (*MPs' Expenses and Allowances: Supporting Parliament, Safeguarding the Taxpayer* (Cm 7724, 2009)); Standards and Privileges Committee Second Report (HC 2009–10, 67)).

IPSA is a statutory body (Parliamentary Standards Act 2009 modified by the Constitutional Reform and Governance Act 2010). It has no jurisdiction over the House of Lords. The Acts go to considerable lengths to make IPSA independent. The members of IPSA must comprise a Chairman (currently Sir Ian Kennedy, a lawyer and seasoned recipient of government patronage), a former senior judge, a qualified auditor and a former MP. Apart from this no MP or former MP may serve. Members hold office for five years, non-renewable, and can be removed only on an Address from both Houses of Parliament. Thus they have similar status to a senior judge.

The members of IPSA are appointed by the Queen on an Address from the Commons on the nomination of the Speaker on the recommendation of the Speaker's Committee (below), subject to the usual mantra of appointment on merit by fair and open competition ('OMFOC'). The Act does not prescribe how the appointment process should be conducted. In fact MPs play no part in the selection of the nominee and the appointment process is subject to the Code for Public Appointments made by the Public Appointments Commissioner. An independent panel is used.

IPSA determines the salaries and expenses of MPs and polices the expenses system. There is a Compliance Officer appointed by IPSA for five years, non-renewable (OMFOC). The Compliance Officer reviews the rejection of an expenses claim by IPSA and investigates misuses of the expenses scheme. An investigation can be carried out on the Compliance Officer's initiative or at the request of the MP concerned or at the request of any individual, including therefore a member of the public. There is a right of appeal from the Compliance Officer to the ordinary tribunal system (see Section 5.4.3). IPSA can recover improper payments through the ordinary courts. There is a penalty of up to £1,000 for failing to provide information to IPSA. MPs' expenses claims must be published, containing such information as IPSA considers appropriate.

IPSA must make an annual report to the House of Commons.

The Speaker's Committee approves appointments to IPSA and that of the Compliance Officer. This Committee comprises the Speaker, the Leader of the House (a government minister), the Chair of the Committee on Standards and Privileges, five backbench MPs, who are nominated by and can be replaced by the House, and three laypersons who have never been MPs. The latter are appointed by resolution of the House (OMFOC).

In *R (Chaytor) v A-G* [2010] (see Section 11.6.2), it was conceded that the expenses scheme as it was before the introduction of IPSA was protected by parliamentary privilege. However IPSA may not be protected by parliamentary privilege. The 2009 Act states that nothing in it affects Article 9 of the Bill of Rights 1688 (s 1) but this in itself does not determine the matter since the question is what Article 9 covers (Section 11.6.3). It is arguable that IPSA is not covered by privilege given its statutory basis and the fact that the expenses system is linked into the general legal system and publicised (see *Rost v Edwards* [1990]).

IPSA is certainly vulnerable to accusations of interfering with proceedings in Parliament under Article 9. For example an MP might complain to the Standards and Privileges Committee that the expenses scheme is so mean that it prevents him from performing his functions. IPSA has already attracted criticism from MPs as being overly bureaucratic, and its staff have been subjected to abuse from some MPs (see *Guardian* 26 August 2010). Its hasty creation and immediate modification may illustrate how constitutional reform can be driven by panic reaction to short-term problems.

11.7.3 Standards in the House of Lords

There is a 'custom' that the House of Lords should not be subject to formal regulation. It is said by its members that it should rely on their 'personal honour' (see Seventh Report of the Committee on Standards in Public Life (Cm 4903, 2000)). However no reason has been offered as to why members of the Lords are more honourable than members of the Commons. With the possible exception of treason, a member could not be deprived of a peerage or expelled for misconduct without statutory authority. Nor can a member resign, although a member can take a leave of absence. The Letters Patent from the Crown that create a peerage confer a legal right to sit in the House of Lords. There may however be a power to suspend a member (see Reports of the Committee for Privileges (HL 2008–09, 87, 88)). It is customary for membership not to be regarded as a full-time commitment and many members have outside interests, including full-time jobs. The present government proposes to introduce a power to remove members of the House of Lords.

There is a House of Lords Code of Conduct (2009) embodying the Nolan Principles of Public Life. This includes a Register of Members' Interests. The register was originally voluntary in respect of non-financial interests. However as a result of the Seventh Report of the Committee on Standards in Public Life (Cm 4903, 2000) it was made compulsory (see HL 1994–95, 90, 98). It is however less stringent than the Commons register.

The Code also provides for an independent House of Lords Commissioner for Standards who investigations allegations against members involving misuse of their position or undisclosed financial interests. A complaint can be made by anyone, including a member of the public. The Commissioner reports to the House of Lords Committee for Privileges, which after a hearing reports to the House. The first Commissioner appointed in May 2010 is a former Chief Constable. IPSA does not apply to the House of Lords, which polices its own expenses claims. Peers now receive a flat rate of £300 per day's attendance.

11.8 The courts and Parliament

As we have seen, the courts do not intervene in the internal affairs of the House. On the other hand, where parliamentary activity involves the rights of persons outside the House, the courts have intervened at least to the extent of deciding whether the privilege asserted by Parliament exists. In a famous eighteenth-century controversy that asserted basic rule of law values the courts held that parliamentary officers have no power to deprive citizens of voting rights: 'where there is a right there is a remedy' (*Ashby v White* [1703]; see also *Paty's Case* [1704]). In *Stockdale v Hansard* [1839] it was held that parliamentary privilege did not protect reports published by order of the House from being the subject of libel actions.

The subject matter of these disputes is only of historical interest. Parliament no longer controls elections and *Stockdale v Hansard* was soon reversed by statute (Parliamentary Papers Act 1840). Nevertheless the general principle about the power of the courts remains valid.

Parliament has never accepted that *Stockdale v Hansard* was correctly decided and has never withdrawn the claim to be the exclusive judge of its own privileges.

In the *Sheriff of Middlesex* case [1840] Parliament imprisoned the two holders of the office of sheriff for enforcing the court's judgment in *Stockdale v Hansard*. Not surprisingly the sheriffs applied to the court for release but the court, including Lord Denman, who had decided *Stockdale v Hansard* itself, held that it was powerless to intervene. Parliament had the undoubted right to commit to prison for contempt and it did not have to give reasons. Unless some improper reason was disclosed on the face of the committal warrant, the court must assume that Parliament was acting lawfully even though the judges knew otherwise.

Therefore by relying on the *Sheriff of Middlesex* case Parliament can arbitrarily imprison anyone it likes. (The Human Rights Act 1998 does not apply to Parliament; see Section 21.5.) Whether this principle will be taken advantage of in modern times rests with Parliament's – or the courts' – political sense. The courts are unwilling to take action that might be considered as trespassing on Parliament's preserves. Parliament too has shown restraint in asserting claims to privilege (eg *Strauss* [1956]; see Section 11.6.3). This standoff could be regarded as an example of the dual sovereignty which it is claimed that the separation of powers requires and also of a constitution abeyance (see Section 3.5). Thus it has been claimed that there is a voluntary, mutual respect between the two institutions (*Hamilton v Al Fayed* [1999] at 333–34). Recently in *R (Chaytor) v A-G* [2010] (see Section 11.6) the Supreme Court held that it was settled that the court can decide the limits of parliamentary privilege. In that case no challenge was made to the court's jurisdiction.

The Nicholls Report (above) suggested the enactment of a code of parliamentary privilege to include modest reforms largely intended to clarify the relationship between Parliament and the courts. These have not formally been implemented but have influenced the evolution of the law. In addition to the recommendations already mentioned, they include the following:

- 'Place out of Parliament' for the purposes of Article 9 should be defined to include courts and tribunals empowered to take evidence on oath but not tribunals of inquiry if both Houses so resolve.
- The offence of abuse of public office should include MPs.
- MPs should be subject to the criminal law relating to corruption.
- Members of the Lords should be compellable before Commons' committees.
- Parliament's 'exclusive cognisance' should be confined to 'activities directly and closely related to the business of the House'.
- Contempt by non-members should be dealt with by the ordinary courts.
- Freedom from arrest should be abolished.

Summary

- Parliament has developed primarily through the party system. It has the competing functions of sustaining the government and holding the government to account. It scrutinises legislation, provides the executive with finance, debates matters of public concern and redresses grievances. The executive is usually too powerful and complex for Parliament to be effective. However at least Parliament is a public forum in which the executive can be forced to justify its actions.
- There is a network of laws and conventions to ensure that Parliament lasts no more than five years, that it meets annually and that it can remove the government. However the Prime Minister can dissolve Parliament subject to the possibility of the overriding powers of the Crown, and MPs cannot hold the government to account during the periods when Parliament is not sitting.
- After the 1688 settlement the House of Lords was regarded as holding the constitutional balance of power, but by the twentieth century it had become subordinate to the elected House of Commons. The Lords was given a new lease of life by the introduction of life peers in the 1960s but the constitutional role of the House remains controversial. By convention and law the Lords must ultimately defer to the Commons. It is primarily a delaying and revising chamber. Since the bulk of the hereditary peers were removed in 1999 the House of Lords has become more aggressive in resisting the executive. The House of Lords is less subject to party pressures than the House of Commons. The rules of procedure and party discipline in the House of Lords are more relaxed than is the case with the Commons. Because of the control over the Commons exercised by the executive, a second chamber is desirable but there is no agreement as to how the hereditary element in the Lords should be replaced. At present the House of Lords is accountable to no one.
- Parliament can protect itself against interference from without and within through the law of parliamentary privilege and its powers to punish for contempt. Parliament can enforce its own privileges free from interference by the ordinary courts. The Committee on Standards and Privileges, which adjudicates on matters referred to it by the House, has been criticised on the grounds of lack of independence and a low standard of procedural fairness.
- The main parliamentary privileges are Parliament's exclusive control over its own affairs and freedom of speech. There are difficulties in terms of what counts as parliamentary proceedings for these purposes. These are probably confined to matters related to the core business of the House and to purely internal matters within the precincts of the House. MPs and the media also have qualified privilege in the law of defamation but this is limited.
- There are safeguards against conflicts of interest for MPs, including the Register of Interests and the Parliamentary Commissioner for Standards. There are similar but less stringent safeguards in the House of Lords. There is no independent mechanism to enforce standards against ministers. IPSA was recently created to determine and police MPs' salaries and expenses but has already run into problems. IPSA does not apply to the House of Lords.
- There has been conflict between the courts and Parliament as to who decides whether a claimed privilege or contempt exists. It is probably recognised that the courts have the power to do so.

Exercises

11.1 'It has been a source of concern to some constitutionalists that the effect of the 1911 Act and more particularly the 1949 Act has been to erode the checks and balances inherent in the British Constitution' (Lord Bingham in *R (Jackson) v A-G* [2005] at 41). Explain and discuss.

11.2 'The virtue, spirit and essence of a House of Commons consists in its being the express image of the feelings of the nation. It was not instituted to be a control on the people. It was designed as a control for the people' (Edmund Burke). 'Parliament really has no control over

Exercises cont'd

the executive. It is a pure fiction' (David Lloyd George). To what extent do these statements represent the contemporary constitution?

11.3 'The executive has undue control over the summoning and dismissal of Parliament.' Discuss.

11.4 'It is not unduly idealistic to regard the integrity of Members' judgement, however constrained it may be by the party system, and the devotion of their time to the job to which they have been elected, as fundamental values worth not only protecting but insisted on' (Sedley). Discuss in relation to the outside interests of MPs and peers.

11.5 In what circumstances is an MP immune from legal action in respect of things he or she says or writes?

11.6 Advise in the following cases whether an action in the courts is likely to succeed:

(i) Dave is an MP. Sam, a constituent, sends Dave a letter accusing the management of a local nuclear power station of negligence in relation to safety standards. Dave, who is employed as a consultant by a company involved in the promotion of renewable sources of energy, passes on the letter to the minister responsible. The manager of the power station hears about the letter and issues writs for libel against Sam and Dave.

(ii) At a local government election, the English National Party (fictitious) publishes a leaflet accusing Cherie, an MP, of receiving gifts from business interests without declaring them. Cherie brings an action for libel against the publishers.

(iii) In a speech in Parliament Dave, an MP, alleges that the Prime Minister has been selling peerages for contributions to party funds. Dave is later asked in a television interview whether he stands by the allegation. He replies, 'You must refer to my speech.'

11.7 Bulldog, an MP, asks Fox, the Minister of Health, in the House of Commons a question in which he strongly criticises the manner in which the National Health Board deals with the problem of 'lengthy waiting lists for hospital treatment and allocation of hospital beds'. In a later letter to Fox, Bulldog makes further and more serious allegations concerning the conduct of an individual hospital manager. The NHB issues a writ for libel against Bulldog while Parliament is in session. Contending that this is a matter of parliamentary privilege over which the court has no jurisdiction, Bulldog refuses to enter an appearance or to defend the action. Meanwhile the House of Commons resolves that any judge, counsel or party who takes part in such proceedings will be guilty of contempt. Discuss the position of Bulldog and any possible action that may be taken against the members of the National Health Board, and any solicitor or counsel who proceeds with the libel.

11.8 Advise in the following cases:

(i) Tony, an MP, is accused by IPSA's Compliance Officer of falsifying his expenses claim. He wishes to challenge the decision in the courts. What would be the position if a member of the House of Lords was similarly accused by the House of Lords Commissioner for Standards?

(ii) Tessa, an MP, is prosecuted in a criminal court for taking a bribe in connection with a recent speech in the House. She claims that the court has no jurisdiction. The police attempt to arrest her at the House of Commons but the Sergeant at Arms refuses them permission to enter.

(iii) Gordon, an MP, claims that IPSA has taken so long to process his claim for reimbursement of expenses that he can no longer afford to attend Parliament.

Further reading

Archer, 'The House of Lords, Past, Present and Future' (2000) 70 Pol Q 396
Blackburn, 'The Summoning and Meeting of New Parliaments in the United Kingdom' (1989) 9 LS 165
Brazier, 'The Constitutional Role of the Opposition' (1989) 40 Northern Ireland LQ 131
Brazier, 'The Financial Powers of the House of Lords' (1998) 17 Anglo-American L Rev 131
Joseph, 'Parliament's Attenuated Privilege of Freedom of Speech' (2010) 126 LQR 568
Lock, 'Parliamentary Privilege and the Courts' [1985] PL 64
Munro, *Studies in Constitutional Law* (2nd edn, Butterworths 2000) ch 7
Oliver and Drewry (eds), *The Law and Parliament* (Butterworths 1998)
Riddall, 'The Second Chamber: In Search of a Complementary Role' (2000) 70 Pol Q 404
Rodgers and Walters, *How Parliament Works* (5th edn, Pearson 2004) chs 1, 2, 5
Royal Commission on the House of Lords, *A House for the Future* (Cm 4534, 2000) [Wakeham Report]
Tomkins, *Public Law* (Clarendon Press 2003) ch 4

Chapter 12

The composition of Parliament and parliamentary elections

Democracy is but the government of a few orators. (Hobbes, *The Body Politic*, ch XXIV, 3)

12.1 Introduction

We have seen that Parliament comprises two Houses which evolved separately and until the early twentieth century shared lawmaking power on broadly equal terms. The upper house, the House of Lords, is not elected but today has less power than the elected lower house, the House of Commons. The House of Commons has exclusive control over public finance. Ministers can be members of either House but the Prime Minister and the Chancellor of the Exchequer must by convention be members of the Commons. Such democracy as exists in the UK consists primarily of the right to vote for members of the House of Commons in accordance with a voting system engineered by the political parties. (Local government elections and jury trials are the other democratic elements.) This single vote indirectly chooses a Prime Minister and a government since the Queen must appoint as Prime Minister the person supported by the House of Commons and the Prime Minister appoints the rest of the government.

The composition of Parliament raises questions about the legitimacy of the constitution. Firstly to what extent does a government chosen in this indirect way have public consent and confidence? Secondly which of the different kinds of democracy outlined in Chapter 2, if any, best captures the UK's arrangements? Can a non-elected element in the legislature be justified? Do the voting rules give fair representation and cater for the different functions of Parliament? Thirdly there are questions concerning the relationship between democracy and other liberal values. What restrictions should there be on the right to vote, stand for election or participate in an election campaign? Liberal freedoms such as freedom of expression may conflict with the aspiration of equality.

12.2 The House of Lords

The dominant feature of the House of Lords is that none of its members is elected, all being chosen by the executive in one form or another. Almost anyone can be a member of the House of Lords. Apart from senior Church of England bishops who sit *ex officio* and certain hereditary members, its members are appointed by the Queen on the advice of the Prime Minister. A member must receive a writ of summons administered by the Lord Chancellor before taking his or her seat. There are certain disqualifications. These are as follows:

1. non-citizens other than Commonwealth and Irish citizens. A non-resident Commonwealth citizen can sit in the Lords but not in the Commons (see Act of

Settlement 1700, s 3 as amended by the Constitutional Reform and Governance Act 2010, s 47);
2. persons under the age of 21 (SO2 – Standing Order);
3. undischarged bankrupts (Insolvency Act 1986, s 426(A));
4. persons convicted of treason until their sentence is served or pardoned (Forfeiture Act 1870, s 2).

As a result of some members of the House of Lords being evasive about their tax position a further restriction has been introduced. A member of the House of Lords, and also a member of the Commons, is deemed to be resident and domiciled in the UK for tax purposes (Constitutional Reform and Governance Act 2010, s 41). In the case of the House of Lords there is a transitional provision which allowed the peer a period of three months from the date the Act came into force to reject the tax status (s 42). If the peer chose to keep non-resident status he or she ceased to be a member; if the peer was a hereditary peer, the place could not be filled and the peer could not stand for election to the Commons for three years.

Otherwise a member of the House of Lords can apparently be removed only by statute. It has been proposed that those convicted of a serious criminal offence should be subject to expulsion from the House but no measures have yet been taken. However the House can suspend a member if he or she abuses his or her position, for example by selling favours (three peers were recently suspended for this; see *Independent* 7 October 2010).

There is no legal limit on the size of the House of Lords. Before the House of Lords Act 1999 there were about 1,349 members, making the House of Lords the largest legislative chamber in the world. The 1999 Act reduced this by removing 654 of the 746 hereditary peers. This still makes the House of Lords, with about 746 members, one of the largest second chambers in the world. Germany's Bundesrat has 69 members and the US Senate 104. Small upper chambers could be justified on the basis that they can be more cohesive and more focused. However attendance in the House of Lords is far from assiduous. In practice only about 400 attend regularly. Reform proposals have suggested reducing the membership to no more than 450 (White Paper, *An Elected Second Chamber* (Cm 7438, 2008)).

Protocol 3 of the European Convention on Human Rights (ECHR) requires states to hold free elections to the legislature. In *Matthieu-Mohun v Belgium* [1988] the ECHR held that this requires at least one chamber to be elected. However one of the judges stated that the elected element must comprise a majority of the legislature and the non-elected element must not have greater powers than the elected element. The present House of Lords violates the majority requirement, there being currently 650 seats in the House of Commons.

The membership of the House of Lords comprises the following three categories:

1. *The Lords Spiritual.* These are the Archbishops of Canterbury and York, the Bishops of London, Durham and Winchester, and 21 other diocesan bishops of the Church of England, these being the senior bishops in order of appointment. Bishops are appointed by the Queen on the advice of the Prime Minister, the practice being that the Prime Minister chooses one from a list of nominations provided by the Church authorities. The bishops vacate their seats in the Lords on ceasing to hold office. They are not peers and can vote in parliamentary elections. (Dignitaries from other faiths may of course be appointed to the House of Lords as ordinary peers.) Reform proposals would remove the bishops from an elected chamber but retain them if

there is to be an appointed element. It is not proposed that representatives from other faiths be entitled to seats. This might be unworkable in practice given the large number of sects who might claim a seat. On the other hand other than on historical grounds it is difficult to see why the Church of England should be so privileged.

2. *Hereditary peers.* Hereditary peers are persons on whose ancestors the monarch has conferred various ranks – dukes, marquises, earls, viscounts and barons – specifying that the peerages can be inherited. Until the House of Lords Act 1999 the hereditary peers formed a majority, thereby biasing the House of Lords in favour of Conservative interests and being difficult to justify rationally. The notion of the 'mixed constitution' could be raised in this context (see Section 7.2). However this presupposes that the peerage is a powerful economic or political force, neither being the case today, particularly as the historical link between peerage and landholding no longer exists (although some peers, such as the Duke of Westminster, are among the largest landowners in the UK).

   At common law a peer cannot surrender his or her peerage (*Re Parliamentary Election for Bristol SE* [1964], an attempt by Tony Benn, then Lord Stansgate). However under the Peerage Act 1963, a hereditary peerage can be disclaimed for life. This would enable the former peer to vote and to stand for election to the Commons. The peerage must be disclaimed within 12 months of succeeding to it (1 month if the new peer is an MP) or within 12 months of coming of age. The succession to the peerage is not affected. A peer who disclaims his or her title cannot again become a hereditary peer but could be appointed a life peer (below).

   As an initial reform measure, the House of Lords Act 1999 provides that no one shall be a member of the House of Lords by virtue of a hereditary peerage. This is subject to an exception, negotiated to prevent the peers from rejecting the Act. Under the exception the House can retain by Standing Order 90 peers, together with the Earl Marshall and the Lord Chamberlain, who are royal officials. Under the relevant Standing Orders a vacancy can be filled by an election by the remaining hereditary members. The elected peers sit for life. They comprise 75 peers elected on the basis of party balance, together with 15 elected as deputy speakers and committee chairs. Peers who are not members of the House of Lords can stand for and vote in elections to the House of Commons (s 4). As a result of the 1999 Act, no single party is likely to command an overall majority in the House.

3. *Life peers.* Life peers (about 600) are appointed by the Crown on the advice of the Prime Minister, with the rank of baron. Originally life peers could not sit in the House of Lords but under the Life Peerages Act 1958, which was enacted in order to regenerate the House of Lords, they can now do so. Unlike a hereditary peerage, a life peerage cannot be disclaimed. Life peerages are intended to enable hand-picked people to play a part in public life. Life peerages are often bestowed on retired public officials who have served loyally or on retired MPs, particularly those who have held high government office. Sometimes a life peerage is created for a person who has performed outstanding public services or whom the Prime Minister wishes to appoint as a minister. This may cause political problems arising out of a lack of perceived legitimacy.

   No reason need be given for the conferring of a peerage and it is unlikely that the conferring of honours or titles is subject to judicial review (see Section 19.7.1). Allegations are made from time to time that peerages are used to bribe supporters or to get rid of dead wood in the House of Commons or even sold. It is unlawful to sell peerages or to offer to do so but this kind of transaction would be very difficult to prove on the standard of criminal liability (Honours (Prevention of Corruption) Act 1925). In an extreme case, where for example a Prime Minister attempts to flood the Lords with his or her cronies, the monarch could perhaps reject the Prime Minister's advice in relation to appointments. Where a Prime Minister seeks to act undemocratically, it is arguable that the monarch has a duty to act as the ultimate constitutional check. On two important occasions the monarch reluctantly agreed to appoint sufficient peers to secure a government majority. These were the Reform Act 1832, which extended the parliamentary franchise, and the Parliament Act 1911, which reduced the powers of the House of Lords. In both cases the House of Lords was threatening to obstruct the Commons. In the case of the 1911 Act George V agreed to appoint the peers only if the government's policy was submitted to a general election.

Pending reform of the House of Lords, the Prime Minister's conventional power to appoint life peers is subject to a non-statutory House of Lords Appointments Commission (see White Paper, *Modernising Parliament: Reforming the House of Lords* (Cm 4183, 1999)). Appointed by and reporting to the Prime Minister, the Commission vets all proposals for political appointments on the ground of propriety and also administers a process for non-party political appointments. However its decisions are only advisory. Any British or Commonwealth citizen over 21 can apply for appointment. The criteria for appointment are a record of 'significant achievement', 'independence of political parties' and 'an ability to contribute to the work of the House'. The last of these criteria invites preference to be given in the manner of a private club to those with whom the existing members feel personally comfortable.

The Commission comprises a cross-bench peer as chair, together with three peers nominated by the main parties and three 'independent' persons. Its terms of reference embody the Nolan Principles of impartiality, integrity and objectivity. Reform proposals favour a statutory commission responsible directly to Parliament.

Former 'Law Lords', members of the Appellate Committee of the House of Lords, which has now been replaced by the Supreme Court, remain members of the House of Lords as life peers, but judges are no longer automatic members, thus underlying the separation of powers.

12.3 Reform of the House of Lords

Attempts to reform the Lords have foundered, mainly because of disagreement as to what proportion of the House should be elected, with consequences for the supremacy of the Commons, and also because the matter has not had high political priority. There is substantial agreement that the second chamber should remain subservient to the House of Commons, with the latter sustaining the government and having the last word on legislation. Mill (1972, ch 13) argued that a second chamber should primarily act as a partial check on the majority and should ideally embody 'the greatest number of elements exempt from the class interests and prejudices of the majority, but having in themselves nothing offensive to democratic feeling'.

Mill thought that in every constitution there should be a centre of resistance to the predominant power 'and in a democratic constitution, therefore, a nucleus of resistance to the democracy'. He recommended including experts in a second chamber, recruited primarily from persons distinguished in the public professions, such as the judiciary, armed forces and civil service. However, although he thought that the question of a second chamber was relatively unimportant, it could be justified (in both liberal and republican terms) on the basis of the corrupting effect of absolute power and as a mechanism for producing compromise. Mill's preferred solution was proportional representation in the House of Commons (below), which would make it more difficult for any majority faction to be dominant.

In a unitary system such as that of the UK, a wholly elected House might either duplicate or rival the House of Commons, thereby weakening the accountability (or power) of the government. On the other hand an entirely appointed chamber would lack public credibility and reinforce the patronage that currently undermines the constitution. Furthermore there is no consensus as to who should make appointments to the House and on what basis. The hereditary element is said to have the advantage of independence but at the price of legitimacy. An attractively democratic possibility would be random selection from the whole adult community, as is currently the case with jury service. However, this raises many practical and economic problems and is probably unrealistic (see Phillipson, 2004). Another possibility would be a House made up of representatives of major community interests such as business, charities, churches, ethnic groups, the professions and local communities. However it could prove impossibly complex and controversial to achieve an acceptable choice of interests and balance between them.

Lord Bingham, a former senior judge, suggested that a second chamber be purely advisory, with no lawmaking powers but designed as a senate of experts to give independent advice to the House of Commons (see Bingham, 2010). He proposed that the composition of the House be similar to its present composition and that it should select its own membership. It is questionable whether such a body would be able to establish public confidence in its political impartiality and, as with the current House, its membership would be likely to be dominated by persons who conform to the interests of those in power. The notion of unbiased expertise is highly questionable.

The Parliament Act 1911 began the process of reform by removing the power of the House of Lords to veto most public bills introduced in the Commons (Chapter 13). The Bryce Conference of 1917–18 (*Conference on the Reform of the Second Chamber* (Cd 9038, 1918)) attempted to tackle the problem of the composition of the House of Lords but was unable to agree. In 1958 the introduction of life peers reinvigorated the House to a certain extent, particularly in relation to the work of its committees. In 1968 an all-party conference proposed removing voting rights from most of the hereditary element and introducing the concept of 'working peers', mainly life peers, who would form a permanent nucleus of the House. The bill to introduce these reforms was abandoned because of backbench opposition from both sides of the House.

The previous Labour government intended to reform the House of Lords in two stages. Stage one comprised the House of Lords Act 1999 (above), the main result of which was to remove most of the hereditary element. Stage two has not taken place. A Royal Commission on the House of Lords (*A House for the Future* (Cm 4534, 2000), the Wakeham Report) examined the composition of the House of Lords in isolation from wider questions of constitutional reform and therefore did not question the role and powers of the House of Commons or those of the executive. Wakeham endorsed the existing roles of the House of Lords as subordinate to the Commons, providing limited checks on the executive, a revising mechanism for legislation and a 'constitutional long-stop' to force the government to have second thoughts. Wakeham's governing principles seem to be:

> the capacity to offer counsel from a range of sources...broadly representative of society in the UK at the beginning of the 21st century...It should give the UK's constituent nations and regions, for the first time, a formally constituted voice in the Westminster Parliament'. (31)

The electorate is not to be trusted to produce these outcomes but must be paternalistically protected from itself.

Wakeham rejected the extremes of an all-elected second chamber and one made up of 'experts'. Wakeham thought that a wholly elected second chamber might produce the 'wrong sort of people', reinforce party political control, result in 'voter fatigue' and either gridlock or rubber stamp the Commons, thus weakening governmental accountability. Wakeham rejected random selection, apparently because of the risk of appointing persons who would not 'fit in'. Wakeham also rejected the notion of a 'council of the wise', recognising that government is about accommodating disagreement and is necessarily political. Perhaps updating the classical 'mixed constitution', Wakeham proposed a balance of representatives from the main interests in the community with about one-third elected. Elections would be on a 15-year cycle, with one-third being elected every five years to ensure that the outcome did not duplicate elections to the Commons. An independent statutory commission would appoint all other members, taking account of regional, ethnic, gender and religious concerns.

Subsequent progress of the reforms is a picture of confusion. Crucial matters have been left open, notably the extent to which there should be an elected element and the method of election. A government White Paper (*The House of Lords: Completing the Reforms* (Cm 5291, 2001)) broadly adopted Wakeham's proposals but weakened them in favour of a larger element of government control over the House of Lords. This was not well received and was followed by proposals from the Public Administration Committee (Fifth Report, HC 2001–02, 494–1), the House of Commons and the political parties for different permutations of elected and appointed members. In 2002 a joint committee of both Houses set out seven options ranging from complete election to complete appointment. None of these was approved by the Commons, while the Lords voted for an all-appointed House (2002–03, HL 17, HC 171).

Revised proposals were set out in a White Paper in February 2007 which remains of value for its historical summary and references (*House of Lords Reform* (Cm 7027, 2007)). These proposals were not well received. The 2007 White Paper was superseded by the White Paper *An Elected Second Chamber* (Cm 7438, 2008). This favoured an elected House with the same functions and powers as the existing House of Lords. However it left open the most contentious matters, namely whether there should be an appointed element of 20 per cent and also the voting system to be used. A form of proportional representation would ensure a different political balance to that of the House of Commons. In order to avoid the political balance of the upper house reflecting that of the Commons, its members would sit for terms of 12–15 years, with staggered elections so that one-third would be elected at the same time as a general election every four to five years.

A more radical proposal in the White Paper is that of 'recall'. This allows a proportion of the electorate to sign a petition which triggers a special election to remove a sitting member. The recall device has a reactionary tendency against the principle of representative democracy in that opinion can most easily be generated against voices for change.

Opinion among the political parties now seems to have moved in favour of an all-elected chamber but without agreement as to the voting system to be used. There were no House of Lords reform provisions in the Constitutional Reform and Governance Act 2010. The Conservative–Liberal Democrat Coalition government which took office in May 2010 is proposing to introduce a second chamber 'wholly or mainly' elected by proportionate representation. The detailed arrangements remain unresolved and, given the desultory history of House of Lords reform, it is doubtful whether reforms will be introduced in the near future. A cross-party committee is currently considering the matter, while a private member's bill seeking to prevent an elected House of Lords is currently before the lords.

12.4 Membership of the House of Commons

Anyone can be a member of the House of Commons, other than the following:

- non-citizens other than Commonwealth citizens with indefinite leave to reside in the UK or citizens of the Irish Republic (Act of Settlement 1700, s 3 as modified by Electoral Administration Act 2006, s 18). Resident EU citizens can sit in the devolved legislatures but not the Commons;
- people under the age of 18 (Election Administration Act 2006, s 17);
- persons detained as mental patients (Mental Health Act 1983; there are special provisions for removing sitting MPs under this Act, involving two medical reports at six-month intervals);
- peers who are members of the House of Lords (peers can sit in the devolved legislatures);
- bishops who sit in the House of Lords (House of Commons (Removal of Clergy Disqualification) Act 2001);
- bankrupts, until five years after discharge unless the discharge certifies that the bankruptcy was not caused by the debtor's misconduct (Insolvency Act 1986, s 426(A));
- persons convicted of election offences (below);
- persons convicted of treason, until expiry of the sentence or pardon (Forfeiture Act 1870);
- persons convicted of an offence and sentenced to prison for more than one year while actually in prison or unlawfully at large (Representation of the People Act 1981, designed to prevent convicted terrorists in Northern Ireland from standing);
- persons holding certain public offices (House of Commons (Disqualification) Act 1975).

The last of these disqualifications is an example of the separation of powers. One element of the seventeenth-century conflict between Crown and Parliament was the Commons' fear that the Crown might bribe members by giving them jobs. The Act of Settlement 1700 therefore provided that nobody who held Crown office or a place of profit under the Crown could sit in the Commons. This would of course have prevented ministers from sitting and the constitution would have had a strict separation of powers. This part of the Act was repealed by the Succession to the Crown Act 1707. However there are limits upon the number of ministers who can be MPs, thus giving the Commons a degree of independence. These are as follows:

1. Under the House of Commons (Disqualification) Act 1975, not more than 95 ministers may sit and vote. There are usually about 20 ministers in the House of Lords.
2. The Ministerial and Other Salaries Act 1975 (as amended) fixed the salaries of the various grades of minister and limits the number of paid ministers of the government to 83, plus about 30 other specialised political office holders such as whips and also four law officers. However a government can increase its loyalists in the House by appointing unpaid parliamentary secretaries.
3. The House of Commons (Disqualification) Act 1975 debars certain other holders of public office from sitting in the Commons. The main examples are as follows:
   - full-time judges of various kinds;
   - regulators of privatised undertakings;
   - civil servants;
   - members of the regular armed services and police (other than specialised forces such as railway police);
   - members of foreign legislatures. However by virtue of the Disqualifications Act 2000 a member of the Irish legislature (the Oireachtas) can be a member of the Commons;
   - members of certain public boards and undertakings;
   - holders of the offices of Steward or Bailiff of the Chiltern Hundreds or the Manor of Northstead. These are meaningless titles in the gift of the Chancellor of the Exchequer. There are no specific rules entitling MPs to resign or retire but a successful application for one of these offices has the same effect.

In the event of a dispute about a disqualification, the Judicial Committee of the Privy Council may make a declaration on the application of any person (1975 Act, s 7). The House may also refer a matter to the Privy Council for an opinion (Judicial Committee Act 1833, s 4). The House has the statutory power to disregard a disqualification if it has been subsequently removed, for example by the MP resigning from a disqualifying post (s 6(2)).

A member of the House of Commons is deemed to be resident, ordinarily resident or domiciled in the UK for tax purposes (Constitutional Reform and Governance Act 2010, s 41).

12.5 The electoral system

Election law is found primarily in the Representation of the People Acts 1983 and 1985 and the Parliamentary Constituencies Act 1986. Important changes were made by the Representation of the People Act 2000, the Political Parties, Elections and Referendums Act 2000 and the Electoral Administration Act 2006.

12.5.1 The purpose of elections

We can assess the electoral system only in relation to its aims. Is it intended (i) to secure fair democratic representation, (ii) to produce effective government, (iii) to produce 'accountable' governments or (iv) to provide a local representative? No electoral system has yet been thought up that successfully combines all these. Underlying these conflicting aims is the difference between 'representative democracy' and 'market democracy' (outlined in Chapter 2). In the case of a market democracy the voter chooses a party from the range on offer in the same way that he or she might buy a car. Protocol 1, Article 3 of the ECHR provides a general and vague standard, limited to representative democracy:

> Free elections at reasonable intervals by secret ballot, under conditions which will ensure the free expression of the opinion of the people in the choice of the legislature.

There is no requirement that the people choose the executive government or that each vote should have equal weight.

Until well into the nineteenth century, the prevalent belief was that only landowners had a sufficient stake in the realm to vote, the majority of the population enjoying 'virtual representation' through the property owners. During the nineteenth century the extension of voting rights to non-property owners was slowly and reluctantly conceded, resisted by liberal arguments that the freedom of talented people to develop themselves would be curtailed by the inflated demands of the masses. Democracy was also resisted on rule of law grounds by the likes of Dicey, who thought that it was unpredictable, and on communitarian grounds by Matthew Arnold (1822–88). Arnold (*Culture and Anarchy* (1869)) believed in a grand overarching concept of the public good and recommended an 'authority of culture', by which he seemed to mean a monarchy or the Platonic ideal of a wise ruling class. This approach is still canvassed in the context of reform of the House of Lords. It was not until 1948 that a universal principle of one-person-one-vote was fully adopted (Representation of the People Act 1948).

There is a conflict between the law of the electoral process and practical politics. The legal basis of democracy in the UK is that the electorate in each constituency chooses an individual to represent the constituency in the House of Commons. However this is distorted by the convention that the executive government and Prime Minster must be supported by the House of Commons and are usually drawn from the majority political party. Thus election candidates are overwhelmingly members of and chosen by political parties. (Exceptionally in the 2010 election the Conservative Party let the whole local community choose one of its candidates.) Elections are therefore fought and funded between the parties on a national battlefield and one vote has to serve three not necessarily compatible purposes, namely choosing a local representative, choosing the governing party and choosing a Prime Minister

The European Convention on Human Rights (Protocol 1, Art 3) requires free elections but does not require any particular kind of electoral system, thus endorsing the principle that elections may have different aims. An electoral system must not discriminate against particular groups of citizens, although a political party cannot apparently challenge the electoral system on the basis that it is at a disadvantage (see *Lindsey v UK* [1979]; *Matthieu-Mohun v Belgium* [1987]; *Liberal Party v UK* [1982]). The courts are likely to adopt a low level of review in relation to electoral machinery because of sensitivity to interfering with the province of Parliament (*R v Boundary Commission for England, ex p Foot* [1983]).

12.5.2 The Electoral Commission

The Electoral Commission is a quango established to regulate the electoral system and the conduct of elections. Created by the Political Parties, Elections and Referendums Act 2000 with wide-ranging functions it was a response to the concerns of the Fifth Report of the Committee on Standards in Public Life (*The Funding of Political Parties in the United Kingdom* (Cm 4057, 1998)) relating to the financing of political parties. This was against a background of reduced public confidence as a result partly of the widespread use of postal voting, with its opportunities for fraud, and partly of worries about the funding of political parties by wealthy business interests.

The Commission has had mixed success and was the subject of the Eleventh Report of the Committee on Standards in Public Life (*Review of the Electoral Commission* (Cm 7006, 2007)). The Committee found that the Electoral Commission was unclear about its role as regulator and was passive and timid in investigating abuses. The report pointed out that the Commission's staff lacked relevant expertise and experience, this being due to the requirement that the Commission be independent, thus raising a familiar tension between efficiency and the appearance of fairness. The report recommended that the Commission's structure and processes should focus more strongly on regulation. In particular its statutory remit as a regulator, as opposed to a monitor, should be clarified.

These recommendations have been implemented by the Political Parties and Elections Act 2009, which has extensively amended the 2000 Act.

The main functions of the Electoral Commission are as follows:

1. It reviews and reports to the Secretary of State such matters relating to elections and referendums as it may determine from time to time.
2. It registers political parties and keeps records of their accounts and of donations to them, thereby bringing what had previously been regarded as private concerns into the open.
3. It has powers to investigate infringements of election requirements and to impose penalties (Political Parties and Elections Act 2009).
4. It provides for public access to information relating to the financial affairs of political parties.
5. It is responsible for periodic reviews of constituency boundaries.
6. It must be consulted on changes in electoral law.
7. It prescribes performance standards for the local authorities who administer elections (Electoral Administration Act 2006).
8. It advises broadcasters in relation to party political broadcasts.
9. It promotes understanding of electoral systems in the UK (Political Parties and Elections Act 2009, s 8).
10. It is involved, together with local authorities, in pilot schemes for alternative methods of voting such as electronic and postal ballots, making voting facilities available in shops or extending voting times.
11. Subject to modifications by the Secretary of State, it can make 'policy development grants' to registered political parties with at least two sitting MPs for the purpose of preparing their election manifestos.

The Electoral Commission has nine or ten members. It is independent of the executive. It is appointed by the Queen on an Address from the House of Commons on a nomination by the Speaker in consultation with the party leaders. The Speaker's Committee, which comprises relevant ministers and backbench MPs (Political Parties, Elections and Referendums Act 2000, Sch 2), must determine the appointment process. A member ceases to hold office if he or she becomes an election candidate and can be dismissed on an Address from the House of Commons on various grounds of incapacity, misbehaviour or failing to perform duties (Sch 1). Members can be reappointed on the recommendation of the Speaker's Committee.

The Commission's members must not be members, officers or employees of political parties or holders of elective office. Nor must they have had such connections or been registered party donors (below) within the last five years. However four commissioners are nominated by the political parties from persons with political experience, one of whom must be from a party other than the three largest parties (Political Parties and Elections Act 2009, s 4).

The Electoral Commission reports to the Secretary of State and is accountable to the Speaker's Committee and an advisory Parliamentary Parties Panel comprising persons appointed by the parties, who must include at least two MPs.

12.5.3 General elections and by-elections

A general election occurs when a Parliament ends. It must be held within about three weeks from the proclamation which summons a new Parliament (Chapter 11). The timetable and other procedural matters are set out in 'Parliamentary Election Rules' in Schedule 1 of the Representation of the People Act 1983 . Writs are sent from the Crown to designated returning officers in each constituency. The returning officers are responsible for the election. There are rules for designating returning officers but where a constituency is a whole county or a whole district, the returning officer is the sheriff of the county or the chairman of the district council. In England this is one of the few remaining duties of the sheriff, who prior to Tudor times was the representative of the Crown in local areas. Registration officers, who are normally local authority chief executives, make the detailed arrangements.

Section 48 of the Constitutional Reform and Governance Act 2010 requires the returning officer to take reasonable steps to begin the count of votes as soon as practicable within four hours of the poll closing at 10 pm. This was a response to statements by some local government officials in relation to the 2010 general election that they would not commence the count until the next day. The constitutional tradition of the UK is that power should be handed over with brutal swiftness. Assuming that a clear majority in favour of another leader emerges, the Prime Minister is expected to resign on the following day.

A by-election takes place when there is an individual vacancy in the House. The House itself decides when to fill the vacancy, and by convention the motion is proposed by the party to which the former member belonged. Unfortunately there is no time limit for this. When the House is not sitting, the Speaker can issue the writ (Recess Elections Act 1975).

12.5.4 Candidates

It is important that any law restricting the ability of people to stand for Parliament does not violate the general principle of free election. An individual with an axe to grind or a single-interest party should be as free to stand as one of the major national parties, despite the undoubted inconvenience to the latter. The law is therefore concerned with fairness between candidates and with preventing fraud, disruption or confusion. To this end it requires clear lines of accountability for the conduct and spending of the parties and candidates. Elections also raise questions of freedom of speech. This might conflict with fairness, for example by enabling well-financed candidates to dominate the media. This is especially important now that elections are largely fought through print and electronic media rather than personally within local communities.

A candidate must provide a deposit of £500 (forfeited if 5 per cent of the vote is not won) and be supported by ten signatures (Representation of the People Act 1983, Sch 1). The nomination paper must state either that the candidate stands in the name of a qualifying registered party under the Political Parties, Elections and Referendums Act 2000 or that they do not purport to represent any party (s 22). The latter applies to candidates standing as independents, to the Speaker seeking re-election or if the nomination paper provides no description. A party is any organisation or person that puts up at least one candidate, so a one-person party is possible (s 40). There is nothing to stop a candidate standing in more than one constituency (cf the devolved regimes).

Each political party must be registered with the Electoral Commission. In order to qualify for registration, the party must provide its name, its headquarters address and the names of its leader, treasurer and nominating officer, although these can be the same person. It can also provide the name of its campaign officer and if it does so the campaign officer will have some of the responsibilities of the treasurer (s 25). It must also have a scheme approved by the Commission for regulating its financial affairs. It can also provide up to 12 descriptions of itself. The Commission can refuse to register a name or description on the following grounds: having more than six words, being obscene or offensive or where publication would be an offence, being misleading, contradictory or confusing, being in a script other than roman or containing words prohibited by the Secretary of State (s 28; Electoral Administration Act 2006, ss 48, 49). This seems to create a significant possibility of executive censorship. Similar rules apply to party emblems (s 29).

A registered political party is subject to accounting and audit requirements (Political Parties, Elections and Referendums Act 2000, Part III; Electoral Administration Act 2006). Accounts must be lodged with the Electoral Commission and must be available for public inspection (s 46). For the first time the law has acknowledged that political parties are more than private clubs and should be subject to external financial controls. However this creates a risk of state interference with political freedom.

12.6 Eligibility to vote

Under section 1 of the Representation of the People Act 2000, to be eligible to vote a person must be:

1. 18 years of age on the date of the poll (the Power Commission (2006) recommended reduction to 16);
2. a British citizen, a citizen of Ireland or a 'qualifying' Commonwealth citizen (ie one who is entitled to reside in the UK). EU citizens can vote in local elections and in elections in the devolved regimes;
3. registered on the electoral register for the constituency. To qualify for registration, a person must be 18 years of age or due to be 18 within 12 months beginning on 1 December following the date of the application for registration and resident in a dwelling in the constituency on the date of the application for registration.

'Residence' means the person is normally living at the address in question as his or her home. This is a question of fact and seems to focus on whether the dwelling is the applicant's home for the time being as opposed to his being a guest or a lodger for some particular purpose. Thus:

> regard shall be had in particular to the purpose and other circumstances, as well as to the fact of his presence at or absence from the address on that date ... for example, where at any particular time a person is staying at any place other than on a permanent basis he may in all the circumstances be taken to be at that time (a) resident there if he has no home elsewhere, or (b) not resident there if he does have a home elsewhere. (Representation of the People Act 2000, s 3; inserting new section 5 in the 1983 Act)

Temporary absence at work or attendance on a course at an educational institution does not interrupt residence if either the applicant intends to return to the actual residence within six months and will not be prevented from doing so by performance of that duty or the dwelling would otherwise be his or her permanent residence and he or she would be in actual residence. Temporary periods of unemployment can be ignored. A student might therefore choose between two possible residencies (*Fox v Stirk* [1970]). Under the Political Parties, Elections and Referendums Act 2000 persons in mental hospitals, unconvicted prisoners and the homeless, as an alternative to establishing residence on normal principles, can make a 'declaration of local connection' in relation to another constituency (s 6).

There are special registration provisions for the benefit of certain people who have to be absent for long periods. These include British citizens resident abroad who have been on the electoral register during the last 15 years (Representation of the People Act 1985), persons in mental hospitals, unconvicted prisoners, merchant seamen, members of the armed forces (service voters; Electoral Administration Act 2006, s 13) and certain other public employees. Detained offenders are not resident where they are detained (ss 4, 5). Applicants to be absent voters must provide a signature and date of birth as a protection against fraud (Electoral Administration Act 2006, s 14).

A problem with the registration arrangements is that registration currently depends on each householder providing the names of eligible voters living in the house. This invites fraud and is to be replaced by individual registration (which could involve fewer people being registered).

Even if they are on the electoral register, the following have no right to vote:

- members of the House of Lords, other than bishops sitting *ex officio*;
- convicted prisoners and persons detained in mental hospitals as offenders (except for contempt of court or refusing to pay a fine), including persons unlawfully at large (Representation of the People Act 2000, s 2). A common law mental capacity test was abolished by the Electoral Administration Act 2006;
- persons convicted of election offences (corrupt practices – for five years; illegal practices – for five years in the particular constituency);
- illegal immigrants and asylum seekers waiting for a decision (Political Parties, Elections and Referendums Act 2000, s 2).

In *Hirst v UK (No 2)* [2004] the European Court of Human Rights held that the blanket exclusion for prisoners violates the right to free elections (above), depriving some 850,000 people of the right to vote. The Court held that an automatic absolute bar was not acceptable, there being no legitimate policy reason for excluding all convicted prisoners irrespective of such matters as the nature of the offence or length of sentence. In *Frodl v Austria* [2010] the Court held that a decision to deny prisoners the franchise should be made by a judge, taking account of the particular circumstances. In particular there must be a link between the offence committed and issues relating to elections and democratic institutions. In March 2010 the Committee of Ministers of the Council of Europe required the UK government to comply with *Hirst*. The government has not changed the law and appears to be defying the European Court.

12.7 The voting system

As we have seen the vote is for a local representative in the House of Commons. In practice however, due to the convention that the person with majority support in the House of Commons forms a government and that this is likely to be the leader of the largest political party, the voter has the conflicting task of choosing the government and choosing a representative to hold the government to account. This is one reason why the parliamentary system is flawed.

There are problems with the workings of voting systems as reflections of democratic values. Firstly a system that always produces a genuine majority government may be impossible to achieve. For example in an election where there are three candidates, different majorities might prefer A to B, B to C and C to A. In the 2010 UK general election no party had an overall majority, although this is relatively rare in the UK, having previously happened in 1973. Until now the electoral system for Parliament has been that of 'first past the post' (FPP), or 'relative majority'. This gives the seat to the candidate with the largest number of votes. This need not be an overall majority.

FPP is particularly defective in terms of democratic representation in that it ignores the votes for all but the winning candidate. Thus in a three-party contest the winner needs only just over one-third of the votes. Under the Parliamentary Voting Systems and Constituencies Act 2011 a referendum was held on 5 May 2011 to decide whether to introduce the AV method of voting for the next general election, in 2015 (see Section 12.7.1; for the outcome see the companion website).

Another reason under FPP why a majority in Parliament may not reflect the majority of the voters is that the constituencies do not contain the same number of voters (below). Moreover in many local areas voters are loyal to family and community traditions favouring particular parties. Thus about three-quarters of parliamentary seats are 'safe seats', so that the MP is effectively chosen by party activists. Thus votes do not translate directly into seats and smaller parties are treated unfairly. The report of the Blake Commission on Electoral Reform (Hansard Society 1976) castigated the voting system as producing flagrant 'minority rule' and at the same time suppressing other minorities. It also encourages 'tactical voting' in favour of the candidate with the best change of affecting the outcome rather than voting according to the political beliefs of the voter.

For example in 2005 Labour won an overall majority of 356 seats with 36.9 per cent of the vote, the Conservatives won 198 seats with 33.9 per cent and the Liberal Democrats won 62 seats with 23 per cent of the vote. In England the Conservatives, with 600,000 more votes than Labour, won 90 fewer seats. Thus most voters voted against Labour. In 2010 there was no overall majority. The Conservatives won 306 seats with 36.1 per cent of the vote, Labour 258 seats with 29 per cent and the Liberal Democrats 57 seats with 23 per cent. This led to the unusual outcome of a coalition government between the Conservatives and Liberal Democrats.

In Parliament itself the members always vote by simple majority in a straight yes/no way between two propositions. The combination of these two forms of voting means that any particular law may command the support of only about 20 per cent of the public.

However the first past the post system is simple and transparent, offering voters a clear choice. It encourages accountable governments that are supported by substantial numbers of voters. A party stands or falls as such at an election and it must answer on its own record. It cannot blame any minority parties and, unlike in systems with proportional representation (below), governments cannot change without the consent of the electorate (below). It also produces a direct link between the constituency and the individual MP, reinforcing accountability.

12.7.1 Other voting systems: the devolved governments

The choice between voting systems is between the incommensurables of strong government, fairness, reflecting the majority will and protecting minorities. Complex systems of proportional representation (PR) are widely used in an attempt to achieve fairness and protect minorities. They rely on various intricate mathematical formulae to make the outcome correspond more closely to the distribution of the vote (see Farrell, *Electoral Systems: A Comparative Introduction* (Macmillan 2000) ch 4). All have advantages and disadvantages, and no voting system has yet been devised that reconciles the competing demands on it.

PR systems favour negotiations between political parties and could produce unstable governments held together by shifting alliances between small and large parties, thus weakening accountability. However Germany and the Scandinavian countries which use PR systems are at least as stable as the UK. Arguably a degree of instability is desirable in a liberal society where there is no agreement as to the right answer to social and political problems.

PR methods are used to elected the European Parliament, the legislatures of the devolved regimes in Scotland, Wales and Northern Ireland and in London elections. The main forms are as follows:

- *The party list*. Under the 'closed list system', the voter chooses only the party, individual seats being allocated by the party in accordance with the party's share of the vote. The party list system has been said to destroy the principle of local representation and to put excessive power into the hands of party leaders. This method is used for elections to the European Parliament. Under an 'open list' system, as used for example in Switzerland, Finland and Luxembourg, the voter can choose between the names on the list, sometimes subject to a preset ranking (eg Sweden, Denmark, Belgium). In Germany a party must achieve at least 5 per cent of the votes or three seats.
- *The additional member system*. This system is used for elections to the Scottish Parliament, the Welsh Assembly and the London Assembly (see Scotland Act 1998, ss 6–8; Government of Wales Act 2006, ss 6–9; Greater London Authority Act 1999, s 4). (A similar system is used in Germany.) A proportion of candidates (73 out of 129 in Scotland, 40 out of 60 in Wales) are elected on the first past the post principle in local constituencies. This is topped up by a second vote either for an individual candidate or on a party list basis, representing eight regions in Scotland and five

regions in Wales. Each region is allocated the same number of seats (eg five in the Welsh regions, seven in the Scottish) and an 'electoral region figure' is produced. The second vote can be for a political party or an individual candidate. In the case of individual candidates, the electoral region figure is the total number of votes cast for that person. In the case of a party, the electoral region figure is the number of votes won by that party divided by the number of seats won by the party's candidates in the local constituency elections plus one. The candidate or party with the highest electoral region figure wins the first seat. The second and subsequent seats are awarded on the same basis, in each case after a recalculation to take account of seats already won. Thus the fewer the seats won by a party in the local constituency elections, the better the chances of winning a seat in the regional election. A person cannot of course take a seat in more than one constituency.

- *The single transferable vote*. This is probably the method that most reflects voting preferences. It is used for elections in Northern Ireland, where the desire to neutralise conflicting political forces dominates the constitutional arrangements (Section 16.3; see Northern Ireland Act 1998, ss 8, 28, 34). Each constituency can elect a given number of members. Votes are cast for candidates in order of preference. There is an 'electoral quota' for each constituency, calculated according to a formula based on the number of voters divided by the number of seats plus one. The quota is the winning post. A candidate who obtains the quota based on first preferences is elected. Any surplus votes over the quota are transferred to other candidates according to the second preference on the winning candidate's voting slips. This may produce more winners who reach the quota. The process is repeated until all the seats are filled. If no candidate reaches the quota, the candidate with the lowest number of votes is eliminated and his or her votes distributed among the other candidates. This system enables voters to choose between different candidates within the same party since all seats within a constituency could be fought by each party. It also prevents wasted votes and protects minorities. On the other hand it weakens the direct link between constituency and member.
- The *alternative vote (AV) system* is a non-PR system that attempts to produce a single candidate with majority support. The candidates are voted for in order of preference and there are several rounds. After each round the candidate with the lowest vote is eliminated and his or her votes distributed among the others until a winner with a clear overall majority emerges. If there is still a deadlock, a winner might then be chosen by lot. This system seems unfair in that it takes account of the second preferences only of those who supported losing candidates. On the other hand it keeps a strong link between the member and the constituency. It is the system used for elections for the Mayor of London (Greater London Authority Act 1999, s 4).

AV was recommended for Britain in 1910 by the Royal Commission on Electoral Systems. In 1998 the Independent Commission on the Voting System (Cm 4090) chaired by Lord Jenkins, a Liberal Democrat victim of the simple majority system, recommended the introduction of the *AV Plus* voting system. This combines the alternative vote in single-member constituencies with a system of topping-up from a party list. Under the Parliamentary Voting Systems and Constituencies Act 2011 a referendum is to be held on 5 May 2011 on whether AV should be introduced into the UK. This is a compromise in favour of a voting method which neither party in the coalition government supports in principle The Liberal Democrat element favour full PR, whereas the Conservative element favour FPP.

- Finally the *double-ballot system* is used in France. A candidate who gets an overall majority in round one is elected. Failing that there is a second ballot which only those who achieved a certain proportion of the vote can enter (in France 12.5 per cent). The candidate with the most votes in the second round wins.

12.8 The constituencies

The outcome of a general election is usually determined by a relatively small number of 'marginal constituencies' in which no one party has a substantial majority. In an ideal election system there would be the same number of voters in each constituency. This is not the case in the UK. The population is not evenly distributed across the country, so each vote does not carry equal weight. Constituency boundaries and voting patterns are significantly influenced by geographical considerations. For example the largest constituency, the Isle of Wight, has about 108,000 potential voters; the smallest, Na h-Eileanan (Western Isles), 21,600. It is tempting for a ruling government to gerrymander, that is to alter the constituency boundaries in favour of its own party. The natural tendency over time is for traditional boundaries to favour right-wing parties since the old industrial conurbations which formed the basis of many constituencies during the early years of electoral politics are losing population in favour of suburbs and rural areas.

There is semi-independent machinery for fixing electoral boundaries (Parliamentary Constituencies Act 1986). This is currently the responsibility of the Secretary of State for Justice, subject to four independent Boundary Commissions for England, Wales, Scotland and Northern Ireland (Parliamentary Constituencies Act 1986). A range of criteria are used and there is some discretion. The dilemma is the conflict between fairness in the sense of equality of votes and the desire that an MP should represent a genuine geographical community.

There must be a review of the number and boundaries of constituencies. Previously this was at intervals of between 8 and 12 years, including provision for public hearings. The last review was in 2007. A review may take several years to complete and once made could well be out of date. However the Parliamentary Elections and Constituencies Act 2011 introduces a requirement for a five-yearly review commencing before 1 October 2013. A report is submitted to the Secretary of State, who is required 'as soon as may be' to lay the report before both Houses of Parliament, together with a draft Order in Council giving effect to it (s 3(5)). Each House must approve the order, which is then submitted to the Queen in Council. It then becomes law.

The main criteria are as follows (Sch 2 as amended by the Parliamentary Voting Systems and Constituencies Act 2011):

1. Currently there are 650 constituencies. The Parliamentary Voting Systems and Constituencies Act 2011 reduces the number of constituencies to 600. This has implications for government control over Parliament since the number of ministers drawn from Parliament need not be reduced.
2. There must be a separate City of London constituency.
3. Each country has an 'electoral quota'. This is a rough average of voters per constituency. It is calculated by dividing the total electorate by the number of constituencies on the date when the Commission begins its review. It cannot be updated during the course of a review. For England the quota is roughly 70,000. The

electoral quota is one factor to be taken into account but because of the many factors that have to be balanced few constituencies correspond to the quota. However the Parliamentary Voting Systems and Constituencies Act 2011 requires that the number of voters in each constituency should vary only between 95 per cent and 105 per cent of the electoral quota, thus favouring equality over community. There are however special provisions for the Isle of Wight and Western Isles of Scotland and for exceptionally low-population areas. No constituency should be larger than 13,000 square kilometres.

4. Other factors to be taken into account, as amended by the 2011 Act, include:
   - existing constituency boundaries and European Parliament constituency boundaries;
   - local ties;
   - the inconvenience involved in altering boundaries;
   - special geographical considerations. These include the size, shape and accessibility of a constituency. (It may be that if modern electronic communications were to be used for voting purposes such geographical factors would be reduced. The current system relies on personal attendance at polling stations or postal voting, which is susceptible to fraud.)

These factors may point in different directions and it is a matter for the Commissions' discretion how to rank them. The Commissions are not required to aim at giving full effect in all circumstances to the rules. However the rules relating to the size of population have the highest priority.

The report and the Order in Council can be challenged in the courts but the chances of success are small. The time factor is important. As we have seen, no court can interfere with parliamentary procedure, so that the Secretary of State could not be prevented from laying an order before the House (*Harper v Home Secretary* [1955]). A court could perhaps require the Secretary of State to lay an order to prevent her or him delaying a report which does not favour the government party. Moreover by virtue of section 4(7) the validity of any Order in Council which purports to be made under the Act and which recites that approval was given by each House 'shall not be questioned in any legal proceedings' (see Section 19.7.2).

A report must therefore be challenged before it is submitted to the Secretary of State. Even here the chances of success are slim because of the Commission's wide discretion. The court will defer to the subjective judgement which the Commission is required to make. It does not require equality to be the primary aim, nor indeed will it rank the various criteria. Even if the Commission does act improperly, for example by ranking the various factors capriciously, the court out of respect for Parliament would not normally make an order that prevents the report from going to Parliament. At most it would make a declaration (a non-binding opinion). *See R v Boundary Commission for England, ex p Foot* [1983]).

12.9 Voting procedures

Voting is traditionally in person at a designated polling station. However any person otherwise qualified to vote can have a postal vote. 'Absent voters' are permitted to vote by post or proxy (Representation of the People Act 2000, Sch 4). A person on the register for that year but no longer resident in the constituency can have an absent vote. A proxy vote also applies in special cases. These include service and overseas voters, disabled people, people with work or education commitments and people who have to make a long journey. The government is currently encouraging the use of postal and electronic voting.

The ballot is secret in the sense that the vote itself is cast in privacy. However there is no protection for postal votes and, by comparing the registration number on the voting slip with the register of electors, it is possible for officials to discover how a voter cast his or her vote. Indeed this is necessary to prevent multiple voting. There are provisions intended to prevent ballot papers being examined except for the purpose of detecting election offences (Representation of the People Act 2000, Sch 1). There was substantial evidence of the misuse of proxy and postal votes in the 2005 election. New offences of stealing such votes were created by the Electoral Administration Act 2006 (s 40). The Eleventh Report of the Committee on Standards in Public Life (Cm 7006, 2007) proposes that registration by households be replaced by individual registration. This is designed to combat fraudulent postal voting whereby one member of a household can return votes on behalf of others.

12.10 Election campaigns

For most purposes the election period begins with the date of the proclamation announcing the dissolution of Parliament and ends with the date of the poll (Political Parties, Elections and Referendums Act 2000, Sch 10) but an election campaign may start well before that (s 72). This chapter is concerned with parliamentary elections but the same principles apply to other elections. The election campaign at constituency level has always been closely regulated by laws designed to ensure fairness between the candidates campaigning in their local arenas. The law was open to the charge that it did not allow for national party politics with its massive financial backing from private donors or for modern methods of campaigning, including the intensive use of the media. The Political Parties, Elections and Referendums Act 2000 attempts to bring the law up to date by addressing this reality (see *The Funding of Political Parties in the United Kingdom* (Cm 4443, 1999)). Reflecting the Nolan Principles of Public Life, the Act attempts to bring greater openness and accountability to the financing of political parties and national campaigns.

12.10.1 Campaign expenses

There are controls over the money spent on the election campaign. They are intended to ensure that no candidate has an unfair advantage or can buy votes (see *R v Jones* [1999]). In the US restrictions upon election expenses have been held to violate freedom of speech (*Buckley v Valeo* [1976]). The counterargument is that equality of resources is a better safeguard of democracy in the long run.

The Power Commission (2006) suggested that political parties should be funded by the state so as to avoid being unduly influenced by wealthy individuals. On the other hand state funding attracts state control, which may also be undesirable. Moreover it is not easy to produce a formula for payments that would be democratically fair and would not favour the status quo. There is currently no general state funding for political parties. However policy development grants of up to £2 million are available from the Electoral Commission to parties with at least two MPs and money is provided by each House of Parliament to opposition parties for their parliamentary duties ('Short Money', after the proposer). (See White Paper, *Party Finance and Expenditure in the UK* (Cm 7329, 2008).) The Committee on Standards in Public Life is currently investigating the general issue of party finance.

The main controls over election expenses are as follows (the Representation of the People Act 1983 applies unless otherwise stated):

1. Every candidate must have an election agent who is accountable for the conduct of the candidate's campaign. A candidate can appoint himself as agent. There are controls over receipts and expenses out of the candidate's own pocket (ss 73, 74).
2. There is a maximum limit upon the amount that can be spent on behalf of any individual candidate in respect of 'the conduct or management of an election' (s 75; Political Parties, Elections and Referendums Act 2000, s 132). This can be varied by statutory instrument. It depends primarily on the size of the constituency and amounts to about £10,000 (SI 2005/269). There is a maximum of £100,000 for by-elections, where there is less national support. There is no fixed definition of an election expense. Some expenditure, for example to canvassers, on posters (except to advertising agents), on hiring vehicles to take people to vote and on broadcasting from abroad, is banned completely (ss 101–12). Reasonable personal expenses can be incurred (s 18).
3. Candidates are entitled to free use of schools and public buildings for meetings (ss 95, 96). Each candidate can send one election address to each voter post-free (s 91).
4. The Political Parties, Elections and Referendums Act 2000 extended controls over 'campaign expenditure' (s 72) by registered political parties at national level (s 79, Sch 9). This applies during the 'campaign period', which is 365 days, ending with polling day. Thus the artificiality of distinguishing between promoting the party and promoting the candidate no longer arises. All campaign expenditure must be authorised by the party treasurer, his or her deputy or another responsible officer delegated by the treasurer (s 75). Campaign expenditure includes party political broadcasts, advertising other than leaflets giving personal information about candidates, market research, rallies, press conferences and transport (Sch 8). There are overall limits on expenditure based on the number of constituencies contested, amounting to about £30,000 for each constituency (s 79). The treasurer must deliver a return of expenditure to the Electoral Commission (s 83), which must be made available for public inspection (s 84).
5. There are provisions regulating payment by third parties, particularly from overseas, on behalf of candidates during the campaign period. No expenditure over £500 can be incurred 'with a view to' promoting a candidate without the authority of the candidate or agent, thus counting as part of the candidate's expenses (Representation of the People Act 1983, s 75; Political Parties, Elections and Referendums Act 2000, s 131; cf *Bowman v UK* [1998]: possible restriction on freedom of expression).

At national level it is an offence to incur 'controlled expenditure' above certain limits unless it is made by a 'recognised third party' (s 94). The limits are £10,000 for England and £5,000 for the other regions. Controlled expenditure is the production or publication of material which is made available to the public and which can reasonably be regarded as intended to promote any candidate (including prejudicing another candidate) even if the material serves some other purpose as well (s 85). For example a leaflet put out by an animal rights pressure group might be controlled expenditure if the concerns of the group feature in the election campaign. Problems might arise however where a pressure group publicises a cause such as reducing poverty by issuing factual material which might be incidental to the election but where no specific intention to influence the election can be shown (cf *R v Inner London Education Authority, ex p Westminster City Council* [1986].

A 'recognised third party' registered with the Electoral Commission has higher limits (£793,500 for England, £108,000 for Scotland, £60,000 for Wales, £27,000 for Northern Ireland; Sch 10). A recognised third party must be an individual resident in the UK or on the electoral register, or a registered political party, company, trade union, building society, friendly society, partnership or unincorporated association. This could include a pressure group (s 88).

There are certain exceptions to these limits on payments by third parties. These include newspaper editorial matter, broadcasts, personal expenses and the value of services provided free by individuals (s 87).

12.10.2 Donations to political parties

Party donations have been a subject of serious concern, mainly in respect of the possibility that wealthy individuals, some resident overseas and non-taxpayers, are in a position to influence political parties by means of gifts and loans which may be anonymous. Controls have been progressively increased but methods of evading them have been exploited. Introduced by the Political Parties, Elections and Referendums Act 2000 controls were tightened by the Electoral Administration Act 2006 and the Political Parties and Elections Act 2009

The controls are not intended to outlaw payments as such but to bring them into the open and ensure accountability. There are no general restrictions on the amount that an individual can donate to a political party. Attempts to impose such restrictions could fall foul of the right to freedom of expression. However under section 10 of the Political Parties and Elections Act 2009 no donation or loan of more than £7,500 can be made in a single calendar year by a non-resident.

Controls apply to donations, loans and credit facilities of more than £200 to political parties. They are not confined to the election campaign. 'Donation' is widely defined to include gifts, sponsorship, subscriptions, fees, expenses and the provision of non-commercial services (s 50). A registered party cannot accept a payment if it is not made by a 'permissible donor' or if it is anonymous (s 54(2); Electoral Administration Act 2006, s 61). In the case of a donation of more than £7,500 there must be a written declaration of its source, including whether the donor is an agent for someone else (Political Parties and Elections Act 2009, s 9)

A permissible donor must be resident and registered to vote in the UK or be a business, trade union or registered political party based in the UK. In the case of a company, the shareholders must have approved the donation and the amount must be disclosed in the directors' report (s 140, Sch 19). There are some exceptions to the duty of disclosure. These include voluntary services provided by an individual, various payments made under statute, payments to MPs by the European Parliament and the hire of stands at party conferences for a payment deemed reasonable by the Commission. It has recently been alleged that the Conservative Party is selling access to ministers to individuals using the device of a social club (see *Guardian* 28 August 2010).

A party must report relevant donations or loans of more than £5,000 regularly to the Electoral Commission (ss 63, 65, 68, 96; Electoral Administration Act 2006, ss 56, 57). This has caused problems since the person responsible for reporting is not clearly identified. The Commission keeps a public register of controlled expenditure although this must not include the address of a donor who is an individual (s 69). Impermissible payments must be returned or, if the donor or lender cannot be identified, given to the Commission (s 56). The court can order a payment to be forfeited (s 58) (see *R (Electoral Commission) v City of Westminster Magistrates Court* [2010]).

12.10.3 Broadcasting and the press

There are rules which attempt to ensure that the parties are treated fairly, which must be balanced against freedom of speech. Campaign publicity has qualified privilege in the law of defamation, so there is no liability if it is published in good faith (*Culnane v Morris* [2006]). The same would apply to the press and broadcasting. There are further controls over the broadcast media, reflecting its power to influence a campaign:

- Political advertising by commercial broadcasters is unlawful except for party political broadcasts made by agreement between the BBC, OFCOM (the Office of Communications) and the main parties (see Communications Act 2003, ss 319–21; *R v Radio Authority, ex p Bull* [1995]). This prevents the worst excesses of wealthy parties. Only registered political parties can make party political broadcasts (Political Parties, Elections and Referendums Act 2000, s 37). Political broadcast programmes do not count as election expenses (Representation of the People Act 1983, s 75(1)).
- There is a general duty on OFCOM to preserve good taste and balance and impartiality in all political broadcasting (Communications Act 2003, s 6). The BBC is not governed by statute but operates under a royal charter and an agreement with the Home Office. However OFCOM can regulate the BBC in accordance with the charter and agreement (Communications Act 2003, s 198). OFCOM forbids the expression of editorial opinion about matters of public policy, excluding broadcasting matters. The independent broadcasters are protected by the ECHR in respect of the right of freedom of expression (Chapter 20). However as a public body the BBC may not be entitled to such protection (Chapter 19). In principle the broadcasters' duties are enforceable by the courts. However the idea of political impartiality is both vague and complex and the courts are reluctant to interfere in party political matters. For example must there be balance within the context of every specific subject? How much coverage should minority parties enjoy? It is unlikely that a court would intervene with the broadcasting authority's decision except in a case of bad faith or complete irrationality (see *R v Broadcasting Complaints Commission, ex p Owen* [1985]; *R (Pro-Life Alliance) v BBC* [2003]).
- Each broadcasting authority in consultation with the parties must adopt a code of practice concerning the participation of the parties in items about the constituency (Representation of the People Act 1983, s 93 as amended).

- It is an illegal practice for a person to 'use or aid, abet, counsel or procure' the use of broadcasting stations outside the UK for electoral purposes except where the matter is to be retransmitted by one of the domestic broadcasting companies (Representation of the People Act 1983, s 93 as amended). However this may not prevent overseas stations from directly broadcasting to voters and does not control the Internet. Indeed considerable political propaganda is now disseminated over the Internet and there seem to be no relevant controls other than the general limits on election expenditure.

12.10.4 Election disputes

There is an Election Court comprising two High Court judges. Either a voter or a candidate may within three months of the election lodge a petition to the court. The court can disqualify a candidate, order a recount or scrutiny of the votes, declare the result, invalidate it and order a fresh election (Representation of the People Act 1983, s 159). The decision takes the form of a report to the Speaker which the House is bound to accept (s 144(7)).

Election offences are either 'corrupt' or 'illegal' practices. These involve the offender being disqualified as a candidate or prevented from sitting in Parliament. The extent of the disqualification depends upon whether it is a corrupt practice (ten years everywhere) or an illegal practice (five years in a particular constituency). 'Innocent' illegal practices can be overlooked (s 167). A corrupt practice involves dishonesty, improper pressure on voters or improper expenditure. Illegal practices concern breaches of various statutory requirements. It is an illegal practice for anyone to make a false statement of fact in relation to a candidate's character or conduct (s 106), a provision that is rarely used but was recently invoked to disqualify a successful candidate for falsely accusing a rival of racism. This provision risks embroiling the judiciary in politics (see *R (Woolas) v Parliamentary Election Court for Oldham East and Saddleworth* [2010]).

Proceedings may also be taken in an ordinary court in relation to the offence. Conviction disqualifies a person from membership of the House and the Speaker must declare the seat vacant. There are also offences concerning misuse of the voting process which are prosecuted in the ordinary courts (Electoral Administration Act 2006).

Summary

- The House of Lords is unelected and with nearly 700 members is one of the largest legislatures in the world. This is thought to be inappropriate to its functions. The composition of the House of Lords is to be further reformed. The government has proposed that the House remain mainly unelected but with an elected element of one-fifth. A further one-fifth should be chosen by an independent commission but most of the House should be nominated by the political parties and appointed by the Prime Minister. As yet no further reforms have been made.
- The voting system for parliamentary elections is currently the simple plurality, first past the post system. Voting systems must cater for the incommensurables of effective government, accountable government and democratic representation. It is questionable whether the electoral system is adapted to its modern task of choosing governments, whether it is truly representative of public opinion and whether it is fair to all candidates. We briefly compared different kinds of voting system, including the alternative vote and proportional representation.

Summary cont'd

Variations of PR are used in elections to the regional legislatures and the European Parliament. This is likely to create political tensions within the UK.

- The machinery for regulating constituency boundaries gives a certain amount of protection against political interference but proposals for changes must be approved by the House of Commons. It is difficult to challenge decisions made by this process in the courts.
- The law governing the conduct of elections, which had previously ignored national politics in favour of the individual election at local level, has been reformed to regulate campaign expenditure at national level, including spending by third parties on election campaigns and sponsorship of political parties. The independent Electoral Commission has wide responsibilities in relation to the finances of political parties and the conduct of elections. This is intended to bring greater openness and accountability to political parties.
- Controls over election broadcasting are designed to ensure fairness between the parties in accordance with their popular support and are more stringent than are restrictions over the press.

Exercises

12.1 'In a democracy there is no point in an upper house of the legislature. If both houses are elected, there is a problem of duplication. If the upper house is not elected then it is not legitimate.' Discuss with reference to current attempts to reform the House of Lords.

12.2 Is democracy in the UK as Hobbes suggested just the rule of a few orators?

12.3 Explain the basis on which parliamentary constituencies are designated. Do the present arrangements contain adequate safeguards against political manipulation?

12.4 Outline arguments for and against giving prisoners the right to vote. What changes in the existing law are needed to comply with the judgments of the European Court of Human Rights?

12.5 To what extent has the law successfully regulated the funding of political parties?

12.6 A general election is expected to take place within the next year. The Campaign for Free University Education proposes to distribute leaflets and hold meetings during the election campaign in various university towns. Jerry, a wealthy businessman resident in the US, wishes to make an anonymous loan of £5 million to any political party that will campaign to withdraw the UK from the EU. He also proposes to advertise in the national press and on TV in favour of encouraging Baseball competitions in the UK. Clive, who is resident in the Channel Islands, wishes to donate £5,000 anonymously to the Get Out of Europe! Party. Discuss the legality of these proposals. What would be the position if Clive wrote to a newspaper stating falsely that Joanna, a candidate for a rival party, was a secret supporter of Get Out of Europe!

12.7 'Reforms of the electoral system through the introduction of a single transferable vote ... would revitalise the operation of political processes and make a major contribution to the development of a more accountable, effective system and a more influential citizenry' (Oliver). Discuss.

Further reading

Bingham, 'The House of Lords: Its Future' [2010] PL 261

Bogdanor, *The New British Constitution* (Hart 2009) ch 6

Committee on Standards in Public Life, Fifth Report, *The Funding of Political Parties in the United Kingdom* (Cm 4057, 1998)

Hansard Society, *The Future of Parliament: Reform of the Second Chamber* (Hansard Society 1999)

Independent Commission on the Voting System, *Report of the Independent Commission on the Voting System* (Cm 4090, 1998) [Jenkins Report]

Lardy, 'Democracy by Default: The Representation of the People Act 2000' (2000) 64 MLR 63

Marriot, 'Alarmist or Relaxed: Election Expenditure Limits and Freedom of Speech' [2005] PL 764

Phillipson, 'The "Greatest Quango of Them All"' [2004] PL 352

Power Commission, *Power to the People: An Independent Inquiry into Britain's Democracy* (Rowntree Trust 2006)

Royal Commission on the Reform of the House of Lords, *A House for the Future* (Cm 4534, 2000) [Wakeham Report]

Russell, *Reforming the House of Lords: Lessons from Overseas* (Oxford University Press 2000)

Russell and Cornes, 'The Royal Commission on the House of Lords: A House for the Future?' (2000) 64 MLR 82

Webb, 'Parties and Party Systems: Modernisation, Regulation and Diversity' (2001) 54 Parl Aff 308

Weill, 'We the British People' [2004] PL 380

Chapter 13

Parliamentary procedure

> **...As no government is more just in the constitution than that of parliaments, having its foundation in the free choice of the people...yet such have been the wicked policies of those who from time to time have endeavoured to bring this nation into bondage that they have in all times, either by disuse or abuse of parliaments, deprived the people of their hopes. (The Large Petition, 1647)**
>
> **In the absence of a written constitution the procedures of Parliament are our constitution. (Simon Carr, *Independent* 10 March 2006)**

13.1 Introduction

Parliamentary procedure may seem to be a dry topic but it is of great importance. It is only through procedures for debating, questioning and voting that the voice of Parliament as a collective institution can make itself known. It will be recalled that there is no strict separation of powers between the executive and the legislature in that all ministers must also be members of Parliament and the most important ministers must be members of the elected House of Commons. This has democratic strengths, ensuring that ministers are directly answerable to Parliament, but where the government has a strong majority it weakens the independence of Parliament. The procedural rules attempt to ensure that Parliament as representative of the people can perform its four sometimes conflicting tasks. These are:

1. making legislation;
2. sustaining the government by providing it with funds and ensuring that government business can be adequately dealt with;
3. holding the executive to account;
4. redressing individual grievances.

The procedural rules also attempt to ensure that the activities of Parliament are public but protected against outside interference.

It is widely acknowledged that the voice of Parliament is to some extent stifled by executive dominance. The reason for this is that the government controls the day-to-day procedures of the House of Commons. Under Standing Order (SO) 14 (HC 2009–10, 539), government business has priority. Twenty days per year are set aside for Opposition business. Private members' bills, that is bills promoted by individual MPs, have priority on 13 Fridays (the House does not otherwise sit on Fridays, so few MPs are likely to be present).

The government also controls the timetable for debating legislation and much legislation is passed with incomplete discussion. The government can also invoke procedures which enable a bill to be passed with little discussion. The government through its whips (party managers) attempts to ensure the party members vote loyally. Most MPs are career politicians who seek advancement through loyalty to their parties, so a majority government can usually be sure of getting its way. The Chief Whip advises the Prime Minister upon the careers of ministers and MPs. It is for the House collectively to control its own procedures, so it could, if it so wished, radically transform itself.

Parliamentary procedure is based upon Standing Orders made by each House, customs and conventions, and rulings by the Speaker of the Commons. The authoritative manual of parliamentary procedure is Erskine May, *Parliamentary Practice* (Butterworths 2004). The finance, administration and staffing of the House of Commons are supervised by the House of Commons Commission, which comprises a group of MPs chaired by the Speaker (House of Commons (Administration) Act 1978). It does not have a government majority and is therefore independent of the executive.

Parliamentary procedure is adversarial, presupposing a government and Opposition constantly in conflict. The rectangular layout of the chamber reflects this. Government and Opposition confront each other on either side and the seats are symbolically arranged two sword lengths from each other. Other European legislative chambers are characteristically semicircular in layout, representing a more conciliatory ethos, with the parties, usually elected by proportional representation, merging into each other. The present government is a coalition of the Conservative and Liberal Democrat parties. As we have seen the 'first past the post' voting system in UK elections means that such an arrangement is unusual (it last occurred in 1945, and before then in 1931) and the processes of Parliament cannot easily accommodate it. In particular, although there are no structural obstacles to a coalition, it is not clear how far the parties in the coalition will be treated separately by the parliamentary procedures.

The adversarial nature of parliamentary procedure is mitigated by what are known as 'usual channels'. These involve informal cooperation between the parties so as to ensure that the procedures operate smoothly and fairly. For example absences from votes may be arranged in 'pairs' so as to maintain party balance. Whips have the responsibility of enforcing party discipline and liaising between the government and backbench MPs. The government Chief Whip, although not a Cabinet member, frequently attends Cabinet meetings.

Time pressures and its majority mean that the government is usually able to dominate the business of the House of Commons and much business gets through without proper scrutiny. In some countries, influenced by the doctrine of separation of powers, there are provisions which prevent the procedure from being controlled by the executive.

The Selection Committee on the Modernisation of the House of Commons has proposed a range of measures to improve the processes of Parliament (see *Modernisation of the House of Commons: A Reform Programme* (HC 2001–02, 1168)). These will be mentioned in context. Some of them, in particular the streamlining of the timetable for debating legislation, seem to enhance governmental control. The *Power Report* (Rowntree Trust 2006) recommended that select committees should get enhanced powers, that there should be limits on the powers of the whips and that Parliament should have greater freedom to initiate legislation, petitions and inquiries independently of the executive.

A Select Committee on Reform of the House of Commons (the Wright Committee) reported in March 2010 (*Rebuilding the House* (HC 2008–09, 1117)). It made several recommendations. These were designed to strengthen the collective power of the Commons, to give individual members greater influence and to make the proceedings of the House more transparent so as to increase public ability to influence and understand parliamentary business.

The Committee's most important recommendations were accepted by the government and the House and implemented by Standing Order. These were:

1. that a backbench business committee should timetable business in the House of Commons. This would initially apply only to non-government business but would eventually extend to most government business;
2. that backbench members should have greater control over the membership of select committees of the House;
3. that more time should be made available to debate select committee reports;
4. that backbenchers should have greater opportunity to initiate debates.

The Wright Committee also recommended that the Opposition should have greater control over the timetabling of the 20 'Opposition days' available for debating subjects of its choosing, that the government should not decide for how long its business should be debated without reference to the House, that aspects of the 'estimates' (see Section 13.4) should be more thoroughly debated and that backbenchers' motions should be voted on. These recommendations have not been formally implemented.

13.2 The Speaker of the Commons

The office of Speaker, 'the first commoner', symbolises the historical development of the House of Commons. The Speaker presides over meetings of the Commons and is the intermediary between the House and the Crown. Originally the Speaker was a Crown servant but since the seventeenth century has asserted independence from the Crown. When Charles I entered the chamber to arrest the Five Members (1642), Speaker Lenthall replied: 'I have neither eyes to see nor tongue to speak in this place but as the House is pleased to direct me, whose servant I am here.' Thus the Speaker represents the rights of the House against the Crown.

Since the nineteenth century it has become established that the Speaker is independent of party, cannot hold ministerial office and takes no part in debate. The Speaker is required to be impartial between the political parties. The Speaker controls the procedure, keeps order and is responsible for protecting the rights of all groups within the House, particularly those of minorities. He or she has considerable discretion. The Speaker makes procedural rulings, decides who shall speak and has summary powers to suspend members or terminate a sitting. In terms of the conduct of particular proceedings, the Speaker need not normally give reasons for decisions. The Sergeant at Arms is the enforcement agency responsible to the Speaker. There is also a Deputy Speaker and deputies to him or her. One of these presides when the whole House is sitting as a committee, as it does in relation to financial matters (Section13.4).

The Speaker is elected by secret ballot from among its members by the House at the beginning of each Parliament. The 'Father of the House', the longest-serving member, runs the election. Traditionally a newly elected Speaker has to be dragged to the chair, a reminder that this was once a dangerous post. The Speaker can be removed by the House. Removal of a Speaker is rare but happened in 2009 when Speaker Martin resigned amid allegations that his conduct was overprotective to the large number of MPs accused of excessive expense claims. He unsuccessfully resisted publication of MPs' expense claims.

13.3 Legislative procedure

Parliament debates each bill in a process that distinguishes between general principles and detail. Parliamentary debates consist of a motion and a question proposed by the chair in the same form as the motion. Following debate the question is put and voted upon, the result being expressed as a resolution or order. At any stage there may be amendments proposed, but in all cases issues are presented to the House one at a time for a yes or no vote by a simple majority. This reflects the confrontational nature of Parliament and also ensures that the voting is on a majoritarian basis. The main distinctions are between public bills and private bills. There are also special arrangements for financial measures.

13.3.1 Public bills

A public bill is a bill intended to alter the general law. The formal procedures in the House are only the tip of the iceberg. Any member can propose a bill (a private member's bill) but almost all public bills are promoted by the government and introduced by ministers. Private members' bills are unlikely to succeed without government support. As we have seen, 13 Fridays are provided in each session on which precedence is given to private members' bills (SO 14(4)). Priority is determined by a ballot held annually, for which only backbenchers are eligible. Only the first six in the ballot have a realistic chance of success because, of the Fridays, five are devoted to bills in their later stages. A private member can also get a bill debated under the 'ten minute rule' (SO 23). This involves a motion twice a week that leave be given to present a bill. A short debate takes place. There is little prospect of the matter going any further, the essential aim being to publicise an issue. Nevertheless some important social reforms have been made by private members' bills, including abortion legislation, the abolition of the death penalty and divorce reform. However all had government support in the form of time allocation and drafting assistance.

Before their formal introduction, public bills go through various processes within the administration involving the formulation of policy and principles and consultation with outside bodies. When these have been completed, the bill is sent to the Parliamentary Counsel for drafting. Some bills, particularly those dealing with commercial matters, are drafted with the aid of outside lawyers. The relationship between the draftsmen and the government is similar to that of lawyer and client. The draftsmen work under considerable pressure of time and there is continuous consultation with government departments. Some bills relating to reform of the general law are prepared by the Law Commission. Important bills may be foreshadowed by Green Papers, which are consultation documents, or White Papers, which state the government's concluded opinions, albeit these often leave matters open for further discussion. Both are published. Recently, as part of the modernisation programme, important bills have been published as draft bills for 'pre-legislative' discussion by Parliament and with public consultation before the formal process is started. Draft bills are considered by a select or standing committee.

The final version of a bill is approved by the Cabinet and then introduced into Parliament. Except for financial measures, which must be introduced by a minister in the Commons, a bill can be introduced into either House. The same stages apply in each House. Relatively uncontroversial bills are likely to be introduced in the House of Lords. The stages of a public bill are as follows:

- *First reading.* A formality which ensures that the bill is printed and published.
- *Second reading.* At which the main principles of the bill are discussed. In theory, once a bill has passed this stage, its principles cannot later be challenged. Occasionally the second reading is dealt with by a special committee. After second reading there is a 'programme motion' timetabling the bill and there may be a vote authorising any expenditure concerning the bill.
- *Committee stage.* The bill is examined usually by a standing committee, with a view to suggesting detailed amendments. Unlike a select committee, which exists for the whole of a Parliament, a standing committee is set up only for the purpose of a particular bill. Its membership of around 50 is based upon the strength of each party in the House, so it is difficult for amendments to be made against the wishes of the government. Opponents of a bill sometimes deliberately cause delays by discussing matters at length in committee. However the chairman has the power to decide which amendments should be discussed and a business subcommittee allocates time for discussion. The parliamentary draftsman may be present and civil servants or experts might be called to give evidence.

  Sometimes a bill is referred to a committee of the whole House. This might happen for example when the bill is uncontroversial or, at the opposite extreme, where it is urgent, highly controversial or a 'major bill of first-class constitutional significance', although the meaning of this is unclear. For example the Bank of England Bill 1997, which transfers power to fix interest rates to the Bank, went to an ordinary standing committee. A government can effectively neutralise the committee stage by obtaining a resolution that a committee of the whole House shall deal with a bill. This means that the bill is unlikely to be examined in detail. This device was used in 2010 for the Academies Bill, which allows qualifying schools to remove themselves from local authority into central control. Occasionally a specialised bill is referred to one of the permanent select committees.
- *Report stage.* The bill is returned to the House, which can then vote upon the committee amendments and consider further amendments. The Speaker can select the amendments to be debated. The report stage can be dispensed with where the bill has been discussed by a committee of the whole House.
- *Third reading.* This is the final vote on the bill. Only verbal amendments are usually possible at this stage (SO 77) but the bill as a whole can be opposed.
- The bill is then sent to the other House. If the Lords veto the bill or make amendments, it is returned to the Commons. If there is continuing disagreement between the two Houses, the Parliament Act procedure can be triggered (Chapters 9, 11). Otherwise the bill is sent for royal assent. This is usually notified by commissioners at the

prorogation ceremony that ends each session (Royal Assent Act 1967). By convention the monarch must always assent, except possibly in the unlikely event of the Prime Minister advising to the contrary. In this case however the government would be at odds with the Commons and so required to resign.

Once a bill has received the royal assent it becomes law. However it is often provided that an Act or parts of it shall take effect only when a minister so orders. A minister's decision whether or not to bring an Act into effect can be subject to judicial review (see *R v Secretary of State for the Home Dept, ex p Fire Brigades Union* [1995]). It is also common for an Act to confer power on ministers to make regulations without which the Act itself cannot operate. These might include a 'Henry VIII clause' under which a minister is empowered to alter the Act or other statutes.

- If a public bill has not become law by the end of a session, it lapses. However some bills can be carried over into the next session (SO 80A (HC 1997–98, 543)). This must be authorised by a resolution of the House, which is of course usually under the control of the governing party.

Some bills can be passed without debate but with scrutiny by a joint committee of both Houses. These are bills of a largely formal nature to consolidate other legislation without making significant changes or to repeal redundant statutes. The Law Commission prepares these bills.

13.3.2 Private bills

A private bill is one directed to particular persons or places, for example a bill to build a new section of railway line. It is not subject to the Parliament Acts. Private bill procedure allows both local and national perspectives to be examined and is therefore suitable for very important private schemes. The procedure includes a special committee stage involving an inquiry open to the interests concerned, who can be legally represented. Although private bill procedure involves outside elements, it is still wholly within parliamentary privilege. Therefore the courts cannot intervene on the ground that the procedure has not been properly followed or even that there has been fraud (*Pickin v British Railways Board* [1974]).

A public bill with a private element is called a 'hybrid bill'. For example the Aircraft and Shipbuilding Bill 1976 nationalised these industries and was, as such, a public bill but it exempted certain named firms from its proposals. A hybrid bill is subject to the public bill procedure until the committee stage, when it is examined by a select committee in the same manner as a private bill.

Private bill procedure has been much criticised, not only because it is slow and antiquated but because it fails to provide opportunities for the public to be directly involved in debating schemes that may have serious environmental impact, for example new railway lines. There are however a range of alternative procedures. The main examples involving Parliament are as follows:

- *The Transport and Works Act 1992* applies primarily to large rail and waterway projects. A Secretary of State authorises projects after consulting local authorities and affected parties and after an environmental assessment. A public inquiry must be held into objections. The Secretary of State can refer proposals of national importance to Parliament for debate.

- *Provisional orders* made by ministers, again following a public local inquiry, are confirmed by a provisional order confirmation bill, the committee stage of which involves a select committee at which interested parties can be heard. It is not subject to the Parliament Acts. This procedure is rarely used.
- *Special parliamentary procedure* involves a ministerial order which is subject to a public inquiry and also to a hearing before a special parliamentary committee. It can be debated on the floor of the House. This procedure is less cumbersome than the procedure for private bills or provisional order confirmation bills. It gives the authority of Parliament to sensitive proposals but is rarely used.

13.3.3 Government control over procedure: cutting short debate

By virtue of its majority and the submissiveness of its supporters, the government is usually in a position to control the timing of debate. Moreover the parliamentary timetable is usually crowded, with the result that many, if not most, clauses of a bill are not discussed at all. As part of the 'modernisation' agenda, the passage of a bill can be timetabled in advance under a 'programme motion' by the government (SO 83A–83I; for background see *Modernisation Select Committee Report* (HC 1997–98, 190); Procedure Committee Report, *Timetabling Legislation* (HC 2003–04, 325): government's response (HC 2003–04, 1169)). This applies to most government bills and increases the government's control over Parliament. There are other procedural devices available to both Houses, but most importantly in the Commons, to cut short the time spent on debate. The main devices are:

- *Closure.* A motion in the House or in a committee that the question now be put. This must be supported by at least 100 members and means that the matter must immediately be voted on (SOs 36, 37). The Speaker can also cut short debate when she or he thinks there has been adequate discussion. Except in the case of private members' bills, closure motions are rare but are important as a last resort.
- *Guillotine.* A minister may propose a timetable for a bill, a motion that cannot be debated for more than three hours (SO 83).
- There is a limited safeguard in that a *business committee* or *programme committee* appointed by the Speaker and chaired by the chair of the Committee of Ways and Means (a senior committee concerned with overseeing the government budget) divides up the time allocated to bills that have been subject to a programme motion (SO 83B) or guillotine (SO 82) in relation to a committee of the whole House or at report or third reading stage.
- *Kangaroo.* The Speaker at report stage or the chairman of a committee selects clauses or amendments for discussion.

13.4 Financial procedure

Financial controls generally have developed pragmatically over the centuries. They are a confusing mixture of statute, convention, parliamentary customs and administrative practice based possibly on royal prerogative powers to control the civil service. They reveal the untidiness of the UK constitution at its worst.

The dependence of the executive on money voted by the people is an essential feature of a democratic constitution. It is a fundamental principle embodied in both law and convention that the House of Commons controls public finance and that proposals for public spending can be initiated only by the Crown: 'The Crown demands money, the Commons grant and the Lords assent to the grant' (May, *Parliamentary Practice* (Butterworths 1997), 732–36). On the other hand modern government finance is so large and complex that parliamentary control may be unrealistic. It is widely accepted that, particularly in relation to advance scrutiny of government demands for money, parliamentary control is ineffective. The Commons can only scrutinise taxation and expenditure proposals very superficially, relying heavily on what the government tells it and having limited resources to carry out independent scrutiny. In practice the most substantial control over government finance is exercised internally by the Treasury (Chapter 15). The independent National Audit Office is effective in relation to scrutiny of past expenditure.

Financial procedure is based on an ancient distinction between 'ways and means' – raising money – and 'supply' – allocating money to the purposes of the executive. This is somewhat artificial since the two are closely related. By virtue of the Bill of Rights 1688 the Crown cannot raise taxation without the consent of Parliament. The basis of the principle that the Crown cannot spend money without the consent of Parliament is partly long-standing custom endorsed by the common law (*Auckland Harbour Board v R* [1924]) and partly statute, in that payments out of the Consolidated Fund, the government's bank account, require statutory authority (Exchequer and Audit Departments Act 1866, s 11).

The Crown comes to the Commons to ask for money in the form of the 'estimates' for each government department. Financial measures can be proposed only by a minister. The Commons can reduce the estimates but not increase them. The survival of a government depends upon the Commons voting it funds, and the refusal of the Commons to do so is equivalent to a vote of no confidence so that the government must resign. By convention the House of Lords cannot amend measures relating to central government finance and, as we have seen in Chapter 11, can delay bills that are exclusively concerned with raising or allocating central government money only for one month.

Taxation and expenditure must first be authorised by resolutions of the House of Commons. Amendments cannot be made outside the terms of the resolution, thus strengthening the government's hand. The enactment of the legislation is a formality, any serious discussion, itself limited, having taken place months earlier when the government presented its public spending proposals according to a timetable of its choosing.

There are three main financial measures (see Brazier and Ram, 2004, chs 1 and 2 for a clear account). Firstly the Finance Act raises taxation. The royal assent to a taxation measure is expressed in the words *La Reyne remercie ses bons sujets, accepte leur benevolence et ainsi le veult* ('the Queen thanks her good subjects, accepts their kindness and thus assents'), as opposed to the normal *La Reyne le veult*. Secondly an Appropriation Act, usually in May, allocates amounts out of the Consolidated Fund to the Crown according to the estimates ('votes') presented for each government department for the current financial year, that is until the following April. It also confirms spending that has been authorised provisionally by other legislation for the current and previous years. Thirdly Consolidated Fund Acts authorise interim spending until the following Appropriation Act and may also authorise additional spending from time to time. These bills have no committee or report stage but go straight from second to third reading.

13.4.1 Taxation procedure

The key taxation event is the annual 'budget' resolution proposed by the Chancellor, usually in March. The 'autumn statement' made in November foreshadows the main features of the budget, so the traditional mystique and prior secrecy of 'budget day' has been reduced. Both speeches set the general economic framework of government policy and proposals for tax changes. The budget resolution is followed by the annual Finance Bill. This includes taxes (notably income tax) that must be authorised afresh each year. These annual taxes are enforced and administered under permanent legislation (Income and Corporation Taxes Act 1988). Some taxes, mainly indirect taxes such as customs duties, are authorised by permanent legislation although their rates can be changed at any time. Constitutional principle is preserved in the case of EU law by the requirement in the European Communities Act 1972 that laws affecting taxation, for example VAT, must be implemented by a statute.

The effect of the budget resolution is that the budget's main tax proposals become law with immediate effect, but they lapse unless embodied in a Finance Act that becomes law by a specified time. This is 5 August if the speech is in March or April, otherwise within four months (Provisional Collection of Taxes Act 1968). The main parts of the Finance Bill are considered by a committee of the whole House. This procedure illustrates the basic constitutional principle that resolutions of the Commons cannot by themselves change the law but need statutory backing (*Bowles v Bank of England* [1913]).

Central government money does not come exclusively from taxation. Governments borrow large sums of money in the form of bonds and on the international money market. Money is also raised from landholding, from investments both in the UK and overseas and from trading activities. These sources of finance are not subject to detailed parliamentary scrutiny, although statutory authority is required in general terms for borrowing (National Loans Fund Act 1968).

13.4.2 Supply procedure

Most public expenditure must be authorised annually by the Appropriation Act which approves the government's estimates. These estimates are made under the supervision of the Treasury. They include 'votes' setting out the government's proposed allocation of funds between departments. Thus the Commons approves both the global sum and the executive's broad priorities. However the Appropriation Act is very short and general, merely listing the broad functions of each department to be financed, allocating a global amount, designating a grant from the Consolidated Fund (the government's main bank account) and setting a limit to 'appropriations in aid', that is money that can be raised from fees and charges and so on. Moreover the Act deals only in cash, so contemporary methods of 'resource accounting', which includes other government assets, may not fall properly within parliamentary controls (see Daintith and Page, 1999, 166).

The Public Accounts Committee admitted in 1987 that parliamentary control over the estimates is largely a formality (HC 1986–87, 98, para 2). The Appropriation Act and Consolidated Fund Acts are usually passed without debate. Debates on the estimates have been replaced by 20 'Opposition days', which allow the Opposition parties to raise anything they wish, and by special 'adjournment debates' following the passage of the Acts. The latter allow issues to be discussed without a vote.

The Act appears to authorise payment to the Crown rather than to the individual department, thus reinforcing the Treasury's power to control other departments by presiding over the internal allocation of funds. However in *R v Lords Comrs of the Treasury* [1872] it was said that the Treasury is obliged to pay the sums in question.

There is an arcane debate as to whether the Appropriation Act alone is sufficient to make lawful particular items of expenditure that fall within its general provisions. This is worth briefly considering as it raises wider concerns as to the role of internal understandings and influences as against legal constraints in the constitution (see Daintith and Page, 1999, 35, 174, 203–06). One view is that in addition to the Appropriation Act, specific powers must be conferred either by statute or under the royal prerogative. In other words the Appropriation Act is addressed only to the executive. It authorises the Crown to use the government's bank account for purposes that are lawful but does not in itself make any purpose lawful. On the other hand if an act of the Crown does not involve interfering with the legal rights of others, why should the Crown require specific powers since as a person it can do anything that the law does not forbid, including, presumably, spending its money? On this argument the Appropriation Act that puts the money into the Crown's hands should be a sufficient legal basis for spending.

Where a statute confers specific spending powers, this cuts down any general power derived from the Appropriation Act (eg *R v Secretary of State for Foreign and Commonwealth Affairs, ex p World Development Movement* [1995]; *R v Secretary of State for the Home Dept, ex p Fire Brigades Union* [1995]). However a later Appropriation Act could possibly validate past unlawful expenditure. A concordat in 1932 between the Treasury and the Public Accounts Committee (see Treasury, Government Accounting, 1989, Annex 2.1) assumed that an Appropriation Act could override limits in other statutes but stated that it was 'proper' that permanent spending powers and duties should be defined by particular statutes. Other government statements are inconsistent (see Daintith and Page, 1999, 205). It may be that the courts would be reluctant to read general provisions in an Appropriation Act as overriding specific provisions in other Acts (see *Fisher v R* [1901]).

Some items of expenditure are permanently authorised by particular statutes. These are called 'Consolidated Fund Services'. They include judicial salaries, royal expenses, EC payments and interest on the national debt. The Government Trading Act 1990 gives permanent authority to the financing of certain commercial services such as the Post Office by means of a Trading Fund. In practice most government spending is the subject of long-term commitments (eg pensions), thus leaving little flexibility.

13.5 Supervision of the executive

Supervision of the executive depends upon the doctrine of ministerial responsibility and relies in the last resort upon the convention that the House of Commons can require the government to resign. In modern times the role of Parliament has been weakened by the party system and the difficulty of obtaining information from the government. It should also be remembered that not all government activity requires formal parliamentary authority. This includes royal prerogative powers such as going to war and other matters concerning foreign affairs (and also commercial and property transactions carried out under ordinary private law powers such as buying and selling weapons). Parliamentary scrutiny is also limited by the practice of transferring government functions to bodies outside the central government. The main procedures for scrutiny of the executive are discussed in this chapter. Particular issues of ministerial responsibility are discussed in Chapter 15.

13.5.1 Questions to ministers

Questions can be written or oral and must be about something for which the minister is responsible. About one hour each day is allowed for oral questions to ministers, the departments being on a fortnightly rota. Questions are selected at random by the Speaker. The Prime Minister has one oral session of 30 minutes each week for which any MP can put down a question. In other cases there is a rota of three ministers per day but members must ballot for the privilege of asking an oral question. Except in the case of Prime Minister's Questions, two weeks' advance notice must be given but a member may ask one unscheduled supplementary question. Civil servants who brief ministers, although required by the Civil Service Code to be as open as possible with Parliament, are skilled in anticipating possible supplementaries, which need only bear a tenuous relationship to the main question. Sycophantic questions by government supporters are frequently asked.

There is provision for an urgent question to be asked without prior warning as a 'private notice' question (SO 8(3)). This must be of an urgent character and relate either to matters of public importance or to the arrangement of business. The Speaker's permission is required and the minister must attend on the same day. For example on 6 September 2010 a question was asked concerning allegations that the Prime Minister's Press Officer had connived in telephone hacking in his previous post as editor of the *News of the World*. There are usually less than a dozen permitted urgent questions per session.

Oral questions are probably of value mainly as a means of ensuring that ministers present themselves in public to acknowledge their personal responsibility for their departments and of assessing the personality and parliamentary skills of the minister. They are of limited value as a means of obtaining information. Written questions, of which there are many thousand per session, can be asked without limit and the answers are recorded in *Hansard*, the official parliamentary journal.

The Ministerial Code (2010) requires that ministers must be as open as possible with Parliament and give accurate and truthful information to Parliament, correcting any inadvertent error at the earliest opportunity (see also Cabinet Office, *Guidance to Officials on Answering Parliamentary Questions*; HC 1996–97, 671, annex C). However, given the government's in-built majority in Parliament, this may carry little weight. The Ministerial Code is enforceable only by the Prime Minister. Moreover ministers can refuse to answer on various grounds, including cost, government efficiency, commercial sensitivity, confidentiality and the 'public interest', and cannot be pressed upon a refusal to answer. Some specific matters are excluded. These include matters relating to the monarchy and personal criticism of a judge. Matters subject to litigation in UK courts cannot be discussed subject to exceptions ruled on by the Speaker in connection with civil litigation relating to ministerial decisions or matters of national importance. Exemptions in the Freedom of Information Act 2000 (see Section 23.2.1) also apply. Reasons must be given for refusing to answer. However answers might be perfunctory or incomplete, although under the Ministerial Code ministers must not 'knowingly' mislead Parliament.

MPs have often expressed frustration that ministers are not always prepared to provide full and timely answers to parliamentary questions. The Public Administration Committee monitors the government's responses to questions. There is no coercive machinery to compel a minister to offer a prompt, relevant and full answer in Parliament and it is unlikely that Parliament would use its contempt powers to compel ministers to answer questions.

13.5.2 Debates

There are various opportunities for debates; all involve limited time. However ministers must respond if required and thus debates require government to present itself in public. The different kinds of debates include:

- *Adjournment debates.* These can be on any matter for which a minister is responsible. The most common is a half-hour daily adjournment debate which can be initiated by a backbencher. There is a weekly ballot (SO 9). There can also be adjournment debates following passage of a Consolidated Fund or Appropriation Act (Section 13.4), emergency adjournment debates (which are rarely permitted) and 'recess' debates, in which miscellaneous topics can be debated for up to three hours. Amendments cannot be moved to adjournment motions, so adjournment motions can be used by the government to restrict the Opposition. Adjournment debates do not result in a formal vote and a minister's response cannot be questioned.
- *Opposition days.* Twenty Opposition days are dispersed through the session which allow the Opposition parties to raise anything they wish.
- *Emergency debates.* The Speaker must hold that the matter is urgent, specific and important and should have urgent consideration. Only three minutes are allowed for the application. If permission is granted there can be a three-hour debate. Urgency debates are rare but could concern such matters as a hospital closure.
- *The debate following the Queen's Speech at the opening of a session.*
- *Censure motions.* By convention a government is expected to resign if defeated on a censure motion (also called a no confidence motion). The government must provide time to debate the motion. Until the 1970s the convention also seemed to include other government defeats on important matters, but the latter seem no longer to require resignation. The possibility that a government can be defeated on a major part of its programme but also remain in office strengthens a weak government by providing a safety valve for dissidents within its party. Since 1964 a government has resigned only once following a censure motion (1979). On that occasion the government was a minority government, again a rare event. A no confidence motion has no particular form. Either government or Opposition can declare any vote to be one of confidence. In today's conditions the procedure seems to be essentially a publicity stunt. However such a vote does require the government to publicly defend itself.

- *The budget debate* (Section 13.4.1).
- *Early day motions*. This procedure allows an MP to put down a matter for debate without a fixed date. Early day motions are hardly ever debated. Their function is to draw public attention to a particular issue. They may be supported by a large number of members across parties, amounting in effect to a petition.
- *Procedural debates such as points of order*. These must nominally relate to the practices of the House but might be used ingeniously to raise a broader issue.
- *Ministerial statements which can be followed by questions and discussion*. The Speaker can require a minister to attend and make a statement.
- *Westminster Hall*. Part of the 'modernisation' programme, this sits in a large committee room on three weekdays. It is a supplement to the main chamber as a forum for debates initiated by backbenchers on less contentious business for which time might not otherwise be easily found. Decisions must be unanimous and otherwise are referred to the main House. Ministers must be available to respond every other week, whereas in the main chamber they must respond if required to any debate.

13.5.3 Select committees

A select committee is appointed from backbenchers for the whole of a Parliament. A select committee must be distinguished from a standing committee, the function of the latter being to scrutinise bills at the committee stage. A select committee is supposed to be independent of government but there is the possibility that committee members would try to curry favour with ministers, for example by discussing proposed committee reports with them.

There are three main kinds of select committee:

1. committees charged with investigating the expenditure, administration and policy of the main departments and reporting to the House (SO 130). There is no Prime Minister's committee as such but the Prime Minister voluntarily appears twice per year before the Liaison Committee, which is composed of the chairs of the other committees. The Security and Intelligence Committee is made up of MPs but is appointed by and reports to the Prime Minister;
2. committees dealing with important general concerns. These include broadcasting, environmental audit, food standards, European scrutiny, public accounts, public administration and regulatory reform;
3. committees dealing with matters internal to the House such as standards and privileges, modernisation and procedure. There is also the Speaker's Committee, which deals with electoral matters (Political Parties, Elections and Referendums Act 2000). Some select committees are joint committees of the Lords and Commons. These include human rights, statutory instruments, financial services and markets, and reform of the House of Lords.

The work of the departmental select committees is coordinated by the Liaison Committee, elected by the House. Previously committees were appointed mainly by party managers. However a result of the recommendations of the Wright Committee (Section 13.1) chairs of departmental and other important select committees are now elected by the House (although the *distribution* of chairs between the parties is still be decided by party managers). Members of select committees are chosen by secret ballot within party groups according to the strength of their representation in the House. Select committees may also recruit outside advisers such as academics.

Committee proceedings are open to the public unless the committee resolves to meet in closed session. Strictly speaking, evidence taken by a select committee cannot be published without the consent of the committee, unless and until it becomes part of the formal record of Parliament. However evidence given in public can be published (SOs 135, 136). Select committee decisions are made in private. Select committees have little ability to probe deeply. Time, party discipline, the doctrine of ministerial responsibility and the rules of parliamentary procedure combine to frustrate their activities (see Liaison Committee, *Shifting the Balance: Select Committees and the Executive* (HC 2000–01, 321)). Relatively minor reforms were made in 2002 to strengthen select committees as a response to a more ambitious agenda from the Modernisation Committee (HC 2001–02, 224). These included paying committee chairs and encouraging committees to monitor the government's response to their reports.

A select committee can issue a report which is published. The government may make a published response, after which nothing is required to happen. A committee has limited powers since enforcement of its report (which the press often misleadingly calls that of a 'powerful' committee) depends on a vote of the whole House. In principle a select committee has power under Standing Orders to send for 'persons, papers and records' at any time, even when Parliament is not sitting, and failure to attend or refusal to answer questions could be a contempt of the House. However the scope of these powers is unclear and enforcement would require a resolution of the House:

- MPs as such can be compelled to attend and produce evidence. This is explicit as regards the Committee on Standards and Privileges (SO 149(6)). Members of the House of Lords, being protected by their own privilege, cannot be required to attend.
- It is not clear whether ministers as part of the Crown can be compelled to attend. In practice, because of the government's majority, compulsion is unlikely. However assurances have been given that ministers will attend and give information to committees (see Section 15.6.2).
- Civil servants attend only with the permission of ministers and cannot be compelled to speak. Their evidence has been limited to describing their actions taken on behalf of ministers as opposed to their conduct generally. Thus civil servants cannot give evidence about the merits of government policy, or the consultation process within government, or the advice they gave to government. Indeed ministers have sometimes forbidden civil servants from appearing, in particular on the grounds of national security, 'good government' and 'excessive cost' (see Cabinet Office, *Departmental Evidence and Response to Select Committees* (2004)). There are also conventions that civil servants should not give evidence about the conduct of other officials or matters before the courts and evidence from papers of a previous government of a different political party. As with questions, exemptions in the Freedom of Information Act 2000 apply (Section 23.2.1).
- Committees have no power to demand papers from government departments. An Address to the Queen (in respect of a Secretary of State) or a formal order from the House may be required.
- Other persons, for example former MPs and the heads of public or private bodies, may be compellable. However this raises the unresolved issue of whether the House has power outside its own internal affairs (see Section 11.8).

- Ministers have relied on these obscurities as a means of shielding the inner workings of government from publicity, slightly tempered by a general undertaking by ministers to cooperate with committees, for example by explaining why evidence cannot be given. However the backbench composition of select committees and their practice of seeking consensus have given them a certain independent status. They have drawn public attention to important issues and have exposed weaknesses in governmental policies and procedures. Their capacity to do this may have a deterrent effect on government departments. However their reports do not necessarily lead to action or even to debate in Parliament.

13.5.4 Supervising expenditure

As we have seen, money raised by central government goes into the Consolidated Fund. The control of spending from the Consolidated Fund is the responsibility of the Commons but given the size and complexity of modern government this is clearly an impossible task for an elected assembly. In practice direct parliamentary control over expenditure is very limited. More substantial if less independent controls are imposed within the government machine itself. These are based on a mixture of statute, royal prerogative, convention, insider networking and the inherent power of any employer to administer its workforce.

In medieval times the Court of Exchequer supervised government spending but the modern courts have relinquished this responsibility in favour of Parliament.

The courts are therefore reluctant to interfere with central government spending decisions which are subject to parliamentary scrutiny (see *Nottinghamshire CC v Secretary of State for the Environment* [1986]). However in *R v Secretary of State for Foreign and Commonwealth Affairs, ex p World Development Movement* [1995] a Foreign Office decision to give a large grant to the Malaysian government for the Pergau Dam project was set aside by the Court of Appeal on the basis that the project had no economic justification and that there was an ulterior political motive. The governing legislation required that the decision be based on economic grounds, which, crucially, the court equated with 'sound' economic grounds. This has the potential to give the courts a wide and possibly undesirable power of review. On the other hand the matter only came to light because of the intensive, adversarial process of the court. The internal process of control had not revealed the misapplication of public funds.

Spending by central departments and other public bodies related to the centre is scrutinised on behalf of Parliament by the Comptroller and Auditor-General, who reports to the Public Accounts Committee of the House of Commons. The Committee carries out an annual scrutiny of government accounts and its report is debated by the Commons (SO 122). It thus provides a key mechanism for government accountability. The Committee's chair is normally a member of the Opposition. The Comptroller is appointed by the Crown on a motion from the House of Commons proposed by the Prime Minister with the agreement of the chair of the Public Accounts Committee (Exchequer and Audit Departments Acts 1866–1957; National Audit Act 1983, s 1). The Comptroller is an officer of the Commons and has security of tenure similar to that of a High Court judge (Exchequer and Audit Departments Act 1866). The Comptroller is not directly concerned with the merits of government policy but only with the efficient and economical use of money (National Audit Act 1983, ss 6, 7). However it is difficult to separate these two concerns.

The Comptroller is supported by the National Audit Office (NAO), which is responsible for scrutinising the accounts of central government departments and also those of some outside bodies dependent on government money, such as universities. The NAO carries out two kinds of audit. 'Certification audit' is based on financial accounting practice. 'Value for money audit' is based on the wider concerns of the 'economy, efficiency and effectiveness' of government expenditure (National Audit Act 1983, s 6). This is not meant to include the substantive merits of government policy, although the line between them may be difficult to draw. The NAO is also concerned with matters of 'regularity, legality, propriety and probity'.

Part V of the Constitutional Reform and Governance Act 2010, Part V has introduced a technical but useful reform intended to make government accounts more transparent. The Act gives the Treasury power to direct that information be included in government accounts coordinating and aligning the different accounting methods used by government departments and designated quangos. (See House of Commons Liaison Committee, *Financial Scrutiny: Parliamentary Control over Government Budgets* (HC 2008–09, 804); Chief Secretary to the Treasury, *Alignment (Clear Line of Sight) Project* (Cm 7567, 2009).)

Financial control over government departments is also exercised internally by the Treasury (see Section 15.6.1).

13.5.5 Scrutiny of delegated legislation

Most delegated legislation is detailed and highly technical. It would be impracticable to subject all delegated legislation to detailed democratic scrutiny, so the law is necessarily a compromise. Thus delegated legislation is subject to a limited degree of parliamentary control by being laid before one or both Houses for approval. Unlike a bill, Parliament cannot usually amend delegated legislation.

Originally the laying process was haphazard but as a result of public concern about 'bureaucratic tyranny' (see *Report of Committee on Ministers' Powers* (Cmd 4060, 1932)), limited reforms were made by the Statutory Instruments Act 1946. A statutory instrument made after the 1946 Act came into force is defined as such either if it is made by Order in Council or if the parent Act expressly provides. Thus there is no legal obligation on governments to comply with the controls in the 1946 Act. However in practice most delegated legislation takes the form of a statutory instrument. Moreover a statutory instrument has to be laid before the House only if its parent Act so requires. The laying procedures typically require only that the statutory instrument be 'laid on the table' of the House in draft or in final form for 40 days subject to annulment by a vote of the House – the 'negative' procedure. The fate of the instrument therefore depends upon the chance of a member seeing the document and securing a debate. Some instruments are required to be laid for information only, Parliament having no power to annul them.

A small number of important statutory instruments are made subject to an 'affirmative' procedure under which there must be a positive vote in order to bring them into effect. Such instruments are usually referred to a standing committee. There are also 'super-affirmative' forms, used occasionally, which require advance consultation and enable the House to propose amendments.

The 1946 Act requires that statutory instruments be published 'as soon as may be' unless there is a special excuse for not doing so (s 3). Failure to publish may not make the instrument invalid but provides a defence to prosecution, provided that the accused was unaware of the instrument and that no reasonable steps had been taken to publicise it (s 3(2); see *R v Sheer Metalcraft Ltd* [1954]).

The Parliament Acts do not apply to delegated legislation, so the House of Lords has the power to veto a statutory instrument. It has done so only on one occasion in the last 30 years, when it vetoed two measures relating to the election for the Mayor of Greater London, one of which would have denied free mailing to candidates (HL Deb 20 February 2000, cols 184–85). The Wakeham Report on Reform of the House of Lords (Section 12.3) and the government have proposed that this power be removed in favour of a delaying power only.

The Joint Committee on Statutory Instruments is responsible for scrutinising statutory instruments laid before Parliament. The Scrutiny Committee is not concerned with the political merits of the instrument but is required to draw the attention of Parliament to specified constitutional matters. These are as follows:

- Does the instrument impose taxation or other forms of charge?
- Does it exclude control by the courts?
- Is it retrospective without the express authority of the parent Act?
- Has there been unjustifiable delay in laying or publishing it?
- Is there doubt as to its legal validity or does it appear to make some unusual or unexpected use of the powers under which it was made?
- For any special reason does its form or purport call for elucidation?
- Does its drafting appear to be defective?
- Any other ground other than those relating to policy or merits.

There is also a House of Lords Scrutiny Committee which looks at the merits of statutory instruments laid before the House.

13.6 Redress of grievances

Members of Parliament have a duty, albeit not enforceable in the courts, and Parliament collectively has a right to seek the redress of the grievances of subjects of the Crown. These flow historically from the Crown's need to ask Parliament for money, which request is granted in return for the redress of grievances. Procedurally this depends upon opportunities being made available to backbench members to raise individual grievances. One problem is the possibility of conflicts with party interests; another is the lack of resources, including time. No parliamentary time is reserved for the redress of grievances as such. An MP is able to give publicity to a grievance by placing it on the parliamentary record. Apart from that, the process is haphazard.

The main procedures available are questions, adjournment debates, early day motions and, perhaps most effective, informal communications with ministers, although the latter are not always protected by parliamentary privilege (see Section 11.6.3). All these suffer from the inability of an individual MP to force disclosure of information. There are other opportunities by way of the debates and motions which we discussed above but these suffer from limited time and the absence of voting.

Finally there are public petitions that members can present on behalf of their constituents (SO 153). In 2009–10 393 such petitions were presented. The right of the subject to petition Parliament dates from the thirteenth century, reflecting the history of the Commons as a means of raising grievances with the monarch. On receipt (each petitioner's name and address must be supplied) petitions can be formally presented to the House or, most commonly, are placed in a green bag behind the Speaker's chair and read out before close of business each day. A petition can be about any subject and is published in *Hansard*. There is no formal machinery for giving effect to petitions, although they are referred for comment to the relevant department and may provide publicity for a cause.

The Procedure Committee (HC 2006–07, 513; HC 2007–08, 136) has suggested that public petitions should be encouraged with the introduction of 'e-petitions'. This is to be the subject of further discussion. The Scottish Parliament and the Welsh Assembly already use e-petitions. A petition can also be presented to the House of Lords but this is very rare, the last such occasion being in 2000.

These examples suggest that a sophisticated knowledge of the procedures of the House can be used tactically to some effect. However it is easy for an MP to avoid following up a complaint from a constituent by passing it to another agency. Members habitually deal with grievances outside the formal parliamentary framework, acting in effect as generalist welfare offices. A letter from an MP is likely to be dealt with at a higher level in the civil service hierarchy than would otherwise be the case.

An MP can also refer a grievance to the Parliamentary Ombudsman (see Section 5.4.4)

13.7 House of Lords procedure

The House of Lords regulates its own procedure, which is less adversarial and party dominated than the Commons. There is also less reliance on formal procedural rules. The Speaker is elected by the House but does not have the disciplinary powers available to the Speaker of the Commons, the only power being to put a question to the vote (SO 18). The House of Lords has no power to suspend or expel a member. Any bill other than one involving government taxation or expenditure can be introduced in the House of Lords. It is not subject to the Parliament Acts. A bill introduced in the House of Commons and passing all its stages goes to the House of Lords. The procedure in the House of Lords is broadly similar except that the committee stage usually takes place before a committee of the whole House. The House can call upon considerable specialist expertise from among its membership even if some of it may be out of date. This is often regarded as a justification for an appointed upper house.

Except for committees of the whole House and some minor committees, all committees in the House of Lords are select committees, which can therefore accumulate expertise. Select committees in the House of Lords deal with subjects rather than departments, reflecting the role of the upper house as a forum for the detailed discussion of important issues free of immediate party pressures. Reports of select committees of the House of Lords, notably those of the European Union Committee, the Science and Technology Committee and the Environment Committee, command considerable respect. On the other hand, as a consequence of the senior judges no longer being members of the House of Lords (see Section 7.7.2), substantial legal expertise over a wide variety of subjects has been lost.

Summary

- Parliament does not embody a strict separation of powers, the executive being in practice the dominant force in Parliament. Parliamentary procedure is designed to ensure that government business goes through but subject to Parliament's duty to control the executive. Recent reforms have attempted to strengthen the independence of Parliament as against the executive.
- We outlined the lawmaking procedure as it applies to public bills and private bills. We then looked at the procedural framework within which the Commons attempts to make legislation, hold the government to account, control public finance and redress citizens' grievances. The timetable is largely under the control of the government, as are procedural devices for cutting short debate. However there are opportunities for backbenchers and the Opposition to intervene.
- There are mechanisms for approving government spending and taxation proposals and scrutinising government expenditure, notably the office of Comptroller and Auditor-General and the Public Accounts Committee. In general however the House of Commons is not equipped for detailed control of government expenditure. In recent years the emphasis has switched to internal controls over expenditure through the Treasury (Chapter 15).
- Other devices for parliamentary control of the executive include specialist select committees and the Parliamentary Commissioner for Administration. These devices have implications for ministerial responsibility (see Section 15.7). This is because they involve investigating the activities of civil servants and they raise questions about the relationship between ministers, civil servants and the House of Commons. Select committees provide a valuable means of publicising issues but have weak powers and are subject to influence by the executive.
- Delegated legislation is often required to be laid before the House, although unless the affirmative procedure is used it may not get serious scrutiny. The Joint Committee on Statutory Instruments monitors delegated legislation on constitutional grounds.
- Procedure in the Commons is dominated by the government through its power to propose business and its control of a majority of votes. Government proposals take up most of the available time. Members of Parliament have no privileged access to government information, so their debate is not especially well informed.
- The House of Lords regulates its own procedure. The presiding officer does not have the disciplinary powers available to the Speaker. Its committees are valued for their expertise.
- The conventional assessment of Parliament is that it has become subservient to the executive, primarily because its members have capitulated to party loyalty, reinforced by the electoral system and the dual role of ministers as members of both executive and Parliament. Parliament, according to this view, is at its worst as a method of controlling government finance, poor at supervising the executive and lawmaking but better at redressing individual grievances, although this owes a lot to the work of members outside the formal parliamentary procedures. On the other hand Parliament provides a forum where the executive must defend itself in public and expose the strengths and weaknesses of its leaders. The possibility of defeat in an election may encourage members to distance themselves from an unpopular government and act as a limited constitutional check.

Exercises

13.1 To what extent has the modernisation programme made Parliament more democratic?

13.2 'The main democratic service provided by Parliament is that it forces the government to defend itself in public.' Discuss.

13.3 'The key to democracy is the power to control public finance.' Are the powers of Parliament adequate in this sense?

13.4 To what extent, if at all, does parliamentary procedure hinder a coalition government from operating smoothly?

13.5 A group of Opposition MPs believe that a senior government minister has been holding secret discussions with a defence equipment company concerning the possibility of engineering a uprising by anti-Western elements in an African state so as to sell weapons to the government of that state. In an answer to a question in the House, the minister denies that the government has any involvement with the state in question. Advise the group as to their chances of obtaining a thorough parliamentary investigation into the matter.

13.6 Compare the strengths and weaknesses of parliamentary questions and select committees as a means of controlling the executive.

13.7 'Parliament in principle can do what it likes but lacks a mechanism independent of the party system controlled by government, in particular to initiate independent inquiries.' Explain and critically discuss.

13.8 Compare the procedures of the House of Commons and House of Lords. To what extent do these reflect the different constitutional functions of the two Houses?

13.9 To what extent can backbench MPs play an effective role in Parliament?

Further reading

Blackburn and Kennon, *Parliament: Functions, Practice and Procedures* (2nd edn, Sweet & Maxwell 2003)
Brazier, *Parliament, Politics and Law Making* (Hansard Society 2004) chs 1–6, 13
Brazier and Ram, *Inside the Counting House* (Hansard Society 2004)
Brazier, Flinders and McHugh, *New Politics, New Parliament? A Review of Parliamentary Modernisation since 1997* (Hansard Society 2005)
Cowley and Stuart, 'Parliament: A Few Headaches and a Dose of Modernisation' (2001) 54 Parl Aff 442
Daintith and Page, *The Executive in the Constitution* (Oxford University Press 1999) ch 4
Davies, 'The Significance of Parliamentary Procedures in Control of the Executive: A Case Study: The Passage of Part 1 of the Regulatory Reform Act 2006' [2007] PL 677
Flinders, 'Shifting the Balance: Parliament, the Executive and the British Constitution' [2002] Pol Stud 50
Jowell and Oliver, *The Changing Constitution* (6th edn, Oxford University Press 2007) ch 7
Judge, 'Whatever Happened to Parliamentary Democracy in the United Kingdom?' (2004) 57 Parl Aff 682
Maer and Sandford, *Select Committees under Scrutiny* (The Constitution Unit UCL 2004)
Nicol, 'Professor Tomkin's House of Mavericks' [2006] PL 467
Oliver, 'Improving the Scrutiny of Bills: The Case for Standards and Checklists' [2006] PL 219
Rogers and Walters, *How Parliament Works* (5th edn, Pearson 2004) chs 6–11, 13
Tomkins, 'Professor Tomkin's House of Mavericks: A Reply' [2007] PL 33
Tomkins, 'What Is Parliament For?' in Bamforth and Leyland (eds), *Public Law in a Multi-Layered Constitution* (Hart 2003)

Chapter 14
The Crown

> **The fool had stuck himself up one day, with great gravity, in the King's Throne; with a stick, by way of sceptre in one hand, and a ball in the other: being asked what he was doing? He answered 'reigning'. Much of the same sort of reign I take it, would be that of our Author's Democracy. (Jeremy Bentham, *A Fragment of Government*, 1776, ch 2, para 34)**

14.1 Introduction: the nature of the Crown

The Queen is the head of state and also head of the executive branch of government. We saw in Chapter 9 that UK law has no concept of the state as such and sometimes uses the notion of the Crown as a substitute. The Crown is an ambivalent concept. The ambivalence derives from the gradual evolution of the constitution from a position where the monarch personally headed the government hierarchy to one where the monarch exercises power only through others. Nevertheless the fiction persists that that power is still monarchical. The term 'Queen' is normally used to refer to the Queen acting personally, whereas the term 'Crown' is used as shorthand for the central government, for example in 'Crown property' or 'Crown immunity'.

As head of state, the Queen has the undefined responsibility of being the ultimate guardian of the constitution. No minister appears to have this responsibility. The fundamental problem about the monarchy is therefore that it is difficult to see how there can be legitimacy and public confidence in the important role of head of state where it is held by a person who is neither elected nor appointed on merit. Furthermore, as we shall see, the monarch inherits the role subject to conditions of religion and blood ties based on the controversies of the seventeenth century.

By convention the Queen must act on the advice of ministers, particularly the Prime Minister, thereby separating the 'dignified' from the 'efficient' constitution and preventing the Prime Minister from pretensions to the role of head of state and ministers from sheltering behind the dignities and privileges of the Crown. Thus Sir Robert Armstrong, the then Cabinet Secretary, said that 'for all practical purposes, the Crown is represented by the government of the day' (Hennessy, 1995, 346).

The Queen is:

- part of the legislature, albeit by convention with no substantive powers. Her formal consent is required for an Act of Parliament and she summons and dissolves Parliament. It has been settled since the *Case of Proclamations* [1611] that, apart from a residue of special royal prerogative powers (see Section 14.6), the monarch has no independent lawmaking powers (see also Bill of Rights 1688);

- as the Crown, formal head of the executive for the UK, the devolved governments and dependent territories. In relation to each government, the Crown has traditionally been regarded as a separate entity. In this sense the Crown is said to be divisible; for example in relation to devolved internal Scottish affairs the Queen should act only on the advice of Scottish ministers (but see Section 6.6 in respect of dependent territories);
- source of the authority of the judiciary, although since *Prohibitions del Roy* [1607] it has been clear that the Queen cannot participate in or interfere with judicial proceedings;
- as the Crown, prosecutor of criminal offences. By statute, the independent Crown Prosecution Service carries out this role under the Director of Public Prosecutions, who is accountable to the Attorney General (Prosecution of Offences Act 1985);
- head of the Church of England;
- head of the armed forces;
- head of the Commonwealth, which is a loose association of former UK territories. The role has symbolic importance no longer especially connected with the UK but carries no legal powers.

Thus, although historically the source of all power was the Crown, a separation of powers has evolved according to which the Crown is mainly the executive arm of government. As the executive, the Crown has a range of important powers collectively known as the 'royal prerogative'. These are common law powers and derive historically from the monarch's personal command of the government and also from the monarch's feudal powers over property. Some of the more draconian prerogatives were abolished in the seventeenth century and all prerogative powers are subject to parliamentary supremacy. The Crown is also in the same position as an individual with the normal powers of an individual to make contracts, own property and so on. Given the resources available to the government, these so-called private law powers are very important.

The historical process of removing power from the monarch (Chapter 4) has left us with ambiguities and confusions concerning the legal nature of the Crown and its relationship with the executive. There is no generally accepted view (see McLean, 2004). It is not clear whether the Crown as the executive means:

- the Queen as an individual;
- or a corporate body with one member, namely the Queen – a corporation sole akin for example to a bishop. (In *Calvin's Case* [1608] it was said that the Crown has two inseparable capacities, one being a 'natural' person, the other a mystical 'body politic' which is immortal (see also *Duchy of Lancaster Case* [1567] at 327). Hence the maxim 'the monarch never dies'. Neither the individual nor the corporation sole theory explains the modern principle that the Crown as the executive acts through ministers. However the corporation sole theory seems to fit the Queen in her role as head of state, separating her from her private capacity);
- or a kind of company together with ministers (corporation aggregate);
- or merely a 'brand name' with no legal identity as such. For example for purposes of civil liability the defendant is a designated government department (see Section 14.5

below). Maitland (1931, 418) regarded the Crown (as opposed to the monarch) as a fiction, a cover for ignorance; Munro (1999, 255) as a convenient abstraction.

Maitland suggested that the best analysis might be to recognise the interplay of law and conventions by treating the Crown as a 'corporate aggregate' akin to a company and acting through many members designated as such by the law, in this case through ministers (Maitland, 'The Crown as Corporation' (1901) 17 LQR 131, 140). This explains not only why the Queen must act on the advice of ministers but also why the prerogative and private law powers are exercised automatically by ministers. (For a useful critical account see Weait and Lester, 'The Use of Ministerial Powers without Parliamentary Authority' [2003] PL 415).

There is also uncertainty about the nature of ministers' powers when acting under the royal prerogative or under the Crown's private law powers. Ministers can automatically exercise these powers, so the convention that the Crown acts on the advice of ministers is not a sufficient explanation. It has been said that the powers of the Crown are 'channelled' through ministers, who for this purpose *are* the Crown (see *R v Secretary of State for Foreign Affairs, ex p Quark Fishing Ltd* [2006] at [12], [19], [78]–[79]). However in *R (Bancoult) v Secretary of State for the Foreign and Commonwealth Office* [2008] at [114] the Court of Appeal turned this on its head, suggesting that ministers govern through the instrumentality of the Crown, thereby making the Crown into a kind of power drill but reflecting the reality rather better. Thus the Crown may be a redundant concept, mysticism obscuring political reality. On the other hand, in the absence of a concept of the state, this is all we have.

The position of statutory powers may be different and more realistic. Statutory powers are usually conferred directly on ministers, who cannot then claim to be acting on behalf of the Crown. In *M v Home Office* [1993] the Home Secretary attempted to rely on Crown immunity in order to deport an immigrant in defiance of a court order. The House of Lords held that he was liable in his official capacity for contempt of court. He was separate from the Crown and was not protected by any Crown immunity. In that case Parliament had conferred the power in question directly upon the Secretary of State. Sometimes however statutory powers are conferred on the Crown as such (eg Bank of England Act 1998, s 1(2): appointment of Governor of Bank). Property is often vested in the Crown as such, since not all government departments have their own legal personality.

In *Town Investments Ltd v Dept of the Environment* [1977] the House of Lords disagreed as to the legal nature of the Crown. The question arose whether an office lease taken by a minister, using the standard formula 'for and on behalf of Her Majesty', was vested in the minister or the Crown, since in the latter case it would be immune from taxation. The House of Lords held that the lease was vested in the Crown. Lord Diplock thought that the Crown was a fiction, a legal shell overlaid by conventions. He seemed to favour the corporation sole model. Lord Simon of Glaisdale said that the expression 'the Crown' symbolises the powers of government that were formerly wielded by the wearer of the crown and reflects the historical development of the executive as that of offices hived off from the royal household. He stated that the legal concept best fitted to the contemporary situation was to consider the Crown as a corporation aggregate headed by the Queen and made up of 'the departments of state including ministers at their heads'. His Lordship added two riders (the second of which may be questionable): 'First the legal concept still does not correspond to the political reality. The Queen does not command those legally her servants. On the contrary she acts on the formally tendered collective advice of the Cabinet.' Secondly, 'when the Queen is referred to by the symbolic title of "Her Majesty" it is the whole corporation aggregate which is generally indicated. This distinction between "the Queen" and "Her Majesty" reflects the ancient distinction between "the King's two bodies", the "natural" and the "politic".'

If we were to abolish the monarchy, a different explanation would have to be found as to the basis of legal power. This could lead to a written constitution. Thus even though the role of the monarch herself is relatively insignificant, the monarchy remains the keystone of the constitution.

14.2 Succession to the monarchy

Under the 1688 settlement Parliament obtained the power to designate who shall be the monarch. The Act of Settlement 1700 (applying to Scotland and Northern Ireland by the Acts of Union 1707 and 1800) is primarily concerned to ensure that Catholics are excluded from the monarchy. It provides that the Crown is to be held by the direct descendants of Princess Sophia (the granddaughter of the deposed James II). The monarch does not apparently have to be a British citizen. However there are provisions designed to prevent a monarch dragging the country into foreign disputes. If the monarch is not 'a native of this kingdom of England', any war for the defence of a foreign country needs the consent of Parliament (s 3). The holder of the crown must be or become a communicating member of the Church of England and must not be or marry a Catholic (s 3). Under the Royal Marriages Act 1772, a member of the British royal family directly descended from George II cannot marry without the consent of the monarch, subject, if over the age of 25, to an appeal to Parliament. The Act of Settlement 1700 might violate the Human Rights Act 1998 since it is discriminatory in relation to religious freedom and the exercise of property rights (the succession being arguably a property right).

The rules of descent are based upon the medieval law governing succession to land. Preference is given to males over females and to the older over the younger. The land law rules required sisters to hold land equally (co-parcenaries). However in the case of the Crown the first-born prevails (although the matter has not been litigated). The succession was last altered when Edward VIII abdicated in 1936 and his brother, the next in line, succeeded (His Majesty's Declaration of Abdication Act 1936). It is not clear whether the monarch has the power to abdicate without an Act of Parliament. Since monarchy is a status conferred by law and without a voluntary act, the answer is probably not. The Crown's titles are also determined by statute (Royal Titles Act 1953).

When the monarch dies, the successor immediately and automatically becomes monarch. A special Accession Council, composed mainly of members of the House of Lords, proclaims the successor. This is confirmed by the Privy Council. Whether these bodies have a power of veto is unclear. One view is that the Accession Council reflects the mythical 'ancient constitution', according to which the monarch was appointed with the consent of the 'people'. The monarch is also required to swear a coronation oath of loyalty (Act of Settlement 1700), although the Coronation Ceremony has no legal significance. It is not clear who resolves the question of a dispute to the succession. Possibly it should be Parliament in its capacity as a court or the Privy Council advising the putative monarch.

If the monarch is a minor, ill or absent abroad, the royal functions are exercised by a regent or councillors of state. These are the persons next in line to the throne (see Regency Acts 1937–53). In such cases certain bills cannot be assented to – most importantly a bill for altering the succession to the Crown.

14.3 Financing the monarchy

Even in her private capacity the Queen is exempt from taxes unless statute specifically provides otherwise. The Queen has however entered into a voluntary agreement to pay tax on current income and personal capital. The expenses of the monarchy and of those members of the royal family who perform public duties are funded from the Civil List in return for the monarch surrendering to Parliament the hereditary income from Crown property. The Civil List is an amount granted by Parliament at the beginning of each reign. It consists of an annual payment that can be increased by statutory instrument made by the Treasury, subject to veto by the House of Commons (Civil List Acts 1952–75). However under the Civil List Act 1975, the Treasury can make additional payments, a practice that would make the monarchy equivalent to an ordinary government department. Many of the royal expenses are funded directly by government departments, such as the upkeep of Crown buildings, security, travel and entertaining political dignitaries. Moreover the Queen has considerable personal wealth, there being no clear line between this and assets derived from the monarchy as an institution.

14.4 The personal powers of the monarch

Since 1688 the personal powers of the monarch have gradually been reduced by the emergence of conventions that require the monarch to act on the advice of Parliament and ministers. The 1688 revolution left the monarch in charge of running the executive but dependent upon Parliament for money and lawmaking power. The monarch retained substantial personal influence until the late nineteenth century, mainly through the power to appoint ministers and influence elections in the local constituencies. Until after the reign of George V (1910–34), monarchs occasionally intervened in connection with ministerial appointments and policy issues. The abdication of Edward VIII (1936) probably spelt the end of any political role for the monarch.

The modern functions of the monarchy can be outlined as follows.

1. *to represent the nation*. For this purpose the monarch participates in ceremonies and public entertainments. It is often said that the popularity and public acceptance of the monarchy is directly related to the fact that the monarch has little political power and is primarily an entertainer. It is not clear why a modern democracy requires a personalised 'leader'. There is a strong element of superstition inherent in the

notion of monarchy, hence the importance of the link between the monarch and the Established Church;
2. *to 'advise, encourage and to warn'*. The monarch has access to all government documents and regularly meets the Prime Minister. The monarch is entitled to express views in private to the government but there is no convention as to the weight to be given to them;
3. *certain formal acts*. These include:
   - assent to statutes;
   - Orders in Council made in the Privy Council (Section 5.7) which give effect to important decisions, laws under the royal prerogative and some statutory instruments regarded as especially important;
   - appointments of ministers, ambassadors, bishops and judges;
   - proclamations, for example dissolving and summoning Parliament or declaring a state of emergency, where the presence of the Privy Council is required;
   - ratifying certain solemn treaties;
   - awarding peerages, honours and medals.

In certain cases it is believed that the monarch can and indeed must exercise personal power. There is little precedent and no principles as to whose advice she should take. There are internal Cabinet Office guidance documents on the matter. The governing principle seems to be that, although the monarch must as far as possible avoid positively intervening in politics, the monarchy is the ultimate guardian of the constitution and must intervene where the normal machinery of government has broken down. The most basic principle here is that the government must have the support of the House of Commons.

Important occasions calling for the intervention of the monarchy are as follows:

- *the appointment of a Prime Minister*. The Queen must appoint the person supported by a majority of the House of Commons. This usually means the leader of the largest party as determined by a general election. Nowadays each party elects its leader. In the event of a majority not being found, as after the election of 2010, the existing Prime Minister must probably be permitted to attempt to form a government. Failing that, the Queen should summon the leader of the largest party. This was the point reached in 2010. If that fails there is disagreement as to what should happen, and in particular as to whether the monarch has any personal discretion. The Queen should not take positive steps at this stage but the politicians should attempt to find someone else capable of commanding a majority. If all else fails the Queen would have to make a personal decision but it is not clear whom she should consult and there is a risk that her choice will be immediately voted out by the House of Commons. Alternatively the Queen should dissolve Parliament, causing another election. The guiding principle seems to be that she must try to determine the electorate's preference without producing instability;
- *the dismissal of a government and the dissolution of Parliament*. If a government is defeated on a vote of confidence in the House of Commons but refuses to resign or advise a dissolution, the Queen could probably dismiss the government. This has not happened in Britain since 1783 but happened in Australia in 1975. In such a case the Opposition, if it could form a majority, could be placed in office or the Queen could dissolve Parliament, thus putting the case to the people through an election. It has been suggested that the Queen could dismiss a government that violates a basic

constitutional principle, for example by proposing legislation to abolish elections. In order to dissolve Parliament, the Queen would require a meeting of the Privy Council. It would therefore be convenient as a temporary measure for her to appoint the Leader of the Opposition as Prime Minister, who would then formally advise her in favour of a dissolution (see *Adegbenro v Akintola* [1963]);

- *refusing a dissolution*. This possibility arises because of the convention that the Prime Minister may advise the monarch to dissolve Parliament (the present government proposes to remove this power). The Queen might refuse a dissolution and appoint another Prime Minister if the Prime Minister is clearly acting unconstitutionally, for example if he or she lost a general election and immediately requested a dissolution, or where a Prime Minister falls personally foul of his or her party. Unfortunately there are no clear precedents. It is likely that the Queen could refuse a dissolution only where there is a viable alternative government and a general election would be harmful to the national interest, although it seems difficult for anyone, let alone the Queen, to make such a judgement. A dissolution has not been refused in Britain in modern times but one was refused by the Governor-General of Canada in 1926. The Governor-General's decision was later rejected by the electorate;
- *refusing a prime ministerial request to appoint peers to the House of Lords*. This might occur where the reason for the request was to flood the Lords with government supporters. The precedents (1832 and 1910–11) suggest that the monarch would have to agree to such a request but only after a general election. This matter is therefore closely connected with the power to dissolve Parliament;
- *the royal assent*. The monarch has not refused assent to legislation since 1709. It appears to be a strong convention that royal assent must always be given. However the Queen might conceivably refuse assent where the refusal is on the advice of the Prime Minister, for example in the unlikely event of a private member's bill being approved by Parliament against the wishes of the government. Here two conventions clash. It is submitted that the better view is that she must still give assent because the will of Parliament has a higher constitutional status than that of the executive. It has also been suggested that the Queen has a residual discretion to refuse consent to a statute that violates fundamental constitutional principles such as abolishing democracy (see Twomey, 'The Refusal or Deferral of Royal Assent' [2006] PL 580). This turns the monarchy into a Supreme Court, which seems unlikely.

14.5 Crown immunities

The Crown has special privileges in litigation. At common law no legal action would lie against the Crown in respect of its property rights and contracts, or in respect of damage or injuries caused by the Crown (torts). This gap in the rule of law was avoided by the Crown's practice of voluntarily submitting to the jurisdiction of the courts. In the case of actions involving property and contract, this was through a procedure called a 'petition of right'. In the case of a tort, the individual Crown servant who committed the tort could be made liable. Where it was not clear who was responsible, the Crown would nominate a defendant, for example where a visitor to military premises was accidentally injured. In either case the Crown would pay the damages.

There is also the obscure maxim 'the King can do no wrong'. This goes beyond the still existing rule that the monarch cannot be made personally liable. It means that wrongdoing or bad faith cannot be attributed to the Crown. For example the Crown at common law could not be liable for wrongs committed by its employees because unlawful acts of its employees were necessarily committed without its authority. However the maxim has never prevented the courts from deciding whether a particular action falls within the lawful powers of the Crown. Invalid acts as such are not wrongful acts (see *Dunlop v Woollahra Municipal Council* [1982]).

The Crown Proceedings Act 1947 subjected the Crown to legal liability as if it were a private person for breaches of contract, for the wrongs of its servants and for injuries caused by defective Crown property. Section 1 permits action for breach of contact against the Crown; section 2 permits action in tort but only where a private person would be liable in the same circumstances. However the Act still leaves the Crown with several special privileges. The most important are as follows:

- No court order can be enforced against the Crown, so the claimant's right to damages depends upon the Crown voluntarily paying up. Similarly no injunction lies against the Crown or against a Crown servant acting on behalf of the Crown (Crown Proceedings Act 1947, s 21). However this applies only in civil law cases involving private rights. In judicial review cases where the legality of government action is in issue and in cases involving the enforcement of EC law ministers cannot claim Crown immunity (*M v Home Office* [1993]; *R v Secretary of State for Transport, ex p Factortame (No 2)* [1991]).
- In an action for breach of contract the Crown can plead 'executive necessity'. This means that it can refuse to comply with a contract where it has an overriding power to take some action in the public interest (*Amphitrite v The King* [1921]; *Comrs of Crown Lands v Page* [1960]). Either there must be some definite prerogative power that overrides the contract or the contract must conflict with a statutory duty. Governments cannot cancel contracts without compensation merely because of policy changes.
- The Crown is not liable in tort for the acts of its 'officers' unless the individual officer was appointed directly or indirectly by the Crown and paid wholly from central government funds (s 2(6)). (The term 'officer' includes all Crown servants and ministers.)
- The Crown is not liable for wrongs committed by 'judicial' officers (s 2(5)), that is judges or members of tribunals. A person exercising judicial functions also enjoys considerable personal immunity (see Section 8.4).
- Until 1987 a member of the armed forces injured on duty by another member of the armed forces or while on military property could not sue the Crown if the injury was pensionable under military regulations (s 10). This caused injustice because it was irrelevant whether or not the victim actually qualified for a pension. The Crown Proceedings (Armed Forces) Act 1987 abolished this rule but the Secretary of State can restore it in times of war or national emergency (see *Matthews v Ministry of Defence* [2003]: immunity does not violate right to a fair trial).
- The Crown is not bound by an Act of Parliament unless it expressly or by necessary implication binds the Crown. Necessary implication is a strict notion. It is not sufficient to show that the Crown is likely to cause unfairness and inconvenience or even that the exemption is against the public interest (*Lord Advocate v Dumbarton DC* [1990]). It has to be established that the statute would be unworkable unless the Crown were bound (see *Cooper v Hawkins* [1904]: speed limit did not bind Crown). It is debatable whether the Crown can take the benefit of statutes even

though it is not bound by them. For example the Crown can evict a tenant free of statutory restrictions, but could the Crown as a tenant resist eviction by a private landlord by relying on the same statutory rights that it can ignore as a landlord?
- The Crown is not liable for injuries caused in connection with bona fide acts of government policy overseas (acts of state), provided that the action is authorised or subsequently ratified by the Crown (see Section 9.7.3).

14.6 The royal prerogative

The royal prerogative comprises special powers, rights and immunities vested in the Crown at common law, and because we have no written constitution is fundamental to the structure of the executive. Identifying each of these powers and their scope is problematic since there is no authoritative source. This uncertainty is a concern because as a matter of constitutional principle those exercising power should be able to identify authority justifying its exercise. The modern prerogative can be explained as the residue of the special rights and powers conferred on the monarch by medieval common law. Some aspects might also be justified in Hobbesian terms (Section 2.3.1) on the basis that a residue of discretionary power is always needed to protect the community against unexpected dangers.

Lord Denning in *Laker Airways Ltd v Dept of Trade* [1977] considered that the Crown had a general discretionary power to act for the public good in certain spheres of governmental activity for which the law had otherwise made no provision. This interpretation is however inconsistent with the rule of law as famously invoked in *Entick v Carrington* [1765]. Here the court emphatically rejected a claim of 'executive necessity' that officers of the state had a general power to enter and search private property. Lord Denning's views were not supported by the other members of the Court of Appeal. The better view is that although the Crown has certain discretionary powers in relation to emergencies, such as the requisitioning of property (Section 14.6.1), the prerogative comprises a finite number of miscellaneous powers rather than one general power to act for the public good.

Some of these powers were based upon the position of the monarch as chief landowner within the medieval feudal system. Others are inherent in the notion of sovereignty, derived from the responsibility of the monarch to keep the peace and defend the realm. This duality may have corresponded to the distinction drawn in seventeenth-century cases between the 'ordinary' and the 'absolute' prerogatives, the latter being discretionary powers vested in the King and arguably beyond the reach of the courts (see *Bates Case* [1606]). From the sixteenth century, theories of absolute monarchy became dominant in Europe but were less influential in England.

In 1611 it was made clear that the King could legislate only within areas of prerogative allowed to him by the existing law (*Case of Proclamations* [1611]). The debate therefore shifted to exploring the limits of the prerogative. The Stuarts attempted to extend the prerogative and to impose taxes and override the ordinary law. However even they submitted themselves to the courts and in a series of famous cases punctuating the political conflicts of the time the scope of the prerogative was inconclusively argued (*Bates Case; R v Hampden* [1637]; *Godden v Hales* [1686]). Given that the judges were dismissible by the Crown, these cases were not always consistent.

The outcome was revolution culminating in the 1688 settlement (Chapter 4), which provides the framework of the modern law. This can be summarised as follows:

- In principle the royal prerogative remains but must give way to statute.
- No new prerogatives can be created (*BBC v Johns (Inspector of Taxes)* [1965]).
- The prerogative can be controlled by the courts, although the extent of such control depends upon the type of prerogative power in question and the context (Section 14.6.4).
- The Bill of Rights 1688 outlawed certain aspects of the prerogative, including the power to suspend laws without parliamentary consent. The Bill of Rights also banned taxation under the royal prerogative. Modern judges have taken this further by refusing to imply a power to raise money in any way unless clear statutory language is used (see *A-G v Wilts United Dairies* [1921]; *Congreve v Home Office* [1976]; *Macarthy & Stone (Developments) Ltd v Richmond upon Thames LBC* [1991]).

14.6.1 The scope of modern prerogative powers

There is no authoritative list of prerogative powers. Prerogatives embrace a variety of subjects, most of the important ones concerning foreign affairs. We shall list them below. In October 2009 the Ministry of Justice published a 'Final Report' on the royal prerogative as it is exercised by ministers (*The Governance of Britain: Review of the Executive Royal Prerogative Powers*; see also Public Administration Committee, *Taming the Prerogative: Strengthening Ministerial Accountability to Parliament* (HC 2003–04, 422)). The Annex contains a list of what the government considers to be the existing prerogative powers. This list does not claim to be comprehensive and of course has no legal significance since only the courts or Parliament can determine the scope of the prerogative. The list distinguishes between powers relating to the internal workings of government, powers relating to justice, powers relating to foreign affairs, powers traditionally involving a formal act of the monarch (albeit on the advice of ministers) and some archaic survivals.

The prerogative powers are as follows. (Those marked * are traditionally performed by the Queen personally, usually on the advice of ministers and sometimes in the Privy Council. Others are exercised directly by ministers.)

In relation to domestic affairs:

- the appointment and dismissal of ministers;*
- the summoning, prorogation and dissolution of Parliament;*
- royal assent to bills;*
- grant of peerages, honours and titles* (some being in the Queen's personal gift);
- the appointment and regulation of the civil service;
- the commissioning of officers in the armed forces;
- security:
  (i) The Crown has a residual power to keep the peace within the realm, for example by deploying the military or issuing the police with weapons (*R v Secretary of State for the Home Dept, ex p Northumbria Police Authority* [1988]; *Chandler v DPP* [1964]);

(ii) The Crown may enter upon, take and destroy private property in an emergency both at home and overseas (*A-G v De Keyser's Royal Hotel Ltd* [1920]). Compensation is payable if property of British subjects anywhere or of anyone within the realm is taken in peacetime (see *Burmah Oil Co v Lord Advocate* [1965]; War Damage Act 1965)

- (possibly) to expel aliens from the UK (see *A-G for Canada v Cain* [1906] at 547);
- the appointment of Queen's Counsel (senior barristers);
- the prerogative of mercy (see *Re Foster* [1965]);
- the granting by the Privy Council of a royal charter to bodies such as universities, learned societies, charities or professional associations that gives the body the status of a legal person and signifies state approval of its activities;
- the regulation of charities;
- the care of the vulnerable: children and the mentally ill;
- the Attorney General's power to institute legal proceedings in the public interest and to stop criminal proceedings.

In relation to foreign affairs:

- the making of treaties;
- the declaration of war;
- the deployment of the armed forces on operations overseas;
- the recognition of foreign states;
- the accreditation and reception of diplomats;
- the governance of some overseas territories (see Section 6.6);
- the granting and revoking of passports.

In relation to security and emergencies the prerogative has largely been superseded by statute (see Chapter 23). Similarly immigration control, the administration of charities and the care of children and the mentally ill are also mainly governed by statute. A framework for the civil service has been enacted by the Constitutional Reform and Governance Act 2010 (see Section 15.7).

Finally there are miscellaneous prerogatives based on feudal landholding. The most important of these are the Crown's ownership of the seashore and tidal waters, and the Crown's rights to bona vacantia, that is property without any other owner, and to ownership of certain living creatures, notably swans.

The 2009 Ministry of Justice Report (above) includes a useful outline of the general law relating to the prerogative and some reform proposals. On the whole the government apparently prefers to leave reform of the prerogative to the traditional evolutionary process. Reforms are vaguely specified and are subject to further discussion. The main ones include increasing parliamentary oversight of treaties, the management of the civil service, war powers and reform of the office of Attorney General (see Section 15.5). Only the first two have so far been implemented (see Sections 15.7, 9.7.1). The current government is considering whether MPs should have the power to decide whether Parliament should be dissolved or recalled. If this reform were enacted it might significantly change the balance between executive and Parliament.

The Public Administration Committee (above) took the view that some prerogative powers, for example the power to press men into the navy, may have lapsed through disuse. Similarly the ancient writ of *ne exeat regno*, which prevents persons from leaving the country, is sometimes regarded as obsolete. However there is no doctrine of obsolescence in English law. Some prerogatives have however been superseded or modified by statute (see Section 14.6.5).

14.6.2 Two kinds of prerogative power?

There is ambiguity as to what a prerogative power is. Blackstone (1723–80), whose view seems to be technically correct, regarded the prerogative as confined to the special powers of the Crown which we have outlined above. Dicey (1915, 429) however described the prerogative as including all the non-statutory powers of the Crown, including the 'private law' powers of ownership, employment, contracting and so on apparently possessed by the Crown as a legal person in common with everyone else. These are sometimes called 'third source' powers or residual powers (eg *Shrewsbury and Atcham BC v Secretary of State* [2008]).

Blackstone's distinction seems unreal in as much as all Crown powers are important politically, and in the way they are exercised are indistinguishable from powers that Blackstone would regard as genuine examples of the prerogative. For example the Crown has enormous economic power (sometimes called dominium power); a defence contract or health service contract made with the Crown could affect the livelihoods of millions. The Crown may be a property owner in common with others but its economic and political power surely put it in a special position and call for additional controls, particularly if, following Locke (Chapter 2), we believe that government holds all its powers subject to public duties. There is much to be said for Dicey's view and for treating all non-statutory powers of the Crown alike.

The matter may be of practical importance in that the exercise of prerogative powers in the narrower or strict sense can be reviewed by the courts whereas it is not clear whether all private law powers are reviewable (see Section 19.5). In principle there should be no difference between the two. The residual powers of the Crown arguably run contrary to the principle that government should have no powers other than those specifically conferred on it by the law. It is true that the residual powers cannot directly violate individual rights but they can nevertheless have serious consequences, for example in terms of livelihood or reputation (eg *R v Secretary of State for Health, ex p C* [2000]: creating sex offenders register).

The modern cases seem to support Dicey. In *Council of Civil Service Unions (CCSU) v Minister for the Civil Service* [1985] (*CCSU*; also known as the GCHQ case) the House of Lords treated the control of the civil service as part of the royal prerogative, holding that they could review the validity of an Order in Council varying the terms of employment of certain civil servants. Lord Diplock expressed the view that the distinction between special and ordinary powers of the Crown is artificial and would regard all common law powers of the Crown as part of the prerogative. In *R v Criminal Injuries Compensation Board, ex p Lain* [1967] a government scheme to pay compensation to the victims of crime was treated as a matter of prerogative, thus enabling the court to review errors of law made by the board set up to run the scheme. The scheme was financed out of money provided by Parliament but was not then statutory. Since anyone can give away money, this scheme would arguably not count as royal prerogative under the Blackstone definition.

14.6.3 Political control over the prerogative

Most prerogative powers are exercised by ministers. These powers include some that are among the most significant powers possessed by government, for example a decision to deploy troops and the power to make a treaty. The constitutional problem concerns a lack of democratic control over officials claiming to act under the prerogative. As common law powers, prerogative powers do not need to be approved by Parliament, so there is a gap in democratic accountability. Decisions taken under the prerogative are essentially decrees with no formal accountability other than the limited possibility of judicial review.

There was for instance no legal requirement for the government to gain parliamentary approval to send British troops to Iraq in 2003. However since approval was in fact sought on that occasion there may now be a convention requiring this. Whether the convention extends to the deployment of troops in a peacekeeping role as opposed to armed conflict is unclear.

The absence of any statutory requirement for parliamentary approval thus raises profound questions in a modern democracy (see Public Administration Committee, *Taming the Prerogative* (HC 2003–04, 422)). Similarly until the enactment of the Constitutional Reform and Governance Act 2010 (see Section 9.7.1) there were few democratic safeguards in relation to the treaty-making power: a ministerial signature, without parliamentary approval, is all that is legally required to make a treaty.

The UK constitution is perhaps unique in allowing government such extensive and imprecise powers that are not granted by the legislature. In some cases however the exercise of a prerogative power must be confirmed by statute. These cases include treaties that alter the existing law and certain EU treaties (see Section 9.7.1).

Some parliamentary control is possible, firstly because all government functions depend on money which must be authorised by Parliament and secondly through the doctrine of ministerial responsibility, although this may be after the event. These methods of control are weak since Parliament has insufficient resources adequately to investigate government spending and there is in any case normally an automatic majority for the executive. Moreover government spending is usually authorised by a blanket departmental allocation or met out of a general contingency fund or a retrospective vote. Although conventionally ministers are responsible to Parliament, at least one Prime Minister has expressed the view that 'it is for individual Ministers to decide on a particular occasion whether and how to report to Parliament on the exercise of prerogative powers' (HC Deb 1 March 1993, col 19W).

By convention the Prime Minister cannot be questioned about advice given to the sovereign concerning certain prerogative powers, such as the granting of honours and appointments and the dissolution of Parliament. The reason is that these powers are exercised personally by the monarch even though the monarch must usually act on the advice of the Prime Minister. In addition ministers sometimes refuse to be questioned about prerogative powers relating to foreign relationships, national security matters and the prerogative of mercy. However Parliament, if it wished, could insist on investigating these. Whether their exclusion is justifiable upon any basis other than the mystique that has traditionally attached to the prerogative is debatable. They involve wide discretionary powers, but that in itself could be an argument for rather than against political accountability.

14.6.4 Judicial control

Historically the courts exercised only limited control over the prerogative. If a prerogative power was disputed, a court could determine whether it existed and (if it existed) what it empowered the executive to do, but the monarch was the only judge of how to exercise the power. For example in the *Saltpetre Case* [1607] the King had the power in an emergency to enter private land and was held to be the sole judge both of whether an emergency existed and what measures to take (see also *R v Hampden; A-G v De Keyser's Royal Hotel Ltd; Chandler v DPP*).

The courts have developed sophisticated rules for judicial review of the exercise of statutory powers based on notions of fairness, reasonableness and relevance. These do not (in theory at any rate) entitle the courts to make the government's decisions for them but are designed to ensure that government keeps within the limits of its powers and complies with basic moral standards. Is there any reason why the same should not apply to the prerogative?

Before the speeches in the House of Lords in *CCSU*, it was assumed that the courts could determine the existence and limits of a prerogative power but could not interfere with how it was exercised. In *CCSU* the House of Lords held that decisions made under prerogative powers are in principle reviewable on the same basis as decisions made under a statutory power. But this does not mean that this jurisdiction will always be exercised. The power must be of a 'justiciable' nature, which means that it must be suitable for the courts' scrutiny. This is no longer resolved by looking at the source of the power (statute or prerogative) but at its subject matter and its suitability in the context of the facts of the case, the particular grounds of review and the political role, expertise and knowledge appropriate to the court. The courts seem to be increasingly reluctant to treat any power as wholly non-justiciable and to take the view that the matter is one of judicial restraint in relation to the particular issue (see *R (Abassi) v Secretary of State* [2002]). Nevertheless a characteristically non-justiciable power is likely be a royal prerogative power, such as the power to deploy the armed forces or make treaties.

For example in *R (Bancoult) v Secretary of State* [2008], the House of Lords held that it had jurisdiction to review a Prerogative Order in Council even though this was primary legislation made by the Queen in Council. Their Lordships were influenced by political reality in the sense firstly that such an Order was in fact made by ministers and secondly that unlike a statute it was not subject to a democratic process. However a majority went on to hold that the Order was valid partly because its particular subject matter was not suitable for the courts to assess (see Section 6.6).

Justiciability will be considered in more detail in the context of judicial review generally (see Section 19.7.1). In summary, in cases where there is a high level of political discretion without guidelines, or where there are considerations outside the proper functions or expertise of the courts, such as in relation to foreign affairs, the threshold of successful challenge is likely to be high. For example powers relating to the dissolution of Parliament and the appointment and dismissal of ministers are central to the democratic process and are unlikely to be justiciable in order to respect the separation of powers. At the other extreme a more intensive standard of review is likely in respect of routine administrative decisions (*R v Secretary of State for Foreign Affairs, ex p Everett* [1989]).

Other prerogative powers have been held to be reviewable on a similar basis. These include the powers to make *ex gratia* payments to the victims of crime (*R v Criminal Injuries Compensation Board, ex p P* [1995]), to compensate farmers affected by the foot and mouth epidemic (*National Farmers Union v Secretary of State for the Environment, Food and Rural Affairs* [2003]) and to issue warrants for telephone tapping (*R v Secretary of State for the Home Dept, ex p Ruddock* [1987]) and the policy of discharging gay men from the armed services (*R v Ministry of Defence, ex p Smith* [1996]).

14.6.5 Prerogative and statute

Since Parliament is sovereign, statute can abolish a prerogative power. How easily can this be achieved in the light of the courts' approach to interpretation? Express words or necessary implication certainly do so. Problems arise where Parliament has enacted statutory provisions dealing with the same subject matter as the prerogative without clearly abolishing the prerogative powers. Where an area of governmental activity is subject both to a statutory and a prerogative power, the statutory power may supersede the prerogative power (see *A-G v De Keyser's Royal Hotel Ltd* [1920]; *Laker Airways Ltd v Dept of Trade* [1977]). Whether or not it does so is a matter of interpretation of the statute. Firstly it depends on whether the statute is intended to bind the Crown (see Section 14.5) and secondly whether the statute is intended to replace the prerogative. If the entire area of governmental activity that was regulated under the prerogative is covered by a statute, the statute probably prevails. However there is a stricter view that the statute prevails only if its exercise is inconsistent with a prerogative power.

In *A-G v De Keyser's Royal Hotel Ltd* [1920] the question concerned whether the property owners were entitled to compensation after their hotel was occupied by the armed forces in wartime. The Crown took possession ostensibly under a statute that conferred an enforceable legal right to compensation. It was nevertheless argued on behalf of the Crown that it had a prerogative power to take possession of land during an emergency and that no compensation was payable as of right under this prerogative power. The House of Lords upheld the property owner's claim, holding that the occupation of the hotel had taken place under statutory powers. The prerogative had been superseded by a comprehensive statute regulating this field of governmental activity and it would be meaningless for the legislature to have imposed limitations on the exercise of governmental power if these could merely be bypassed under the prerogative. In *Shrewsbury and Atcham BC v Secretary of State* [2008] the Court of Appeal held that the common law powers of the Crown could not be exercised where Parliament legislated comprehensively covering that ground. However in the circumstances the Act had retrospectively validated the

Crown's action, which had been to make preparations for a reorganisation of local government in advance of the coming into force of the statute. It might have been different if the use of the common law power had seriously disadvantaged the claimant.

On the other hand in *R v Secretary of State for the Home Dept, ex p Northumbria Police Authority* [1988] the prerogative was not overridden. Here it was held that the Home Secretary could use a prerogative power to supply the police with weapons even though statute placed local authorities in charge of providing police resources. The court said that the prerogative power was suspended only when its exercise was actually inconsistent with a statutory power. *De Keyser's* was treated as an example of inconsistency (see also *Laker Airways Ltd v Dept of Trade* [1977]). Purchas J suggested that the *De Keyser's* principle is qualified where executive action under the prerogative is designed to benefit or protect the individual. In such cases the exercise of prerogative power for this purpose will be upheld unless statute unequivocally prevents this.

However prerogative power is subject to the important limitation that it must not be exercised in a manner which, in substance, conflicts with the intention of Parliament. In *R v Secretary of State for the Home Dept, ex p Fire Brigades Union* [1995] the Secretary of State had power to make a commencement order bringing legislation into force intended to establish a particular regime for compensation for victims of crime. It was held that he could not refuse to bring the statute into effect in order to establish a different scheme under the prerogative. However, as their Lordships remarked, the case is not strictly an example of a conflict between statute and prerogative. The statute was not yet in force and the gist of their Lordships' reasoning was that by committing himself to the prerogative scheme the minister had disabled himself from bringing the statute into force.

It is not clear whether repeal of the statute may revive the prerogative (see *A-G v De Keyser's Royal Hotel Ltd* at 539; *Burmah Oil Co v Lord Advocate* at 143). Occasionally a statute will specifically preserve a prerogative power (eg Immigration Act 1971, s 33(5)).

14.6.6 Prerogative and human rights

The Human Rights Act 1998 provides that an Order in Council made under the royal prerogative is 'primary legislation' for the purposes of the Act (s 21). This means that the court cannot set aside an Order in Council that conflicts with a right protected under the European Convention on Human Rights but would be limited to making a 'declaration of incompatibility' (s 21(2)).

A further consequence of section 21 is that a public authority is only bound to act in accordance with convention rights unless conflicting primary legislation requires it to act otherwise (s 6). Since an Order in Council is primary legislation, a public authority that acts in accordance with its terms would not violate the Human Rights Act 1998 (see further Billings and Ponting, 'Prerogative Powers and the Human Rights Act: Elevating the Status of Orders in Council' [2001] PL 21).

However, like any other executive action, an Order in Council can be challenged in the courts on other grounds (see *R (Bancoult) v Secretary of State*). In this connection a majority in *Bancoult* seemed to suggest that a clearly worded Order in Council can override a fundamental right, whereas Lord Bingham's and Lord Mance's dissenting speeches suggested that only statute can do so. Other prerogative powers can be challenged both on human rights grounds and on domestic grounds.

Summary

- In this chapter we first discussed the meaning of the term 'Crown'. The Queen as head of state, the monarchy, must be distinguished from the Crown as the executive. The legal nature of the Crown is unclear but the dominant view is that the Crown is analogous to a company (corporation aggregate), its members being ministers. Ministers exercise the powers of the Crown directly (see also Section 6.6).
- Succession to the monarchy depends on statute, thus reinforcing the subordinate nature of the monarchy.
- The monarch has certain personal political powers which should be exercised in times of constitutional crisis. These include the appointment of a Prime Minister, the dissolution of Parliament and the appointment of peers.
- At common law the Crown was immune from legal action. Some of this immunity has been reduced by the Crown Proceedings Act 1947, but the Crown is still immune from enforcement and has certain special defences. There is however no general doctrine of state necessity as justifying interference with private rights. Certain acts of the Crown give rise to immunity from legal liability.
- The Crown's executive powers derive from three sources:
  - (i) statutes;
  - (ii) the royal prerogative that is, the residue of special common law powers peculiar to the monarch;
  - (iii) powers possessed by virtue of the fact that the Crown is a legal person with basically the same rights and duties as an adult human being. The Crown can therefore make contracts, own property, distribute money and so on. There is a dispute as to whether this kind of power is part of the royal prerogative.
- The prerogative cannot be used to make law or raise taxation.
- No new prerogative powers can be created.
- Prerogative powers can be reviewed by the courts unless they concern a 'non-justiciable' subject matter or issue such as foreign relationships.
- While prerogative powers are subject to some parliamentary scrutiny, in practice political control over prerogative power is limited.
- The prerogative must give way to statute, although the scope and extent of this is unclear. The matter depends on the interpretation of the particular statute

Exercises

14.1 Compare the royal prerogative with parliamentary privilege (Chapter 11), with reference to (i) its purposes, (ii) its history and sources and (iii) the extent to which it can be controlled by the courts.

14.2 Which analysis of the nature of the Crown best fits the law?

14.3 The UK has a constitutional monarchy. Explain and critically discuss.

14.4 'For all practical purposes, the Crown is represented by the government of the day' (Sir Robert Armstrong, former Cabinet Secretary). Is this a correct statement of the law?

14.5 To what extent are royal prerogative powers subject to control by Parliament?

14.6 Advise the Queen in the following cases:

(i) There has just been a general election in the UK. The existing government has obtained the largest number of seats in the Commons but without an overall majority. The Opposition is negotiating with a minority party to form a government. The Prime Minister refuses to resign.

(ii) What would be the position if the Opposition had obtained the largest number of seats in the Commons and the government was negotiating with the minority party?

(iii) The government is defeated in a vote on the annual Finance Act. The Prime Minister refuses to resign.

(iv) The Prime Minister has just been sacked as party leader. However due to an agreement with the Opposition and a minority party, he could still command a small majority in the Commons.

14.7 Parliament has recently enacted a statute that requires all UK passport holders to swear an oath of loyalty to the Crown. The statute is to be brought into effect by a ministerial order at an unspecified future date. Before the statute is brought into effect there is a change of government. The new government states that it will continue to issue passports indefinitely without requiring the taking of any oath but has no time available to propose the repeal of the statute. Advise the Royalist Society, which wants to challenge this policy in the courts.

Further reading

Blackburn, 'Monarchy and the Royal Prerogative', in Blackburn and Plant (eds), *Constitutional Reform* (Longman 1999)

Bogdanor, *The Monarchy and the Constitution* (Oxford University Press 1995)

Harris, 'The Third Source of Authority for Government Action Revisited' (2007) 123 LQR 225

Hennessy, *The Hidden Wiring* (Gollancz 1995) ch 2

Maitland, *The Constitutional History of England* (Cambridge University Press 1931)

McLean, 'The Crown in Contract and Administrative Law' [2004] OJLS 129

Munro, *Studies in Constitutional Law* (2nd edn, Butterworths 1999) ch 8

Sunkin and Payne (eds), *The Nature of the Crown: A Legal and Political Analysis* (Clarendon Press 1999)

Tomkins, *Public Law* (Clarendon Press 2003) ch 3

Vincenzi, *Crown Powers, Subjects, Citizens* (Pinter 1998)

Chapter 15

Ministers and departments

> **Institutions tend to protect their own and to resist criticism from wherever it may come. (Lord Hope in *R v Shaylor* [2002] at 509)**
>
> **Provided that ministers act 'in good faith' ministerial responsibility for gross errors of judgment is written in water – except at election time. (Anthony Lester QC, *Guardian* 3 August 2004)***

15.1 Introduction

This chapter concerns one of the central issues of the constitution, namely the accountability of government. We shall be concerned with conventions more than with law in the strict sense. The structure and powers of the central executive depend on powers being channelled from Parliament and the Crown, usually to ministers, and upon the general principle, which combines law and convention, that ministers can exercise power through civil servants. Many of the inherent prerogative powers of the Crown can automatically be exercised by ministers. The relationship between ministers, civil servants and Parliament (see Section 14.6.1) is therefore at the centre of the constitution.

There are few legal controls over the organisation of government departments or the relationship between ministers, civil servants and Parliament. The size and structure of the executive has not normally been regarded as a matter of constitutional significance, although it is of course central to the role of government. The most important matters are governed by convention. This aspect of the constitution has been relatively untouched by reform, and the problems raised during the 1990s remain largely unresolved.

The Constitutional Reform and Governance Act 2010 has finally given statutory effect to the basic principles of the civil service but without changes of substance. Some general principles are published in the Ministerial Code (revised 2010) and the Civil Service Code (revised 2006). The Ministerial Code, having no legal basis, is not enforceable in the courts (see *R (Hemmings) v Prime Minister* [2006]). However the Civil Service Code may be enforceable.

The relationship between ministers, civil servants and Parliament is governed by the conventions of collective and individual ministerial responsibility but there is no consensus as to what these mean and no method of enforcing them other than by Parliament itself. While Parliament has the power for example to call civil servants to account, it does not have the will to do so, preferring to defer to ministers, who in practice control its proceedings.

15.2 Appointment of the Prime Minister

The powers of the Prime Minister have evolved since the middle of the eighteenth century, corresponding to the decline in the powers of the monarch. The office, which dates from the early eighteenth century, was originally that of Cabinet chairman, deputising for the monarch and acting as an intermediary between the monarch and the government. The main principles relating to the office are wholly matters of convention and are somewhat murky and secretive.

The Prime Minister is appointed by the Queen subject to the following conventions:

- The Prime Minister must be a member of and enjoy the support of the House of Commons. The size of the popular vote is constitutionally irrelevant but may be politically influential.
- As far as possible the Queen must not influence the outcome.
- The monarch normally acts on the advice of the existing Prime Minister.
- The Prime Minister can advise the monarch to dissolve Parliament at a time of his or her choosing, thereby reapplying for his post. This convention is currently subject to reform proposals (see Section 24.3).
- The existing Prime Minister has the first right to try to form a government by seeking the support of the Commons.

There are a number of possible problems. These would be alleviated if a principle similar to that in Scotland applied, where the Scottish Parliament formally votes for the Chief Minister (see Section 16.2).

In practice the Prime Minister is usually the leader of the party with the largest number of seats in the Commons. This is normally determined by a general election and usually means that his or her party has a majority in the Commons. However in the case of a 'hung Parliament', where no single party has an overall majority, a leader might gain the support of the Commons by forming a coalition between two or more parties, as is presently the case with the Conservative and Liberal Democrat parties. Alternatively a minority government might be possible with the looser support of other parties. The outcome of an election is usually clear (see Section 12.5). Where this is not the case, as in 2010, informal discussions between political leaders supported administratively by civil servants, including the Queen's officials, seem to be the only mechanism for gauging Parliament's support.

The usual process is as follows. If the existing government has won the election it continues in office. Otherwise the existing Prime Minister approaches the Queen and advises her as to the succession, that is to appoint the candidate with majority support in the Commons. The Queen must normally act on the outgoing Prime Minister's advice. The successor then approaches the Queen, who requests him or her to form the government.

At the 2010 general election Gordon Brown, the incumbent Prime Minister, gained fewer seats in the Commons than the Conservative Party. No party achieved a majority. Having negotiated with other parties over five days but failing to secure support, Brown advised the Queen to appoint David Cameron, the Conservative Party leader, as Prime Minister, even though it was at the time not certain that he could gain the support of the Commons. During that time the Conservatives were negotiating with the Liberal Democrat Party, which was also negotiating with Labour. There is no constitutional objection to a minority government or to a coalition government made up of the smaller parties; however a political reason why the present government is a coalition of the Conservative and Liberal Democrat parties is that a combination of Labour and the Liberal Democrats, even though ideologically closer, might have been more unstable given that the Conservative Party held the largest number of seats and also the largest share of the popular vote. Similarly a minority government would depend on the support of other parties on an issue-by-issue basis and would be vulnerable to being dismissed by a vote of confidence.

This elaborate protocol reflects the 'dignified' element of the constitution (see Section 5.1), namely that the government is the Queen's government but also that the monarch takes no political initiative. There is no formal timetable for forming a government, although the practice is to act quickly. Where there is a clear election winner, any change of government is dramatically quick, taking place immediately after the election results are known. In 2010, when there was no overall majority, the process took five days.

There are some problematic situations:

- If the outgoing Prime Minster failed to advise the Queen as to Parliament's wishes and for example advised her to dissolve Parliament so as to rerun the election, it seems that the Queen would be entitled to refuse the request in favour of the stronger convention that Parliament must be respected (see Section 14.4). It is not clear on whose advice she should act.
- Another scenario is if Parliament could not support any candidate. In this case the Prime Minister should advise the Queen to dissolve Parliament.
- The Commons approves or rejects a new government's programme in a vote on the Queen's Speech after the government is formed. This is the same as a vote of confidence, so that if the government is defeated it must collectively resign. This starts the process of choosing a Prime Minister again. Normally the Prime Minister must advise the Queen to dissolve Parliament, triggering a new general election. However if an alternative government could command the support of the Commons, the Queen could perhaps refuse a dissolution on the advice of the leader of the alternative government. This would be especially compelling if the Prime Minister had triggered the immediately previous election and was now asking for a second dissolution to cling to power. The disruption of two elections close together might also be relevant. In this scenario of course the monarchy would be becoming involved in the political process and would have to choose between two conventions.
- Different considerations might apply where a government survived for a time but was eventually defeated on a vote of confidence. This could be the case with the present Conservative–Liberal Democrat coalition government. If say the Liberal Democrat Party joined forces with the Labour Opposition in circumstances where an alternative government was viable, the Prime Minister should perhaps advise the Queen to appoint the Leader of the Opposition. Only if there was no

alternative government with the support of the Commons should he ask for a dissolution, triggering an election. However it is arguable that the defeated Prime Minister would be entitled anyway to ask for a dissolution so as to give the electorate a choice. In this situation, where there is a time lag following the previous election, it should not matter whether the same Prime Minister had triggered the previous election.

- Should a Prime Minister resign or retire during the course of a Parliament the Queen would normally seek advice from him or her as to the succession. However there might be no clear alternative candidate enjoying the support of the Commons. In such a case, in law the matter seems to fall within the discretion of the Queen. This violates the convention that the monarch should not make political choices. It is not clear what action she should take or whom she should consult (see Vennard, 2008). Her first course would probably be to seek a consensus among the senior members of the majority party. Failing such consensus she should probably dissolve Parliament on the advice of the outgoing Prime Minister.

In the above scenarios much depends on the Prime Minister at the time sticking closely to the conventions. Should he or she fail to do so, there seems no alternative to the monarch entering the political arena (see Section 14.4).

15.3 The powers of the Prime Minister

The powers of the Prime Minister are mainly derived from convention. They are also scattered in statute, custom and practice, royal prerogatives and 'nods and winks' derived from the British culture of sycophancy. The Prime Minister exercises the most important prerogative powers. Apart from political powers (below) these include overall responsibility for security, control of the civil service and the mobilisation of the armed forces. The Prime Minister also has statutory powers in sensitive political areas (eg Police Act 1997, s 9; Intelligence Services Act 1994, s 2; National Minimum Wages Act 1998; National Audit Act 1983, s 1). In recent years Prime Ministers have also assumed control over foreign policy, which has the attraction of providing opportunities for self-promotion without the chore of detailed administration.

The main conventions that secure the pre-eminent power of a Prime Minister are as follows:

- The Prime Minister appoints and dismisses all government ministers and determines their status and pecking order. She or he also has powers of appointment in relation to many other important public posts (a mixture of statute and convention).
- By convention the Prime Minister controls the Cabinet agenda, formulates its decisions and allocates government business. In this way Cabinet discussion can be bypassed and matters entrusted to selected prime ministerial supporters, smaller groups of ministers or advisers, or indeed anyone since there are no controls over a Prime Minister taking advice.
- Except for the unlikely event of intervention by the monarch, impeachment by Parliament or removal by his or her party under its rules, there is no formal machinery to get rid of a Prime Minister. A vote of no confidence in the House of Commons can only bring down the government as a whole.

- The Prime Minister may advise the Queen to dissolve Parliament. Thus the Prime Minister can choose the date of a general election, holding his or her colleagues' careers to ransom. This power is subject to removal in a current bill (see Section 11.3)
- The Prime Minister is also Minister for the Civil Service.
- The Prime Minister is head of the internal security services.
- The Prime Minister is the channel of communication between Queen and government.
- The Prime Minister is the main spokesperson for the nation and as such has unique access to the media. The Prime Minister's press office holds a key position. There is a danger that, in terms of public perception and therefore legitimacy, the Prime Minister is perceived as a head of state, thereby eclipsing the monarchy. Ministers' energies are centred upon their own departmental interests. Few have the time or knowledge to concentrate upon issues outside their departmental concerns.

The main limits upon the power of a Prime Minister lie in limited checks and balances that prevent the Prime Minister using powers arbitrarily. In the main they rely on the unlikely event of the Prime Minister's supporters turning against him. Their inadequacy can be illustrated by the then Prime Minister's decision to invade Iraq in 2003, where, despite limited information being given both to the Cabinet and Parliament, a vote in the Commons endorsed the decision. The checks and balances include:

- defeat of the government in a vote of confidence in the Commons;
- the Queen's power to intervene in extreme cases (see Section 14.4);
- the risk of dismissing Cabinet ministers who may enjoy political support in their own right. In practice, a Prime Minister's freedom to appoint ministers may be limited by party considerations. The Cabinet is full of rivals for power. A Prime Minister could not impose his or her will over a united Cabinet that enjoyed substantial support in the Commons. If a Prime Minister requested the Queen to dissolve Parliament in such circumstances, she might be entitled to refuse the request (Section 14.4);
- the absence of a separate prime ministerial department (apart from a Private Office). However Prime Ministers may have a substantial staff of independent special advisers brought in from outside the regular civil service;
- the possibility of a Prime Minister being deposed as party leader and therefore losing the support of the Commons. The influence of senior backbench MPs may be significant. The resignation of Margaret Thatcher in 1989 provides an example.

15.4 The Cabinet

The Cabinet is the policy-making body which formally coordinates the work of government departments. It comprises all Secretaries of State and certain other senior ministers. It is doubtful whether it is underpinned by convention or is merely a creature of practice. Its proceedings are confidential.

The Cabinet originated in the seventeenth century as a group of trusted Privy Counsellors called together to give confidential advice to Charles II. The term was originally one of abuse and referred to the King's 'closet' or anteroom. An attempt was made in the Act of Settlement 1700 to prevent 'inner caucuses' from usurping the functions of the Privy Council, but the provisions were never implemented and were later repealed. George I (1714–27) leaned particularly heavily on party leaders and from his reign onwards the monarch ceased to attend Cabinet meetings, substituting the Prime Minister. During the reign of George III (1760–1820) the convention emerged that the monarch should generally consult the Cabinet. The eighteenth-century Cabinets served the vital purposes of ensuring that the executive could command the support of the Commons and presenting the monarch with a united front. From a mid-nineteenth-century perspective, Bagehot regarded the Cabinet as the 'buckle' that held the government together.

The Cabinet has no legal powers as such. However statute law recognises the status of the Cabinet by protecting Cabinet secrecy (Health Service Commissioners Act 1983, s 12; Parliamentary Commissioner Act 1967, s 8(4)), and sometimes powers can be exercised only by a minister of Cabinet rank (eg Data Protection Act 1998, s 28(10)).

According to the Ministerial Code (2010) the business of the Cabinet and ministerial committees consists in the main of (i) questions which significantly engage the collective responsibility of the government because they raise major issues of policy or are of critical importance to the public and (ii) questions on which there is an unresolved argument between departments. Cabinets usually comprise between 20 and 30 ministers, including the heads of the main government departments and certain other senior office holders. Other ministers and civil servants often attend Cabinet meetings for particular purposes, notably the Chief Whip, who forms a link between the government and its backbench supporters.

Cabinet business is frequently delegated to committees and subcommittees or informal groups of ministers and other persons such as civil servants and political advisers. This is an inevitable consequence of the complexity of modern government and is an important method by which the Prime Minister can control the decision-making process. There are two kinds of formal Cabinet committee: (i) ad hoc committees set up on a temporary basis to deal with particular problems and (ii) named permanent committees, for example defence and overseas policy, economic strategy and legislation. The names and membership of these committees are published (www.cabinetoffice.gov.uk). The Butler Report (Section 15.7.1) criticised the contemporary practice of policy making by informal groups and individuals selected by the Prime Minister without written records and without the Cabinet being fully informed.

Collective Cabinet responsibility (Section 15.7.1) ensures that every member of the government is bound by decisions approved by the Cabinet whether or not the full Cabinet has discussed them. Thus it is sometimes said that the Cabinet has become merely a rubber stamp or 'dignified' part of the constitution. The secrecy surrounding the workings of the Cabinet is also an aspect of collective responsibility and makes objective analysis difficult. Other practical limits upon Cabinet power are that its meetings are relatively short (about two hours per week), its members have departmental loyalties and its agenda and procedure are controlled by the Prime Minister.

The Cabinet Office services and coordinates the work of the Cabinet and records its decisions for implementation by departments. It comprises about 100 civil servants headed by the Cabinet Secretary, who also coordinates other Whitehall committees, designates most of their chairmen and, as head of the civil service, reports to the Prime Minister. Arguably these three roles create fundamental conflicts of duty. The Ministerial Code (2010) issued by the Cabinet Office provides a general framework for the conduct of ministers which we shall draw upon in context.

15.5 Ministers

A minister is defined by section 8 of the Ministers of the Crown Act 1975 as an office holder under Her Majesty. It is for the Queen on the advice of the Prime Minister to designate the number and titles of ministers and to appoint and dismiss ministers. Some ministers have separate legal personality as corporations sole. By convention a minister must be a member of Parliament and most ministers, particularly those in major spending departments and the Treasury, must be members of the House of Commons. In principle any number of ministers can be appointed. However there are statutory limits on the number of ministers who can sit in the Commons and also the number of paid ministers in either House (see Section 12.4). There are about 100 ministers, ranked as follows:

- *Cabinet ministers*. Most Cabinet ministers head departments but some offices are traditionally without departments and can be assigned to special or coordinating work by the Prime Minister. These include the Chancellor of the Duchy of Lancaster and the Lord President of the (Privy) Council. The Leader of the House of Commons is responsible for managing government business in the House. The most important departments are traditionally headed by Secretaries of State. These are the successors of the powerful officials created by Henry VIII to control the central government.
- *Ministers of state and parliamentary under-secretaries of state* (where the head of the department is a Secretary of State). The two law officers, the Attorney General and the Solicitor General, who deals primarily with internal matters, are also of this rank.
- *Parliamentary secretaries*. These are mainly recruited from the House of Commons and assist more senior ministers with political and administrative work.
- *Parliamentary private secretaries*. These are members of Parliament who act as unpaid assistants to individual ministers.
- *Whips*. The whips control party discipline and provide a channel of communication between government and backbenches. They are formally officers of the royal household. The Chief Whip is not a member of the Cabinet but attends Cabinet meetings and consults with the Prime Minister on matters such as the appointment of ministers.

By convention a minister must head each government department in order to ensure ministerial responsibility to Parliament. Ministers are often appointed for their political or parliamentary skills or for reasons of political balance and reward for loyalty. They do not necessarily have the skills, interest or experience to run complex departments. Unlike the position with most other parliamentary systems there is a practice in the UK of 'reshuffling' ministers at roughly two-yearly intervals so that only exceptionally does the same person hold office for the duration of a Parliament. During a reshuffle ministers may be sacked or reallocated and junior ministers or backbench MPs promoted. This is a prime ministerial tool to enforce party loyalty and perhaps to deflect public attention from policy failures. It also underpins incompetent government by inexperienced politicians who are likely to leave office without taking responsibility for the consequences of their failings.

15.6 Government departments

There are no constitutional requirements relating to the organisation of government departments. They can be freely created, abolished or amalgamated by the Prime Minister. The only statutory limitations concern restrictions upon the number of ministers who can sit in the House of Commons (Section 12.4) and provisions relating to particular offices, notably the Lord Chancellor (Constitutional Reform Act 2005). The Treasury also has a special position. The organisation of departments is sometimes regarded as one of royal prerogative but could also be the right of the Crown, as of any private organisation, to organise itself as it wishes, thus illustrating a possible weakness in our non-statist constitution. In the nineteenth century committees of the Privy Council or special bodies were set up to deal with new governmental responsibilities but as the work of government increased separate permanent departments headed by ministers were created. These have been expanded, abolished, split up or combined as circumstances dictated without apparent constitutional constraints.

Some government departments and ministers, notably the Treasury and the Lord Chancellor, trace their origins back to medieval times. The Home Office and Foreign Office are nineteenth-century creations of the royal prerogative. Other departments are either statutory or more commonly set up by using the prerogative to create a Secretary of State, at least in relation to his statuotry powers over them. Some departments, such as the Revenue and Customs Department, a non-ministerial government department (see Section 5.2.7), have substantial administrative and financial independence, with powers conferred directly upon them. They are known as non-ministerial departments. However a minister remains constitutionally responsible for them, at least in relation to any statutory powers he possesses in respect of them.

Because English law has no umbrella concept of the state (Chapter 9), government property is sometimes held by the Crown, often through the Crown Estates Commission, and sometimes by ministers and sometimes by departments created with legal personality. This has caused problems in deciding in what capacity a given asset is held (see eg *Town Investments v Dept of the Environment* [1977]; Section 14.1). Provision must also be made for transferring rights and liabilities between ministers and from ministers to other agencies. Under the *Carltona* principle (Section 15.8.3) functions entrusted to a minister can be exercised by a civil servant in his own department but not transferred to other ministers or to anyone else. These matters are dealt with by standardised legislation (eg Ministers of the Crown Act 1975; Deregulation and Contracting Out Act 1994). Under the Civil Service (Management Functions) Act 2002 a minister can transfer the management of civil servants to any other Crown servant. This is intended to allow ministers to create semi-independent 'executive agencies' (see Section 5.2.7).

For the purposes of litigation a list of appropriate departments is maintained by the Treasury. In cases of doubt the Attorney General represents the Crown (Crown Proceedings Act 1947, s 17). There is a curiosity that since the office of Secretary of State is in law a single office, the various Secretaries of State can interchange functions and assets without the need for legislation.

15.6.1 The Treasury

The Prime Minister is the First Lord of the Board of the Treasury, a body that never meets. By convention the Chancellor of the Exchequer is the responsible minister. The Treasury is an overlord and coordinating department in that it is responsible for the economy as a whole, allocates finance to government departments, supervises their spending and is responsible for the tax-gathering agencies and the Bank of England.

The Treasury has special constitutional significance and its activities provide a good illustration of the mix of legal and informal controls that typify the UK constitution and make the exercise of power obscure. There is a general 'understanding', the basis of which lies in internal practices based on 'ancient authority', that the Treasury both authorises and polices departmental expenditure (see Daintith and Page, 1999, 109–26). The support of the Public Accounts and Public Administration Committees of the House of Commons also authorises Treasury power. Article 10 of the Ministerial Code requires government departments to consult the Treasury in relation to spending proposals. Thus the Treasury can strongly influence if not control the spending priorities of other departments.

The Treasury also plays the role of gatekeeper to Parliament, in which it authorises and presents government spending and taxation proposals. Parliament depends on an initiative from the Treasury since (by convention) the Crown's recommendation is required for all taxation and public expenditure. Moreover it is arguable that Parliament votes money to the Crown rather than to any particular department (Chapter 13). This gives the Treasury a powerful lever since it can approve allocations to individual departments. The Treasury fixes the overall levels of expenditure for each department and can set objectives against which the effectiveness of spending is measured. It approves spending proposals by departments either in general or in relation to especially sensitive items. Thus a strong Chancellor can concern himself with the business of every government department as a rival power centre to the Prime Minister. This was apparently the case during the Labour government led by Tony Blair, leading to confusion and hostility within the government organisation.

Treasury pre-eminence is backed by specific legal powers. Firstly the Treasury has statutory power to approve payments from the Consolidated Fund and the National Loans Fund (the government's main bank accounts) and to place limits on other sources of income such as fees and charges (Government Resources and Accounts Act 2000, ss 2, 3). Secondly the Treasury approves the form and method of the accounts of government departments (ss 5, 7). Under these powers the Treasury is in a position to decide what count as public assets and expenditure and thereby to determine the extent to which public bodies can raise private money. Thirdly the Treasury can authorise additional payments to departments (s 6) and many items of expenditure require Treasury consent under particular statutes. It is unlikely that in the absence of a plain violation of statute matters of economic policy would be subject to judicial review (see *R v HM Treasury, ex p Smedley* [1985]: payments contrary to statute).

The Treasury appoints an Accounting Officer for each department who is responsible for the management of the department (Exchequer and Audit

Department Act 1866, s 22). This is usually the head (Permanent Secretary) of the department and in the case of an executive agency, its chief executive. The Comptroller and Auditor General examines departmental accounts and reports unauthorised expenditure to the Treasury, which can either authorise it or report the matter to Parliament (Exchequer and Audit Departments Act 1921, s 1).

Under the Fiscal Responsibility Act 2010 the Treasury has certain duties to control public finances. It must ensure that the level of government borrowing is reduced year by year. After 2016 it must make an Order imposing on itself a duty to ensure 'sound public finance' (until 2016 it may do this). It must report annually to Parliament but its performance or non-performance of these duties 'does not affect the lawfulness of anything done by any person' (s 4). This formula would prevent judicial review of a failure to perform the duty, although the court is unlikely to decide what counts as sound public finance (see Section 19.7.1).

The Bank of England has some independence. A statutory body, it administers the government's bank account and in conjunction with the Treasury and the Financial Services Authority regulates other banks (Bank of England Act 1998). Subject to the statutory objectives of maintaining price stability, supporting the economic policies of the government and complying with inflation targets set by the Treasury, it is responsible for monetary policy (primarily fixing interest rates) and for issuing currency. Its directors are appointed by the Crown and can be dismissed on prescribed grounds with the consent of the Chancellor of the Exchequer, and 'in extreme economic circumstances' it is subject to directions from the Treasury. The Bank is also subject to scrutiny by the Treasury Select Committee and is required to publish the minutes of its Monetary Policy Committee, an annual report and an annual inflation report.

The Office for Budget Responsibility, currently a non-statutory body of a kind familiar in the UK, is appointed by and reports to the Chancellor. It makes financial forecasts which feed into Treasury processes. It has been criticised as not being sufficiently independent of the Treasury.

15.6.2 The law officers

As party politicians closely bound up with the legal process, the law officers raise questions about the separation of powers. The Attorney General is the chief law officer and is assisted by the Solicitor General. The Attorney and Solicitor are ministers and therefore members of Parliament. Like all ministers they are appointed and dismissed on the advice of the Prime Minister. By convention they are not members of the Cabinet but the Attorney attends Cabinet meetings as required. The Attorney can delegate any of his functions to the Solicitor (Law Officers Act 1997).They are entitled to consult other ministers but by convention act independently.

The Attorney General has the following main functions:

- representing the government in legal proceedings, including intervening in any legal proceedings to put the government's view;

- giving confidential legal advice to the government. The government has no obligation to obtain independent legal advice;
- political responsibility for the Crown Prosecution Service, the Serious Fraud Office and powers under various statutes to consent to the prosecution of certain offences and under the prerogative power to interfere to prevent a prosecution (*nole prosequi*);
- bringing legal proceedings on behalf of the general 'public interest', either on his or her own initiative or on the application of any member of the public (a relator action). This might include an action against a public authority. The Attorney General's decision whether or not to intervene cannot be challenged in the courts (*Gouriet v Union of Post Office Workers* [1978]);
- referring questions of law to the Court of Appeal where an accused person has been acquitted of a criminal offence or requesting a more severe sentence for a convicted person.

By tradition the Attorney is also Leader of the Bar, even though it is important that the legal profession should be seen to be independent of government.

The extent to which the Attorney General (A-G) is influenced by political considerations is obscure. In relation to legal actions against government officers and government attempts to suppress the media, the A-G's two roles as government lawyer and representative of the public interest are potentially in conflict. For example in 2007 the A-G was required to obtain an injunction preventing the BBC from reporting allegations relating to the Prime Minister's Office selling peerages. We have only the predictable assertions of successive A-Gs that they can be trusted – a notion offensive at least to republicans (see Section 2.5) but a recurring theme in the UK constitution.

In 1924 the government fell because the A-G acted on instructions from the government in relation to a prosecution of an anti-government journalist. The Scott Report (*Report of the Inquiry into the Export of Defence Equipment and Dual Use Goods to Iraq and Related Prosecution* (HC 1995–96, 115)) revealed an official culture in which the advice of the A-G was treated as if it had legal force, a practice condemned by the court in *R v Brown* [1993]. Moreover the A-G is regarded as having a private lawyer–client relationship with the government, so that his or her advice can be made public only with the consent of the government.

The combination of these principles allowed the government to claim that it was lawfully entitled to invade Iraq in 2002 on the basis of advice from the A-G over which he changed his mind. His report were never fully disclosed. At first he rejected the legality of the invasion but subsequently became confident that it would be lawful, having apparently accepted advice from the US but not revealing what it was (see Lord Goldsmith's evidence to the Chilcott Inquiry, January 2010). Lord Bingham, a former senior Law Lord, argued that the invasion of Iraq was clearly unlawful and that the A-G's advice was fundamentally flawed (*Grotius Lecture*, British Institute of International and Comparative Law, 17 November 2008).

Recent reform proposals to comply with the separation of powers have not been implemented (see Select Committee on the Constitution, *Reform of the Office of Attorney General* (HC 2007–08, 93)).

15.7 Ministerial responsibility

Ministerial responsibility defines both the relationship between ministers and Parliament and that between ministers and civil servants. Ministerial responsibility has two aspects:

- Firstly all members of the government are *collectively* responsible to Parliament for the conduct of the government.
- Secondly each minister is *individually* responsible to Parliament for the conduct of his or her department.

Ministerial responsibility developed during the eighteenth and nineteenth centuries, corresponding to the rise of the House of Commons and the decline in the power of the Crown. Its original purpose was as a weapon against the monarch by achieving coherence among politicians with divergent views. Ministerial responsibility is a matter of convention, although it is recognised by the law (eg Freedom of Information Act 2000, s 36(2)(a)(i); see Section 23.2.1).

While the rule of law might be the cornerstone of the legal constitution, ministerial responsibility is the cornerstone of the political constitution. Ministerial responsibility in a broad sense gives the constitution a republican element (see Section 2.5). However it is arguable that the doctrine is so nebulous and so damaged by executive domination of Parliament that it currently has little value as a constitutional principle.

Parliament may from time to time make grand pronouncements in favour of ministerial responsibility but these are seldom translated into action (see Tomkins, 2003, 134, who is more optimistic). In particular Tomkins identifies three 'fault lines' in the doctrine. These are firstly a lack of openness in government; secondly 'ownership', in the sense that the government itself can influence the meaning and enforcement of the doctrine; and thirdly, and most importantly, the pressures of party domination. These work together to weaken Parliament.

'Responsibility' is sometimes used interchangeably with 'accountability'. Both terms have a range of meanings (see Public Service Committee, Second Report (HC 1995–96, 313) paras 14–21, 32). They include obligations to provide explanation, information, acknowledgement, review and redress. Sometimes resignation may also be expected. The particular combination appropriate to any given case depends on the circumstances. In addition to ministerial responsibility as such, there are instruments such as the Freedom of Information Act 2000, the Codes of Conduct for MPs and civil servants and the *Guidance to Officials on Drafting Answers to Parliamentary Questions* which inform the notion of openness and accountability. More generally the openness and accountability of government is required by the fourth and fifth Principles of Public Life, namely accountability and openness, set out by the Committee on Standards in Public Life (see Section 5.9).

Ministerial responsibility does not mean that Parliament (except through a statute) can give orders to ministers or lay down policies. Parliament does not itself govern and to this extent there is a separation of powers. Ministerial responsibility means only that ministers must discharge their duties in a manner that has the continued support of the Commons and they must give an account of their actions and decisions. If the Commons so votes on a motion of confidence, the government collectively must resign.

Opposition MPs as well as those of the minister's own party influence ministers in their decisions and exert pressure for changes in government policy. Ministerial responsibility also provides information to arm opponents in the adversarial conduct of British political debate. Indeed it is a characteristic of the parliamentary system of government that there is a continuing struggle on the part of MPs to gain more information than ministers are willing to provide.

On its face the convention can be acclaimed as a device to ensure accountable government. An alternative view is that the convention favours 'strong' government because it allows ministers to govern with little effective parliamentary supervision or interference since Parliament has neither the will nor the resources to hold ministers effectively to account (see Flinders, 2000). Ministerial responsibility may also be out of line with the practices of modern government, in particular the techniques of privatisation and devolved public management. In this context the convention actually shields government from public accountability because the impugned decision may have been taken in an agency that has been hived off from central government. Although in principle the minister remains fully responsible, the vague meaning of responsibility enables ministers more easily to evade blame the further away they are from the location of decision making. The party system and the tradition of secrecy within the civil service have also played a part in breaking the chain of accountability through Parliament to the electorate.

15.7.1 Collective responsibility

Collective responsibility applies to the Cabinet and probably to all government ministers. It was developed originally so that government and Parliament could put up a solid front against the King. It suggests collegial government that is at odds with the legal basis of government with powers given to individual ministers. Collective responsibility has four aspects:

1. It requires all ministers to be loyal to the policies of the government whether or not they are personally concerned with them (solidarity). Collective responsibility therefore applies even though many important decisions are made elsewhere and are not fully discussed by the Cabinet as a whole. Resignation is required before a minister can speak out on a particular issue. Nevertheless as a convention collective responsibility may be adapted to new circumstances. The Prime Minister can apparently modify it over a particular issue (such as membership of the EEC in 1975).
2. It requires the government as a whole to resign if it is defeated on a vote of confidence in the House of Commons or if the Prime Minister resigns.
3. It requires that Cabinet and government business be confidential (see Ministerial Code (2005) para 6.17).
4. It protects ministers against personal responsibility since collective responsibility can be used to justify individuals' avoiding blame. For example the Butler Report into intelligence failures relating to Iraq (*Review of Intelligence on Weapons of Mass*

Destruction: Report of a Committee of Privy Counsellors (HC 2004, 898)) absolved all ministers and civil servants from blame for misleading the public on the basis that the various falsehoods were 'collective'. (Butler himself was a former head of the civil service.) Collective responsibility and individual responsibility (Section 15.7.2) are therefore in conflict.

The drastic sanction of a vote of confidence is the only method by which Parliament can enforce collective responsibility but governments have rarely been defeated in this way in modern times. In 1924 Ramsay MacDonald's Labour government resigned, and in 1979 so did James Callaghan's Labour government. Both were minority governments.

The relationship between Prime Minister and Cabinet has an important impact on how well collective responsibility works in practice. The collegial model of government, which emphasises the participation of all Cabinet ministers in decision making, disguises the dominance of the Prime Minister in the formulation of policy, which tends to blur the difference between a parliamentary and a presidential system. There are no formal checks and balances. The extent to which the Prime Minister can exercise an authoritarian style depends on the composition and mood of the Cabinet, the attitude and cohesion of the party and of the Commons, the temper of the electorate and not least the personal style of the Prime Minister. If undue reliance is placed on a select group of senior ministers (the 'inner cabinet') or unelected 'cronies', if too many 'private deals' are struck with individual ministers or if too many controversial policies are effectively formulated in Cabinet subcommittees, ministers may feel less inclined to loyalty. Serious embarrassment can result where senior ministers resign, having concluded that the workings of the Cabinet have strayed unacceptably far from the collegial model. Michael Heseltine resigned during the Westland affair in 1986. Similarly Geoffrey Howe's resignation over EC policy in 1990 resulted from his concern about the Prime Minister's apparent distaste for collective decision making. This resignation played a pivotal role in ending Mrs Thatcher's tenure of No 10 Downing Street in 1990.

It could be argued that collective responsibility is no different from the solidarity expected within any organisation. Ministers can discuss policy differences in private, confident that all will support the decision which is eventually reached. The presentation of a single view also adds authority to the government's position because it disguises the coalition nature of many governments. This argument begs the question whether government can be compared with, say, a large private sector company. Given that an important value of democratic government is to manage disagreement without suppressing it, it may be desirable for government not to speak with a single voice but to recognise the provisional nature of any decision reached. It can also be argued that the doctrine of collective responsibility could contribute to a general public disenchantment with politics if ministers were seen to vote in support of policies they were believed not to support.

15.7.2 Individual responsibility

Sir Edward Bridges, the Permanent Secretary to the Treasury, expressed the classical interpretation of the doctrine of individual responsibility in 1954, after the Crichel Down affair (see Public Service Committee, Second Report (HC 1995–96, 313) para 8). He stated that a minister is responsible to Parliament for the exercise of all executive powers and every action taken in pursuance of those powers. This emphasises that a minister must always answer questions and give a full account of the actions of his or her department. This is so whether or not the minister is personally at fault for what has gone wrong and has been subject to only limited exceptions, related among other things to commercial confidence, national security and some macroeconomic issues.

Individual ministerial responsibility is concerned with a chain of accountability from Parliament through ministers to civil servants. Ministerial responsibility protects civil servants from direct public responsibility since they owe their loyalty to the government and especially to the minister in charge of their department. Thus civil servants appear before Parliament only with the permission of ministers and on terms set by ministers.

Beyond that, its meaning and scope are unclear: firstly in respect of what 'responsibility' entails and secondly in respect of what actions the minister is responsible for. Ministerial responsibility is primarily enforced by Parliament. Most specifically it requires that ministers provide information to Parliament by means of answers to parliamentary questions, evidence to select committees, formal ministerial statements and letters to MPs. Within the executive the Prime Minister is responsible for enforcing ministerial responsibility and therefore, indirectly, for defining it.

Ministers are certainly responsible for their departments, less clearly so in relation to executive agencies sponsored by their departments. There does not seem to be direct responsibility for non-ministerial government departments or for quangos, although in both cases ministers are responsible for their specific functions in relation to these bodies (see Sections 5.7, 5.8).

Ministers have attempted to limit their responsibility by making various distinctions and by seeking to ensure that their civil servants are not subject to direct scrutiny by Parliament. On the whole Parliament has pandered to ministers in these respects rather than asserting its undoubted right to have the last word.

Firstly it has been claimed that responsibility applies only to 'policy' matters as opposed to 'operational' matters, which are deemed to be failures properly to implement policy. This has been particularly evident following the radical restructuring of government in the 1990s, with the majority of civil servants working in semi-detached executive agencies under the day-to-day direction of chief executives with only limited departmental control (see Section 15.8.4). This restructuring has tended to confuse lines of accountability.

Similar problems arise where a quango stands between the minister in charge of policy formulation and the delivery of a service. It seems however that ministers do not always escape blame where serious errors occur in such cases (see McCaig, 'School Exams: Leavers in Panic' (2003) 56 Parl Aff 471).

The policy/operational dichotomy is a vague one. Indeed the two are often inextricably interconnected. The effect has been to make it more difficult for Parliament to find out who is to blame when problems arise. For example is prison overcrowding policy or operation? Furthermore, even if a matter can be classified from the outset as 'policy', as soon as adverse political consequences arise, the same matter may mutate into one of 'operation', causing confusion as to whether (and if so when) responsibility shifts between a chief executive and a minister. Thus ministers can exploit confusion by intervening where they perceive electoral gains, as in the events leading up to the dismissal of Derek Lewis, the head of the prison service, following allegations of interference by the Home Secretary in the detailed administration of the service (see *Review of Prison Service Security in England and Wales and the Escape from Parkhurst Prison on Tuesday 3rd January 1995* (Cm 3020, 1995) (the Learmont Report); Report of the House of Lords Public Service Committee (HL 1997–98, 55) para 341).

Ministers may also interfere in 'operational' matters while declining to answer questions about them, claiming that such matters fall within the responsibility of the chief executive. Moreover, since it is the minister who decides what is policy and what is operation, ministers can effectively determine the extent of their constitutional responsibilities. The House of Lords Public Service Select Committee concluded that it was not possible effectively to separate policy from operations and that such a division was not desirable (HL 1997–98, 55, para 348).

Secondly ministers have distinguished between 'accountability' and 'responsibility'. This seems to divorce the circumstances in which a minister must give to the House an explanation of the actions of his department (accountability) from cases in which a minister must accept the blame for departmental mistakes and resign (responsibility). In *Taking Forward Continuity and Change* (Cm 2718, 1995, 27–28) the government stated that Parliament can always call a minister to account for all that goes on in his department but it added that a minister cannot be responsible in the sense of having personal knowledge and control of every action taken and cannot be personally blameworthy when delegated tasks are carried out incompetently or errors of judgement are made at an operational level. Coupled with this is a reluctance by ministers to subject civil servants to independent scrutiny, thereby creating an 'accountability gap' (see Section 15.8.3).

The accountability/responsibility distinction was rejected in 1996 by the Public Service Committee of the Commons (above) but accepted by the Scott Report on the Arms to Iraq affair (HC 1995–96, 115). It demands that ministers be prepared to offer a complete explanation of any error to Parliament but not to take the blame. The duty embraces an obligation to offer reasons by way of justification in the face of criticism. Experience reveals however that ministers have not always been willing to give a full account of their actions. Notoriously the conclusion of the Scott Inquiry (Section 15.6.2) was that there were numerous examples of ministers failing to give full information about the policies, decisions and actions of government regarding arms sales to Iraq (HC 1995–96, 115, K8.1, para 27) and that this had undermined the democratic process (D4.56–D4.58). Answers to parliamentary questions in the affair had been 'designedly uninformative' because of a fear of adverse political consequences if the truth were revealed (D3.107).

Following revelations of this kind, it became clear that there should be a renewed commitment to the doctrine of individual responsibility combined with a need to clarify the obligations entailed by it, and in particular to ascertain the matters about which ministers must answer questions. This led to resolutions of the House of Commons and House of Lords on ministerial accountability (HC Deb 19 March 1997, vol 292, cols 1046–47; HL Deb 20 March 1997, cols 1055–62).

These resolutions led to the adoption by the government of the Ministerial Code (2010), which now incorporates a 'Ministerial Code of Ethics'. The Code sets out the following principles of ministerial conduct (which are mostly in the terms of the resolutions):

1. Ministers must uphold the principle of collective responsibility.
2. Ministers have a duty to Parliament to account, and be held to account, for the policies, decisions and actions of their departments and Next Steps agencies.
3. It is of paramount importance that ministers give accurate and truthful information to Parliament, correcting any inadvertent error at the earliest opportunity. Ministers who knowingly mislead Parliament will be expected to offer their resignation to the Prime Minister.
4. Ministers should be as open as possible with Parliament and the public, refusing to provide information only when disclosure would not be in the public interest, which should be decided in accordance with the relevant statutes and the Freedom of Information Act 2000.
5. Ministers should similarly require civil servants who give evidence before parliamentary committees on their behalf and under their direction to be as helpful as possible in providing accurate, truthful and full information in accordance with the duties and responsibilities of civil servants as set out in the Civil Service Code.

However there is no independent method of enforcing the Code, which has no legal force. It states that it is not an enforceable rule book (para 1.3). It is not policed by the Cabinet Secretary or by the Parliamentary Committee on Standards since this has jurisdiction only over MPs as such. Part 1 of the Code reminds ministers that they can only continue to hold office for as long as they have the support of the Prime Minister. The Code states that the Prime Minister 'is the ultimate judge of the standards of behaviour expected of a Minister and the appropriate consequences of a breach of those standards'. This suggests that the Code envisages that the Prime Minister is both a setter of standards and responsible for their enforcement. For that reason the statement reads rather oddly in the light of the resolutions.

The respective resolutions of each House are of fundamental importance because ministerial responsibility is no longer an unwritten convention which can be varied at will by the government of the day; ministerial responsibility is now a rule of Parliament. The terms of the resolutions are not however without difficulty. As Woodhouse (1997) observes, satisfying them may not be unduly burdensome. Ministerial judgement will still govern what it means to be 'as open as possible' and when disclosure 'would not be in the public interest'. This means that the problems of interpretation remain and that the doctrine of ministerial responsibility is still somewhat elusive. However, subject to substantial exceptions, the Freedom of Information Act 2000 gives legal backing to requests for information from ministers (see Section 23.2.1).

15.7.3 Ministerial resignation

Ministerial resignation engages both collective and individual responsibility. This is because where resignation takes place it saves fellow ministers from having to offer support for the beleaguered minister under the principle of collective responsibility. The classical doctrine does not resolve the question of when, as a constitutional requirement, a minister's 'responsibility' also entails a duty to take the blame for departmental errors if necessary by resignation. One interpretation of the convention is that resignation is required for every serious departmental error regardless of the personal blame of the minister. Characteristically of conventions, such a convention if it ever existed seems to have been destroyed by disuse. The Crichel Down affair (Cmd 9220, 1954), which involved serious official misconduct in relation to government confiscation of land, was once thought to have required resignation but is not now considered to support such a wide proposition. Sir Thomas Dugdale's resignation in that case probably owed more to political misjudgement and a lack of parliamentary support.

It seems that resignation is only constitutionally required in three categories of case:

1. where a minister has knowingly misled Parliament (except in the very limited cases where this is justified: Public Service Committee, Second Report (HC 1995–96, 313) para 32). However an honest even though unreasonable belief in the accuracy of information given to Parliament can be a lifeline to beleaguered ministers. The Scott Inquiry found that William Waldegrave unreasonably clung to the view that government policy governing the sale of arms to Iraq had not changed (HC 1995–96, 115, D4.1–D4.7). Waldegrave did not resign. Similar questions arose after Lord Falconer's refusal in 2001 to resign in respect of the funding and sale of the Millennium Dome;
2. where the minister is personally to blame for a serious departmental error (Sir Richard Butler in evidence to the Scott Inquiry, 9 February 1994, Transcript 23–24);
3. in the case of personal dishonesty or wrongdoing, at least when the minister is politically vulnerable. Examples include Peter Mandelson, who in 1998 did not disclose that he had received a substantial private loan from a fellow minister whose business affairs were subject to investigation by Mandelson's department, and David Laws in 2010 for breaching rules on MPs' expenses at a time when the matter was the subject of considerable public agitation. Private misconduct unrelated to a minister's duties might also lead to resignation but perhaps only where the minister becomes politically vulnerable (eg David Mellor in 1992 following adverse publicity about his private life).

However raw politics and media attention rather than constitutional obligation may be the best explanation of ministerial resignations. Even in cases of personal misjudgement or serious policy failure, resignation will be influenced by pragmatic concerns of the gravity of the issue, party support for the beleaguered minister, the timing of the discovery of the error, the support of the Prime Minister and Cabinet and the public repercussions of the fault. For example David Laws' resignation in 2010 involved a technical breach of expenses rules but in circumstances of massive public anger at MPs' conduct generally. Woodhouse argues that personal indiscretions fall within the ambit of conventional requirements because they affect the public credibility of the minister concerned ('Ministerial Responsibility in the 1990s: When Do Ministers Resign?' (1993) 46 Parl Aff 277).

15.8 The civil service

The civil service is a professional, permanent and independent part of the executive, giving the constitution continuity and stability, and a source of expert advice. Its purpose is to assist the government in formulating its policies, to carry out decisions of the government and to administer services for which the government is responsible. In the last resort where ministers fail the civil service must keep the government functioning.

There is no authoritative legal definition of a civil servant. The Constitutional Reform and Governance Act 2010, following the report of the Tomlin Commission on the Civil Service (Cmd 3909, 1931), unhelpfully refers to 'the civil service of the State'. This may include every person who serves the Crown other than the military, ministers and holders of judicial offices. The armed forces are of course also Crown servants but are subject to a distinctive legal regime. The police are not civil servants because they are not employed by the Crown. Thus the best definition of a civil servant is partly negative, meaning a Crown servant other than those falling into special categories (see Sandberg, 'A Whitehall Farce? Defining and Conceptualising the British Civil Service' [2006] PL 653).

Management of the civil service is currently vested in the Prime Minister, who is also Minister for the Civil Service. The Cabinet Office and the Treasury supervise the civil service, with each department or agency being managed by its Accounting Officer, usually of the highest rank of Permanent Secretary. The Accounting Officer's activities can be examined by Parliament by means of the Public Accounts Committee and the Comptroller and Auditor General. According to the Ministerial Code (Art 5.4) the Accounting Officer is personally responsible for the department, thus raising the question of ministerial responsibility (Section 15.7).

There is particular tension from two directions. On the one hand the civil service must offer impartial advice and expertise to governments of all political colours (Civil Service Code (2006) paras 1, 13). On the other hand it is required loyally to carry out government instructions. The argument that UK civil servants should have wider duties to the Crown as distinct from duties to the government of the day has not succeeded (see House of Commons Public Service Committee, Second Report (HC 1995–96, 313) para 169).

Ministers (perhaps weak ones) may complain that they are dominated or subverted by their civil servants. Civil servants may complain about political interference with the impartiality and influence of the civil service, for example through ministerial involvement in appointments and the influence of special advisers and other persons recruited informally by ministers.

15.8.1 The statutory framework

Following persistent recommendations by the Committee on Standards in Public Life (Ninth Report, *Defining the Boundaries within the Executive* (Cm 5775, 2003)), the Constitutional Reform and Governance Act 2010 has enacted a framework of principles regulating the civil service. This replaces the previous mixture of royal prerogative rules and conventions. The Act does not however remove the royal prerogative power to regulate the civil service (see Civil Service Order in Council 1995, as amended; Civil Service Management Code; Civil Service Code (2006)). The 2010 Act does not apply to the security services, the Northern Ireland civil service or civil servants serving wholly outside the UK.

Most importantly the Act has nothing to say about the detailed relationship between civil servants, ministers and Parliament, so the disagreements surrounding these conventions remain (see Institute for Public Policy Research (2006), recommending a statutory framework).

The main provisions of the Act are as follows:

- The Civil Service Commission, previously existing under the royal prerogative, is established as a corporate body with its own legal identity. The Commission hears complaints relating to violations of the Civil Service Code and disciplinary and recruitment matters but has no enforcement powers. It also monitors recruitment practices (ss 2, 9, 11, 12, 14).
- Management of the domestic civil service is vested in the Minister for the Civil Service. The Foreign Secretary manages the diplomatic service. The managers must 'have regard to the need to ensure that civil servants who advise ministers are aware of the constitutional significance of Parliament and of the conventions governing the relationship between Parliament and government' (s 3). Unfortunately the Act does not state what these are.
- The Civil Service Code must be published and laid before Parliament (s 5). The Code must require civil servants to carry out their duties with integrity, honesty, objectivity and impartiality. However special advisors (see Section 5.7) need not be objective or impartial (s 7). In addition the Ministerial Code (2010), which is not statutory, requires ministers to uphold the impartiality of the civil service and to give due consideration to its advice.
- The Minister for the Civil Service must publish a Special Adviser's Code, which must be laid before Parliament (s 8). Special advisers cannot authorise expenditure from public funds or manage other civil servants, except other special advisers, or exercise statutory or prerogative power (s 8(5)). This of course raises the question whether the 'ordinary' common law powers of the Crown, such as contractual powers, should be regarded as prerogative powers (see Section 14.6.2). A special adviser must be appointed by the minister personally, subject to the approval of the Prime Minister (s 15). The terms of the appointment require the consent of the Prime Minister and the Minister for the Civil Service (usually the same person).
- Civil servants, other than special advisers and statutory Crown appointments such as the Governor of the Bank of England, must be appointed by a fair and open competition (s10). The recruitment process is supervised by the Civil Service Commission, which must publish recruitment principles (s 11). These can create exemptions from the open competition requirement, for example when someone with a particular expertise or experience is needed. In such cases the Commission must approve the appointment and can participate in the appointment process. In the case of senior appointments ministers can be consulted but by convention do not make the decision. Under the recruitment principles senior appointments must be approved by the Civil Service Commission.

- However ministers can appoint anyone they wish to advise them outside the civil service, there being no safeguards in place. For example in 2010 Lord Browne, a former chairman of BP, was enlisted to advise the Prime Minister in relation to reducing the costs of running the executive. There was no formal appointment process or apparently any element of competition. It is arguable that business persons are unlikely to be successful government appointees, often being authoritarian and unfamiliar with the practices of consultation, openness and detailed accountability that are desirable in a democracy.

15.8.2 Discipline

According to one view, a civil servant, being subject to the royal prerogative, has no contract of employment and cannot enforce the terms of his employment other than those laid down by statute. At common law the Crown can dismiss a civil servant 'at pleasure', that is without notice and without giving reasons (*Dunn v R* [1896]). This is consistent with the view that there is no contract. On the other hand it has been held that there can be a contract between the Crown and a civil servant but that as a matter of public policy the contract can be overridden by the Crown's power to dismiss the civil servant at pleasure (*Riordan v War Office* [1959], but see *Reilly v R* [1934]). On this second analysis other terms of employment such as pay and conditions are enforceable against the Crown.

Modern cases have stressed that there is no inherent reason why the relationship cannot be contractual (see *Kodeeswaren v A-G for Ceylon* [1970]; *R v Civil Service Appeals Board, ex p Bruce* [1988]; *R v Lord Chancellor's Dept, ex p Nangle* [1992]). The Employment Act 1988 deems there to be a contract between the Crown and a civil servant for the purpose of making a civil servant liable for industrial action (s 30). Whether or not there is a contract it seems clear that the Crown can still dismiss at pleasure and that a contractual term which says otherwise is not enforceable. This can be regarded as a matter of public policy.

Civil servants, like other citizens, may be protected by judicial review. However in Nangle it was held that judicial review did not apply to internal disciplinary decisions unless a formal adjudicative process is involved (but see *Bruce* and *R v Civil Service Appeals Board, ex p Cunningham* [1991]). Moreover internal remedies must be used before resorting to the courts. Most civil servants are also protected by statutory unfair dismissal rules administered by industrial tribunals (Employment Rights Act 1996, s 191).

Special machinery applies to security issues. A minister can, by issuing a certificate, remove any category of Crown employee from the employment protection legislation on grounds of national security (Employment Rights Act 1996, s 193). A civil servant who is suspected of being a security risk is given a special hearing, but without the normal rights of cross-examination and legal representation, before a panel of 'three advisers'. These usually comprise two retired senior officials and a High Court judge.

Problems arise when a civil servant considers that his or her integrity is compromised, for example by being required to act for politically partisan purposes or possibly to break the law. Obeying the orders of a superior is not a defence in English law. The orthodox doctrine is that civil servants owe an absolute duty of loyalty to ministers (Section 15.7.2) and the Civil Service Code imposes a lifelong duty not to disclose official information without authority.

There are internal mechanisms to enable civil servants to express issues of conscience. These include a right of appeal to the independent Civil Service Commission (above) and special provisions relating to the Official Secrets Act (Chapter 21). Judicial review may also be available (see *R v Shaylor* [2002]).

Civil servants cannot be members of Parliament (House of Commons (Disqualification) Act 1978). The political activity of civil servants is also restricted according to the level of the individual in the policy-making hierarchy. The majority are unrestricted except while on duty or in uniform or on official premises. An 'intermediate' group can take part in political activities with the consent of their head of department. This group includes clerks, typists and officials performing specialist non-political jobs. A 'restricted' group of senior officials directly involved in policy making cannot take part in national politics at all but can indulge in local politics with the consent of their head of department. However whole departments can be exempted. Civil servants are also prohibited from taking gifts or doing other things that could create a conflict between their private interests and their official duties. A retired civil servant requires government approval before accepting employment with private sector organisations that are likely to have dealings with the government (see Treasury and Civil Service Committee, Fifth Report, Civil Service Pay and Conditions Code (HC 1989–90)).

15.8.3 Civil servants and ministerial responsibility

Under the *Carltona* doctrine (*Carltona v Comr for Works* [1943]) a minister can lawfully exercise any of his statutory powers through a civil servant in his department and need not personally exercise any power unless statute specifically so requires (eg Immigration Act 1971, s 13(5); Regulation of Investigatory Powers Act 2000, s 59). The decision remains that of the minister – the civil servant and the minister being indivisible in law (see also *Bushell v Secretary of State for the Environment* [1981]; *R (Alconbury Developments Ltd) v Secretary of State for the Environment, Transport and the Regions* [2001]). It is not clear how far this principle depends on the power of control over civil servants available to ministers, the convention of ministerial responsibility itself or simply the unreality of ministers being capable of acting personally in every case. Possible limits to the principle might be influenced by such matters. In *Oladehinde v Secretary of State for the Home Dept* [1990] the House of Lords held that a deportation decision could be made by an immigration officer on behalf of the Secretary of State. However Lord Templeman remarked (at 397) that the person exercising the power must be 'of suitable seniority in the Home Office for whom the minister accepts responsibility'. In *R v Minister of Agriculture, ex p Hamble Fisheries* [1995] Sedley J suggested (at 732) that the *Carltona* principle does not apply to the making of policy. However in *Re Golden Chemical Products Ltd* (1976) the court rejected any distinction between powers that a minister must exercise personally and those that can be delegated.

The *Carltona* principle does not apply to delegation to other ministers or outside the civil service. Thus statute is required to give a minister wider powers of delegation (eg Extradition Act 2003, s 101: decisions to senior officials in civil and diplomatic services).

The classical doctrine has been that as civil servants have no powers of their own and so cannot take decisions or do anything except and in so far as they are subject to the direction and control of ministers, a civil servant has no direct responsibility to Parliament and cannot be called to account by Parliament. Civil servants are therefore accountable to ministers, and ministers accountable to Parliament. In particular advice given to ministers by civil servants cannot be disclosed without the permission of ministers (see Freedom of Information Act 2000, s 35). According to the government, civil servants appear before parliamentary committees only with the consent of their ministers. Ministers therefore shield civil servants from outside scrutiny. In return civil servants are loyal to ministers and owe no other allegiance, thus emphasising the minister's own accountability to Parliament.

The relationship between ministers and civil servants can cause an 'accountability gap'. This is because accountability can break down where a minister blames a civil servant for some failure and subsequently directs that individual not to appear before a select committee (this is permitted under the Cabinet Office document *Departmental Evidence and Response to Select Committees* (2005)). Notoriously the Secretary of State for Trade and Industry refused to allow the civil servants involved in aspects of the Westland affair to appear before the Commons Defence Select Committee (see HC 1985–86, 519 (Cmnd 9916, 1986)). This problem has in part been addressed in the parliamentary resolutions. Although civil servants still give evidence to select committees under the direction of ministers, the minister must insist that civil servants be as helpful as possible in providing accurate, truthful and full information (HC Deb 19 March 1997, vol 292, cols 1046–47, para iv). However Parliament still lacks power to compel ministers to answer questions and cannot require civil servants to give evidence to select committees (see Section 13.6.3).

The Scott Inquiry (Section 15.6.2) revealed how civil servants have sometimes acted independently of ministers or in the expectation of subsequent ministerial ratification of their actions (HC 1995–96, 115, para D3.40). This exposed the constitutional fiction that civil servants only give advice to ministers. Civil servants concealed important questions from ministers and may even have defied ministerial instructions. Moreover, as we saw above, ministers have attempted to pass responsibility to civil servants, firstly by distinguishing between policy and operational matters and secondly by distinguishing between 'accountability' as a duty to explain and 'responsibility' as liability to take the blame (Treasury and Civil Service Select Committee, Fifth Report, *The Role of the Civil Service* (HC 1993–94, 27) para 120).

It has long been accepted that as Accounting Officer the permanent head of a department must appear before the relevant parliamentary committee. It has never been settled whether select committees can require other civil servants to attend to answer questions. In 1986 the Defence Select Committee claimed the absolute right to secure attendance from civil servants (HC 1985–86, 519). However a compromise has been arrived at whereby ministers are enjoined to permit civil servants to appear but subject to restrictions (see Cabinet Office, *Departmental Evidence and Response to Select Committees* (January 1997) para 37, replacing the so-called Osmotherly Rules). This document exhorts civil servants to be as forthcoming as possible in providing information.

Moreover civil servants cannot disclose or discuss the advice they gave to ministers, only the action they took on behalf of ministers. However the Ministerial

Code provides some protection to the civil service. If the Accounting Officer considers that a minister's action breaches requirements of propriety, regularity or value for money he or she may set out objections in writing and, if the minister decides to override the objections, the Accounting Officer may 'seek' written instructions and the Comptroller and Auditor General must be notified (Art 5.4).

15.8.4 Executive agencies and ministerial responsibility

The reorganisation of government departments into a fragmented model copied from private business, coupled with the privatisation of some governmental activities (the 'hollowing out' of the state), has further placed the classical model under strain. This is most notably the case in the relationship between ministers and chief executives of executive agencies (see Section 5.2.7). In principle ministerial responsibility applies equally to the work of executive agencies but the policy/operational distinction discussed above complicates the matter.

The principle underlying the respective functions of the agencies and the departments is that autonomy for service delivery should reside with the agency, while policy matters should be reserved for the department acting under ministerial control. Framework agreements made between the agency and the sponsoring department (sometimes with the Treasury as a party) constitute the relationship between the two. The framework agreement contains the corporate strategy and financial arrangements under which the agency will work.

A chief executive is appointed, usually for a fixed term, to be responsible for the day-to-day management of the agency. The chief executive is responsible to the minister but as Accounting Officer also appears before select committees to answer MPs' questions about the functioning of the agency. MPs have also been encouraged to approach chief executives directly on behalf of their constituents and chief executives answer written parliamentary questions. The answers are published in *Hansard* to avoid the bypassing of Parliament which might occur if chief executives responded directly to individual MPs.

It is therefore unclear how far ministers have been involved with this process. For example chief executives are subject to the direction of their minister, which would limit their competence as witnesses and Parliament's ability to investigate. However the House of Commons Public Service Committee has stated emphatically that ministers remain accountable for what goes on in agencies just as in their departments (see Public Service Committee, Second Report (HC 1995–96, 313) paras 84–91, 109–23; Cabinet Office, *Modernising Government* (Cm 4310, 2002)).

Finally the *Carltona* principle (Section 15.8.3) seems to apply to executive agencies when they are exercising functions delegated by a minister by means of the normal framework agreement (see *R v Secretary of State, ex p Sherwin* [1996]; cf Freedland, 'The Rule against Delegation and the *Carltona* Doctrine in an Agency Context' [1996] PL 19, arguing that this should only be the case where there is a clear line of decision making from the minister). In *Williams v Home Office (No 2)* [1981] the court drew a distinction between acts done by civil servants in the exercise of statutory functions conferred on ministers and routine management matters, saying that the latter are not to be regarded as the act of ministers. This is questionable in terms of the traditional doctrine of ministerial responsibility but perhaps represents a more realistic view of the nature of modern government. In *Sherwin* Brightman J thought that there might be activities of an executive agency which no one would reasonably connect with the minister but gave no example.

15.8.5 Non-ministerial government departments and ministerial responsibility

It seems that ministerial responsibility is limited in the case of a non-ministerial government department such as the Serious Fraud Office or HM Revenue and Customs to circumstances where the minister possesses specific statutory powers in relation to the department (see Section 5.2.7). This is appropriate since bodies of this kind frequently exercise quasi-judicial powers akin to those of courts or tribunals so that it is important that politicians maintain a separation in order to preserve the independence of the non-ministerial government department.

Summary

- The Prime Minister has large powers under the royal prerogative, pre-eminently to dissolve Parliament, appoint and dismiss ministers and control the government agenda. However these are largely convention, and determined political opposition could control a Prime Minister.
- As a body the Cabinet has been reduced in power in recent years, with decisions effectively being made by smaller groups within and outside the Cabinet and by departments of the executive.
- There are few constitutional laws or conventions concerning the detailed distribution of functions between departments. Political and administrative considerations rather than constitutional principle determine the number, size, shape and interrelationship of government departments. The creation of bodies outside the framework of the Crown is of greater constitutional and legal significance.
- The convention of ministerial responsibility is central to the UK constitution. Collective responsibility means that all members of the government must loyally support government policy and decisions and must not disclose internal disagreements. Individual responsibility means that each minister is answerable to Parliament for all the activities of the department under his control. It also means that civil servants are not personally accountable. From these principles follow (i) the traditional notion of the civil service as anonymous and politically neutral, having a duty to serve with unquestioning loyalty governments of any political complexion, and (ii) the secrecy that pervades the British system of government.
- The traditional doctrine of ministerial responsibility may be out of line with the practices of modern government and effectively shields the government from accountability. In particular (i) Cabinet decisions are rarely made collectively; (ii) many government bodies are not directly controlled by ministers, the creation of executive agencies reinforcing this; (iii) civil servants are increasingly expected to make political decisions and to be responsible for the financial management of their allotted activities; (iv) public functions are increasingly being given to special bodies or private bodies. Thus the traditional chain of accountability between Parliament, ministers and civil servants is weakened.
- In law civil servants are servants of the Crown. They can be dismissed 'at pleasure', that is without notice and without reason being given. However the modern cases suggest that there

Summary cont'd

can be a contractual relationship between the Crown and a civil servant and that a civil servant can be protected by the law of judicial review.

- In the light of the convention relating to ministerial responsibility civil servants are regarded as servants of the government of the day with an absolute duty of loyalty to ministers. Their advice to ministers is secret and they appear before Parliament only with the consent of ministers. They are supposed to be non-political and neutral, responsible for giving ministers objective advice and for carrying out ministerial orders. However 'special advisers' need not be neutral or appointed on merit. Their existence creates tensions within the civil service.
- The internal arrangements for the carrying out of government business involve entrusting individual civil servants with considerable decision-making responsibility and in recent years with financial accountability within the government machine. Many civil servants work in executive agencies, hived off from the central departmental structure and outside the direct control of ministers. This has led to tensions between traditional ideas of ministerial responsibility and the actual channels of accountability and has raised problems in connection with the supposed distinction between policy and operational matters.

Exercises

15.1 Consider whether the relevant laws and conventions support Bagehot's view that the Cabinet is the central institution of the UK constitution.

15.2 A general election has just been held. The Prime Minister's party has won the largest number of votes but has only 45 per cent of the seats in the Commons. The Solidarity Party, with 10 per cent of the seats. is willing to support the Prime Minister's party but only if he resigns in favour of a candidate supported by the Solidarity Party. Advise the Queen as to the constitutional position.

Suppose the Solidarity Party and the Prime Minister's party form a coalition but the coalition's programme is defeated in a vote on the Queen's Speech. The Prime Minister requests the Queen for a dissolution. Advise the Queen

What would be the position if the Opposition party had won the election and formed the coalition with the Solidarity Party but the facts were otherwise as in the above two scenarios?

15.3 'Ministerial responsibility is, in practice, an obstacle to the availability of information and to the holding of government to account' (Oliver). Discuss.

15.4 To what extent can Parliament and the public scrutinise the activities of a civil servant?

15.5 When should a minister resign?

15.6 Critically evaluate the constitutional significance of special advisers.

15.7 The government creates an executive agency to regulate motorway service areas. The Secretary of State for Consumption delegates to the agency his statutory powers to ensure the 'adequate provision of motorway services'. Under a contract made with the Secretary of State the agency promises to achieve certain targets, including a clean environment. The agency employs Grasper plc to run the Crusty Group of service areas. Due to cuts in its funding from the Secretary of State the agency does not check Grasper's performance but increases its chief executive's annual performance bonus by 100 per cent. A newspaper subsequently discovers that many of the catering staff employed by the Crusty Group are illegal immigrants and several of them have contracted food poisoning. In response to a parliamentary question, the Secretary of State asserts that the matter is no concern of his and he knows nothing about it. He also refuses to permit the agency chief executive to appear before the Select Committee for Consumption. Discuss.

Further reading

Benn, 'The Case for a Constitutional Premiership' (1980) 33 Parl Aff 7

Brazier, *Constitutional Practice: The Foundations of British Government* (3rd edn, Oxford University Press 1999) chs 2–7

Daintith and Page, *The Executive in the Constitution* (Oxford University Press 1999) chs 1–6

Dowding, *The Civil Service* (Routledge 1995) chs 1, 2, 5, 6, 8

Flinders, 'The Enduring Centrality of Individual Ministerial Responsibility within the British Constitution' (2000) 6 JLS 73

Harden, 'Money and the Constitution, Financial Control, Reporting and Audit' (1993) 13 LS 16

Hennessy, *The Hidden Wiring* (Gollancz 1995) chs 3–5, 8

Hough, 'Ministerial Responses to Parliamentary Questions: Some Recent Concerns' [2003] PL 211

Institute for Public Policy Research, *Whitehall's Black Box: Accountability and Performance in the Senior Civil Service* (2006)

Jowell and Oliver (eds), *The Changing Constitution* (6th edn, Oxford University Press 2007) chs 8, 15, 18

Power Commission, *Power to the People: An Independent Inquiry into Britain's Democracy* (Rowntree Trust 2006)

Sampson, *Who Runs This Place?* (John Murray 2004) chs 1–4, 7, 8

Thompson and Ridley (eds), *Under the Scott-Light: British Government Seen through the Scott Report* (Oxford University Press 1997)

Tomkins, *Public Law* (Clarendon Press 2003) ch 5

Vennard, 'Prime Ministerial Succession' [2008] PL 302

Woodhouse, *In Pursuit of Good Administration: Ministers, Civil Servants and Judges* (Clarendon Press 1997)

Chapter 16
Devolution

> **The England Team is the only team playing in the World Cup that is not a nation state: there is no political or cultural outlet for England's feeling of national identity. (*Observer* 13 June 2004)***

16.1 The general nature of devolution in the UK

This chapter discusses the devolution provisions for Scotland, Northern Ireland and Wales. It is not appropriate in a general book to discuss the internal systems of government within those countries in depth. We shall therefore concentrate on two general themes: (i) a comparison of the devolved regimes with the constitutional arrangements for the UK as a whole; (ii) a comparison of the extent of the powers conferred on the three regimes. The main aim is to introduce readers to the role which devolution plays in the wider UK constitution.

The UK is a union of what were the separate states of England, parts of Ireland and Scotland. Wales is a nation within the UK but has never been a state in its own right. Before the introduction of devolved government in 2000, the internal affairs of Scotland, Northern Ireland and Wales were governed by the UK central executive with what have sometimes been regarded as overtones of colonialism. This took the form of 'administrative devolution' to ministers for each territory. There was no specific democratic power base or accountability mechanism linking the ministers to their regions since the relevant minister might have an English constituency. Scotland and Northern Ireland have separate legal systems but the Supreme Court is the final court of appeal for all the UK jurisdictions except Scottish criminal cases.

In 1973 the Royal Commission on the Constitution (Cmnd 5460) asserted that government in the UK was overcentralised and recommended devolved government. Referendums were subsequently held in Scotland and Wales which foundered because they failed to obtain the required two-thirds majorities in favour of change. The Labour government that took office in 1997 was supportive of devolved government as part of an agenda of constitutional reform in favour of dispersing power. Further referendums (this time requiring only a 51 per cent majority) produced considerable public support for devolution in Scotland and significant but less support for devolution in Wales. Legislation was then enacted to give devolved powers to a Scottish Parliament (Scotland Act 1998), a Northern Ireland Assembly (Northern Ireland Act 1998) and, to a lesser extent, a Welsh Assembly (Government of Wales Act 1998). The powers of the Welsh Assembly were later expanded (Government of Wales Act 2006) but are still less than those of Scotland and Northern Ireland.

The devolution statutes could be regarded as embodying a constitution for the territory in question. The basic devolution arrangements are entrenched in statute so that they cannot be altered by the devolved regimes. On the other hand the devolution arrangements are not stable in that they can be altered by Parliament at any time. The

Welsh provisions in particular have been substantially altered, so Welsh devolution has the appearance of an experiment.

The devolution arrangements for the three territories have many features in common but there are important differences in relation to each region. In all cases the devolved structure is modelled on the UK parliamentary system but with different voting systems which make strong executive governments less likely. In the cases of Scotland and Northern Ireland the Acts do not specify the powers of the devolved governments but specify what they cannot do. They can legislate on any other matter. Wales by contrast can legislate only on matters specifically assigned to it in the legislation. Scotland, with its history as an independent state, has the greatest devolved powers. Provisions for ensuring that the devolved regimes keep within their powers are similar in all three cases, relying heavily on the courts. To this extent devolution has 'juridified' the constitution. The devolved governments have very limited tax-raising powers. They are funded mainly by block grants from the UK Parliament. The Scotland and Northern Ireland governments have certain limited tax-raising powers and only the Northern Ireland government has borrowing powers. Thus there is incomplete accountability to voters.

In the case of Northern Ireland there is provision for an inclusive form of democracy reflecting the divisive history of the province. Devolution in Northern Ireland raises more fundamental issues than is the case elsewhere. This is partly because the arrangements are concerned with fundamental disputes about the legitimacy of the state itself and partly because they are influenced by the international concerns of relationships with the neighbouring Republic of Ireland. The devolved powers of Wales currently fall below those in the other regions and it is not clear what the purpose of devolution is. Wales does not have a separate legal system. However there is a mechanism for evolutionary expansion (see Section 16.4). There are also requirements for substantive economic and social aspirations of a communitarian nature. These represent a paternalistic approach to Welsh devolution.

There is no federal element. The devolution arrangements do not affect the unlimited legal power of the UK Parliament to make laws for the devolved regions and to override laws made by the devolved regimes (eg Scotland Act 1998, s 28(7)). The UK government retains ministers responsible for each of the devolved regimes. The devolved arrangements, including the structure of the executive and the proceedings of the legislative assemblies, cannot be changed by the devolved bodies. Thus there is limited room for evolution generated by the wishes of people in the devolved areas, the progress of devolution remaining centralised in the UK.

Although the law is not federal there are political mechanisms which give protection to the devolved governments. Under the 'Sewel Convention' (1999), the UK Parliament does not legislate for a devolved territory without the consent of its legislature (see HL Deb 1998, vol 592, col 791). There are also non-legally binding 'concordats' between each UK government department and the devolved administrations. These put in place principles for coordinating the activities of the governments, for example through a joint ministerial committee, and may buttress the kind of secretive informality characteristic of the UK constitution (see *Memorandum of Understanding and Supplementary Agreements* (Cm 4444, 2001; Cm 4806, Cm 5420, 1999); Poivier, 'The Function of Intergovernmental Agreements' [2001] PL 134; Rawlings, 'Concordats of the Constitution' (2000) 116 LQR 257).

The courts are responsible for ensuring that the limits of the devolved powers are respected. The devolution legislation therefore marks a change in our constitutional arrangements away from reliance upon informal and political methods and towards juridification, although devices such as the Sewel Convention make this far from complete. This leads to the question of whether the devolution arrangements can be regarded as 'constitutional' and so subject to a special approach to interpretation (Chapter 1). We might invoke matters such as the importance of the devolved arrangements with respect to the fundamental concerns of the particular community. On this basis the Northern Ireland arrangements have a particularly strong claim to be regarded as constitutional. Indeed in *Robinson v Secretary of State for Northern Ireland* [2002], Lord Hoffmann asserted (at [33]) that the Northern Ireland Act 1998 is to be construed:

> against the background of the political situation in Northern Ireland and the principles laid down by the Belfast Agreement for a new start. These facts and background form part of the admissible background to the construction of the Act just as much as the Revolution, the Convention and the federalist papers are the background to construing the Constitution of the USA.

It is important that there are provisions for dealing with issues that cross boundaries and for settling disputes between the different layers of government. Characteristic of the UK constitution these tend to be political rather than strictly legal, although some are formal in the sense that they are contained in published documents such as concordats (above). There are also legal arrangements for interaction between the different levels. These allow functions to be shared or transferred in both directions between the UK government and the devolved regimes (see eg Scotland Act 1998, ss 63, 108, 109).

The following sections discuss the main features of each regime. Unless stated otherwise the relevant provisions in Wales and Northern Ireland are similar to those in Scotland. The detailed matters that are devolved to each regime are significantly different but will not be discussed here. They are set out in schedules to the statutes.

16.2 Scotland

Scotland was a separate nation state from 1010 until 1706, although after 1603 the Crowns of England and Scotland were united. Since the sixteenth-century Reformation there had been some cultural assimilation between the two countries but also quarrels between Catholics and Protestants. In 1689 Scotland offered its Crown to William and Mary on the same revolutionary terms as in England (Chapter 4). After quarrels between the two Parliaments, the Treaty of Union 1706 agreed to abolish the separate Scottish and English Parliaments and to create a Parliament of Great Britain.

The Union was unpopular but was brought about by economic interest in Scotland and fear of invasion in England. The treaty was confirmed by separate Acts of each Parliament (Act of Union with England 1706; Act of Union with Scotland 1706). Scottish rebellion on behalf of the Stuarts' claim to the throne continued until defeat at Culloden in 1746. The Acts of Union are still in force. They preserve the separate Scottish legal system and Church and safeguard the private rights of Scottish subjects. Scotland has its own judicial system, and its Church, although not 'established' in the sense that the Crown and Parliament are not part of its governance, enjoys independence by statute (Church of Scotland Act 1921). There is an argument that the UK Parliament cannot override these aspects of the Acts of Union, although section 37 of the Scotland Act 1998, which makes the Acts of Union subject to the 1998 Act, assumes that the UK Parliament can do so (see Section 8.4.2).

The Scotland Act 1998 creates the greatest freedom of the three regimes. It is modelled more closely on the UK's parliamentary system than is the case with the other devolved regions, the Act giving legal force to provisions akin to those which in the UK constitution are conventions. There is a Scottish Parliament and a Scottish executive responsible to it. The Scottish executive has somewhat less power in relation to the Parliament than its UK counterpart.

Scottish devolution claims to uphold four basic aspirations (*Shaping Scotland's Parliament* (HMSO 1999); see Procedures Committee, *The Founding Principles of the Scottish Parliament* (Third Report 2003, SP Paper 818)). These are political guidance rather than legally enforceable provisions. They are:

- sharing of power between the people, Parliament and the executive (but there is no legal provision other than periodic general elections to enable the people to exercise power);
- accountability of the executive to the Parliament and the Parliament to the people;
- access and participation;
- equal opportunities.

However the structure of the devolution legislation is closely modelled on that of the UK parliamentary system with its reliance on a central executive responsible to Parliament and with no direct involvement of the people other than voting in party-oriented elections. On the other hand the introduction of proportional representation and the relatively stronger powers of the Parliament in relation to government appointments may marginally alter the balance in favour of Parliament.

16.2.1 The Scottish Parliament

The Scottish Parliament can make Acts on any matter other than those specified in the 1998 Act (below). The Parliament comprises 129 members, of whom 56 are elected by proportional representation in eight regions (see Section 12.7.1). There is therefore more likely to be a coalition government involving more than one party in Scotland than is the case in the UK, where the present coalition is relatively unusual.

Entitlement to vote is based on that for local government elections (s 11). It includes adult resident citizens of the UK and EU citizens. (EU citizens cannot vote in UK parliamentary elections.)

Before 1998 Scotland was entitled to at least 71 seats in the UK Parliament, thus making it overrepresented in terms of its population. Section 86(1) of the Scotland Act 1998 abolishes this entitlement and places Scotland under the same regime as England in terms of the criteria for defining constituencies (Chapter 12). This has reduced the number of Scottish MPs to 59. Originally the constituencies for the Scottish Parliament were the same as those for the UK Parliament. However, by virtue of the Scottish Parliament (Constituencies) Act 2004, the link between the two has been severed.

Membership of the Scottish Parliament is subject to similar disqualifications to those applying to the UK Parliament, mainly the holding of certain public offices (s 15; see Section 12.4). There is no residence requirement in either case. However, unlike in the UK Parliament, a citizen of an EU country can be a member of the Scottish Parliament (MSP) (s 16). The same person cannot be a candidate in more than one constituency but, unlike the case in Wales, can stand in both a regional election and a local constituency election in the same region (s 5). The constituency election has priority. If the candidate wins the constituency he or she must be excluded from of the regional count. The same person can be a member of the Scottish Parliament and the UK Parliament.

The Presiding Officer, elected by the House for the duration of the Parliament (s 19), has a formal constitutional role. This includes submitting bills for royal assent (below), recommending the appointment of the First Minister, advising a dissolution (below) and proposing the date of the general election.

The Scottish Parliament sits for four years, after which it is automatically dissolved. A general election must be held on the first Thursday in May in the fourth year after the previous ordinary general election, after which the Parliament must meet within seven days (s 2). The Presiding Officer may vary this by up to one month (s 2). The Parliament can be dissolved earlier by the Queen following a two-thirds majority vote – an unlikely event – or following a proposal from the Presiding Officer where the Parliament fails to designate a First Minister within 28 days (below) (s 3). This might arise where an administration finds itself deadlocked because of tensions within a coalition government. Thus, unlike the case with the UK Parliament, the First Minister cannot trigger a general election (similar arrangements are currently being proposed for the UK Parliament; see Section 11.3). The electoral system combines the traditional 'first past the post' method with a 'party list' system (Chapter 12).

The Scottish Parliament can legislate generally, including altering Acts of the UK Parliament, subject to the restrictions in the Act (ss 28–30, Sch 4). These concern both subject matters and particular UK statutes, mainly those of constitutional importance, including of course the Scotland Act 1998 itself. Thus Scotland cannot change the devolved arrangements. The UK Parliament retains its full power to legislate for Scotland, thus overriding the devolution provisions (s 28(7)). However this may be politically unreal. Indeed, according to the Sewel Convention (Section 16.1), the UK Parliament will not intervene in a devolved area without the consent of the Scottish Parliament. (The normal procedure is a 'Sewel Resolution'.)

Acts of the Scottish Parliament require royal assent (Scotland Act 1998, s 28). Although sometimes called 'primary' legislation, Acts of the Scottish Parliament are strictly subordinate legislation, owing their validity only to the Scotland Act 1998 (see Human Rights Act 1998, s 21: not primary legislation under Act). They can be set aside by the courts if they are outside the devolution provisions and also perhaps under the ordinary law of judicial review, for example if they are 'unreasonable'. However the courts are unwilling to find that a decision made by a democratic body is unreasonable. Thus in the case of *In Petition of Axa Insurance* (2010) the Court of Session accepted that judicial review applied but the claim failed because the legislation at issue did not pass the threshold of what is unreasonable, which depends on the circumstances of each case (see Section 17.1). The court took into account that unlike for example local government, which can act only within specific statutory powers, the Scottish Parliament has wide lawmaking powers which should be respected.

The validity of the procedure leading to an enactment does not affect the Act's validity (s 28(5)) but otherwise Acts of the Scottish Parliament that are outside its competence 'are not law' (s 28). Thus, unlike UK statutes (see Section 20.3), Scottish legislation that violates the Convention rights set out in the Human Rights Act 1998 is of no effect. Where a measure is ambiguous it must be interpreted narrowly in favour of its validity (s 101).

The following are the main limits on the power of the Scottish Parliament (s 29):

- Although it can alter UK statutes it cannot, except in minor respects, amend the Scotland Act 1998 itself or various UK statutes, including the parts of the Act of Union dealing with free trade (Sch 4). (Possibly neither the Scottish nor the UK Parliament can amend the Act of Union in as far as it includes certain basic rights; see Section 8.4.2.)
- It cannot alter any law which 'would form part of the law of a country or territory other than Scotland, or confer or remove functions exercisable otherwise than in or as regards Scotland'. The UK government can specify these functions (s 30(3)). This is of particular significance in relation to fishing.
- It cannot override European law or rights under the European Convention on Human Rights incorporated by the Human Rights Act 1998. However the specific procedures applicable under the Human Rights Act itself do not apply to Scotland, so Scottish courts have the potential to develop their own scheme of remedies for human rights violations (see *Somerville v Scottish Ministers* [2007]; see further Beatson *et al*, 2008, ch 8). However UK ministers have the exclusive power to bring EC law into effect (ss 52, 54, 57(2)).
- It has taxation powers limited to altering the basic rate of income tax by three pence in the pound (s 73). However most of its finance is derived from the UK government. These taxation limits are currently being reconsidered by the government with a view to increasing the powers of the Scottish Parliament.
- There are 'reserved matters' on which only the UK Parliament can legislate (s 30, Sch 5). They include the most basic functions of government and important constitutional matters. The main reserved matters are matters affecting the Crown (but not the exercise of the royal prerogative); the civil service; electoral arrangements (an important control); the registration and funding of political parties; the Union with England; the UK Parliament; the higher Scottish courts; international relations; defence and national security; treason; fiscal, economic and monetary policy; currency; financial services and markets; money laundering; border controls; transport safety and regulation; media policy; employment regulation; certain health matters; the regulation of key professions; and social security. Reserved matters can be altered by Order in Council (s 30(2)).

There are provisions for guarding against *ultra vires* legislation. A member of the Scottish executive in charge of a bill must, on or before the introduction of the bill in Parliament, state that in his view the provisions of the bill would be within the legislative competence of Parliament (s 31(1)). The Presiding Officer, who submits bills for royal assent (s 32), must on or before its introduction 'decide whether or not in his view' the bill is within the powers of the Parliament (s 31(2)). This statement does not block the bill. These provisions generate political accountability but have no legal effect on the bill since only a court can decide what a law means. The Advocate General, the Lord Advocate or the UK Attorney General can require a bill to be referred to the Supreme Court (s 33).

Somewhat controversially due to the 'colonial' flavour of such a power, the Secretary of State can prohibit a bill from being sent for royal assent where she or he 'has reasonable ground to believe' that the bill would be incompatible with international obligations or the interests of national security or defence or would have an adverse effect on the law relating to reserved matters (s 35). (See also section 58 in relation to the Scottish executive.)

The UK government can make subordinate legislation remedying *ultra vires* Acts of the Scottish Parliament and the Scottish executive (s 107). The court can protect people who may have relied on invalid laws by removing the retrospective effect of the invalidity or suspending the invalidity to allow the defect to be corrected (s 102).

The Parliament and its members do not enjoy parliamentary privilege, although its members do have absolute privilege in defamation (s 41; see Section 11.7). Parliament's power to control its own procedure is limited by the Act (s 22) but it does have the right to require any person, including ministers, to attend, give information and disclose documents in relation to matters for which the Scottish executive has responsibility (ss 23–25). This contrasts with the murkiness of the practices surrounding ministerial responsibility in the UK. In practice however the Scottish Parliament seems to have followed the Westminster model, according to which the executive dominates parliamentary processes and decides what information to disclose.

There have been innovations in practice which have made the Scottish Parliament more proactive than the UK Parliament. Scottish committees not only scrutinise the executive and revise legislation but may initiate legislation and conduct inquiries that involve direct engagement with the people. A public petitions system has been introduced and there are Internet-based information and discussion mechanisms.

After a slow start the Scottish Parliament has enacted a substantial amount of legislation, particularly concerning social matters and public services, which has markedly distinguished the regime from its English counterpart. These include free personal care for the elderly, greater support for students, rescue packages for fisheries and the victims of foot and mouth disease, land reform, mental health and freedom of information.

16.2.2 The Scottish executive

The Scottish executive comprises a First Minister, ministers, junior ministers and law officers (Lord Advocate and Solicitor General (Scotland Act 1998, ss 44–50)). The Crown is the formal head of the Scottish executive. The capacity of the Crown in relation to Scotland is separated from that of the Crown in relation to the UK, in effect treating the two as separate entities so that they can enter into property transactions with each other for example (s 99).

Within the devolved areas the Scottish Parliament can confer functions on Scottish ministers either individually or collectively (s 52). Statutory and royal prerogative powers previously exercised by UK ministers are automatically transferred to Scottish ministers (s 53). In order to provide flexibility additional functions outside devolved matters can be given to Scottish ministers either alone or jointly with UK ministers by Order in Council (s 63), for which they are presumably accountable to the UK Parliament.

The principles for forming and dismissing the Scottish executive are broadly similar to the conventions applying to the UK Parliament. Since matters such as the appointment and dismissal of ministers and the dissolution of the Scottish Parliament are covered by statute it is not clear whether the Queen has any residual personal power in relation to these matters (see Section 14.4). The Scotland Act 1998 is not explicit as to whether it entirely replaces any relevant royal prerogative powers (see Section 14.6.5). The Scottish rules are more structured, give a larger role to Parliament and give a significant role to the Presiding Officer, whereas the conventions in the UK rely heavily on the outgoing Prime Minister when there is a change of government, and no other office holder except the monarch has a formal role. The detailed provisions are compared in the following box.

Scotland: forming and removing governments

- Everything is statutory (Scotland Act 1998). The rules cannot be changed by the Scottish Parliament. (The UK relies mainly on conventions, but the UK provisions are subject to reform proposals (see Section 11.3).)
- The Parliament ends after four years. This triggers a general election on the first Thursday in May (s 2). (In the UK Parliament must end after five years from first meeting (Parliament Act 1911). This triggers a general election under statutory arrangements.)
- The monarch dissolves the Parliament after a two-thirds majority vote. This triggers an 'extraordinary' general election (s 3). The First Minister has no power to dissolve the Parliament. (There is no UK equivalent. By convention the monarch must dissolve Parliament on the advice of the Prime Minister. This triggers a general election under statutory arrangements.)
- The Parliament is also dissolved if no First Minister is nominated within 28 days of a 'trigger' event (below). This also triggers an 'extraordinary' general election (s 3). (Under the UK convention the monarch dissolves Parliament if no leader can command a majority in the Commons or at any time on the advice of the Prime Minister.)
- The new Parliament must meet with seven days of the general election (ss 2(3)(b), 3(2)(c), 4). (In the UK there is no fixed date. The proclamation dissolving Parliament summons the successor on a specified date, which is usually about one week later. By convention Parliament must meet annually.)
- The monarch appoints the First Minister on the nomination of the Parliament (s 46). The Presiding Officer recommends the nomination to the Queen (s 46(4)). Presumably she must accept. (By convention in the UK the monarch appoints the Prime Minister on the advice of the outgoing Prime Minister. This must be the person commanding a majority in the Commons.)
- The Parliament must nominate the First Minister within 28 days of a 'triggering' event (s 46):
  (i) a general election or extraordinary general election;
  (ii) the resignation of the First Minister. The First Minister can resign at any time and must do so if the government is defeated on a vote of confidence. The First Minister remains in office until a successor is appointed (s 45(3)).
  (iii) the First Minister ceases to be a member of the Scottish Parliament, except on dissolution, when the trigger event is (i).

If there has been no nomination after 28 days the Parliament is dissolved, leading to an extraordinary general election and thus starting the process again. (There is no UK equivalent here.)

- If the First Minister cannot act or the office is vacant, the Presiding Officer appoints an acting First Minister from among MSPs (or former MSPs in the event of a dissolution; s 45(4), (5)). (There is no UK equivalent; Cabinet makes the arrangements.)
- The monarch appoints other ministers and law officers (the Lord Advocate and Solicitor General) on the nomination of the First Minister with the agreement of the Parliament (ss 47–49). All ministers but not the law officers must be MSPs (ss 47, 48). (The UK convention is that the monarch appoints all ministers and law officers on the advice of the Prime Minister. All must be MPs or members of the House of Lords.)
- The First Minister can dismiss ministers (ss 47(3), 49(4)). The First Minister can dismiss law officers only with the approval of the Parliament (s 48(1)). (Under the UK convention the monarch can dismiss ministers and law officers on the advice of the PM.)
- Ministers and law officers can resign at any time and must resign if they are defeated in a vote of confidence (ss 47(3), 48(2), 49(4)). They lose office immediately, except that the Advocate General continues in office for essential functions until a replacement is appointed (ss 47(3)(d), 49(4)(d), 48(3)). (The UK has a similar convention but after a vote of confidence ministers and law officers probably do not lose office until they are replaced.)
- Ministers lose office if they cease to be MSPs, except on dissolution, when they stay in office until the election (ss 47(2)(e), 49(4)(e)). (The UK convention is that ministers must resign if they cease to be MPs, except on dissolution.)

- The law officers are the Lord Advocate and the Solicitor General for Scotland. They can be but need not be MSPs. They can participate but cannot vote in the Parliament (s 27). Unlike ministers they cannot be dismissed without the agreement of the Parliament (s 48(1)). The Parliament cannot interfere with the independence of the Lord Advocate as head of the criminal prosecution and investigation of death systems (ss 29(2)(e), 48(5)). (The UK law officers are ministers and members of Parliament and dismissible by the Prime Minister (see Section 15.6). There is also an Advocate General for Scotland, who is responsible for giving advice on Scottish matters to the UK government (s 87).)
- Ministers in the UK government cannot hold office in the Scottish executive (s 44(3)). However MSPs can sit in the UK Parliament and be UK ministers.
- In relation to the continuing role of the UK government in respect of Scotland, there are special committees in Parliament to examine Scottish affairs and a Secretary of State for Scotland accountable to the UK Parliament.
- The civil service is part of the UK civil service and subject to the UK law regulating the civil service. Management of the civil service is not a devolved matter. Civil servants are however appointed by and presumably responsible to Scottish ministers (s 51). Thus there may be a conflict of loyalty. However since the Crown

in relation to the Scottish executive is a different entity from the Crown in relation to the UK government (s 91), their primary loyalty is to Scottish ministers. They are however responsible to Scottish ministers only in relation to functions exercised by those ministers. Conflicts of loyalty might therefore still arise in relation to functions exercised jointly by Scottish and UK ministers.

- Ministerial accountability may be more effective in the Scottish Parliament than is the case in the UK Parliament. The Scottish Parliamentary Standards Commissioner Act 2002 permits the Parliamentary Standards Commissioner to investigate complaints that an MSP has breached the Code of Conduct and report the findings to the Scottish Parliament. A complaint by an aggrieved MSP that a minister has breached the Scottish Ministerial Code by improperly refusing to disclose information may be made to the First Minister. If this avenue is not fruitful, the complaint can be referred by the MSP to the Presiding Officer as a dispute between MSPs. If the Presiding Officer were either unwilling or unable to resolve the matter, he or she might decide to refer it to the Scottish Parliament's Standards and Public Appointments Committee, which could by motion recommend that a member's rights and privileges be withdrawn if the complaint were upheld. However ministerial openness seems less controversial than in Westminster.

16.2.3 The courts

Scotland has its own court system. However civil appeals are decided by the Supreme Court, which has jurisdiction over the whole of the UK, while criminal appeals are decided wholly within the Scottish courts. Scottish criminal law is markedly different from that in England. However there need not be uniformity in the civil law (see *Mackintosh v Lord Advocate* [1876]; *R v Manchester Stipendiary Magistrate, ex p Granada Television Ltd* [2001] at 304).

The most senior judges (the Lord President of the Court of Session and the Lord Justice Clerk) are appointed by the monarch on a recommendation from the Prime Minister on the nomination of the First Minister (s 95). Other judges are appointed on the recommendation of the First Minister. In some respects Scottish judges appear to have stronger protection against political interference than their UK counterparts (Chapter 8). Senior judges can be dismissed for inability, neglect of duty or misbehaviour only on a recommendation by the First Minister following a resolution of the Parliament (s 95). The resolution can be made only on the basis of a written report from a tribunal, chaired by a member of the Privy Council who has held high judicial office, concluding that the judge is unfit for office on one of these grounds. In the case of the Lord President and the Lord Justice Clerk, the Prime Minister must be consulted.

The courts have a special role in relation to 'devolution issues'. These are (Sch 6):

- whether the Parliament has exceeded its powers;
- whether a member of the executive has acted outside his or her devolved competence or violated rights under the Human Rights Act 1998 or European Community law;
- any other question about whether a function is within devolved competence;
- any other question arising by virtue of the Act about reserved matters.

Devolution issues can arise in any legal proceedings. A devolution issue is ultimately decided by the Supreme Court, either on appeal or by way of a reference from a lower court. In addition the Lord Advocate or the Advocate General can directly refer to the Supreme Court any devolution issue, including perhaps hypothetical issues – an innovation in the UK. In English and Welsh courts the UK Attorney General can bring proceedings and in Northern Ireland courts the Advocate General for Northern Ireland. So far the devolution cases have mainly concerned human rights issues that do not involve the devolution arrangements as such (but see *In Petition of AXA Insurance* [2010]; see Section 16.2.1).

16.3 Northern Ireland

Devolved powers are more limited in Northern Ireland than in Scotland. The history of Ireland is complex and raises fundamental political issues about the sharing of political power in Northern Ireland and its relationship with the UK. Disagreements centre on divisions between the Catholic and Protestant communities and on a history of imposed settlement from England and Scotland. Broadly speaking the majority Protestant community prefers to remain an integral part of the UK, while the Catholic community would prefer union with the neighbouring Republic of Ireland.

Ireland had been nominally subject to the English Crown from the tenth century. According to the English story, laws made by the Irish Parliament had been subject to English statutes and approval by the King in Council since 1494 ('Poyning's Law'). However until Tudor times England effectively controlled only an area around Dublin called the Pale. Henry VIII and Elizabeth I attempted to extend English administration to the whole of Ireland, precipitating rebellion followed by confiscation of land and extensive settlement by English and Scots Protestants in what is now Northern Ireland. Cromwell's regime during the 1650s consolidated this policy with large-scale massacres. The conquest of Ireland was completed in 1690 when William III, in alliance with France and supported by the Pope, defeated the deposed Catholic King of England, James II, at the Battle of the Boyne.

After a series of violent rebellions against Protestant supremacy, the Acts of Union of 1800 joined Britain and Ireland into the UK, thus creating the UK Parliament. The Irish Parliament was abolished in favour of Irish representation in the UK Parliament. The Acts of Union declared that the Union was to last 'forever'. They also protected the United Church of England and Ireland, but the repeal of this provision by the Irish Church Act 1879 has been upheld (*Ex p Canon Selwyn* (1872)).

Unrest punctuated by periods of violence continued throughout the nineteenth and twentieth centuries. In the late nineteenth and early twentieth centuries the question of 'Irish home rule' was among the most important questions in UK politics. It had profound constitutional implications. It weakened the personal authority of the monarch, who unwisely took sides in the dispute and generated dispute about the most fundamental principles of the constitution, including the nature of the UK Parliament. It was a fundamental reason for the enactment of the Parliament Act 1911 (see Section 11.6), which removed the House of Lord's power to veto a bill approved by the Commons. The Government of Ireland Act 1914 gave internal home rule to Ireland.

From 1916 there was a period of violent rebellion in favour of complete independence from the UK. The UK attempted to impose a compromise in the form of the Government of Ireland Act 1920. This partitioned Ireland between what is now the Republic of Ireland and the six counties of Northern Ireland. The Act introduced a devolved government in Northern Ireland. The Irish Free State (Constitution) Act 1922 purported to give the rest of Ireland internal self-government.

Both measures were ignored in the Republic of Ireland, which created its own constitution based upon the sovereignty of the people. This constitution applied to the whole of Ireland, although it was ineffective in the north. As a result there were conflicting legal orders, each being valid from its internal viewpoint. Eventually the UK recognised the independence of the Republic (Ireland Act 1949) but provided that 'in no event will Northern Ireland cease to be part of the UK without the consent of the Parliament of Northern Ireland' (s 1(2)).

From 1972, following continuing violence resulting from perceived discrimination against Catholics, direct rule from Westminster was imposed and, characteristically of UK government, stringent emergency legislation was introduced. A series of agreements attempted to engineer a compromise by creating machinery for inter-community negotiations (Anglo-Irish Agreement 1985; 'Downing Street Declaration' (Cm 2422, 1994)). These led to the Belfast, or Good Friday, Agreement (Cm 3883, 1998) between the two governments and the main political parties in Northern Ireland. This provides for the restoration of devolved government, the amendment of the Irish constitution to accept that Northern Ireland is currently controlled by the UK, and the creation of various consultative bodies representing the interests of the UK, Northern Ireland and the Republic of Ireland (North/South Ministerial Council, British–Irish Council, British–Irish Intergovernmental Conference). The Good Friday Agreement was endorsed by 71 per cent of voters in Northern Ireland and 94 per cent in the Republic of Ireland in separate referendums and led to the present devolution arrangements.

The Northern Ireland Act 1998 attempts to ensure a balance between the competing communities. It is sometimes characterised as an example of deliberative democracy and liberal pluralism (Chapter 2). It restricts the political freedom of the legislature and executive to a greater extent than is the case in the rest of the UK. The overriding power of Parliament to make law for Northern Ireland is not affected (s 5(6)). Ministers are directly elected by the Assembly in accordance with the balance of the parties within it. Thus the system is very different from the UK's traditional system, which concentrates power in the leader of the largest party. The Northern Ireland devolution settlement also provides for the people to vote in a referendum to leave the UK and for the Republic of Ireland to participate in the affairs of Northern Ireland. The Assembly's powers are more limited than is the case with Scotland, and the UK Secretary of State has stronger powers.

The following are the main provisions of the Act:

- Northern Ireland remains part of the UK and the status of Northern Ireland will be altered only with the consent of a majority of its electorate (s 1). If a referendum favours a united Ireland, the Secretary of State is required to 'make proposals' to implement this by agreement with the Irish government (s 1).
- The Northern Ireland Assembly is elected by a single transferable vote (see Section 12.7.1).
- The Assembly sits for a fixed four-year term but can be dissolved on a resolution supported by two-thirds of its members, or by the monarch on the advice of the Secretary of State, or if a Chief Minister or Deputy Chief Minister cannot be elected within six weeks of the first meeting of the Assembly (ss 16, 32). (See *Robinson v Secretary of State for Northern Ireland* [2002].)
- If 30 members petition the Assembly in relation to any matter to be voted on, the vote shall require cross-community support (s 42).

- The Assembly can legislate generally in relation to matters exclusively within Northern Ireland except in relation to matters which are excluded (s 6). As in Scotland the Assembly's powers are subject to EC law and to the rights protected by the Human Rights Act 1998. It can raise certain taxes but not the main taxes that apply generally throughout the UK. Unlike in Scotland excluded matters are of two kinds: 'excepted' matters and 'reserved' matters, listed in Schedules 2 and 3. The Assembly cannot legislate on excepted matters unless ancillary to other matters. It can legislate on reserved matters and on ancillary matters with the consent of the Secretary of State (ss 6, 8, 10). Policing and justice finally became devolved matters in 2010. Discrimination on the grounds of religious belief or political opinion is outside the competence of the Assembly, and certain statutes (European Communities Act 1972; Human Rights Act 1998; parts of the Justice (Northern Ireland) Act 2002) cannot be altered (s 7).
- The Presiding Officer introduces bills to the Assembly. If the Presiding Officer decides that a bill is outside the powers of the Assembly he must refuse to introduce it (s 10). (Cf Scotland, where the bill is not blocked.)
- Acts of the Assembly require royal assent (s 5). Unlike the case in Scotland, where this is a matter for the Presiding Officer, the Secretary of State submits bills for royal assent (s 14). He can refuse to submit a bill if he thinks it is outside the competence of the Assembly or contains provisions incompatible with international obligations, the interests of defence or national security, or the protection of public safety or public order, or would have an adverse effect on the operation of the single market within the UK.
- The First Minister lacks the discretionary power of a UK Prime Minister to appoint or dismiss other ministers or dissolve the legislature. Instead there is a bipartisan arrangement for power sharing, ensuring that both unionists and nationalists play a part. The First Minister and Deputy First Minister are elected jointly by the Assembly from its members. This requires a majority of the Assembly and also separate majorities of unionists and nationalists (s 16). The First and Deputy First Ministers must both lose office if either resigns or ceases to be a member of the Assembly. Subject to a maximum of ten, which can be increased by the Secretary of State (s 17(4)), and to the approval of the Assembly, the First and Deputy First Ministers jointly decide on the number of Northern Ireland ministers heading departments and forming a Cabinet. Ministers are then nominated by the political parties from members of the Assembly in accordance with a formula designed to reflect the balance of parties in the Assembly (s 18). Assembly committees must also reflect party strengths.
- A minister can be dismissed by his or her party's nominating officer and loses office on ceasing to be a member of the Assembly other than after a dissolution (s 18). Ministers collectively lose office when a new Assembly is elected, where a party is excluded on a vote of confidence, where a new determination as to the number of ministers is made or as prescribed by Standing Order (s 18).
- Ministers and political parties can be excluded for up to 12 months (renewable) by the Assembly on the grounds that they are not committed to peace or have otherwise broken their oath of office (s 30). The motion must have the support of at least 30 members (from a total of between 96 and 108) and must be moved by the First and Deputy First Ministers jointly or by the Presiding Officer of the Assembly if required to do so by the Secretary of State. The Secretary of State must take into account the

propensity to violence and cooperation with the authorities of the excluded person. The resolution must have cross-party support.

- Ministers must take a pledge of office which includes a Ministerial Code of Conduct (s 16(10), Sch 4). The Code requires the 'strictest standards of propriety, accountability, openness, good community relations and equality and avoiding or declaring conflicts of interest'. Any direct or indirect pecuniary interests that members of the public might reasonably think could influence ministers' judgement must be registered. The Code is similar to the Ministerial Code for UK ministers and requires compliance with the Nolan Principles of Public Life (Chapter 5). In Northern Ireland, unlike the rest of the UK, it might therefore be enforceable in the courts.
- The Attorney General for Northern Ireland is the government's principle legal adviser and representative. Although the Attorney General cannot be a member of the Assembly, he or she can participate in its debates but cannot vote. The Attorney is appointed for a single term of five years, and dismissed, by the First Minister and Deputy First Minister jointly. The office has greater security than its Scottish equivalent in that dismissal is only on the ground of misbehaviour or inability and requires a proposal from a special tribunal (s 24). There is also an Advocate General for Northern Ireland, who shares certain functions with the Attorney General. The post of Advocate General must be held by the UK Attorney General (Justice (Northern Ireland) Act 2002, s 27, Sch 7). Thus governmental legal arrangements are less independent than is the case in Scotland since the Advocate is appointed and dismissed by the UK Prime Minister without safeguards.
- As in Scotland, devolution issues can arise in any legal proceedings and can also be referred directly to the Supreme Court. In Northern Ireland courts the power to do so and to defend legal proceedings lies with the Attorney General for Northern Ireland and the Advocate General for Northern Ireland; in England and Wales the UK Attorney General can bring proceedings, and in Scotland the Advocate General (Sch 10).
- There is a separate civil service for Northern Ireland but the functions of the Civil Service Commissioners (dealing with appointments and standards) are reserved matters (Sch 3).
- There are human rights and equal opportunities commissioners with powers to advise government and support legal proceedings.

16.4 Wales

Wales was never a separate state but consisted of a number of principalities which were gradually assimilated by the English. Until Tudor times there was continuing hostility between the English Kings and the Welsh rulers. The largest of the principalities passed into English rule in 1084 (Statute of Wales) and the English local government system was imposed by the Statute of Rhuddlan (1284), when much of north Wales had been conquered by Edward I. England claimed control over the whole of Wales by the sixteenth century and imposed the English language and administration (Act of the Union of Wales 1536). In 1543 a system of Welsh courts was introduced to apply English law. There were Welsh representatives in the English Parliament and a separate Welsh Assembly was abolished in 1689. A single court system for England and Wales was introduced in 1830.

Although there have always been voices in favour of Welsh independence the political pressures are less clear than in the case of Scotland, and in economic terms Wales and England are more closely assimilated. Earlier proposals for Welsh devolution in the Wales Act 1978 were defeated by a referendum and the current proposals were only narrowly approved.

The system of devolution created by the Government of Wales Act 1998 is a weaker form of devolution than the forms in Scotland and Northern Ireland. Unlike the Scottish Parliament and the Northern Ireland Assembly, the Welsh Assembly can legislate only on prescribed subjects. Thus it requires a positive power to make law as opposed to being able to do anything that is not forbidden.

Originally all powers, both lawmaking and executive, were vested in the Assembly itself, with flexible powers for delegation to committees and secretaries. Wales has no separate judicial system. The Welsh system was a hybrid of a local government model based on committees formed out of an elected assembly, a parliamentary model and an administrative model based on the former Welsh Office of the UK government. The Assembly was confined to making subordinate legislation under powers that were previously exercised by UK ministers under particular statutes or were subsequently conferred on it by statute.

However the Government of Wales Act 2006 has substantially increased the powers of the Assembly and creates a system of ministers responsible to the Assembly on a similar basis to that in Scotland. The Act therefore introduces a separation of powers between legislature and executive. It replaces most of the 1998 Act.

Under the 2006 Act the Welsh Assembly can do anything that could be done by an Act of Parliament on any of the subjects designated by the Act. Thus the need for a positive power to make a law still applies. The designated subjects include agriculture, ancient monuments, economic development, education, environment, food, fisheries, health, highways and transport, housing, local government, the National Assembly, public administration, social welfare, sport, tourism, town and country planning, water supply and sewage, and the Welsh language. Measures must take effect exclusively within Wales, or in the case of enforcement and incidental matters in England and Wales (s 94). As in Scotland this is subject to EC law and to human rights under the Human Rights Act 1998 and also to restrictions limiting the creation of criminal offences and the alteration of certain statutes.

Initially the extended power takes the form of 'Assembly Measures', each of which requires the consent of the Queen in Council and the approval of Parliament. The Assembly therefore must apply to the UK government to make legislation on any given topic. Measures must be bilingual unless otherwise prescribed by Standing Order (s78(5)).

There is further provision for the Assembly to enact 'Acts of the Assembly' with similar scope (s 106). Unlike Measures, Acts will require only the formal royal assent, as in Scotland, and will not need individual approval from the UK government. The general power to enact Acts is triggered by an Order in Council approved by Parliament and requiring a referendum of the Welsh people. The referendum can be triggered either by the UK government or by the Assembly on the proposal of a Welsh minister. In both cases a two-thirds majority of the Assembly is required. Where the Assembly initiates the process the Secretary of State can refuse to make the Order for the referendum but must give reasons. Following a favourable referendum vote a Welsh minister is empowered to bring the power to enact Acts of the Assembly into effect (ss 103–06).

Section 114 empowers the Secretary of State to veto an Assembly Act on public interest grounds, including interference with the English water supply.

The system created by the 2006 Act is closer to the parliamentary system than was previously the case. The Welsh Assembly of 60 members is elected by a method similar to that in Scotland, with 20 members elected in five regions and 40 in local constituencies (Section 12.7.1). However, unlike in Scotland, a person cannot stand in both regional and local constituency elections (ss 7, 17). The Assembly sits for a fixed term of four years but, unlike the position under the 1998 Act, can be dissolved earlier by a two-thirds majority or if a First Minister is not nominated within 28 days, as in Scotland (ss 5, 47) (see Section 16.2.2).

A First Minister is chosen by the Assembly and appoints and dismisses other ministers and deputy ministers from Assembly members (ss 46–51). However the approval of the Assembly is not required for ministerial appointments. Instead the total number of ministers and deputy ministers is limited to 12.

A Council General, responsible for giving legal advice to the government, must also be appointed and can be removed by the First Minister with the agreement of the Assembly. The Council General loses offices when a new First Minister is appointed (s 49). Safeguards for the independence of the law officer are therefore less than in Scotland and Northern Ireland. She or he can be but need not be an Assembly member.

Welsh ministers are financially responsible to the Assembly, for which purpose there is an Auditor General (ss 143, 145). However, unlike the position in Scotland, their accounts are regulated by the UK Treasury and can be examined by the UK Comptroller and Auditor General. The UK Secretary of State for Wales represents Welsh affairs at national level and in the Council of Ministers of the EU.

As regards accountability, the Committee on Standards of Conduct receives and investigates complaints referred to it by the Presiding Officer relating to the conduct of any member of the National Assembly for Wales. If the complaint is substantiated, in its report to the Assembly the Committee may 'recommend' action in appropriate cases. In addition the Code of Practice on Members' Access to Information (2004) confers on members of the National Assembly for Wales more extensive rights of access to information than those available under the UK Freedom of Information Act 2000. The National Assembly Commissioner for Standards can investigate complaints that any Code of the Assembly has been breached.

The 2006 Act has a communitarian edge. Welsh ministers are empowered to promote or improve the economic, social and environmental well-being of Wales (s 60) and under the rubric of 'inclusiveness' must consult widely, advance various social and cultural concerns and prepare strategies dealing with sustainable development, the voluntary sector, equal opportunities and the Welsh language. There must also be a 'Partnership Council' comprising ministers and local authority representatives (s 72).

There is no separate Welsh court system, although there is a division of the Administrative Court in Cardiff dealing with Welsh governmental issues. This could develop distinctive constitutional principles in the Welsh context. There are provisions similar to those in Scotland and Northern Ireland for the Supreme Court to deal with devolution matters. The Council General is responsible for referring devolution issues to the Supreme Court, the provisions being similar to those for Scotland (s 96).

There is a Public Services Ombudsman (Public Services Ombudsman (Wales) Act 2005). This is a stronger version of the Ombudsman mechanism than the various English and UK equivalents. The Ombudsman can receive complaints directly from the public and has jurisdiction over the Assembly and government, local authorities, health authorities and social landlords. The Ombudsman may publish his or her report and the authority concerned must also do so unless the Ombudsman excludes publication in certain circumstances on public interest grounds (s 21). In the event of non-compliance, the Ombudsman can refer the matter to the High Court.

16.5 England

England, comprising 85 per cent of the population of the UK, has neither elected institutions of its own nor indeed a legal identity. England is governed by the central UK government. Therefore Scottish, Welsh and Northern Ireland members of the UK Parliament are entitled to vote in debates affecting exclusively English matters for which they are not accountable to their own voters. Similarly a UK government might be kept in power on the strength of Scottish votes. For example in 2004, by a majority of five, the Labour government won the vote in favour of increasing university tuition fees in England by virtue of its Scottish supporters.

This problem (often called 'West Lothian question' after the constituency formerly represented by Tam Dalyell, a relentless pursuer of the matter) is an inevitable result of the UK Parliament having exclusive jurisdiction over English affairs. It can be resolved adequately only by creating a separate lawmaker for England, a proposal for which there is little public interest. Indeed the same problem arose without solution in relation to the Irish Home Rule Bills between 1886 and 1914.

A possible compromise solution of creating a procedure under which Scottish MPs cannot vote on 'English' matters is fraught with problems relating to how English matters are to be identified and disentangled from UK matters, particularly in relation to finance (see Hazell, 2006). Moreover Scottish, Welsh and Northern Ireland voters are represented in the UK Parliament roughly in proportion to their population. This means that the UK Parliament is dominated by English MPs who can vote on Scottish matters, including devolved matters such as the amount of money to be given to Scotland from the UK government.

It is often suggested that there should be a devolved assembly for England. Central government powers relating to the English regions, such as land use, transport and economic development, are divided between different government departments, the names and functions of which are constantly changing. There are nine regional offices of central government charged with a coordinating role. There are also eight quangos – Regional Development Agencies (RDAs) (mainly composed of private businesspeople) appointed by the Secretary of State. RDAs are charged with advancing economic development, business efficiency, investment, competitiveness, employment and sustainable development. They have certain, albeit minor, powers and also power to distribute funds provided by the EC (Regional Development Agencies Act 1998).

These arrangements are characteristic of the dislike of democracy that pervades political culture in the UK. A sketchy proposal for an elected regional assembly for northeastern England was defeated by 78 per cent in a referendum in 2004 (see Regional Assemblies (Preparations) Act 2003, *Your Region, Your Choice: Revitalising the English Regions* (Cm 5511, 2002)). The present government proposes to abolish RDAs and to disband regional offices of the central government in favour of local consultative councils and increased powers for local authorities.

There is a limited form of regional devolution for the London region in the form of an elected Mayor and Assembly (Greater London Authority Act 1999). The Assembly is elected on the basis of 'first past the post' (Chapter 12), together with an 'additional member' from a party list in accordance with the party's share of the vote, thereby reflecting public opinion to a greater extent than is the case with local government and Parliament. The Mayor and Assembly have certain executive powers in relation mainly to transport, policing, land use planning, housing and local amenities.

Summary

- Legislative and executive power has been devolved to elected bodies in Scotland and Northern Ireland but without significant tax-raising powers. The UK Parliament has reserved the power to legislate in respect of many matters and has a general power to override the devolved assemblies. Their legislation is subordinate legislation, which is invalid if it exceeds the limits prescribed by the devolution statutes and also on judicial review grounds, although the courts will be circumspect in reviewing the acts of an elected body (see Section 19.6.1). In particular, unlike a UK statute, legislation violating the rights protected by the Human Rights Act 1998 is invalid.
- A more limited devolution applies to Wales. The Welsh Assembly can legislate only on matters specifically assigned to it, whereas Scotland and Northern Ireland can legislate on any subject other than those specifically excluded.
- Elections to the devolved bodies are partly by proportional representation. Citizens of EU countries resident in the UK can be candidates for and vote in elections to the devolved bodies.
- The Scottish and Welsh executives are structured according to the UK parliamentary system. However the balance of power is more in favour of the Parliament than is the case in the UK system. The Northern Ireland system is primarily concerned to achieve a balance between different political factions and is more restrictive than is the case with Scotland.
- There is no devolved government in England. Representatives from the devolved countries can therefore vote in the UK Parliament on purely English matters.

Exercises

16.1 To what extent is Wales a 'poor relation' in relation to devolution?

16.2 Compare the rules governing the appointment and removal of the Scottish and Northern Ireland First Ministers. Which is the more democratic?

16.3 Compare the methods in the UK and Scotland for dealing with a hung Parliament.

16.4 Compare the positions of the law officers in the devolved governments from the point of view of their independence.

16.5 To what extent can a majority in the Northern Ireland Assembly control the executive?

16.6 What are the constitutional problems, if any, of Scottish devolution in respect of England? How would you address them?

16.7 What safeguards are there in the devolved regimes (i) for ensuring that the devolved lawmakers do not exceed their powers and (ii) for ensuring that the UK government respects the independence of the devolved governments?

16.8 What are the powers of the Supreme Court in relation to the devolved regimes?

Exercises cont'd

16.9 On 4 May, elections take place in Scotland. The Socialist Party gets the largest number of seats in the Scottish Parliament (40 per cent). The Freedom Party, which came third with 15 per cent, agrees to support the Socialists in order to nominate Cherie, the leader of the Socialists, as the next First Minister. The Socialists and the Freedom Party together hold 55 per cent of the seats of the Parliament. In response to its support, Cherie promises to appoint two members of the Freedom Party as ministers.

On 4 June, the Parliament nominates Cherie for appointment as First Minister. The Conservatives, who came second in the election, oppose the nomination. The General Secretary of the Socialist Party, on behalf of the Scottish Parliament, submits the nomination to the UK Prime Minister, who advises the Queen to accept it.

Once Cherie is appointed as the First Minister, she decides to appoint as ministers exclusively members of her political party, irrespective of whether they have been elected as members of the Scottish Parliament. Nick, the leader of the Freedom Party, claims that the First Minister has breached her promise and warns her that she will face severe consequences and that he will use the most drastic measures at his disposal.

After this controversial commencement, the Socialist government declares that it is going to develop an extremely ambitious programme for Scotland. In its electoral programme, the Socialist Party had promised a stronger voice for Scotland in both the UK and Europe, and therefore the government announces a bill concerning legally binding international agreements between Scotland and other European States. This bill will be introduced in the Scottish Parliament by Dave, a Scottish Minister. The Secretary of State for Scotland informs Edinburgh that he will block this bill if they decide to put it forward.

Discuss the constitutional position in respect of each of these events.

16.10 Elections in Wales are to be held on the first Thursday of May. Huw is very pleased because this is the first time he is entitled to vote. In his polling station in the local constituency of Ynys Môn he is planning to cast two votes for two different political parties, Hope for Wales and Welsh People Together. In Huw's opinion both offer what the Welsh nation needs for further political development and he hopes that they will govern together.

Catrin, an enthusiastic woman who is a personal friend of Huw's, is standing to be the Assembly member for Ynys Môn. She lives in London and is a member of the party Welsh People Together. Catrin also wishes to be a candidate in the regional constituency in Wales where she spent her childhood.

Dyfed, who is standing to be the Assembly member for the local constituency of Caernarfon, is a member of the political party United Celtic Nations, which aims to unify Scotland, Wales and Northern Ireland and secure their independence from the United Kingdom. His Italian friend Fabrizio and his American friend Ron, both of whom are very keen on Dyfed's political ideas, have decided to vote for him.

Comment on the legal issues which may arise.

Further reading

Beatson, Grosz, Hickman, Singh, *Human Rights: Judicial Protection in the United Kingdom* (Sweet & Maxwell 2008) ch 8 [devolution cases]

Bogdanor, *The New British Constitution* (Hart 2009) ch 4

Cornes, 'Devolution and England: What Is on Offer?' in Bamforth and Leyland (eds), *Public Law in a Multi-Layered Constitution* (Hart 2003)

Hadfield, 'Devolution, Westminster and the English Question' [2005] PL 286

Hazell, *The English Question* (Manchester University Press 2006)

Hazell and Rawlings (eds), *Devolution, Law Making and the Constitution* (Imprint Academic 2005)

Himsworth, 'The Domesticated Executive in Scotland' in Craig and Tomkins (eds), *The Executive and Public Law* (Oxford University Press 2005)

Himsworth and O'Neill, *Scotland's Constitution: Law and Practice* (LexisNexis 2003)

House of Lords Select Committee on the Constitution Committee, *Devolution: Inter-Institutional Relations in the United Kingdom* (HL 2002–03, 147)

Jowell and Oliver (eds), *The Changing Constitution* (6th edn, Oxford University Press 2007) chs 9–11

Merinos, 'Democracy, Governance and Governmentality: Civic Public Space and Constitutional Renewal in Northern Ireland' (2001) 21 OJLS 287

Rawlings, 'Hastening Slowly: The Next Phase of Welsh Devolution' [2005] PL 824

Tierney, *Constitutional Law and National Pluralism* (Oxford University Press 2004)

Trench, 'The Government of Wales Act 2006: The Next Steps in Devolution for Wales' [2006] PL 687

Winetrobe, 'Collective Responsibility in Devolved Scotland' [2003] PL 24

Part V

Administrative law

Chapter 17

The grounds of judicial review, I: illegality and *ultra vires*

In modern Britain, where no agreement exists on the ends of society and the means of achieving those ends, it would be disastrous if courts did not eschew the temptation to pass judgement on an issue of policy. Judicial self-preservation may alone dictate restraint. (Lord Parker LCJ 1959)

To avoid a vacuum in which the citizen would be left without protection against a misuse of executive powers the courts have had no option but to occupy the dead ground in a manner and in areas of public life, which could not have been foreseen 30 years ago. (Lord Mustill in *R v Secretary of State for the Home Dept, ex p Fire Brigades Union* [1995] at 267)

17.1 Introduction: the constitutional basis of judicial review

Judicial review has ancient origins (see *Keighly Case* [1609]) but has become prominent only since the 1970s. Sometimes called the 'supervisory jurisdiction', it is the High Court's power to police the legality of decisions made by public bodies. An accommodation must be struck between competing aspects of the separation of powers. On the one hand the rule of law and the principle of checks and balances require that the legality of government action be subject to review by independent and impartial tribunals: 'The principles of judicial review give effect to the rule of law. They ensure that administrative decisions will be taken rationally in accordance with a fair procedure and within the powers conferred by Parliament' (per Lord Hoffmann in *R (Alconbury Developments Ltd) v Secretary of State for the Environment, Transport and the Regions* [2001] at 981; see also *R (Cart) v Upper Tribunal* [2010] at [34]–[37]: eulogy for rule of law).

On the other hand judicial review operates within the context of the parliamentary accountability of the executive. From this perspective the functional separation of powers pulls in the other direction by requiring the court to avoid trespassing into the political territory of the government and Parliament. Judicial review is regarded as a last-resort method of challenge and there are procedural barriers intended to prevent it being too easily taken up (Chapter 19). Other and cheaper methods of challenging government decisions exist, for example through tribunals, statutory regulators, ombudsmen and MPs. However these may be questionable either because of the absence of enforcement or investigatory powers or because of a perceived lack of independence (see *R v Secretary of State for the Home Dept, ex p Fire Brigades Union* [1995], Lord Mustill at 267).

The courts claim not to be concerned with the 'merits' of government action, that is whether it is good or bad, but only with whether governmental decisions fall within their authorising legislation and meet legal standards of fairness and 'reasonableness' (see Laws J in *R v Somerset CC, ex p Fewings* [1995]). However as *Fewings* illustrates (disagreement as to whether morality should be taken into account in relation to a decision to ban hunting), these principles are vague, shading into questions of merit, and there is considerable room for debate as to the proper limits of the courts' powers.

Judicial review applies to all public bodies, including courts and tribunals other than the High Court itself and equivalent bodies. However a minister can designate a tribunal other than the High Court to deal with human rights matters (see Section 21.1). As with all legal proceedings judicial review is subject to parliamentary privilege (see Section 11.6). Judicial review cases are decided by the Administrative Court, part of the Queen's Bench Division of the High Court. Section 15 of the Tribunals, Courts and Enforcement Act 2007 also confers judicial review jurisdiction upon the Upper Tribunal created by that Act (see Section 5.4.3). The Administrative Court will be discussed in chapter 19.

Judicial review applies to government decisions and actions that affect individual rights and interests and also to general statements of government policy (see *Gillick v West Yorkshire CC* [1986]). However some matters are 'non-justiciable', meaning not appropriate for investigation by the courts (see *Council of Civil Service Unions (CCSU) v Minister for the Civil Service* [1985]). There are various reasons for this self-restraint (see Section 19.7.1). Firstly the court may lack the expertise or practical competence to deal with the matter; secondly the legal process may be unsuitable because of the nature and range of matters involved or because there are no objective laws available; thirdly matters of high political policy may be involved concerning the separation of powers. Examples, mostly involving the royal prerogative, include the dissolution of Parliament, the appointment of ministers, the granting of honours, the making of treaties and the decision to go to war. The court's constitutional role concerns focused disputes between particular parties and it is not equipped to deal with wide-ranging policy issues or interests which may not be represented in court. Those matters are the concern of elected assemblies or those who act on their behalf.

Moreover the judicial review principles are flexible in that the intensity of review, the range of grounds available and the selection of remedies vary with the context. While not excluding review entirely the courts may allow a wide discretion to the government decision maker in relation to a particular issue. There is no definitive list; the matter depends on the circumstances. This is often referred to as 'deference' to the decision maker (or 'due deference', indicating that the court will focus on the particular issue). The courts also respect the sphere of Parliament, although some judges are more deferential to this than others (see the disagreement in *R v Secretary of State, ex p Fire Brigades Union*; Section 7.8.1) and as early as 1911 judicial doubts about ministerial responsibility were raised (see *Dyson v A-G* [1911]). The court will be influenced by the extent to which the decision maker is democratically accountable, the status of the decision maker, the extent to which subjective evaluations are involved and the relative expertise of the decision maker and the court.

The Human Rights Act 1998 (HRA) has added a further dimension to judicial review. It creates separate grounds for challenge in addition to those provided by the general law (although some of them overlap). The main principles of the Act will be dealt with in Chapter 21. In this chapter and the next we shall introduce aspects of the HRA that particularly affect the grounds of judicial review.

17.1.1 The legal basis of judicial review

The legal basis of judicial review is disputed, reflecting the wider debate as to the nature of our constitution. There is a large but somewhat repetitive literature on this issue (the main viewpoints are collected in Forsythe, 2000). One perspective bases judicial review upon the common law, according to which powerful bodies must act in accordance with rule of law values of fairness and rationality (*Dr Bonham's Case* [1610]; *Bagg's Case* [1615]; *Cooper v Wandsworth Board of Works* [1863]). This draws inspiration primarily from liberal ideas and from the history of the common law as applying community-based values of fairness and justice.

The other perspective gives greater emphasis to parliamentary supremacy, democracy and the separation of powers. It is republican in tone (see Section 2.5). It assumes that because most government powers are created by Act of Parliament, the courts' role is confined to ensuring that powers do not exceed the limits set out by Parliament: the *ultra vires* doctrine. The underlying principle is that of parliamentary supremacy. The courts must obey a statute. Conversely acts outside a statute have no legal effect. To its supporters this provides a more substantial basis for judicial review than does the vague rule of law idea. Rather tediously, both approaches can be made to fit the facts, and the historical evidence is inconclusive.

Both approaches conform to possible meanings of the separation of powers and the rule of law. The *ultra vires* approach is more heavily biased towards the functional aspect of the separation of powers; the common law approach towards checks and balances. One difference between the two approaches is that the *ultra vires* approach would not permit the courts to override an Act of Parliament. The common law approach is in itself neutral on this issue. However some of its adherents claim that the courts might be able to override a statute in an extreme case (see Section 8.4.5).

Another difference between the two approaches is that the common law approach has less difficulty with freeing up judicial review to apply to bodies whose powers do not derive from statute. For example royal prerogative powers and other non-statutory powers exercised by public bodies are subject to judicial review (*CCSU*; *R v Panel on Takeovers and Mergers, ex p Datafin plc* [1987]). The common law might also be the basis for extending judicial review principles, similar to those applied to government, to powerful private bodies (eg sports regulatory bodies and powerful commercial companies) which exercise control over aspects of public life (eg *McInnes v Onslow-Fane* [1978]). Proponents of the *ultra vires* doctrine accommodate this possibility by suggesting that there need not be a single basis for judicial review. Thus the extent of judicial review depends on political choice rather than an abstract conceptual theory.

Even the *ultra vires* approach accepts that the judges are developing their own principles in accordance with the 'amplified' or 'extended' versions of the rule of law and the principle of legality according to which basic rights cannot be infringed unless Parliament uses very clear language (see Sections 6.5, 6.6). The *ultra vires* approach claims that Parliament intended these principles to be implied into the exercise of statutory powers because Parliament can be assumed to respect the rule of law as developed by the courts. In other words the *ultra vires* doctrine concerns an assumed intention of Parliament as opposed to a specific intention as to the meaning of given legislation.

Forsythe (1996) suggests that the *ultra vires* doctrine is a useful 'fig leaf' which gives constitutional respectability to what is happening and at least reminds us that Parliament has the last word. There are many presumptions of statutory interpretation which require courts to assume that Parliament intended to act fairly while allowing the court considerable room to decide what this means. Judicial review may be regarded as an application of this. The difference between the two approaches is that according to the common law view Parliament *tolerates* judicial review, whereas on the *ultra vires* view Parliament somehow *authorises* judicial review.

Forsythe's fig leaf could be taken to hide something we would prefer not to see, namely that the *ultra vires* doctrine is an empty vessel for whatever happens to be the prevailing judicial fashion. The common law version claims to be more honest. It does not ignore the intention of Parliament. Firstly a decision which is *ultra vires* in the sense that it violates a statute is invalid under both theories. Secondly the common law approach is perfectly consistent with the view that Parliament can exclude any ground of judicial review just as Parliament can change any other common law rule. There is therefore no inconsistency with parliamentary supremacy.

There is substantial judicial support for the *ultra vires* doctrine as the basis of judicial review (eg *Boddington v British Transport Police* [1999]; *Credit Suisse v Allerdale BC* [1996] at 167; *Page v Hull University Visitor* [1993] at 107). On the other hand in *CCSU* Lord Diplock famously abandoned the *ultra vires* doctrine by classifying the grounds of judicial review under the three broad heads of 'illegality, irrationality and procedural impropriety', claiming that the law should not pursue 'fairy tales'.

17.2 Appeal and review

Judicial review must not be confused with an appeal. An appeal is a procedure which exists only under a particular statute or, in the case of a voluntary body, by agreement. An appeal allows the appellate body to decide the whole matter again unless the particular statute or agreement limits the grounds of appeal (see Tribunals and Inquiries Act 1992, s 11: questions of law only). An appeal therefore may involve a thorough reconsideration of the whole decision, whereas judicial review is concerned only with ensuring that legal standards are complied with. Depending on the particular statute, an appellate body might be a court, tribunal, minister or indeed anyone. A claim for judicial review is possible only in the High Court or the Upper Tribunal.

An appellate body can usually substitute its decision for the first instance decision, although in some cases its powers are limited to sending the matter back to be decided again by the lower body. In judicial review proceedings, unless there is no doubt as to the right decision, the court cannot make the decision itself but must send the matter back to the decision maker with instructions as to its legal duties.

Unlike a right of appeal, which can be raised only in the body specified, the invalidity of government action can be raised not only in the Administrative Court but also, by way of 'collateral challenge', in any proceedings where the rights of a citizen are affected by the validity of government action (eg *Boddington v British Transport Police* [1998]: defence to prosecution for smoking contrary to railway bylaws alleged to be *ultra vires*). This is because an unlawful government decision is of no effect in law (void/nullity) and can be ignored, thus vindicating the rule of law (*Entick v Carrington*

[1765]). In the case of an appeal, the offending decision is fully valid until the appeal body changes it.

17.3 Nullity: void and voidable decisions

According to the rule of law and also the *ultra vires* doctrine, an invalid government act should be a nullity (*void*) and have no legal consequences. Indeed this has been emphasised by the courts (eg Lord Reid in *Ridge v Baldwin* [1964] and *Anisminic Ltd v Foreign Compensation Commission* [1969] at 171, 195, 207; Lord Irvine LC in *Boddington v British Transport Police* [1999]; *Secretary of State for the Home Dept v JJ* [2008] at [27]). On the other hand it may be impractical simply to ignore a decision since its invalidity can be exposed only once a court has ruled as much. In that sense a decision is only *voidable*: valid until set aside by a court. This is reinforced by the fact that all the judicial review remedies are discretionary, so in judicial review proceedings the court does not have to set aside even an *ultra vires* decision (*Credit Suisse v Allerdale BC* [1996] at 167). By contrast, where a decision is challenged collaterally, for example as a defence to a prosecution, the court has no discretion (*Credit Suisse v Allerdale BC*), so a different outcome is possible depending solely on which route is taken for the challenge.

If a decision is held in judicial review proceedings to be a nullity then in principle it will be treated as never having had legal effect and its consequences will be unwound. For example in *Ridge v Baldwin* a Chief Constable dismissed without a hearing was held still to be in office and so entitled to his pension rights. In *Secretary of State v JJ* it was held that a void Control Order made by the Home Secretary under anti-terrorist legislation could not be amended to make it lawful but must be set aside.

The concept of nullity does not always lead to a just solution. In *DPP v Head* [1959] a woman was improperly detained in a mental hospital as a result of an invalid medical procedure. A man charged with having sexual relations with a patient 'detained' under the Mental Health Acts was able to argue that because the patient's detention order had not been made according to the required formalities, she was not 'detained' under the relevant Acts. On the same analysis the officials who administered the hospital would have made numerous decisions affecting the detainee on the assumption that the initial order was valid. If, due to the initial infection of the invalid decision, all consequential acts had to be unpicked the result would be chaos. In *Credit Suisse v Allerdale BC* a local authority successfully relied on the argument that a guarantee which it had given was *ultra vires* to prevent the guarantee being enforced against it (see subsequently Local Government (Contracts) Act 1997). Similarly, would everyone granted a driving licence under a regulation which later turned out to be invalid for some procedural reason find themselves guilty of an offence?

There are various ways of attacking this problem, none of them entirely satisfactory.

1. to argue that only the most serious defects make a decision void, while others make it only voidable in the sense that it might be set aside for the future only (see *Bugg v DPP* [1993] at 493). This was rejected by the House of Lords in *Anisminic*, who took the view that all defects make the decision a nullity (cf Lords Browne Wilkinson and Slynn in *Boddington*);
2. to claim that there is a 'presumption of validity', meaning that until it is set aside a decision must be treated as valid but if successfully challenged it can be set aside

retrospectively, that is treated as if it never existed (see *Hoffmann-La Roche v Secretary of State* [1974]). In that sense all decisions would be voidable. This does not address the problem of third parties who rely on a decision before it is set aside;

3. using judicial discretion. This sits uncomfortably with the rule of law;
4. treating the matter as one of statutory interpretation in the particular context (see *Seal v Chief Constable of South Wales Police* [2007]). Of course a statute can prevent a decision being treated as void but this approach abandons any general principle. It was favoured by Lord Hoffman (dissenting) in *Secretary of State v JJ*;
5. Professor Wade deals with the conundrum by using the concept of 'relative nullity', meaning that an invalid decision is indeed a nullity but only if challenged in the right court by the right person in the right way ('Unlawful Administrative Action: Void or Voidable?' (1968) 84 LQR 95). For example a claimant may be out of time, in which case the decision must stand and a third party can rely on it. Again this does not deal with the position of third parties who rely on the decision if it is set aside (see also *Agricultural Training Board v Aylesbury Mushrooms Ltd* [1972]);
6. Forsythe (1998) suggests a distinction between an act valid in law and an act that exists in fact. This refers to the situation where an invalid decision has a chain of consequences where it is relied upon by other officials or citizens – the 'domino effect' and 'the theory of the second actor', that is an official who makes a decision on the assumption that a previous decision is valid (see also Beatson and Matthews, *Administrative Law: Text and Materials* (3rd edn, Oxford University Press 2005) 94–101). According to Forsythe the crucial question is whether the validity *in law* of the first act is a precondition to the validity of the second decision or whether a decision *in fact* is sufficient. For example in *R v Wicks* [1998] the House of Lords held that a developer could be prosecuted for disobeying a planning enforcement notice even though the notice was invalid since the statutory requirement was only for a notice that existed in fact, that is one that appeared to be valid. This approach (which harks back to an old notion of a document which is defective 'on its face'; see *Smith v East Elloe RDC* [1956]) begs the question of how we know which category applies to the given case;
7. distinguishing between the decision itself and the preliminary steps leading to it. These are not necessarily void (see *Shrewsbury and Atcham BC v Secretary of State* [2008] at [57]–[58]).

17.4 Classification of the grounds of review

Unfortunately there is no general agreement on how to classify the grounds of judicial review, and textbooks take different approaches. The grounds themselves are broad, vague and overlapping, a conspicuous example of this being *Wheeler v Leicester City Council* [1985] (see Section 18.1). I shall organise the grounds of judicial review on the basis of Lord Diplock's classification in *Council of Civil Service Unions (CCSU) v Minister for the Civil Service* [1985], that is under the three heads of 'illegality, irrationality and procedural impropriety'. However the Diplock categories tell us little in themselves and do not avoid overlaps. Indeed the House of Lords has emphasised that the heads of challenge are not watertight compartments but run together (*Boddington v British Transport Police* [1999]). In this chapter, we shall discuss illegality. The other grounds are discussed in Chapter 18.

It might be helpful at this point to provide a checklist:

1. *Illegality*
   - 'narrow' *ultra vires*, or lack of jurisdiction, in the sense of straying beyond the limits defined by the statute;
   - errors of law and (in certain cases) errors of fact;
   - 'wide' *ultra vires*, or acting for an ulterior purpose, taking irrelevant factors into account or failing to take relevant factors into account;
   - fettering discretion.
2. *Irrationality*
   - *Wednesbury* unreasonableness. This could stand alone or be the outcome of taking an irrelevant factor into account;
   - proportionality, at least under the Human Rights Act 1998.
3. *Procedural impropriety*
   - violating important statutory procedures;
   - bias;
   - lack of a fair hearing;
   - failure to give reasons for a decision.

17.5 Illegality: 'narrow' *ultra vires*

Illegality concerns *ultra vires* in its basic sense, namely a requirement that the decision conform to the statute that confers the power. This is not merely a matter of reading the statute but involves various presumptions which the court brings to the task of statutory interpretation. A decision is *ultra vires* if it is outside the language of the statute that authorises the decision to be made. Many government bodies are entirely statutory; for example local authorities and tribunals and most central government powers are conferred by statue on individual ministers. In the case of courts and judicial tribunals, the terminology of 'lack' or 'excess' of jurisdiction is often used. (Jurisdiction means 'area of power' and 'lack' or 'excess' of jurisdiction means here the same as *ultra vires*).

Here are some famous examples of *ultra vires*. In *A-G v Fulham Corporation* [1921] a local authority had power to provide a 'wash house' for local people. It interpreted this as authorising the provision of a laundry service for working people, who could leave washing to be done by staff and delivered to their homes. This was held to be unlawful in that 'wash house', according to the court, meant a place where a person can do their own washing. This raises questions as to the assumptions that the courts bring to the task of interpreting statutes. For example the court might have been influenced by a prejudice against local bodies spending taxpayers' money on welfare services. If the court had read the statute against an assumption of democratic freedom, the outcome might have been different. More recently in *Bromley LBC v GLC* [1983] the House of Lords held that an obligation to provide an 'efficient and economic' public transport service meant that the Council could not subsidise the London Underground for social purposes. Among other lines of reasoning, it was held that 'economic' meant that there was an obligation to break even financially (see also *Prescott v Birmingham Corporation* [1955]: free transport for pensioners held *ultra vires* under a power to charge such fares as the Council thought fit). *Roberts v Hopwood* [1925] ('wages' should not include a social welfare element) is a similar case where the court might be suspected of political bias.

These cases suggest that the courts take a narrow approach and are reluctant to read a statute as authorising a local authority to be guided by wide political ideologies. Similarly in *R v Somerset CC, ex p Fewings* [1995], Laws J held that a decision to ban hunting on local authority land could not take into account the moral views of the counsellors, even though supported by public opinion, unless the statute clearly authorised this. Democracy was nothing to do with it.

Where the scope of a statute is unclear, the courts rely on presumptions of interpretation. These can reflect the courts' perception of community values, although this does not mean public opinion. Examples include *R v Secretary of State for the Home Dept, ex p Simms* [1999] at 412 (freedom of expression); *Congreve v Home Office* [1976] and *Macarthy & Stone v Richmond upon Thames LBC* [1991] (no taxation without statutory authority); *R v Secretary of State for the Home Dept, ex p Pierson* [1998] (retrospective use of powers); *Raymond v Honey* [1983] (prisoner's rights); *Anisminic Ltd v Foreign Compensation Commission* [1969] and R v *Lord Chancellor's Dept, ex p Witham* (1997) (access to the courts). These presumptions have been reinforced by the Human Rights Act 1998, which imposes a strong obligation to interpret all legislation so as to conform with rights embodied in the European Convention on Human Rights (ECHR) (Chapter 21). Many of these presumptions appeal to individualistic liberals (red light) but some of them have been criticised by 'welfare liberals' as attempts to counter policies based on the collective public interest (green light) (see Section 1.6).

There is some leeway in the *ultra vires* doctrine in favour of the government. The courts will permit an activity which, although not expressly authorised by the statute, is 'reasonably incidental' to something that is expressly authorised. Section 111 of the Local Government Act 1972 applies a similar principle to local authorities. For example in *Akumah v Hackney LBC* [2005] the House of Lords held that it was lawful to clamp cars in a car park attached to a block of local authority flats under a scheme which required tenants to obtain parking permits at a cost of £2. The Council had statutory power of 'management, regulation and control' over the 'dwelling houses' and this should be interpreted broadly to include the regulation of car parking since this affects the quality of life of the residents. This was the case even though the Council could have made parking regulations under other, more specific legislation. However the House of Lords was not asked to rule on the legality of the particular scheme, thus leaving it open whether making a charge or clamping was lawful.

A narrow approach was taken in *Macarthy & Stone*, where a charge for giving advice in connection with planning applications was held not to be incidental to the authority's planning powers. Giving advice was not expressly authorised and was itself an incidental function. The House of Lords took the view that something cannot be incidental to the incidental. Moreover there is a presumption dating from the Bill of Rights 1688 that taxation cannot be imposed without clear statutory authority (but is a charge for a service taxation?). (See also *A-G v Crayford UDC* [1962]: voluntary household insurance scheme reasonably incidental to the power to manage council housing because it helped tenants to pay the rent; *Hazell v Hammersmith and Fulham LBC* [1992]: interest swap arrangements – made by several local councils to spread the risk of future changes in interest rates – were not incidental to the Council's borrowing powers because they concerned debt management rather than borrowing as such.)

17.6 Errors of law and fact

By 'error' or 'wrong' in this context I mean a mistake. A typical error of law would be to misunderstand the meaning of a legal rule (eg what is meant by 'residence' in a dwelling). A typical error of fact is a mistake about something happening in the real world (eg whether a person was actually in the dwelling). Sometimes the term 'error' is used loosely to mean any unlawful act. This broad meaning should be avoided here.

The question of whether the court can review decisions on the ground of legal or factual errors has caused problems. There is a clash of principle. On the one hand if the court could intervene merely because it considered that a mistake had been made, it would be trespassing into the merits of the case, showing disrespect for the deciding body and violating the separation of powers. Thus it has been said that if a body has jurisdiction to go right it has jurisdiction to go wrong (Lord Reid in *R v Governor of Brixton Prison, ex p Armah* [1968] at 234). From this perspective the question is not whether there was a mistake but who should have the last word in deciding whether a mistake has been made. It is not obvious that a reviewing court is in a better position than the original decision maker to decide what the facts are (see *R v Nat Bell Liquors* [1922]: false evidence not reviewable). On the other hand the rule of law surely calls for a remedy if a decision maker makes a clear mistake. The courts have therefore adopted a compromise. Almost all errors of law and some errors of fact can be challenged. However they have reached this position only after much technical wrangling.

A rationale that was popular in the nineteenth century is the doctrine of the 'jurisdictional' or 'collateral' or 'preliminary' question. According to this doctrine, if a mistake relates to a state of affairs which the court thinks that Parliament intended should exist objectively as a condition of the official having power to make the decision, then the court will interfere if it thinks that the required state of affairs does not exist. The decision is *ultra vires*, or outside jurisdiction. This applies both to mistakes of law and to mistakes of fact. For example in *White and Collins v Minister of Health* [1939] the Secretary of State had power to acquire land 'other than a garden or parkland'. It was held that the court could interfere if it thought that the minister had wrongly decided whether the claimant's land was parkland. The doctrine can be justified on the rule of law ground that a minister should not be allowed to expand his own powers (see Farwell J in *R v Shoreditch Assessment Committee, ex p Morgan* [1910] at 880). However there seems to be no logical way of deciding which of many issues that a decision maker has to decide are 'preliminary' in this sense. Nevertheless the doctrine still exists (see Section 17.6.1).

A second device, which flourished during the 1960s but has largely been superseded, is the doctrine of 'error of law on the face of the record', or patent error (*R v Northumberland Compensation Appeal Tribunal, ex p Shaw* [1952]). This allows the court to quash a decision if a mistake of law can be discovered from the written record of the decision without using other evidence. This could not be squeezed into the *ultra vires* doctrine and decisions tainted by patent error may only be 'voidable', that is valid unless and until formally quashed by the court (see Section 17.3). The face of the record principle provides a practical compromise by allowing obvious mistakes to be rectified without reopening the whole matter. Many bodies are required to give written reasons for their decisions as part of the record (eg Tribunals and Inquiries Act 1992, s 10) and the courts were liberal in what material they regarded as part of the record. However mistakes of fact could not be challenged at all.

Most importantly, as a result of the speeches of the majority of the House of Lords in *Anisminic Ltd v Foreign Compensation Commission* [1969], the older doctrines have been made largely redundant in relation to errors of law. *Anisminic* appears to have made all errors of law reviewable, at least in principle. Before *Anisminic* it was widely believed that a jurisdictional error was an error committed at the outset of the decision-making process which made the tribunal go entirely outside its allotted sphere ('excess of jurisdiction') and that errors committed subsequently (errors within jurisdiction) could not be reviewed unless they were 'on the record'. For example suppose a tribunal has power to fix the rent for a 'furnished dwelling'; in order to decide whether it had jurisdiction it must first decide whether the dwelling in front of it is 'furnished'. A mistake about this would go to its jurisdiction. Mistakes which it committed later, for example in calculating the rent, would not. In *Anisminic* a majority of their Lordships rejected this approach as arbitrary and held that defects at any stage in the process could go to jurisdiction.

> The Foreign Compensation Commission (FCC) was established to adjudicate on claims to compensation for war damage in connection with an Arab–Israeli war. Under the complex regulations it had to decide many questions, one of which was that the owner of the damaged property and the owner's successor in title must be British subjects. The FCC had interpreted the term 'successor in title' as including a purchaser. This led it to refuse compensation to the claimant, who had sold its property to an Egyptian company. The House of Lords held that as a matter of law a purchaser was not a successor in title because the term 'successor in title' in this context was intended to mean only someone who succeeds to property on the death or winding up of its original owner. Therefore an irrelevant matter had been taken into account that Parliament did not intend, namely the nationality of the Egyptian company. According to a majority of their Lordships, this made the decision not just wrong but outside the FCC's jurisdiction.

Anisminic has been widely taken as deciding that any mistake of law makes a decision *ultra vires* (see *Re Racal Communications* [1981]; *O'Reilly v Mackman* [1982]; *Page v Hull University Visitor* [1993]; *Boddington v BTC* [1999] at 158). The reason for this seems to be the loose way in which the majority characterised a jurisdictional error as taking an irrelevant matter into account, failing to take a relevant matter into account or 'asking the wrong question'. All mistakes could logically be presented under those heads. However there are dicta in *Anisminic* itself denying that all errors of law are jurisdictional, and Lord Morris strongly dissented (see 174, 189, 195, 209; see also *Pearlman v Governors and Keepers of Harrow School* [1979]; *South East Asia Fire Brick Sdn Bhd v Non-Metallic Mineral Products Manufacturing Employees Union* [1981].

The courts have to some extent drawn back from *Anisminic.* They have recognised that some matters raise specialised issues outside the court's competence or involve a mixture of matters of law, fact and opinion which the tribunal or government decision maker is better equipped to decide than the court. For example in *Re Racal Communications* Lord Diplock suggested that *Anisminic* did not apply to decisions of courts where questions of law and questions of fact were inextricably mixed up. In *Page v Hull University Visitor* it was held that the specialised rules of universities should be conclusively interpreted by the university visitor. In both these cases it was recognised that unfair or unreasonable decisions could be reviewed.

Recently in *R (Cart) v Upper Tribunal* [2010] the Court of Appeal held that the Upper Tribunal, which hears appeals on points of law from a wide range of tribunals, was subject to judicial review. However out of respect for the independence and competence of the tribunal its decisions would not be reviewed for error of law on *Anisminic* grounds but only where it exceeded its jurisdiction in the pre-*Anisminic* sense ('outright excess of jurisdiction') or committed 'a denial of procedural justice'. Sedley LJ asserted that 'there is a true jurisprudential difference between error in the course of an adjudication and conducting an adjudication without lawful authority' (at [36]). (This case is currently before the Supreme Court.)

17.6.1 Errors of fact

More generally *Anisminic* has not been applied to mistakes of *fact,* which arguably should not be reviewable because the primary decision maker is usually in a better position than the court to discover the facts.

It is not always easy to distinguish between questions of law, questions of fact and questions of opinion. A question of law basically involves the meaning and usually the application of a rule. A question of fact involves the existence of some state of affairs or event in the world outside the law and depends on evidence. A question of opinion is where on the same evidence more than one view can reasonably be taken (*Lord Luke of Pavenham v Minister of Housing and Local Government* [1968]: whether a building 'harmonised' with its surroundings was a matter of opinion).

However the courts may treat some apparently legal questions of interpretation as matters of fact or opinion where they concern broad everyday notions or involve value judgements or matters of degree where no sharp line is possible. The following are characteristic: *Pulhoffer v Hillingdon BC* [1986] ('homeless'); *R v Monopolies and Mergers Commission, ex p South Yorkshire Transport* [1993] ('substantial' part of the UK); *Edwards v Bairstow* [1956] ('trade'); *Brutus v Cozens* [1973] ('insulting'); *R v Radio Authority, ex p Bull* [1997] ('political nature'); *Shah v Barnet LBC* [1983] ('ordinarily' resident); *BBC v Sugar* [2007] ('journalism, art or literature').

Errors of fact are not normally reviewable since the courts regard the initial decision-making body as in the best position to find the facts. However there are exceptions.

These might be explicable on the basis that the particular error could be brought within another head of review

The doctrine of the preliminary question (see Section 17.6) applies to errors of fact, where it is sometimes called the 'precedent fact' doctrine. This allows the court to decide the question of fact itself. For example in *Khawaja v Secretary of State for the Home Dept* [1983] the Home Secretary could deport an 'illegal immigrant'. The House of Lords held that the court could decide whether the appellant was in fact an illegal immigrant and was not limited to deciding whether the minister's decision was unreasonable. The problem is to decide what kind of case falls within the doctrine. This depends upon the statutory context. In *Khawaja* the court was influenced by the fact that the decision involved personal freedom, so that a high level of judicial control was required. By contrast in *Bugdaycay v Secretary of State for the Home Dept* [1987] the question was whether the applicant was a genuine asylum seeker. Here the decision was heavily laden with subjective political judgement and the court was not prepared to treat the matter as one of precedent fact. *R (A) v Croydon LBC* [2009] concerned a provision making an asylum seeker eligible for housing only if there was a child in need. It was held that the court could interfere where there was an objectively right or wrong answer (ie whether there was a child) but not on the question of need. It was also held that the court would look at the quality of the initial decision-making process: the better it was, the less willing the court would be to interfere. This is an important feature of judicial review which emphasises the way a decision is reached rather than the outcome in isolation.

A finding of fact which is completely unreasonable in the sense that it has no evidential basis is reviewable (*Ashbridge Investments v Minister of Housing and Local Government* [1965] at 1326). In *R v Criminal Injuries Compensation Board, ex p A* [1999] at 344 Lord Slynn said that 'misunderstanding or ignorance of an established and relevant fact' is reviewable but emphasised that this is no more than an application of ordinary review principles (see also *Secretary of State for Education and Science v Tameside Metropolitan BC* [1977] at 1017). By contrast judicial review does not include a reinvestigation of disputed facts unless the decision is perverse (*Adan v Newham LBC* [2002]). In other words the courts will not attempt to investigate factual disagreements or to weigh evidence but will intervene in clear cases.

In general it might be preferable in cases both of law and of fact to allow judicial review only where the decision is an *unreasonable* one, for example where proper consideration was not given to the matter. This provides a safeguard without infringing the competence of the decision maker. A right of appeal can be provided by statute where a more detailed scrutiny is required.

17.6.2 Errors and the ECHR

Article 6 of the ECHR, which applies to UK law under the Human Rights Act 1998, confers a right to a fair trial where 'civil rights and obligations' are in issue. This includes a right to challenge an administrative decision before a body with 'full jurisdiction'. In deciding whether there has been a fair trial, the court will look at the process as a whole, including any right of judicial review (*Albert v Belgium* [1983]). The question arises whether the limited review on questions of fact available in an English court satisfies this.

The first question is what is meant by a 'civil right and obligation'. Although some judges, notably Lord Hoffmann (*R (Alconbury Developments Ltd) v Secretary of State for the Environment, Transport and the Regions* [2001]), prefer to confine the term to disputes about private law rights such as property rights, the European Court has taken a broader view. The ability to hold and deal with property is certainly included (eg *Winterwerp v The Netherlands* [1979]: mental incapacity; removal of property rights). However the concept of civil rights is 'autonomous', meaning a self-contained concept. It is not limited to rights recognised as such by domestic law. It includes some claims to benefits from government. The underlying principle seems to be that for a civil right the decision in question must have a serious effect on existing individual interests or must involve a claim to some kind of entitlement. There is no civil right where entitlement depends on the exercise of discretionary evaluation of the claim. A civil *obligation* arises where there is a legal duty towards the state, for example to pay taxes.

- In *Ali v Birmingham Corporation* [2010] a claim to be housed under homelessness legislation did not create a civil right because there was a substantial element of discretion. In *Runa Begum v Tower Hamlets LBC* [2003] the House of Lords had assumed but specifically did not decide that a similar decision engaged civil rights. However in *Ali* it was pointed out that Lord Hoffmann in *Runa Begum* intimated that the concept of civil rights should not include discretionary decisions (see also *R (A) v Croydon LBC*: provision of accommodation for children: no civil right).
- In *Feldbrugge v The Netherlands* [1986] and *Salesi v Italy* [1993] claims to health insurance from the state on proof of certain facts were held to concern civil rights.
- The removal of an existing benefit will normally engage a civil right. In *Tre Tractorer Aktebolag v Sweden* [1989] it was held that the revocation of a liquor licence engaged a civil right (see also *Bentham v The Netherlands* [1986]: petrol storage licence affecting operation of business).
- In *R (G) v Governors of X School* [2010] it was held that the dismissal of a teacher engaged a civil right of professional practice, as for similar reasons did the placing of a care worker on a blacklist (*R (Wright) v Secretary of State for Health* [2009]).
- If a decision is purely advisory in its effect, a civil right may not be engaged (see *R (Hammond) v Secretary of State for the Home Dept* [2006] at [11], [28]).

The limited scope of judicial review in relation to findings of fact has sometimes been held to satisfy Article 6. The courts have reduced the notion of 'full jurisdiction' to the virtually meaningless 'full jurisdiction to deal with the case as the nature of the decision requires' (see Lord Bingham in *Runa Begum* at 736). They have made a distinction between on the one hand a decision where a citizen has a definite entitlement on proof of certain facts (eg to a pension based on prescribed contributions) and on the other hand a decision where the facts are part of a larger policy or politically oriented process where the decision maker has to balance facts against competing considerations and has a discretion as to the outcome (eg a decision to widen a motorway; *Alconbury*). In *Runa Begum* (at [5]) Lord Bingham remarked that the more elastic the interpretation give to 'civil rights' the more flexible must be the approach to the requirement of an independent review. This is in order to prevent the decision-making process becoming too formal and expensive.

In the first, 'factual' kind of case, the reach of judicial review into the facts is not far enough, so unless the initial decision is made by a body fully independent of government, such as a tribunal, an independent procedure is required which can examine all questions of fact (*Runa Begum*; *Tsfayo v UK* [2009]). In the second, 'policy' kind of case, it has been held that in the interests of democracy and respect for the machinery chosen by Parliament judicial review may suffice as a safety net (see *Alconbury*: land use planning decisions). It can be decided which category a case falls within only by looking closely at the particular decision-making process and its goals. It is clear however that the wider the view taken on the question of the meaning of 'civil right', the more likely it is that the case will fall within the 'policy' category.

In cases where other human rights are engaged, such as the right to respect for home and family life (Article 8), the limited scope of judicial review in relation to findings of fact has been held to provide inadequate protection (*Connors v UK* [2004]; *R (Wright) v Secretary of State*).

17.7 'Wide' *ultra vires*: improper purposes and relevance

These aspects of illegality arise in the context of discretionary powers where the governing statute does not define the extent of the powers precisely. They are sometimes labelled 'abuse of discretion'. Even though the decision maker keeps within the express language of the statute:

- it may act for an unauthorised purpose; or
- it may be influenced by irrelevant factors; or
- it may fail to take relevant factors into account.

These grounds apply even where the statute appears to give the decision maker an unrestricted, subjective discretion, using such expressions as 'if the minister thinks fit', since even the widest discretionary power is in principle reviewable. It is for the court to decide what factors are relevant and what are the purposes of the Act (*Padfield v Minister of Agriculture, Fisheries and Food* [1968]: a minister acting under a particular statutory power must not be influenced by wider political considerations that do not advance the policy of the Act).

As always the starting point is the language of the statute but where wide discretionary powers are concerned this may not be helpful. Sometimes it will be clear from the statutory context what factors are relevant. This was the case in *Padfield*, where the statute concerned pricing arrangements for agricultural products. Sometimes the legislation is unhelpful. For example the Town and Country Planning Act 1990 requires decision makers to have regard to 'material considerations' without saying what these are (see *Tesco Stores v Secretary of State for the Environment* [1995]: apparently taking the view that anything could be relevant unless clearly irrelevant). The courts therefore have leeway to impose their own view as to what is relevant. Thus the concept of relevance sets out conditions of proper decision making.

For example in *R v Somerset CC, ex p Fewings* [1995] the Council had banned hunting on its land for ethical reasons. Laws J held that freedom could not be interfered with by a public authority without clear statutory language and that the statute in question, which was for land management purposes, did not explicitly authorise ethical factors to be taken into account. The Court of Appeal took a different view, holding that the Council could take ethical factors into account unless barred by the statute. However they agreed with Laws J that the decision was flawed since the Council had not taken the statute into account at all but had assumed that they could do what they liked on their own land. It is of course fundamental that a statutory authority can act only in accordance with statute.

In *R v Parliamentary Comr for Administration, ex p Balchin* [1997] Sedley J suggested that that any consideration is relevant if, had it been taken into account, the decision maker might have reached a different conclusion (in that case a local council's attitude to the acquisition of some land). This seems to beg the question of what *should* be taken into account.

In deciding what factors are relevant, the court can look at background evidence, for example official reports that influenced the legislation in question and also things said in Parliament as to government policy. However statements made in Parliament cannot be used as evidence that a minister has acted in bad faith since this would violate the protection given to parliamentary proceedings by Article 9 of the Bill of Rights 1688 (Chapter 11). An unequivocal statement as to the scope of a provision might however prevent a minister subsequently from attempting a different explanation (*R v Secretary of State for the Environment, Transport and the Regions, ex p Spath Holme* [2001]: were rent control powers limited to anti-inflation measures or of wider scope?).

A decision maker must also take into account all relevant government policies and guidance, including international obligations, even though these do not necessarily have the force of law. Indeed such policies might create a 'legitimate expectation' (Section 17.9) that they will be followed. Moreover factors which are relevant must be clearly explained. For example if a policy refers to 'exceptional circumstances' the authority must be able to indicate as far as possible what these might be (*R (Rogers) v Swindon Primary Health Care Trust* [2006]: refusal to provide drug).

The relevant consideration doctrine can be used to protect important interests. In *R (Bulger) v Secretary of State for the Home Dept* [2001] the court, drawing on international obligations, held that in fixing the length of time a convicted child offender must serve, the Secretary of State must take into account the welfare of the child and keep the child's progress and rehabilitation under review. In *R v Secretary of State for the Home Dept, ex p Venables* [1997] it was held that public opinion, in the shape of an opinion poll in the *Sun* newspaper, was not relevant where the Secretary of State was charged with the judicial duty of reviewing the sentence in a notorious child murderer case, since his judicial function must be exercised using his independent judgement.

The courts have also held that local authorities should concern themselves with local issues as opposed to general issues of national or international politics (see *R v Lewisham LBC, ex p Shell UK Ltd* [1988]). The courts are therefore policing the boundaries of the democratic process. In earlier cases the courts appeared to be restricting the powers of local authorities in order to compel them to conserve taxpayers' money by adopting 'business principles' in fixing wages, fares and prices at the expense of local democratic freedom (see *Roberts v Hopwood* [1925]; *Prescott v Birmingham Corporation* [1955]; *Bromley LBC v GLC* [1983]). However it has also been stressed that the scope of what is relevant should be responsive to changing community values (see *Pickwell v Camden LBC* [1983]).

In *R v Secretary of State for Foreign and Commonwealth Affairs, ex p World Development Movement* [1995] the court perhaps went too far into the merits of government action (see Irvine, *Human Rights, Constitutional Law and the Development of the English Legal System* (Oxford University Press 2003) 164–65). The government had statutory power to give financial aid to other countries for 'economic' purposes. It decided to give a grant to Malaysia for the Pergau Dam project. The Court of Appeal held that Parliament must have intended the word 'economic' to include only 'sound' economic decisions, so the court was entitled to infer that the decision had been made primarily for an ulterior purpose (perhaps of facilitating an arms sale arrangement). This seems to come near to interfering with the merits of the decision since the court could deepen its investigation into any statutory function by saying that Parliament must have intended that function to be carried out 'soundly'. On the other hand parliamentary scrutiny had been ineffective, so the court's role may be justifiable as the only available constitutional check.

The relevance principle does not mean that the decision maker must give any particular weight to a given matter. In general the appropriate weight to be given to a factor is a political matter that is not for the court. The decision maker can choose which of the competing factors to prefer, provided that a relevant consideration is not completely ignored. For example in *Tesco Stores v Secretary of State* the House of Lords held that in accordance with a government circular, a planning authority must take into account an offer from Tesco to contribute to the building of a new road in the area in return for planning permission. However it could give the offer 'nil' weight in influencing its decision. On the other hand the court is not entirely excluded from matters of weighting.

1. A statute might expressly or implicitly indicate that special weight be given to some factors.
2. The courts themselves have decided that special weight must be given to the fundamental rights of the individual (eg *R v Secretary of State for the Home Dept, ex p Simms* [1999]).
3. Similarly matters falling within the Human Rights Act 1998 attract the 'proportionality' principle, which is essentially one of weighting, requiring as it does a strong reason to override a human right.
4. A legitimate expectation might also be given special weight (Section 17.9).
5. More generally the court can interfere if the decision maker has acted irrationally in relation to matters of weighting (see Section 18.1.).

There is some flexibility since the courts respect the expertise and political independence of the decision maker.

Firstly the court will not set aside a decision if the irrelevant consideration would not objectively have made any difference to the outcome. In this sense the line between legality and merits is blurred (see *R v Inner London Education Authority, ex p Westminster City Council* [1986]; *R v Secretary of State for Social Services, ex p Wellcome Foundation* [1987]). In the context of improper purposes, this is sometimes expressed as the 'dominant purpose' test. The following are illustrations.

- In *Westminster Corporation v London and North Western Railway* [1905] the local authority had power to construct public lavatories. It incorporated a subway into the design of its lavatories and it was objected that this was its real purpose. This was held to be lawful on the basis that the subway was merely incidental. Although it could be used by people to cross the street, it was also an appropriate method of reaching the lavatories. By contrast in *Webb v Minister of Housing and Local Government* [1965] the local authority had power to construct coast protection works. It incorporated a promenade into a scheme, compulsorily acquiring a number of houses for the purpose. This was held to be unlawful on the ground that more land was acquired than was needed for a coastal protection barrier. The whole scheme was invalid and the good part could not be separated from the bad.
- In *R v Lewisham LBC, ex p Shell UK Ltd* [1988] the Council decided to boycott Shell's products on the ground that Shell had interests in South Africa, which at the time was subject to apartheid. It was held that the policy could have been lawfully justified on the ground of promoting good race relations in the borough. However as the Council had tried to persuade other local authorities to adopt a similar policy, it had gone too far, its purpose being to put pressure on Shell.

It may be that if the decision maker's *subjective motive* is predominantly improper then the decision is always invalid, irrespective of whether it could be objectively justified, so as to encourage good standards of conduct. In *Porter v Magill* [2002] the leader of a local authority had embarked upon a policy of selling off the authority's housing. This in itself was a lawful policy. However sales were concentrated in marginal electoral wards with a view to attracting votes for the Conservative Party. The House of Lords held that the policy could not be justified on the basis of legitimate housing purposes. A democratic body can hope for an electoral advantage as the incidental outcome of its policies (and probably choose between alternative legitimate policies for electoral reasons) but it cannot distort policies in order to seek electoral advantage. However where the decision maker comprises many people acting collectively, such as a council or committee, it may be impossible to identify a predominant purpose, so an objective approach may be preferable.

Secondly, in relation to general factors such as hardship or expense, political or moral considerations, unless the statute plainly requires otherwise, the decision maker may have discretion to decide what is relevant in the particular circumstances. The court will interfere only where the authority exercises its discretion unreasonably. For example in *Fewings* the Court of Appeal took the view that had the Council properly addressed the statute, it could – but did not have to – take into account the moral question of cruelty (see also *R (Khatum) v Newham LBC* [2004]; *Ashby v Minister of Immigration* [1981] at 224: 'obligatory' and 'permissible' considerations).

In *R v City of Westminster Housing Benefit Review Board, ex p Mehanne* [2001] legislation required the housing benefit authority to reduce a claim when it considered that the rent was unreasonably high, 'having regard in particular to the cost of suitable accommodation elsewhere'. The board interpreted this as preventing it from taking into account the claimant's personal circumstances, including his wife's pregnancy and his reduced income as an asylum seeker. The House of Lords held that personal circumstances were relevant, pointing out that the phrase 'in particular' invited other factors to be considered. Lord Bingham said that 'in the absence of very clear language I would be very reluctant to conclude that the board were precluded from considering matters which could affect the mind of a reasonable and fair minded person' (at 617).

Cases where the court does not decide for itself what is or is not relevant but applies an unreasonableness test relate particularly to the notion of *justiciability*, where the increasing tendency of the courts is not to exclude particular areas from review completely but to interfere only where the decision maker acts in bad faith or irrationally or wholly without evidence. These cases involve wide discretionary powers where for various reasons judicial intervention is not considered appropriate (see Section 19.7.1). In the present context these reasons include matters involving wide political discretion where it is difficult to determine what factors should be relevant (see eg *R (Al Rawi) v Secretary of State* [2007]): Foreign Office refused to make representations concerning UK residents imprisoned by the US army in Guantanamo Bay; the Court would not decide what factors were relevant).

Problems have arisen when it has had to be decided whether a decision maker is entitled to take financial costs into account, for example when a local authority fails to provide a welfare benefit on the ground that it does not have sufficient resources and must prioritise between different kinds of needs. If the court were to order the authority to provide the benefit, the rule of law would be asserted and political pressure put on the government to come up with the necessary resources. There may also be inequity where different standards are applied in different local areas. On the other hand the court cannot command the impossible. Moreover the imposition of a duty inhibits democratic choice. Different priorities between areas reflect the workings of democracy. Thus in *Southwark LBC v Tanner* [2001] at 9–10, Lord Hoffmann warned against judicial intervention in a field which is so very much a matter of the allocation of resources in accordance with democratically determined priorities.

The courts are required to interpret the statute in order to determine whether the duty to provide the benefit is intended to be absolute (mandatory) or permissive. Words such as 'shall' or 'may' are indicative but not conclusive and the whole statutory context must be examined. The importance of the matter, the desirability of uniformity and resource implications are taken into account (see *R (M) v Gateshead Council* [2007]). For example in *R (G) v Barnet LBC* [2004] the House of Lords held that the duty imposed on local authorities by the Children Act 1989 to safeguard and promote the welfare of children in need provided only broad aims which the authority should bear in mind. This is sometimes labelled a 'target duty', reflecting the fact that not all needs can realistically be met in full. The Act therefore gave the authority a discretion to choose between competing demands and to take cost into account, and the court will interfere only if the discretion is exercised unreasonably. By contrast in *R (Conville) v Richmond on Thames LBC* [2006] the Court of Appeal held that a statute which required the Council to give a tenant a 'reasonable opportunity' to secure other accommodation did not allow it to take its own circumstances into account in deciding what was reasonable (see also *R v Gloucestershire CC, ex p Barry* [1997]; *R v East Sussex CC, ex p Tandy* [1998]; *R v Sefton Metropolitan BC, ex p Help the Aged* [1997]; R *v Newham LBC, ex p Begum* [2000]).

17.8 Fettering discretion

Officials fetter their discretion by binding themselves in advance to decide in a particular way, without being prepared to consider all the circumstances of an individual case on its merits. Thus this is an extreme example of a failure to take relevant factors into account.

Discretion can be fettered in many ways since administrators may find this is an attractive method of disposing of cases without too much effort or responsibility. Examples of unlawful fetters include the following:

- rigid application of rules, 'guidance' or policies made within the government hierarchy. Unless the rule is made legally binding by a statute or subordinate legislation, it is unlawful to treat it as binding (*R v Port of London Authority, ex p Kynoch* [1919]). An official can of course take into account guidelines drawn up within the government. Indeed government would be impracticable without them. Moreover fairness requires that people be treated equally, thereby requiring general guidelines. No more is required than that the decision maker always keep an open mind by considering whether in any given case an exception to the guideline should be made. This is a vital protection for the individual against official intransigence. In *British Oxygen Co v Ministry of Technology* [1971] there was a valid policy that grants would be payable only in respect of products above a certain size. Nevertheless the possibility of making an exception should have been considered. As Lord Reid put it:

  > a Ministry or large authority may have had already to deal with a multitude of similar applications and then they will almost certainly have evolved a policy so precise that it could well be called a rule. There can be no objection to that, provided that the authority is always willing to listen to anyone with something new to say. (at 625)

  Thus in this kind of case, assuming that we are dealing with a discretionary power, two questions arise and must be kept separate. Firstly is the rule or policy lawful in itself on the basis of the *ultra vires* principles discussed above? Secondly has the discretion been unlawfully fettered? For example in *R v Secretary of State for the Home Dept, ex p Hindley* [2000] a 'whole life tariff' set by the Home Secretary for a convicted murderer was lawful, provided that it was open to periodic review;
- rigid application of party political policies without making an independent judgment (*R v Waltham Forest LBC, ex p Baxter* [1988]);

- electoral mandates (*Bromley LBC v GLC* [1983]). These can of course be given great weight (cf *Secretary of State for Education and Science v Tameside Metropolitan BC* [1977];
- agreements and contracts that contradict a statutory obligation (*Ayr Harbour Trustees v Oswald* [1883]; *Stringer v Minister of Housing and Local Government* [1971]). Contracts are always binding and so inevitably fetter the future exercise of a discretion. However the principle seems to be that a contract is invalid only if it is inconsistent with a clear statutory obligation (see *R v Hammersmith and Fulham LBC, ex p Beddowes* [1987]);
- advice given by officials (*Western Fish Products v Penwith DC* [1981]: developer wrongly told that he would not need planning permission). Thus the doctrine of estoppel familiar in private law areas such as contract, under which in certain circumstances a person is bound by a promise or statement on which another relies, does not apply to governmental decisions made under statute. (This was the eventual outcome of an attempt over many years by Lord Denning to apply principles of estoppel in public law.)

  The justification for this harsh principle is the public interest that government decisions should be made according to law. On the other hand a citizen who is misled by an official is the victim of unfairness. To some extent the concept of a 'legitimate expectation' (Section 17.9) attempts to compromise between these competing considerations. There is of course no unlawful fetter where the decision-making power has been validly delegated to the official in question (see Section 18.2). Here the decision will be binding;
- acting under the dictation of another body (*Lavender & Son Ltd v Minister of Housing and Local Government* [1970]). But consulting another body and even relying on the decision of another body unless an objection is raised is lawful (see *R v GLC, ex p Blackburn* [1976]).

17.9 Legitimate expectations

By ensuring that the decision maker takes all relevant factors into account, the fettering discretion doctrine sometimes protects the citizen. However it also protects the general public interest by allowing a public body to change its mind or put right a mistake if the public interest so requires. This is one of the most important democratic principles. On the other hand it may be unjust to the individual if the decision maker disregards a previous promise or announced policy, particularly where the individual has re-arranged his or her affairs in reliance on the undertaking. Suppose for example a student gives up a job or pays fees for a course on the strength of a government announcement that a student of her category will be given a grant. The government later withdraws the announcement. Thus the law creates a dilemma in which fairness to the individual and legal certainty are in conflict with the public interest in democratic freedom.

The developing concept of 'legitimate expectation' confronts this dilemma. There is much uncertainty about its rationale and limits. First recognised by Lord Denning in *Schmidt v Secretary of State for Home Affairs* [1969], a legitimate expectation arises where the citizen has been led to believe by a statement or other conduct of the government that he is singled out for some benefit or advantage of which it would be unfair to deprive him. The expectation might be generated by a promise or assurance either announced generally or given specifically to an individual (eg *R v Secretary of State for the Home Dept, ex p Khan* [1985]: Home Office circular stated that adoptions of children from abroad would be allowed in certain circumstances; *Preston v IRC* [1985]: letter concerning tax affairs). A legitimate expectation might also be generated by a consistent practice whereby people in the same position as the applicant have been given a benefit in the past (*Council of Civil Service Unions v Minister for the Civil Service* [1985]).

A legitimate expectation must single out the claimant or a group the claimant including. It usually depends on a statement or promise and cannot be inferred merely from the general context (*Re Westminster City Council* [1986]). Nor can unofficial statements such as an election address or media interviews create a legitimate expectation (*R v Secretary of State for Education, ex p Begbie* [2000]). There may be a legitimate expectation that the government will honour an international treaty obligation which it has ratified (*R (Abassi) v Secretary of State* [2002], but cf *R v DPP, ex p Kebeline* [1999]).

Although Article 9 of the Bill of Rights 1688 prevents the courts from holding a minister liable for anything said in Parliament, a statement in Parliament might be used as evidence in judicial review proceedings and might create a legitimate expectation (see *Wilson v First County Trust* [2003] at [140]). Article 9 does not seem to be violated since the minister is not being *penalised* for anything said in Parliament (see Section 11.6.2).

Where an assurance is given to an individual, the individual must have disclosed all relevant information (*R v IRC, ex p MFK Underwriting Agents Ltd* [1990]). The statement that gives rise to the expectation must be clear and unambiguous and it must be reasonable for the claimant to rely upon it (see *Preston v IRC*: letter not sufficiently clear; see also *R (Bancoult) v Secretary of State for the Foreign and Commonwealth Office (No 2)* [2008]). *Abassi* provides an example of the need to define exactly what the legitimate expectation is. Lord Phillips explained that a legitimate expectation can be of 'a regular practice that the claimant can reasonably expect to continue' (at [82], [92]). However the expectation in that case was only that the Foreign Office would *consider* making diplomatic representations about the treatment of prisoners in Guantanamo Bay not that it would actually do so.

A legitimate expectation cannot arise if the decision in question would be *ultra vires* (see *Rowland v Environment Agency* [2003]: assurance given that stretch of river was private but public rights existed over it) since statute cannot be overcome. Thus the legitimate expectation doctrine is about a valid government statement or practice which the government subsequently withdraws either because it was made by mistake or because it has changed its mind. However where personal freedom or property rights are in issue, as was the case in *Rowland*, law might violate the wider principles of the ECHR since it is clearly unfair that that public body should be able to rely on its own illegality so as to override the interests of the individual (see *Stretch v UK* [2004]). In *Rowland* the Court of Appeal reached its conclusion reluctantly, being constrained by the *ultra vires* doctrine. It required the authority to do what it could within the law to mitigate the injustice to the claimant.

17.9.1 Reliance

It is sometimes suggested that the individual must rely on the statement that creates the legitimate expectation by incurring expense or other detriment. In practice this will often be the case. It must certainly be *reasonable* to rely on the statement. For example in *Odelola v Secretary of State* [2009] the claimants were Nigerian doctors who had applied to work in the UK. While their applications were in progress the government changed immigration policy. The change meant that only doctors with UK qualifications would now be admitted. The court rejected the claimants' argument that the application should be assessed under the rules as they were when the application was made. There was no legitimate expectation that the policy would not change because the claimants should have realised that immigration policy frequently does so. It would however be irrational and 'conspicuously unfair' not to return the claimants' fee.

Where the individual is relying on a general government policy, the statutory context might exclude a legitimate expectation if it is directed to concerns inconsistent with the interests of the claimant (eg *Findlay v Secretary of State for the Home Dept* [1985]: change in parole policy intended to protect the public interest).

However the need for actual reliance has been denied (see *R v Minister of Agriculture, Fisheries and Food, ex p Hamble (Offshore) Fisheries* [1995]). Indeed in the Australian case of *Minister of State for Immigration, ex p Teoh* [1995] it was suggested that the individual need not even know of the statement. This was the case in *R (Rashid) v Secretary of State* [2005], where the Court of Appeal condemned as 'conspicuous unfairness' (at [52]) a refusal to give asylum to a group of Kurds fleeing Iraq. Neither the officials concerned nor the asylum seekers knew about a government policy that relocation to an apparently safe part of Iraq should not defeat an asylum claim (but see *R v MoD, ex p Walker* [2000]; *R (A) v Secretary of State for the Home Dept* [2006]). In *R (Bancoult) v Secretary of State*, Lord Bingham suggested (at [73]) that *detriment* was required but not reliance.

This raises the question of what the purpose of the legitimate expectation doctrine is. In support of *Teoh* and *Rashid* it might be suggested that it is to ensure good administration and consistency. It is wrong for government to disregard serious assurances that it has given. On the other hand the purpose of the doctrine could be to redress injustice suffered by the individual. On this basis the principle of equality indicates that the individual should not get special treatment without a good reason, namely that he or she has suffered in some way as a result of the government statement.

Perhaps a distinction can be drawn between statements made to particular individuals and statements made more generally. Where the undertaking in question is given to a particular individual, there is a strong argument that his or her interests deserve special consideration even if he or she has not suffered in reliance upon it. However an expectation is often generated by a general policy announced in a circular or a general practice. It is arguable that where the claimant relies on an announcement or practice directed to the public at large, the claimant must show that she or he can be distinguished from the public at large by acting on the expectation so as to incur expense or other detriment (see *R v Jockey Club, ex p RAM Racecourses* [1993] at 236–40). Perhaps detrimental reliance may be one aspect of a wider principle of fairness, something to be taken into account but not conclusive (see *Begbie*; *R (Bibi) v Newnham LBC* [2002]).

R v Secretary of State for Education, ex p Begbie [2000] provides a useful illustration of the ingredients of a legitimate expectation.

- The Education (Schools) Act 1997, introduced after the general election of 1997, abolished the 'assisted places' scheme, which funded children from low-income families in private schools. Children already in the scheme would be funded only until the end of primary education unless the minister decided otherwise at his discretion.

- The position of children at 'all-through' schools was in doubt. There was a pre-election announcement by the Opposition leader and letters from MPs saying that funding would continue. These were not government statements, so they could not create a legitimate expectation.
- There was also a newspaper article by the Prime Minister stating that the funding would continue. This could not create a legitimate expectation because it was contrary to the statute and was also unclear.
- There was an official letter from the minister to a grandparent. This also contradicted the statute and was unclear. Moreover it was corrected later, so there could be no reliance upon it.

Thus incompetent government can get away with it.

17.9.2 Consequences: procedural or substantive

The legitimate expectation doctrine does not prevent a policy from being changed for the future. It concerns only the possible injustice to those who have already been affected by it. It is clear that a legitimate expectation does not create a fully enforceable right (*O'Reilly v Mackman* [1982]: prisoners' expectation of early release). What then are its consequences?

1. At the very least a legitimate expectation is a relevant consideration which must be taken into account in making a decision (*R (Theophilus) v Lewisham BC* [2002]: student grant to study abroad). In *R (A) v Secretary of State* Collins J said: 'Legitimate expectation is grounded in fairness. The courts expect government departments and indeed all officials who make decisions affecting members of the public to honour statements of policy. To fail to do so will ... mean that the decision maker has failed to have regard to a material consideration' (at [29]). On this basis, as long as the expectation is taken into account, the court will interfere only if the decision is completely unreasonable (see *R v North and East Devon HA, ex p Coughlan* [2000] at [57]).
2. A legitimate expectation may also entitle the claimant to a fair hearing and perhaps require reasons to be given before the benefit is refused or withdrawn (*Khan*). Indeed the expectation itself may be only of a hearing (eg *A-G for Hong Kong v Shiu* [1983]: to consider applications for citizenship on their individual merits; *R v Liverpool City Council, ex p Liverpool Taxi Fleet Operators Association* [1975]: undertaking to consult). This is called a 'procedural' expectation. It may however be that some other factor, for example national security, might override the duty to give a hearing (see Section 18.3).
3. Where the expectation is that of an actual benefit (a 'substantive' expectation) the court may go further and in certain cases require the authority to give the citizen the benefit itself (substantive protection). However the circumstances where this will be so are unclear. In *R v Secretary of State for Health, ex p US Tobacco International Inc* [1992] it was held that a legitimate expectation could not override the government's statutory discretion. The government had encouraged the company to manufacture snuff in the UK. After the company had incurred expense on its investment, the government withdrew its permission on medical advice. It was held that the

government could withdraw its invitation. The company was entitled only to a hearing on the health issue giving it an opportunity to persuade the government to change its mind.

There are however cases supporting substantive protection. In *Khan*, where the government stated by letter that certain policies concerning overseas adoptions would be followed, Lord Parker CJ suggested that 'vis-à-vis the recipient of such a letter, a new policy can only be implemented after such recipient has been given a full and serious consideration whether there is some overriding public interest which justifies a departure from the procedures stated in the letter' (at 48). The main issue which has divided the courts is whether the court itself decides what the public interest is or whether it is for the authority to do so. The latter would be the traditional approach.

- In *R v Minister of Agriculture, Fisheries and Food, ex p Hamble (Offshore) Fisheries* [1995] Sedley J suggested that a legitimate expectation created a binding obligation that could be overridden only if in the court's view it was necessary to do so to achieve the objectives of the statute. The case concerned a claim to retain a fishing licence on the basis of a previous announcement in the face of a change in a policy designed to conserve fishing stocks. However, on the facts, giving effect to the expectation would seriously have disrupted government fishing policy, so the expectation was not honoured. In *R v Secretary of State, ex p Hargreaves* [1997] (at 412) this approach was described as heresy as it went beyond the normal limits of judicial review.
- In *R v North and East Devon HA, ex p Coughlan* [2000], which remains the only case where substantive protection was unequivocally given, the Court of Appeal held that a severely disabled resident of a local authority nursing home could hold the local authority to a previous assurance that it would be her home for life. The authority proposed to close the home in order to transfer nursing care to the local authority. It was held that the assurance created an enforceable legitimate expectation that only an overriding public interest could displace. The scope of this is not clear. In particular the right to respect for home and family life (ECHR, Art 8) was in issue, thereby raising the threshold of review. Moreover, although the decision to close the home had financial consequences, it did not raise general policy issues. Lord Woolf suggested that the court should weigh the expectation against any overriding interest required by the change of policy. This balancing exercise invites the court to scrutinise the merits of the decision beyond the usual limits of judicial review. It is however similar to the doctrine of proportionality which applies in human rights cases. Lord Woolf also formulated a more conventional test, namely where 'to frustrate the expectation is so unfair that to take a new and different course will amount to an abuse of power'. Lord Woolf also distinguished between statements made to a few individuals or to a group with a common interest and statements made to large numbers of people or to diverse groups. Substantive protection may be less appropriate in the second kind of case.

- In *R v Secretary of State for Education, ex p Begbie* [2000] Laws LJ said that decisions which affect wide-ranging policy issues or indefinite numbers of people should not be overridden since the court would be usurping the democratic process and would not be sufficiently aware of the consequences of its decision.
- In *R (Rashid) v Secretary of State* [2005] Dyson L recognised circumstances where it would be 'an abuse of power' to override an expectation (at [50]). In particular the court should not usually interfere where the matter raised issues in the 'macro-political field' that affected large numbers of people or had long-term consequences. Even here a seriously unfair decision would probably be invalid.
- In *R (Wheeler) v Office of the Prime Minister* [2008] it was claimed that government announcements gave rise to a legitimate expectation that the Lisbon Treaty, which increased EU powers, would not be ratified without a referendum. The court refused to give effect to any expectation on the ground that this was a macro-political matter appropriate only to Parliament and would involve improper interference by the judiciary with Parliament.

The cases are therefore inconclusive. The legitimate expectation debate sets the individual claim to respect against the public good. The law cannot combine these incommensurable values and so reaches an untidy accommodation, usually by offering the individual a hearing that might persuade the authority to change its mind. Another compromise solution would be to pay compensation to the victim. Unfortunately there is no right to compensation in UK law for unlawful administrative action as such.

Summary

- Judicial review is constitutionally ambivalent. On the one hand it supports the rule of law, parliamentary supremacy and democracy by enabling the courts to police the limits of government power. On the other hand the courts are open to the complaint based on the separation of powers that they are interfering with the decisions of democratically elected bodies. The basis of this complaint is that the courts interpret the legislation in question in the light of their own values and presumptions of interpretation which are not necessarily democratic.
- Judicial review is not concerned with the merits of a government decision but with whether the decision maker has kept within legal limits and followed broad principles of fairness and rationality. The grounds of judicial review are loosely classified under the heads of illegality, irrationality and procedural impropriety.
- The constitutional basis of judicial review is contested. According to one view, it depends on the *ultra vires* doctrine. The alternative view is that judicial review is a freestanding part of the common law but subject to parliamentary supremacy. Proponents of the *ultra vires* doctrine cater for the fact that much of the law is actually judge made by claiming that Parliament intends and so implicitly authorises legislation to be interpreted according to principles of judicial review
- A statutory decision maker must act within the limits of the statute, including what is 'reasonably incidental' to the statute. The courts apply presumptions of statutory interpretation, notably 'the principle of legality', in policing the limits of statutory powers.

Summary cont'd

- Review for mistakes of fact is limited since this might involve a reviewing court going outside its proper sphere. Clear errors of fact may be reviewable and an error of fact might also fall within one of the other grounds, for example irrationality (Chapter 17). The interpretation of broad subjective terms in a statute may be classified as mixed questions of law and fact to limit review. Limitations on review for mistakes of fact may raise the question of the right to a fair trial under the ECHR, which in cases where civil rights or obligations are in issue requires an independent decision on factual matters.
- A decision maker also acts *ultra vires* by acting for an improper purpose, taking an irrelevant factor into account or failing to take a relevant factor into account where this affects the outcome of the decision. Matters directly related to the statute must always be taken into account. Broader factors can be taken into account.
- Fettering discretion concerns the application of a self-created rigid rule, policy or undertaking in a case where, under a statute, the decision maker must exercise a discretion. A decision maker can adopt guidelines but cannot treat them as absolutely binding.
- The doctrine of 'legitimate expectation' attempts to deal with the injustice arising where a decision maker departs from a lawful undertaking, policy statement or practice which it is reasonable for the citizen to rely upon. It is not settled how far an individual must actually rely on the expectation. Basically a legitimate expectation does no more than entitle the individual to a hearing to persuade the decision maker to give effect to its previous statement. In some cases the court may require the authority to honour its previous statement by weighing the interests of the individual against the public interest. Matters of general policy are unlikely to be so restricted.

Exercises

17.1 'The simple proposition that a public authority may not act outside its powers (*ultra vires*) might fitly be called the central principle of administrative law' (Wade and Forsythe, *Administrative Law*). Discuss.

17.2 When can mistakes of law and fact be challenged in the courts? To what extent has the Human Rights Act 1998 affected the position?

17.3 Pleasantville District Council has statutory power to 'manage dwelling houses designed for elderly persons'. The Council owns a block of 10 flats with accommodation for a warden on the outskirts of Pleasantville that it lets to persons over the age of 60. Experiencing financial difficulties, it makes the following arrangements:

(i) It advertises the sale of three of the flats to persons under 60.

(ii) It bans all car parking in the precincts of the flat unless a residents parking permit is purchased at £50 per annum or a visitors permit at £20 for 10 visits.

(a) Advise the residents of the flats, who object to both these arrangements.

(b) Advise George, who is 48 and has purchased one of the three flats.

17.4 The (imaginary) Higher Education Act 2011 provides that local authorities 'may award grants to university students in accordance with criteria approved by the Secretary of State'. In March 2009 the Secretary of State issues guidance in a circular sent to all secondary schools stating that grants will be awarded to anyone whose family income is less than £15,000 or if there is evidence of hardship. Peter, who has read the guidance, and Wendy, who has not, decided to

Exercises cont'd

leave their current employment to take up university places in September 2009. Their family incomes are £10,000 and £12,000 respectively. Fi wishes to take a university course in Surfing Studies from September 2009. Her family income is in excess of £15,000 but her family refuse to support her as they want her to study Law. An official from the local authority writes to Fi informing her that this constitutes hardship and that she is eligible for a grant.

In June 2009 the Secretary of State issues new guidance. This states that 'due to a funding shortfall, grants will be awarded only where family income is less than £8000 or where there is evidence of "exceptional hardship"'. The official now writes to Fi telling her that her circumstances do not constitute exceptional hardship and that she will not receive a grant. Peter and Wendy are also refused grants.

Advise Peter, Wendy and Fi as to the likelihood of a successful challenge to these decisions in the courts and whether they are entitled to grants.

17.5 Under the Sports Act 2002 (fictitious) the Minister of Sport has power 'where he considers it necessary in the interest of public safety and good order, to require the admission of paid spectators to any sporting event to be subject to showing membership cards at the entrance'. The minister, interpreting 'sport' as including any activity that is competitive, has made an order requiring entrance to chess competitions to be subject to the showing of membership cards. There has been some evidence of disorder at the events. The minister has been advised that chess events are an important source of the Opposition party's finances. In another case the minister has revoked the membership cards of all the members of a football club because the club has failed to provide an all-seater stadium. The club is in the third division and the present stadium is very rarely more than half full. Discuss.

Further reading

Allan, 'Constitutional Dialogue and the Justification for Judicial Review' (2003) 23 OJLS 129

Atrill, 'The End of Estoppel in Public Law?' [2003] CLJ 3

Barber, 'The Academic Mythologians' (2001) 21 OJLS 369

Craig, 'The Common Law, Shared Power and Judicial Review' (2004) 24 OJLS 237

Craig and Bamforth, 'Constitutional Principle, Constitutional Analysis and Judicial Review' [2001] PL 763

Craig and Tomkins (eds), *The Executive and Public Law* (Oxford University Press 2006)

Forsythe, 'Of Fig Leaves and Fairy Tales: The *Ultra Vires* Doctrine, the Sovereignty of Parliament and Judicial Review' (1996) 55 CLJ 122

Forsythe (ed), *Judicial Review and the Constitution* (Hart 2000) [includes articles cited here]

Forsythe and Elliot, 'The Legitimacy of Judicial Review' [2003] PL 286

Forsythe *et al* (eds), *Effective Judicial Review: A Cornerstone of Good Governance* (Oxford University Press 2010)

Halpin, 'The Theoretical Controversy concerning Judicial Review' (2001) 64 MLR 500

Hannett and Busch, '*Ultra Vires* Representations and Legitimate Expectations' [2005] PL 729

Hare, 'Separation of Powers and Error of Law' in Forsythe and Hare (eds), *The Golden Metwand and the Crooked Cord* (Clarendon Press 1998)

Harlow and Pearson, *Administrative Law in a Changing State* (Hart 2008)

Jowell, 'Of Vires and Vacuums: The Constitutional Context of Judicial Review' [1999] PL 448

Further reading cont'd

Knight, 'Expectations in Transition: Recent Developments in Legitimate Expectations' [2009] PL 519

Poole, 'Legitimacy, Rights and Judicial Review' (2005) 25 OJLS 697

Sales and Steyn, 'Legitimate Expectations in English Public Law: An Analysis' [2004] PL 564

Steele, 'Substantive Legitimate Expectations: Striking the Right Balance' (2005) 121 LQR 300

Tomkins, 'The Role of the Courts in the Political Constitution' (2010) 60 U Toronto LJ 1

Tucker, 'Legitimate Expectations and the Separation of Powers' (2009) 125 LQR 233

Williams, 'When Is an Error Not an Error? Reform of Jurisdictional Review of Errors of Law' [2007] PL 793

Woolf, 'Judicial Review: The Tensions between the Executive and the Judiciary' (1998) 114 LQR 579

Chapter 18

The grounds of judicial review, II: beyond *ultra vires*

> **The indispensable requirement of public confidence in the administration of justice requires higher standards today than was the case even a decade or two ago. The informed observer of today could perhaps be expected to be aware of the legal traditions and culture of this jurisdiction... But he might not be wholly uncritical of that culture.**
>
> **(Lord Steyn in *Lawal v Northern Spirit* [2004] at [22])**

This chapter continues the discussion in Chapter 17. It concentrates on grounds of review that are less directly linked to the notion of *ultra vires* and which therefore especially raise issues of the proper limits of the courts' role.

18.1 Irrationality/unreasonableness

Irrationality or 'unreasonableness' is an overriding ground of review. It can be used to challenge the exercise of discretion or findings of law and fact (see Section 17.6). Although the question of what is reasonable must, as always, be decided in the context of the particular statutory power, this ground of review operates as an external control in that it draws on values not directly derived from the statute itself. Indeed the notion of 'unreasonableness' is so vague that it seems to invite the court to impose its own opinion of the merits in place of that of the decision maker.

Against this, the separation of powers coupled with practical considerations suggests that the courts should be cautious in interfering with the decisions of the executive on vague grounds such as unreasonableness. The former Lord Chancellor Lord Irvine (1996) suggested that three broad reasons lay behind this: firstly respect for Parliament, which had conferred decision-making power on the body in question; secondly limited judicial expertise in matters of policy concerning the general public interest; thirdly what he called the 'democratic imperative', namely that government is judged by the electorate every few years. Lord Irvine's third rationale seems ludicrous since the electorate cannot vote in respect of individual decisions and his first begs the controversial question as to whether *ultra vires* is the basis of judicial review and if so what Parliament intends (see Section 17.1).

The courts have struggled to give the notion of unreasonableness a limited meaning. The main result has been to create a multi-level approach in which the intensity of judicial scrutiny varies with the context, the main factors being the seriousness of the decision in relation to the rights of the individual and, pulling in the other direction, the extent to which the decision maker's powers involve controversial social, economic, political or moral judgements.

The starting point and baseline is usually called '*Wednesbury* unreasonableness' after Lord Greene's speech in *Associated Provincial Picture Houses Ltd v Wednesbury*

Corporation [1948]. Lord Greene MR emphasised that the court will interfere only where a decision is 'so unreasonable that no reasonable authority could have made it', not merely because it thinks it is a bad decision. In that case the court upheld a condition that no child should attend a cinema in the town on a Sunday. (Of course perceptions of what is unreasonable may change over time.)

Other attempts have been made to capture this elusive idea. For example the decision must be 'beyond the range of responses open to a reasonable decision maker' (*R v Ministry of Defence, ex p Smith* [1996] at 263; *R v Chief Constable of Sussex, ex p International Trader's Ferry Ltd* [1999] at 157). In *Council of Civil Service Unions (CCSU) v Minister for the Civil Service* [1984] Lord Diplock said that the courts will interfere only where a decision has no rational basis or 'is so outrageous in its denial of accepted moral standards that no sensible person who has applied his mind to the question to be decided could have arrived at it' (at 951). Errors of reasoning or misunderstanding of evidence make a decision *Wednesbury* unreasonable (eg *R (AB) v Secretary of State for Justice* [2010]: refusal to transfer transgender prisoner to woman's prison: misunderstanding of expert advice [82]–[85]).

Lord Diplock's formulation is often used to justify not interfering with a decision. For example in *Brind v Secretary of State for the Home Dept* [1991] the government banned live media interviews with supporters of the Irish Republican Army (IRA). The House of Lords held that although the ban was probably misguided it had some rational basis as a means of denying publicity to terrorists and was therefore valid (see also *R v Radio Authority, ex p Bull* [1997] at 577). On the other hand although successful challenges for unreasonableness are rare, they seem to fall short of irrationality in the extreme sense suggested above. For example in *Hall & Co Ltd v Shoreham-by-Sea UDC* [1964] a local authority planning condition required the plaintiff to dedicate a road to the public. This was held to be 'unreasonable' because it amounted to the confiscation of property without compensation. However the condition was hardly perverse or irrational, given that the plaintiff stood to make considerable profit out of the permission.

In *R v Secretary of State for the Home Dept, ex p Daly* [2001] Lord Cooke described *Wednesbury* as 'an unfortunately retrogressive decision in English administrative law, in so far as it suggested that only a very extreme degree [of unreasonableness] can bring an administrative decision within the scope of judicial invalidation' (at [32]). He emphasised that the level of interference should vary with the subject matter: 'It may well be, however, that the law can never be satisfied in any administrative field merely by a finding that the decision under review is not capricious or absurd.'

A more flexible approach to unreasonableness is to ask whether a reasonable decision maker *in the light of the material properly before him* could reasonably justify his decision, or whether a decision shows 'conduct which no sensible authority acting with *due appreciation of its responsibilities* would have decided to adopt' (see Lord Cook in *International Trader's Ferry* at 452). This formula enables the court to apply different levels of scrutiny in different contexts and to evaluate the quality of the decision maker's reasoning (see eg *R (Rogers) v Swindon and District NHS Trust* [2006]: decision to withhold drug treatment not based on financial considerations but no alternative rationale given). However it comes perilously close to enabling the court to interfere merely because it disagrees with the decision.

Where important interests of the individual are at stake, the level of review is sometimes called 'heightened *Wednesbury*'. It requires the decision maker to show that it has placed particularly close attention – 'anxious scrutiny' – to the interests in question (see *Bugdaycay v Secretary of State for the Home Dept* [1987] at 952; *R v Ministry of Defence, ex p Smith*; *R v Lord Saville of Newdigate* [1999]). Heightened *Wednesbury* in itself does not mean that the court will intervene. For example in *R v Ministry of Defence, ex p Smith* the Court of Appeal refused to interfere with a decision to ban practising homosexuals from serving in the army. The court recognised that the decision affected fundamental rights and therefore called for 'anxious scrutiny' but also thought that the court was not in a position to assess the specialist needs of military service and should therefore defer to the views of the military establishment. The decision of the UK courts was later held to violate the European Convention on Human Rights (ECHR) (see Section 18.1.1).

At the other end of the scale, where a decision depends on broad social, economic or political factors or matters remote from ordinary judicial experience, the court has been cautious in interfering. This is an application of the general notion of 'deference' which underlies much of the law (see Section 17.1). In cases of this kind, at least where human rights interests are not an issue, the courts may apply a standard even lower than Lord Diplock's rationality test, interfering only where a decision is entirely capricious – an approach sometimes called 'super-*Wednesbury*'. This also applies where separation of powers issues are at stake, in particular where the decision in question is one that has been approved after a debate in Parliament.

Thus in *Hammersmith and Fulham LBC v Secretary of State for the Environment* [1990] (central grants to local government), Lord Bridge said:

> since the statute has conferred a power on the Secretary of State which involves the formulation and implementation of national economic policy and which can only take effect with the approval of the House of Commons, it is not open to challenge on the ground of irrationality short of the extremes of bad faith, improper motive or manifest absurdity. Both the constitutional propriety and the good sense of this restriction seem to me to be clear enough. The formulation and implementation of national economic policy are matters depending essentially on political judgment. The decisions which shape them are for politicians to take and it is in the political forum of the House of Commons that they are properly to be debated and approved or disapproved on their merits. If the decisions have been taken in good faith within the four corners of the Act, the merits of the policy underlying the decisions are not susceptible to judicial review by the courts and the courts would be exceeding their proper function if they presumed to condemn the policy as unreasonable. (at 637)

(See also *Nottinghamshire CC v Secretary of State for the Environment* [1986].)

It must be emphasised that Lord Bridge's remarks apply only to unreasonableness. Where a decision is *ultra vires* on some other ground, then approval by Parliament (other than in the form of a statute) does not validate it or prevent the court scrutinising it in the ordinary way. Thus the separation of powers works in both directions (see *R v Secretary of State for the Home Dept, ex p Fire Brigades Union* [1995]). It must also be emphasised that the fact that a matter may be controversial is not in itself a reason for deference.

Sometimes the statute itself may require that a decision maker act 'reasonably' or 'have reasonable cause' to believe or do something. In this kind of case the court may decide for itself what is reasonable in the ordinary, non-*Wednesbury* sense (see eg *Nakkuda Ali v Jayaratne* [1951]). On the other hand if a wide political discretion is involved the court may apply the *Wednesbury* approach even here. The matter depends on the particular context (see eg *Secretary of State for Education and Science v Tameside MBC* [1977]: Secretary of State could interfere with local school decisions on reasonable grounds: *Wednesbury* applied).

Unreasonableness may overlap with other grounds of review. In *Wheeler v Leicester City Council* [1985] a local authority refused to allow a rugby club to use its playing field. This was because the club had not prevented certain of its members from touring in South Africa during the apartheid era. The House of Lords held that the Council had acted unlawfully. This could be regarded as an unreasonable infringement of individual freedom, as a decision based upon an improper political purpose or as an unfair decision in that the matter had been prejudged. Today *Wheeler* would probably be explained on human rights grounds, a perspective that was raised in the Court of Appeal but which the House of Lords avoided.

18.1.1 Proportionality

At least in cases subject to the Human Rights Act 1998 (Chapter 21) and in EC law, a more stringent standard of review applies in the form of the doctrine of 'proportionality'. Broadly speaking a decision is proportionate only if it meets an important public goal (a 'pressing social need') and in doing so violates the right in question as little as possible. As Lord Diplock ponderously put it in *R v Goldsmith* [1983], proportionality 'prohibits the use of a steam hammer to crack a nut if a nutcracker would do' (at 155). In *CCSU* Lord Diplock suggested (at 950) that proportionality might at a future date become a ground of domestic judicial review in its own right. This has not yet been fully realised, although proportionality is closely related to unreasonableness and often overlaps with it.

The requirements of proportionality set out by the Privy Council in *De Freitas v Ministry of Agriculture, Fisheries and Housing* [1999] have been widely adopted. These are whether:

- the legislative objective is sufficiently important to justify limiting a fundamental right. It is a difficult question as to whether the court or an elected body should decide this but, under the Human Rights Act 1998, unless the language of the statute makes it impossible to interpret it other than as violating the right, the court has the last word (Chapter 19);
- the measures designed to meet the legislative objective are rationally connected with it;
- the means used to impair the right or freedom are no more than is necessary to accomplish the objective.

Before the Human Rights Act 1998 English judges had objected to proportionality on the ground that it takes the court too far into the political merits (see *Hone v Maze Board of Prison Visitors* [1988] at 327–29; *Brind v Secretary of State*; *Tesco Stores v Secretary of State for the Environment* [1995]). Therefore English law sometimes fell foul of the ECHR because it failed to reach the standard of necessity required by the proportionality doctrine. For example *Smith* was condemned by the European Court of Human Rights in *Smith and Grady v UK* [2000]. It was held that even heightened *Wednesbury* failed to satisfy the ECHR because it excluded any consideration of whether the interference with the applicant's rights answered a pressing social need or was proportionate to the national security and public order aims pursued.

Proportionality overlaps with unreasonableness but will sometimes produce a different outcome, as in *Smith and Grady*. In many cases however the two are likely to produce the same outcome. For example in *R v Barnsley Metropolitan BC, ex p Hook* [1976] a market trader was dismissed by the market manager for the relatively minor wrong of urinating in the street. This was held to be an unreasonably severe penalty. In *Daly* it was government policy that a prisoner's confidential correspondence with his lawyer could be examined in the prisoner's absence. The House of Lords held that although the policy satisfied the bare rationality test and was administratively convenient it was contrary to Article 8 of the ECHR (respect for correspondence). A reasonable minister could not have concluded that the policy was necessary for the legitimate goal of keeping order in prisons. Lord Bingham based his reasoning firstly on the common law, heightened *Wednesbury* approach. However he also said that under the Human Rights Act 1998 'domestic courts must go beyond the ordinary standard and themselves form a judgment whether a Convention right has been breached, conducting such an inquiry as is necessary to form that judgment' (at 455). Lord Steyn applied the proportionality test, emphasising that it went beyond *Wednesbury* by requiring the court itself to decide whether the right 'balance' had been struck between the conflicting interests. Lord Steyn also said that there had not been a shift to merits review, the respective roles of judges and administrators remaining 'fundamentally distinct' (although how this distinction should be drawn is elusive).

It is sometimes suggested that proportionality should not be confined to human rights cases but should be considered as an aspect of unreasonableness. It is generally accepted, sometimes reluctantly, that the two approaches, although overlapping, are not merged. Thus in *R (Alconbury Developments Ltd) v Secretary of State for the Environment, Transport and the Regions* [2001] Lord Slynn emphasised that proportionality was different from *Wednesbury* but that 'the difference in practice is not as great as is sometimes supposed' (at 976). He thought that proportionality and *Wednesbury* should not be kept in separate compartments and that 'even without reference to the 1998 Act the time has come to recognise that this principle is part of English administrative law, not only when judges are dealing with Community acts but also when they are dealing with acts subject to domestic law'. (But see *R (Association of British Civilian Internees; Far East Region) v Secretary of State* [2003] at [35]–[37]: suggesting that *Wednesbury* be replaced by proportionality but bound by authority to apply *Wednesbury* meanwhile.) This leaves unexplained what other situations might attract the proportionality test. One such might be the case of a 'substantive' legitimate expectation (see Section 17.9.2).

18.2 Procedural impropriety: statutory procedural requirements

This topic illustrates the elastic nature of contemporary judicial review. Failure to comply with a procedural requirement laid down by statute (such as time limits, consultation or giving required information or notice) could make a decision *ultra vires* and so void. However the courts are reluctant to set aside a decision on purely technical grounds. Traditionally the courts have tried to rationalise this by distinguishing between 'mandatory' (important) and 'directory' (unimportant) procedural requirements by reference to the language of the governing statute (see eg *R v Clarke and McDaid* [2008]). They also take a flexible response to the particular context. Using their discretionary power to withhold a remedy, the courts will set a decision aside for procedural irregularity only if the harm or injustice caused to the applicant by the procedural flaw outweighs the harm to the government or to innocent third parties in setting the decision aside (see eg *Coney v Choyce* [1975]; *London and Clydeside Estates Ltd v Aberdeen DC* [1979]; *Wang v IRC* [1995]; *R v Immigration Appeal Tribunal, ex p Jeyeanthan* [1999]).

On the other hand the courts will not allow administrative convenience to override a statutory right of the public to be consulted. In *Berkeley v Secretary of State for the Environment* [2000] the House of Lords held that a local authority was required to make environmental information relating to a planning application for a football stadium available to the public even though the Council successfully argued that it already had adequate environmental evidence to enable it to make a proper decision. Lord Hoffmann in particular, reflecting the broad concept of democracy, suggested that public consultation was an end in itself and not merely an instrument of effective decision making (see also *R (Boyejo) v Barnet LBC* [2009]: consultation must be genuinely interactive: providing an opportunity for questions not sufficient).

Another important statutory procedural requirement is the rule against delegation. An official (or indeed anyone) who is entrusted with power to make a decision affecting the rights of individuals should not transfer that power to someone else (*delegatus non potest delegare*; *Barnard v National Dock Labour Board* [1953]). However applying this principle strictly would cause administrative breakdown and many exceptions have been made. Nevertheless public bodies have sometimes ignored the requirement. For example the Housing Corporation (now abolished) had done so for more than 40 years without anyone complaining until the matter was put right by retrospective legislation (Housing Corporation Act 2006).

Exceptions to the rule against delegation are as follows:

- Under the *Carltona* doctrine a minister can act through a civil servant in her or his department (see Section 15.7.3). This can be rationalised as not a true exception in that constitutionally the minister and civil servant are one, the minister being responsible to Parliament for the act of the civil servant (see *R (Alconbury Developments Ltd) v Secretary of State for the Environment, Transport and the Regions* [2001]). On the other hand why should political responsibility affect the legal position, particularly as we have seen that ministerial responsibility is weak and uncertain. Nevertheless unless the method of delegation is entirely unreasonable it seems that the courts cannot interfere (*Re Golden Chemical Products* [1976]; *R v Secretary of State for the Home Dept, ex p Olahinde* [1991], but see Section 15.7.3). *Carltona* does not apply to government agencies outside the central civil service such as the police or the local government or independent statutory bodies (but see *R (Chief Constable of the West Midlands Police) v Birmingham City Justices* [2002]: basing the rule on a wider rationale of implied statutory authority and distinguishing between normal decision making within the organisational hierarchy and cases where the statute requires a named official to act personally).

- Many local authority functions can be delegated by statute to committees, subcommittees, officers and other authorities but not to individual councillors or outside bodies unless authorised by statute (see Local Government Act 1972, s 101; *R v Port Talbot BC, ex p Jones* [1988]). A committee cannot comprise one person.
- Many governmental functions can be transferred to private bodies (Deregulation and Contracting Out Act 1994, ss 61, 69).
- Functions involving little independent discretion can be delegated. Indeed the courts seem ready to imply statutory authority to delegate in cases where it would be inconvenient for the decision maker to do everything her or himself (*Provident Mutual Life Assurance Association v Derby City Council* [1981]; see also *R (Chief Constable of the West Midlands Police) v Birmingham City Justices*).
- Fact finding, making recommendations and giving advice can be delegated but the decision maker must not merely 'rubber stamp' the advice she or he is given. The decision maker must have enough information before him or her, for example a summary of evidence, to make a genuine decision (*Jeffs v New Zealand Dairy Production and Marketing Board* [1967]).

18.3 Procedural impropriety: the right to a fair hearing

This ground of review is of ancient common law origin and is central to the idea of the rule of law. It is called in aid by those who claim that judicial review is based on a freestanding common law (see Section 17.1). Until the early twentieth century the courts applied a broad principle traceable to the seventeenth century and usually labelled 'natural justice', namely that anyone whose rights were affected by an official decision was entitled to advance notice of a decision and a fair hearing before an unbiased judge (eg *Bagg's Case* [1615]; *Dr Bonham's Case* [1610]; *Cooper v Wandsworth Board of Works* [1863]).

The advance of the democratically supported administrative state produced a more cautious judicial approach. *Local Government Board v Arlidge* [1915] marks a turning point where Dicey felt that the rule of law itself was at risk. In *Arlidge* the House of Lords held that in the case of administrative decisions (in that case a house closure order), provided that it complies with minimum standards of fairness, the government can decide for itself what procedures to follow, the citizen's protection lying not in the courts but in ministerial responsibility to Parliament (see also *Board of Education v Rice* [1911] at 182, but cf *Dyson v A-G* [1911]).

The courts then refused to apply natural justice to decisions other than those which they labelled 'judicial'. For this purpose 'judicial' means the impartial application of rules to settle a dispute about the parties' existing rights, narrowly defined – essentially what a court does. Thus the courts took a crude separation of powers approach that removed natural justice from political, discretionary and policy-oriented decisions, which the court labelled 'administrative'. This excluded much of the welfare state from natural justice since the conferring of benefits such as education and housing does not strictly affect existing rights. It also excluded government powers such as planning, compulsory purchase and other forms of licensing which, although they affect rights, are usually discretionary. The main area left for natural justice was where a formal tribunal or inquiry determined a specific dispute, but even this caused problems in the case of public inquiries held as part of a larger discretionary process leading to a political decision, for example to build a new road (see eg *Franklin v Minister of Town and Country Planning* [1948]).

However in *Ridge v Baldwin* [1964], a landmark case that marks the beginning of the contemporary renaissance of judicial review, the House of Lords returned the law to its older rationale. The Chief Constable of Brighton had been dismissed by the local police authority without a hearing. The authority had statutory power to deprive him of his position for incapacity or misconduct but not otherwise. The House of Lords held that he was entitled to a hearing for two reasons: (i) he had been deprived of an important right; (ii) the power to dismiss was limited by statute, so the authority did not have a complete discretion. Lord Reid emphasised that irrespective of whether it is judicial in the above sense a government decision that causes serious harm to an individual ought in principle to attract the right to be heard. Moreover it was emphasised that the right to be heard applies irrespective of how clear-cut the outcome appears to be. Indeed the protection of a hearing may be most necessary in what seems to be an open-and-shut case.

Since *Ridge v Baldwin* the right to a hearing is no longer limited to judicial functions. The courts have extended the right to a hearing into most areas of government, including for example prison management (*R v Hull Prison Visitors, ex p St Germain* [1979]; *Leech v Parkhurst Prison Deputy Governor* [1988]). Although the expression 'natural justice' is still occasionally used it has become interchangeable with 'fairness' (see *Re HK* [1967]). The concept of 'judicial' is still relevant since a judicial decision will certainly attract a right to a hearing and this may be of a higher procedural standard than in the case of an administrative decision. A legitimate expectation (see Section 17.9) is also ground for a right to be heard in order to persuade the decision maker to honour the expectation (*A-G for Hong Kong v Ng Yuen Shiu* [1983]; *R v Secretary of State for the Home Dept, ex p Khan* [1985]).

However the courts have introduced limits to the right to be heard. These are based on pragmatic factors. They include the following:

- 'Fairness' concerns the protection of persons who are adversely affected by government action and not the idea of democratic participation in government. Thus the right to be heard may not include access to policy information (see *Bushell v Secretary of State for the Environment* [1981]; *Hammersmith and Fulham LBC v Secretary of State for the Environment* [1990]).
- Advisory or preliminary governmental decisions do not attract a right to be heard unless the decision has direct adverse consequences for the individual's rights (*Norwest Holst v Trade Secretary* [1978]: decision to start an investigation, no right to be heard; cf *Furnell v Whangarie High Schools Board* [1973]: suspension of teacher pending investigation, hearing required).
- A judicial decision to remove existing legal rights usually attracts a hearing but the refusal of a discretionary benefit in the public interest, where the claimant has no specific entitlement, may not (see *Schmidt v Secretary of State for Home Affairs* [1969]: extension of immigration permit; *McInnes v Onslow-Fane* [1978]: refusing a referee's licence; *Findlay v Secretary of State for the Home Dept* [1985]: parole, change in policy). However a decision to refuse a benefit that can only be made on limited grounds or involves accusations of misconduct or bad character or affects a legitimate expectation will attract a hearing (see *R v Gaming Board, ex p Benaim and Khaida* [1970]; *R v Secretary of State for the Home Dept, ex p Fayed* [1997]).

- Other factors might override or limit the right to a hearing, in particular national security considerations (*Council of Civil Service Unions (CCSU) v Minister for the Civil Service* [1985]). The need to act quickly in an emergency will also exclude at least a prior hearing (*R v Secretary of State for Transport, ex p Pegasus Holidays* Ltd [1989]: air safety; *Calvin v Carr* [1980] (below)). A hearing might be excluded where large numbers compete for scarce resources, for example applications for university places, or in respect of general decisions such as school closures. On the other hand where a policy decision, for example to close an old people's home, directly affects the existing rights of the persons concerned there may be a collective right to be consulted, although not necessarily a hearing in individual cases (see *R v Devon CC, ex p Baker* [1995]).
- Although the courts have sometimes warned against this (eg *Ridge v Baldwin*; *John v Rees* [1969]) a hearing may be excluded when the court thinks that the outcome of the decision was not affected, so a hearing would be futile (*Cheall v Apex* [1983]). In *Cinnamond v British Airports Authority* [1980] the Court of Appeal upheld a decision to withdraw licences without a hearing from a group of Heathrow Airport taxi drivers who had been repeatedly warned about allegations of misconduct but had not responded.
- The same flexible concept of 'fairness' also determines the ingredients of a hearing. There are no fixed requirements. Subject to any statutory requirements, a decision maker can fix its own procedure provided that it is 'fair' in the circumstances of the particular case (see *Lloyd v McMahon* [1987]). Perhaps the law has become too flexible, with the disadvantage that 'fairness' does not necessarily imply a definite right to a hearing. For example in *Calvin v Carr* the plaintiff, a racehorse trainer, was suspended from the course because of accusations of tampering with the horses before a race. The Privy Council held that a combination of factors meant that he was not entitled to be heard. These included the need to act quickly to preserve the integrity of the sport, the fact that he could appeal, when he would be given a full hearing, and the fact that he had agreed to the regulations under which the decision was made.

The following factors are particularly important:

- The more serious the consequences for the individual, the higher the standard of hearing that is required. To this extent the notion of a judicial decision remains important. At one end of the scale preliminary investigations at best entitle a person to be told only an outline of any accusations against him or her and answer them (*Maxwell v Dept of Trade and Industry and Others* [1974]; *R v Commission for Racial Equality, ex p Cottrell and Rothon* [1980]). At the other end of the scale a person accused of misconduct or whose rights are in issue is normally entitled to see all the evidence and cross-examine witnesses (*R v Army Board, ex p Anderson* [1992]). This is endorsed by the right to a fair trial under Article 6 of the ECHR (see eg *Roberts v Parole Board* [2006]). Administrative convenience cannot justify refusing to permit a person to call witnesses, although the tribunal does have a residual discretion in the matter (*R v Hull Prison Visitors, ex p St Germain (No 2)* [1979]).

- Fairness is a minimum standard to be balanced against the government's right to decide its own procedure. An oral hearing is not necessarily required even under the ECHR, although an absolute rule excluding an oral hearing is not permitted (*Lloyd v McMahon* [1987]). The importance of the matter and the nature of the particular issues should be taken into account to decide whether the matter can be fairly determined without an oral hearing (see *R (Smith) v Parole Board* [2005]; *R (Dudson) v Secretary of State for the Home Dept* [2006]). Formal rules of evidence are not required. Fairness demands only that the evidence be relevant and that the parties have a chance to comment on it (*Mahon v Air New Zealand* [1984]). There is no automatic right to legal representation but the decision maker must not adopt an absolute rule on the matter and must allow representation where a person cannot effectively present his or her own case (*Hone v Maze Prison Board of Visitors* [1988]; cf *Enderby Town Football Club v Football Association* [1971]). However under the ECHR a person subject to a severe penalty akin to a criminal charge is entitled to legal representation (see *R (G) v Governors of X School* [2010]: dismissal of teacher).
- Problems arise where an individual is confronted with those who claim inside knowledge but are reluctant to have this challenged. An expert decision maker can rely on his own accumulated experience without having to disclose this to the parties. Expert assessors are sometimes used to help judges and other decision makers; they need not disclose their advice in advance. However where the judge disagrees with an assessor on an important matter he should give the parties a chance to comment (*Ahmed v Governing Body of Oxford University* [2003]). If an inquiry is held the decision maker cannot subsequently take new evidence or advice received from an outside source into account without giving the parties an opportunity to comment (see *Elmbridge BC v Secretary of State for the Environment, Transport and the Regions* [2002]; *AMEC Ltd v Whitefriars City Estates* [2005]). However advice given to a minister by a civil servant in his or her department does not count as outside advice and by virtue of the doctrine of ministerial responsibility need not be disclosed (*Bushell v Secretary of State for the Environment* [1981]).

18.4 Procedural impropriety: bias

An impartial and independent judge is a fundamental aspect of the rule of law. However complete impartiality is impossible to realise. Not only is bias inherent in human nature but many kinds of decision-making process inevitably involve conflicts of interest. The law therefore has to compromise, and has done so by distinguishing between different kinds of decisions and different kinds of biases.

The decision maker need not actually be biased – this would fall under the head of irrelevant considerations (Chapter 17). The bias rule is importantly concerned with the risk or appearance of bias, hence the dictum of Lord Hewart in *R v Sussex Justices, ex p McCarthy* [1924] that 'justice must not only be done but must manifestly and undoubtedly be seen to be done' (at 259). The rationale is not only that of fairness to the parties but also that of public confidence in the integrity of the decision-making process. A decision maker who becomes aware that he or she is subject to a biasing factor must disqualify him or herself, irrespective of the cost, delay or inconvenience that may result (*AWG Group v Morrison* [2006]). However the parties can consent to the bias in question (waiver) (see *Smith v Kvaener Cementation Foundations Ltd* [2006]).

The main principles are as follows:

- *financial interests.* A direct personal financial interest, however small, will automatically disqualify the decision maker, the law conclusively presuming bias (*Dimes v Grand Junction Canal Co* [1852]: Lord Chancellor held shares in company appearing before him; *R v Hendon RDC, ex p Chorley* [1933]: local councillor had financial interest in development for which planning permission was sought; see also *R v Camborne Justices, ex p Pearce* [1955] at 47);
- *parties to the case.* In *R v Bow Street Stipendiary Magistrate, ex p Pinochet (No 2)* [1999] the House of Lords extended automatic disqualification to a case where a judge is a member of an organisation that is party to the case even though there is no financial interest. Lord Hoffmann, a Law Lord, was an unpaid director of a charitable subsidiary of Amnesty International, a human rights pressure group, which was a party to an appeal concerning whether to extradite the former President of Chile to Spain to face charges of torture and genocide. *Pinochet* has been criticised on the ground that there is an important distinction between 'interest', where the judge stands to gain personally, so he is a judge in his own case and should automatically be disqualified, and 'favour', where the judge might prefer a particular outcome, where a more flexible approach is appropriate (Olowofoyeku, 2000). Other common law jurisdictions have confined automatic disqualification to strictly financial interests and, bearing in mind that *Pinochet* was a case of special political significance, it is unlikely that its rationale will be extended (see *Locobail (UK) Ltd v Bayfield Properties Ltd* [2000]);
- *other personal connections.* These are too various to list. Examples include social, family or professional relationships with the parties, previous involvement with the same decision-making process, the holding of opinions or the membership of groups related to the issues. Here a more flexible approach is taken. The courts have tried to find a formula which on the one hand reflects the interest of public confidence in the impartiality of the decision maker and on the other hand blocks challenges for flimsy or ill-informed suspicions. The current formula asks whether in the view of a 'fair-minded and informed observer' taken as knowing all the circumstances there is a 'real possibility' or 'real danger' of bias (*Porter v Magill* [2002]).

  This formula emerged from *R v Gough* [1993], which replaced two earlier tests (albeit often producing the same outcome). These were firstly a strict 'reasonable suspicion' test according to which any suspicious factor as it appeared to a reasonable hypothetical observer might disqualify the judge, even though if all the circumstances were known the observer might be reassured; secondly the more liberal 'real likelihood' test allowed the reviewing court to decide for itself whether in all the circumstances bias was likely. *Gough* tried to compromise between the two. It did not include the device of the hypothetical outsider but neither did it require an overall balance, only a 'real danger' of bias. However *Gough* seemed to be out of line with the ECHR and the practice in other English-speaking countries (see Olowofoyeku, 2000). In particular the court might be too trusting of other decision makers, sharing the 'insider' view of public life which is endemic among the clannish professional and official elite.

The Gough test was modified by *Re Medicaments (No 2)* [2001], which reintroduced the imagined standpoint of a hypothetical reasonable outsider. It is questionable whether this makes any difference since the outsider who knows all and is fair-minded seems to be no more than an idealised avatar for the judge (see *Virdi v Law Society* [2010]). Each case depends on its particular circumstances. Generally speaking substantial conflict of interest is required. The following are examples.

- In *R v Gough* [1993] the accused's brother was a neighbour of a jury member, who did not however recognise him. The jury was not disqualified.
- In *R v Abdrocar* [2005] it was held that the presence of a policeman and a prosecuting solicitor on a jury was acceptable in the light of the normal understandings of what citizenship entailed.
- In *Re Medicaments (No 2)* [2001] a lay member of the Restrictive Practices Court was applying for a job with a firm one of whose members often appeared as an expert witness before the court. The Court of Appeal held that she was disqualified even though she had taken steps to minimise the conflict of interest.
- In *Locobail (UK) v Bayfield Properties* [2000] the Court of Appeal stressed that general objections based on religious, racial, ethnic or national characteristics, gender, age, class, political views, membership of organisations, income and sexual orientation would not normally disqualify. Specific connections might include personal friendships or animosity but making adverse remarks on a previous occasion would not in itself be sufficient. The court disqualified a judge who had written polemical articles in legal journals attacking the practices of insurance companies in circumstances similar to those in the case before him. However it did not disqualify a judge who had been a member of a solicitors' firm acting for one of the parties since he had not been personally involved, or a decision to give a licence to a betting shop where the judge was a director of a company of which the shop was a tenant. Nor did the court disqualify the chair of a tribunal that had decided both a preliminary application to proceed in a sexual harassment case and the full case later.
- In *R (Al-Hasan) v Secretary of State for the Home Dept* [2005] a deputy prison governor who had been present while the governor gave an allegedly unlawful order to carry out an intimate body search on a prisoner was held to be disqualified from participating in the hearing into the complaint.
- In *AMEC Ltd v Whitefriars City Estates* [2005] the reappointment of the same adjudicator to re-determine a previous flawed arbitration constituted bias.
- In *Gillies v Secretary of State for Work and Pensions* [2006] prior experience and specialist knowledge were not a disqualification.

Allegations of bias are often successfully met by the claim that professional practices ensure integrity; in other words we should trust those in power. For example in *Porter v Magill* a local government auditor investigating allegations of bribery had made a provisional press announcement endorsing the allegations. His later formal report confirmed his findings. The House of Lords held that he was not disqualified since the reasonable observer could assume that an experienced professional was impartial. Similarly in *Helow v Secretary of State for the Home Dept* [2009] a judge who was a member of the International Association of Jewish Lawyers was presiding over an asylum application by a supporter of the Palestine Liberation Front. The House of Lords held that the fair-minded and informed person would not conclude that there would be a real possibility of bias. It would require extreme words or conduct identifying with a partisan cause to justify such a conclusion. Even though this was a campaigning organisation it could be assumed that when he put his judicial hat on the judge would put any private views aside.

In *Taylor v Lawrence* [2002] it was held that a judge was not disqualified where a solicitor appearing before him had recently transacted family business on his behalf. Lord Woolf remarked that an informed observer can be expected to be aware of 'the legal traditions and culture of this jurisdiction' (at [61–64]), with the implication that this would be reassuring. In *Virdi v Law Society*, in a disciplinary hearing by the Law Society, the clerk, who was a Law Society employee, retired with the tribunal and drafted its report. The Court of Appeal held that there was no danger of bias because the 'well-informed reasonable person' would know that there was no impropriety.

Lawal v Northern Spirit [2004] suggests a less complacent approach. The claimant appealed to the Employment Appeal Tribunal in respect of an allegation of racial discrimination by his employer. The senior counsel for the employer had previously sat as a part-time judge with one of the lay members of the Tribunal. The House of Lords held that the reasonable outsider might well suspect that the relationship could bias the lay member. Lord Steyn warned against complacent assumptions of professional integrity, pointing out that:

> the indispensable requirement of public confidence in the administration of justice requires higher standards today than was the case even a decade or two ago. The informed observer of today could perhaps be expected to be aware of the legal traditions and culture of this jurisdiction ... But he might not be wholly uncritical of that culture. (at [22])

The bias rule is overridden where there is an unavoidable conflict of interest, in which case Parliament must be taken to have impliedly authorised the bias (*Wilkinson v Barking Corporation* [1948]; see also Supreme Court Act 1981, s 11: judges as taxpayers). In the case of administrative decisions taken by politicians, conflicts of interest arising out of political policies or competing responsibilities may be built into the system by statute. The same applies in organisations, such as prisons and universities, where officials have a mixture of administrative and disciplinary functions.

Conflicting interests inevitably built into the decision-making structure do not invalidate the decision unless the decision maker actually acts unfairly by closing his mind to relevant factors (eg *R v Frankland Prison Board of Visitors, ex p Lewis* [1986]: prison visitors having both judicial and investigatory roles; *R v Secretary of State for the Environment, ex p Kirkstall Valley Campaign Ltd* [1996]: local authority had interest in developing land for which it also had to decide whether to grant planning permission). This approach has been held to satisfy the ECHR (Section 18.6). A decision may also be upheld if there is no unbiased decision maker available (see *R v Barnsley Licensing Justices* [1960]: all justices members of the local Co-op).

18.5 Procedural impropriety: reasons for decisions

There is no general duty to give reasons for decisions, although many statutes impose such a duty (see *R v Criminal Injuries Compensation Board, ex p Moore* [1999]; *Stefan v GMC* [1999]; Tribunals and Inquiries Act 1992, s 10). The absence of a duty to give reasons has been justified on the grounds of cost, excessive formality, the difficulties of expressing subjective reasons and because in the case of collective decisions it may be impossible to identify specific reasons (see *McInnes v Onslow-Fane* [1978]; *R v Higher Education Funding Council, ex p Institute of Dental Surgery* [1994]; *Stefan v GMC*).

The main justification for the giving of reasons is respect for human dignity and equality so that those who purport to exercise power must be accountable. Even an admission that a decision is based on subjective judgement fulfils this requirement. The giving of reasons also strengthens public confidence in the decision-making process, concentrates the mind of the decision maker and helps identify problems.

However the courts have required reasons to be given in certain cases based on the principle of fairness which allows the court to take all the circumstances into account. In *R v Secretary of State for the Home Dept, ex p Doody* [1993] Lord Mustill referred to 'a perceptible trend towards an insistence upon greater openness in the making of administrative decisions' (at 107; see also Lord Bingham in *R v Ministry of Defence, ex p Murray* [1998]). The dominant view seems to be that a duty to give reasons must either be expressed or implied in the relevant statute or there must be some special justification for giving reasons. In *Institute of Dental Surgery* Sedley J held that arguments which applied to all cases were not sufficient, for example the difficulty of challenging a decision in the absence of reasons. Examples of cases where there is a duty to give reasons include the following:

- judicial decisions analogous to those of a court (*Murray* [1998]);
- cases that involve very important interests where if reasons were not given the individual would be at a disadvantage (eg *Doody*: fixing of minimum sentence for life prisoner; *Stefan v GMC*: risk of loss of livelihood, unrepresented defendant);
- cases where the particular decision is unusual or a severe penalty is involved (eg *R v Civil Service Appeals Board, ex p Cunningham* [1991]: compensation award out of line with that given in analogous cases by industrial tribunal; *R v DPP, ex p Manning* [2000]: decision not to prosecute after coroner's finding of unlawful killing);
- a legitimate expectation might also generate a duty to give reasons for overriding the expectation (*R v Secretary of State for Transport, ex p Richmond upon Thames BC (No 4)* [1996]);
- if an appeal is provided this may point to a duty to give reasons where the appeal would otherwise be pointless (*Stefan v GMC*). On the other hand a comprehensive appeal that reopens the whole case may point against a duty to give reasons at first instance;
- in *Padfield v Minister of Agriculture, Fisheries and Food* [1968] the House of Lords suggested that if a minister refuses to give reasons, the court can infer that he has no proper reasons for his decision. However in *Lonrho v Secretary of State for Trade and Industry* [1989] the House held that a failure to give reasons does not in itself justify the drawing of an adverse inference but is at most supportive of other evidence that the decision is improper.

Reasons need not be detailed or comprehensive, provided that they enable the parties to understand the basis of the decision (see *South Bucks DC v Porter* [2004]).

A duty to give reasons arises after the decision is made and should be distinguished from failing before the decision is made to disclose grounds in the sense of allegations against the applicant. Failure to disclose such grounds would normally be unfair as a breach of the right to a hearing. Moreover once an applicant has obtained leave to apply for judicial review there is a duty of full and frank disclosure. The authority 'owes a duty to the court to cooperate and make candid disclosure of the relevant facts and the reasoning behind the decision challenged' (Lord Walker in *Belize Alliance of Conservation NGOs v Dept of the Environment* [2003] at [86]; *R v Lancashire CC, ex p Huddlestone* [1986]). However this is of no help in finding grounds for challenge in the first place.

18.6 The European Convention on Human Rights

Article 6(1) states that:

> in the determination of his civil rights and obligations ... everyone is entitled to a fair and public hearing within a reasonable time by an independent and impartial tribunal established by law. (see Section 20.3)

The requirements of Article 6(1) are usually sufficiently flexible to be satisfied by the common law of procedural propriety (see *Bentham v Netherlands* [1986]; *R v DPP, ex p Kebeline* [1999]). However an irreducible core of fairness is required by Article 6, whereas the common law duty is less strict, involving a broader balance between fairness and the public interest (*Re Officer L* [2007]; *Secretary of State for the Home Dept v MB* [2008]). Thus, except in connection with the right to a hearing in public, which can be excluded in certain circumstances (Article 6(1)), the right to a fair trial cannot be overridden by other factors, although particular aspects might be modified to deal for example with security matters (see Section 23.3) or a grave social problem (*Brown v Stott* [2001]). The common law does not necessarily require a public hearing. Under Article 6 there are additional requirements in criminal cases, including a right to legal representation (see *R (G) v Governors of X School* [2010]).

As we saw in Section 17.6.1, not every decision of a public authority affects civil rights and obligations. For example in *R (M) v Secretary of State for Constitutional Affairs* [2004] it was held that a district judge could make an interim Anti-Social Behaviour Order against youths suspected of drug dealing without notice or a hearing. Because the order only had temporary effect and was subject to review and confirmation at a later hearing, it did not affect civil rights (cf *R (Wright) v Secretary of State for Health* [2009]: placing on Child Abuse Register).

Apart from Article 6 some Convention rights may require a hearing in themselves. In cases involving deaths in government custody the relatives of the victims have a right under Article 2 (right to life) to an open and public investigation to establish blame, a matter closely related to the rule of law (see *R (Middleton) v West Somerset Coroner* [2004]; *R (Amin) v Secretary of State for the Home Dept* [2002]). This may also apply to Article 3 (torture and inhuman and degrading treatment). (Cf *R (Gentle) v Prime Minister* [2008]: no right to inquiry concerning military deaths in Iraq war, partly because the risk was voluntary; however the issue of inadequate resources was not raised.)

As regards the bias rule the ECHR approach is similar to that of domestic law. In particular there is a broad distinction between policy decisions and judicial decisions.

In *R (Alconbury Developments Ltd) v Secretary of State for the Environment, Transport and the Regions* [2001] a variety of decisions made by the Secretary of State were challenged as violating Article 6 on the ground of bias. These included decisions to confirm compulsory purchase orders relating to road and rail schemes in which the government had an interest. Apart from the Human Rights Act 1998, the arrangement could not be challenged because it was authorised by statute. The House of Lords held that in order to satisfy the test of impartiality the process as a whole should be examined, including the protection given by judicial review. Overruling the lower courts, the Lords held unanimously that the process satisfied Article 6. They held that the jurisprudence of the ECHR supported a fundamental democratic distinction between policy or political decisions, for which the minister is answerable to Parliament, and judicial decisions made by courts and similar bodies. Provided that there is judicial review, 'a government minister can be both a policy maker and hear appeals without violating Article 6' (per Lord Hutton at 1018). The position is otherwise where a decision turns on findings of law or disputed facts as opposed to policy, where further safeguards such as independent fact finding might be necessary (see Lord Hoffmann at 992; Section 17.6.1). Thus the House of Lords endorsed the traditional English approach against a stricter application of the separation of powers.

Finally, as regards the giving of reasons, the ECHR has confined itself to holding that the courts, as the citizen's last protection, must give reasons for their decisions but has not required administrative bodies to do so (*Van de Hurk v The Netherlands* [1984]; see also *Helle v Finland* [1998]: detailed reasons not necessary).

Summary

- The doctrine of *Wednesbury* unreasonableness comes near to interfering with the merits of a decision. The threshold of unreasonableness varies with the context on a sliding scale determined by the impact of the decision on the individual and whether the decision involves political factors with which a court should not interfere. At one extreme a bare 'rationality' test is applied. At the other extreme where the Human Rights Act 1998 applies the court itself may weigh the competing considerations, exercising what is effectively an appeal function. Between these extremes the test appears to be whether the outcome is within the range of reasonable responses to the particular context. In effect the court is drawing upon widely shared social and moral values.
- The principle of proportionality is applied in the human rights context and may extend to other contexts such as legitimate expectations. This requires the court to weigh the competing factors on the basis that the interference with the right must be no greater than is necessary to achieve a legitimate objective (in the case of some rights protected by the ECHR 'a pressing social need').
- Natural justice or fairness requires that a person adversely affected by a decision be entitled to a hearing. The requirements of a hearing are flexible and depend on the circumstances.

Summary cont'd

In order to respect the interests of government efficiency, fairness is regarded as the minimum necessary to do justice. The courts are increasingly requiring reasons to be given for decisions.

- A decision maker must also be free from the appearance of improper bias. This too depends on the circumstances. A direct financial interest automatically disqualifies the decision maker, as perhaps does membership of an organisation which is a party to the case. In other cases the test is whether a hypothetical, reasonable and fully informed observer would consider there to be real danger of bias.
- The rules of natural justice or procedural fairness are underpinned by the Human Rights Act 1998, although what amounts to a fair trial depends on the context and in particular the extent to which the decision is a policy-oriented political decision.

Exercises

18.1 'I think the day will come when it will be more widely recognised that the *Wednesbury* case was an unfortunately retrogressive decision in English administrative law' (Lord Cooke). What does he mean and do you agree?

18.2 'The difference in practice [between *Wednesbury* unreasonableness and proportionality] is not as great as is sometimes supposed ... even without reference to the 1998 Act the time has come to recognise that this principle is part of English administrative law, not only when judges are dealing with Community acts but also when they are dealing with acts subject to domestic law' (Lord Slynn). Do you agree?

18.3 'Judicial review is mainly concerned with the way in which a decision is reached rather than with its outcome.' Do you agree?

18.4 The (fictional) Environmental Penalties Act 2009 provides that 'the Secretary of State may make regulations for the purpose of ensuring that household waste is recycled on a sustainable basis'. The Secretary of State makes the following regulation: 'Each household must produce if required to do so by an authorised officer a standard-sized bin containing a reasonable amount of recyclable waste. Failure to do so will incur a penalty at the discretion of the authorised officer.'

(i) Alf fails to produce a bin. He claims that his bin was recently stolen. The authorised officer tells him that he has no choice but to impose a penalty.
(ii) Bill produces a bin containing only a small amount of waste. He explains that he has recently been absent abroad. The officer, who considers that Bill is lying and who has fallen behind his performance target, imposes a penalty on Bill.
(iii) Clara's bin is filled to overflowing. The officer imposes a penalty on her on the ground that the amount of waste produced is unreasonable.

Advise Alf, Bill and Clara as to any grounds on which they can challenge the regulations and the decisions in their individual cases.

18.5 The local Council is given statutory power to 'regulate the operation of cinemas'. The Council introduces a system of licences for cinemas. It imposes the following conditions:

(i) Children are prohibited from attending any performance on a Sunday.
(ii) No refreshments are to be sold at the cinema.

The Chairman of the Council owns a fast food shop next to the cinema and is a well-known Evangelical preacher.

(a) A local cinema wishes to challenge conditions (i) and (ii). Advise it.

Exercises cont'd

(b) Another local cinema is accused of breaching condition (i), and without giving it a hearing the Council orders it to close. Advise the Council. What would be the position if a councillor had said to the cinema manager, 'Between ourselves, we are not likely to enforce the condition where a child is accompanied by a parent,' and the manager had followed that advice?

18.6 The Sports Commission is a (fictitious) statutory body. It is required to 'encourage and assist the provision of sporting facilities in local communities'. The statute requires that the Commission comprise a panel of five people chosen by the Secretary of State on the basis of their 'established international reputation in sporting activities'. The Commission decides to set up a scheme to give grants to darts clubs based in public houses. It delegates the power to award the grants to local agents chosen from pub landlords. Advise as to the legality of the scheme. Are there further facts you need to know?

18.7 Does the bias rule strike a reasonable balance between efficiency and justice?

18.8 Under the (imaginary) Landlords Act 2008 no person can do business as a residential landlord without first obtaining a licence from the local authority certifying that he or she is a 'fit and proper person' to be a landlord. Ed applies to the local authority in writing for a licence, giving the required information, including the fact that he has no criminal record. An official writes to him informing him that there 'will be no problem' with his application. However when the relevant committee of the local authority considers his application they are informed by one of their members (a competitor of Ed's) that the police once charged Ed with intimidation. Another member of the Committee remembers Ed as a pupil at the school of which she was head teacher and that he was a 'trouble maker'. Ed's application for a licence is refused. Ed wishes to explain that the charge against him had been withdrawn as being without evidence. The Committee refuses to reconsider the matter. Ed now seeks judicial review. Advise him.

Further reading

Allan, 'Procedural Fairness and the Duty of Respect' (1998) 18 OJLS 497

Craig, 'Substance and Procedure in Judicial Review' in Andenas and Fairgrieve (eds), *Tom Bingham and the Transformation of the Law* (Oxford University Press 2009)

Elliot, 'Has the Common Law Duty to Give Reasons Come of Age Yet?' [2011] PL 56

Hickman, 'The Reasonableness Principle: Reassessing Its Place in the Public Sphere' (2004) 63 CLJ 166

Hunt, 'Sovereignty's Blight: Why Contemporary Public Law Needs the Concept of Due Deference' in Bamforth and Leyland (eds), *Public Law in a Multi-Layered Constitution* (Hart 2003)

Irvine, 'Judges and Decision Makers: The Theory and Practice of *Wednesbury* Review' [1996] PL 59

Jowell, 'Beyond the Rule of Law: Towards Constitutional Judicial Review' [2000] PL 671

Jowell, 'Judicial Deference: Servility, Civility or Institutional Capacity' [2003] PL 592

Olowofoyeku, 'The *Nemo Judex* Rule: The Case against Automatic Disqualification' [2000] PL 456

Poole, 'The Reformation of English Administrative Law' [2008] CLJ 67

Rivers, 'Proportionality and Variable Intensity of Review' [2006] CLJ 174

Taggart, 'Reinventing Administrative Law' in Bamforth and Leyland (eds), *Public Law in a Multi-Layered Constitution* (Hart 2003)

Taggart, 'Proportionality, Deference, *Wednesbury*' [2008] New Zealand LJ 423

Tomkins, *Public Law* (Clarendon Press 2003) ch 6

Walker, 'What's Wrong with Irrationality?' [1995] PL 556

Wong, 'Towards the Nutcracker Principle: Reconsidering the Objections to Proportionality' [2000] PL 92

Chapter 19

Judicial review remedies

> **For this is not the liberty which we can hope, that no grievance ever should arise in the Commonwealth, that let no man in this world expect; but when complaints are freely heard, deeply considered, and speedily reformed, then is the outmost bound of civil liberty attained that wise men look for. (Milton, *Areopagitica*, 1644)**

19.1 Introduction

It could be argued that the courts provide the only open and universal means by which the individual can challenge government action. Ministerial responsibility to Parliament is of little use to the citizen directly in that it can be called upon only by members of Parliament, who are unlikely to be independent. The Committee on Standards in Public Life plays a valuable monitoring role but has no enforcement powers. The 'ombudsman' institution which investigates citizens' complaints against government is free to complainants and its powers of investigation into facts are more extensive than those of the courts. However its jurisdiction is limited to maladministration and many public bodies are excluded, it has no enforcement powers and it does not hold public hearings (see *R v Local Comr for Administration, ex p Liverpool City Council* [2001]).

Until 1977 there was no distinctive legal process for judicial review. The powers of the courts to review government action developed historically in different courts through a variety of remedies, some of which were general remedies applying also to private disputes. As we saw in Section 6.4.1, one aspect of the 'rule of law' emphasised by Dicey was that the common law does not distinguish between public law and private law but applies the same principles to government and citizen alike, so that an official is in no better position than a private individual. However since Dicey's day the powers of government have expanded enormously and this approach has become inadequate both to protect the citizen and to reflect the democratic interest in the effective delivery of government policy.

Since 1977 the various remedies have been concentrated in a single section of the High Court, part of the Queen's Bench Division and now called the Administrative Court. Originally the Administrative Court sat only in London but it now sits in Cardiff and other major cities. The workload of the Administrative Court is substantial. Further flexibility is added by the Tribunals, Courts and Enforcement Act 2007, under which the Upper Tribunal, which also hears appeals from the main tribunals, has a judicial review jurisdiction in types of case (other than those concerning the Crown Court) designated by the Lord Chief Justice or another judge designated by him or her (ss 15, 18). The Upper Tribunal has the same status as the High Court but includes other senior judicial officers (see Section 5.4.3).

The law is governed by section 31 of the Supreme Court Act 1981 and Part 54 of the Civil Procedure Rules 1998 (CPR) (see *Practice Direction* [2000] 1 WLR 1654). There is a unified procedure for all the remedies. This replaces numerous technical rules which had developed over the years in relation to individual remedies. These had made challenge to government action complex and sometimes unjust, with litigants having to traverse a minefield of procedural niceties and sometimes being frustrated by choosing an inappropriate remedy in the wrong court. A Law Commission Report in 1976 (Law Com No 6407) led to the main reforms. A further Law Commission Report (No 226, 1994) led to further, relatively minor changes.

A claim for judicial review means a claim to review the lawfulness of (i) an enactment or (ii) a decision, action or failure to act in relation to the exercise of a public function (CPR 54.1). The procedure as a whole is characterised by wide discretionary powers which allow the court to choose the most appropriate remedy from the whole range. It also embodies principles concerned with the special nature of disputes between government and citizen.

These principles are of three kinds:

1. The remedies are designed to set aside unlawful government action and to send the matter back to the decision maker or to restrain an unlawful act but not, normally, to allow the court to make a new decision itself, thus complying with the separation of powers. However the court might exceptionally correct a drafting mistake made for example in a statutory instrument where it is plain that the mistake was inadvertent and when the purpose of the instrument is clear (*R (Confederation of Passenger Transport (UK)) v Humber Bridge Board* [2004]). Moreover where there is only one possible decision that could lawfully be made the court can make it itself (CPR 54.19).
2. The procedure reflects the limited role of the courts. In particular the procedure is normally based on written statements since the court is not primarily concerned with factual disputes. However there is power to hear witnesses if justice so requires.
3. The procedure contains barriers designed to safeguard the public interest in protecting government against improper challenges (Section 19.3). To a certain extent judicial review could be regarded as part of the political process since it provides a public platform for grievances against the government so that, to a well-funded partisan, even hopeless litigation might be attractive as a means of publicising a cause. On the other hand any restriction on the right to go to court might be seen as an affront to the rule of law. However in cases where a person's ordinary private rights are at stake, for example if a public authority interferes with private property, an action or defence can be brought in any court, thus reflecting the traditional idea of the rule of law.

19.2 The range of remedies

Historically there are two groups of remedies suitable for judicial review. Firstly from the seventeenth century the courts developed the 'prerogative orders' (so called because in theory they issue on the application of the Crown). These were *mandamus*, *prohibition* and *certiorari*. They enabled the High Court to police the powers and duties of 'inferior bodies', that is lower courts and government officials. *Mandamus* ordered a body to perform its duty. *Prohibition* was issued in advance to prevent a body from exceeding its jurisdiction. *Certiorari* summoned up the record of an inferior body to be examined by the court and the decision was set aside and sent back if it was invalid. These orders remain the basis of the modern law of judicial review but are now called mandatory orders, prohibiting orders and quashing orders respectively (CPR 54.1). These remedies are available only in the Administrative Court (CPR 54.2).

The second group of remedies comprises declarations, injunctions and damages (Supreme Court Act 1981, s 31(2)). These are also available in other courts and are primarily private law remedies. A claimant may apply for these in the Administrative Court and must do so if he or she is seeking these remedies in addition to a prerogative order (CPR 54.3). A declaration is a statement of the legal position which declares the rights of parties (eg 'X is entitled to a tax repayment'). Declarations are not enforceable but a public authority is unlikely to disobey one. Indeed a declaration is useful where an enforceable order would be undesirable, for example in the case of a draft government order before it is considered by Parliament or an advisory government opinion. It might for example be used to avoid offending Parliament (see *R v Boundary Commission, ex p Foot* [1983]). The former prerogative orders do not lie against the Crown as such but the declaration does. However this is relatively unimportant because most statutory powers are conferred on ministers and the prerogative orders lie against individual ministers.

An injunction restrains a person from breaking the law or orders a person to undo something done unlawfully (a mandatory injunction). An interim injunction can restrain government action pending a full trial. In *M v Home Office* [1993] the House of Lords held that an injunction can be enforced against a minister of the Crown (see also *R v Minister of Agriculture, Fisheries and Food, ex p Monsanto plc* [1998]). This overturns a long tradition that the Crown and its servants cannot be the subject of enforceable orders (see Crown Proceedings Act 1947, s 21, which still applies to ordinary civil law actions involving contract, tort or property issues). However it was stressed that injunctions should be granted against ministers only as a last resort. Injunctions cannot be granted against the Crown itself.

Claimants often apply for more than one of the remedies, which may well overlap. For example a quashing order has the same effect as a declaration that the offending decision is void. The court can issue any of the remedies in any combination and is not limited to those for which the claimant has applied (Supreme Court Act 1981, s 31(5)).

A claimant cannot seek a financial remedy, damages, restitution or the recovery of a debt alone in judicial review proceedings but must attach it to a claim for at least one of the other remedies (CPR 54.3(2)). Moreover even in the Administrative Court damages are not available in respect of unlawful government action as such but can be awarded only in respect of conduct and losses which are not authorised by statute and which would be actionable in an ordinary civil action (Supreme Court Act 1981, s 31(4); Tribunals, Courts and Enforcement Act 2007, s 16 (6)). In other cases damages must be sought in an ordinary civil action.

The law relating to the liability for damages of public authorities is complex and cannot usefully be discussed without prior knowledge of the law of tort. We will not attempt to discuss the matter here other than to remark that the courts are reluctant to impose liability in damages upon bodies exercising statutory powers in respect of purely public functions on the basis of negligence or a failure of a public duty (see eg *X (Minors) v Bedfordshire CC* [1995]; *Marcic v Thames Water Utilities Ltd* [2004]; *Cullen v Chief Constable of the RUC* [2004]; *Anufrijeva v Southwark LBC* [2004]). This is because the risk of paying damages might inhibit the decision maker from exercising its powers independently (but see *Connor v Surrey CC* [2010]: existing duty in private law, public law duties should conform to this).

In four kinds of case however damages may be awarded on the basis of unlawful government action:

1. under the *Francovich* principle in EC law (see Section 10.3.3);
2. under the tort of 'misfeasance in public office' where an authority has a specific intention to injure or knowingly acts outside its powers, being reckless as to the consequences, and causes material damage (see *Dunlop v Woollahra Municipal Council* [1982]; *Calverley v Chief Constable of Merseyside Police* [1989]; *Racz v Home Office* [1994]; *Three Rivers DC v Bank of England (No 3)* [2003]; *Watkins v Secretary of State for the Home Dept* [2006]);
3. where a right protected by the Human Rights Act 1998 is infringed (see *D v East Berkshire Community Health NHS Trust* [2005]);
4. where there has been a breach of a duty specifically intended to be enforced by the person to whom it is owed. However the courts are reluctant to interpret statutes as imposing such enforceable duties on a public authority (*Marcic v Thames Water Utilities Ltd*).

There is also the ancient prerogative writ of habeas corpus ('produce the body'). Habeas corpus is not part of the judicial review procedure. The grounds for issuing it are probably the same as those of judicial review. However there is authority that habeas corpus applies only where a decision is *ultra vires* in the narrow sense (*R v Secretary of State for the Home Dept, ex p Cheblak* [1991]).

Habeas corpus can be sought in the High Court and has priority over other business. It requires anyone detaining a person to bring the prisoner immediately before a judge to justify the detention. According to Dicey (1959, 199) habeas corpus is 'worth a hundred constitutional articles guaranteeing civil liberty' (even though Parliament had suspended it several times).

Habeas corpus may be of little practical importance today, when judicial review can provide a speedy way of challenging unlawful detention. Indeed because it cannot be used to challenge facts, habeas corpus has been held not to provide an effective remedy under Article 5 of the European Convention on Human Rights (ECHR): right to liberty (*X v UK* [1982]). (See Le Sueur, 'Should We Abolish the Writ of Habeas Corpus?' [1992] PL 13; Shrimpton, 'In Defence of Habeas Corpus' [1993] PL 24; Law Com No 226, 1994, Part XI.)

19.3 The judicial review procedure: public interest safeguards

The judicial review process contains mechanisms designed to protect the public interest against improper challenges. In attempting to do this, it is vulnerable to objections relating to the right of access to the courts and the right to a fair trial under Article 6 of the ECHR. As so often, a balance between competing values must be struck and the court has a wide discretion.

The judicial review process must also be set in the wider context of the 'Woolf' reforms in civil procedure introduced in 1999 (Woolf, *Access to Justice: A Final Report to the Lord Chancellor* (HMSO 1996)). These reforms include the following general aspirations in respect of which the parties are under an obligation to assist the court (CPR 1.1):

(a) ensuring that the parties are on an equal footing;

(b) saving expense. In this connection 'a protected costs order' can put limits on the exposure of the parties in cases involving the public interest (see eg *R (Boggis) v Natural England* [2010]);
(c) dealing with the case in ways which are proportionate
    (i) to the amount of money involved;
    (ii) to the importance of the case;
    (iii) to the complexity of the issues;
    (iv) to the financial position of each party;
(d) ensuring that the case is dealt with expeditiously and fairly;
(e) allocating to the case an appropriate share of the court's resources while taking into account the need to allot resources to other cases.

The main distinctive features of the judicial review procedure are as follows:

- Permission to apply is required from a judge before proceedings can be commenced in or transferred to the Administrative Court (Supreme Court Act 1981, s 31(3); CPR 54.4). The procedure is *ex parte*; that is the government side need not appear, although it must be given the opportunity to do so. At this stage the applicant merely shows that she or he has a chance of success, so as to discourage spurious challenges and help the court to manage an ever increasing caseload by filtering out hopeless cases. There is a right to renew the application for permission before another judge in open court, and in the case of a refusal in open court, before the Court of Appeal, and then with leave to the Supreme Court. If the Court of Appeal gives permission it often then proceeds to deal with the whole matter. After permission has been granted, interim relief preventing the implementation of the government action in question can be granted pending the full hearing either by injunction (Section 19.2) or under section 31 of the Supreme Court Act 1981.
- At the full hearing the court has a discretion in relation to procedural matters. The case is normally decided on the basis of affidavits (sworn written statements) but the court may order discovery of documents, witnesses and cross-examination 'where the justice of the case so demands' (CPR 54.16(1)). In *Tweed v Parade Commission for Northern Ireland* [2007] it was held that this was a broad principle which should take account of all the circumstances and that there may be a greater need to examine evidence in cases where the doctrine of proportionality applies. Moreover the government is obliged to make full and frank disclosure of all relevant material (see *R v Secretary of State for Foreign and Commonwealth Affairs, ex p Quark Fishing Ltd* [2006]; Lord Walker in *Belize Alliance of Conservation NGOs v Dept of the Environment* [2003]). With the agreement of the parties, the court can decide the whole matter without a hearing (CPR 54.18). It is arguable that in view of the broad policy issues that may arise in judicial review cases, particularly under the Human Rights Act 1998, it would be desirable that a more expansive process be used, at least in cases of major importance. One suggestion has been to appoint an Advocate General or Director of Civil Proceedings with the duty of representing the public interest before the court.
- Procedural flexibility is enhanced in that the Administrative Court can transfer cases to the ordinary trial process and vice versa (CPR 54.20).

- There is a shorter time limit than the periods of three or six years applicable to ordinary civil litigation. The law is contained in a somewhat confusing combination of section 31(6–7) of the Supreme Court (Senior Courts) Act 1981 and CPR 54.5(1)(b). The former is without prejudice to any enactment or rule of court which specifies a time limit (cf Tribunals, Courts and Enforcement Act 2007, s 16(4–5), which seems to be comprehensive).

  Under section 31(6) the court may refuse leave to make the application or refuse to give a remedy if 'undue delay' results in 'substantial hardship to any person, substantial prejudice to the rights of any person, or would be detrimental to good administration'. However by virtue of CPR 54.5(1) the claim must be filed (i) promptly and (ii) not later than three months after the ground to make the claim first arose. In the case of a quashing order, this means the date of the decision. The time limit cannot be extended by agreement and is subject to any shorter time limit in a particular statute (CPR 54.6). The time limit can however be extended by the court (CPR 3.1(2)).

  The combined effect of these provisions is a two-stage filter mechanism. Firstly a failure to apply for permission promptly, even within three months, is undue delay. The court might then extend the time limit. Secondly, if it does so, it can still refuse relief but only on the grounds specified in section 31(6). These considerations are usually examined at the full hearing stage (see *Caswell v Dairy Produce Quota Tribunal for England and Wales* [1990]).
- The court can refuse to grant a remedy in its discretion even when a decision is *ultra vires* and strictly speaking void. By contrast in ordinary litigation an *ultra vires* decision is treated as a nullity (*Credit Suisse v Allerdale BC* [1996]; see Section 17.2). The court will not set aside a decision where for example no injustice has been done, where the interests of third parties would be prejudiced or where intervention would cause serious public disruption (eg *R v Secretary of State for the Home Dept, ex p Swati* [1986]; *R v Secretary of State for Social Services, ex p Association of Metropolitan Authorities* [1986]; *Coney v Choyce* [1975]). The court might also prefer a declaration to an enforceable order where enforcement might be impracticable or hinder the governmental process (see eg *R v Panel on Takeovers and Mergers, ex p Datafin plc* [1987]; *Chief Constable of North Wales Police v Evans* [1982]; *R v Boundary Commission for England, ex p Foot* [1983] at 1116). The court will also take into account whether the claimant has made full disclosure of all relevant circumstances (*R v Lancashire CC, ex p Huddleston* [1986]).
- A particularly important aspect of the court's discretionary power is that judicial review is intended as a remedy of last resort. The court will not normally permit judicial review if there is another remedy which is at least equally appropriate. The court's approach is flexible and pragmatic. It will take account not only of the interests of the parties but of whether the matters to be decided raise issues of general importance, in which case judicial review would be more appropriate. The rule of law and the general presumption in favour of access to the courts is of particular concern. Thus in exceptional cases other remedies do not have to be exhausted. These include claims by asylum seekers due to their unique position, excess of jurisdiction in the pre-*Anisminic* sense (see Section 17.6) and denial of procedural justice. (See *R v Chief Constable of the Merseyside Police, ex p Calverley* [1986]; *R (Sivasubramaniam) v Wandsworth BC* [2003]; *R (G) v Immigration Appeal Tribunal* [2004]; *R (Weatherspoon) v Guildford BC* [2007].) *R (RK (Nepal)) v Secretary*

of State for the Home Dept [2009] illustrates the harshness of the general principle. It was held that where a system of appeals was provided, judicial review would be permitted only in limited and exceptional cases. Here an appeal could be made only from outside the country.

Secretary of State for Justice v Jones [2009] illustrates the limitations of the judicial review procedure in doing justice and more generally of judicial review in respect of decisions in the context of limited government resources. Under the Criminal Justice Act 2003 persons serving indeterminate sentences could be considered for release by the Parole Board if they could demonstrate that they were no longer a danger to the public. Due to lack of resources the Secretary of State had failed to provide the necessary training and support facilities to enable prisoners to do this. This failure was held to be unlawful. Nevertheless the claimant had no remedy.

Firstly damages are not available in respect of invalid government action as such and his detention was still lawful since he had no right to be released.

Secondly there was no breach of Article 5 of the ECHR (deprivation of liberty) since the detention was lawful. It was not arbitrary since the Parole Board hearings were not wholly an empty exercise.

Thirdly the Parole Board hearings themselves were not unfair since the Board was doing the best it could in the circumstances.

19.4 Standing (*locus standi*)

The applicant must show that he has 'sufficient interest' in the matter to which the application relates (Supreme Court Act 1981, s 31(3)). Before the 1977 reforms the law was complex and diffuse, depending primarily upon which remedy was being sought. In some cases standing was limited to a person whose legal rights were affected by the decision in question.

However in *IRC v National Federation of Self-Employed and Small Businesses Ltd* [1982], sometimes called 'Fleet Street Casuals' or the 'Mickey Mouse Case', the House of Lords, although holding that the applications had no standing on the facts, significantly liberalised the law. The applicants were members of a pressure group representing certain business interests. They challenged a decision of the Inland Revenue not to collect arrears of tax from casual print workers who were alleged to have made false claims (in some cases under the name of Mickey Mouse) on the ground that the decision was politically motivated. The following propositions were laid down:

- The question of standing must be decided both at the preliminary leave stage, with a view to filtering out obvious busybodies and troublemakers, and at the full hearing where the entitlement to a particular remedy is in issue.
- Standing is not limited to a person whose legal rights are affected by the decision in question.
- A majority held that 'sufficient interest' depends on the nature of the interests relevant to the statute under which the decision was made. Here the applicants failed since under the tax legislation a taxpayer's affairs are confidential and not the concern of other taxpayers, whether individuals or groups.

Lord Diplock, with some support from the others, took a broader approach based on the importance of the matter from a public interest perspective, suggesting that the more important the matter, the more generous should be the standing requirement. In some cases affecting the whole community, any citizen should have standing. Standing should not be separate from the substance of the case. It is not clear what this means since the two matters are conceptually distinct. It probably means that the stronger the merits, the more generous the standing test. Indeed Lord Diplock would have given the applicants standing had they produced evidence in support of their allegations.

Upholding the rule of law is also important, so a low threshold might be appropriate if there is no other way of calling the decision maker to account (see Rose J in *R (Bulger) v Secretary of State for the Home Dept* [2001]).

As a result of this case standing has become substantially a matter of discretion and is generous. It may be that standing will be given to anyone with a serious issue to argue and where a useful purpose would be served (eg *R (Feakins) v Secretary of State for the Environment, Food and Rural Affairs* [2004]; *R v North Somerset DC, ex p Dixon* [1998]). (The narrower approaches taken in *R v Somerset CC, ex p Garnett* [1998] and *R v Secretary of State for the Environment, ex p Rose Theatre Trust* [1990] are probably now unreliable.) However where a contribution can more effectively be made by others, standing may be denied (eg *Bulger*).

The courts have given standing to pressure groups certainly when they are 'associational' (see Cane, 2003), meaning that they represent people as a group who have an interest in the matter (see *R v Inspectorate of Pollution, ex p Greenpeace (No 2)* [1994]; *R (Edwards) v Environment Agency* [2004]). By contrast what Cane calls 'surrogate' groups, representing others who themselves could have standing, are less likely to succeed (see *R v Legal Aid Board, ex p Bateman* [1992]), although even here an important matter might succeed (eg *R (Quintavalle) v Human Embryology and Fertilisation Authority* [2005]: pressure group representing a patient, but standing not contested). A third category according to Cane comprises groups or individuals representing the general public interest. These have standing at least where there is no other way of challenging the decision (eg *R v HM Treasury, ex p Smedley* [1985]: taxpayer; *R v Secretary of State for Foreign and Commonwealth Affairs, ex p World Development Movement* [1995]: campaigning organisation; *R v Secretary of State for Foreign and Commonwealth Affairs, ex p Rees-Mogg* [1994]: concerned citizen (former editor of *The Times*); *R (Quintavalle) v Secretary of State for Health* [2003]: anti-abortion group). Indeed the contribution of pressure groups has been welcomed as adding a valuable dimension to judicial review (*R v Secretary of State for Trade and Industry, ex p Greenpeace* [1998]).

The particular remedy is also a factor. For example in *R v Felixstowe Justices, ex p Leigh* [1987] a newspaper editor had standing for a declaration that magistrates should not hide behind anonymity, but not *mandamus* to reveal the identity of magistrates in a particular case.

Even where the claimant lacks standing the court may consider the substantive issues, albeit without granting a remedy (eg *Bulger; Rose Theatre*). Moreover even where a person has no standing in their own right the court has a discretion in an action brought by someone with standing to hear any person, thereby broadening the scope of the process and allowing interest groups to have a say (CPR 54.17).

19.5 Choice of procedure: public and private law

The judicial review procedure applies only to 'public functions' (CPR 54.1). This implies that not all activities of government bodies are necessarily public functions and opens the possibility that some functions carried on by bodies outside government might nevertheless be public functions. Indeed contemporary political fashion favours using private bodies to deliver public services. It seems anomalous that a body carrying out functions on behalf of government should not be subject to judicial review (see the dissenting speeches of Lord Bingham and Lady Hale in *YL v Birmingham City Council* [2007]). There is no clear definition of 'public', and what is public in one context may not be so in another (see Section 6.2). Indeed it is often suggested that judicial review should be about controlling any concentration of power rather than government as such. The debate about the legal basis of judicial review reflects this (see Section 17.1.1).

The remedies provided by the Human Rights Act 1998 are also triggered in some cases by a 'public function' (see Section 21.5). The courts have warned that the meaning of public function in the two contexts is not necessarily the same since the purpose of the Human Rights Act is the narrower one of applying certain provisions of the ECHR in domestic law and the purpose of judicial review is contested. On the other hand cases in either context can be used as guidance and the same outcome has invariably been chosen (eg *Weaver v London and Quadrant Housing Trust* [2009]; *YL v Birmingham City Council*; *Hampshire CC v Beer* [2003]).

The courts have refused to apply a single test but have indicated a number of factors which make a function 'public'. They have taken a relatively flexible if cautious approach. It is relevant but not enough that the function in question is exercised in the public interest or that the body is important or that the decision has serious consequences for those affected by it. The main factors are as follows:

- Firstly where a power exercisable for public purposes is conferred directly by statute or royal prerogative it will normally be regarded as a public function (see *R v Panel on Takeovers and Mergers, ex p Datafin plc* [1987]; *Scott v National Trust* [1998]). However a body, such as an insurance company, which exercises commercial functions of a kind similar to those exercised by private bodies and happens to have been created by statute is not regarded as exercising public functions (*R (West) v Lloyds of London* [2004]).
- Secondly a function which is intermeshed with or 'underpinned' by government may be public in the sense that government bodies have control over its exercise or participate in its activities (*Poplar Housing and Regeneration Community Association Ltd v Donoghue* [2001]: housing association formed by local authority). How much government involvement is required is a matter of degree in the particular circumstances, making this approach highly uncertain. Relevant factors are the degree of involvement of government through finance, control or regulation and the extent to which the body in question has special powers. The following are the main examples:

In *R v Panel on Takeovers and Mergers, ex p Datafin plc* [1987], which is the seminal case, it was held that the Takeover Panel, a self-regulating voluntary body which acted as a City 'watchdog', was exercising public law functions. This was because it was set up in the public interest, it reported to the government and although it did not have statutory powers itself was supported by the statutory powers of the Department of Trade.

In *Hampshire CC v Beer* [2003] the Court of Appeal held that a farmers' market run by a farmers' cooperative was exercising public functions both for human rights and for judicial review purposes. This was for two reasons, each of which alone would have apparently sufficed. Firstly it had control over a public space in the street; secondly it had previously been run by the local authority, which had now handed it over to the cooperative.

In *Weaver v London and Quadrant Housing Trust* [2009] a majority of the Court of Appeal held that a housing association that was not formed by the local authority but which received government funding in return for delivering government housing policy and was intensively regulated by the government was exercising public functions both for judicial review and for Human Rights Act 1998 purposes in respect of decisions to evict tenants since these could not be separated from its public function of allocating social housing according to government policy. It was also relevant that the association had certain special powers and was under a statutory duty to cooperate with local authorities. However some of its functions, such as contractual arrangements with repair firms, could be private. The position of tenants who receive unsubsidised housing and pay a market rent is unclear.

The dissent took a radically different approach, regarding a function as private if it used private law powers such as a landlord's power to evict a tenant. Housing associations have no special powers of eviction. (Cf *YL v Birmingham City Council* [2007], a human rights case: privately run care home where individual residents funded by local authority but without direct public control not exercising public function; see Section 21.3.1.)

In the light of *Weaver* most universities would be bodies exercising public functions. Like housing associations almost all UK universities have chosen to submit to government direction and control in return for money.

- It has been held, sometimes reluctantly, that a power which is based exclusively on contract, for example the disciplinary power exercised by sports or professional associations, is a private law power (see *R v Disciplinary Committee of the Jockey Club, ex p the Aga Khan* [1993]; *R v Football Association, ex p Football League* [1993]; *R (Heather) v Leonard Cheshire Foundation* [2002]: retirement home owned by a charity). This seems artificial since many such bodies exercise their powers for the purpose of protecting the public in much the same way as the Takeover Panel. In cases such as *Aga Khan* the reality is that the individual has no choice but to submit to the jurisdiction since the alternative is to be excluded from an area of public life. Even in the context of government it has been held that judicial review does not apply to a purely contractual relationship (compare *R v East Berkshire HA, ex p Walsh* [1985]: nurse employed under contract, with *R v Secretary of State for the Home Dept, ex p Benwell* [1985]: prison officer employed directly under statute). However where there is an additional element of statute or governmental policy or if the decision affects persons beyond the contractual relationship the court may treat the matter as one of public law (*McLaren v Home Office* [1990]; see also *Weaver*; Hoffmann LJ in *Aga Khan*).

- Another possible test is whether if the body in question did not exist the government would have to intervene (see *R v Advertising Standards Authority* [1990]; *R v Chief Rabbi, ex p Wachmann* [1993]). However this is not reliable or conclusive since there is no agreement on what functions are necessary in this sense (see eg *Aga Khan*). Indeed it could apply to anything of importance. For example if all food shops closed, no doubt the government would intervene.

19.6 Exclusivity

Although originally important and controversial, this issue has now faded into the background and will be considered only briefly. Assuming that a decision concerns a public function, must the judicial review procedure always be used or can judicial review grounds be raised in another court, such as a local county court in respect of the eviction of council tenants? The Act does not say that challenges in other courts are forbidden and the remedies of declaration, injunction and damages are available in any court. When the judicial review procedure was introduced in the late 1970s the courts were initially concerned that it should not be avoided because it is geared to the special concerns of challenging government action. The procedure was unfamiliar to lawyers, some of whom may have been reluctant or too slow to use it. The judicial review procedure, although relatively speedy and flexible, is in some ways more restrictive than an ordinary action, particular in respect of the need for permission to apply and its three-month time limit. Thus the new procedure could be regarded as a threat to the rule of law. During the 1980s and 1990s several cases reached the House of Lords solely on this matter, so the new procedure looked as unfriendly as the old methods.

The seminal case was *O'Reilly v Mackman* [1982], where prisoners sought to challenge a decision not to give them remission for good behaviour. They were outside time for judicial review and attempted to bring an ordinary civil action for a declaration. Lord Diplock emphasised that a prisoner has no legal right to remission, which was an 'indulgence' from the government, but at most a legitimate expectation that his or her case would be considered fairly. This was a matter solely of public law (see Section 6.2). The House of Lords struck out their claim as an abuse of the court's process. Lord Diplock said that the judicial review procedure should normally be used in public law cases because of its safeguards which protected the government against 'groundless, unmeritorious or tardy harassment'.

However the issue seems to have become less important. The Administrative Court is now more accessible, having recently been extended to centres outside London. The Woolf reforms (Section 19.3) have narrowed the gap between judicial review and other civil actions by giving all courts wider powers to control proceedings and by requiring the parties to cooperate with the court in expediting proceedings. Although permission to apply is not required in an ordinary civil action, Part 24 of the CPR empowers the court to strike out a civil action at an early stage if the defendant can show that it has no reasonable chance of success. (In judicial review proceedings however the onus is on the *claimant* to establish a reasonable chance of success.) Moreover cases can be transferred at any time between the Administrative Court and another court.

The courts have emphasised that unless the procedure chosen is clearly inappropriate they will not disturb it. For example in *Kay v Lambeth LBC* [2006], concerning the eviction of a former tenant, the House of Lords held that methods of redress available in other courts can be used where appropriate but that in some cases (eg where the matter does not involve ordinary private rights, such as welfare benefit and immigration cases) no other forum is available (at [30]–[31]). Thus in *Clark v University of Lincolnshire and Humberside* [2000] a student brought an ordinary action for breach of contract against a decision by the University to fail her. It was argued that she should have brought a judicial review claim within the three months' time limit. The Court of Appeal held that she was entitled to bring a civil action. Even if judicial review was appropriate, the court would not strike out a claim in another court unless the court's processes were misused or the chosen procedure was unsuitable.

Here follows a brief summary of the main cases in order to track what seems to be an unfortunate diversion in the law. These cases illustrate how a bad decision can be sidelined or undermined by later cases.

In *O'Reilly v Mackman* [1982] Lord Diplock suggested that there should be exceptions to the exclusivity principle but did not fully identify them. He did indicate that the judicial review procedure would not be exclusive in cases of 'collateral' challenge, where the validity of government action arises incidentally in litigation.

In *Cocks v Thanet DC* [1983] the House of Lords applied *O'Reilly* harshly to hold that a claimant who had been refused housing under homelessness legislation must use judicial review rather than a more convenient action in a local county court. This was because the claimant had no right to a home, the decision being one of discretion. The county court now has what amounts to a judicial review function in homelessness cases (Housing Act 1996; see *Runa Begum v Tower Hamlets LBC* [2003] at [7]).

But in *Davy v Spelthorne BC* [1984] Lord Wilberforce expressed his distaste for the *O'Reilly* rule: 'The expressions "private law" and "public law" have recently been imported into the law of England from countries which unlike our own have separate systems concerning public law and private law. No doubt they are convenient expressions for descriptive purposes. In this country they must be used with caution for, typically, English law fastens, not upon principles but upon remedies' (at 276).

The courts soon began to back away from *O' Reilly* by exploiting Lord Diplock's exceptions, particularly as regards collateral challenge. Thus a citizen can raise a defence in any relevant proceedings against an unlawful government claim (*Wandsworth LBC v Winder* [1985]: rent arrears; *Boddington v British Transport Police* [1998]: prosecution for smoking). An ordinary civil action might also be appropriate if the issues are mainly factual or where the public law aspects are peripheral (*Mercury Communications v Director General of Telecommunications* [1996]; *D v Home Office* [2006]). Indeed to deny a citizen access to the court to protect legal rights could be regarded as violating the rule of law.

Roy v Kensington, Chelsea and Westminster Family Practitioner Committee [1992] further weakened *O'Reilly*. A doctor was seeking a discretionary 'practice allowance' from the NHS. He had established entitlement to some kind of allowance but not how much. The House of Lords suggested that whenever a litigant was protecting a 'private law right' he need not use the judicial review procedure. Alternatively it was held that the circumstances were so closely analogous to a private claim that as matter of discretion the action should go ahead. (See also *Trustees of the Dennis Rye Pension Fund v Sheffield City Council* [1997]; *British Steel v Customs and Excise Comrs* [1997]; *Cullen v Chief Constable of the RUC* [2004], illustrating how this may turn on complex questions of statutory interpretation.)

Cases where there is no alternative to judicial review because no legal rights are involved include discretionary government decisions to grant benefits or permissions, many immigration, prison and homelessness claims, and challenges to government investigations or inquiries that do not produce legal consequences.

19.7 The exclusion and limitation of judicial review

19.7.1 Justiciability

Some matters are non-justiciable, meaning that they raise issues that the courts prefer not to engage with. There are several reasons for this. They concern the nature and purpose of the courts and so raise separation of powers issues. It is difficult to pinpoint exactly what makes a matter non-justiciable and there is no recognised formula. (In another sense non-justiciability means that the courts will obviously not enforce directly any rules which are not law, for example constitutional conventions (see Section 3.4.2) or treaties (see Section 9.7.1), although these can be taken into account to help interpret and apply the law.)

Two preliminary matters can be emphasised. Firstly the fact that an issue is politically controversial or important, although a relevant factor, is not sufficient reason to exclude judicial review. Secondly there is a distinction between a matter which is wholly non-justiciable in the strict sense of being outside the court's jurisdiction and matters where the court shows 'deference' in the sense that it is unwilling to intervene except in very strong cases. It is arguable however that every case is one of discretion in the particular circumstances and that there are no areas that the courts can never investigate. However in *R (Cart) v Upper Tribunal* [2010] Sedley LJ asserted (at [28]) that the scope of judicial review is a matter of law.

Matters held to be wholly outside the court's jurisdiction are relatively few. They include the following:

- decisions of the High Court;
- proceedings in Parliament (this is statutory see Section 11.6);
- certain acts of state, including the making, ratification and content of treaties (see Section 9.7);
- disputed questions of international law (see Section 9.7);
- probably political decisions at the highest level of government, such as the dissolution of Parliament and the appointment of ministers. Matters of 'high policy' are often said to be non-justiciable (see *R (Gentle) v Prime Minister* [2008]);
- the Attorney General's power to commence legal actions (*Gouriet v Union of Post Office Workers* [1978]). However the Privy Council has hinted that this might be reconsidered (*Jeewan Mohit v DPP of Mauritius* [2006] at [21]);
- perhaps the deployment of the armed forces. In *R v Jones (Margaret)* [2006] the House of Lords was influenced by the reluctance of the courts to investigate the deployment of the armed forces in holding that the international war crime of aggression was not an offence in domestic law. Lord Bingham regarded the

matter as one of self-restraint. He took the view that the courts would be slow to interfere with the conduct of foreign policy or the deployment of the armed forces but did not rule it out (at [30]). Lord Hoffmann however treated it as a 'constitutional principle' that the Crown's discretion to go to war was not justiciable (at [65]). In *Gentle* the House of Lords refused to investigate whether the decision to invade Iraq was lawful in international law (see Section 9.7.1) but did not rule out intervention altogether. However in *R (Smith) v Secretary of State for Defence* [2010] Baroness Hale said that the deployment of the armed forces was essentially non-justiciable.

As *Gentle* suggests, the courts seem reluctant to treat a government power as wholly non-justiciable on a blanket basis. Recent cases have preferred to look more flexibly at specific issues or particular grounds of review. In these cases the court can either refuse to go into a specific matter, intervene only in a very clear or important case or apply some grounds of review but not others. Thus the principle is that of self-restraint, or what Hunt (2003) calls 'due deference'. In *R (ProLife Alliance) v BBC* [2003] Lord Hoffmann criticised the term 'deference'. He pointed out that the matter concerns the separation of powers, namely the distinction between the role of the courts and those of the other branches of government. According to Lord Hoffmann, the courts are deferring to no one but are upholding their constitutional function (see also Lord Bingham in *A v Secretary of State for the Home Dept* [2005]: 'institutional competence'). The issue of deference arises especially in human rights cases, where even a statute might be in issue (see Section 21.5.2).

Examples of deference include:

- diplomatic representations concerning prisoners in Guantanamo Bay (*R (Abbasi) v Secretary of State* [2002]; *R (Al Rawi) v Secretary of State* [2007]);
- the decision to invade Iraq (*R (Gentle) v Prime Minister* [2008]; *R (CND) v Prime Minister* [2006]; *R v Jones (Margaret)* [2006]) (but see box above);
- controversial matters of morality and taste and decency (*R (ProLife Alliance) v BBC* [2003] (see Section 22.3); *R (Countryside Alliance) v A-G* [2008] (see Section 20.3));
- a decision not to allow a person into the UK on public interest grounds (*R (Farrakhan) v Secretary of State* [2002]);
- high-level expert tribunals and other specialist bodies: no review for error of law (*Page v Hull University Visitor* [1993]; *R (Cart) v Upper Tribunal* [2010]; see Section 17.5); review only for difficult issues of general significance (*R (Sinclair Gardens Investments) v Lands Tribunal* [2005]);
- discretionary resource allocation: no review for unreasonableness except in an extreme case (*Hammersmith and Fulham LBC v Secretary of State* [1990]; *R (Douglas) v North Tyneside MBC* [2004] at [62]; *R v Cambridge HA, ex p B* [1995]; see Section 18.1);

- in the interests of the separation of powers the courts are reluctant to interfere with the decisions of independent prosecutors but will do so exceptionally where the grounds for doing so are strong and clear (*R (Corner House Research) v Director of the Serious Fraud Office (No 2)* [2008] at [30]–[32], [58]);
- decisions which are approved by Parliament also rate deference, especially in respect of unreasonableness (see *Nottingham CC v Secretary of State* [1986]; *R v Lichniak* [2003]; cf *R v Secretary of State for the Home Dept, ex p Fire Brigades Union* [1995]; see Section 7.8.4);
- national security was once considered a wholly non-justiciable area (*The Zamora* [1916] at 107) but this is no longer the case, although deference is still given (see Section 24.1).

Before *Council of Civil Service Unions (CCSU) v Minister for the Civil Service* [1985] it was widely believed that royal prerogative powers were wholly non-justiciable. The House of Lords rejected that approach, holding that it was the content rather than the source of the power that mattered. In that case the prerogative power to control the civil service was used to ban strikes at GCHQ (the base for intelligence interception of overseas broadcasts) without complying with an established practice of consulting the trade unions. The House held that the power was reviewable. However because the matter was one of national security, the court would not interfere since the government must be the judge of what national security requires. However the court did not regard the matter as wholly non-justiciable. It was held that the government must provide supporting evidence that the matter was genuinely one of national security, which in that particular case was of course easy to do.

In accordance with *CCSU* a Prerogative Order in Council, the highest expression of royal prerogative power, was held to be reviewable in *R (Bancoult) v Secretary of State (No 2)* [2008]. However their Lordships disagreed as to the extent to which deference should be shown to the government (see Section 6.6). The power to issue a passport was held to be reviewable because it is an administrative decision affecting the right of individuals as opposed to a matter of 'high policy' (*R v Secretary of State for Foreign and Commonwealth Affairs, ex p Everett* [1989]).

In *CCSU* Lord Roskill listed subjects he regarded as wholly non-justiciable because their nature or subject matter was not amenable to the judicial process. These included the making of treaties, defence, the prerogative of mercy, the grant of honours, the dissolution of Parliament and the appointment of ministers.

Lord Roskill's list has not stood the test of time. The prerogative of mercy has been held to be reviewable (*R v Secretary of State for the Home Dept, ex p Bentley* [1993]; *A-G of Trinidad and Tobago v Lennox Phillips* [1995]). As we have seen defence matters may be justiciable to some extent. On the other hand, the dissolution of Parliament and the appointment and dismissal of ministers are pre-eminently non-justiciable. They are functions of the highest level of government and are central to the democratic process. The legal process is clearly unsuitable for their resolution and the separation of powers requires the courts to refrain. Moreover these matters are governed by conventions which are not legally enforceable.

What general principles identify non-justiciable issues or matters calling for deference? There have been various attempts to identify them. Jowell (2009) distinguishes between two types of deference, these being firstly on constitutional principles relating to the separation of powers and democracy and secondly pragmatic matters based on the practical limitations of the judicial process, bearing in mind that UK judges, unlike judges in some other countries, have limited experience of political or administrative matters. Thus in *R v Ministry of Defence, ex p Smith* [1996] Lord Bingham said that 'the greater the policy content of a decision and the more remote the subject is from ordinary judicial experience the more hesitant the court must necessarily be in holding a decision to be irrational' (at 556).

Under the first head are matters, such as security, which are inherently the responsibility of the government (see *R (Mohamad) v Secretary of State for Foreign and Commonwealth Affairs* [2010]), matters of general policy which affect large numbers of people (polycentric) and the application of broad social values, especially when these decisions are taken by elected and democratically accountable bodies. The court's function in this kind of case is limited to ensuring that statutory requirements are complied with (see Lord Hoffmann in *R (Alconbury) v Secretary of State* [2001] at [76]). To this might be added foreign affairs, which raises issues of respect for sovereign governments beyond the reach of the courts.

Under the second head are specialist assessments and decisions where there are no objective standards on which the court can form a judgement and where an expert or a democratic body has greater legitimacy. These include professional judgements, aesthetic judgements such as architectural merit, moral evaluations, academic standards or security matters, where judges lack training, resources and experience to choose between the competing arguments or where another body is more suitable (see Lord Hoffmann in *R (ProLife Alliance) v BBC* at [76]: 'taste and decency'; *R (Countryside Alliance) v A-G* [2008] at [45]: the morality of hunting; *Cart*: specialist tribunal). Discretionary decisions involving the allocation of scarce resources, such as medical treatment, where competing considerations of money and welfare raise agonising dilemmas, require deference under both heads (see *R v Cambridge HA, ex p B* [1995] at 906). In these cases review for unreasonableness is likely to be limited to cases of clear irrationality (see Section 18.1). The court will also defer to another tribunal out of respect for its expertise and experience in specialised areas (see *Cart*).

The second head also takes account of the limitations of the court's adversarial procedures in terms of the parties before the courts, problems of delay and the availability of information to the court (*R (G) v Immigration Appeal Tribunal* [2004]: delay). In particular the court should concern itself with defined, specific issues. For example in *Copsey v WBB Devon Clays Ltd* [2005] at [39], it was said that the court should not decide controversial general matters such as whether an employer can keep a workforce secular since it lacks expertise and the necessary consultative procedures. (See the classic article by Fuller, 1978.)

Emphasising that it is the particular *issue* that falls to be considered not the power itself, Endicott (2009, ch 7.3) suggests four reasons why the court should defer to another body. These are expertise, political responsibility, effective processes and respect for the fact that the law has allocated the power to an administrative body. Endicott's fourth reason applies to all decision-making powers and underlies the basic principle that judicial review does not concern the merits of a decision (see Section 17.1). From a deference perspective, respect for a *democratic* decision maker is especially important.

R (Farrakhan) v Secretary of State [2002] provides an example of Endicott's approach. This was a decision by a minister to ban a visit by an overseas religious leader with a history of causing disturbances. In deciding not to interfere the court took account of the international principle that states can control their borders, that the decision was made by the Secretary of State personally after careful consideration, that the Secretary of State has greater expertise and information than is available to the court and that the Secretary of State is democratically accountable for the decision.

There are of course limits to deference. Indeed 'deference' may not be a separate doctrine at all but may merely reflect the fact that the judicial review principles are flexible and sensitive to context (see *Huang v Secretary of State* [2007] at [14]). As a minimum the courts can ensure that government processes are fair and reliable, that the decision maker is acting within its powers, that decisions have a rational basis and that fundamental rights are respected. The more serious the impact on individual rights, the less deference will be shown. At a very general level it may be the uncertainty of the absence of objective standards, together with the need to deal with incommensurable principles or values, that deters the courts from interfering (see Section 1.6).

19.7.2 Statutory exclusion of judicial review

Sometimes a statute attempts to exclude judicial review, thereby confronting a fundamental tenet of the rule of law that the exercise of power should be controlled by independent courts. The courts are reluctant to accept this and construe such statutes narrowly. Clear words are required to exclude judicial review, and there are even dicta, albeit unreliable, that Parliament cannot do this at all (see *Cart* at [38]). For example a provision stating that a decision shall be 'final' does not exclude review but merely prevents the decision maker from reopening the matter and excludes any right of appeal that might otherwise apply (*R v Medical Appeal Tribunal, ex p Gilmore* [1957]). Even a provision stating that a 'determination of the tribunal shall not be questioned in any court of law' is ineffective to prevent review where the tribunal exceeds its 'jurisdiction' (powers). This is because the tribunal's act is a nullity and so not a 'determination'. Given that a government body exceeds its jurisdiction whenever it makes an error of law (see Section 17.5) this neatly sidesteps the 'ouster clause' (*Anisminic v Foreign Compensation Commission* [1969]).

However given Parliament's ultimate supremacy, a sufficiently tightly drafted 'ouster clause' could surmount *Anisminic*. The court will take the policy of the Act into account. Here are some examples:

- A clause often found in statutes relating to land use planning and compulsory purchase allows challenge within six weeks and then provides that the decision 'shall not be questioned in any court of law'. The courts have interpreted this provision literally, on the ground that review is not completely excluded and that the policy of the statute is to enable development of land to be started quickly (see *R v Cornwall CC, ex p Huntingdon* [1994]).
- A provision stating that a particular act such as entry on a register or a certificate shall be 'conclusive evidence' of compliance with the Act and of the

matters stated in the certificate may also be effective since it does not exclude review as such but makes it impossible to prove invalidity. However this may leave open the possibility of review for unfairness or unreasonableness (see *R v Registrar of Companies, ex p Central Bank of India* [1985]).

- In certain cases, mainly involving security, special tribunals are given judicial review powers (see Sections 23.4, 23.5). Clear statutory language is required to prevent their decisions themselves being reviewable in the Administrative Court (see *R (Cart) v Upper Tribunal* [2010]). For example, under the Anti-Terrorism, Crime and Security Act 2001 an asylum seeker can appeal to the Immigration Appeal Tribunal against a decision of an adjudicator but only with the permission of the Tribunal (s 101). A decision to refuse permission can be challenged by a 'paper review' by a High Court judge, which is significantly more limited than normal judicial review. It was held in *R (G) v Immigration Appeal Tribunal* [2004] that in the absence of express words in a statute, judicial review could not completely be excluded. However given the intention of Parliament to deal with the serious problem of delays arising from the processing of asylum cases, the court would permit judicial review only in exceptional cases.

  Under the same Act there is a right of appeal to the Special Immigration Appeals Commissioners (SIAC), who include a High Court judge, against a decision of the Home Secretary to certify that a person is an 'international terrorist'. The proceedings of the commissioners are in private and evidence is sometimes not revealed to the complainant. The Act provides that any action taken by the Home Secretary may be questioned in legal proceedings only by this method (s 30). It was held in *Cart* that the SIAC, not being the equivalent of the High Court, was subject to full judicial review.
- Sometimes Parliament creates a new right and at the same time designates exclusive machinery for deciding disputes about it. This is not strictly a case of excluding judicial review since the right and the machinery are inseparable. However the court will scrutinise the machinery to establish whether it is as good as judicial review and, if this is not the case, judicial review will be available (see *A v B* [2010] at [21]): Investigatory Powers Tribunal for complaints against intelligence services under Human Rights Act 1998; see Section 23.5).
- Statutes dealing with surveillance and the security services feature a clause stating that a decision cannot be challenged even on jurisdictional grounds (see Security Services Act 1989, s 5(4); Regulation of Investigatory Powers Act 2000, s 67(8)). These may exclude judicial review completely, although they do provide a right to complain to special commissioners.

Where judicial review is excluded, Article 6 of the ECHR may be invoked on the ground that the ouster clause prevents a fair trial in relation to a person's 'civil rights and obligations'. The fairness of the proceedings as a whole must be considered, including the judicial review stage. It is arguable that the limited rights of challenge conferred by legislation dealing with security matters would be regarded as a proportionate response since 'fairness' is a flexible concept. Nevertheless in *Re MB* (2006) (control order over a suspected terrorist) the Administrative Court held that section 3 of the Prevention of Terrorism Act 2005 violated Article 6. It was conspicuously unfair in limiting judicial review to the lawfulness of the Secretary of State's decision on the basis only of the material before the Secretary of State, which the claimant was unable to see or challenge.

Summary

- There is a special procedure for challenging decisions of public bodies in the Administrative Court. It is highly discretionary. The procedure provides the citizen with a range of remedies to quash an invalid decision, prevent unlawful action and require a duty to be complied with. Damages may sometimes be available but under restricted circumstances. It provides machinery for protecting government against improper or trivial challenges. Leave to apply is required and judicial review will be refused where there is an equally convenient alternative remedy.
- Standing is flexible and increasingly liberal, although a third party may not be given standing where others are in a better position to challenge the decision.
- Judicial review applies only to public law functions, which usually include powers exercised by a wide range of bodies connected to the government or exercising statutory powers but does not usually exclude powers derived exclusively from contract or consent. In some cases the citizen may challenge public law powers outside the judicial review procedure on the basis of the rule of law principle that, where private rights are at stake, unlawful government action can be ignored.
- The remedies and procedure for judicial review are discretionary, so that even though an unlawful government decision is strictly speaking a nullity, the court may refuse to intervene. Delay, misbehaviour, the impact on third parties and the absence of injustice may be reasons for not interfering. Public inconvenience or administrative disruption are probably not enough in themselves but they might be relevant to the court's discretion when coupled with another factor such as delay.
- Some kinds of government power are inherently non-justiciable but more commonly the courts are deferential to certain issues for reasons relating to the separation of powers or the limitations of judicial procedures or expertise. In these cases judicial review may be limited to clear abuses of power.
- Sometimes statutes attempt to exclude judicial review. The courts are reluctant to see their powers taken away and interpret such provisions strictly. The Human Rights Act 1998 reinforces this.

Exercises

19.1 What are the advantages and disadvantages of the judicial review procedure from the point of view of the citizen? When may government action be challenged in the courts by means of an ordinary action?

19.2 'The expressions "private law" and "public law" have recently been imported into the law of England from countries which unlike our own have separate systems concerning public law and private law. No doubt they are convenient expressions for descriptive purposes. In this country they must be used with caution for, typically, English law fastens, not upon principles but upon remedies' (Lord Wilberforce). Discuss in the light of *O'Reilly v Mackman* [1982] and subsequent cases.

Exercises cont'd

19.3 Claire, a civil servant working in the Cabinet Office, has evidence that the Prime Minister has been selling peerages to rich businesswomen in return for promises to make donations to charities specified by the Prime Minister's wife. Claire informs the head of her department, who replies that 'it's not possible, my dear'. Claire now seeks judicial review. Advise her.

19.4 James, as the father of a soldier, wants to challenge the Prime Minister's decision to reduce the number of troops fighting in Afghanistan, on the ground that the troops there are not sufficiently supported and lack resources. Advise him.

19.5 Forever Open Housing Association provides sheltered accommodation for vulnerable people. It is a charity owned by a religious sect and is part-funded and regulated by the Housing Corporation, a government agency. Mary lives in a residential home owned by Forever Open, her accommodation being paid for by the local authority under its statutory obligation to arrange for care provision for the elderly. When Mary took up residence Forever Open told her that she now had 'a home for life'. Forever Open now proposes to close the home. Advise Mary whether she can challenge this proposal in the Administrative Court.

19.6 By statute (fictitious) the NHS is required to provide 'an effective healthcare service for all residents of England and Wales'. The statute also provides that 'the actions of any NHS hospital in relation to the provision of any service to the public shall not be questioned in any court on any ground whatsoever'. St Dave's Hospital in the English town of Holby is short of money and trained staff because of government financial cuts. The Secretary of State has issued a circular to all hospitals stating, among other things, that no further patients are to be admitted for sex-change operations and that hip replacement operations should normally be performed only on patients who play an active part in the economic life of the community.

(i) The Holby Transsexual Rights Society, a local pressure group, objects to the circular. It discovers the contents six months after it came into effect. Advise the Society as to its chances of success in the courts.

(ii) Frank, who is an unemployed resident in a hostel for the homeless, is refused a hip replacement operation. He wishes to bring an action in his local county court. Advise St Tony's Hospital.

(iii) The Welsh Nationalist Party want to challenge the circular. Advise the Party.

Further reading

Allan, 'Deference, Defiance and Doctrine: Defining the Limits of Judicial Review' (2010) 60 U Toronto LR 41

Cane, 'Accountability and the Public/Private Distinction' in Bamforth and Leyland (eds), *Public Law in a Multi-Layered Constitution* (Hart 2003)

Endicott, *Administrative Law* (Oxford University Press 2009) chs 7.3, 10, 15.5, 15.6

Fordham, 'Judicial Review: The New Rules' [2001] PL 4

Fuller, 'The Forms and Limits of Adjudication' (1978) 92 Harvard LR 353

Halliday, *Judicial Review and Compliance with Administrative Law* (Oxford University Press 2004)

Harris, 'Judicial Review, Justiciability and the Prerogative of Mercy' (2003) 62 CLJ 631

Hunt, 'Sovereignty's Blight: Why Contemporary Public Law Needs the Concept of "Due Deference"' in Bamforth and Leyland (eds), *Public Law in a Multi-Layered Constitution* (Hart 2003)

Jowell, 'Judicial Deference: Servility, Civility or Institutional Incapacity?' [2003] PL 592

Jowell, 'What Decisions Should Judges Not Take?' in Andenas and Fairgrieve (eds), *Tom Bingham and the Transformation of the Law* (Oxford University Press 2009)

Further reading cont'd

King, 'Institutional Approaches to Judicial Restraint' (2008) 28 OJLS 409
Miles, 'Standing in a Multi-Layered Constitution' in Bamforth and Leyland (eds), *Public Law in a Multi-Layered Constitution* (Hart 2003)
Rivers, 'Proportionality and the Variable Standard of Review' (2006) 65 CLJ 172
Taggart (ed), *The Province of Administrative Law* (Hart 1997) chs 1, 2, 10

Part VI

Fundamental rights

Chapter 20

Human rights and civil liberties

The absurd device of a bill of rights. (Michael Oakeshott)

Democracy is the will of the people but the people may not will to invade those rights which are fundamental to democracy itself. (Lady Hale in *R (Countryside Alliance) v A-G* [2008])

20.1 Introduction: the nature of human rights

The concept of human rights concerns attempts to identify fundamental human interests which have a special status in the sense that they should not be violated, either at all or only in extreme circumstances. These rights concern basic needs such as personal freedom, privacy and freedom of religion; political interests such as freedom of expression and association; and fairness and justice, such as the right to a fair trial before an independent judge. Some of these rights conflict with others, for example freedom of the press and respect for privacy. Some may conflict with social goals such as security and the fair distribution of wealth. Human rights did not become a prominent legal issue in the UK until the aftermath of the Second World War, which produced a worldwide reaction against the atrocities of the Nazis.

The expression 'bill of rights' is often used when talking about human rights. A bill of rights strictly speaking is a list of rights, usually contained in a written constitution, which cannot be overridden by the lawmaker except in circumstances spelled out in the bill of rights. The rights in a bill of rights need not be what we might think of as human rights but depend on the culture of the state in question. For example the right to bear arms is part of the US Bill of Rights. The UK has no bill of rights. The Human Rights Act 1998, which will be discussed in the next chapter, is the nearest we have. This Act makes certain rights taken from the European Convention on Human Rights (ECHR) part of UK law.

Three interrelated issues underlie human rights law. Firstly what is a human right? Is it anything other than a political claim? Attitudes to this question influence the importance we attach to human rights law. The classic Enlightenment writers, notably Locke (see Section 2.3.2), thought that there were certain natural rights given by God which it is the state's duty to protect. In his case these were life, health, liberty and property. For Hobbes by contrast there are no rights other than those created and enforced by law. To Hobbes natural rights are based on the universal human interests of gain, safety and reputation and are essentially rational reasons for action rather than rights as such. They include primarily self-defence, 'do-as-you-would-be-done-by' and the honouring of promises. From a utilitarian perspective, Bentham regarded the notion of rights as 'nonsense on stilts' except in the sense of interests protected by particular laws.

There is no agreement as to how we identify human rights. Some claim that they are revealed by God, others that they are based upon the idea that humans have a special 'dignity', others that they are self-evident, being derived from basic human needs. For example the UN Universal Declaration of Human Rights (Cmd 7226, 1948) is founded on the 'inherent dignity...of all members of the human family', equality, rationality and 'brotherhood' (Preamble Article 1). However in the absence of a religious belief it is difficult to see where this 'dignity' comes from. Some, for example Hume (Section 2.3.3), claim that human rights are driven by our natural sympathy for others and that we create customs underpinning particular ways of life which we desire to preserve. Others, following Kant, derive them from apparently self-evident rational truths such as 'equality' or 'autonomy'. For example Dworkin (*Freedom's Law* (Oxford University Press 1996)) argues that certain interests, such as freedom of expression and the right to a fair trial, are non-negotiable conditions of a democratic society because they underpin equality, this being the nearest we can get to a bedrock principle.

Such grandiose assertions face the difficulty that they may be too vague to be directly applied. Indeed politicians and officials drafting laws or international treaties might take refuge in vagueness as a way of producing agreement, while leaving the hard questions to be decided by others such as the courts ('constitutional abeyance'; see Section 3.5). Indeed this was the case with the ECHR (see Marston, 'The UK's Part in the Preparation of the ECHR' (1993) 42 ICLQ 796).

Moreover claims to universality face the problem of multiculturalism. Some rights, for example private property, may not be recognised in every culture, and different cultures may understand particular rights and their limits in different ways. In the UK this feeds into a debate as to whether our human rights law should be confined by the limits of the ECHR or whether we should develop our own notion of human rights. At present the UK courts stick closely to ECHR jurisprudence (see Section 21.1).

This leads to the second issue. What is the legal basis for a statement of fundamental rights? The UK relies on the ECHR and the European Court of Human Rights. The Convention came into force in 1953 as an international treaty under the auspices of the Council of Europe, which was established in 1949 and has 41 members. It derives from the Universal Declaration of Human Rights, a resolution of the UN General Assembly (1948) which is not in itself legally binding. As a response to Nazi atrocities the ECHR concentrates on the protection of individual freedom against state interference rather than on what are known as 'second- and third-generation rights', these being respectively social claims such as housing and collective interests such as environmental quality. The ECHR is something of a bland compromise with many exceptions. An alternative claim relates to Dicey's version of the rule of law (Section 6.4.2), namely that human rights are implicit in the common law, which does not need the support of an international treaty (see Section 20.2).

The third issue is who should have the last word in human rights disputes? In particular should there be a bill of rights protected against being overridden by the democratic lawmaker? Even if we accept that the concept of human rights is meaningful and should be embedded in the law, nothing follows automatically from this as to what is the best mechanism for protecting it. The ultimate decision maker might for example be a court as in the US, an elected lawmaker as in the UK or a special body as in France.

Human rights disputes differ significantly from those with which the courts traditionally deal. There is fundamental and apparently never-ending disagreement about the meaning and application of human rights concepts. Human rights cases often require the judge to assess the validity of a legal rule or government decision against a vague aspirational concept such as 'freedom of expression' and to decide the extent to which a right should be sacrificed to some important public goal, for example personal freedom against the suppression of terrorism.

Thus a human rights dispute often raises wide issues affecting society as a whole, going beyond the interests of the particular parties. As we saw in Section 1.6 there are different perspectives upon political values which are incommensurable, lacking any overriding principle against which they can be assessed. For this reason it is often doubted whether the legal process with its limited sources of information and its authoritative solution imposed from above is an appropriate way of deciding human rights disputes. A court is limited by the circumstances and parties in a particular case and the legal process is not comfortable with wide-ranging debate. The legal process is also vulnerable to the republican attack that it gives the judge the power of arbitrary domination.

It is often claimed that the courts are most likely to produce the 'best' outcome, being independent, open and guided by intense rational analysis as a forum for public debate. However arguments about what is the best outcome merely repeat the disagreement. Unless we agree as to what counts as a best outcome, we cannot agree what mechanism is most likely to produce it. A court is attractive to those who wish to impose philosophical master principles on others but less so to those who rely on a pragmatic accommodation between competing interests. While judges are good at interpreting and applying linguistic formulae, conflicts between fundamental rights and other important interests go beyond legal rules into territory where judges have no special expertise, requiring them either to be political philosophers or politicians or to resort to semantic evasion. For example, in *Secretary of State for the Home Dept v JJ* [2008] disagreement in the House of Lords turned upon the semantic question of the line between a 'deprivation of liberty' and a 'restriction on liberty', the former but not the latter being a violation of a Convention right.

The main role of a court based on the separation of powers is to apply a legal rule made by others to a specific case using methods which are supported by substantial public confidence. In human rights cases these are the very matters on which there is often intractable disagreement. Moreover in a human rights case there is not usually a rule to be applied since the right, even if can be clearly defined, has to be 'weighed' against a competing public interest. Since there is no objective way of doing this, or at least one which commands widespread support, the task may be more appropriate to a democratic body which may be able to negotiate a solution acceptable to most of those involved. Many of the cases have produced sharp disagreements between the judges.

The favourite liberal argument in favour of a court is fear of what De Toqueville called 'the tyranny of the majority'. The argument runs that 'democracy' is more than just the will of the majority and must be policed by certain basic rights of equality and freedom protected against the volatility, corruption or foolishness of the majority (see Lord Hoffmann in *R (Alconbury Developments Ltd) v Secretary of State for the Environment, Transport and the Regions* [2001] at [70]). Thus handing over power to a court is not anti-democratic but a prudent 'pre-commitment' of a majority anxious to guard against its own weaknesses, for example a panic overreaction to a supposed threat such as that of terrorism. By removing fundamental rights from its control, the majority lessens the risk that it will misuse its power. In particular a court can protect unpopular minorities.

However Waldron draws on the republican argument (see Section 2.5) that we sacrifice dignity, equality and control over our lives by letting unelected judges decide whether laws are valid. The appropriate question is what mechanism can most appropriately manage disagreement? Arguably this should be a democratic assembly in which the whole community can participate on equal terms. Moreover even if a democratic body gives this power to the judges, the exercise of the power does not thereby become democratic, any more than if a democratic body handed over its power to a dictator (see Waldron, *Law and Disagreement* (Oxford University Press 1999)).

The Human Rights Act 1998 recognises this irreducible disagreement by trying to accommodate both sides. It uses the advantages of the courts in applying the law even to the extent of scrutinising statutes for compatibility with the ECHR. On the other hand the Act upholds democracy by leaving the final word with Parliament while empowering the courts to put pressure on Parliament, thereby creating an accommodation in accordance with the separation of powers. In this way the Human Rights Act 1998 is sometimes said to create a 'constitutional dialogue'. (See also Ghosh, 'Deliberative Democracy and the Countermajoritarian Difficulty: Considering Constitutional Juries' (2010) 30 OJLS 327, suggesting that juries representing deliberative democracy might decide constitutional questions.)

20.2 The common law

English lawyers have traditionally used the terminology of negative freedom (see Section 2.4) and civil liberties rather than the positive language of rights. The traditional common law standpoint has been residual, namely that everyone is free to do whatever the law does not specifically prohibit. In Hobbes' language, 'freedom lies in the silence of the laws'. However, in a constitution based on unlimited parliamentary power that can readily be harnessed by political parties in thrall to vested interests, the problem lies in ensuring that the laws are indeed silent. Moreover the notion of negative freedom assumes that all freedoms are of equal value. For example, Dicey may appear complacent:

> English law no more favours and provides for the holding of public meetings than for the giving of public concerts...A man has a right to hear an orator as he has a right to hear a band or eat a bun. (1915, 500)

The common law's residual approach therefore depends on trusting the lawmaker not to enact intrusive laws and trusting the courts to interpret laws in a way sympathetic to individual liberty. This violates republican ideas by treating us as 'happy slaves' content with a kind master.

Recently however the judges have held that some common law principles amount to fundamental rights and enjoy especial protection. The rule of law has been invoked in this connection in the form of the 'principle of legality', which requires clear statutory language or perhaps necessary implication is required to override fundamental rights so that Parliament is compelled to face up to what it is doing and to be accountable (see Sections 6.6, 8.4.5, 17.4). However this cannot surmount the creeping erosion of liberty by the accumulation of statutes, which, taken individually, are relatively innocuous but which add up to a formidable armoury of state powers. Numerous statutes were enacted on behalf of the governments of 1997–2010 restricting individual liberty and increasing surveillance in order to combat antisocial behaviour and terrorism (Some of these are currently proposed for removal in the Protection of Freedoms Bill 2011). Moreover legislation enacted to deal with a particular problem may be used for other purposes. The Terrorism Act 2000 for example was used to remove an elderly heckler from the 2005 Labour Party Conference, and the Serious Organised Crimes and Police Act 2005 to arrest a demonstrator for possession of an article in *Vanity Fair* critical of the government (see HL Deb 1 February 2006, cols 231, 239; *Guardian* 29 June 2006).

It is also claimed that the common law, being open to any argument and treating all parties as equals, is especially suitable for a liberal society (Allan, *Constitutional Justice* (Oxford University Press 2001)). Indeed until the Human Rights Act 1998 the UK had resisted incorporation of the ECHR on the basis that the common law provided equivalent protection (see *Brind v Secretary of State for the Home Dept* [1991]; Lord Goff in *A-G v Guardian Newspapers (No 2)* [1998] at 660). In *R v Secretary of State for the Home Dept, ex p Simms* [1999] Lord Hoffmann set out to show that the common law can protect individual rights without recourse to the Act.

However the two approaches are different in important respects. Firstly the ECHR requires special justification to override a right, whereas in the common law any sufficiently clearly worded statute will do. Secondly the common law, sometimes described as unprincipled, is multifactoral and utilitarian in the sense that it depends on accumulating factors pointing to or against a particular conclusion without necessarily organising these within a formal hierarchy of principles.

20.3 The European Convention on Human Rights

The ECHR has three roles under the UK constitution:

1. Individuals can petition the European Court of Human Rights in Strasbourg alleging that the state has violated their rights under the Convention. The court may award compensation and require the state to change its law. However its decisions are binding only in international law under the Convention itself and have no direct binding force in domestic law. The court sometimes gives a 'margin of appreciation' to the state. This acknowledges the liberal value of diversity and allows the Convention to be applied flexibly in the light of particular variations in the values and needs of different countries. The court does not require domestic courts to be bound by its decisions and does not itself follow a strict doctrine of precedent. Without this room for manoeuvre it would be difficult to obtain general acceptance of the court's jurisdiction (see *Handyside v UK* [1976]: pornography; *Leander v Sweden* [1987]: security). The margin of appreciation is of course limited. States cannot disregard fundamental values and standards supported by a consensus among member states and the court will review the reasonableness of the state action (see eg *Funke v France* [1993] at [55]–[57]; *Marper v UK* [2008] at [102]).
2. As a treaty the Convention should be taken into account by domestic courts when interpreting statutes, at least where they are ambiguous. The common law should probably also be developed in the light of the Convention (see *A-G v Guardian Newspapers Ltd (No 2)* [1998]).
3. The Human Rights Act 1998 incorporates the main rights listed in the Convention, *but not the Convention itself*, into UK law and provides a special mechanism for applying them and for drawing upon the jurisprudence of the European Court of Human Rights. Points (1) and (2) are not affected by the Act. As Lord Bingham pointed out in *R (Al-Skeini) v Secretary of State* [2007] at [10], rights *under* the Convention differ from rights created by the 1998 Act *by reference to* the Convention. The Human Rights Act 1998:
   - provides remedies against a public authority that violates a Convention right;

- requires the court to interpret legislation in accordance with Convention rights;
- enables the courts to assess whether an Act of Parliament is compatible with a Convention right;
- provides mechanisms for Parliament and the executive to accommodate human rights issues.

The court has no power under the Act to overturn an Act of Parliament, so the traditional doctrine of parliamentary supremacy is preserved. Arguably this is a quibble since a court ruling that a statute does not comply with the Convention has great political force, particularly where Parliament lacks moral authority. The mechanics of the Act will be discussed in Chapter 21.

The ECHR is primarily concerned with 'negative' rights protected against state interference as opposed to positive rights requiring state action to give effect to the right. Sometimes however a positive right exists. There are two kinds of positive right. The first is where the right requires the state to provide some positive benefit or facility such as welfare services or formal acceptance of a minority status (see *Rees v UK* [1986]: transsexuality). In a democracy courts are reluctant to impose this kind of duty on the state since it may involve choices about public spending that are regarded as more appropriate to an elected body (see Section 19.7.1).

Moreover liberals may object to the impact of positive rights on the free market and the likely conflict with individual liberty and initiative (see Sunstein, 'Against Positive Rights' (1993) 2 EECR 35). This raises the irreducible clash between positive and negative freedom (see Section 2.4). Only in cases of extreme destitution does the ECHR enter the territory of positive rights in this sense. There are however other international treaties dealing with social and political rights of a positive kind, notably the UN International Covenant on Economic, Social and Cultural Rights (1976). These have not been incorporated into domestic law and contain no enforcement machinery. Some constitutions, notably those in states associated with the former Soviet Union, contain a range of economic and social rights.

The second kind of positive right is where the state is required to ensure not only that it respects the right in question but also that private bodies do so. It is not enough that the state does not interfere with the right. It must also take active steps to protect the right (see Lord Steyn in *R (Ullah) v Special Adjudicator* [2004] at [34]; Fredman, 'Human Rights Transformed: Positive Duties and Positive Rights' [2006] PL 562). Such positive obligations are unlikely to be absolute and the state will be afforded a margin of discretion in carrying them out (Section 21.5.2; see *R (Pretty) v DPP* [2002] [15]). Particular examples include the right to life, respect for privacy and family life and press freedom. Thus the state must ensure not only that the media is free to inform the public but also that the privately owned press respects the privacy of individuals.

20.4 The main Convention rights

The structure of the Convention rights is as follows. Many Convention rights can be *overridden* on defined grounds relating to the public interest and the rights of others (see Arts 7–11; Art 14 (indirectly); Protocol 1, Art 1). Articles 2, 5 and 7 are *absolute*, subject to designated *exceptions*. Articles 3, 4(1), 6 and 12 and Protocol 1, Articles 2 and 3 are absolute without exceptions, albeit vaguely expressed. Indeed even in the case of the absolute rights the courts may use public interest arguments when they define the meaning and scope of the right, thereby blurring the separate issues of whether there is a right and whether it has been violated (eg *Austin v Metropolitan Police Comr* [2009]; see Section 20.4.1). This is justified by the assertion that a principle of 'fair balance' between individual rights and the wider interests of society runs through the whole Convention (eg Lord Bingham in *Kay v Lambeth LBC* [2006] at [32]; *Sporrong and Lonnroth v Sweden* [1982] at [52]). It has also been proclaimed that the ECHR is a 'living instrument' to be interpreted in the light of changing values and circumstances (*Tyrer v UK* [1978]). An extreme example of this approach would be to suggest that torture for a good purpose is lawful. Moreover the European Court has held that a right may be qualified by another international obligation such as compliance with a UN resolution (see *R (Al Jedda) v Secretary of State for Defence* [2008]).

The question of overriding protected rights will be discussed in Chapter 21 in relation to the Human Rights Act 1998. In this section we shall outline the rights themselves.

Under Article 15 of the Convention, states can 'derogate' (completely opt out) or 'reserve' (partly opt out) from many rights under the Convention 'in time of war or other public emergency threatening the life of the nation' but 'only to the extent strictly required by the exigencies of the situation' (see Section 23.6). This does not apply to Article 2 (right to life), except in respect of a lawful act of war, Article 3 (torture and inhuman or degrading treatment or punishment), Article 4(1) (slavery or servitude) or Article 7 (retrospective punishment). The Human Rights Act 1998 reflects this (see ss 14–16).

The following provisions of the ECHR are incorporated into the Human Rights Act 1998 (s 1).

20.4.1 Absolute rights subject to exceptions

Article 2: right to life

> Except for capital punishment following criminal conviction, defence against unlawful violence, lawful arrest or prevention of unlawful escape, lawful action for quelling riot or insurrection.

Article 2 requires the state not to take life in any circumstances outside the designated exceptions. It also requires the state to provide a positive framework of laws to protect life. The state must also hold an open, effective and thorough investigation into an unexplained death or serious injury to someone in state custody. Failures of this kind have generated considerable public concern.

> See *R (Middleton) v West Sussex Coroner* [2004]; *R (Hurst) v North London District Coroner* [2007]; see also *R (D) v Secretary of State for the Home Dept* [2006]: supervision of suicide risk; *Thompson and Venables v News Group Newspapers Ltd* [2001]: protection of offender; *Van Colle v Chief Constable of Hertfordshire Police* [2006]: protection of witness; *R (Reynolds) v IPPC* [2009] at [20]–[25]: serious injury in police custody; *R (JL) v Secretary of State* [2009]: where there is evidence of egregious failures there should be a public hearing and legal representation; *R (AM) v Secretary of State* [2009]: privately run detention centre; allegations must be investigated.

In so far as there is a duty to prevent loss of life it is narrow, requiring a real and immediate risk objectively verified and a failure to take reasonable precautions (*Re Officer L* [2007]; *R (Gentle) v Prime Minister* [2008]: right to life of soldiers not engaged by decision to go to war in Iraq but issue of inadequate resources not addressed). Article 2 has been interpreted narrowly so as not to authorise voluntary euthanasia (*R (Pretty) v DPP* [2002]: the right to life is the right not to be killed, not to have control over one's own life). The court emphasised that the Convention is not meant to intervene in controversial moral issues around which there is no consensus. This is one way in which the court deals with the problem that it lacks democratic legitimacy.

Article 4(1): slavery, 4(2): forced or compulsory labour

Exceptions (to 4(2) only) are prison or parole, military service, emergency or calamity and 'normal civic obligations'.

Article 5: liberty and security of person

Except in prescribed cases in accordance with a procedure prescribed by law, this is an absolute right that cannot be overridden. The main exceptions are criminal convictions, disobedience to a court order, control of children, infection, mental health, alcoholism, drug addiction, vagrancy and in order to prevent illegal immigration or with a view to deportation or extradition. There are safeguards to ensure a speedy trial and adequate remedies against unlawful detention. A person arrested must be informed promptly of the reasons for the arrest, shall be brought promptly before a court and 'shall be entitled to take proceedings by which the lawfulness of his detention shall be decided speedily by a court and his release ordered if the detention is not lawful'. The right to personal liberty is given especially high importance (see eg *Secretary of State for the Home Dept v JJ* [2008] at [37], [107]).

Outside the exceptions Article 5 is absolute. However it has been weakened by drawing a distinction between deprivation of liberty and restrictions upon liberty. The latter do not fall within Article 5 but fall within Protocol 4, Article 2, which the UK has not ratified, and so do not apply.

In *Austin v Metropolitan Police Comr* [2009] the House of Lords held that police confinement of a crowd for two hours within a cordon on the road in uncomfortable conditions was only a 'restriction' on liberty and so was not unlawful. The distinction between restriction and deprivation is one of degree by way of comparison with the core case of complete confinement in a small space. The court will take into account the circumstances of the individual and the context (at [21]). This includes the type, duration, effect and manner of implementation of the interference with liberty. Even though Article 5 is absolute and its exceptions must be interpreted narrowly (at [13]), their Lordships also thought the purpose of the police action to be relevant, in this case the important purpose of public order (at [34]–[35], [39], [45]–[46]).

Thus *Austin* is an example of a public interest balancing test even where the Convention does not expressly so provide. Similarly (perhaps echoing the distinction between positive and negative freedom; see Section 2.4) the European Court of Human Rights held that the placing of a child in a foster home was not a deprivation of liberty since it was done by a responsible authority in the child's own interests (*HM v Switzerland* [2002]).

In *Gillan v UK* [2010] the House of Lords had held that a police 'stop and search' involving complete coercion for 30 minutes was not a deprivation of liberty. The European Court condemned the police action under Article 8 (see Section 23.7.4) and did not decide this particular point. However it was suggested (see [57]) that complete coercion of this kind did fall within Article 8, thus throwing doubt on *Austin*.

'Control Orders' under anti-terrorism legislation include confinement in the home for many hours. These also raise the distinction between deprivation and restriction of liberty. The matter depends particularly upon the impact on the victim's ability to live a normal life (cf *Secretary of State for the Home Dept v JJ* [2008]; *Secretary of State for the Home Dept v MB* [2008]; *Secretary of State for the Home Dept v E* [2008]; see Section 23.7.5). In this connection a restraint that does not amount to deprivation of liberty might fall foul of Article 8 (privacy).

Article 7: no retrospective criminal laws

> Except in respect of acts which were criminal when committed according to the general principles of law recognised by civilised nations.

20.4.2 Rights with no exceptions

Article 3: torture or inhuman or degrading treatment or punishment

This is an absolute right which cannot be overridden (see eg *Tyrer*; *Costello-Roberts v UK* [1993]: severe corporal punishment; *Ireland v UK* [1978]: interrogation of suspected terrorists; sensory deprivation not torture but inhuman treatment). Article 3 was applied to a government decision to withdraw welfare support from asylum seekers where to do so would result in destitution, thereby imposing a positive duty (*R (Limbuela) v Secretary of State for Social Security* [2007]). However it was emphasised that Article 3 does not confer a right to be provided with welfare services as such. In *Limbuela* the inhuman treatment resulted from a specific exclusion of failed asylum seekers from the normal provision. The House of Lords emphasised that Article 3 was engaged only when, taking account of all the claimant's circumstances, age, health, gender, other means of support and so on, the claimant was reduced to a sense of despair and humiliation, for example by having no access to toilet or washing facilities. (See also *N v UK* [2008]: no duty to ensure medical care.)

The government cannot use evidence which might have been obtained by torture in other countries in legal proceedings here. In *A v Secretary of State for the Home Dept (No 2)* [2006] the House of Lords held that, in principle, evidence obtained by torture was not admissible, regarding this as a 'constitutional principle'. However their Lordships disagreed as to the standard of proof. A majority held that it must be shown on balance of probabilities that the evidence was tainted, whereas the minority thought that it was enough to show that there was a 'real risk'. (See also *Secretary of State for the Home Dept v Rehman* [2002]; *R v Secretary of State for the Home Dept, ex p McQuillan* [1995]; *R v*

Secretary of State for the Home Dept, ex p Adams [1995].) However the government might still use evidence obtained by torture overseas as part of its investigations (see Section 23.3.3).

The government must not participate in or condone torture by others (see *R (Mohamed) v Secretary of State for Foreign and Commonwealth Affairs* [2010]; Section 23.3.3). It also has a positive duty to ensure that private persons do not violate Article 3 rights, for example by beating a child (*A v UK* [1998]). Under Article 3 a person cannot be deported to a country where he or she would be at risk of torture or inhuman or degrading treatment by the state or condoned by the state (*Chahal v UK* [1996]). However in *R (Wellington) v Secretary of State* [2008] (the return of suspected offenders to a requesting state; in this case to the US) the House of Lords held that Article 3 should be construed less strictly in cases involving extradition. Otherwise extradition arrangements might be at risk. (See also UN Refugee Conventions (Cmd 9171, 1954; Cmnd 3906, 1967); Section 9.7.1.)

In *R (Ullah) v Special Adjudicator* [2004] the House of Lords extended this principle to the risk of serious violations of other Convention rights. This raises problems most obviously in relation to Article 8 (respect for family life) and Article 9 (religion) because of the cultural and social differences involved. For example in *HJ (Iran) v Secretary of State for the Home Dept* [2010] the Supreme Court held that a person could not be expelled to a country where he or she would be unable openly to live as a homosexual. It was emphasised that the Refugee Convention was not intended to guarantee all the human rights standards that are part of our own culture but to make a judgement on the failure of a state in relation to one of the core entitlements recognised by the international community. Thus some Convention rights are more fundamental than others.

There is also the consideration that the ECHR should not impose a general duty on the government to provide medical or other welfare services. The matter seems to be one of degree. Contrast *R (Razgar) v Secretary of State for the Home Dept* [2004] (serious mental illness if Kurdish refugee returned to Germany; upheld under Article 8 (Baroness Hale dissenting)) with *N v Secretary of State for the Home Dept* [2005] (likelihood of earlier death from AIDS if deported to Uganda due to lower level of treatment available; refused under Article 3). The fact that medical treatment or other support is worse than in the UK does not engage Convention rights except in exceptional cases (eg *D v UK* [1997]: final stages of AIDS and no family support). According to Lord Steyn in *Ullah* in cases other than Article 3 there must be a 'real risk of a flagrant violation of the very essence of the right' (at [50]).

Article 6: right to a fair trial

In relation to civil rights and obligations and the determination of any criminal charges against them, individuals have a right to a fair trial in public before an independent and impartial tribunal established by law. Judgment shall be pronounced publicly. The press and public may be excluded from all or any part of the proceedings in the interests of morals, public order or national security in a democratic society, where the interests of juveniles or the protection of the private lives of the parties so require, or to the extent strictly necessary in the opinion of the court in special circumstances where publicity would prejudice the interests of justice.

As we have seen, 'civil rights and obligations' has a wide meaning, including loss of employment opportunities and other important social and economic interests (see Section 17.6.1; *R (Wright) v Secretary of State* [2009]: placing on Child Abuse

Register). In a criminal case there must be further safeguards. These include a right 'to be informed promptly and in a language he understands and in detail, of the nature and cause of the accusation', adequate time and facilities to prepare a defence, a right to choose a lawyer and free legal assistance 'when the interests of justice so require', a right to call witnesses and to examine opposing witnesses on equal terms and a right to an interpreter. However 'charged with a criminal offence' has been defined narrowly to exclude matters relating to sentencing and bail (*Phillips v UK* [2001]; *R (DPP) v Havering Magistrates Court* [2001]).

The right to a fair trial cannot be overridden by public interest concerns. However individual ingredients can be modified as long as the trial overall is fair. For example in *Brown v Stott (Procurator Fiscal Dunfermline)* [2001] the Privy Council held that the requirement of section 172(2) of the Road Traffic Act 1998 to disclose the name of the driver was not in breach of the right against self-incrimination. The reason for this was the clear public interest in reducing the high rate of death and injury on the roads. And in *O'Halloran and Francis v UK* [2007] (speed cameras, duty to give information as to identity of driver) it was held that fairness requires the circumstances to be considered, including the public responsibilities of all drivers.

Nevertheless the trial overall must be fair, so any shortfall in one respect must be compensated by scrupulous fairness in others. The court will look at the entire process. Thus where a decision maker is not itself independent and impartial, as in the case of administrative policy decisions, then judicial review may provide a sufficient safeguard (see Section 18.6; *R (Alconbury) v Secretary of State* [2001]). In cases involving claims to state secrecy evidence may sometimes be withheld from an accused person but if the safeguards for fairness are insufficient the trial may not go ahead (see Section 23.3.3).

Article 6 is primarily concerned with procedural matters. It may sometimes be difficult to distinguish procedural matters from matters of substantive law which might engage other parts of the Convention but not Article 6. For example in *Z v UK* [2002] a local authority was held to be in breach of Article 3 for failing to protect children but not in breach of Article 6. The domestic law of negligence had failed to protect the children, not because of any procedural immunity but because of the limited scope of negligence law itself in relation to the duties of public bodies (see Section 19.2). The same applies to the non-liability of the Crown in certain cases (*Matthews v Ministry of Defence* [2003]; Section 14.5).

Article 12: right to marry and found a family according to national laws governing the exercise of the right

In *R (Baiai) v Secretary of State for the Home Dept* [2007] it was held that the courts must be vigilant to protect the right to marry but that it carries less weight than the fundamental rights of personal liberty, freedom of expression and access to the courts. In that case a requirement of Home Office consent for non-Anglican marriages by immigrants was held invalid on the basis that the immigration authority could only interfere with the right to marry in the case of a sham marriage and it must be shown that the marriages targeted made substantial inroads into the scheme of immigration control. Moreover 'marriage' has been narrowly interpreted as referring only to traditional marriages between biological men and women (*Rees*: transsexuals), leaving it to individual states to determine policy on this sensitive issue (eg *Wilkinson v Kitzinger* [2006]: civil partnerships).

Protocol 1, Article 2: education

> No person shall be denied the right to education. In the exercise of any functions which it assumes in relation to education and to teaching, the State shall respect the right of parents to ensure such education and teaching is in conformity with their own religious and philosophical convictions.

This is a limited right. It does not confer a right to be educated as such. Its primary purpose is to combat state discrimination and indoctrination. It does not require the state to provide education. It means only a right not be excluded from whatever education the state chooses to provide (*A v Head Teacher and Governors of Lord Grey School* [2004]). Nor does it include a right to state funding (*R (Douglas) v North Tyneside DC* [2004]).

It also raises the conflict between individualistic liberalism and liberal pluralism (Chapter 2) since religious education might favour repression against individuals. It also treats the right as that of the parent rather than that of the child itself, an attitude that could be regarded as misplaced. It probably prevents the state from outlawing 'faith schools' but is subject to the limits on the manifestation of religion mentioned in Section 20.4.3. (*R (Williamson) v Secretary of State for Education and Employment* [2005]).

Moreover the UK has made a reservation:

> only so far as compatible with 'the provision of efficient instruction and training and the avoidance of unreasonable public expenditure'.

Protocol 1, Article 3: free elections to the legislature at reasonable intervals by secret ballot

See *Hirst v UK (No 2)* [2004]: blanket disqualification of convicted prisoners outlawed (see Section 12.6).

Protocol 6: abolition of the death penalty in peacetime

Although this Protocol was not itself incorporated into the Human Rights Act 1998, the Act abolished the last remaining death penalty provisions in the UK (s 21(5)).

20.4.3 Rights subject to being overridden

As we shall see (Section 21.5) the court is required according to the principle of 'proportionality' to weigh the importance of the right in question both to the person who is being interfered with and to the public interest against the public interest claimed by the state to justify overriding the right. Moreover this group of rights is vague and difficult to define. For these reasons the judicial process is especially problematic in this area.

Article 8: respect for privacy, family life, home and correspondence

> Overrides. There shall be no interference by a public authority with an Article 8 right except such as is in accordance with the law and is necessary in a democratic society in the interests of national security, public safety or the economic well being of the country, for the prevention of disorder or crime, for the protection of health or morals, or for the protection of the rights and freedoms of others.

Article 8 is especially vague and wide ranging. Indeed, unlike most of the other rights which are phrased as definite entitlements, Article 8 gives only an entitlement to 'respect', whatever that means.

Article 8 has three interlinking aspects. Firstly it protects against intrusion, surveillance and disclosure of information about oneself (*R (c) v MPC* [2010]). Secondly it concerns intimate family relationships. Thirdly it embraces respect for personal autonomy and identity, including reputation, community relationships, gender, sexual preferences, culture and lifestyle: 'those features which are integral to a person's identity or ability to function socially as a person' (Lord Bingham in *R (Razgar) v Secretary of State for the Home Dept* [2004] at [9]; see also *S v UK* [2008] at [19]: 'the manner in which a person presents himself to the state and to others'; *von Hanover v Germany* [2005] at [50]: 'a person's physical and psychological integrity; ... the development, without outside interference, of the personality of each individual in his relations with other human beings'. There is therefore a social zone in a public context, which may fall within the scope of 'private life'.

See for example *Gwillan and Quinton v UK* [2010]: police 'stop and search' of journalists (see Section 23.7.2); *Wainright v Home Office* [2003]: strip searches; *R (Purdy) v DPP* [2009]: disability and the manner of one's death; *S v UK* [2008]: police retention of DNA samples; *Chapman v UK* [2001]: ethnic groups; *Autronic AG v Switzerland* [1990]: immigrant lifestyle; access to satellite TV from overseas; *R (AB) v Secretary of State* [2010]: refusal to transfer transsexual prisoner to woman's prison; goes to heart of identity; *HM Advocate v Murtogh* [2010]: police records; *R (L) v Metropolitan Police Comr* [2010]: 'enhanced criminal record certificate'; *Von Hanover v Germany* [2005]: celebrity on holiday (see Section 22.6); *Aguila Quila v Secretary of State for the Home Dept* [2011]: immigrant's right to settle and marry.

Article 8 applies to nuisances and environmental pollution, although the courts are likely to give considerable weight to the limited resources of public authorities in this context (see *Guerra v Italy* [1998]; *Hatton v UK* [2003]; *Marcic v Thames Water Utilities* [2004]). It applies to the restriction of employment, where there is a stigma or social exclusion (*R (Wright) v Secretary of State for Health* [2009]: Child Abuse Register.

Article 8 is therefore very wide and susceptible to the different customs and values of individual states. It broadly reflects Mill's version of liberalism, namely that in the context of the good of society as a whole, people are happier when they choose for themselves what form of life and lifestyle to adopt (see Section 2.3.3). The European Court therefore gives a 'margin of appreciation' to the individual state as to how it applies Article 8 provided that the state does not violate widely shared values (eg *Rees v UK* [1986]: transsexual; *Olsson v Sweden* [1988]: child care).

By contrast in *Marper v UK* [2008] the policy of retaining DNA samples from people arrested or charged by the police but subsequently held to be innocent was held to be in violation as going beyond practices elsewhere and lacking safeguards. (The Crime and Security Act 2010 responds to this by introducing a selective scheme, also applying to fingerprints, based on the gravity of the accusation, the necessity for the action and the age of the offender.)

The UK courts seem reluctant to treat Article 8 liberally.

In *M v Secretary of State for Work and Pensions* [2006] Lord Nicholls and Lord Mance (at [24]–[29]) took the view that 'family life' did not include same-sex couples on the ground that there was no Europe-wide consensus on this matter and that Article 8 does not confer a general right to self-determination.

In *Marper v UK* [2008] the European Court condemned the UK practice of retaining indefinitely DNA samples from people arrested or charged with offences irrespective of whether they were subsequently convicted. A majority of the House of Lords had upheld the practice under *R (S) v Chief Constable of South Yorkshire Police* [2004]. It was held that the practice was not a significant enough intrusion to fall within Article 8 and in any case was overridden by the public interest in detecting crime. The European Court held that the UK policy was more extreme than practices elsewhere in Europe. The difference between the two courts seems to lie mainly in the English judges placing less importance on the offence to human dignity involved (Lady Hale dissenting), giving greater weight to the policing advantages of the practice and having greater confidence in the integrity and competence of the police not to misuse the power. (See also *Gwillan and Quinton v UK* [2010]: police stop and search powers.)

In *R (Countryside Alliance) v A-G* [2008] it was argued that the Hunting Act 2004, which outlaws hunting wild mammals with dogs, violated Article 8 in that there was a right to participate in hunting as an aspect of countryside life and as a social activity integral to the personality. The House of Lords held that the Act does not attract Article 8. It was accepted that in principle sporting and cultural activities, such as playing music, could fall within Article 8 since these were an important aspect of human nature and self-development. Hunting fell outside Article 8 because it was carried out in public and was a spectator sport open to all. At the heart of Article 8 is the idea of the personal and intimate. Moreover hunters were not a distinctive group so as to claim an identity analogous to an ethnic group. Some of the claimants were workers who serviced the hunt. It was held that Article 8 can apply to loss of livelihood but only where the loss of a job seriously impinges upon other aspects of Article 8 protection affecting the person's social relationships and status in society as a whole or involving loss of a home.

In *Norris v USA* [2010] the Supreme Court held that only the greatest interference with family life would override the public interest in complying with an extradition request from the US.

Article 8 protects the inviolability of the home but does not normally confer a positive right to be provided with a home or welfare benefits but only a right to be protected as to the use of an existing home, against eviction for example, thus illustrating that the Convention's primary concern is with existing interests rather than welfare (*Kay* at [191]–[193]; *Harrow LBC v Qazi* [2004] at [50]; *N v Secretary of State for the Home Dept*). However in cases involving especially vulnerable people Article 8, referring as it does to 'respect', may impose a positive duty to provide a benefit (see eg *Chapman v UK* [2001]: gypsies; *R (Bernard) v Enfield LBC* [2002]: disabled with children; *Anufrijeva v Southwark LBC* [2004]: asylum seekers). However there must be culpability in the sense of a deliberate or negligent failure to act which has foreseeably serious consequences (*Anufrijeva*).

There is a positive obligation on the state to enable the expression of personal lifestyles and to protect Article 8 rights against violation by private bodies (see Lord Hope in *Qazi*; *Campbell v MGN* [2004]: press intrusion; *Von Hannover v Germany* [2005] at [57]). In *YL v Birmingham City Council* [2007] Lady Hale emphasised that the state has such a positive duty in relation to the care of the elderly. However as we saw in Section 21.4.1 she was dissenting in her view that a private care home should be treated as having public functions so as to bring it directly within the ambit of the Human Rights Act 1998. The state might however be required to regulate private care homes so as to ensure that they respect the Article 8 rights of their residents.

In at least one respect Article 8 may be weaker than the other protected rights. In *Qazi* a majority of the House of Lords held that property rights, in that case a right to evict a tenant, always overrode a right based only on Article 8 and that personal circumstances were not relevant. However Lord Steyn (dissenting) remarked:

> It would be surprising if the views of the majority ... withstood European scrutiny ... The basic fallacy in the approach is that it allows domestic notions of title, legal and equitable rights and interests, to colour the interpretation of Art. 8 (1). The decision of today does not fit into the new landscape created by the 1998 Act. (at [27])

And so it proved. In *Connors v UK* [2004] the European Court held that a decision by a local authority to evict gypsies from a site that it owned was contrary to Article 8. In *Kay* the House of Lords modified *Qazi* to the extent that, in exceptional cases, personal circumstances could be taken into account. *Connors* was such a case since gypsies are vulnerable minorities. Another case might be where the victim has special personal circumstances, such as ill health. However Lord Bingham emphasised that personal circumstances which were catered for by statutory welfare services should not be relevant (at [38]).

Article 8 is also usually overridden by the right to a fair trial (see *HM Advocate v Murdoch* [2010]: police records concerning a witness).

Article 9: freedom of thought, conscience and religion

> Overrides. Freedom to manifest one's religion or beliefs shall be subject only to such limitations as are prescribed by law and are necessary in a democratic society in the interests of public safety, for the protection of public order, health or morals or for the protection of the rights and freedoms of others.

This includes a right to manifest religion or belief in worship, teaching, practice and observance. In order to avoid intolerance the courts have not attempted to define religion, which includes any kind of spiritual belief, including for example vegetarianism and pacifism, or to assess the validity of a religious belief beyond deciding whether it is genuinely held. However while the 'holding' of a belief is entirely subjective, the 'manifestation' of belief has been subject to a broad objective threshold based on 'seriousness, coherence and consistency with human dignity' (see *Williamson*). Thus despite the importance of respect for minority beliefs there is a tendency towards imposing orthodoxy by assessing the claimant's practices against those of dominant groups within the sect in question (eg *R (Begum) v Head Teacher and Governors of Denbigh High School* [2007]: extreme version of Muslim dress lawfully forbidden in school) or by giving a broad margin of distinction to the majority opinion represented by Parliament (eg *Williamson* at [50]–[51]: 'light' corporal punishment in school in pursuance of fundamentalist Christianity outlawed; *Otto Preminger Institut v Austria* [1994]: majority Catholic susceptibilities protected against offensive film). Moreover although in *Denbigh* Lord Bingham emphasised (at 111) the pluralistic, multicultural nature of our society, religion despite being important is regarded – as in the Protestant tradition but certainly not universally – as essentially a private matter (see *Williamson* at [15]–[19]).

In the employment sphere the right to manifest religion has been held to be violated only where the employer fails to take reasonable steps to accommodate the religious requirements of the employee with its own interests. In *Copsey v WBB Devon Clays Ltd* [2005] an employee was dismissed for refusing to work on a Sunday. The employer had compelling economic reasons for Sunday working, had engaged in a long consultation process on the matter and had offered the employee an alternative position which was refused. The Court of Appeal held that in these circumstances Article 9 had not been violated. Mummery LJ appeared to go further, indicating that Article 9 was not engaged at all by requiring work which interfered with the manifestation of religion. These cases provide another illustration of the avoidance of confronting a clash between a right and other public interest concerns by defining the right narrowly (see Section 20.4).

Article 10: freedom of expression.

> This right shall include freedom to hold opinions and to receive and impart information and ideas without interference by public authority and regardless of frontiers. This article shall not prevent states from requiring the licensing of broadcasting, television or cinema enterprise.
>
> Overrides. The exercise of these freedoms, since it carries with it duties and responsibilities, may be subject to such formalities, conditions, restrictions or penalties as are prescribed by law and are necessary in a democratic society in the interests of national security, territorial integrity or public safety, for the prevention of disorder or crime, for the protection of health or morals, for the protection of the reputation or rights of others, for preventing the disclosure of information received in confidence or for maintaining the authority and impartiality of the judiciary.

Freedom of expression is discussed in Chapter 22.

Article 11: freedom of peaceful assembly and association

> Everyone has the right to freedom of peaceful assembly and to freedom of association with others, including the right to form and to join trade unions for the protection of his interests.
>
> Overrides. No restrictions shall be placed on these rights other than such as are prescribed by law and are necessary in a democratic society in the interests of national security or public safety, for the prevention of disorder or crime, for the protection of health or morals or for the protection of the rights and freedoms of others. This article shall not prevent the imposition of lawful restrictions on the exercise of those rights by members of the armed forces, of the police or of the administration of the state.

Freedom of assembly is discussed in Chapter 22.

Protocol 1, Article 1: private property

> Every natural or legal person is entitled to the peaceful enjoyment of his possessions. No one shall be deprived of his possessions except in the public interest and subject to the conditions provided for by law and by the general principles of international law. The preceding provisions shall not, however, in any way impair the right of a State to enforce such laws as it deems necessary to control the use of property in accordance with the general interest or to secure the payment of taxes and or other contributions or penalties.

This protects property rights against confiscation without compensation but does not confer a positive right to acquire property (see *Marckx v Belgium* [1979]). Restrictions on the use of property imposed in the public interest, for example environmental and rent controls, are valid without compensation, although the line between use and confiscation may be difficult to draw (*Mellacher v Austria* [1989]). Moreover the courts are not willing to use the Convention in cases where a property right is restricted by the exercise of other property rights (see *Aston Cantlow and Wilmcote with Billesley Parochial Church Council v Wallbank* [2003]: charge to repair church roof taking effect as a common law right). Property rights probably have a lower level of protection than the other human rights and the rights of the state to override them are wider and less specific. (The concept of 'fair balance' rather than proportionality is used: see *Fredin v Sweden* [1991]; *R (Countryside Alliance) v A-G* [2008]).

20.4.4 Discrimination

Article 14: discrimination

> The enjoyment of the rights and freedoms set forth in this Convention shall be secured without discrimination on any ground such as sex, race, colour, language, religion, political or other opinion, national or social origin, association with a national minority, property, birth or other status.

The ECHR does not outlaw all discrimination. Article 14 applies only where discrimination takes place in relation to one of the other Convention rights, although no such right need actually have been violated. For example although there is no right to be housed, refusing housing for discriminatory reasons is unlawful (*R (Morris) v Westminster City Council* [2005]: refusal of housing because dependent child had no immigration rights; *Ghaidan v Mendoza* [2004]: inheritance by gay partner). However a tenuous link will not suffice (*M v Secretary of State for Work and Pensions* [2006]: differential maintenance payments). Article 14 was described by Lord Nicholls in *Ghaidan v Mendosa* as fundamental to the rule of law and calling for close scrutiny (at [9], [19]) and by Lady Hale in the same case as 'essential to democracy which is founded on the principle that each individual has equal value' (at [132]).

Since it refers to 'such as' Article 14 extends to forms of discrimination other than those listed (eg *A v Secretary of State* [2005]: nationality; *Ghaidan v Mendoza*: sexual orientation; *Douglas*: age; *Wandsworth LBC v Michalack* [2002]: family membership). It is not easy to identify its limits. In *R (S) v Chief Constable of South Yorkshire Police* the House of Lords took the view that the discrimination must relate to a 'personal characteristic or status' shared by the disadvantaged group as opposed to a matter of behaviour only. Article 14 was therefore not engaged by a policy of retaining DNA samples taken lawfully from suspects who were later found to be innocent since the general category of 'innocent persons' was not capable of being a protected category. (When the European Court rejected this decision in *Marper v UK* (see Section 20.4.3) it did not decide the discrimination point.) In another instance 'rough sleeper' was held not to be a protected category (*M v Secretary of State for Work and Pensions*), nor was the hunting community (*Countryside Alliance*; see also *R (Clift) v Secretary of State* [2007]: seriousness of offences qualify for release of prisoners on licence).

On the other hand 'overseas resident' and 'person responsible for a child under a residence order' have been held to be protected as having different legal rights and duties from UK residents and natural parents respectively (*R (Carson) v Secretary of State for Work and Pensions* [2006]: claim to pension; *Francis v Secretary of State for Work and Pensions* [2006]: maternity grant). A protected category can therefore be something voluntarily assumed.

It is difficult to see an underlying rationale in these cases such as protecting a sense of identity. However certain 'suspect categories', race and sex being pre-eminent, which are central to identity and over which the victim has no choice, enjoy a high standard of protection in that especially strong reasons are required to justify discrimination on those grounds (see Lord Walker in *Carson*; see also Lord Carson at [15]–[17], [32]; *Walker v UK* [2006]).

Although Article 14 has no express overrides, discrimination can nevertheless be justified on the basis of the overrides which apply to the Articles on which Article 14 is parasitic (see *Belgian Linguistics Case* [1968]). One way of rationalising this is to argue that 'discrimination' in itself means making an *unjustified* distinction so as to violate the principle of equality. However once again this has the danger of confusing whether a right has been breached with whether it should be overridden. Another is to rely on the principle of balance which is said to underlie the Convention as a whole (Section 20.4). Moreover by virtue of Article 16: 'Articles 10, 11 and 14 shall not prevent a state from imposing restrictions on the political activities of aliens.'

The meaning of discrimination is not clear. The courts have applied the following guidelines in Article 14 cases (see *Michalack*; cf *Carson*), recognising however that they overlap:

1. Do the facts fall within the ambit of one or more of the substantive Convention provisions?
2. If so, was there differential treatment as respects that right between the complainant on the one hand and the other persons put forward for comparison (the chosen comparators) on the other?
3. Were the chosen comparators in an analogous position to the complainant's situation?
4. If so, did the difference in treatment have an objective and reasonable justification in accordance with proportionality?

In *A v Secretary of State* [2005] a statute failed the fourth test. The Anti-Terrorism, Crime and Security Act 2001 authorised the indefinite detention of a foreign national whose presence in the UK the Home Secretary reasonably believes is a risk to national security and whom he reasonably suspects is a terrorist, unless the person voluntarily leaves the country. The government claimed that these powers were necessary because a non-national could not be deported to a place where he or she would be at risk of torture or inhuman or degrading treatment (*Chahal v UK* [1996]). The government argued that it would otherwise be impossible to deal with suspects who were too dangerous to be at large but against whom no criminal charges could be brought. The House of Lords held by an 8 to 1 majority that the derogation was discriminatory and without justification in singling out foreign nationals since the threat was no less from British terrorists. In response to *A*, the Prevention of Terrorism Act 2005 put restrictions of movement, 'Control Orders', on non-nationals and nationals alike (see Chapter 23).

Summary

- The human rights debate involves attempts to accommodate competing and incommensurable values without any coherent overarching principle to enable a choice to be made. It is therefore arguable that an elected body rather than a court should have the last word. The Human Rights Act 1998 has attempted a compromise by leaving Parliament the last word but giving the court power to influence Parliament.
- Freedom in the common law is residual in the sense that one can do anything unless there is a specific law to the contrary. I suggested that this is an inadequate method of safeguarding important liberties. There is a debate as to the extent to which the common law embodies the principles of the ECHR and it is suggested that there are important differences in the approaches of the two systems.
- The ECHR as such is not strictly binding upon English courts but can be taken into account where the law is unclear or where a judge has discretionary powers. The individual can petition the European Court of Human Rights, the decisions of which are binding in international law but, unlike those of the European Court of Justice (in relation to European Union law), are not legally binding in domestic law.
- The Human Rights Act 1998, while not incorporating the Convention as such, has given the main rights created by the ECHR effect in domestic law. UK legislation must be interpreted to be compatible with Convention rights but parliamentary supremacy is preserved.
- Most Convention rights are negative rights which restrain the state from interfering with them. Some have a positive aspect by imposing a duty on the state to ensure that the right in question is respected.
- Some rights, notably deprivation of liberty, are narrowly defined; others, notably privacy and family life, are broad and vague.
- Some of the rights are absolute and cannot be overridden by public interest considerations, although they might be defined narrowly in the light of the public interest. Other rights are subject to exceptions, and an important group of rights can be overridden on prescribed grounds of the public interest or of other rights.
- Some rights, notably the right to life, protection against torture and against deprivation of liberty, freedom of expression and non-discrimination have an especially high status. The right to property may have a lower level of protection than other rights.

Exercises

20.1 'Human Rights are permeated with irresolvable disagreement as to what they mean, how they apply, and as to the nature of disputes about them. The courts are therefore a hopelessly inadequate mechanism for resolving human rights problems.' Discuss.

20.2 Jones is holding a group of people in a secret location. The police arrest him. He says that his prisoners will be blown up by a bomb in one hour. Can the police use techniques of simulated drowning ('waterboarding'), which they believe to have been recommended by military intelligence services worldwide, to discover the whereabouts of the prisoners?

20.3 Parliament passes an Act offering a reward to any citizen who gives evidence in confidence to the authorities that a household is harbouring illegal immigrants. Does this violate the ECHR and if so how would you modify the Act to make it conform?

Exercises cont'd

20.4 Explain the scope of Article 14 of the ECHR. Does it go far enough in combating discrimination?

20.5 'Democracy is the will of the people but the people may not will to invade those rights which are fundamental to democracy itself' (Lady Hale in *R (Countryside Alliance) v A-G* [2008]). Discuss.

20.6 (i) What is meant by a deprivation of liberty under the ECHR?

(ii) Jack, who suffers from memory loss, is an outpatient at an NHS hospital. After his latest visit the hospital authorities lock Jack in a small office for three hours in order to prevent him from leaving the hospital until his wife arrives to take him home. Advise Jack, who strongly objects to this. What additional facts might influence your answer?

20.7 You are the leader of a pressure group representing the hunting community. What arguments could you raise to challenge the decision of the Law Lords in *R (Countryside Alliance) v A-G* [2008]?

Further reading

Alder, 'The Sublime and the Beautiful: Incommensurability and Human Rights' [2006] PL 697

Amos, *Human Rights Law* (Hart 2006)

Arden, 'On Liberty and the European Convention on Human Rights', in Andenas and Fairgrieve (eds), *Tom Bingham and the Transformation of the Law* (Oxford University Press 2009)

Campbell, Ewing and Tomkins (eds), *Sceptical Essays on Human Rights* (Oxford University Press 2001) chs 3, 6, 7

Gearty, *Can Human Rights Survive?* (Hamlyn Lectures, Cambridge University Press 2006)

Harvey, 'Talking about Human Rights' (2004) EHRLR 500

Hickman, 'The Substance and Structure of Proportionality' [2008] PL 694

Hill and Sandberg, 'Is Nothing Sacred? Clashing Symbols in a Secular World' [2007] PL 488

Hooker, 'Griffin on Human Rights' (2010) 30 OJLS 193

Laws, 'The Constitution: Morals and Right' [1996] PL 622

Leader, 'Freedom and Futures: Personal Priorities, Institutional Demands and Freedom of Religion' (2007) 70 MLR 713

Mahoney, 'Marvellous Richness of Diversity or Invidious Cultural Relativism' (1998) 19 HRLJ 1

McCormick, *Institutions of Law* (Oxford University Press 2007) ch 11

Sales, 'The General and the Particular: Parliament and the Courts under the Scheme of the European Convention on Human Rights' in Andenas and Fairgrieve (eds), *Tom Bingham and the Transformation of the Law* (Oxford University Press 2009)

Williams, 'Human Rights and Law: Between Sufferance and Insufferability' (2007) 123 LQR 133

Chapter 21

The Human Rights Act 1998

21.1 The scope of the Act

As we saw in Chapter 20 the Human Rights Act 1998 (HRA) does not incorporate the European Convention on Human Rights (ECHR) as such. It gives rights taken from the Convention and listed in Schedule 1 the status of 'Convention rights', with defined consequences in UK law. All legislation must be interpreted in accordance with Convention rights and the Act provides remedies enforceable in the courts against public authorities that violate Convention rights. The Act does not however override parliamentary supremacy. Decisions and opinions of the European Court of Human Rights must be taken into account, but they are not binding on the UK court (s 2(1)). The Act has not incorporated Article 1 (duty to secure to everyone within the jurisdiction the rights and freedoms under the Convention) or Article 13 (effective domestic remedies for breach of the Convention), it being claimed that the Act itself achieves these aims even though Convention rights must give way to Acts of Parliament. This claim therefore seems dubious.

The Act is sometimes described as a 'partnership' or a 'constitutional dialogue' between the three branches of government. It respects the separation of powers by making specific provisions concerning the relationship between the three branches (see Lord Hobhouse in *Wilson v First County Trust* [2003]). According to Lord Bingham the court's role under the Act is democratic because Parliament has given the courts 'a very specific wholly democratic mandate' (*A v Secretary of State for the Home Dept* [2005] at [42]; but see Section 20.1).

The extent to which the Human Rights Act 1998 is radical is controversial. On the one hand according to Lord Hoffmann (*R v Secretary of State for the Home Dept, ex p Simms* [1999] at 412–13) the Act does little more than reinforce the existing law. It has three aims. These are firstly to provide a specific text, much of it in his view reflecting existing common law principles; secondly to enact the existing 'principle of legality' (see Section 6.6), according to which fundamental rights can be overridden only by explicit statutory language or necessary implication; and thirdly to force Parliament to face squarely what it is doing. In *R (Alconbury Developments Ltd) v Secretary of State for the Environment, Transport and the Regions* [2001] he remarked that the Act 'was no doubt intended to strengthen the rule of law but not to inaugurate the rule of lawyers' (at [129]), relating the Act to the characteristics of UK parliamentary government, where policy decisions are taken by politicians.)

Similarly in *R v Lambert* [2001] at 603, Lord Hope emphasised the need (i) to respect the will of the legislature so far as this remains appropriate and (ii) to preserve the integrity of our statute law so far as this is possible. In the same case Lord Bingham described the Act as a 'complement' to the processes of democratic government (at 703). On the other hand in *R v DPP, ex p Kebelene* [1999] Lord Hope emphasised that a generous approach should be taken to the scope of fundamental rights and freedoms, and in *Lambert* Lord Slynn remarked:

> it is clear that the 1998 Act must be given its full import and that long or well entrenched ideas may have to be put aside, sacred calves culled. (at 581)

Over the past 10 years, a restrained approach has been predominant, with the courts closely following the case law of the European Court. It has been asserted that an action cannot be unlawful under the HRA unless the UK would be liable in Strasbourg, so that the UK courts cannot develop their own human rights principles or augment the Convention. The courts have frequently emphasised that the European Court must be followed even to the extent of trying to ascertain what the court might do in the future unless there are special reasons concerned with important principles of our constitution or legal system not to do so.

- In *R (S) v Chief Constable of South Yorkshire Police* [2004] the House of Lords considered that the application of the ECHR should be decided on a uniform basis throughout member states. This rejected the approach taken in the Court of Appeal that English law might develop its own higher standard of human rights. (Their Lordships' actual decision was rejected by the European Court in *Marper v UK* [2008] partly on the ground that UK practice did not conform to European standards (see Section 20.4.3).)
- In *R (Begum) v Head Teacher and Governors of Denbigh High School* [2006] at [29] it was said that the purpose of the Act was not to enlarge human rights but to apply the Convention in domestic law.
- In *R (Pretty) v DPP* [2002] it was said that the purpose of the Convention was to reflect a European consensus and not to lead opinion.
- In *R (Ullah) v Special Adjudicator* [2004], regarded as the leading case, the House of Lords held that 'the duty of national courts is to keep pace with the Strasbourg jurisprudence as it evolves over time: no more but certainly no less', and to follow a clear and consistent line of Strasbourg cases (at [20]). In *R (Al-Skeini) v Secretary of State for Defence* [2007] Lord Brown put this as 'no less but certainly no more' on the ground that a restrictive approach but not a generous one could be challenged in Strasbourg. In *R (Gentle) v Prime Minister* [2008] Lady Hale said that the domestic court was not free to develop Convention rights going 'way beyond anything which we can reasonably foresee Strasbourg might do' (at [56]).
- See also as examples *R (Clift) v Secretary of State for the Home Dept* [2007]; *R v Secretary of State for Foreign and Commonwealth Affairs, ex p Quark Fishing Ltd* [2006] at [24], [34] (see Section 9.6); *R (Countryside Alliance) v A-G* [2008]; *R (Purdy) v DPP* [2009]; *A v B* [2010] at [30]; *R (Animal Defenders International) v Culture Secretary* [2008]; *R (Al Jedda) v Secretary of State for Defence* [2008]; *R v Horncastle* [2010]; *R (Smith) v Secretary of State for Defence* [2010] at [60].

Thus, the Act is not a springboard for the UK to develop its own bill of rights.

However what has become known as the '*Ullah* principle' is contestable and leaves some room for manoeuvre. The Human Rights Act 1998 is not an enactment of the ECHR as such. Moreover the European Court does not enforce a doctrine of precedent and sometimes allows a 'margin of appreciation' to individual states to apply the Convention to their own circumstances (see Section 21.5.2). This allows a state to apply the Convention in accordance with its own values and constitutional traditions (see Lord Hoffman in *Alconbury*). Thus in *Re G (Adoption) (Unmarried Couple)* (2009) the House of Lords accepted that at least where Strasbourg permits a 'margin of appreciation' the court can develop its own principles. Nevertheless the court must follow 'clear and consistent' settled Strasbourg jurisprudence and (more dubiously) must not make any finding on a matter that has not yet been positively addressed by Strasbourg (at [25], [31]–[38], [53]).

A recent Scottish case, *In Petition of Axa Insurance* [2010], is more radical. A distinction was drawn between cases where the European Court had made a definite ruling and those where there was no clear guidance from Europe. In the latter case there seems to be no reason why the UK courts should not develop their own jurisprudence. Moreover except perhaps where the whole rationale of the previous case has been undermined, courts below the House of Lords must follow domestic cases even if they are inconsistent with Strasbourg rulings (*Lambeth LBC v Kay* [2006] at [43]–[45]).

In general the court's approach to human rights issues does not display a clear overall philosophy. This is no more than one might expect from the pragmatic common law tradition coupled with the loose evasive nature of the Human Rights Act 1998 itself. Some judges, notably Sir Stephen Sedley (1995), Sir John Laws (1996) and Lord Steyn (retired), appear to take a traditional liberal standpoint and welcome the notion of constitutional rights, which they claim depends on the common law as much as the Human Rights Act. Others such as Lady Hale, Lord Hope, Lord Bingham (deceased) and Lord Hoffman (retired) also take an overtly liberal stance but may take a more pragmatic view in relation to the importance of democratic decision making, although these differences are probably only matters of emphasis (see also Sections 8.4.5, 8.4.6). Academic commentators disagree. Ewing (2010) for example regards the Act as futile since it is permeated with discretion, whereas perhaps a majority of the commentators appear to support judicial developments which of course increase the influence of the legal profession as an elite (see eg Allan, 2006; Hickman 2008; Lester, 2005; Kavanagh, 2009; Young, 2009).

It might tentatively be suggested that possible reasons why, despite the Human Rights Act 1998, the verdicts of UK courts are frequently rejected by the European Court is that the UK approach to 'balancing' seems to be broadly pragmatic and utilitarian in the sense that the court weighs the *consequences* on either side and tries to choose the least harmful overall solution. The UK courts may also tend to underplay the importance of relatively limited or temporary restriction on freedom The European Court by contrast is more likely to stress the value of the right in principle. Moreover the UK courts seem to have a tendency to trust the discretion of the police and other officials and to accept informal safeguards, whereas the European Court requires stronger safeguards (see eg *Gillan v UK* [2010] (Sections 20.4.1, 23.7.4); *Marper* (Section 20.4.3)).

The HRA applies to all legislation whether made before or after it came into force in October 2000 (s 3(2)(a)). However the Act is not in general retrospective. It applies only to *events* that took place after it came into force. This seems to be strictly applied (see *R (Hurst) v North London District Coroner* [2007]: death occurring before Act came into force but a decision not to resume inquest made after Act came into force: Act not applicable (Lady Hale and Lord Mance dissenting)). There is an exception in the case of a defence to proceedings brought by a public authority. Here it applies whenever the action complained of took place.

21.2 Extraterritorial application

The Human Rights Act 1998 has limited effect outside UK territory. It has been consistently emphasised that the Act is regional and unified in scope, respects international law and applies only exceptionally outside the UK. The ECHR imposes a duty on states to secure the rights in respect of everyone 'within their jurisdiction'. There is an argument that international relations might be destabilised if the courts interfered with matters occurring abroad.

In *R (Al-Skeini) v Secretary of State for Defence* [2007] the House of Lords held that the Act could in principle apply outside UK territory but that it applied only where the UK was exercising governmental powers as a sovereign state in respect of territory under its control. Thus it was held (Lord Bingham dissenting) that the Act applied to the death of an Iraqi prisoner in custody on a British base in Iraq. The Act probably applies to diplomatic and other activities recognised in international law as cases where there is sovereign territorial jurisdiction overseas (see *R (B) v Secretary of State for Foreign and Commonwealth Affairs* [2005]: diplomatic premises: Act applies). By contrast in *R (Smith) v Secretary of State for Defence* [2010] the right to life did not apply to the death of a British soldier from heatstroke while on active service in Iraq. Nor did the Act apply to the handing over of a prisoner to the Iraqi government where the UK was acting as an agent of that government and not exercising sovereign powers (see *R (Al Saadoon) v Secretary of State for Defence* [2009]).

Acts of the government carried out within the UK but which have some effect outside the UK should in principle be subject to the Act, for example where a person is expelled to a country where he or she is at risk of a violation of a Convention right (see Section 20.4.2).

The Act seems to have limited application to UK dependent territories. In *R v Secretary of State for Foreign and Commonwealth Affairs, ex p Quark Fishing Ltd* [2006] (see Section 9.6) the Secretary of State had ordered the Commissioner of South Georgia and South Sandwich Islands (SGSSI) to refuse a fishing licence to the claimant. The claimant sought compensation under the Human Rights Act 1998 but their Lordships held that the Act did not apply since it has effect only in relation to the UK itself. The ECHR can be extended to dependent territories (Art 56) but had not been so in this case. However their Lordships did not agree as to whether this would suffice to attract the Human Rights Act. Lords Bingham and Hoffmann took the view that, irrespective of the scope of the treaty, the Human Rights Act applies only to the UK government as such, but Lord Nicholls opined that the matter depended on whether the ECHR applied to the territory. Lady Hale thought that the Act should apply wherever the territory in question was governed by the UK.

21.3 The Human Rights Act and Parliament

The Human Rights Act 1998 makes clear that the court cannot set aside an Act of Parliament or other 'primary' legislation (see ss 3(2)(b), 6(2)), thereby preserving parliamentary supremacy. For this purpose primary legislation includes, in addition to statutes, measures of the Church Assembly and the General Synod of the Church of England and delegated legislation that brings into force or amends primary legislation. A Prerogative Order in Council is also primary legislation even though the courts can set it aside in judicial review proceedings on domestic grounds (see Section 14.6.6). Acts of the Scottish Parliament and Northern Ireland Assembly are not primary legislation (s 21). The court can set aside subordinate legislation and other government decisions unless primary legislation makes it impossible to do so (s 3(2)).

If an Act of Parliament violates a Convention right, the court must therefore enforce it. However the court can make a 'declaration of incompatibility' (s 4) which invites Parliament or the executive to change the law (Section 21.3.2). This is often described as a 'constitutional dialogue' between the two branches but if so it is a limited and formalised one. As with other aspects of the separation of powers the practical relationship between the courts, Parliament and the executive depends on political forces and the relative moral authority each is able to command. It has been suggested that this kind of 'parliamentary' Bill of Rights differs little in its effect from an 'entrenched' bill of rights that empowers courts to overturn legislation. The court is likely to enjoy greater public respect than the government and legislation is likely to be drafted with judicial review in mind (see Hiebert, 'Parliamentary Bills of Rights: An Alternative Model' (2006) 69 MLR 7).

21.3.1 The interpretative obligation

At the heart of the Act is the requirement that:

> So far as it is possible to do so, primary legislation and subordinate legislation must be read and given effect in a way which is compatible with Convention rights. (s 3(1))

The limits of the section 3 obligation to interpret in line with the Convention are not precise and depend primarily on the judges' attitude to the constitutional limits on their function. The court has to keep to the right side of the border between interpretation and legislation. The government did not introduce a strong formula of the kind used in Canada, under which a statute must expressly state that it overrides the Bill of Rights (Home Office, *Rights Brought Home: The Human Rights Bill* (Cm 3782, 1997) para 2.10). Nevertheless section 3(1) was apparently intended to be a strong provision. The court is not confined to cases where the provision is ambiguous (*R v A* [2001]; *Ghaidan v Mendoza* [2004]).

In *Wilson v First County Trust* [2003] the House of Lords emphasised that the normal assumption of statutory interpretation, namely that the court is seeking the intention of Parliament, does not apply and that it is for the court to make an independent judgment as to whether the language of the statute can be read in a way to make it compatible with the Convention (see also *Secretary of State for the Home Dept v MB* [2007]; Section 23.7.5). Nor does the court apply the normal principle that the ordinary meaning of the statute must prevail. In *Harrow LBC v Qazi* [2004] Lord Bingham said:

> The court has to arrive at a judicial choice between two possibilities, a choice which transcends the business of finding out what the legislation's words mean. (at [23])

For example in *Ghaidan v Mendoza* [2004] a statutory provision entitled a person who had lived with a tenant 'as husband and wife' to succeed to the tenancy on the tenant's death. A majority of the House of Lords held that a homosexual relationship fell within the phrase 'living as husband and wife', which they made Convention-compatible by inserting the words 'if they were' after 'as'. The House held that even if the ordinary meaning of the statute is clear, the court could still distort its language or read in additional wording in order to achieve a meaning that complied with the Convention (at [33]).

The boundary of the court's power depended on two factors. Firstly the interpretation must not go against the grain of the legislation in the sense of contradicting its underlying purpose. The courts must look beyond the language itself and consider the policy context and legislative history of the statute in order to identify the essential features of the statutory scheme in question, which they must not violate. Secondly the courts must not make decisions for which they are not equipped in the sense of producing an interpretation that raises social or economic issues that are best left to Parliament. This relates to the issue of 'deference' (see Section 19.7.1).

The language of the statute is however a side constraint. Although the court can stretch or add to the language of the statute it cannot repeal, delete or contradict the statutory language. The courts have been warned to refrain from 'judicial vandalism' (*R (Anderson) v Secretary of State for the Home Dept* [2002] at 1089: Home Secretary's power to interfere with sentencing process could not be circumvented; see Nicol, 2004; Kavanagh, 2004). In *Ghaidan* Lord Millett gave the example of the word 'cat' in a statute (at [72]). In some circumstances 'cat' might be read to include 'dog', for example where the care of pets was the underlying concern. However if the legislation had originally stated 'Siamese cats' and later been amended to 'cats', this route would not be possible.

The following are examples (see also the table provided by Lord Steyn in *Ghaidan v Mendoza* [2004]).

- *R (Hurst) v North London Coroner* [2007]. The governing statute required a coroner to investigate 'how' a deceased came by his death. In the case of deaths prior to the Human Rights Act 1998 'how' is construed narrowly to mean 'by what means'. In the case of post-HRA deaths, 'how' means 'in what circumstances', thereby allowing a wider-ranging inquiry into deaths in custody.
- *R v Lambert* [2001]. Under section 28 of the Misuse of Drugs Act 1971 it is a defence to a charge of possessing drugs for the accused to 'prove' that he neither knew of nor suspected nor had reason to suspect some fact alleged by the prosecution. This conflicts with the presumption of innocence (HRA, Art 6(2)). The House of Lords gave the phrase 'to prove' the unusual meaning of 'to give sufficient evidence'. Thus the prosecution still has the general burden of disproving the accused's claim. Lord Hope emphasised (at 604) that great care must be taken to make the revised meaning blend in with the language and structure of the statute. 'Amendment' seems to be possible as long as it does not make the statute unintelligible or unworkable (cf [80] and [81]). (See also *R (H) v London North and East Region Mental Health Review Tribunal* [2001]: reverse burden of proof but no room for manoeuvre.)
- *R v A* [2001] (perhaps the most radical example). The Youth Justice and Criminal Evidence Act 1999 prohibited evidence in rape cases of the alleged victim's previous sexual experience without the court's consent, which could be given only in specified circumstances (s 41(1)). It was held that the court could construe the Act so as to permit evidence necessary to make the trial fair since that was

the general object of the Act. Thus additional provisions, 'subject to the right to a fair trial', could be implied into unambiguous language beyond the normal limits of statutory interpretation even if this strained the normal meaning (see Lord Steyn's speech). However the court cannot override provisions that specifically contradict Convention rights.

- *S (Children) (Care Plan)* [2002]. The power of the court to intervene in local authority care proceedings could not be added to the Children Act 1989; the court cannot depart substantially from a fundamental feature of a statutory scheme, particularly if it has practical consequences which the court cannot evaluate (s 38). Similarly in *Poplar Housing and Regeneration Community Association v Donoghue* [2001] the term 'reasonable' could not be inserted into a statute which gave a landlord an absolute right to evict a tenant.
- *Bellinger v Bellinger* [2003]. A statute could not be interpreted so as to treat a transsexual as female for marriage purposes since this would raise wide social issues that a court is not equipped to confront (cf Gender Recognition Act 2004).
- *Cachia v Faluyi* [2002]. A provision in the Fatal Accidents Act 1976 that not more than one 'action' shall lie in respect of the same subject matter arose when a firm of solicitors issued a writ in respect of the death of the claimant's wife in a road accident but then disappeared before it could be served. A second firm issued a new writ several years later. Under domestic law the second writ would probably be invalid. However under the HRA the Court of Appeal read 'action' in an unorthodox way to mean 'served process'. Brooke LJ remarked that this was a very good example 'of the way in which the 1998 Act now enables English judges to do justice in a way that was previously not open to us' (at [20]).

Section 3 seems to assume that the meaning of the Convention is a given against which UK law can be measured. However, even though the decisions of the European Court give some assistance, the meaning and scope of a Convention right is often vague. Indeed as a 'living instrument' (Section 21.5) the meaning of the Convention is always evolving. Thus interpretation is against a moving target. The enterprise may be self-defeating since a Convention provision could be 'read down' to conform to existing UK law as well as a UK law being 'read up' to conform to the Convention.

21.3.2 Declaration of incompatibility

Where it is not 'possible' to interpret primary legislation in line with a Convention right, the Supreme Court, the Court of Appeal, the High Court and certain other courts of equivalent status may – but are not required to – make a 'declaration of incompatibility' (s 4). This is at the heart of the accommodation between law and democracy made by the Act. A declaration of incompatibility invites Parliament to consider whether to change the law. It has no effect on the validity of the law in question and is not binding on the parties (s 4(6)).

A declaration of incompatibility triggers a 'fast-track' procedure that enables a minister, by statutory instrument subject to the approval of Parliament, to make such amendments as he or she considers necessary to remove the incompatibility.

A declaration of incompatibility is a last resort (*R v A* at [108]) and should not be used in order to avoid the task of interpreting the statute to comply with the Convention (Lord Steyn in *Ghaidan* at [39]).

The fast-track procedure can also be used where an incompatibility arises because of a ruling by the European Court of Human Rights and a minister considers that there are 'compelling reasons' for proceeding (s 10). It does not apply to measures of the Church of England. Also subordinate legislation that conflicts with a Convention right can be quashed by the court and reinstated in amended form under this procedure. Ministers are not bound to obey a declaration of incompatibility but judicial review may lie in respect of a refusal to do so.

The declaration of incompatibility therefore gives the court a constitutional role detached from the outcome of the particular case. However in two cases a declaration of incompatibility was refused on the narrow ground that the outcome of the cases did not damage the interests of the claimant (*R (H) v Secretary of State for Health* [2006]; *Secretary of State for the Home Dept v Nasseri* [2009]). This seems questionable.

21.3.3 Statement of compatibility

Under section 19 a minister in charge of a bill in either House of Parliament must, before the second reading of the bill, (i) make a statement to the effect that in his or her view the provisions of the bill are compatible with Convention rights (a 'statement of compatibility') or (ii) make a statement to the effect that although he or she is unable to make a statement of compatibility the government nevertheless wishes the House to proceed with the bill. The statement must be in writing and published in such manner as the minister considers appropriate.

Apart from putting political pressure on the government, the effect of a statement of compatibility is not clear. As a statement of the opinion of the executive, the courts should not defer to it when interpreting the legislation in question (*Wilson v First County Trust*). Indeed a statement of compatibility means little where the statute in question confers a wide discretion on the executive or the police. Moreover because the statement applies only to the second reading it does not cover amendments that might be included at later stages.

21.4 The executive and judiciary: remedies

A 'public authority', including the executive and the courts, is liable in the courts for failing to comply with a Convention right unless this is required by a statute or other primary legislation. By virtue of section 6(1) 'it is unlawful for a public authority to act in a way which is incompatible with a Convention right' except where (i) 'as a result of one or more provisions of primary legislation, the authority could not have acted differently' or (ii) 'in the case of one or more provisions of, or made under, primary legislation which cannot be read or given effect in a way which is compatible with the Convention rights, the authority was acting so as to give effect to or enforce those provisions'.

For this purpose an 'act' includes a failure to act but does not include a failure to introduce or lay before Parliament a proposal for legislation or make any primary legislation or remedial order (s 6(6)). This effectively adds another ground to judicial review in respect of governmental decisions except those necessarily authorised by a statute or a Prerogative Order in Council. It links with the interpretative obligation in section 3 (Section 21.3.1) in that an action which is required by a UK statute or a Prerogative Order in Council is not unlawful on human rights grounds, although a declaration of incompatibility may be made in relation to the primary legislation.

The Human Rights Act 1998 must be applied by all courts. However a minister can make rules designating an 'appropriate court or tribunal' for the purposes of an action under the Act (see s 7(1)(a), (2), (9)). For example a special tribunal can be designated to deal with security matters. The designated court or tribunal may not have the power to issue a declaration of incompatibility (see Section 21.3.2). However the ordinary courts can ensure that the designated tribunal provides an adequate process for protecting the right in issue (see *A v B* [2010]: publication of book by former member of the security services: Investigatory Powers Tribunal held appropriate given the flexibility of its rules to accommodate security issues; see Sections 19.7.2, 23.3).

Section 7 entitles a 'victim' to bring proceedings in respect of an act which is unlawful under section 6 and also to rely on Convention rights in any legal proceedings. However the Secretary of State can make rules designating an appropriate court or tribunal for particular purposes (ss 7(1)(a), 9(1)(c)). The Secretary of State has exercised this power principally in relation to special tribunals concerning immigration, asylum and other cases involving national security matters. Reflecting the concerns of judicial independence, in relation to the judicial functions of a court or tribunal, proceedings must be by appeal or judicial review or otherwise as provided for by rules made by the Lord Chancellor or Secretary of State.

The onus is on the claimant to show that a law or decision does not comply with the Convention (*Lambeth BC v Kay* [2006]) and that he or she is a 'victim'. 'Victim' has the same meaning as in cases brought before the ECHR (s 7(7)). The claimant or a close relative must be directly affected, or at least very likely to be affected, by the action complained of (see *Klass v Federal Republic of Germany* [1979]; *Open Door and Dublin Well Woman v Ireland* [1992]). There is no standing for non-governmental organisations (NGOs) representing collective or public interests unless possibly the NGO is composed of victims (*Director General of Fair Trading v Proprietary Association of Great Britain* [2001]). Thus in a judicial review case an NGO can challenge a decision only on domestic grounds (s 7(3)). It appears that a public authority cannot be a victim against another public authority since in ECHR terms both are part of the 'state' (see *Aston Cantlow and Wilmcote with Billesley Parochial Church Council v Wallbank* [2003]). In ordinary judicial review law the courts can review decisions of central government against public bodies such as local authorities. In principle this restriction seems unjustifiable.

Under Section 8 the court can award any of the remedies normally available to it 'as it considers just and appropriate'. Damages can be awarded only by a court which has power to award damages or order compensation in civil proceedings (eg not criminal courts and other specialist courts) and then only if the court is satisfied that 'the award is necessary to afford just satisfaction to the person in whose favour it is made' (s 8(4)). The phrase 'just satisfaction' is part of the jurisprudence of the ECHR and the court must take into account the principles applied by the ECHR in awarding compensation (s 8(4)). However apart from insisting that there must be substantial loss or injury these do not give clear guidance and the court has considerable discretion (see *Z v UK* [2002]; *Damages under the Human Rights Act 1998* (Law Com No 266, 2006); *Cullen v Chief Constable of the RUC* [2004]). In order to safeguard judicial independence, where an action for damages is brought in respect of a judicial act, meaning in this context an act of a court, there is no liability in respect of an act in good faith except for an unlawful arrest or detention. The action must be brought against the Crown with the judge concerned being made a party (HRA, s 9(3)–(4)).

21.4.1 Public authorities

The European Convention on Human Rights applies to states, and some of its articles, notably Articles 8 and 10, are directed explicitly to public authorities. The Human Rights Act 1998 can be directly enforced only against a public authority (s 6(1)). For the purposes of the HRA 'public authority' includes a court or tribunal (s 6(3)). However Parliament or a person exercising functions in connection with proceedings in Parliament is not a public authority (s 6(3)). An individual can be a public authority (*A v Head Teacher and Governors of Lord Grey School* [2004]).

'Public authority' also includes anybody 'certain of whose functions are functions of a public nature' (s 6(3)b). Thus there are two kinds of public authority. Firstly there are bodies, such as central and local government and the police, which are inherently public. These are known as 'core' public authorities. All the activities of these bodies fall within the HRA. Secondly there are 'functional' or 'hybrid' public authorities. These include private or voluntary bodies whose activities interrelate with those of the government. Functional public authorities may perform some functions on behalf of the government but also perform private functions. The 'private acts' of hybrid public bodies do not fall within the HRA (s 6(5)).

Thus in the case of hybrid public authorities the court must look not only at the particular *function* but also at the particular *act* within that function which is claimed to invade a Convention right. For example the provision of social housing under government control was held to be a public function, as was the act of evicting a tenant in furtherance of government policy. It was suggested however that other acts within the same overall function, such as managing repair contractors, might not be public acts (*Weaver v London and Quadrant Housing Trust* [2008]).

This can be compared with the approach taken in domestic judicial review cases (see Section 19.5). In judicial review contexts the function as a whole must be looked at in the case both of core and of hybrid bodies. In both cases the *function* itself attracts public status. However, although the courts have emphasised that the purpose of the two regimes is not the same, they have usually applied the same authorities in both contexts.

It has been argued that a broad view should be taken of what is a public function so as to subject a wide range of powerful bodies to the Act. This has been endorsed by the Joint Committee on Human Rights (Seventh Report, 2003–04, HL 39, HC 382). On the other hand it has been suggested that private bodies should be subject to less onerous obligations than public bodies narrowly defined (see Oliver, 'Functions of a Public Nature and the Human Rights Act' [2004] PL 329; cf Sunkin, 'Pushing Forward the Frontiers of Human Rights Protection' [2004] PL 643).

The approach of the ECHR seems to be based on whether the particular act is carried out under the control of the government or on behalf of the government (see *Sigurjónnson v Iceland* [1993]). The UK courts have broadly followed this approach. They have also been influenced by the belief that a body which is a public authority cannot itself claim human rights against another branch of the government. This is particularly significant in relation for example to religious bodies and charities that protect vulnerable minorities. The matter remains controversial and there are fundamental disagreements among the judges.

In *Aston Cantlow and Wilmcote with Billesley Parochial Church Council v Wallbank* [2003] the House of Lords held, overruling the Court of Appeal, that a parochial church council of the Church of England is not a core public authority even though the Church of England has a close connection with the state and has many special legal powers and privileges. A core public authority must be 'governmental' in the sense that its activities are for the benefit of the general public interest, whereas the Church of England primarily benefits its own members.

However some aspects of the Church of England might fall into the category of *functional* public authority, for example functions in connection with marriages and funerals since these involve public rights. The case itself concerned the statutory right of a parochial church council to force a house owner to pay for the repair of a church roof under an obligation acquired with the property. A majority held that this was a private function, being the enforcement of a property right for the primary benefit of churchgoers. Lord Scott, dissenting, thought that this was a 'public' function in that it involved historic conservation for the benefit of the community enforced by special powers.

Wallbank illustrates the artificiality and uncertainty of attempting to distinguish between the public and the private and that the matter depends on a combination of factors. These include in particular public benefit and the operational connection between the body in question and another acknowledged public authority.

YL v Birmingham City Council [2007] is the other main authority. The House of Lords held that a privately owned care home was not exercising a public function for human rights purposes in relation to a resident who was placed there and financed by a local authority acting under a statutory duty to care for the vulnerable. The majority took the view that there was not a sufficiently close connection between the home and the government to attract the Human Rights Act 1998. The home had no special powers and was not acting as the agent of the government, and the relationship between the home and its resident was the same whether or not the resident was supported by the local authority. The local authority funded the individual resident and not the home as a whole.

Lord Bingham and Lady Hale dissented, taking a fundamentally different approach. This was based on the principle that the state had taken on itself the function of caring for the elderly and that it should make no difference so far as human rights were concerned whether this was done through a private agency or directly by the state itself. Lady Hale emphasised the positive duty of the state to ensure that Article 8 rights were protected, arguing that this can best be achieved by imposing liability directly on the private agency. This leads to the question of 'horizontality' (Section 21.4.2).

In *Weaver v London and Quadrant Housing Trust* [2009] a majority of the Court of Appeal held that a housing association that was not formed by the local authority but which received government funding in return for delivering government housing policy and was intensively regulated by the government and under a statutory duty to cooperate with local authorities was exercising public functions both for judicial review and HRA purposes in respect of decisions to evict tenants since these could not be separated from its public function of allocating social housing according to government policy. It was also relevant that the association had certain special powers and was under a statutory duty to cooperate with local authorities. However some 'acts', such as contractual arrangements with repair firms, could be private and the position of tenants who receive unsubsidised housing and pay a market rent is unclear. The dissent took a radically different approach, regarding a function as private if it used private law powers such as a landlord's power to evict a tenant. Housing associations have no special powers of eviction.

21.4.2 Horizontal effect

On the face of it the Human Rights Act 1998 gives a remedy only against a public authority. According to section 6 the primary liability under the HRA is that of a public authority. However it is arguable that the Act sometimes has 'horizontal effect' in the sense that private persons as well as public bodies may be required to respect human rights. Even private legal relationships are created and defined by the state, which could therefore be regarded as responsible for ensuring that the law meets the minimum standards appropriate to a democratic society. For example it would be anomalous if there were a right of privacy against an NHS hospital and not a private hospital. Unfortunately the UK courts have not yet directly ruled on the question of horizontal effect and have sometimes ignored the issue (see eg *Aston Cantlow* and *YL v Birmingham City Council* [2007]; Section 21.3.1).

These are some of the more technical arguments for and against horizontality. According to section 7 a claim under the Act can be made only by a person who would be a 'victim' for the purposes of Article 34 of the Convention if proceedings were brought in Strasbourg (s 7(1)(b), (7)). Under Article 34 a claim in Strasbourg can be made only against a party to the Convention, usually a state. It has therefore been argued that since the purpose of the HRA is to give effect to the ECHR, by their nature Convention rights are directed only against the state (Buxton, 2000). Moreover the Act does not include Article 1 of the ECHR, which requires states to 'secure to everyone within their jurisdiction' the rights and freedoms conferred by the Convention. On the other hand it can be recalled that the Human Rights Act 1998 does not incorporate the Convention as such but makes certain rights taken from the Convention enforceable in the courts (s 1). Moreover section 7 merely defines 'victim' by reference to hypothetical proceedings under the Convention. Such proceedings can it is true only be brought against the state but if the state were to defend itself by claiming that the perpetrator was a private body the claimant would surely still be a victim, although the state would escape liability.

The main arguments in favour of horizontal effect are as follows:

- All legislation must be interpreted according to the Convention, even that applying to private relationships. In *Ghaidan v Mendoza* [2004] the House of Lords applied Article 14 (discrimination) to legislation which discriminated against homosexual couples occupying property owned by private landlords (see also *Wilson v First County Trust* [2003]).
- By virtue of section 6 the courts are public authorities. It is arguable that a court would act 'unlawfully' if it did not apply Convention rights in every case before it, even between private persons (see Sedley LJ in *Douglas v Hello!* [2001]; Section 22.6). However, the victim's right would be against the court itself, not directly against the other private party. It is therefore difficult to see how the court could award damages. Moreover section 6 could also be interpreted as applying only to the court's own practice and procedure.
- A less extreme version of the above is that while section 6 cannot create a new cause of action against a private body, it can require the court to apply Convention rights in the context of *existing* causes of action or in respect of the court's own powers to make orders and grant remedies (see *Wilson v First County Trust* at [174]; Baroness Hale in *Campbell v MGN Ltd* [2004] at [133]). The matter would therefore have to arise in the course of other legal proceedings into which a human rights dimension could be implied. For example a court might be entitled to refuse to give a possession order to a private landlord who attempted to evict a tenant from her home (*R (McLellan) v Bracknell Forest BC* [2002] at [42]). The weakness of this approach seems to be that it is random in that it depends on the matter falling into an existing category of UK law. In *Kay v Lambeth LBC* [2006] the House of Lords specifically refused to decide whether the Act would apply in cases involving a private landlord.
- Particular Convention rights may include a positive obligation on the state to protect the right and to require private persons to respect it (see *Kroon v The Netherlands* [1995]). This has been recognised in the case of Article 2 (right to life), Article 3 (torture and inhuman or degrading treatment: *Z v UK* [2002]; *X and Y v Netherlands* [1985]; *A v UK* [1998]), Article 8 (privacy: *Douglas v Hello!* at [91]; *Thompson v News Group Newspapers* [2001]) and Article 9 (freedom of religion: *R (Williamson) v Secretary of State for Education and Employment* [2005] at [4], [86]; cf *Re GA (A Child)* [2001]). However this positive obligation is not absolute and the court will give the government a substantial margin of discretion in relation to the measures it takes (see Section 21.5.2).
- Particular provisions of the Act itself may have horizontal effect in their own right, notably section 12, which requires the court to have regard to the interests of press freedom (Section 22.3).
- The courts might develop the common law on the basis that the ECHR encapsulates values of general import. In *Campbell v MGN Ltd* the House of Lords used Articles 8 and 10 of the ECHR to reconfigure the common law in respect of privacy in relation to press freedom (see Section 22.6). The majority did not seem to think that the matter strictly fell within the Human Rights Act 1998 (see [17]–[19], [26], [49]).

21.5 Overriding protected rights

Any workable code of fundamental rights must be expressed in general language and with sufficient filters or exceptions to permit governments to act in the public interest or to resolve conflicts with other rights. Several methods are available to accommodate competing concerns and to adjust the law to changing circumstances. The ECHR has been described as a 'living instrument', meaning that the rights themselves and their ranking against other factors change with the times (eg *Ghaidan v Mendoza* [2004]: homosexual partners).

It is tempting to seek an overarching principle that would balance or combine the human right with the competing interest under some overall concept of common good. However it is doubtful whether any such overriding principle is possible. Indeed in *R (S) v Chief Constable of South Yorkshire Police* [2004] Sedley LJ in the Court of Appeal pointed out that the notion of 'balancing' individual rights against the public interest means that the latter will always prevail (see also Lord Steyn in *Brown v Stott* [2001] at 118).

Moreover there are competing approaches as to what human rights are about. On one view, that of liberal individualists, human rights concern a zone of individual freedom which might exceptionally be overridden in the public interest, but recognising the sacrifice involved. On the other hand communitarians and republicans, favouring 'positive freedom', might argue that human rights in themselves are valuable only by virtue of their contribution to some greater good. For example in *Gough v Chief Constable of Derbyshire* [2001] Laws LJ said:

> rights are divisive, harmful, ultimately worthless, unless their possession is conditional upon the public good. (at 321)
>
> it is inherent in the nature of the right itself that the individual who claims its benefit may have to give way to the supervening weight of other claims ... the right's practical utility rests upon the fact that there can be no tranquillity within the state without a plethora of unruly individual freedoms. (at 320)

There are two ways of accommodating competing public interest considerations. Firstly the right itself could be narrowly defined. Secondly many of the rights are made subject to specific justifications for overriding them (overrides).

In *R (Begum) v Head Teacher and Governors of Denbigh High School* [2007] the House of Lords took both approaches. It was held that a ban on the wearing of a strict form of Muslim dress at school was not an unlawful interference with freedom of religion (Art 9). A majority held that the right to religious freedom was not infringed at all. The child concerned had chosen to attend the school in question and could have attended another, more flexible school. Perhaps uncomfortable with the reality of this, Lord Nicholls and Baroness Hale held that the right had been infringed but that the decision was 'objectively justified' under one of the prescribed overrides, namely 'the rights of others', these being the social purpose of fostering a sense of community by means of a dress code. This case provides an illustration of the subjective and impressionistic nature of the balancing exercise and also the importance of mainstream opinion. Thus it was stressed that great weight should be given to the professional judgement of the head teacher and mainstream Muslim groups (at [34]).

The technique of defining the right narrowly can be seen in respect of the meaning of 'deprivation' of liberty as opposed to 'restriction' of liberty (see Section 20.4.1). Sometimes this works against the claimant since the onus is on the claimant to bring him or herself within the scope of the right in question, whereas in the case of the separate public interest overrides it is for the state to justify interfering with the right. On the other hand sometimes this might work in the claimant's favour since, as Lord Hoffmann pointed out (at [44]) in *Secretary of State for the Home Dept v JJ* [2008], a narrow definition of deprivation of liberty may make it more difficult for the state to justify overriding it.

The law might react to political pressures. For example the meaning of 'torture or inhuman and degrading treatment' might be redefined according to changing sensibilities (*Chalal v UK* [1996]; *Z v UK* [2002]). 'Fairness' and 'discrimination' in themselves embody the notion of a reasonable balance between competing concerns and are receptive to changing attitudes. In *R (Williamson) v Secretary of State for Education and Employment* [2005] the House of Lords refused to define 'religion' in a restrictive way or pronounce on the validity of a religion but indicated that the 'manifestation' of religion, meaning the interaction with others, was subject to implicit limits based on 'seriousness, cogency and compatibility with human dignity' (at [64], [76]). Other rights are sometimes defined in ways to the point of having little meaning (eg Art 12: right to marry in accordance with the laws of the particular state).

Under Articles 8–11 and Protocol 1, Article 1 the court is required to balance the right against a specified override, which might be another right or a more general public concern. The overrides vary with the particular article but in all cases include public safety, public order, the prevention and detection of serious crime, the protection of health and morals and the protection of the rights of others. This is broadly understood to include the rights of the public generally to have fair, reasonable and effective laws (*Kokkinakis v Greece* [1993]). Sometimes one human right may conflict with another, for example freedom of expression and privacy, but the Convention contains no guidance as to any ranking order. Freedom of expression is often said to have special importance but it readily seems to give way to other rights (Chapter 22).

There are certain threshold requirements. Firstly the restrictions must be 'prescribed by law' or 'in accordance with the law', terms which apparently mean the same. This imports traditional rule of law ideas. Thus the restrictions must be authorised by domestic law but, more than that, they must not involve wide discretion and must be made in accordance with a regular, democratic and accessible lawmaking process and preferably not by judicial extension of the law (see *R (Purdy) v DPP* [2009]: guidance as to prosecution policy for assisted suicide; *R (Laporte) v Chief Constable of Gloucestershire* [2007] at [52]: policing demonstrations (see Section 22.8.1); *Gillan v UK* [2010]: stop and search powers (see Section 23.7.4)). The applicant must be able reasonably to foresee that the conduct in question would be unlawful and there must be adequate safeguards, including independent and accessible courts. The common law is particularly vulnerable to claims of uncertainty (see *R v Goldstein* [2006]; *Sunday Times v UK* [1979]; *Klass v Germany* [1979]).

Secondly the restrictions must be 'necessary in a democratic society'. The concepts of 'necessary' and 'democratic' are vague, inviting the judge to impose his or her personal views. They take their meaning from the context. Necessity is closely related to proportionality (Section 21.5.1) in the sense that the more serious the interference with the right, the stronger must be the justification. It usually means an important interest, sometimes called a 'pressing social need', which is more than merely 'useful', 'reasonable' or 'desirable' (*Handyside v UK* [1976]; *R (Laporte) v Chief Constable of Gloucestershire* [2007] at [52]; *Brown v Stott*: combating drink driving; *Williamson* at

[79]: child welfare; *R (Begum) v Head Teacher and Governor of Denbigh High School* [2007]: social cohesion). In some cases, notably the question of whether a state is entitled to derogate from the Convention, it may come near to meaning 'indispensable', although the court may defer to the government's judgement as to whether this is the case (see Section 21.5.2).

21.5.1 Proportionality

We considered proportionality in Section 18.1.1. In the human rights context the main role of proportionality concerns how the 'fair balance' is struck between a right and the public interest or between two competing rights. Proportionality also applies where the state has a positive duty to protect a right in order to avoid placing undue burdens on the government. This applies even to the 'absolute' rights (*R (Pretty) v DPP* [2002] at [90]).

The court will ask:

1. whether the restriction is imposed for a proper and practicable purpose, to meet a 'pressing social need'. In most cases the court will accept the government's view as to the existence of such a need. In particular an international treaty is unlikely to be questioned (*R (Bermingham) v Serious Fraud Office* [2006]);
2. whether the interference with the right is a rational way of achieving the purpose. This is stricter than ordinary *Wednesbury* unreasonableness (Section 18.1). For example in *A v Secretary of State for the Home Dept* [2005] legislation authorising the indefinite detention of non-British terrorist suspects was not sufficiently focused upon the emergency which the government claimed to be tackling, namely the threat posed by al-Qaeda. The measure, although satisfying the *Wednesbury* test since it had a reasonable purpose which it partly achieved, went too far in some respects and not far enough in others. On the one hand it included people whose activities did not relate to al-Qaeda. On the other hand British terrorists were no less a threat than foreign ones and the detainees were free to leave the UK to harm UK interests from overseas. (See also *Aguila Quila v Secretary of State for the Home Dept* [2011]: immigration restriction on young adults to combat forced marriages was *Wednesbury* reasonable but too wide to be proportionate.)
3. whether the restriction is 'necessary' whether there are safeguards (see *R v Shaylor* [2002]; *Gaskin v UK* [1990]). In *McVeigh v UK* [1983] the European Court held that an emergency restriction on travel did not justify a refusal to let the claimants contact their wives. Proportionality also requires that the restrictions must not be discriminatory in the sense that like cases must be alike (*Marckx v Belgium* [1979]).

Proportionality might therefore require restricting the right or limiting the extent to which the public interest is met. For instance an important aspect of freedom of expression is whether there are alternative outlets for what the claimant wishes to communicate (Chapter 22; see also *R (Szluk) v Governor of Full Sutton Prison* [2004]). In *RJR Macdonald v Canada* [1995] the Canadian Supreme Court was divided over the extent to which tobacco advertising should be restricted in order to meet the public interest in health. It is not clear that the courts are well equipped for this kind of task. It has been held that a right can be overridden on the ground of the public cost in giving effect to it only in clear and weighty cases (see *R (AB) v Secretary of State for Justice* [2010]: refusal to move transsexual prisoner to woman's prison).

Moreover it has been held that, at least in Article 8 cases, in dealing with legislation concerning matters of general social or economic policy, the question of proportionality should be decided at the 'macro' level of the legislation in general and only in exceptional circumstances at the 'micro' level of the facts of the individual case (*Wandsworth LBC v Michalak* [2002]; *Harrow LBC v Qazi* [2004]; *Wilson v First County Trust* [2003]; *Kay v Lambeth BC* [2006]). On the other hand according to the separation of powers the court's role is precisely at the level of application.

Sometimes the competition is between two individual protected rights of equal status, for example privacy (Article 8) and freedom of expression (Article 10). Each right is looked at in turn, comparing the consequences to the individual and the public interest of violating each right and choosing the lesser evil (see eg *R (L) v Metropolitan Police Comr* [2010]: publication of 'enhanced criminal record certificate protecting children's privacy'; *Campbell v MGN* [2004]; Section 22.6).

Thus in the end proportionality is a subjective judgement, raising the question of whether the courts are in the best position to make it (see Section 20.1).

21.5.2 Margin of discretion/deference

Normally the court decides whether the state action complained of is proportionate. The concept of the 'margin of appreciation' was developed by the European Court as a safety valve in cases where there are significant national differences in political, religious or moral values or practices. Where the margin of appreciation applies, the European Court will not substitute its views for those of the state but asks itself only whether the national authorities were reasonably entitled to think that the interference was justifiable (see *Handyside v UK*; *Open Door and Dublin Well Woman v Ireland* [1992]; *Buckley v UK* [1997]). Different communities may have different but justifiable blends of values and attitudes and if an international tribunal intervened it might forfeit respect.

The doctrine of margin of appreciation as such has no application in domestic cases (see *R v DPP, ex p Kebilene* [2000] at 380–81). However, by whatever name, the courts sometimes leave a discretionary area of judgement to ministers and Parliament. This is the concept of 'deference', which we encountered in Section 19.7.1. The courts do not wish to exceed their proper constitutional role or to interfere in matters where they have no experience or expertise or to which legal processes are unsuited.

Thus in *R (Mahmood) v Secretary of State for the Home Dept* [2001], Lord Phillips MR said that:

> the court will bear in mind that, just as individual states enjoy a margin of appreciation which permits them to respond, within the law, in a manner that is not uniform, so there will often be an area of discretion permitted to the executive of a country before a response can be demonstrated to infringe the Convention ... The court will ask the question, applying an objective test, whether the decision maker could reasonably have concluded that the interference was necessary to achieve one or more of the legitimate aims recognised by the Convention. (at [38])

Because all public authorities are obliged to respect Convention rights unless overridden by primary legislation (see Section 21.2) there seems to be no place in human rights cases for any matter to be strictly non-justiciable and deference may be more limited than in other judicial review cases. Nevertheless the margin of discretion applies to the question of whether the government is entitled to override the right on a public interest ground (*R (S) v Chief Constable of South Yorkshire Police* [2004] at [27], [64]). It also applies to the government's positive duty to ensure that human rights are protected (see *Pretty* at [15]; *Rees v UK* [1986]: transsexuals). In cases where a right is vaguely defined it could influence the court's decision as to extent of the right (see *R (Gentle) v Prime Minister* [2008]: decision to invade Iraq; did not engage right to life).

The width of the margin of discretion varies according to the importance of the right, the importance of the public interest in question and the democratic content of the decision. In *Gough v Chief Constable of the Derbyshire Constabulary* [2001] it was said (at [78]) that the margin of discretion is greater, perhaps akin to the *Wednesbury* test, when the decision maker is the primary legislator. In *R (S) v Chief Constable of South Yorkshire Police* [2004] Lord Woolf said:

> I regard it as being fundamental that the court keeps at the forefront of its consideration its lack of any democratic credentials. (at [16])

The guide to deference provided (at [83]–[87]) by Laws LJ (dissenting) in *International Transport Roth GmbH v Secretary of State for the Home Dept* [2003] is often cited. The case concerned a scheme to fine truckers for every illegal immigrant discovered in their vehicles. A majority of the Court of Appeal held that this violated the right to a fair trial under the Human Rights Act 1998. Laws LJ took account of the following factors to justify refusal to intervene in decisions made by what he called 'the democratic powers':

- great deference paid to an Act of Parliament as the highest level of authority;
- more scope for deference where the Convention itself requires a balance to be struck than in the case of the unqualified rights, but even here there may be some scope for deference in defining the right, for example deprivation of liberty (see Section 20.3);
- greater deference in relation to matters peculiarly within the responsibility of the executive such as security, defence and immigration. Less deference in relation to matters directly concerning the courts;
- deference to matters especially within the expertise of the democratic powers such as macro-economic policy.

The margin of discretion is particularly strong in areas involving controversial political or ethical issues which depend on moral or political value judgements (eg *R (Countryside Alliance) v A-G* [2008]: hunting; *R (ProLife Alliance) v BBC* [2003]: taste and decency). It is also strong in relation to legislation intended to meet general welfare goals such as the provision of social housing, these being matters of priority appropriate to democratic decision. In *Poplar Housing and Regeneration Community Association v Donoghue* [2001]. Lord Woolf LCJ remarked that:

> the economic and other implications of any policy in this area are extremely complex and far reaching. This is an area where in our judgement the courts must treat the decisions of Parliament as to what is in the public interest with particular deference. (at [69])

(See also *R (Animal Defenders International) v Secretary of State for Culture, Media and Sport* [2008]: censorship of political advertising: important that issue had been fully debated in Parliament.)

On the other hand some matters are so fundamental or closely related to legal issues as to fall outside any margin of discretion. Here the court will do the interest balancing itself. These include discrimination (Baroness Hale in *Ghaidan v Mendoza*), the right to a fair trial (*R v A* [2001]), personal liberty (Lord Bingham in *A v Secretary of State for the Home Dept* [2005] at [39]–[42]) and serious restrictions on freedom of political expression (Chapter 22). In *A*, a majority of the House of Lords deferred to the government as to whether the current terrorist threat amounted to an emergency so as to justify derogating from the detention without trial provisions of the ECHR since this was matter of political judgement. However it was held (Lord Walker dissenting) that the court could decide whether the detention powers themselves were proportionate since personal liberty was directly in issue.

The margin is not applied automatically. The government must provide some rational support for its actions (*Shaylor* at [61]; *Matthews v Ministry of Defence* [2003]). In the context of the 'margin of appreciation' the Strasbourg Court has emphasised that it may depend upon whether the matter has been subject to considered democratic deliberation as opposed to 'unquestioning and passive adherence to a historic tradition' (*Hirst v UK (No 2)* [2004]; Section 12.6). If this were to apply in domestic law, the court might be influenced by the extent to which a controversial government decision has been debated in Parliament or is supported by international Conventions, expert opinion and so on (see *Williamson*).

Judicial review on domestic principles and judicial review under the HRA overlap particularly in relation to the principle of legality and the right to a fair trial (see Sections 6.6, 18.3) but there are differences. The main differences are:

- Breach of most Convention rights focuses essentially on the effect of a decision, while judicial review primarily concerns the decision-making process. (But see blurring of this in eg *R (Begum) v Head Teacher of Denbigh High School* (see Section 20.4.3): court took into account consultation process used.)
- *Locus standi* for judicial review is wider (see Section 19.4).
- Damages can be obtained under the HRA but only exceptionally in domestic judicial review (see Section 19.2).
- Prerogative Orders in Council can be set aside in domestic judicial review proceedings but not under the HRA.
- A minister can designate an exclusive tribunal for HRA purposes. Only the High Court and the Upper Tribunal have judicial review powers.
- The right to a fair trial under the HRA is narrower in scope than the domestic requirement of fairness (see Section 18.3).
- The application of the two regimes to private bodies may differ, although the same cases have usually been applied to both. The HRA applies to 'public authorities'; judicial review to 'public functions' (see Section 19.5). Under the HRA the notion of a 'public function' is only relevant to 'hybrid' bodies.
- The HRA does not apply to dependent territories (see Section 9.6).

Summary

- The Human Rights Act 1998, while not incorporating the European Convention on Human Rights as such, has given the main rights created by the ECHR effect in domestic law. UK legislation must be interpreted to be compatible with Convention rights, and public bodies other than Parliament must comply with Convention rights. The courts must take the decisions of the ECHR into account but are not bound by them. However the UK courts take a cautious approach and follow Strasbourg closely.
- The Act is territorial and applies outside the UK only exceptionally.
- Parliamentary supremacy is preserved in that Convention rights must give way where they are incompatible with a statute. The courts have taken a moderate approach in relation to the obligation to interpret statutes, 'so far as it is possible to do so', to be compatible with Convention rights. However there are differences of emphasis between judges as to the assumptions on which interpretation should be approached, in particular the extent to which established English law should be respected.
- Where primary legislation is incompatible the court can draw attention to violations by making a declaration of incompatibility. There is a 'fast-track' procedure available in special circumstances to enable amendments to legislation to be made. The government must be explicit as to any intention to override Convention rights.
- The HRA can be directly enforced only against public authorities and by a 'victim' defined in accordance with the case law of the European Court.
- 'Public authority' includes all the activities of government bodies proper and courts and tribunals, but in relation to bodies that have a mixture of public and private functions (eg social landlords) only to their public 'acts'. The courts seem to be taking a similar approach to the question of what constitutes a public function as in judicial review cases.
- 'Horizontal effect' may be direct, where the court is required to enforce a right against a private person, or indirect, where the state is required to protect against violations by private persons. It is not clear how far the Act has horizontal effect, although there are several devices that might enable it to do so.
- Some Convention rights can be overridden by prescribed public interest concerns or other rights and a principle of fair balance runs through the Convention as a whole. The courts are guided by the concept of proportionality. While these devices help to structure and rationalise decision making they do not remove the need for the court to make a subjective political judgement.
- The courts have applied the notion of 'margin of appreciation' or 'margin of discretion', particularly in the context of decisions made by elected bodies (see also Section 19.7.1). The width of the margin depends on various factors, chief among which are the importance and extent of the particular right that is violated in relation to the seriousness of the public harm if the right were not overridden, and the extent to which the matter involves controversial political, social or economic choices. It remains controversial whether the courts provide the best method of protecting fundamental rights.

Exercises

21.1 What is meant by describing the Human Rights Act 1998 as creating a 'constitutional dialogue'? Do you agree with this description?

21.2 According to Lord Bingham the court's role under the Act is democratic because Parliament has given the courts 'a very specific wholly democratic mandate' (*A v Secretary of State for the Home Dept* [2005]). Do you agree?

21.3 'Rights under the Convention differ from rights created by the 1998 Act by reference to the Convention' (Lord Bingham in *R (Al-Skeini) v Secretary of State for Defence* [2007]). Explain and critically discuss.

21.4 Compare the legal effect in domestic law of the ECHR with that of the EU Treaties.

21.5 Explain and compare the constitutional significance of the declaration of incompatibility and the statement of compatibility.

21.6 'My impression is that two factors are contributing to a misunderstanding of the remedial scheme of the 1998 Act. First there is the constant refrain that a judicial reading down or reading in would flout the will of Parliament. The second factor may be an excessive concentration on linguistic factors of the particular statute' (Lord Steyn in *Ghaidan v Mendoza* [2004]). Explain and critically evaluate this statement.

21.7 The Commune of the Many Names of the Lord is a religious community which believes that all life is sacred and that animal life is as valuable as human life. It cares for a number of animals at a small sanctuary. Among these animals is Clive the Golden Eagle. Under the imaginary Animal Health Act 2009 the local authority has power to order the slaughter of any bird which displays a positive reaction to the test for Avian Flu. Clive has tested positive and the local authority has ordered his slaughter. The Commune has evidence from a number of expert veterinarians that Clive could be successfully isolated and treated for the condition. Jobsworth, a vet in private practice whom the government had contracted to make the decision, gave the following reasons for the decision to order the slaughter: (i) in her opinion Clive's condition represents a serious threat to human health; (ii) an outbreak of Avian Flu would have disastrous effects for the local economy.

Advise the Commune as to the possibility of challenging the order in the courts.

21.8 Advise on the chances of success of challenges to each of the following under the Human Rights Act 1998:

(i) the policy of a private care home not to accommodate gay couples;

(ii) the ransacking of a hotel in Iraq by British soldiers during a counter-insurgency operation and the beating up of several of its staff for refusing to provide the soldiers with food and drink;

(iii) the placing of a building worker on a 'blacklist' by a government-funded housing association.

21.9 'The court will bear in mind that, just as individual states enjoy a margin of appreciation which permits them to respond, within the law, in a manner that is not uniform, so there will often be an area of discretion permitted to the executive of a country before a response can be demonstrated to infringe the Convention' (Phillips LJ in *R (Mahmood) v Secretary of State for the Home Dept* [2001]). Explain, illustrate and discuss critically.

21.10 Advise on the chances of success of challenges to each of the following:

(i) a decision by the NHS to refuse a life-extending drug to elderly people suffering from certain terminal illnesses on the grounds that the cost is not worth the benefit and the funding is desperately needed for medical supplies in support of military interventions against non-democratic states;

Exercises cont'd

(ii) a decision to deport a family to a country where they claim that their child, who has learning difficulties, will be compulsorily detained in a mental hospital and subject to electric shock treatment rather than receive behavioural therapy in the home which is available in the UK.

Further reading

Allan, 'Parliament's Will and the Justice of the Common Law in Constitutional Perspective' (2006) 59 CLP 27

Allan, 'Human Rights and Judicial Review: A Critique of "Due Deference"' (2006) 65 CLJ 695

Beatson, Grosz, Hickman and Singh, *Human Rights: Judicial Protection in the UK* (Sweet & Maxwell 2008)

Buxton, 'The Human Rights Act and Private Law' (2000) 116 LQR 116

Buxton, 'The Future of Declarations of Incompatibility' [2010] PL 261

Clapham, *Human Rights Obligations of Non State Actors* (Oxford University Press 2006)

Clayton, 'Judicial Deference and Democratic Dialogue: The Legitimacy of Judicial Intervention under the Human Rights Act 1998' [2004] PL 33

Ewing, *Bonfire of the Liberties: New Labour, Human Rights and the Rule of Law* (Oxford University Press 2010)

Ewing and Than, 'The Continuing Futility of the Human Rights Act' [2008] PL 668

Fenwick, Phillipson and Masterman (eds), *Judicial Reasoning under the Human Rights Act* (Cambridge University Press 2007)

Gearty, 'Reconciling Parliamentary Democracy and Human Rights' (2002) 118 LQR 248

Hickman, 'Constitutional Dialogue, Constitutional Theories and the Human Rights Act 1998' [2005] PL 306

Hickman, 'The Courts and Politics after the Human Rights Act' [2008] PL 84

Hickman, 'The Substance and Structure of Proportionality' [2008] PL 694

Jowell, 'Judicial Deference and Human Rights: A Question of Competence' in Craig and Rawlings (eds), *Law and Administration in Europe* (Oxford University Press 2003)

Kavanagh, 'The Elusive Divide between Interpretation and Legislation under the Human Rights Act 1998' (2004) 24 OJLS 259

Kavanagh, 'The Role of Parliamentary Intention in Adjudication under the Human Rights Act 1998' (2006) 26 OJLS 179

Kavanagh, *Constitutional Review under the Human Rights Act* (Cambridge University Press 2009)

Kavanagh, 'Judging the Judges under the Human Rights Act' [2009] PL 287

Kay, 'The ECHR and the Control of Private Law' (2005) 5 EHRR 466

Klug, 'A Bill of Rights: Do We Need One or Do We Already Have One?' [2007] PL 701

Lakin, 'How to Make Sense of the Human Rights Act 1998: The Ises and Oughts of the British Constitution' (2010) 30 OJLS 399

Laws, 'The Constitution: Morals and Right' [1996] PL 622

Lester, 'The Utility of the Human Rights Act: A Reply to Keith Ewing' [2005] PL 249

Lester and Beattie, 'Human Rights and the British Constitution' in Jowell and Oliver (eds), *The Changing Constitution* (Oxford University Press 2007)

Lewis, 'The European Ceiling on Human Rights' [2007] PL 720

Further reading cont'd

Masterman, 'Taking the Strasbourg Jurisprudence into Account: Developing a Municipal Law of Human Rights under the Human Rights Act' (2005) 54 ICLQ 907
Nicol, 'Statutory Interpretation after Anderson' [2004] PL 273
Nicol, 'Law and Politics after the Human Rights Act' [2006] PL 722
Phillipson, 'Deference, Discretion and Democracy in the Human Rights Era' (2007) 40 CLP 57
Poole, 'Of Headscarves and Heresies: The *Denbigh High School* Case and Public Authority Decision Making under the Human Rights Act' [2005] PL 685
Sales, 'The General and the Particular: Parliament and the Courts under the Scheme of the European Convention on Human Rights' in Andenas and Fairgrieve (eds), *Tom Bingham and the Transformation of the Law* (Oxford University Press 2009)
Shah and Poole, 'The Impact of the Human Rights Act on the House of Lords' [2009] PL 347
Steyn, 'Deference: A Tangled Story' [2005] PL 346
Symposium, 'Can Human Rights Survive?' [2007] PL 209
Wicks, 'Taking Account of Strasbourg: The British Judiciary's Approach to Interpreting Convention Rights' (2005) 11 EPL 405
Wilde, 'The Extraterritorial Application of the Human Rights Act' (2005) 65 CLI 47
Wright, 'Interpreting Section 2 of the Human Rights Act: Towards an Indigenous Jurisprudence of Human Rights' [2009] PL 595
Young, 'In Defence of Due Deference' (2009) 72 MLR 554
Young, 'A Peculiarly British Protection of Human Rights' (2005) 68 MLR 858

Chapter 22

Freedoms of expression and assembly

> **A free press is not a privilege but an organic necessity in a great society. Without criticism and reliable and intelligent reporting, the government cannot govern. (Walter Lippmann, journalist, 1889–1974)**

22.1 Introduction: justifications for freedom of expression

A range of arguments can be advanced in support of freedom of expression. These have been placed into two broad groups (Dworkin, *Freedom's Law* (Oxford University Press 1996) 199–201). The first identifies freedom of expression as an end in itself as a defining characteristic of a human being. Dworkin argues that freedom of expression is an essential and 'constitutive' feature of a just political society in which the government treats all its members, except those who are incompetent, as responsible moral agents. Those upon whom the right to freedom of expression is conferred are regarded as capable of 'making up their own minds about what is good or bad in life or in politics, or what is true and false in matters of justice and faith' and are properly entitled to 'participate in politics' and to 'contribute to the formation of [their] moral or aesthetic climate'. Like Kant, who uses 'reason' in much the same way, Dworkin seems to regard freedom of expression as a badge of moral worth (see also Freeden, *Rights* (Oxford University Press 1991) 8–59). This might be regarded as merely a recital of liberal faith (Chapter 2) and easily rejected for example from a religious perspective. It is moreover uncomfortable for those whom Dworkin regards as incompetent.

The second group of justifications regards freedom of expression as instrumentally valuable, that is valuable as a means by which to pursue some other valuable end. This approach, popular among the professional elite in the UK, could make freedom of expression conditional upon the approval of some authority such as themselves designated to decide what the valuable end is and whether it is being sought. The ends in question were identified by Mill (see Section 2.3.3) as democracy, self-fulfilment and the testing of truth.

As regards democracy Lord Steyn in *R v Secretary of State for the Home Dept, ex p Simms* [1999] emphasised freedom of expression in informing debate as a safety valve to encourage consent and as a brake on the abuse of power. Democracy can only flourish in circumstances where a free press with access to government proceedings can offer information and comment which the public has a right and perhaps a duty to receive. Lord Bingham in *McCartan Turkington Breen v Times Newspapers Ltd* [2001] stressed the importance of a free, active, professional and inquiring media to a modern participatory democracy, pointing out that ordinary citizens cannot usually participate directly but can do so indirectly through the media (at 290–91).

Free expression requires not only the right to criticise government and challenge orthodoxy but also fair opportunities at elections and other public debates (*Handyside v*

UK [1976]; *Bowman v UK* [1998]; *Castells v Spain* [1992]) and access to official information and to the proceedings of public bodies, including courts, in order to ensure that they are properly impartial. In *Hector v A-G of Antigua and Bermuda* [1990] Lord Bridge said that 'in a free democratic society ... those who hold office in government must always be open to criticism. Any attempt to stifle or fetter such criticism amounts to political censorship of the most insidious and objectionable kind' (at 106). Moreover, apart from rejecting censorship, freedom of expression imposes a duty on the media to disseminate ideas and information.

The liberal argument that freedom of expression provides a means to the end of self-actualisation has been advanced by, among others, John Stuart Mill (see Section 2.3.3) and Thomas Emerson. Its starting point is the proposition that the proper end of humanity is the realisation of individual potential, which cannot flourish without freedom of expression. However human development also requires protection for privacy, so there is a conflict between these fundamental human needs (see *Von Hannover v Germany* [1995]).

Mill was concerned that people should be free to experiment with different lifestyles, provided only that they did not harm others. Mill distinguished between causing harm and causing offence, which should not be prohibited. Indeed being offended or shocked might be considered good, as stimulating thought. However it is not clear what counts as harm. Mill took harm to mean interfering with someone's rights or interests but of course this begs the questions of what counts as a right and who decides? Am I not harmed if I am seriously upset or offended by someone exercising freedom of expression by attacking my religion?

The argument that freedom of expression facilitates the pursuit of truth and the acquisition of knowledge suppressed by official orthodoxy has a long history. It was expressed in the seventeenth century by John Milton in his *Areopagitica*. Mill supported it, arguing that 'truth', which he equated with the general good, can best be discovered and preserved by constant questioning. However this provides relatively weak support since there is no reason to suppose that truth is always conducive to the general welfare. Moreover in the marketplace of ideas is there any reason to suppose that truth rather than the loudest and best-paid voice will prevail? According to the philosopher of science Karl Popper, free critical discussion provides a means by which to eliminate errors in our thinking and thus to move towards ever more plausible working hypotheses but never incontrovertible truths (*The Open Society and Its Enemies* (Routledge 1996)).

In the political sphere, at least from a liberal perspective, the point of freedom of expression is arguably to keep diversity and disagreement alive. Thus Bollinger suggests that freedom of expression facilitates 'the development of [a] capacity for tolerance' ('The Tolerance Society' [1990] CLR 979). A capacity for tolerance weakens 'a general bias against receiving or acknowledging new ideas' (ibid). Secondly as Locke recognised (*On Tolerance* (1698)) it is particularly valuable as a means of keeping the peace in large and complex societies containing people with varied beliefs and interests.

It is widely accepted that freedom of expression is not absolute and that not all aspects of it are equally important. This leads to the danger, identified by Berlin (see Section 2.4), of freedom of expression being regarded as a 'positive freedom' conditional upon those in power assessing its worthiness.

The interests with which freedom of expression might conflict are open ended and difficult to define. Some are also human rights. They include security, public order, confidential relationships, the fairness and independence of court proceedings, respect for religious groups and for minorities, and the protection of children and of reputation and personal privacy.

'Hate speech' which insults or denigrates others is particularly controversial since it can be justified on all the grounds outlined above. It has often been emphasised that in a liberal society, freedom of expression is especially important where it involves controversial statements which might shock and offend, for example in relation to the religious, moral or cultural susceptibilities of others (see *Handyside*; Hoffmann LJ in *R v Central Independent Television plc* [1994]). On the other hand tolerance requires a certain degree of respect for the values of others. A further issue is whether it is possible to protect other interests without inhibiting the public interest in press freedom. Vaguely defined limits to freedom of expression might have a 'chilling' effect on the press by discouraging bold investigations (see *Campbell v MGN Ltd* [2004]).

The protection of free expression has other dangers. In *R v Shaylor* [2002] Lord Hutton suggested, redolent of the 'dignified constitution' (see Section 5.1), that freedom of expression might undesirably weaken confidence in those who govern us (although the opposite might be said). It could be argued most obviously in relation to elections that freedom of expression allows the loudest voice to prevail. Hence there are curbs on the funding of political parties and provisions about balance in the media (see Section 12.10).

It has been suggested that protection against state interference encourages indirect censorship by private commercial and social forces which are intolerant of minority opinions. A free press is necessarily influenced by commercial concerns: the need to sell newspapers or advertising space. This leads to the press violating privacy by including trivial or sensational personal stories to attract customers or publishing material that suits the prejudices of the majority. According to this view society is polarised between a deeply conformist majority and marginalised dissenters, and the protection of minorities might be improved through greater state intervention. There is also the possibility in a free market culture that control of an uncomfortably large share of the media might be concentrated in a single owner. To some extent this is regulated by the Communications Act 2003, which empowers the Secretary of State to refer a takeover or a merger to the Office of Fair Trading, which in turn can refer the matter to the Competition Commission.

We should not suppose that limits on freedom of expression should always be imposed by law. This is because we may not be able to trust lawmakers or officials to exercise the delicate power of censorship wisely or honestly. In addition fear of an expensive legal action might have a chilling effect on the media whereby liability rules encourage writers and other commentators to censor themselves rather than risk litigation. Moral constraints are equally important and we might question whether we should entrust any public official with large power in relation to so fundamental a matter as freedom of expression. For example in relation to press freedom there is reliance on self-regulation by means of the Press Complaints Commission (see Blom-Cooper, 2008).

22.2 The legal status of freedom of expression

Article 10 of the European Convention on Human Rights (ECHR) defines freedom of expression as:

> freedom to hold opinions and to receive and impart information and ideas without interference by public authority and regardless of frontiers. This article shall not prevent states from requiring the licensing of broadcasting, television or cinema enterprise.

Freedom of expression is protected by the common law 'principle of legality' as well as by the Human Rights Act 1998 (see Section 6.6) and some judges have claimed that freedom of expression has an especially high status (eg Lord Steyn in *R v Secretary of State for the Home Dept, ex p Simms* [1999] at 407–08: 'the primary freedom'; Lord Nicholls in *R (ProLife Alliance) v BBC* [2003] at [6]). However as we shall see privacy may be given equal weight.

The extent of freedom of expression is influenced by the sort of expression approved of by the state. Thus some kinds of expression are given greater weight than others. The greatest weight is given to political expression through the media since this is regarded as essential to the processes of democracy (see Lord Bingham in *McCartan Turkington Breen v Times Newspapers* [2001] at 290–91). Less weight is given to commercial expression such as advertising and possibly the least weight is given to lifestyle matters such as pornography. In *R v Secretary of State for the Home Dept, ex p Simms* [1999] a prisoner was held entitled to have access to a journalist in order to publicise his claim that he was wrongly convicted. Lord Steyn thought that he would not have had such access to indulge in pornography or even in a general political or economic debate (see also *Campbell v MGN Ltd* [2004]; *R (British American Tobacco UK Ltd) v Secretary of State for Health* [2004]: advertising; *'Miss Behavin' v Belfast City Council* [2007]: sexual services).

It is not clear how much weight is given to non-political cultural matters such as theatre and works of art. However where these conflict with religious susceptibilities, at least those of influential sections of the community, it seems that the latter carry greater weight (see *Otto Preminger Institut v Austria* [1994]).

There is probably a positive obligation on the state to protect freedom of expression against interference by private bodies (see Section 21.3.2; Lord Scott (dissenting) in *R (ProLife Alliance) v BBC*). Some statutes give specific protection to freedom of expression. The main examples are the Bill of Rights 1688, the Parliamentary Papers Act 1841 and the Defamation Act 1952, which protect parliamentary proceedings and related reporting (see Sections 11.6.3.2, 11.6.3), and the Education (No 2) Act 1986, which imposes a duty on universities to protect freedom of speech on their premises. Sometimes statute protects freedom of expression against some general restriction (eg Environmental Protection Act 1990, s 79(6A): noise controls: political demonstrations exempted).

A distinction is often drawn between banning expression entirely, which is not acceptable, and regulating the time and place at which it can be carried out, which might be (eg *R (ProLife Alliance) v BBC*).

Article 10 confers the right of freedom of expression subject to 'duties and responsibilities'. These entitle the state to limit freedom of expression for the following purposes:

- national security;
- territorial integrity or public safety;
- prevention of disorder or crime;
- protection of health or morals;
- protection of the reputation or rights of others;
- preventing the disclosure of information received in confidence;
- maintaining the authority and impartiality of the judiciary.

In particular freedom of expression may be compromised by the right to a fair trial (Art 6), privacy (Art 8) and freedom of religion (Art 9).

Numerous statutes and common law principles have restricted freedom of expression for the following main purposes. These conform to Article 10 in principle. However any restriction must be proportionate in the specific circumstances (see Section 21.5).

- security (see Section 23.3);
- public order and safety (Section 22.8);
- reputation (Section 22.5);
- privacy (Section 22.6);
- sexual morality (Obscene Publications Act 1959: 'deprave and corrupt' subject to defence of artistic merit);
- child protection, particularly in relation to reporting court proceedings (Children Act 1989, s 97(2); Magistrates Courts Act 1980, s 69(2)(c); see *Pelling v Bruce-Williams* [2004]; *Re Webster (A Child) (No 1)* [2006]);
- combating racial, religious and sexual hatred (Section 22.7);
- the independence of judicial proceedings. Press comment is restricted on pending trials that create a 'substantial risk' that the course of justice will be seriously impeded or prejudiced (Contempt of Court Act 1981, s 2; see *Re Lonrho plc* [1990]). There is an important defence that the publication contains a discussion in good faith of public affairs where the risk of prejudice is merely incidental to the discussion (see *A-G v English* [1983]). Contempt law indirectly restrains free expression when it requires the identity of press informants to be disclosed (Section 22.4);
- protection against misleading advertising and professional claims;
- intellectual property rights such as copyright.

22.3 Press freedom and censorship

Press freedom is not a separate right but is an aspect of the general right to freedom of expression whereby the media exercise the right on behalf of the public. There is a two-way relationship in that the public have a right to receive information and the press a duty to give it. As we have seen political expression is especially important, so attacks on the government are subject to restriction only in extreme cases.

The media enjoys a high level of protection because it is a watchdog over government on behalf of the public. In *Lingens v Austria* [1986] the European Court said that 'freedom of the press…affords the public one of the best means of discovering and forming an opinion of the ideas and attitudes of political leaders. More generally, freedom of political debate is at the very core of the concept of a democratic society which prevails throughout the Convention'. (See also *Castells v Spain* [1992]; *Jersild v Denmark* [1994]; *A-G v Punch* [2003].) For example in *Re Webster (A Child) (No 1)* [2006] the press but not the public were permitted to attend a high-profile case involving childcare proceedings (see Ministry of Justice, *Confidence and Confidentiality: Openness in Family Courts – A New Approach* (CP 10/07, 2007)).

It is also important for democratic participation and for liberal pluralism that there be a wide variety of media outlets (see *Informationsverein Lentia v Austria* [1993]). Thus in *Binyam Mohammed v Foreign Secretary* [2009] it was emphasised that Article 10 embraces a public right to information provided by the press as the watchdog of the public. (See also *Re S (A Child)* [2004] at [602]–[604]; *LRT v Mayor of London* [2001]). However in the outcome the value of press freedom was outweighed by national security concerns (see Section 23.3.3).

The European Court has consistently emphasised the importance of press freedom, including the need to give some journalistic latitude in order to prevent the chilling effect of legal restrictions discouraging frankness and openness (see *Thomas v Luxemburg* [2003] at 373; *Fressoz v France* [1999] at 656; *Selisto v Finland* [2006] at 161).

In the eighteenth century Blackstone introduced the distinction between 'prior restraint – censorship', requiring government approval in advance, and punishing the speaker after the event (*Commentaries* (1765) III, 17). Prior restraint is regarded as an especially serious violation of freedom of expression because it removes from the public sphere the possibility of assessing the matter, whereas punishment may be regarded as a legitimate compromise between competing goods. Prior restraint should therefore be only a last resort. The ECHR subjects prior restraint to a high level of scrutiny, particularly in the case of news, 'which is a perishable commodity' (see *Observer and Guardian Newspapers v UK* [1992]). Indeed in *Open Door and Dublin Well Woman v Ireland* [1992] five judges thought that prior restraint should never be tolerated. In *VGT v Switzerland* [2002] a ban on political advertising was condemned. In *R (Laporte) v Chief Constable of Gloucestershire* [2006] Lord Bingham emphasised (at [32]) that prior restraint in the context of public demonstrations should be subject to careful scrutiny (Section 22.8.1).

On the other hand where Parliament has established a special regulatory censorship mechanism the courts are reluctant to impose their own judgments, short of reviewing unreasonable decisions (*R v Broadcasting Standards Commission, ex p BBC* [2001]). In this context the courts are reluctant to impose their own views of what is appropriate.

In *R (ProLife Alliance) v BBC* [2003] the House of Lords was asked to decide whether an obligation imposed on the BBC to ensure that its programmes do not offend 'good taste and decency' overrode the right to freedom of expression of the Alliance, who wished to include in an election broadcast vivid but accurate and unsensationalised images of the process of abortion. A majority of the House refused to intervene on the grounds that deciding the limits of good taste is not appropriate to a court and that the BBC has a margin of discretion which it had exercised reasonably. By taking this line the Court accepted the principle that free expression could be restricted on the ground of taste alone. Indeed Lord Hoffmann emphasised the pervasive influence of television, with the implication that protective measures are especially justified.

A distinction was drawn between banning someone altogether from what he or she wished to say and refusing to give someone a platform to disseminate offensive material (see also *Appelby v UK* [2003]; *DPP v Collins* [2006]). Just as no one has a right to have his or her work published by a particular publisher, no one has a right to appear on television. This analogy may seem unreal given the importance of television as a medium of political communication and the state's positive duty to ensure the dissemination of opinion.

Lord Scott dissented on classical liberal freedom of speech grounds. The difference between his approach and that of the majority was that he gave greater weight to the democratic importance of an election broadcast. Far from wishing to protect the public against offence he thought that 'the public in a mature democracy are not entitled to be offended by the broadcasting of such a programme' and that a ban would be 'positively inimical to the values of a democratic society to which values it must be assumed that the public adheres' (at [98]). His Lordship also remarked in the context of 'voter apathy' that:

> a broadcaster's mindset that rejects a party election television programme on the ground that large numbers of the voting public would find the programme 'offensive' denigrates the voting public, treats them like children who need to be protected from the unpleasant realities of life, seriously undervalues their political maturity and can only promote [voter apathy]. (at [99])

Since the abolition in 1695 of state licensing of printing presses the government has no censorship powers over the printed word, although in characteristically British fashion there are non-enforceable mechanisms presided over by committees of insiders for the purpose of self-censorship in security matters (Defence Advisory (DA) Notices).

Broadcasting raises particular problems because of the variety of broadcast media that now exist at an international level and the ease with which material can be pirated (see eg *Autronic AG v Switzerland* [1990]). There is significant state regulation over broadcasting (but not the Internet), including a general power to require announcements or to ban broadcasts exercisable by the Secretary of State (Broadcasting Act 1990, s 10; BBC Licence Agreement). There are also specific requirements, including impartiality and taste, policed by the Office of Communications (OFCOM), which replaced a variety of other bodies (Communications Act 2003). Under the Cinemas Act 1985 local authorities have a power to license cinema performances. There are also controls over the distribution of videos and DVDs (see Video Recordings Act 2010, the result of a botched earlier measure).

The courts have prior restraint powers in the form of an injunction, disobedience to which attracts imprisonment for contempt of court. The Attorney General can seek an injunction in the name of the public interest, most notably in the case of publications that risk prejudicing legal proceedings such as newspaper comments on matters related to pending litigation (contempt of court) and in the interests of government confidentiality or national security (Chapter 21). A temporary injunction pending a full trial can be granted on the basis that there is an arguable case, since once material is published there is no turning back. A temporary injunction prevents anyone, whether a party or not, publishing the material with the intention to impede the court's purpose in granting the injunction (*A-G v Observer Ltd* [1988]; *A-G v Times Newspapers Ltd* [1991]). However an injunction will be granted only if it serves a useful purpose. Once material becomes public, even if unlawfully, the press has a duty to disseminate it and comment on it and further restraint cannot be justified (see *Observer and Guardian Newspapers*).

UK law had previously violated the ECHR because injunctions had been used in a manner disproportionate to the risk of harm. For example in *Sunday Times v UK* [1979] the ECHR held that contempt law could inhibit freedom of expression only where this was necessary to ensure a fair trial, for example to prevent influence on juries or witnesses. The test is whether there is a 'substantial risk' that the course of justice will be impeded or prejudiced (Contempt of Court Act 1981, s 2)

Even after the Human Rights Act 1998 the courts have taken a generous approach to injunctions. In *A-G v Punch* [2003] a magazine published a series of articles by David Shaylor, a former member of the security services against whom a prosecution under the Official Secrets Act was pending for disclosing information about intelligence operations. An injunction prevented publication of any material obtained by Mr Shaylor in the course of or as a result of his employment in the security services. Although critical of this wide injunction because of the chilling effect on freedom of expression of restrictions that are not precisely targeted (at [61]–[63]), the House of Lords upheld it, rejecting the editor's argument that he did not intend to damage national security on the ground that this was irrelevant to the court's purpose in granting the injunction and the editor should have realised this. Moreover this was not censorship by the Attorney General, who under the terms of the injunction could clear publication, since the matter was in the control of the courts.

In 2009 an application was made to obtain a 'super-injunction' which would have prevented the *Guardian* (i) from publishing material concerning possible environmental offences committed by an oil company even though this was contained in a parliamentary question and (ii) from reporting even the existence of the injunction. The application was withdrawn, leaving the position of super-injunctions unclear (see Section 11.6.3). A committee has now been set up by the Justice Department under the chairmanship of the Master of the Rolls to examine the issue.

The importance of press freedom has been reinforced by section 12 of the Human Rights Act 1998. This provides firstly that a court order limiting the 'Convention right of freedom of expression' cannot normally be granted in the absence of the respondent. This affects interim injunctions which might be sought as an emergency measure against the media. Secondly section 12 prevents an interim order being made unless the applicant is likely to establish that publication should not be allowed. Thirdly section 12 requires the court to have particular regard to freedom of expression and,

> where the proceedings relate to material which the respondent claims or which appears to the court to be journalistic, literary or artistic material (or to conduct connected with such material), to [have regard to] (a) the extent to which (i) the material has, or is about to, become available to the public; or (ii) it is, or would be, in the public interest for the material to be published; and (b) any relevant privacy code

(eg that made by the Press Complaints Commission).

However section 12 has been held not to privilege freedom of expression above other Convention rights such as privacy. In *Douglas and Zeta-Jones v Hello! Ltd* [2001] the Court of Appeal held that it merely ensures that the competing rights in question are taken into account at the interim stage. In *Cream Holdings v Banerjee* [2004] the House of Lords held that where section 12 applies the normal threshold is that the applicant would 'more likely than not' succeed at the trial. However the approach must be flexible; for example if publication would cause serious harm, a lower threshold would be justified. In *Thompson and Venables v News Group Newspapers Ltd* [2001] the claimants (the notorious killers of James Bulger) sought indefinite injunctions restraining the press from disclosing their (new) identities on release from custody. Since the circumstances of the case were exceptional in that they involved the right to life, Dame Butler-Sloss granted the injunctions. She stated that it will only be necessary to grant injunctive relief where it can be 'convincingly demonstrated' that the requirements of Article 10(2), as to overrides, can be satisfied.

22.4 The free flow of information

The European Court has held that the public has a right to receive information, ideas and opinions, so the state has a positive duty to safeguard the free flow of information and opinion. Moreover Article 10 of the ECHR imposes duties on the media to ensure the free flow of information. The relationship between the duties of the press to inform the public and open justice significantly influenced the Court of Appeal in *R (Mohamed) v Secretary of State for Foreign and Commonwealth Affairs* [2010] when it overturned a claim by the Foreign Office that certain pages from a previous court judgment be 'redacted' (removed) in order to protect communications with the US government concerning the alleged involvement of the UK in the torture of terrorist suspects (see Section 23.3.3). It was emphasised that under Article 10 a diverse press should be free to report court proceedings from its different political points of view (at [180]).

Jersild v Denmark [1994] concerned a television interview with representatives of an extremist political group. The interview was edited to highlight abusive remarks made about ethnic groups within Denmark. The TV interviewer, who did not challenge the racist remarks, was charged with aiding and abetting the offence of 'threatening, insulting or degrading a group of persons on account of their race, colour, national or ethnic origin or belief'. The court held, with seven dissenters, that the interview was protected by Article 10 because of the duty of the press to report controversial opinions in its role of public watchdog and the corresponding right of the public to be informed. It was not for the court to decide how journalists presented their material, provided that taken in its whole context the broadcast did not support the views put forward. In these circumstances restricting the press was not necessary in a democratic society, as required by Article 10 (see also *Castells v Spain* [1992] at [43]; *Lingens v Austria* [1986] at [41]).

It is important that the confidentiality of those who supply information to the press is protected. In *R v Central Criminal Court, ex p Bright, Alton and Rusbridger* [2001] the Court of Appeal quashed a production order sought by the Crown against the editors of the *Guardian* and the *Observer* to disclose information received from David Shaylor, a former MI5 agent. It was held that disclosure would inhibit press freedom without there being a compelling reason for the disclosure.

The press also has statutory protection. Section 10 of the Contempt of Court Act 1981 protects the anonymity of a publisher's sources of information except where the court thinks that disclosure is necessary on the grounds of the interests of justice, national security or the prevention of crime and disorder. Section 10 enables the court to exercise a discretion between the competing concerns. Before the Human Rights Act 1998 the courts interpreted the exceptions broadly against the press, influenced by the common law idea that the press should have no special privileges (eg *X Ltd v Morgan Grampian Publishers Ltd* [1991]: commercial interest outweighed press freedom). This was strongly criticised by the European Court in *Goodwin v UK* [1996] on the ground that the protection of journalistic confidentiality is crucial to press freedom, interference with which requires the most careful scrutiny. It has also been held that where national security or wrongdoing is involved the court will usually order disclosure (*X v Morgan Grampian; Ashworth Hospital v MGN Ltd* [2001]). However in *John v Express Newspapers Ltd* [2000], which concerned the leaking of legal advice, it was held following *Goodwin* that a confidential source should be publicly disclosed only as a last resort (see also *Financial Times v UK* [2009]: sources should be protected unless clear evidence of damage or harmful intent).

22.5 Press freedom and reputation: defamation

Defamation concerns reputation, which is protected by the ECHR (Art 8) (see Lord Nicholls in *Reynolds v Times Newspapers Ltd* [2001]: 'reputation [as] an integral and important part of the dignity of the individual' (at 201)). Apart from its role in ensuring that those who rule us are accountable, freedom of expression is also part of individual dignity. Moreover both interests secure autonomy by providing protection against arbitrary interference. Hence agonising and politically controversial choices must be made between incommensurable rights (see Section 1.6).

Material is defamatory if it reflects on the claimant's reputation so as to lower him or her in the estimation of right-thinking members of society generally (*Sim v Stretch* [1936]) or tends to cause the claimant to be shunned or avoided (*Youssoupoff v Metro-Goldwyn-Mayer Pictures Ltd* [1934]) or would bring the claimant into ridicule or contempt (*Dunlop Rubber Co Ltd v Dunlop* [1921]).

A claimant must prove that the relevant material (i) is defamatory, (ii) has been published and (iii) refers to him or her. Publication means merely communication to another person, so each time an item is passed on (eg from journalist to newsroom to a newspaper seller to the public) there is a separate publication.

Defamatory publications take one of two forms: namely, libel and slander. Material is libellous if it is published in a permanent form, for example writing or another recorded medium. It is slanderous if it takes a less than permanent form, for example word of mouth.

In general the press is subject to the law of defamation in the same way as anyone else. English law is widely regarded as relatively unsympathetic to the press and English courts are often chosen as a forum for defamation actions as opposed for example to the US, where freedom of expression has a higher level of protection as enshrined in the Constitution. The main relevant difference is that in English law the defendant media have to prove the truth of any allegations they make, whereas more usually the onus is on the claimant to prove that the allegation is false. Moreover in the US a public official cannot sue for defamation. Given the expense and uncertainty of litigation this may have a chilling effect on the flow of information. The government has promised reforming legislation but the details of this are not yet known.

Defamation law recognises the importance of freedom of expression. To this end there are various defences. These include:

1. *truth (or justification).* Subject to an exception under section 8 of the Rehabilitation of Offenders Act 1974 this can be pleaded even where a defendant has been actuated by malice (ie spite or ill will). The publication as a whole must be considered, so the truth of part is no defence;
2. *absolute privilege.* Liability cannot be imposed in the course of:
   (i) parliamentary proceedings (see Section 11.6.3);
   (ii) judicial proceedings;
   (c) official communications (*Chatterton v Secretary of State for India* [1895]);
3. *qualified privilege.* Traditionally this defence applies where a defendant who honestly believes what he or she says to be true meets the following two requirements (see Lord Nicholls in *Reynolds* at 194–95, 200):
   (i) the defendant has an interest or a duty (legal, social or moral) to communicate the relevant material to another or others;
   (b) the recipient of the material must have a corresponding interest or duty to receive it.
   (eg *Clift v Slough BC* [2011]: circular about anti-social staff member circulated more widely than necessary: right of privacy must be balanced). This important defence is discussed further below (Section 22.5.3);
4. *fair comment (recently renamed 'honest comment').* This protects honest expressions of *opinion* on matters of public interest. Judges sometimes identify it as a bulwark of free expression (see eg Lord Denning MR in *Slim v Daily Telegraph Ltd* [1968] at 170). As with qualified privilege a plea of honest comment can be defeated by a showing that the defendant was actuated by malice. Important support to freedom of expression was provided in *British Chiropractic Association v Singh* [2010]. The Court of Appeal held that a statement in a scientific journal concerning contested scientific conclusions was to be treated as an expression of opinion not a statement of fact. Thus the defendant would not be faced with the virtually impossible task of proving that the statement was true. The Court remarked that to treat matters of scientific controversy as matters of fact would be a disproportionate interference with freedom of expression: an Orwellian Ministry of Truth (see [18]–[23]). Similarly in *Joseph v Spiller* [2010] the Supreme Court held that the comment need not identify the facts on which it was based in detail but must identify in general terms what led the commentator to make the comment so that the reader could understand what it was about and call for further explanation;
5. *reportage.* A person is liable if he or she repeats a defamatory statement made by another. This applies to the press as much as to anyone else. However there is a defence if it can be shown clearly that when read as a whole the author did not in any way associate himself with or support the statement in question. Thus very careful journalistic writing is required (see *Chapman v Orion Publishing Group* [2008]; *Galloway v Telegraph Group* [2006]).

Two further features of the law protect freedom of expression. First the institution of the jury and second the limited availability of an injunction. Defamation actions (which are heard in the High Court) are usually tried with a jury, which is regarded as providing a safeguard against official repression (see Fox's Libel Act 1792). However in *Grobbelaar v News Group Newspapers Ltd* [2001] the Court of Appeal took the (apparently) ground-breaking step of overturning a jury's findings of fact on the ground that they were perverse and unreasonable.

The judiciary has long been reluctant to grant injunctions in defamation cases. Hence this remedy will not be granted unless the plaintiff can satisfy a number of exacting conditions, in particular that there is no ground for supposing that the defendant may avoid liability by pleading truth, privilege or fair comment (*Bonnard v Perryman* [1891]). Furthermore judges are grudging in their readiness to grant interim (or interlocutory) injunctions which restrain the offending expression pending a full trial (ibid). Such injunctions are only granted where (i) a court is satisfied that publication will result in immediate and irreparable injury and (ii) damages would not provide an adequate remedy (*Monson v Tussauds Ltd* [1894]; see also HRA 1998, s 12 (Section 22.3)).

The current government proposes to introduce a Defamation Bill along the lines of a bill prepared by Lord Lester. This would strengthen press freedom by introducing a defence of responsible publication on a matter of public interest, would allow the truth defence to be raised in relation to part of a publication and would replace the defence of fair comment with one of 'honest opinion'.

22.5.1 Public bodies

In recent years three features of defamation law have been modified by the judiciary with a view to establishing a balance between press freedom and reputational interests compatible with the ECHR. These concern public bodies, damages and qualified privilege.

In *Derbyshire CC v Times Newspapers Ltd* [1993] the House of Lords held that a local authority and other public bodies cannot sue in defamation. The Council sued following the publication in the *Sunday Times* of an allegation of mismanagement of pension funds. Lord Keith explained that: 'it is of the highest public importance that a democratically elected body... should be open to uninhibited public criticism' (at 1017). Hence the law could not be allowed to exert a chilling effect on expressive activity. The House of Lords did not base its decision on the ECHR but found support in 'the common law of England'. Lord Keith did however conclude that English common law was 'consistent' with the ECHR's requirements. The same principle applies to political parties (see *Goldsmith v Bhoyrul* [1997]).

However one feature of the case suggests that Lord Keith's commitment to democracy may be half-hearted. Lord Keith indicated that individual public officials can sue in defamation on the same basis as private individuals. The House of Lords has been criticised for failing to follow the US Supreme Court's lead in *New York Times Co v Sullivan* [1964] by introducing the 'actual malice' rule into UK defamation law in relation to individuals. This rule protects statements against both public institutions and individual public officials made in the absence of malice and with knowledge that they are false. This would have helped to protect political expression and would have brought the law of defamation into closer alignment with the European Court of Human Rights. This treats Article 10 as requiring three distinctions; namely political figures should receive less protection from defamation law than private individuals and governmental bodies (and political parties) should receive even less protection from the law than political figures (see *Lingens v Austria* [1986]; *Castells v Spain* [1992]; *Oberschlick v Austria* [1995]).

22.5.2 Damages

Damages are the principal remedy for defamation. Plaintiffs are entitled to damages for both reputational and economic injury, for example loss of employment. Juries determine the amount and until recently they were not furnished with clear guidance as to the appropriate sum to award. This sometimes led to very large awards, a factor which helped make the UK courts the forum of choice for many overseas claimants. Such awards are open to objection on at least two grounds. Firstly they are a disproportionate response to a defendant's wrongdoing. Secondly the prospect of having to pay such a sum may exert a powerful chilling effect.

However under section 8 of the Courts and Legal Services Act 1990 the Court of Appeal has the power, where a jury has awarded 'excessive' compensation, to substitute a lower sum. This power was first exercised in *Rantzen v Mirror Group Newspapers Ltd* [1994], where the Court substituted an award of £110,000 for the jury's award of £250,000. While the Court based its decision on the Act, it also justified it by reference to Article 10 of the ECHR. Neill LJ stated that the Convention required that damages should not exceed the level 'necessary to compensate the plaintiff and re-establish his reputation' (at 994; see *Tolstoy Miloslavsky v UK* [1995]).

In *John v Mirror Group Newspapers Ltd* [1996] the Court of Appeal restricted the range of circumstances in which a plaintiff can recover exemplary or punitive damages. The Court stated that awards of this sort could only be recovered where the plaintiff offers 'clear' proof of the two following things (Lord Bingham at 58): first the defendant knowingly or recklessly published untruths; second the defendant proceeded to publish the relevant untruths having cynically calculated that the profit accruing from the publication would be likely to exceed any damages award made against him or her. The Court buttressed its decision by reference to Article 10, which, according to Lord Bingham, requires that 'freedom of expression should not be restricted by awards of exemplary damages save to the extent shown to be strictly necessary for the protection of reputations' (ibid).

22.5.3 Responsible journalism

As we saw above the defence of qualified privilege has traditionally required a reciprocal relationship between the publisher of the statement and the recipient, namely that there must be an interest or duty (legal, social or moral) to communicate the material and a corresponding interest or duty to receive it. For example a reference written by a tutor to a student's prospective employer would qualify. Newspapers have experienced difficulty in establishing reciprocity vis-à-vis material communicated to the public at large. This is because judges have been reluctant to bestow on newspapers and other media organs an open-ended 'public interest' defence. However *Reynolds* marks a movement in this direction.

In *Reynolds v Times Newspapers Ltd* [2001] the House of Lords held that qualified privilege can in some circumstances be pleaded where political material is disseminated to the general public. However their Lordships emphasised that such material would still have to fall within the criteria for reciprocity (Lord Nicholls at 200, 204). Their Lordships also rejected the gloss placed on the qualified privilege defence by Lord Bingham LCJ in the Court of Appeal, who stated that the press would have to satisfy an additional condition, namely what Lord Bingham termed 'the circumstantial test' (at 909). To satisfy this test defendants were required to show that 'the nature, status and source of the material and all the circumstances of its publication' were such that the publication should 'in the public interest' be protected (at 912).

However their Lordships (rather equivocally) identified 'circumstances' as a highly relevant consideration. Lord Nicholls stated:

> through the cases runs the strain that, when determining whether the public at large had a right to know the particular information, the court has regard to all the circumstances. The Court is concerned to assess whether the information was of sufficient value to the public that, in the public interest, it should be protected by the privilege in the absence of malice. (at 195)

To this his Lordship added a (non-exhaustive) list of considerations relevant to the question of whether the qualified privilege defence should be available, namely (i) the seriousness of the allegation(s); (ii) the nature of the information and the extent to which the matter is a matter of public concern; (iii) the source of the information; (iv) the steps taken to verify the information; (v) the status of the information; (vi) the urgency of the matter; (vii) whether comment was sought from the claimant; (viii) whether the relevant publication contained the gist of the claimant's side of the story; (ix) the tone of the article; and (x) the circumstances of the publication (at 205).

Reynolds is open to at least two criticisms. Firstly where judges draw on the considerations listed by Lord Nicholls they will be defining standards of good journalistic practice. It is far from obvious that this is a task that they are well equipped to undertake. Secondly the House's decision can be expected to produce uncertainty and so the chilling effect.

By contrast in *Lange v Atkinson and Consolidated Press NZ Ltd* [1998] the New Zealand Court of Appeal, invoking Article 10 of the ECHR, held that defendants can plead qualified privilege vis-à-vis politically significant material communicated to the public. As well as expanding the qualified privilege defence, the Court also sought to forestall the danger of chilling effects. To this end it stated that plaintiffs must, in order to defeat a plea of qualified privilege, prove that the defendant lacked an honest belief in the truth of his or her statements. The decision was subsequently appealed to the Privy Council. The Privy Council remitted the case to New Zealand for rehearing, thus affording the New Zealand Appeal Court the opportunity to consider Reynolds (*Lange v Atkinson* [1998]). While prepared to 'amplify' its earlier decision, the New Zealand Appeal Court declined to follow *Reynolds*. One of the reasons it gave for this decision was the greater readiness of the New Zealand press, as compared with the British press, to behave responsibly (at 398).

Later cases have perhaps redefined the *Reynolds* defence as in effect one of 'responsible journalism' and have emphasised that the law should be regarded as liberalising in favour of press freedom. It has been suggested that there is no longer a need to show a reciprocal duty/interest relationship in relation to the particular material. The public can be assumed to have a general interest in receiving material from the media and the press a corresponding duty to disseminate it. (See *Jameel v Wall Street Journal Europe* [2006]; *Chapman v Orion*.)

There is no agreement as to whether *Reynolds* signals a completely new defence or is merely an extension of the traditional qualified privilege defence with all its baggage. It has been emphasised that the *Reynolds* list of the requirements of good journalistic practice should not be regarded as an obstacle course or applied strictly and pedantically but should be treated as providing general guidelines, allowing latitude for editorial judgement (*Jameel* at [46], [50], [57]). In *Flood v Times Newspapers* [2011] the defence failed since journalists investigating allegations of police corruption did not check their sources adequately and failed to remove the offending article from a website once it became known that the allegations were false.

22.6 Press freedom and privacy

Article 8 of the ECHR states that 'everyone has a right to respect for his family and private life'. Privacy relates among other things to dignity, independence and self-respect and the desire to control personal information (see Section 20.3). There is therefore a clash with Article 10. Before the Human Rights Act 1998 English law had no separate right to privacy and was accordingly in violation of the ECHR (see *Malone v UK* [1984]). At best privacy was regarded as a value that influences specific causes of action, most importantly breach of confidence (see *Wainright v Home Office* [2003]; *Kaye v Robertson* [1991]). Breach of confidence protects secrets and personal information. It concerns wrongful disclosure of information arising out of a confidential relationship. It relates to a range of concerns, some being matters of efficiency, for example commercial and professional confidentiality, others relating to dignity, for example intimate relationships and feelings.

Article 8 forbids a 'public authority' from interfering with privacy. Newspapers are privately owned, so the protection of privacy against the press is an example of a positive obligation imposed on the state to ensure that private bodies also respect human rights (see Section 20.3). In recent years the law of confidence has arguably become assimilated into the more general right of privacy by becoming detached from the need to show a specific confidential relationship. Indeed it is sometimes argued that confidentiality and privacy have been given too much weight in relation to freedom of expression.

An injunction can be obtained for breaches of confidence where the following three conditions are satisfied (*A-G v Guardian Newspapers (No 2)* [1998]):

1. The information is confidential in character. In *Campbell v MGN Ltd* [2004] the House of Lords held that privacy lay at the root of breach of confidence. It was suggested that information is confidential whose disclosure violates 'a reasonable expectation of privacy'. This test was preferred to the stronger one used in some jurisdictions that the disclosure be highly offensive to a person of ordinary susceptibilities (see [21]–[22], [83], [134]–[135]). This includes not only the content of the information but also the situation or relationship in which it is revealed, for example in the home or in a diary. A matter might still be protected even in a public place.
2. The information must have been imparted in circumstances imposing an obligation of confidence; for example it was imparted for a limited purpose. Earlier cases requiring a specific confidential relationship such as family or employment no longer

apply (see *Campbell v MGN*), although such a relationship, for example between ministers and civil servants, will still be sufficient (see Section 23.3.2). The claimant must however establish that the relevant information was acquired in circumstances where a reasonable person would have realised that it was confidential. For example in *HRH Princess of Wales v MGN Ltd and Others* [1993] photographs acquired by the press of the plaintiff exercising in a semi-public gymnasium were held to be subject to a duty of confidentiality.

3. There must be an unauthorised use of the relevant information by the confidant or a third party with knowledge of the confidence and for a purpose other than that for which it was imparted (eg *Prince of Wales v Associated Newspapers* [2006]: diaries written by the Prince making disparaging remarks about overseas dignitaries).

There is a defence (i) that disclosure of the relevant material was in the public interest and (ii) that this outweighs the interest in preserving confidentiality. In cases involving press intrusion privacy is currently given a high level of protection (see *Von Hannover v Germany* [2004]).

Privacy must also be balanced against the right to freedom of expression. As a starting point the courts treat the competing rights as having equal weight, although why this is so is obscure. The clash with freedom of expression is acute in that there seems to be no overarching general principle capable of comparing the two so as to balance the harms caused when one violates the other. Thus the familiar proportionality principle seems to be of little help.

The main technique used by the courts when a conflict arises, for example in relation to press intrusion into the personal lives of public figures, is to look at the impact on each right in turn, asking whether the harm done to the privacy interest is in its own terms more serious than the harm done to freedom of expression taking all the consequences into account, most importantly the effect on the public interest. An important distinction here seems to be between matters which concern the public and matters which the public are merely interested in, such as the private lives of famous people. For example in *Moseley v Mirror Group Newspapers* [2008] what would otherwise have been protected as a private sex party was lawfully made public on the basis that the court considered it to have Nazi overtones.

Again this rough utilitarianism founders upon the problem that there is no common denominator against which to compare the harms and no agreement as to the proper relationship between a person's private and public lives. It is sometimes believed that privacy has been strengthened at the cost of restricting press freedom. On the other hand the public interest in open justice has been strongly asserted. As usual the judges must make a subjective choice. The uncertainty generated by this risks inhibiting freedom of expression.

In *Campbell v MGN Ltd* [2004] the *Daily Mirror* had published information and photographs about the treatment for drug addiction undergone by a famous fashion model. The newspaper's and indirectly the public's right to freedom of expression was balanced against the claimant's right to privacy. The House of Lords regarded these rights as of equal importance and looked closely at all the circumstances with the aim of producing the least harmful outcome. Lord Hoffman remarked (at [51]) that the law had shifted in emphasis from the notion of good faith to that of protecting autonomy and dignity and the control of information about one's private life (see also *Von Hannover v Germany* [2004]). It was held firstly that the fact the claimant had been a drug addict was not protected since she had repeatedly told the media that she was not on drugs, and to that extent had given up her privacy. However it was also held that the details of her treatment should not have been published since these were inherently confidential in nature. Importantly there were no political or democratic values in issue of a kind which supported press freedom. Lords Nicholls and Hoffmann dissented, taking a wider view of press freedom, that a newspaper should be able to add colour and detail to its reporting and that journalists should be entitled to some latitude in the wider interests of a healthy press. A restrictive approach might inhibit the press and so hamper democracy.

In *HRH Prince of Wales v Associated Newspapers* [2007] the Court of Appeal prohibited the press from publishing extracts from the personal journals of the Prince of Wales. These contained his impressions of the appearance and character of the Chinese leaders during an official visit to China. The Court held firstly that the right to privacy arose where there is a 'reasonable expectation' of privacy; secondly that the test is 'whether in all circumstances it was in the public interest that the duty of confidence be breached'. Factors to be taken into account include the fact that the information was leaked by an employee in breach of contract. It is a matter of public interest in itself that confidential employment relationships be protected. It was also relevant that the information made only a 'minimal' contribution to the public interest.

In *Re S (A Child)* [2004] the competition was between press freedom in reporting the identity of the parties in court proceedings and the privacy of a child in care whose mother had been convicted of murdering his brother. The Court of Appeal preferred the press interest. It held that the importance of open justice and drawing public attention to child abuse outweighed the child's interest since the additional publicity would cause relatively limited upset over and above that which had already occurred.

In *Attorney General's Reference (No 3 of 1999)* [2010] the Court permitted the BBC to publish the name of a person who was subject to a retrial for rape as a result of a previous trial in which DNA evidence had been wrongly excluded. Again the public interest in open justice outweighed the harm to the claimant's reputation. The issue of DNA evidence was one of public concern and there were procedures available to safeguard the right to a fair trial.

In *Re Guardian News and Media Ltd* [2010] the Supreme Court overturned an anonymity order which had prevented publication of the names of terrorist suspects whose assets had been frozen by the court. The information was of general public interest and any damage to reputation was not specific. It was assumed that the public are capable of understanding the difference between accusation and guilt.

In *JIH v News Group Newspapers Ltd* [2011] the Court of Appeal said that no special treatment should be given to public figures or celebrities. However where publication of the information was permitted an anonymity order could be made, but only where there was a clear case for doing so.

Breach of confidence protects privacy up to a point but it may be undesirable to shoehorn privacy law into the category of breach of confidence since the two serve different purposes. The purpose of breach of confidence is to protect the information; that of privacy to protect the person. For example the quality of confidence is lost once the material has been released into the public domain, so the claimant cannot get an injunction in respect of publication after that time (*Guardian Newspapers (No 2)*). However a claimant might still be awarded damages, for example where photographs that have been published with the claimant's permission are stolen and republished without permission (see *Douglas and Zeta-Jones v Hello! Ltd (No 3)* [2005]). This is more consistent with a general privacy law than with breach of confidence.

22.7 'Hate Speech'

Hate speech involves attacks on racial, ethnic, religious or cultural groups, including lifestyle matters such as sexuality. Freedom of expression therefore comes into particular conflict with Article 8 (privacy), Article 9 (thought, conscience and religion) and on a secondary level Article 14 (discrimination). Hate speech also involves matter that shocks or offends, thereby raising the overrides of public morality and the rights of others and providing a hard test of the rationales for freedom of expression. It could be argued along with Mill that being offended or shocked is not harmful since it challenges orthodoxy and does not limit freedom. On the other hand there is an argument for suppressing the expression of opinions that offend others where there is a risk to public safety or the welfare of vulnerable groups. However this leads to oppressive or lazy enforcement since it is often cheaper and easier to suppress a speaker than to police those who cause a disturbance because they are offended.

The notion of ideas and information as underlying freedom of expression has enabled it to be claimed that some forms of hate speech should not be protected since they contain no worthy ideas (see *Otto Preminger Institut v Austria* [1994] (Section 22.7.2)). Pornography is also susceptible to this argument. For example the publication of material that is likely to deprave and corrupt a significant proportion of those exposed to it is prohibited (the 'harm' principle) but subject to a defence of literary or artistic merit (Obscene Publications Act 1959). However this elevates the truth rationale for freedom of expression at the expense of that of self-fulfilment and comes close to Berlin's fear of 'positive freedom' (see Section 2.4).

As usual the law must find an accommodation. One way of achieving this is by attempting to distinguish between expressing opinions, however distasteful, and inciting unlawful or harmful behaviour. However in the case of particularly vulnerable groups this line is breached and some forms of expression that are offensive to such groups are also prohibited. The law is sensitive to particular historical circumstances and is not entirely consistent. For example there is protection in respect of racial or ethnic hate expression and to a lesser extent in respect of religion but not in relation to gender or class hate expression as such. There is no known rational solution and public opinion is the ultimate arbiter.

22.7.1 Racism

Racism has been so widely condemned throughout Europe as to amount to a special case. Freedom from discrimination as such is not protected under the ECHR, which expressly prohibits discrimination only in respect of the other protected rights (see Section 20.4). However the International Convention on the Elimination of All Forms of Racial Discrimination (1965) (CERD) has been ratified by most members of the Council of Europe (not Ireland, Lithuania or Turkey). Article 4 of this Convention requires signatories to create offences in relation to:

> all dissemination of ideas based on racial supremacy or hatred, incitement to racial discrimination, as well as acts of violence or incitement to such acts against any race or group of persons of another colour or ethnic origin.

Article 4 also requires states to have 'due regard' to (among other things) the right to freedom of opinion and expression.

Racist expression is not entirely outside the protection of Article 10 but has a low level of protection, usually being outweighed by the need to protect the rights of others and prevent disorder. In *Jersild v Denmark* [1994] the objective reporting by the media of racist abuse was held to be protected by Article 10. The reason for this is the role of the media as a watchdog against obnoxious elements in society. Measures to combat racism are reinforced by Article 17, which aims at preventing reliance on a Convention right to undermine another. It is unlikely therefore that UK law contravenes the ECHR.

The main offences are contained in sections 17–23 of the Public Order Act 1986. A person is guilty if he or she uses:

> threatening, abusive or insulting words or behaviour or displays written material which is threatening, abusive or insulting if (a) he intends to stir up racial hatred or, (b) having regard to all the circumstances, such hatred is likely to be stirred up thereby. (s 18)

Race includes colour, race, nationality, and ethnic or national origins (s 17). An ethnic group can be defined by cultural as well as physical characteristics (see *Mandla v Dowell-Lee* [1983]: Sikhs; *Commission for Racial Equality v Dutton* [1989]: gypsies but not other travellers).

The offences can be committed in public or private places except exclusively within a dwelling (s 18(2)(4)). Public disorder is not required nor is the presence at the time of any member of the targeted racial group. For example the offence could apply to an academic paper read to an audience in a university or club. However there is a defence if the accused did not intend to stir up racial hatred and did not intend his or her words or behaviour to be, and was not aware that it might be, threatening, abusive or insulting (s 18(2)(5)).

It is also an offence to publish or distribute written material in the same circumstances (s 17) and to possess racially inflammatory material (s 23). Similar provisions apply to a public performance of a play (s 20), to distributing, showing or playing recordings and to broadcasting or cable services except from the BBC and ITC (ss 22(7), 23(4)). Broadcasting bodies are governed by special systems of regulation. Contemporaneous reports of parliamentary, court or tribunal proceedings are exempted (s 26).

The offences are arrestable and the police have wide powers of entry and search (s 24). The consent of the Attorney General is required for a prosecution, which might be regarded as a safeguard for freedom of expression (s 27)

There are increased sentences for offences of assault, criminal damage, public order and harassment committed wholly or partly with religious or racial motivations (Crime and Disorder Act 1998, ss 28, 32). At the time of committing the offence or immediately before or after, the offender must demonstrate hostility towards the victim based on the victim's membership (or presumed membership) of a racial or religious group.

22.7.2 Religion

In the context of religion, causing offence seems to justify restricting freedom of expression. Religion is defined to include any spiritual belief but its 'manifestation' must be cogent, serious, cohesive and important. It is not confined to belief in a supernatural entity (*Campbell and Cozens v UK* [1982]; *R (Williamson) v Secretary of State for Education and Employment* [2005]). This invites the decision maker to impose his or her own view as to what is important (see also Charities Act 2006, s 2(3): need not involve belief in a god). Article 9 of the ECHR concerns freedom of religion (see Section 20.4.3). This overlaps with Article 10 but the two may conflict where freedom of expression is used to pressurise a religion or its supporters. The Human Rights Act 1998 requires courts to have particular regard in matters involving religious organisations to the importance of freedom of thought, conscience and religion (s 13). This could be read as authorising religious organisations to violate other rights such as privacy or to discriminate on religious grounds.

The European Court appears to give states a wide margin of discretion in respect of religious matters. In *Otto Preminger Institut v Austria* the state seized a film depicting Christ and his mother as in league with the Devil which offended the Roman Catholic majority in the Tyrol. The Court held that the seizure was lawful for the purpose of protecting the rights of others. Recognising that there are differences in religious sensibilities between states and regions, the Court said that:

> in the context of religious opinion and beliefs ... may legitimately be included an obligation to avoid as far as possible expressions that are gratuitously offensive to others and thus an infringement of their rights, and which therefore do not contribute to any form of public debate capable of furthering progress in human affairs.

This seems to come close to censorship based on majority sentiment. (See also *Wingrove v UK* [1997]: homoerotic imagery discomforting to some Christians; ban upheld with strong dissent.) In this kind of case it is difficult to see how such images prevent a person from manifesting or practising a religion as required by Article 9 but Christianity at least seems to be given a privileged status (cf *Choudhury v UK* [1991]: state not required to criminalise verbal attacks on Islam).

Although the Church of England is closely associated with the state, Christianity as such is not part of English law (*Bowman v Secular Society* [1917]). The main restriction on freedom of speech concerning religion was the offence of blasphemy. This ancient common law offence penalises attacks upon Christianity. It was originally used to enforce loyalty to the state. The common law offences of blasphemy and blasphemous libel were finally abolished by the Criminal Justice and Immigration Act 2008 (s 79).

The Racial and Religious Hatred Act 2006, adding Part 3A to the Public Order Act 1986, creates various offences of intention to stir up religious hatred similar to those already applying to racial hatred (Section 22.7.1). Religious hatred means hatred towards a group of persons defined by reference to religious belief or lack of religious belief. Thus atheists are protected by the Act. Religion is not defined. Threatening words or behaviour are required and, as with other public order offences, conduct taking effect entirely within a private dwelling is excluded.

The Act attempts to protect freedom of expression by stating that:

> nothing in this Part shall be read or given effect in a way which prohibits discussion, criticism or expressions of antipathy, dislike, ridicule, insult, or abuse of particular religions or the beliefs or practices of their adherents, or of any other belief system or the beliefs of its adherents, or

proselytising or urging the adherents of a different religion or belief system to cease practising their religion or belief system.

Since the offence requires threatening words or behaviour it may be that this provision limits the offence to personal abuse. Can threats of hellfire be used as part of an evangelising recruitment drive? Moreover it is arguable that the other public order offences (Section 22.8) adequately protect religious groups. Under the Anti-Terrorism, Crime and Security Act 2001 the penalties for certain offences involving assault, property damage, public order and harassment are increased where there is a religious motivation along the same lines as those applying to racially aggravated offences (s 39).

Under section 74 of the Criminal Justice and Immigration Act 2008 this group of offences has been extended to stirring up hatred on the ground of sexual orientation. Again there is some protection for freedom of expression. By virtue of Schedule 16 the discussion or criticism of sexual conduct or practices or the urging of persons to refrain or modify such conduct or practices shall not be taken of itself to be threatening or intended to stir up hatred.

22.7.3 Political protest

Under the ECHR the limits of permissible criticism are wider with regard to the government than in relation to a private citizen or even a politician (*Castells v Spain* [1992] at [46]).

The old common law offence of seditious libel consists of publishing material with the intention to incite hostility towards the government or its institutions or possibly to promote hostility between different classes of 'Her Majesty's subjects' (*R v Burns* [1886]). During the eighteenth century, which was punctuated by fear of popular uprising, seditious libel was used as a tool of state control in that judges had a wide power to decide what was seditious. Under Fox's Libel Act 1792 this was made a matter for the jury, thus providing a safeguard for the individual in that judges cannot direct a jury to convict and juries do not have to give reasons for their decisions. Seditious libel has now been abolished but echoes remain in the broad discretionary powers that modern law gives to the police (see Section 22.8) under which disagreement with government policy might be regarded by a police officer as evidence of unlawful intent.

There are other offences related to sedition that are little used but because of their vague language remain potential threats against political dissenters. The Incitement to Disaffection Act 1934 makes it an offence maliciously and advisedly to endeavour to seduce any member of the armed forces from his or her duty or to aid, counsel or procure him or her to do so. The Police Act 1996 creates a similar offence in relation to the police (s 91) and the Aliens Restrictions (Amendment) Act 1917 prohibits an alien from attempting to cause sedition or disaffection and also from promoting or interfering in an industrial dispute in an industry in which he or she has not been employed for at least two years immediately before the offence. It is questionable whether these provisions, particularly the latter, are compliant with the Human Rights Act 1998.

Anti-terrorism legislation imposes wide restrictions on political expression by virtue of its broad definition of terrorism (Terrorism Act (TA) 2000; see Section 23.7.1). Terrorism includes any act or the threat of an act that involves serious violence against a person or property or which endangers life or creates a serious risk to the health or safety of the public or a section of the public or seriously disrupts or interferes with an electronic system. The action must be intended to advance a political, religious or ideological cause. (The Counter Terrorism Act 2008 adds 'racial' to this list.) The action must be designed to influence the government or coerce the public or a section of it or an international governmental organisation (added by TA 2006, s 34).

The Terrorism Act 2006 outlaws the publication or dissemination of a statement which directly or indirectly encourages terrorism (ss 1, 2). Encouragement includes 'glorifying' (which includes praising or celebrating) the commission or preparation (whether in the past or in the future or generally) of acts of terrorism in such a way that members of the public could be expected to infer that they should emulate the conduct in question in existing circumstances. However the accused must intend or be reckless as to the consequences of publication and there is a defence that the statement did not express his or her views and did not have his or her endorsement. The offence can be applied to Internet service providers (s 3).

22.8 Demonstrations and meetings

Article 11 of the ECHR confers a right to freedom of assembly and association, with the following overrides: national security or public safety, the prevention of disorder or crime, the protection of health or morals, or the protection of the rights and freedoms of others. Also, 'this article shall not prevent the imposition of lawful restrictions on the exercise of those rights by members of the armed forces, of the police or of the administration of the state'.

Freedom of assembly should be given high protection, being closely related to freedom of expression. Indeed the right to meet in public is particularly important because, unlike many other forms of expression which depend on access to the media and therefore on money or influence, this right is open to all. However public order issues, in respect of which the executive is often conceded a wide discretion, are closely related to freedom of association). Freedom of assembly applies mainly to assembly for political purposes but not to assemblies for sports or other recreational purposes (*R (Countryside Alliance) v A-G* [2008] at [58], [119]; see also *Anderson v UK* [1997]).

The law has developed as a series of pragmatic responses to particular problems and political agendas and has become relentlessly more restrictive in recent years. For example the Public Order Act 1936 was a response to fears of fascism and communism. It was superseded by the Public Order Act 1986, which was provoked by race riots. Further legislation has been aimed at miscellaneous targets of the government of the day. These included anti-nuclear demonstrations, hunt saboteurs, travellers, 'stalkers', football hooligans, anti-war demonstrators, terrorists and animal rights groups (see Criminal Justice and Public Order Act 1994, ss 60, 60AA; Protection from Harassment Act 1997; Crime and Disorder Act 1998; Football (Offences and Disorder) Act 1999; Football (Disorder) Act 2000; Serious Organised Crime and Police Act 2005; Terrorism Acts 2000, 2006). Whether or not all of these are legitimate causes for concern the legislation may be drafted loosely enough to include wider political activities, thereby attracting human rights arguments based on uncertainty, proportionality and discrimination.

This illustrates the weakness of the traditional residual approach to liberty under which according to Dicey the right to hold a public procession is in principle no different from the right to eat a bun. The development of this subject is an example of the creeping erosion of civil liberties of a kind that Dicey did not anticipate. Taken individually each provision may be desirable but taken together they amount to a range of restrictions which, being loosely drafted, could be used for purposes other than those for which they were originally intended.

The notion that everything is permitted unless forbidden is particularly ironic in the case of public meetings. All meetings and processions take place on land. All land, even a public highway, is owned by someone, whether a private body, a local authority, the Crown or a government department. Holding a meeting without the consent of the owner is likely to be a trespass (see *Harrison v Duke of Rutland* [1893]). Trespass as such is not a criminal offence. However the offences of 'aggravated trespass' and 'trespassory assembly' (Section 22.8.1) put a powerful weapon into the hands of the police to remove demonstrators from land. The police can also remove 'travellers' from land under pain of criminal penalties (Criminal Justice and Public Order Act 1994, ss 61, 61A; see *R (Fuller) v Chief Constable of Dorset* [2002]).

The essential question is what are the public's rights in relation to the highway (which includes roads and their verges, footpaths, bridleways and waters over which there is a public right of navigation)? The traditional view has been that the public has a right only to 'pass or repass' on a highway (ie to travel) and also to stop on the highway for purposes that are reasonably incidental such as 'reasonable rest and refreshment' (*Hickman v Maisey* [1900]). In *Hubbard v Pitt* [1976] for example the Court of Appeal held that peaceful picketing by a protest group who distributed leaflets and questionnaires was not a lawful use of the highway. Dicey thought that a procession, but not a static meeting, would usually be lawful because processions comprise a large number of individuals exercising their right to travel at the same time. However the procession could become unlawful if it paused.

In *DPP v Jones* [1999] the House of Lords upheld a right of peaceful demonstration in a public place, although the limits of this are not clear. The defendant was part of a group of environmentalists who were arrested during a demonstration at Stonehenge. The demonstration was peaceful and nobody was obstructed. Lord Irvine LC asserted that the law should now recognise that the public should have a right to enjoy the highway for any reasonable purpose provided that the activities did not constitute a nuisance and did not obstruct other people's freedom of movement. Lords Hutton and Clyde agreed but took a narrower approach, emphasising that not every non-obtrusive and peaceful use of the highway is necessarily lawful. Lord Hutton said:

> the common law recognises that there is a right for members of the public to assemble together to express views on matters of public concern and I consider that the common law should now recognise that this right, which is one of the fundamental rights of citizens in this country, is unduly restricted unless it can be exercised in some circumstances on the public highway.

Lords Hope and Slynn dissented, Lord Hope because of the effect of such a right on property owners who were not before the Court to defend their interests, Lord Slynn because of a reluctance to unsettle established law.

The law of trespass might be used to restrict political activity in premises such as shopping malls. Although the public have access to these places, they are not in law public places and are privately owned, often by commercial companies. The owner can therefore require anyone to obey whatever restrictions the owner wishes to impose and can exclude anyone from the premises. Whether the Human Rights Act 1998 applies to impose a positive duty on the state to protect freedom of expression in such places is questionable. In *Appelby v UK* [2003] the European Court held that the owner of a shopping mall could prevent environmental campaigners from setting up a stall and distributing leaflets. However the Court stressed that they had other means of communicating their concerns. Moreover restrictions must have a rational justification.

Under the Serious Organised Crimes and Police Act 2005 it is an offence to trespass on a site in England and Wales or Northern Ireland designated by the Secretary of State (s 128). Except in the case of land owned by the Crown, which covers most central government land, and by the Queen or the immediate heir to the throne in their private capacity, this power can be used only in the interests of national security. However the courts are reluctant to interfere with the government's view as to what national security requires.

22.8.1 Statutory police powers

The police have wide powers to regulate public meetings and processions. These are supplemented by powers relating to particular places (Seditious Meetings Act 1817, s 3: meetings of 50 or more people in the vicinity of Westminster when Parliament is sitting; Serious Organised Crime and Police Act 2005). The main general police powers are as follows:

- The organiser of a public procession intended (i) to demonstrate support for or opposition to the views or actions of any person or body of persons, (ii) to publicise a campaign or cause or (iii) to mark or commemorate an event must give advance notice to the police (Public Order Act 1986, s 11). There are certain exceptions. These include:
  - (i) processions commonly or customarily held in the area. This only applies if the route remains the same. It is not enough that the time and place of commencement are the same (*Kay v Metropolitan Police Comr* [2007]: mass cycle ride through London);
  - (ii) funeral processions organised by a funeral director in the normal course of business;
  - (iii) cases where it is not reasonably practicable to give advance notice (eg a spontaneous march).
- There is no power to ban a procession for failing to give notice. However, if a 'senior police officer' reasonably believes (i) that any public procession may result in serious public disorder, serious damage to property, or serious disruption to the life of the community or (ii) that the purpose of the organisers is to intimidate people into doing something they have a right not to do, or not doing something they have a right to do, the senior officer can impose such conditions as appear to him or her to be necessary to prevent such disorder, damage, disruption or intimidation, including conditions as to the route of the procession or to prohibit it from entering any public place specified in the directions (Public Order Act 1986, s 12). A 'senior police officer' is either the Chief Constable, Metropolitan Police Commissioner or the senior officer

present on the scene (s 12(2)). Intimidation requires more than merely causing discomfort and must contain an element of compulsion.

- All public processions or any class of public procession can be banned if the Chief Constable or Metropolitan Police Commissioner reasonably believes that the power to impose conditions is not adequate in the circumstances (Public Order Act 1986, s 13). The decision is for the local authority with the consent of a Secretary of State (in practice the Home Secretary), thus injecting a nominal element of democracy.
- There are police powers to impose conditions upon public meetings for the same purposes as in the case of processions (Public Order Act 1986, s 14). For this purpose a public assembly is an assembly of 20 or more people in a public place which is wholly or partly open to the air (s 16). Unlike processions the police have no general power to ban a lawful assembly but can control its location and timing and the numbers attending.
- Section 70 of the Criminal Justice and Public Order Act 1994 (inserting ss 14A–C into the Public Order Act 1986) confers power on a local authority with the consent of the Secretary of State to ban certain kinds of assembly in a place to which the public has no right of access or only a limited right of access. This includes private land and buildings where the public is invited, for example ancient monuments such as Stonehenge, meeting rooms, shops, sports and entertainment centres and libraries. The Chief Constable must reasonably believe that an assembly (i) is a trespassory assembly likely to be held without the permission of the occupier or to exceed the limits of his or her permission or of the public's rights of access and (ii) may result in serious disruption to the life of the community or, where the land or a building or monument on it is of historical, architectural or scientific importance, may result in significant damage to the land, building or monument. A ban can last for up to four days within an area of up to five miles. The ban covers all trespassory assemblies and cannot be confined to particular assemblies.
- Under section 30 of the Anti-Social Behaviour Act 2003 a police officer of the rank of superintendent or above can make an order valid for up to six months within an area defined in the order: a 'dispersal zone'. An order can be made where the officer has reasonable grounds to believe that the presence or behaviour of any persons is likely to result in any member of the public being intimidated, harassed, abused or distressed where there have previously been complaints of such behaviour. An Anti-Social Behaviour Order empowers a constable to disperse any group of two or more people where the constable has reasonable grounds to believe that the behaviour of those persons is likely to result in any member of the public being intimidated, harassed, abused or distressed. There are exceptions for lawful picketing under trade union legislation and for lawful processions under section 11 of the Public Order Act 1986. This power is mainly directed at hooligans but has also been used against political protestors.
- The Serious Organised Crime and Police Act 2005 adds further controls in the case of areas designated by the Secretary of State within one kilometre of Parliament Square (ss 132–38). These are ostensibly intended to protect access to Parliament but also deter effective political protest. In view of the proximity of Parliament this power has a special symbolic resonance as an act of governmental arrogance. However a bill to remove this power is currently before Parliament.

Under the 2005 Act it is an offence to organise or take part in a demonstration within a designated area without police permission, for which written notice must be given if reasonably practicable at least six clear days in advance and in any case not less than 24 hours in advance. In relation to 'taking part' a demonstration can be by one person. If proper notice is given the police must give authorisation but this can be subject to conditions, including limits on the number of people who may take part, noise levels and the number and size of banners and placards. These provisions do not apply to public processions which fall within the Public Order Act 1896 or to lawful trade union activity.

22.8.2 Common law police powers

Apart from the specific statutory powers outlined above, where a breach of the peace is taking place or imminent the police have a wide common law power to arrest anyone who refuses to obey their reasonable requirements (*Albert v Lavin* [1982]). The power to prevent a breach of the peace includes a power to remove a speaker (*Duncan v Jones* [1936]) and a right of entry to private premises (*Thomas v Sawkins* [1935]). A charge of obstructing the police is also possible (Police Act 1996, ss 8, 9(1)) and magistrates can 'bind over' a person to keep the peace.

Before the Human Rights Act 1998 the courts were reluctant to interfere with police discretion. The main consideration was efficiency in giving the police the power to control the disturbance as they saw fit within the resources available to them. Therefore even where a peaceful and lawful meeting is disrupted by hooligans or political opponents the police could prevent a likely breach of the peace by ordering the speaker to stop in preference to controlling the troublemakers (*Duncan v Jones*).

Although the police must act even-handedly (*Harris v Sheffield United Football Club* [1988] at 95) there is a risk that they will exercise their discretion in favour of interests supported by the government or at least supported by public opinion. For example during the miners' strike of 1983 the police restricted the activities of demonstrators in order to protect the 'right to work' of non-strikers, going as far as to escort non-strikers to work and spending vast sums of money on police reinforcements. A cheaper and less provocative policy would have been to restrain the non-strikers (see also *R v Coventry City Council, ex p Phoenix Aviation* [1995]: duty to protect business interests). On the other hand in *R v Chief Constable of Sussex, ex p International Traders Ferry Ltd* [1999] and *R v Chief Constable of Devon and Cornwall Constabulary, ex p Central Electricity Generating Board (CEGB)* [1981] police restrictions on lawful business activities favoured animal rights and anti-nuclear protestors respectively. In both cases it was held that the matter was one of discretion (in the Sussex case this resulted in a breach of EC law).

In *CEGB* Lord Denning MR said (at 832) that there is a breach of the peace 'wherever a person who is lawfully carrying out his work is unlawfully and physically prevented by another from doing it' (protesters lying in front of a drilling machine). Thus passive resistance might be a breach of the peace. However today the meaning of breach of the peace is almost certainly confined to violence or threatened violence (see *R v Howell* [1982]; *R (Laporte) v Chief Constable of Gloucestershire* [2006] at [27]). In *McLeod v UK* [1998] the European Court held that breach of the peace can satisfy the test of legality (see Section 20.4.3) only where the individual causes or is likely to cause harm or acts in a manner the natural consequences of which would be to provoke violence in others.

As a result of the Human Rights Act 1998 the courts have adopted a more interventionist stance. Under the ECHR, the police are required to give priority to freedom of expression as long as the person concerned does not himself commit a wrongful act, unless there is a serious risk of disruption. In *Plattform 'Arzte fur das Leben' v Austria* [1988] the ECHR held, in the context of an anti-abortion demonstration, that there was a positive duty to protect a peaceful demonstration even though it might annoy or give offence to persons opposed to the ideas and claims which it is seeking to promote (see also *Ezelin v France* [1991]; *McLeod v UK* [1998]).

The courts have recently given mixed protection to the right to demonstrate. In *R (Laporte) v Chief Constable of Gloucestershire* [2006] the House of Lords reviewed the police common law powers to prevent a breach of the peace. The police had stopped, searched and then turned back with a police escort a coachload of anti-Iraq war protesters who were travelling to a demonstration at a military site. Although this took place several miles from the site, the police claimed that their powers extended to taking action whenever they reasonably anticipated that a breach of the peace was likely, whether committed by the persons in question or by others. The House of Lords, invoking the importance of freedom of expression and emphasising the increasing legislative constraints on public protest, held that the common law power to prevent a breach of the peace was confined to a situation where the breach of peace was actually taking place or was imminent. Moreover a breach of the peace must involve violence. If this was not the case the police had no power even to take lesser action. It was also held that the police action was disproportionate, in that freedom of expression should be limited only as a last resort and the police should attempt initially to target the actual trouble makers. Lord Bingham regarded *Moss v McLachlan* [1985], where demonstrators were also turned back, as a borderline example of imminence, recognising that the police must have some discretion.

In *Wood v Metropolitan Police Comr* [2009] it was held that the retention by the police of photographs of people not suspected of any offence was an unlawful infringement of privacy (a *Guardian* investigation revealed that the police had been targeting thousands of political campaigners over many years: see *Guardian* 27 October 2009). Lord Collins stressed the chilling effect of the practice on the exercise of lawful rights such as the right to protest.

But in *Austin v Metropolitan Police Comr* [2009] the police detained a crowd, including bystanders, behind a cordon on the highway for two hours in conditions of discomfort in order to prevent a violent demonstration ('kettling'). It was held that the actions of the police did not constitute a deprivation of liberty under the ECHR but only the lesser 'restriction' of liberty (see Section 20.4.1). However in the light of *Gillan v UK* [2010] (see Sections 20.4.1 and 23.7.4) it may be that the exercise of this power violates the Convention as lacking sufficient safeguards.

The police action was also lawful at common law as necessary to keep order at the time. It was stressed however that the lawful exercise of rights can be curtailed only as a last resort and in extreme and exceptional circumstances. The action must be reasonably necessary and proportionate. However once this power is justified the actions of individual policeman can be challenged only if they are unreasonable in the *Wednesbury* sense (see Section 18.1). It is unclear how far the police have a margin of discretion, in particular the extent to which police resources can be taken into account in assessing the necessity of the police action. It was left open whether an arrest can be justified under Article 5(1)(b) of the ECHR (to fulfil an obligation prescribed by law) on the basis that there is a general obligation to obey police orders.

22.8.3 Public order offences

Specific public order offences strike primarily at people who intentionally cause violence, but sometimes go beyond that. They overlap, allowing police discretion in relation to the penalties. Moreover the police and in some circumstances police support officers can arrest on the basis of reasonable suspicion for any offence (Police and Criminal Evidence Act 1984 (PACE), s 24, as modified by Serious Organised Crimes and Police Act 2005). Even minor punishments or disciplinary measures might be condemned under the ECHR as disproportionate or uncertain and so chilling the right of assembly (*Ezelin v France* [1991]).

The main offences are as follows:

1. Under the Highways Act 1980 it is an offence to obstruct the highway and the police can remove the offender (s 137). It is not necessary that the highway be completely blocked or even that people are inconvenienced. Here the accused's intentions are irrelevant (*Arrowsmith v Jenkins* [1963]; *Homer v Cadman* [1886]; *Hirst and Agu v West Yorkshire Chief Constable* [1986]). However as a result of *DPP v Jones* [1999] a reasonable peaceful demonstration would probably not be unlawful. There are also numerous local statutes and bylaws regulating public meetings in particular places.
2. The Public Order Act 1986 creates several offences, replacing a clutch of ancient and ill-defined common law offences (rout, riot, affray and unlawful assembly). However the old case of *Beatty v Gillbanks* [1882], often cited as an endorsement of freedom of assembly, may still apply to them. A temperance march by the Salvation Army was disrupted by a gang, known as the Skeleton Army, sponsored by brewery interests. The organisers of the march were held not to be guilty of the offence of unlawful assembly (replaced by the Public Order Act 1986) on the ground that their behaviour was in itself lawful and the disruption was caused by their opponents. Thus even though in one sense the Salvationists were provoking their opponents the court was in effect ascribing moral blame.

   The offences under the Public Order Act 1986 are as follows (in descending order of seriousness):

   - *riot* (s 1). Where 12 or more people act in concert and use or threaten unlawful violence for a common purpose, each person using violence is guilty of the offence;
   - *violent disorder* (s 2). At least three people acting in concert and using or threatening unlawful violence;
   - *affray* (s 3). One person suffices. Using or threatening unlawful violence is sufficient, but threats by words alone do not count;

     The above offences may be committed in public or in private and the conduct must be such 'as would cause a person of reasonable firmness present at the scene to fear for his personal safety'. No such person need actually be on the scene. The defendant must either intend to threaten or use violence or be aware that his or her conduct may be violent or threaten violence (s 6). 'Violence' is broadly defined to include violent conduct to property and persons and is not restricted to conduct intended to cause injury or damage (s 8);
   - *fear or provocation of violence* (s 4). This offence is wider and includes freedom of expression generally. A person is guilty who uses 'threatening, abusive or insulting words or behaviour or distributes or displays any writing, sign or

visible representation that is threatening, abusive or insulting'. The offence can be committed in a public or a private place except exclusively within a dwelling or between dwellings (s 8). The meaning of 'threatening, abusive or insulting' is left to the jury (see *Brutus v Cozens* [1973]) but the accused must be aware that his words are threatening, abusive or insulting (s 6(3)). The act must be aimed at another person with the intention either to cause that person to believe that immediate unlawful violence will be used or to provoke that person into immediate unlawful violence. Alternatively the accused's conduct must be likely to have that effect even though he or she does not so intend.

In *R v Horseferry Road Metropolitan Stipendiary Magistrate Court, ex p Siadatan* [1991] Penguin Books was prosecuted under section 4 in relation to the publication of Salman Rushdie's book *Satanic Verses*. It was alleged that the book was likely to provoke future violence because it was offensive to Muslims. It was held that the violence must be likely within a short time of the behaviour in question. However whether the other person's reaction is reasonable is irrelevant, so the principle that a speaker 'takes his audience as he finds it' seems to apply. Thus provoking a hostile or extremist audience, as in *Beatty v Gillbanks*, would be an offence, provided that the words used or act performed is to the knowledge of the accused threatening, abusive or insulting to that particular audience (*Jordan v Burgoyne* [1963]);

- *threatening, abusive or insulting behaviour or disorderly behaviour with intent to cause harassment, alarm and distress where harassment, alarm or distress is actually caused* (s 4A) (inserted by the Criminal Justice and Public Order Act 1994). This offence and section 5 threaten freedom of expression in that they move away from the important safeguard that the conduct in question must be threatening, abusive or insulting, applying also to 'disorderly behaviour', an expression which is not defined;
- *harassment, alarm, or distress* (s 5). Section 5 also applies to threatening, abusive or insulting behaviour or disorderly behaviour. It requires only that a person who actually sees or hears the conduct must be likely to be caused harassment, alarm or distress and does not require an intent to cause harassment or alarm or actual harassment, alarm or distress. Violence is not involved. However there are the defences that (i) the accused had no reason to believe that any such person was present; (ii) he did not intend or know that his words or actions were threatening, abusive or insulting, or disorderly (see *DPP v Clarke* [1992]) and (iii) his conduct was 'reasonable'.

The police have a summary power of arrest in relation to all the above offences but under section 5 must first warn the accused to stop. The conduct before and after the warning need not be the same.

It is unlikely that the offences under sections 1–4 are contrary to the ECHR in that they aim at preventing violence. Sections 4A and 5 are more vulnerable. In addition to 'threatening' behaviour they target abusive, insulting and disorderly behaviour which leads to no more than distress. This arguably runs counter to the view of the European Court that conduct which shocks and offends is a price to be paid for democracy (see Section 22.7).

3. Section 1 of the Public Order Act 1936 prohibits the wearing of political uniforms in any public place or public meeting without police consent, which can be obtained for special occasions. 'Uniform' includes any garment that has political significance,

for example a black beret (*O'Moran v DPP* [1975]). Political significance can be identified from any of the circumstances or from historical evidence.

4. Aggravated trespass, aimed originally at anti-hunting protestors, occurs where a person who trespasses on land in the open air does anything (such as shouting threats, blowing a horn or erecting barricades) which in relation to any lawful activity that persons are engaging or about to engage in on that land or on adjoining land is intended to have the effect (i) of intimidating those persons or any one of them so as to deter them or any one of them from engaging in that lawful activity; (ii) of obstructing that activity or (iii) of disrupting that activity (Criminal Justice and Public Order Act 1994, s 68). For this purpose a lawful activity is any activity that is not a criminal offence or a trespass (s 68(2)). There is no defence of reasonableness and violence is not an ingredient. The police can order a person who is committing or has committed or intends to commit an offence to leave the land (s 69). The police can also order two or more people who are present with the common purpose of committing the offence to leave the land. In both cases it is an offence to return within three months. Given the above examples, it is not clear whether passive conduct such as lying down would be an offence. It is likely that this offence would not be subject to a Human Rights Act 1998 challenge in that it derives from property rights, which the courts appear to be keen to protect (see Section 20.4.3).
5. Under the Protection from Harassment Act 1997 as amended by the Serious Organised Crime and Police Act 2005 a course of conduct (meaning conduct on at least two occasions relating to one person or on one occasion relating to each in the case of two or more persons) which the perpetrator knows or ought to know amounts to or involves the harassment of another is an offence. The test is whether a reasonable person in possession of the same information as the accused would think the conduct likely to cause harassment (s 1(2)). Aimed originally at animal rights activists, this provision can be used against political demonstrations in general. Harassment is a wide term. It includes a course of conduct intended to persuade any person not to do something lawful or to do something unlawful and can include 'collective' harassment by a group (Criminal Justice and Police Act 2001, s 44). Thus the anti-abortion protesters in *DPP v Fidler* [1992], who were acquitted because they intended to persuade rather than to prevent women entering an abortion clinic, would now probably be convicted. There are defences of preventing or detecting crime and acting under lawful authority and a broad defence of 'reasonableness' (s 1(3)(c)). This may allow the press to claim that its duty to inform the public overrides the victim's right of privacy. It may also allow religious enthusiasts to evangelise (cf Human Rights Act 1998, s 13; Chapter 19).

Summary

- The justifications for freedom of expression concern the advancement of truth, the protection of democracy and the rule of law, and self-fulfilment. Press freedom is particularly important in a democracy. Freedom of expression involves the state not only abstaining from interference but in some cases, particularly in relation to the press, taking positive steps to protect freedom of expression.
- Freedom of expression may conflict with other rights, notably religion and privacy. It may also be overridden by public interest concerns such as the integrity of the judicial process.

Summary cont'd

- We distinguished between prior restraint (censorship) and punishments after the event. UK law has some direct censorship by the executive in relation to the broadcast and film media. More general powers of censorship are available by applying to the courts for injunctions. These may be too broad in the light of the Human Rights Act 1998.
- Defamation protects a person's interest in reputation. Public bodies are not protected by the law of defamation, although, perhaps unjustifiably, individual public officials are. The protection of qualified privilege is available to the press, although its scope is uncertain.
- English domestic law has no distinct right of privacy which protects interests in self-esteem, dignity and autonomy. Breach of confidence covers some but not all of the ground. However under the Human Rights Act 1998 freedom of expression must be balanced against privacy as an independent right. Both have equal weight in the abstract and the court will compare the seriousness of the consequences in the individual circumstances. Protection for press freedom is based on establishing a public interest in disclosure.
- The relationship between freedom of expression and offence is particularly difficult. Although offence is generally not protected against freedom of speech, this may not apply to religious feelings.
- There are specific protections against hate speech in relation to race, religion and sexual orientation. These have savings to protect freedom of expression but the line is difficult to draw.
- The law relating to public meetings and processions sets freedom of expression and assembly against public order. This is characterised by broad police discretion. A range of statutes responding to perceived threats have created various offences that restrict freedom of expression and give the police extensive powers to regulate public meetings and processions and demonstrations by individuals and groups. The police also have wide common law powers to prevent imminent breaches of the peace. Under the Human Rights Act 1998 these powers must be exercised in accordance with the principle of proportionality in order to safeguard freedom of expression and association.

Exercises

22.1 'Freedom of expression is a trump card that always wins' (Lord Hoffmann). Does this reflect the present state of the law in relation to issues of press intrusion on privacy?

22.2 'In the context of religious opinion and beliefs ... may legitimately be included an obligation to avoid as far as possible expressions that are gratuitously offensive to others and thus an infringement of their rights, and which therefore do not contribute to any form of public debate capable of furthering progress in human affairs' (*Otto Preminger Institut v Austria* [1994]). Discuss the implications of this for freedom of expression.

22.3 'The common law recognises that there is a right for members of the public to assemble together to express views on matters of public concern and I consider that the common law should now recognise this right, which is one of the fundamental rights of citizens in this country, is unduly restricted unless it can be exercised in some circumstances on the public highway' (Lord Hutton in *DPP v Jones* [1999]). Discuss whether there is such a right and what its limits are.

22.4 Jim, a member of the Cabinet, has often written articles in the press explaining the moral merits of vegetarianism. A journalist working for the *Daily Graft* learns from a well-known chef that Jim regularly has lunch at a famous steak restaurant under a false name. The *Graft* publishes this story on its gossip page and on its website. Advise Jim, who denies the story. Also advise him on the basis that the story is true.

Exercises cont'd

22.5 'A function of free expression is to invite dispute. It may indeed best serve its purpose when it induces a condition of unrest, creates dissatisfaction with conditions as they are and even stirs people to anger' (Mr Justice Douglas in *Terminiello v Chicago* [1949]). To what extent does English law recognise this?

22.6 A prominent Bishop has been invited to address a rally which the local diocese holds each year at various locations following a procession. This year the rally is to be held in Phear Park. Police permission has not been sought. A press release announces that the Bishop will argue that homosexuals should be expelled from the Church. He will also claim that Christianity is a distinctively European religion. A rival group, Christians for Tolerance (CT), proposes to attend the rally. CT hires a coach for the occasion. Fearing that there may be violence at the rally, the police stop the CT coach at a motorway service area some five miles from Phear Park. They refuse to allow any passengers to disembark and detain the coach for about three hours, by which time the rally has finished. Discuss the legality of these events.

22.7 Every Sunday George parades outside a local church and addresses passers-by. He urges them to attend the church services, among other things announcing that atheists are unfit to participate in the community. Advise the local Humanist Society, which wants to prevent George's activities.

22.8 Members of the Freedom for Peace Party distribute leaflets in a shopping mall in Westchester every Saturday morning. The leaflets include appeals to the armed forces to refuse to fight in Iraq and praise the seventeenth-century Leveller movement, which was prepared to fight for equality and democracy. Last week security guards employed by the owners of the mall, an insurance company, ordered the leaflet distributors to leave and when they refused to do so removed them by force. Discuss the legality of these events.

Further reading

Ahdar and Leigh, *Religious Freedom in the Liberal State* (Oxford University Press 2005)
Barendt, *Freedom of Speech* (2nd edn, Oxford University Press 2005)
Blom-Cooper, 'Press Freedom: Constitutional Right or Cultural Assumption?' [2008] PL 260
Errera, 'The Twisted Road from *Prince Albert* to *Campbell*, and Beyond: Towards a Right of Privacy?' in Andenas and Fairgrieve (eds), *Tom Bingham and the Transformation of the Law* (Oxford University Press 2009)
Fenwick, 'Marginalising Human Rights: Breach of the Peace, "Kettling", the Human Rights Act and Public Protest' [2009] PL 737
Greenawalt, 'Free Expression Justifications' (1989) 89 CLR 119
Hare, 'Crosses, Crescents and Sacred Cows: Criminalising Incitement to Religious Hatred' [2006] PL 52
Moreham, 'Privacy in the Common Law: A Doctrinal and Theoretical Analysis' (2005) 121 LQR 628
Morgan, 'Privacy in the House of Lords Again' (2004) 120 LQR 563
Nicolson and Reid, 'Arrest for Breach of the Peace and the ECHR' [1996] CLR 764

Chapter 23

Exceptional powers: security, state secrecy and emergencies

The words 'national security' have acquired over the years an almost mystical significance and the mere incantation of the phrase of itself instantly discourages the court from satisfactorily fulfilling its normal role of deciding where the balance of public interest lies. (Sir Simon Brown, 1994)

23.1 Introduction: security and the courts

The rule of law requires that government powers be defined by clear laws and that there should be safeguards for individual freedom. Liberal democracy requires that laws be made by means of a democratic debate and that citizens should be fully informed as to what government is doing. As against this the Hobbesian minimum duty of the state is to safeguard human life by keeping order (see Section 2.3.1). This may involve facing unpredictable events and acting quickly. Hobbes believed that the people must entrust open-ended and absolute powers to government. He thought that the risk of government abusing its power was a price worth paying for security.

Wide emergency powers are particularly prone to abuse. For example political pressures may encourage a government to introduce legislation that removes normal legal safeguards on the ground that the seriousness of the threat requires speedy and decisive action. The 'precautionary principle' developed in relation to environmental protection applies to other risks by insisting that a lack of certain knowledge should not inhibit the taking of steps to combat serious or irremediable harm. This could be a cloak for satisfying the mob, particularly where the emergency involves threats from outsiders or minorities. Moreover it is easier and cheaper to bypass the rule of law than to raise policing standards. History tells us that governments may use the excuse of an emergency as a means of reinforcing their own positions. Marshal J (in *Skinner v Railway Labor Executives' Association* [1989]) remarked:

> When we allow fundamental freedoms to be sacrificed in the name of real or perceived exigency, we invariably come to regret it. (at [635]–[636])

Emergency laws may violate the rule of law and democracy in several respects:

- There may be a temptation to use oppressive methods such as torture or detention without trial in order for example to prevent terrorist attacks. Torture is absolutely prohibited by the European Convention on Human Rights (ECHR) (see Section 20.4.2).
- Parliamentary scrutiny of legislation may be rushed or truncated so that the laws are effectively made by a small group within the executive without the wide process of consultation and checks and balances which both the rule of law and democracy require.

- Vaguely defined powers may target ill-defined groups because the needs of an emergency favour flexibility. The judicial review doctrine that powers must be used reasonably and for proper purposes may be frustrated by the wide terms in which the powers are conferred.
- Safeguards such as judicial review might be restricted.
- Requirements of secrecy in court proceedings may lead to exclusion of the press.
- Evidence in legal proceedings may be restricted, for example by allowing evidence taken by oppressive means or uncorroborated statements by anonymous informers or by altering the burden of proof.
- Jury trial has been removed in some cases (Northern Ireland (Emergency Provisions) Act 1978).
- Random stop and search powers might be implemented.
- Intrusive surveillance is authorised. For example, on the pretext of community protection against local anti-social behaviour, in 2009 the West Midlands police established large-scale CCTV surveillance in a predominantly Muslim area of Birmingham without local oversight and concealing its true purpose, which was national counter-terrorism (see *Guardian* 1 October 2010).
- Powers of detention without going before a court might be extended.
- Minorities might be targeted on the basis that those who do not support majority values are a security risk. For example Lord Rooker, a Home Office minister, stated that:

  > in a tolerant liberal society, if we are not guarded we will find that those who do not seek to be part of our society will use our tolerance and liberalism to destroy that society. (HL Deb 27 November 2001, col 143)

- Measures originally introduced to meet an emergency become permanent. Typically emergency measures are temporary and should contain a 'sunset clause' under which the measure expires on a given date unless renewed by Parliament.
- The executive is given power to alter existing laws.
- Measures intended to deal with serious threats are used against trivial offences or for political purposes. Laws cast in wide terms are not necessarily ambiguous, so ministerial reassurances about the scope of the legislation cannot be used as an aid to interpretation under the *Pepper v Hart* doctrine (see Section 7.8.5).

The rhetoric of human rights that there must be a 'proportionate response' expresses a benevolent aspiration but does not rule out any particular violation of individual rights. The rhetoric of 'balancing' the interests of security and the rights of the individual is also of limited assistance since there is no objective measure to tell us where the balance should be struck. This has led to famous judicial disagreements (eg *Liversidge v Anderson* [1942]).

A state can derogate from some Articles of the European Convention on Human Rights in times of war or other public emergency threatening 'the life of the nation' (Art 15; Human Rights Act 1998, ss 1(2), 14, 15). The state must show that the threat is current or imminent, that the measures do not go beyond a necessary response to the emergency and that other international obligations are not violated. There must also be the safeguard of judicial review by an independent court (*Chahal v UK* [1996]). However protection ultimately depends on the extent to which the court is prepared to accept the government's word as to the needs of the situation. This is a context where the government is given a margin of discretion (see Section 21.5.2). Article 2 (the right to life) cannot be derogated from except in respect of deaths resulting from lawful acts of war, nor can Article 3 (torture and inhuman and degrading treatment). A state cannot itself torture or condone or participate in torture by others (see Section 20.4.2). Article 4(1) (slavery), Article 7 (retrospective punishment) and Protocol 6 (capital punishment) cannot be derogated from.

The definition of 'emergency' is not clear. The European Court has given a wide margin of discretion to member states (see *Brannigan and McBride v UK* [1993]). The criteria are that the threat be actual or imminent, that its effects involve the whole nation, that the organised life of the community is at risk and that the crisis be exceptional so that normal measures are plainly inadequate (see *Lawless v Ireland (No 3)* [1961]; *A v Secretary of State for the Home Dept* [2005]). The last criterion suggests that the crisis must be temporary, although it might be indefinite.

The UK had previously derogated in respect of measures in Northern Ireland. In 2003 it derogated from Article 5 (liberty and security) in order to enable it to detain those suspected of terrorism for relatively long periods without being tried before a court.

In *A v Secretary of State for the Home Dept* [2005], a majority of the House of Lords were prepared to defer to the government on the question of whether an emergency existed but not on the proportionality of the measures (see Section 20.4.4). Lord Hoffmann took a different view. He suggested that an emergency existed only when the basic principles of democracy and the rule of law were threatened and that a high risk of terrorist attack was not in itself evidence of this. Indeed he suggested that government measures of the type in issue were a greater threat to democracy.

Derogation is from the ECHR as such. If as is often suggested the ECHR reflects rights that are inherent in the common law then derogation would not necessarily prevent the courts applying similar principles. However common law rights can be overridden by clear statutory language, short of the 'impossibility' principle that applies to Convention rights under the Human Rights Act 1998 (see Section 21.3.1).

In deciding whether an exceptional interference with a Convention right is justified, the courts are particularly concerned with safeguards to prevent an abuse of power. These try to strike a balance by requiring certain non-negotiable standards based on the rule of law. They include:

- powers being defined in detail by clear publicly announced laws (see *R (Gillan) v Metropolitan Police Comr* [2006] at [31]);
- the safeguards of access to a lawyer and judicial supervision;
- the right to a fair trial, including the right to challenge evidence (*Secretary of State for the Home Dept v MB* [2008]);

On the other hand the courts are prepared to accept evidence given in secret and the use of 'special advocates', state-approved lawyers appointed to act on behalf of suspects (see Section 23.3.4). The suspects themselves may be denied access to witnesses and evidence.

The courts have traditionally been reluctant to interfere with national security matters. This is on separation of powers grounds since, as Hobbes argued (see Section 2.3.1), security matters are pre-eminently the responsibility of the government. The courts also show deference because they have limited access to the specialised knowledge that security matters require, some of which must be secret (see *R (Mohamed) v Secretary of State for Foreign and Commonwealth Affairs* [2010]; Section 23.3.3).

Traditionally the UK courts have regarded matters of national security as non-justiciable, relying on ministerial accountability to Parliament as a safeguard. According to Lord Diplock in *Council of Civil Service Unions (CCSU) v Minister for the Civil Service* [1985], 'national security is par excellence a non-justiciable question. The judicial process is totally inept to deal with the type of problems which it involves.' (See also *Liversidge v Anderson*, although Lord Atkin's famous dissent in favour of individual liberty is now widely acknowledged as preferable to the views of the majority; *A v Secretary of State for the Home Dept* [2005]). However even in the *CCSU* case the government had to show that it was acting in good faith and that the matter (the effectiveness of GCHQ, the government's centre for the interception of electronic communications) was genuinely one of national security.

On the other hand the European Court has emphasised the need for safeguards against abuse as being necessary in a democratic society. It has however given a wide margin of discretion and been reluctant to attribute improper motives to a government (see *Lawless v Ireland (No 3)*; *Klass v Federal Republic of Germany* [1979]; *Malone v UK* [1984]; *Aksoy v Turkey* [1996]; *Brogan v UK* [1989]).

In recent years the UK courts have been more willing to interfere with national security powers, at least on the level of broad principle. The jurisprudence of the European Court of Human Rights has invited the courts to apply the proportionality principle, thus increasing the intensity of review. On the other hand at the level of detail the 'margin of discretion' enables the courts to defer particularly to the government's use of information, its assessment of risk and its use of secrecy since these are matters with which judicial experience is not comfortable (see Poole, 2008).

23.2 State secrecy: access to information

There are two aspects to state secrecy. The first concerns a right of access to information held by government. This relates to the general accountability of government and also, acutely, the right to a fair trial when government withholds evidence in court or inquiry proceedings. Arguments in favour of 'open government' include the following:

- *democratic accountability*: officials should be accountable to well-informed public opinion;
- *autonomy*: people should be able to exercise informed choice in relation to their own affairs;
- *justice*: in being able to correct false information;
- *direct public participation*: in decision making, as a republican idea based on equality and dignity;
- *public confidence*: in government.

Arguments in favour of government secrecy are primarily efficiency based and include the following:

- release of certain kinds of information might cause serious harm, for example to national security, crime prevention, childcare and some economic information;
- expense and delay, bearing in mind that seekers of information may be cranks, enemies or maniacs;
- freedom of information perhaps weakening ministerial responsibility to Parliament;

- frankness within government, for example the danger of policy making being inhibited by premature criticism or the quality of debate being diluted by the temptation to play to the gallery;
- public panic if disclosures are misunderstood;
- self-importance and self-protection by public officials: without secrecy it might be more difficult to make public appointments;
- the mystique of government (the 'dignified constitution'), emphasised by Bagehot as a source of stability (see Section 5.1);
- contemporary policies of privatisation and encouraging public bodies to follow commercial practices, including 'commercial confidentiality', also militate against openness in favour of a protective, defensive culture.

Apart from cases where the principles of natural justice apply (see Section 18.3) the common law gives no right to information. Indeed in *Burmah Oil Co Ltd v Bank of England* [1980] at 1112, Lord Wilberforce did not believe that the courts should support open government. There are however certain statutory rights to information, of which the Freedom of Information Act 2000 is the most general. There are also particular doctrines, such as public interest immunity (Section 23.3.3) and the absence of a general duty to give reasons for government action (see Section 18.5), that reinforce state secrecy.

Access to government information as such is not protected by the ECHR. Article 10 has been said to protect people who wish to disclose information and does not force anyone to do so (see *Leander v Sweden* [1987]). However this takes no account of the democratic interest in the free flow of information which the ECHR has recognised in the context of press freedom (see Section 22.4). There is however a right to information under Article 6 (right to a fair trial) and Article 8 (respect for family life; see *Guerra v Italy* [1998]: environmental risks; *Gaskin v UK* [1990]: adoption records; applied restrictively in *Gunn-Russo v Nugent Care Housing Society* [2001]).

The second aspect of secrecy concerns claims by the state to suppress information held by others, such as the media. Here the state is interfering with common law rights and also the right of freedom of expression under Article 10 of the ECHR. The onus is therefore on the state to justify its intervention. In relation to government information secrecy is reinforced by statutes, notably the Official Secrets Act 1989 forbidding disclosure of certain information, by the civil law of breach of confidence and by employment contracts.

23.2.1 The Freedom of Information Act 2000

The scope of the Freedom of Information Act 2000 is potentially wide. Subject to many exemptions, the Act requires public authorities in England, Wales and Northern Ireland (see also Freedom of Information (Scotland) Act 2002) to disclose information on request and also to confirm or deny whether the information exists (s 1). This is supervised and enforced by an Information Commissioner, who also has advisory and promotional functions. As so often in the UK constitution the Act depends heavily on the ability of the Information Commissioner, a government appointee, to stand up to the government and to be adequately resourced by government. The Act does not prevent an authority from disclosing any information (s 78).

Under Schedule 1 central government departments (but not the Cabinet, the royal household or the security services), Parliament, the Welsh Assembly (but not the Scottish government (s 80)), local authorities, the police, the armed forces, state educational bodies and NHS bodies are automatically public authorities, as are a long list of other specified bodies, including companies which are wholly owned by these bodies (s 6)

The Secretary of State may also designate other bodies, office holders or persons as public authorities which appear to him to be exercising 'functions of a public nature' or who provide services under a contract with a public authority whose functions include the provision of those services (s 3(1)). This might include a voluntary body acting on behalf of a government agency. The designation is controversial in relation to bodies, such as Network Rail (not currently listed), constituted as private companies and run on business lines but with the government holding an interest The Secretary of State can however limit the kind of information that the listed bodies can disclose (s 7). For example journalistic material held by the BBC is exempt. Where a body holds information for mixed purposes only some of which are exempt there need be no disclosure (*BBC v Sugar* [2010]).

The Act gives a right to any person to request in writing (s 8) information held by the authority on its own behalf or held by another on behalf of the authority (s 3(2)). The person making the request is entitled to be told whether or not the authority possesses the information (duty to confirm or deny) and to have the information communicated to him or her (s 1(1)). Reasons do not normally have to be given for the request. However disclosure can be refused if the applicant has not provided such further information as the authority reasonably requires to enable the requested information to be found (s 1), although the authority must provide reasonable advice and assistance (s 16). A request can also be refused if the cost of compliance exceeds a limit set by the Secretary of State or where the request is vexatious or repetitive (s 14). A fee regulated by the Secretary of State can be charged (s 9). The authority must respond promptly and within 20 working days, although there is no penalty for failure to do so (s 10). However if the matter might involve an exemption there is no time limit other than a 'reasonable' time to make a decision. Thus the right to information is far from absolute and there is considerable scope for bureaucratic obfuscation and delay and for lying as to the existence of a document.

The Information Commissioner can require the authority to disclose information either on her or his own initiative (enforcement notice, s 52) or on the application of a complainant whose request has been refused (decision notice, s 50). Reasons must be given for a refusal and the Commissioner can where appropriate inspect the information in question and also require further information. An authority can refuse to disclose to the Commissioner any information which might expose it to criminal proceedings other than proceedings under the Act itself. Both sides may appeal to the Information Tribunal on the merits, with a further appeal to the High Court on a point of law (s 57). The right to information can be enforced by the courts through the law of contempt but no civil action is possible (s 56).

The right to information under the Act is subject to many exemptions (Part II). These apply both to the information itself and usually to the duty to confirm or deny (but in looking at each exemption the distinction should be borne in mind). Some exemptions are absolute exemptions for whole classes of information. Others require a 'prejudice' test relating to the particular document. However this is less onerous for the government than the 'substantial prejudice' that was originally envisaged in the White Paper (*Your Right to Know: Freedom of Information* (Cm 3818, 1997)). Some exemptions are vague, encouraging delaying tactics by officials.

The absolute exemptions are as follows:

- information which is already reasonably accessible to the public even if payment is required (s 21);
- information supplied by or relating to the intelligence and security services (s 23). A minister's certificate is conclusive, subject to an appeal to the Tribunal by the Commissioner or the applicant, which in respect of the reasonableness of the decision is limited to the judicial review grounds (s 60);
- information contained in court records widely defined (s 32);
- information protected by parliamentary privilege (s 34). In *Corporate Officer of the House of Commons v Information Comr* [2009] an attempt to prevent disclosure of MPs' expenses claims on the grounds of parliamentary privilege was unsuccessful (see Section 11.6.2). However information held by Parliament is exempt if the Speaker or in the case of the House of Lords the Clerk of the Parliaments so certifies (s 34(1));
- information that would prejudice the conduct of public affairs in the House of Commons or the House of Lords (s 36);
- certain personal information, although some of this is available under the Data Protection Act 1998 (s 40(1)(2));
- information the disclosure of which would be an actionable breach of confidence (s 41);
- information protected by legal obligations such as legal professional privilege or European law (s 44);
- communications with the sovereign, the heir to the throne and the second in line to the throne (see below).

In other cases the exemption applies only where it 'appears to the authority' that 'the public interest in maintaining the secrecy of the information outweighs the public interest in disclosure' (s 2(1)(b)). The balance is therefore tipped in favour of disclosure. However because this test is subjective the Commissioner's powers may be limited to the grounds of judicial review.

The main exemptions of this kind are as follows:

- information which is held at the time of request with a view to being published in the future (s 22). No particular time for publication need be set although it must be reasonable that the information be withheld;
- information required for the purpose of safeguarding national security. There is provision for a minister's certificate as under section 23 (above);
- information held at any time for the purposes of criminal proceedings or investigations which may lead to criminal proceedings or relate to information provided by confidential sources (s 30). This would include many inquiries into matters of public concern;
- information the disclosure of which would or would be likely to prejudice defence, foreign relations, relations between the UK devolved governments, the House of Commons or the House of Lords, law enforcement widely defined to include many official inquiries, the commercial interests of any person including the public authority holding the information, or the economic interests of the UK (ss 26–29, 31);

- audit functions;
- communications with the royal family. However the Constitutional Reform and Governance Act 2010 has removed the public interest test as regards communications with the sovereign, the heir to the throne and the second in line to the throne, thus giving these communications absolute exemption. Presumably this change in the law protects correspondence from the Prince of Wales, who, according to press reports and a recent judicial comment (see *Guardian* 26 June 2010), has attempted with some success to lobby private and official decision makers, arguably in abuse of his constitutional obligation to avoid partisan politics;
- health and safety matters;
- environmental information (this is subject to special provisions; see Section 23.2.2);
- information concerning the 'formulation or development' of government policy (s 35). This includes all communications between ministers, Cabinet proceedings, advice from the law officers and the operation of any ministerial private office. It also seems to include advice from civil servants. However once a decision has been taken statistical background information can be released;
- other information which 'in the reasonable opinion of a qualified person' would or would be likely to prejudice collective ministerial responsibility or which would or would be likely to inhibit 'free and frank' provision of advice or exchange of views or 'would otherwise prejudice or be likely to prejudice the effective conduct of public affairs' (s 36). This would again ensure that civil service advice remains secret. A 'qualified person' is the minister or other official in charge of the department. Because the test is subjective it appears that the Commissioner would have no power to intervene except where the qualified person's decision was 'unreasonable'. A question here would be whether the minimal *Wednesbury* version of unreasonableness (see Section 18.1) would apply.

Ministers also have power to override the Commission's enforcement powers. In the case of information held by the central government, the Welsh Assembly and other bodies designated by the Secretary of State, an 'accountable person' (a Cabinet minister or the Attorney General, or their equivalents in Scotland and Northern Ireland) can serve a certificate on the Commissioner 'stating that he has on reasonable grounds formed the opinion' that there was no failure to comply with the duty to disclose the information (s 53). Reasons must be given and the certificate must be laid before Parliament. The certificate would also be subject to judicial review.

23.2.2 Other statutory rights to information

Other statutory rights to information are characterised by broad exceptions and weak or non-existent enforcement mechanisms. None of them gives access to the contemporary inner workings of the central government. The most important of them are as follows:

- historical records. Part VI of the Freedom of Information Act 2000 has replaced a series of Public Records Acts. A government document becomes a historical record after 20 years (reduced from 30 years by the Constitutional Reform and Governance Act 2010, Sch 7). At which point, subject to certain exemptions (mainly relating to matters such as legal proceedings and other investigations which directly affect individuals), the document is placed in the National Archives available to the public;

- personal information relating to the applicant held on computer or in structured manual records (Data Protection Act 1998). However the Act exempts much government data, including national security matters, law and tax enforcement matters and data 'relating to the exercise of statutory functions';
- local government information. The Local Government (Access to Information) Act 1985 gives a public right to attend local authority meetings, including those of committees and subcommittees, and to see background papers, agendas, reports and minutes. There are large exemptions, which include decisions taken by officers, confidential information, information from central government, personal matters excluded by the relevant committee and 'the financial or business affairs of any person'. The Act appears to be easy to evade by using officers or informal groups to make decisions. It is not clear what counts as a background paper;
- the Public Bodies (Admission to Meetings) Act 1960 gives a right to attend meetings of parish councils and certain other public bodies. The public can be excluded on the grounds of public interest (see *R v Brent HA, ex p Francis* [1985]);
- the Access to Personal Files Act 1987 authorises access to local authority housing and social work records by the subject of the records and in accordance with regulations made by the Secretary of State (see also Housing Act 1985, s 106(5));
- the Environmental Information Regulations 2004 (SI 2004/3391) implementing EC Directive 2003/4/EC require public authorities to disclose certain information about environmental standards and measures. The information must be made available within 20 days on request but there are no specific requirements as to how this is to be done. A charge can be made. Requests can be refused on grounds including manifest unreasonableness or a too general request, confidentiality, increasing the likelihood of environmental damage, information voluntarily supplied unless the supplier consents, international relations and national security. Under the Aarhus Convention (*Access to Information, Public Participation in Decision Making and Access to Justice in Environmental Matters* (Cm 4736, 1998)) the government is required to make regulations giving a general right to environmental information subject to exceptions on public interest grounds.

23.3 Disclosure of government information

23.3.1 The Official Secrets Act 1989: criminal law

The Official Secrets Act 1989 protects certain kinds of government information from unauthorised disclosure. It was enacted in response to long-standing and widespread criticism of section 2 of the Official Secrets Act 1911, which covered all information, however innocuous, concerning the central government and allowed no defence on public interest grounds (see *Departmental Committee on Section 2 of the Official Secrets Act 1911* (Cmnd 5104, 1972), the Franks Report). A series of controversial prosecutions culminated in the trial of Clive Ponting in 1995, where a civil servant who gave information to an MP concerning alleged governmental malpractice during the Falklands War was acquitted by a jury against the judge's summing up. Ponting's acquittal meant that the government could no longer resist reform.

Section 1 of the 1911 Act, which concerns spying activities, remains in force but section 2 has been repealed. The Official Secrets Act 1989 is narrower but more sharply focused.

It identifies four protected areas of government activity and provides defences which vary with each area. The aim is to make enforcement more effective in respect of the more sensitive areas of government. In each case it is an offence to disclose information without 'lawful authority'. In the case of a Crown servant or 'notified person' (below) this means 'in accordance with his official duty' (s 7). In the case of a government contractor, lawful authority means either with official authorisation or disclosure for the purpose of his or her functions as such, for example giving information to a subcontractor.

In the case of other persons who may fall foul of the Act, such as a former civil servant, lawful authority means disclosure to a Crown servant for the purpose of his or her functions as such (ss 7(3)(a), 12(1)), for example to a minister or the Director of Public Prosecutions but not a member of Parliament or the police since these are not Crown servants. Alternatively lawful authority means in accordance with an official authorisation, presumably by the head of the relevant department (s 7(3)(b), 7(5)).

The protected areas are as follows:

- security and intelligence (s 1). This applies (i) to a member or former member of the security and intelligence services; (ii) to anyone else who is 'notified' by a minister that he or she is within this provision; (iii) to any other existing or former Crown servant or government contractor. In the cases of (i) and (ii) any disclosure is an offence unless the accused did not know and had no reasonable cause to believe that the information related to security or intelligence. The nature of the information is irrelevant. In the case of (iii) the disclosure must be 'damaging' or where the information or document is of a kind where disclosure is likely to be damaging (s 1(4)). 'Damaging' does not concern the public interest generally but means only damaging to 'the work of the security and intelligence services'. This might include for example informing MPs that security agents are breaking the law. It is a defence that the accused did not know and had no reasonable cause to believe that the disclosure would be damaging;

In *R v Shaylor* [2002] the House of Lords held that section 1 did not violate the right to freedom of expression. The accused, a former member of the security services, had handed over documents to journalists which according to him revealed criminal behaviour by members of the service, including a plot to assassinate President Gaddafi of Libya. His motive was to have MI5 reformed in order to remove a public danger. The House of Lords held that the interference with the right to freedom of expression was proportionate. The main reason for this was that the restriction was not absolute. It allowed information to be released with 'lawful authority', thereby inviting the claimant to approach a range of 'senior and responsible crown servants' such as the Metropolitan Police Commissioner and the Security and Intelligence Commission (at [103]). The consent of the Attorney General is required for a prosecution, although it is questionable whether this provides independence.

Lord Hutton (at [99]–[101]) went further than the others in stressing that the need to protect the secrecy of intelligence and military operations was justified as a 'pressing social need' even where the disclosure was not itself harmful to the public interest (cf Lord Scott at [120]). This was to protect confidence in the security services both among its own members and among those who dealt with them. Moreover an individual whistleblower may not be sufficiently informed of the consequences of his actions. Lord Hutton (at [105]–[106]) also rejected the argument that senior officials or politicians might be reluctant to investigate complaints of wrongdoing, holding that the court must assume that the relevant legislation is being applied properly. By contrast Lord Hope asserted that 'institutions tend to protect their own and to resist criticism from wherever it may come' (at [70]).

Their Lordships also stressed the safeguard of judicial review and that a reviewing court would apply a strong proportionality test to a refusal to disclose. Lord Bingham (at [34]) said that he could not envisage circumstances where disclosure would be refused to a qualified lawyer on a claimant's behalf even where this had to be limited to a special counsel appointed by the court (see also Lord Hope (at [73]); Lord Hutton (at [108]–[116]). The Court of Appeal had left open the possibility that a defence of necessity might apply to the Official Secrets Act 1989. This would apply only in extreme circumstances where disclosure was needed to avert an immediate threat to life or perhaps property. The House of Lords did not comment on this issue.

2. defence (s 2). This applies to any present or former Crown servant or government contractor. In all cases the disclosure must be damaging. Here damaging means hampering the armed forces, leading to death or injury of military personnel or leading to serious damage to military equipment or installations. A similar defence of ignorance applies as under section 1;
3. international relations (s 3). Again this applies to any present or former Crown servant or government contractor. Two kinds of information are covered: (i) any information concerning international relations; (ii) any confidential information obtained from a foreign state or an international organisation. The disclosure must again be damaging. 'Damaging' here refers to endangering the interests of the UK abroad or endangering the safety of British citizens abroad. The fact that information in this class is confidential in its 'nature or contents' may be sufficient in itself to establish that the disclosure is damaging (s 3(3)). There is a defence of ignorance on the same basis as under section 1 (s 3(4));
4. crime and special investigation powers (s 4). This applies to present or former Crown servants or contractors and covers information relating to the commission of offences, escapes from custody, crime prevention, detection or prosecution work. 'Special investigations' include telephone tapping under a warrant from the Home Secretary and entering on private property in accordance with a warrant under the Security Services Act 1989 (see Section 23.4). Section 4 does not require that the information be damaging as such because damage is implicit in its nature. There is however a defence of 'ignorance of the nature' of the information (s 4(4)–(5)).

Section 5 makes it an offence to pass on protected information, for example by the press. Protected information is information falling within the above provisions which has come into a person's possession as a result of (i) having been 'disclosed' (whether to him or another) by a Crown servant or government contractor without lawful authority; or (ii) entrusted to him in confidence; or (iii) disclosed to him by a person to whom it was entrusted in confidence. This does not seem to cover someone who receives information from a former Crown servant or government contractor. If this is so the publisher of the memoirs of a retired civil servant may be safe, although the retired civil servant herself will not (but see *Lord Advocate v The Scotsman Publications Ltd* [1990], where section 5 was applied). Nor does the section seem to apply to a person who accidentally finds protected information (eg a civil servant leaves her briefcase in a restaurant). Could this be regarded as a 'disclosure'? It is an offence for a Crown servant or government contractor not to look after the protected information and for anyone to fail to hand it back if officially required to do so (s 8).

The Crown must prove that the accused knew or had reasonable cause to believe that the information was protected under the Act and that it came into his or her possession contrary to the Act. In the case of information in categories (1), (2) and (3) above the Crown must also show that disclosure is 'damaging' and that he or she knew or had reasonable cause to believe that this was so.

23.3.2 Civil liability: breach of confidence

As we saw in Chapter 22 the publication of information given in confidence can be prevented by means of an injunction. As a legal person the Crown can take advantage of this. However a public authority must show positively that secrecy is in the public interest, which the court will balance against any countervailing public interest in disclosure. A public authority can rely on a public interest in disclosure in order to override private confidentiality even where the information has been given only for a specific purpose (see *Hellewell v Chief Constable of Derbyshire* [1995]; *Woolgar v Chief Constable of the Sussex Police* [1999]).

A civil action for breach of confidence may be attractive to governments since it avoids a jury trial, can be speedy and requires a lower standard of proof than in a criminal case. Indeed under the common law a temporary injunction, which against the press may destroy a topical story, could be obtained from a judge at any time on the basis merely of an arguable case (see *A-G v Guardian Newspapers* [1987]).

In *A-G v Guardian Newspapers Ltd (No 2)* [1990] (*Spycatcher*) the House of Lords in principle supported the interests of government secrecy. Peter Wright, a retired member of the security service, had published his memoirs abroad revealing possible malpractice within the service. Their Lordships refused to grant a permanent injunction but only because the memoirs were no longer secret, having become freely available throughout the world. It was held that in principle publication was unlawful since the relationship between the member of the security service and the Crown was inherently one of confidence and that the Crown could probably obtain compensation from Wright and from newspapers in respect of publication in the UK before the memoirs had been published abroad.

The position is probably the same under the Human Rights Act 1998, subject to the limited protection provided by section 12 (see Section 22.3). In *Observer and Guardian Newspapers v UK* [1992]) the ECHR, with a strong dissent from Morenilla J, held that in the area of national security an injunction is justifiable to protect confidential information even where the content of the particular information is not in itself harmful (see also *Sunday Times (No 2) v UK* [1992]; *A-G v Jonathan Cape Ltd* [1975]).

Spycatcher also confirmed that members of the security services have a 'lifelong duty of confidence'. In *A-G v Blake* [1998] a former civil servant had been convicted of spying but escaped to Moscow, where he published his memoirs. The House of Lords held that even though the contents of the memoirs created no danger to national security and were no longer confidential Blake was liable to account for his royalties to the government on the ground that he should not be permitted to profit from his wrong.

The exposure of 'iniquity' (serious wrongdoing or crime) by government officers can justify disclosure (see eg *Lion Laboratories v Evans* [1985]). In *Spycatcher* serious iniquity was not established and it remains to be seen whether 'iniquity' overrides national security. The method of disclosure must be reasonable and the discloser must probably complain internally before going public (*Francombe v Mirror Group Newspapers* [1984]). This suggests that a high standard of evidence is required, given that *Spycatcher* involved allegations of criminal activity against security service members, including a plot to destabilise the Labour government.

A common response by UK officials to those who disclose official wrongdoing is to condemn the whistleblower (see Committee on Standards in Public Life, consultation paper, *Getting the Balance Right*, 2003). For example Steve Moxon, a civil servant who had revealed irregularities in the processing of immigration visas to the press leading to the resignation of the responsible minister, was dismissed for 'an irretrievable breakdown in trust' (*Independent*, 2 August 2004).

The Public Interest Disclosure Act 1998 (Employment Rights Act 1996, Part 4A) protects employees against unfair dismissal in certain cases. 'Qualifying disclosures' are those which the whistleblower reasonably believes relate to the commission or likelihood of commission of any of the following: criminal offences, breaches of legal duties, miscarriages of justice, danger to health and safety or danger to the environment. Internal disclosure in good faith to an employer or responsible superior is protected and also disclosure to a minister or to a person prescribed by a minister. However there is no protection where the disclosure is an offence, for example under the Official Secrets Act 1989, and employees working in national security areas can be excluded (s 11). Exceptionally, an employee can make a disclosure to another person or even to the press. However this must be 'reasonable' and applies only where either the matter is exceptionally serious or the discloser reasonably believes either that she or he will be victimised or that evidence will be concealed, or there is no prescribed person or the matter has already been disclosed to the employer. In the public sector the Act has mainly been used by NHS employees.

23.3.3 Public interest immunity

An important aspect of government secrecy concerns the doctrine once called 'Crown privilege' and now 'public interest immunity' (PII). A party to a legal action is normally required to disclose relevant documents and other evidence in his or her possession. Where PII applies, such information need not be disclosed. In deciding whether to accept a claim of PII, the court is required to 'balance' the public interest in the administration of justice against the public interest in confidentiality. At one time the courts would always accept the government's word that disclosure should be prohibited. However as a result of *Conway v Rimmer* [1968] the court itself does the balancing exercise.

Public interest immunity applies both to civil and to criminal proceedings (see Criminal Procedure and Investigations Act 1996, ss 3(6), 7(5)). Any person can raise a claim of PII. Claims are often made by ministers following advice from the Attorney General, ostensibly acting independently of the government. It appears that a minister is not under a duty to make a claim even if he or she believes that there is a public interest at stake but must personally do an initial balancing exercise. In *R v Brown* [1993] the court emphasised that it was objectionable for a minister automatically to accept the Attorney General's advice.

Where a PII certificate is issued the person seeking disclosure must first satisfy the court that the document is likely to be necessary for fairly disposing of the case, or in a criminal case of assisting the defence – a less difficult burden (see *Air Canada v Secretary of State for Trade (No 2)* [1983]; *Goodridge v Chief Constable of Hampshire Constabulary* [1999]; Criminal Procedure and Investigations Act 1996, s 3). The court can inspect the documents at this stage but is reluctant to do so in order to discourage 'fishing expeditions' (see *Burmah Oil Co Ltd v Bank of England* [1980]). An important aspect of this concerns the duty of anyone mixed up with wrongdoing, even innocently, to make the material available to the court if requested (see *Norwich Pharmaceuticals v Customs and Excise Comrs* [1974]). This raises a dilemma for example when information from informers or from foreign governments is given to the government in confidence (see *R (Mohamed) v Secretary of State for Foreign and Commonwealth Affairs* [2010] (below)).

The court will then 'balance' the competing public interests involved, at this stage inspecting the documents. The court will give great weight to statements by ministers, particularly in relation to security issues, where the separation of powers and the court's relative lack of expertise require deference to the executive (see Section 23.1). The decision is however for the court, taking into account all the circumstances (*Mohamed*).

Grounds for refusing disclosure include for example national security, the protection of anonymous informers or covert surveillance operations (*Rogers v Secretary of State for the Home Dept* [1973]; *D v NSPCC* [1978]), financially or commercially sensitive material, in particular communications between the government and the Bank of England and between the Bank and private businesses (*Burmah Oil*), and the protection of children and relationships with foreign governments.

It has also been said that preventing 'ill-informed or premature criticism of the government' is in the public interest (*Conway v Rimmer*). There is no automatic immunity for high-level documents such as Cabinet minutes but a strong case must be made for their disclosure (see *Burmah Oil*; *Air Canada (No 2)*).

The desire to protect candour and frankness within the public service is arguably not a sufficient justification (*Conway v Rimmer* at 957, 976, 993–95; *R v West Midlands Chief Constable, ex p Wiley* [1994]; *Williams v Home Office (No 2)* [1981] at 1155; *Science Research Council v Nasse* [1980] at 1970: candour a 'private' interest; but *Burmah Oil* at 1132 disagrees).

A distinction has been made between 'class claims' and 'contents claims'. In a class claim, even if the contents of a document are innocuous, the document should still be protected because it is a member of a class of documents whose disclosure would prevent the efficient working of government, such as policy advice given by civil servants or diplomatic communications.

In *R v West Midlands Chief Constable, ex p Wiley* [1994] it was claimed that evidence given to the Police Complaints Authority was protected by class immunity. The House of Lords rejected this blanket claim, holding that immunity depended on whether the contents of the particular document raised a public interest, which on the facts they did not. It is not clear whether the notion of a class claim as such survives this decision since their Lordships rejected the claim only in relation to that particular class of document. However Lord Templeman remarked (at 424) that the distinction between a class and a contents claim loses 'much of its significance'.

A successful PII claim means that there could be unfairness to the individual. Before the Human Rights Act 1998, at least in civil cases, the court did not give special weight to the interests of justice but applied a balance of probabilities test, treating both sides equally. In both respects therefore PII may violate the right to a fair trial under Article 6 of the ECHR. Article 6 contains no overrides except to the extent that the press or public may in certain circumstances be excluded from a trial. Indeed in *R v DPP, ex p Kebilene* [1999] Lord Bingham remarked that 'I can conceive of no circumstances in which, having concluded that that feature rendered the trial unfair, the court would not go on to find a violation of article 6.'

In *Kostovski v Netherlands* [1989] the European Court of Human Rights refused to allow the state to protect the anonymity of witnesses. It applied a test of whether the exclusion placed the accused at a substantial disadvantage. The Court emphasised that the right to a fair trial cannot be sacrificed to expediency. Nevertheless PII as such has been held not to violate the Convention provided that the trial overall is 'fair' (*Edwards and Lewis v UK* [2003]; *Rowe and Davies v UK* [2001]; *Jasper v UK* [2000]; *Fitt v UK* [2000]). In *R v H and C* [2004] Lord Bingham emphasised that PII must never imperil the overall fairness of the trial.

In *R v H and C* the House of Lords specified principles that must be applied, at least in a criminal case, to minimise unfairness. The government must show a pressing social need that cannot be met by less intrusive means. The parties must be given an opportunity to argue the reasons for the claim in open court and also for the procedure to be adopted. However this may not be possible without revealing the information itself. As much as possible of the material must be disclosed, although there may be extreme cases where it cannot be revealed even when a PII application is being made. Where a criminal conviction is likely to be unsafe as a result of PII the trial must probably be discontinued. Lord Bingham remarked that it is axiomatic that if a person charged with a criminal offence cannot receive a fair trial, he should not be tried at all.

R (Mohamed) v Secretary of State for Foreign and Commonwealth Affairs [2010] provides an illustration of the balancing exercise in a security context. In a series of cases the claimant, a British prisoner in Guantanamo Bay, sought judicial review of a refusal by the Foreign Office to reveal the contents of information which it had obtained from the US relevant to the claimant's defence against a prosecution in the US for terrorism. In particular the information might have suggested that UK officials turned a blind eye to torture carried out by US officials. The Foreign Office sought a PII in respect of certain passages in the court's judgment in previous cases which included the information in question.

The Court of Appeal emphasised that only in exceptional circumstances would it override a ministerial statement in a security matter but these were such circumstances. The rule of law and freedom of the press in relation to open justice strongly required disclosure. Moreover the government's reasons for its claim were inaccurate and misleading. According to Lord Judge LCJ there was nothing secret in the material, which carried no threat to national security since it contained nothing that would help a terrorist. Moreover the government's claim that, if it revealed the information, the US would not cooperate in intelligence matters in future had no basis, particularly as the information had already been published in legal proceedings in the US. (This therefore seems to have been a relatively easy balancing exercise since there was a blatant abuse of power by the government.)

23.3.4 Closed proceedings and special advocates

In PII cases and other proceedings involving secret evidence, for example from undercover agents or informers, such as security cases decided by the Special Immigration Appeal Commission (SIAC), terrorism cases and hearings by the Parole Board, the court can use material not disclosed to the accused. This denial of open justice confronts not only the rule of law in the form of the right to a fair trial but also the right of freedom of expression under Article 10 of the ECHR in the sense of the public right through the press to be informed of what is being done in its name. Closed proceeding have long been used in judicial review cases and in *Al Rawi v Security Service* [2009] it was held that closed proceedings could be used in civil claims for damages. There are limits to the use of closed material. The minimum requirements of a fair trial must be satisfied. In particular a defendant must always have access to enough material to be able to answer the allegations against him.

A method of accommodating these conflicting concerns is the device of a 'special advocate'. This is a lawyer appointed by the court and subject to security vetting who acts on the accused's behalf and might see the material but without disclosing it to the parties. A special advocate has no duty to give information to the claimant or to take instructions from the claimant. This device creates serious problems of fairness and raises ethical issues relating to the confidence inherent in the lawyer–client relationship.

In *M v Secretary of State for the Home Dept* [2004] the Court of Appeal reluctantly endorsed the closed process. Lord Woolf remarked (at 868) that the undoubted unfairness involved in this secretive procedure can be necessary because of the interests of national security but that so far as possible the disadvantage must be avoided or, if it cannot be avoided, minimised by the appointment of a special advocate who can object to evidence and to the need for secrecy.

In *Secretary of State for the Home Dept v MB* [2008] the Secretary of State had made a control order under the Prevention of Terrorism Act 2005 (see Section 23.7.5) restricting the claimant's movements. The Secretary of State relied on powers in the Act to exclude the claimant and his lawyers from the proceedings and to exclude material, without giving full particulars of his reasons. The House of Lords held that the power to make control orders was not a criminal matter, so that Article 6 of the ECHR (fair trial) was to be applied less rigorously. Article 6 did not confer absolute rights but allowed a 'fair balance' to be struck between the interests of the community and those of the individual. The use of a special advocate was justifiable on that basis. Nevertheless there was probably an irreducible minimum of fairness, so that if access to the excluded material was essential to enable a person to defend himself or herself the court would be entitled to quash the control order.

In *Secretary of State for the Home Dept v AF* [2008] the Court of Appeal gave guidance on when a trial would be unfair where evidence was not disclosed in respect of a control order. However the approach taken by their Lordships seems to make the matter largely one of discretion. It was held that that as much information as possible should be disclosed but that there was arguably no irreducible minimum beyond which a trial would automatically be unfair. The overall test was whether the person concerned would be exposed to significant injustice. A special advocate can be used. Relevant factors include the nature of the case, what steps had been taken to explain to the controlled person the detail of the allegations and a summary of the closed material, how effectively the special advocate was able to act on behalf of the controlled person and what difference disclosure would make.

It seems that a control order cannot be made on the ground of closed evidence alone. In *BM v Secretary of State for the Home Dept* [2010] the minister ordered the claimant to move to another city under a control order, alleging that there was a risk that he might abscond. The court set aside the minister's decision on the ground that the 'open material' showed no support for the allegation.

In *R (Roberts) v Parole Board* [2006] the House of Lords upheld the use of special advocates in principle but with strong reservations. It could not be decided as a general principle whether the use of a special advocate satisfied the right to a fair trial but depended on the particular circumstances. An accused person must have the opportunity to challenge all the evidence against him. Lord Steyn thought that the special advocate was always a violation as being conspicuously unfair. Lord Bingham described the device as 'taking blind shots at a hidden target' (at [18]) and thought that it could be used only where no serious unfairness was involved, for example where the relevant information could be edited or was not relied upon (at [19]).

(See also *A v UK* [2009]; *Home Secretary v AF* [2009]; Commons Constitutional Affairs Committee, *The Operation of SIAC and the Use of Special Advocates* (Seventh Report, HC 2004–05, 323-I).)

23.4 The security and intelligence services

The 'secret services' comprise the security services, the intelligence services and the government communications centre, GCHQ. Traditionally they have operated under the general law without special powers other than the possibility of royal prerogative power. They were in principle accountable to ministers, ultimately the Prime Minister, but there was no formal mechanism for parliamentary accountability. Their role has been primarily that of information gathering. Where powers of arrest or interference with property were required, the assistance of the police was requested. However the *Spycatcher* litigation (see Section 23.3.2) brought to a head recurrent concerns that security agents were out of control and unaccountable and they have now been placed within a statutory framework. This relies heavily on the discretionary powers of ministers but contains certain safeguards, albeit judicial review is restricted.

The security services (formerly MI5) deal with internal security (Security Services Act 1989 as amended by Intelligence Services Act 1994). They report to the Prime Minister. Their responsibilities include

> the protection of national security and, in particular, its protection against threats from espionage, terrorism and sabotage, from the activities of agents of foreign powers, and from actions intended to overthrow or undermine parliamentary democracy by political or violent means. (s 1)

Section 1(3) includes the safeguarding of 'the economic well-being of the UK against threats posed by the actions or intentions of persons outside the British Islands'. This is extremely wide and could extend for example to the lawful activities of environmental non-governmental organisations (NGOs). The Security Services Act 1996 extends the functions of the security services to include assisting the police in the prevention and detection of serious crime. This includes the use of violence, crimes resulting in substantial financial gain, conduct by a large number of persons in pursuit of a common purpose or crimes carrying a sentence of three years or more. This is wide enough to include political public order offences and industrial disputes and may violate ECHR notions of clarity and proportionality.

The intelligence services (formerly MI6 now SIS and GCHQ) deal with threats from outside the UK. They are governed by the Intelligence Services Act 1994. They are under the control of the Foreign Office but also report to the Prime Minister. Their functions are 'to obtain and provide information relating to the actions and intentions of persons outside the British Islands' and 'to perform other tasks relating to the actions and intentions of such persons'. GCHQ monitors electronic communications and 'other emissions' and can provide advice and information to the armed forces and other organisations specified by the Prime Minister. Reflecting the ECHR their powers are limited to national security, with particular reference to defence and foreign policies, the economic well-being of the UK in relation to the actions and intentions of persons outside the British Islands and the prevention and detection of serious crime (ss 1(2), 3(2)).

Neither service must take action to further the interests of any political party (Security Services Act 1989, s 52(2); Intelligence Services Act 1994, s 2(3)).

Under sections 5 and 6 of the Intelligence Services Act 1994 all the intelligence agencies can enter property or interfere with wireless telegraphy under a warrant issued by the Secretary of State or Scottish ministers. Contravention is 'unlawful' but not a criminal offence. In the case of SIS and GCHQ a warrant cannot relate to property in the UK but the Secretary of State can authorise SIS and GCHQ to carry out actions overseas that would be a crime or civil wrong in the UK (s 7). (This does not of course affect any liability in the overseas country concerned.) In relation to the police support role of the security service a warrant can be issued only in the case of more serious crimes (see Security Services Act 1994, s 5 as amended by Security Services Act 1996). The security services also have powers to intercept communications (Section 23.5).

23.5 Surveillance

The problem of the state amassing information about individuals is of increasing concern because of computer technology which enables large amounts of information to be stored, collated, speedily accessed and transferred without apparent safeguards. Thus proposals innocuous in themselves, such as the introduction of identity cards (Identity Cards Act 2006), are viewed with suspicion not only because of the risk of abuse of power but also because of the risk of errors and accidents.

There is no common law right to privacy as such (see Section 22.6). Provided that no trespass occurred the use by the police of telephone tapping and other covert surveillance devices were therefore lawful (*Malone v Metropolitan Police Comr* [1979]). As a general rule unlawfully obtained evidence is admissible in court subject to a test of reliability (Police and Criminal Evidence Act 1984, s 78; *Schenk v Switzerland* [1988]; *R v Sang* [1979]; *R v Khan* [1997]; *Jones v University of Warwick* [2003]). However evidence obtained by telephone tapping cannot be used in court (see below).

The right to privacy now depends on the Human Rights Act 1998. The European Court of Human Rights has held that under Article 8 of the ECHR (privacy) there must be safeguards in respect of surveillance. These must include clearly defined limits on the power and supervision by an independent court (*Malone v UK* [1984]; *Khan v UK* [2001]). Moreover retaining data falling within Article 8 after it has been used for the authorised purposes is a violation unless there is a particular reason for suspicion against that person (*Amman v Switzerland* [2000]). In *Halford v UK* [1997] it was held that the UK was in breach of Article 8 by failing to regulate the use of interception devices by employers. In *JH Ltd v UK* [2001] the European Court held that bugging in a police station was a violation of the right to privacy.

The Regulation of Investigatory Powers Act 2000 (RIPA), which largely supersedes the Interception of Communications Act 1985, responds to the ECHR. It includes not only the police and intelligence services but also the revenue and military services and can be extended by the Secretary of State to other public bodies such as local councils. RIPA authorises telephone tapping and intercepting electronic data such as emails and websites both on public and private systems. It also creates new powers of surveillance by making clear that certain forms of interception and uses of information are lawful, including bugging devices. However, notwithstanding the Act, eavesdropping upon lawyer–client communications may still be unlawful as an affront to the rule of law (see *R v Grant* [2005] at [52]).

RIPA does not apply to CCTV cameras used in public places, these being outside specific statutory regulation. The use of CCTV cameras by local authorities is authorised by section 163 of the Criminal Justice and Public Order Act 1994. The use of CCTV cameras by private persons might arguably be restricted in particular circumstances by the developing law of privacy on the basis that there may not be a sufficiently strong public interest supporting their use (see Section 22.6.; *Campbell v MGN* [2004]; *Peck v UK* [2003]). In its Protection of Freedoms Bill the present government proposes to bring CCTV cameras under regulation based on proportionality as part of its promise to repair the damage to civil liberties allegedly committed by the previous government.

RIPA distinguishes between 'directed surveillance' which is covert surveillance undertaken as part of a specific operation to obtain private information about a person (s 26) and 'intrusive surveillance'. Intrusive surveillance is covert surveillance carried out in relation to anything taking place on residential premises or in a private vehicle where there is an individual planted or a covert surveillance device is used. Intrusive surveillance can be carried out only in the interests of national security or for preventing or detecting serious crime or in the interests of the economic well-being of the country. RIPA also regulates the use of covert human intelligence (ss 26, 29). This includes undercover officers, spies and informers.

Intrusive surveillance must be authorised by the heads of the government agency in question. In the case of the police and customs agencies there must also be the approval of a Surveillance Commissioner (s 36). Authorisation by the armed services, the intelligence services and the Ministry of Defence requires the approval of the Secretary of State. The authorising officer can appeal to the Chief Surveillance Commissioner against a refusal by a Commissioner, but not by the Secretary of State, to approve an authorisation. A person 'aggrieved' by an authorisation can complain to the Investigatory Powers Tribunal (s 65).

Directed surveillance and use of covert human intelligence can be authorised by a range of public bodies designated by the Secretary of State, including government agencies, the police and local authorities (see SI 2003/3171). It can be used if 'necessary' and 'proportionate' for a wide range of purposes within the overrides to Article 8 of the ECHR (s 28). These purposes include national security, the prevention and detection of serious crime, the safeguarding of the economic well-being of the country and – but only in the case of conduct other than interception – the safeguarding of public health, public safety, tax collection, protecting life and health in emergencies and 'other purposes specified by the Secretary of State' (s 22). There is a evidence that low-level public bodies such as local councils may apply powers casually. Local authorities allegedly used directed surveillance powers more than 8,500 times during 2008 and 2009 to combat relatively trivial matters such as dropping litter, car parking and sickness claims. Less than 5 per cent resulted in prosecutions (see *Guardian* 24 May 2010).

By virtue of section 1(1) of RIPA it is an offence intentionally and without lawful authority to intercept a communication while it is being transmitted by means of a public postal service or a public telecommunications system, including email. It is also an offence intentionally and without lawful authority to intercept a communication transmitted through a private telecommunications system (eg a company network, cordless phone or pager) except by the controller of the system or with his or her consent (see *R v Sargent* [2003]).

The obtaining and use of electronic 'communications data' (emails) can be authorised by a wide range of officials without prior judicial control (RIPA, Part 1, ch 2). Communications data does not include the content of a message but includes 'traffic information' such as billing data and the source and destination. The Secretary of State can require persons operating public postal or telecommunications systems (which includes Internet service providers) to keep a reasonable 'interception capability' (s 12(1)) and to provide traffic data to designated public officials on demand (s 22(4)). Under section 102 of the Anti-Terrorism, Crime and Security Act 2001 the Secretary of State can issue codes of practice authorising retention of communications data and making it admissible in court for the purposes of safeguarding national security, the prevention and detection of crime or the prosecution of offenders. However blanket storage of personal information unrelated to a specific investigation may violate the ECHR.

RIPA empowers anyone in lawful possession of intercepted information to require the disclosure of the key to protected (encrypted) data on the grounds of national security, serious crime and, more dubiously, that it is necessary for the performance of a public function (s 49). The UK is the only leading democracy to allow this. A disclosure notice must be authorised by a circuit judge, who must be satisfied that there is no other means of obtaining the required information and that the direction is proportionate to what is sought to be achieved. A disclosure notice requested by the police, the security services or the customs and excise commissioners can also contain 'tipping off' provisions imposing a lifelong secrecy requirement as to the existence of the notice (s 54).

The ordinary courts are largely excluded. Evidence cannot normally be given suggesting that there has been telephone tapping, lawful or otherwise (RIPA, ss 17, 18). Information obtained by telephone tapping is not therefore admissible, thus encouraging the government to seek to detain terrorist suspects without trial (see Section 23.7.5). Information obtained from telephone tapping can be used in police interviews and presumably by the executive for other purposes (*R v Sargent* [2003]). Information obtained from overseas surveillance is admissible (*R v P* [2001]), as is information obtained by bugging devices, CCTV and undercover agents (*R v Khan (Sultan)* [1996]).

There are limited independent safeguards. The Secretary of State is responsible for ensuring that interception warrants are issued for proper purposes (s 15). The Directors General of each of the security and intelligence services are responsible as both poacher and gamekeeper for the efficiency of their service and for making 'arrangements' for securing that information is neither obtained nor disclosed 'except in so far as is necessary for the proper discharge of its functions' or, in the case of disclosure, for the prevention or detection of serious crime.

There is an Intelligence Services Commissioner who reviews the exercise of the various powers of investigation and use of material under the legislation (Regulation of Investigatory Powers Act 2000, ss 57, 59). The Commissioner, who must be a senior judge, has no enforcement powers and reports to the Prime Minister, who must lay the Commissioner's annual reports before Parliament. Interception Commissioners and Surveillance Commissioners have similar status and functions. There is also an Intelligence and Security Committee composed of backbench members of Parliament, which examines the spending, administration and policy of the intelligence services (Intelligence Services Act 1994, s 11). However this is appointed by and reports to the Prime Minister and is not strictly speaking a committee of Parliament with a duty to Parliament itself. Its annual report is laid before Parliament but can be censored by the Prime Minister after consultation with the Committee.

RIPA creates an Investigatory Powers Tribunal to hear allegations of misuse of power by the security and intelligence services and also in relation to the interference with property, interception of communications, covert surveillance or misuse of information by the police and other bodies (s 65). The Tribunal is also concerned with claims based on human rights, for which it has been designated as the only forum (see Human Rights Act 1998, s 7). The Tribunal may award compensation and quash warrants or authorisations and order records to be destroyed (ibid). The Tribunal is required to apply judicial review principles (s 67). In view of the wide powers involved this affords only a low level of review. However the designation as the only forum has been upheld as proportionate because the tribunal's procedure is flexible enough to protect the right in question. (See *A v B* [2010]: former security services member wishing to publish book.)

Decisions of the Tribunal and the Commissioners cannot be questioned in the courts even on jurisdictional grounds (Intelligence Services Act 1994, s 5(4); RIPA, s 67(8)). In the case of the intelligence services, the Tribunal may, where it does not decide in favour of the complainant, refer a matter to the Commissioner to investigate 'whether the service has in any other respect acted unreasonably in relation to the complainant or his property'. The Commissioner may then report to the Secretary of State, who can make an award of compensation (Schedule 1(7)).

The use of covert surveillance devices by the police is also regulated by the Police Act 1997 and the two regimes overlap. Part III of the 1997 Act authorises the police to interfere with property for the purpose of preventing or detecting 'serious crime'. For this purpose serious crime means crimes involving the use of violence, substantial financial gain or conduct by a large number of persons in pursuit of a common purpose (s 93(4)). Thus political demonstrators may be vulnerable. In a gesture towards human rights language the action must be 'necessary' and 'proportionate'. The action taken can include maintaining or retrieving surveillance equipment authorised under RIPA. The exercise of the power must be authorised by a designated senior police officer, military officer, customs and revenue officer or officer of certain other law enforcement agencies.

In certain cases the authorisation must be by a Commissioner (above). This includes dwellings, hotel bedrooms and offices and matters likely to involve legal professional privilege, confidential personal information or confidential journalistic material. Where residential premises are involved these would also constitute 'intrusive surveillance' under RIPA. The 1997 Act also imposes duties on private communication providers such as Internet service providers to cooperate with the authorities.

23.6 Emergency powers

As we saw in Chapter 22 the police have a general power to prevent a breach of the peace. There is no legal obstacle to the armed forces or indeed anyone else being used in support of this. Indeed perhaps everyone has a duty to aid the civil power in quelling a disturbance (*Charge to the Bristol Grand Jury* [1832]). An individual, whether policeman, soldier or private person, acting in self-defence is however liable for the excessive use of force, thus illustrating Dicey's version of the rule of law (see Section 6.4.2). The force used must be no more than is reasonable in the circumstances for self-defence or the defence of others (see Criminal Law Act 1967, s 3). In deciding what is reasonable the court will take into account the pressure of the circumstances (see *Attorney General for Northern Ireland's Reference (No 1)* [1975]; *McCann v UK* [1995]). However obedience to orders as such is probably not a defence (*Keighley v Bell* [1866]) but should be taken into account as an aspect of reasonableness.

Under the royal prerogative the armed forces can be deployed at the discretion of the Crown and the Crown can also arm the police (see Section 14.6.1). The Crown may also enter private property in an emergency but must pay compensation for any damage caused other than in wartime (War Damage Act 1965; *Saltpetre Case* [1607]; *A-G v De Keyser's Royal Hotel* [1920]). The Secretary of State for Defence is politically accountable to Parliament for the use of these powers.

Beyond this is the possibility that where there is such a serious disruption to public order that the courts cannot function, the military may assume control under a state of martial law. Dicey denied that martial law is part of English law (1915, ch 8). However the concept has been used and indeed applied where the courts were still sitting in relation to colonial territories (*Marais v General Officer Commanding* [1902]). Martial law was declared in Ireland in 1920 and the House of Lords accepted the possibility that the courts could in principle control the activities of the military under martial law (*Re Clifford and O'Sullivan* [1921]). It is arguable that martial law is no more than an application of the broad doctrine of necessity which justifies the deployment of the armed forces. The courts are unlikely to interfere with such decisions (*Chandler v DPP* [1964]; see Section 19.7.1).

Exceptional executive powers can be conferred by emergency regulations (Civil Contingencies Act 2004). This might override any overlapping prerogative powers (see Section 14.6.5). Regulations can be made by Order in Council (or if this would cause serious delay by a senior minister) if the relevant authority is satisfied that an emergency exists or is imminent, that there is an urgent need to deal with it and that existing legislation is inadequate for the purpose. The regulations must be in 'due proportion' (ss 20, 21). Thus there need be no declaration of a formal state of emergency or approval by Parliament to trigger the powers. However the powers lapse unless approved by Parliament within 7 days (s 27) and must be renewed at 30-day intervals (s 27(4)).

An emergency is more widely defined than for the purpose of derogating from the ECHR (see Section 23.1). An emergency means:

> an event or situation which threatens serious damage to human welfare or the environment in the United Kingdom or in a part or region, or war or terrorism which threatens serious damage to the security of the United Kingdom. (s 19(1))

These threats are widely drawn. Human welfare includes loss of life, illness or injury, homelessness, property damage, disruption of supplies of money, food, water, energy and fuel, or disruption of a communication system, facilities for transport or health services. Environmental damage is limited to biological, chemical or radioactive contamination or disruption to or destruction of plant or animal life (s 19(2)–(3)). An emergency might include for example a general strike, a natural disaster or epidemic or terrorist threat.

Parliament must meet within 5 days and the regulations lapse unless approved by Parliament within 7 days and in any event after 30 days. In both cases they can be renewed (ss 26, 27).

The Act allows ministers to alter statutes. It confers powers to deploy the armed forces, to require people to perform unpaid functions and to provide information, to restrict freedom of movement and assembly, to take or destroy property without compensation (s 22) and to extend the power to detain without trial. There are safeguards based on the ECHR. These include proportionality and compliance with Convention rights. The powers can be used only for the specific purpose of dealing with the threats created by the emergency. There can be no military conscription or outlawing of industrial action. No offence can be created except one triable summarily by magistrates or the Sheriff's Court in Scotland and not punishable with more than three months' imprisonment. Criminal procedure cannot be altered, nor the Human Rights Act 1998 (s 23). Judicial review is not specifically preserved but 'regard' must be had to its importance (s 22(5)).

The emergency regulations are delegated legislation and as such are subject to the general law of judicial review and to the Human Rights Act 1998. Thus although somewhat unfocused the emergency regime is subject to traditional safeguards.

23.7 Anti-terrorism measures

The UK's anti-terrorism laws illustrate the phenomenon of 'creep' as increasingly wide powers introduced in response to specific events become absorbed into the general law. They also illustrate the importance of safeguards comprising access to independent courts, monitoring bodies and parliamentary mechanisms. However these reassuring forms may help to legitimise harsh laws.

Since terrorist actions usually constitute ordinary crimes such as murder there is a problem in treating terrorism as a special case calling for special powers, even though certain features of terrorism, notably large-scale secretive and undiscriminating attacks, call for exceptional investigation and enforcement activity and for offences to be defined so as to prevent harm in advance. The problem lies in giving terrorism a political dimension in order to justify special measures. The rhetoric of 'war on terrorism' is substituted for that of law enforcement. This rhetoric may encourage the very terrorism that it seeks to combat. It has been widely recognised that:

> situations involving mass and flagrant violations of human rights and fundamental freedoms ... may give rise to international terrorism and may endanger international peace and security. (UN General Assembly Resolution A/RES/40/61, 9 December 1985, para 9)

Raising the political temperature may also lead to hasty, impetuous dramatic gestures that result in inadequate evidence for a successful prosecution and may create martyrs. For example in 2008 a failure to obtain a conviction in relation to an alleged plot to bomb aircraft was at least partly the result of US agencies prematurely detaining a suspect currently under surveillance by British police (see *Guardian* 10 September 2008).

Moreover the width of the powers means that they may be used against non-violent people whose activities the government dislikes or whom the police or local officials find it convenient to target. For example anti-terrorist legislation was used to remove a member who objected to the invasion of Iraq from a Labour Party conference (see *Guardian* 8 October 2005).

Special anti-terrorism laws were originally enacted as emergency provisions in response to the conflict in Northern Ireland. The Northern Ireland (Emergency Provisions) Act 1978 (EPA) and the Prevention of Terrorism (Temporary Provisions) Act 1974 (PTA) created new offences and wider police investigation powers. These Acts created two distinct anti-terrorism regimes in the UK since there were now additional measures in Northern Ireland (eg trial without a jury and detention without trial). The EPA and PTA were intended to be temporary and only apply to terrorism cases but between 1973 and 2000 these Acts were repeatedly re-enacted, extended and modified. The PTA 1984 was expanded to cover international terrorism associated with Northern Ireland, and further offences and police powers were added. During this period some of the powers in the PTAs and EPAs were mirrored in new laws to deal with ordinary crime. Thus the extraordinary powers had become ordinary.

In response to the peace process in Northern Ireland a review of the anti-terrorism laws was undertaken to ensure they were suitable for countering future terrorism threats. In 1996 the Lloyd Report (*Inquiry into Legislation against Terrorism* (Cm 3420, 1996)) recommended wide-ranging changes, including the harmonisation of anti-terrorism laws across the UK, the expansion of these powers to all domestic and international terrorism and a new definition of terrorism. Many of these recommendations were enacted in the Terrorism Act 2000 (TA) which applied to the whole of the UK.

After the attacks in the US in September 2001 the TA was considered to be inadequate. In 2001 the Anti-Terrorism, Crime and Security Act 2001 (ATCSA) was enacted in unseemly haste. It was controversial, in particular introducing indefinite detention of non-UK nationals (s 23), and not all the powers were restricted to terrorism investigations. Because of its controversial nature, indefinite detention was subject to a 'sunset provision', automatically expiring after a prescribed time (see s 29: 15 months). This is one of the fundamental safeguards against the misuse of emergency powers since it ensures democratic debate.

The government's inability to secure the re-enactment of indefinite detention led to the enactment of the Prevention of Terrorism Act 2005, which introduced an alternative: control orders. However these have proven almost as controversial and are currently being reconsidered (see Section 23.7.5). The hasty and panic-fuelled retreat from human rights norms that typifies anti-terrorism legislation has generated considerable litigation and has been continued in the legislation introduced after the London bombings in July 2005. The Terrorism Act 2006 extended pre-charge detention (s 23) and introduced new offences that are widely feared to restrict free speech (ss 1–3) (see Section 22.7.3). It also introduced the offences of preparation of terrorist acts (s 5) and training for terrorism (s 6). The Treasury has power to freeze the assets of suspected terrorists (ATCSA 2001; see Section 23.7.6). The Counter Terrorism Act 2008 introduced measures which largely tightened up existing powers.

23.7.1 Definition of terrorism

The definition of terrorism (TA 2000, s 1) is complex, 'sweepingly broad and extraordinarily vague' (Richards J in *R (Kurdistan Workers' Party) v Secretary of State for the Home Dept* [2002]). It has three elements.

Firstly there must be an act or the threat of an act that falls into one of five categories:

- serious violence against a person;
- serious violence against property;
- endangers life;
- serious risk to the health or safety of the public or a section of the public;
- seriously disrupts or interferes with an electronic system.

Secondly the action must be intended to advance a political, religious or ideological cause. (The Counter Terrorism Act 2008 adds 'racial' to this list.)

Thirdly the action must be designed to influence the government or coerce the public or a section of it or an international governmental organisation (added by TA 2006, s 34). It is not necessary for the action to be carried out on UK soil, against a UK citizen or property owned by a UK citizen.

The breadth of the definition means that attacks or threats against any government anywhere can be investigated by British police. This would include people resident in the UK who are active political agitators against other states. Thus it is possible that the TA could be used to police international politics, raising grave questions of traditional liberties. The vagueness of the definition means that it could include a wide variety of actions and persons, some of which might not necessarily be a significant threat to national security. For example the definition could apply to environmental protestors who chain themselves to trees in order to obstruct the building of a motorway through a wildlife habitat.

This breadth of definition would therefore permit the use of the legislation in situations where the low threat of violence does not justify specialised powers and offences. During the Terrorism Bill's passage through Parliament, Jack Straw, the Home Secretary, conceded that the definition granted considerable discretion to the enforcement agencies (SC Deb (D) 18 January 2000, col 22). Given the breadth of the definition, the ministers and the police have the key roles in deciding who is or is not a terrorist.

23.7.2 Proscription

One of the key elements of the anti-terrorism regime is the banning of terrorist organisations. It is an offence to belong to or to support a proscribed organisation (TA 2000, ss 11, 12). The proscribed organisations are listed in Schedule 2 of the TA 2000 or have the same name as one listed or are proscribed by statutory instrument. The organisation remains proscribed irrespective of any change in name (TA 2006, s 21).

The Home Secretary can add other organisations to the list if she believes the organisation is 'concerned in terrorism' (TA 2000, s 3; TA 2006, s 21). This means committing or participating in acts of terrorism, preparing for terrorism, promoting, encouraging or unlawfully 'glorifying' terrorism or otherwise being concerned with terrorism. Glorifying terrorism, which includes praise or celebration, is unlawful if it can reasonably be inferred to refer to conduct that should be emulated in present circumstances. The Home Secretary does not apparently have to show reasonable grounds for her belief.

It is an offence to be or to profess to be a member of a proscribed organisation (s 11) or to invite support for a proscribed organisation (s 12) (see *Attorney General's Reference (No 4 of 2002)* [2005]). In the case of Northern Ireland a statement by a senior police officer that in his opinion the accused belongs to a proscribed organisation, although it is not sufficient by itself, is sufficient supporting evidence to justify a conviction (s 108). However this may contravene the right to a fair trial under the Human Rights Act 1998.

The organisation or someone affected by the proscription can apply to the Secretary of State to de-proscribe the organisation. There is a further right of appeal to the Proscribed Organisations Appeal Commission (POAC) established under the TA 2000 but this appeal can only apply the rules of judicial review (s 5). The POAC is appointed by the Lord Chancellor and includes an appellate court judge. The Lord Chancellor can make rules permitting its proceedings to be held in secret and for evidence to be withheld from the parties and their representatives (TA 2000, Sch 3). There is a further right of appeal to the Court of Appeal but this requires the permission of the Court (s 6). Judicial review is otherwise excluded (see *Kurdistan Workers' Party*).

It is an offence to express support or invite support for a proscribed organisation, to address a meeting (of three or more persons) with the purpose of encouraging support for a proscribed organisation or furthering its activities, or to arrange or help to arrange a meeting which the person knows supports or furthers the activities of a proscribed organisation or which is addressed by a person who belongs to or professes to belong to a proscribed organisation, irrespective of the subject of the meeting (s 12). In the case of a private meeting there is a defence that the person has no reasonable cause to believe that the address would support a proscribed organisation or further its activities.

A remnant of the legislation's roots in the Northern Ireland conflict (where mass parades were held with men and women in paramilitary uniforms of flak jackets and berets) is the crime of wearing clothing or an item in public that would arouse reasonable suspicion the person is a member of a proscribed organisation (s 13). These laws on proscription are serious restrictions on freedom of expression and were controversial when they were first enacted but have come to be viewed as necessary and are among the least problematic of the anti-terrorism laws.

23.7.3 Arrest and pre-charge detention

A constable may arrest without warrant and search a person whom he reasonably suspects to be a terrorist, that is someone who has committed a terrorist offence or is concerned in the commission, preparation or instigation of acts of terrorism (ss 41, 43(2)). It is not clear whether 'reasonably suspects' has the same meaning as 'suspects on reasonable grounds', which is the text for an ordinary arrest. Arguably 'reasonably' in this context means in accordance with proportionality. Unlike ordinary powers of arrest this power does not tie the arrest to a specific offence (*R v Officer in Charge of Police Office Castlereagh Belfast, ex p Lynch* [1980]). Significant in the context of liberal values of human dignity, the officer does not need to disclose to the arrestee the grounds for his suspicions (*Oscar v Chief Constable RUC* [1992]).

Once the person has been arrested he or she can be detained for questioning without charge for up to 28 days (Sch 8 as extended by TA 2006, s 23). Extended pre-charge detention originated under the Northern Ireland legislation, where the police could detain a suspect for up to 7 days with permission from the Home Secretary. In *Brogan v UK* [1989] the European Court of Human Rights held this power to be in breach of the Convention requirement that a suspect must be brought promptly before a court (Art 5). The Court decided that a suspect should be brought before a judge within a maximum of 4 days after their arrest. The UK therefore derogated from the ECHR.

Section 23 of the Terrorism Act 2006 was intended to end this difficulty and is in accordance with a narrow interpretation of *Brogan*. The Act creates a series of increasing powers. A suspect can be detained for up to 48 hours by the police alone. To detain a person from 48 hours up to 14 days, the police must apply to court (a senior district judge or his deputy in England, a sheriff in Scotland or a county court judge or designated resident magistrate in Northern Ireland). For detention up to 28 days they must apply to a senior judge (Sch 8). Permission can be granted if the detention is necessary to obtain or preserve evidence or to carry out an examination or analysis and the investigation is being conducted diligently and expeditiously (ibid) but again the police investigation does not need to be tied to a specific crime. The detention must be reviewed regularly. The accused is entitled to legal representation but can be excluded from any part of the hearing and sensitive material can be withheld from the accused and his or her advisors (Sch 8; see *Ward v Police Service of Northern Ireland* [2008]). The Act includes provision for questioning a terrorist suspect after being charged, which does not apply to ordinary charges (ss 22–24).

However the continued ability to detain a suspect for up to 28 days flouts a wider understanding of *Brogan*. This narrow interpretation of the ruling illustrates the state's ambivalence towards protecting terrorist suspects' human rights. There is a weekly democratic 'sunset' provision (s 25) under which the 28-day extension from 14 days ceases to have effect after one year unless the Secretary of State renews the extension. The provision has currently not been renewed pending government reconsideration of the whole matter in accordance with its policy of undoing previous restrictions on liberty.

23.7.4 Stop and search

Under section 43 of the Terrorism Act 2000 a constable may stop and search anyone whom he reasonably suspects to be a terrorist. Under sections 44–45 a policeman in uniform can stop and search at random any person within an area authorised by a senior officer for articles of a kind that could be used in connection with terrorism. Reasonable grounds need not be shown. By contrast except after an arrest search powers normally require a warrant specifying the nature of the material to be searched for (see Police and Criminal Evidence Act 1984, Part II). Safeguards include a requirement for confirmation by the Home Secretary and a provision that the order has a limited life of 28 days. Moreover the police must use the power circumspectly and only in relation to terrorism. No more than outer clothing can be removed in public.

In *R (Gillan) v Metropolitan Police Comr* [2006] a policeman used section 44 against a student demonstrator and a journalist at an arms sale fair supported by the government. The House of Lords held that this limited and temporary restraint was not a deprivation of liberty within Article 5 of the ECHR and as an interference with privacy was justified because the proportionality test should be applied lightly in terrorist cases. *Gillan* was subsequently condemned by the ECHR (*Gillan and Quinton v UK* [2010]). It was held that section 44 engaged at least Article 8 of the ECHR as a clear interference with privacy. It was held that the power was too vague and lacked essential safeguards, including judicial supervision. It was not therefore 'in accordance with the law'. The current Protection of Freedoms Bill proposes to place restrictions on the exercise of this power and to require a stronger rationale for its exercise (see companion website).

Under section 42 a magistrate may issue a search warrant for the search of any premises if a constable has reasonable grounds to suspect that a person whom the constable reasonably suspects to be concerned with the commission, preparation or instigation of acts of terrorism is to be found there. (Under the general law a search can be carried out either under a warrant or in premises where a person is arrested or which is occupied or controlled by a person who has been arrested (Police and Criminal Evidence Act 1984, ss 18, 32).) The Counter Terrorism Act 2008 adds a power to remove documents, including electronic data, for examination and retain them for up to 96 hours (s 1).

Under section 89 a member of the armed forces on duty or a constable may stop any person so long as it is necessary in order to question him for the purpose of ascertaining that person's identity or movements and what he or she knows about a recent explosion or incident.

23.7.5 Control orders

Detention without trial ('internment') was introduced in Northern Ireland in 1971. It was an unmitigated disaster, triggering far more violence than had previously occurred. Nevertheless indefinite detention for certain foreign terrorist suspects was reintroduced by the Anti-Terrorism, Crime and Security Act 2001 (ss 21–23). For this purpose the UK was obliged to derogate from Article 5 of the ECHR (SI 2001/3644) (see Section 20.4.1). The government attempted to justify this on the basis of *Chahal v UK* [1996], where the European Court held that if there was a real risk that a person's Article 3 (freedom from torture, degrading and inhuman treatment) rights might be abused they could not be deported to their home country even if they were a risk to national security. The UK argued that indefinite detention was necessary because *Chahal* had made it impossible to deal with suspects who were too dangerous to be at large but against whom no criminal charges were brought.

The indefinite detention regime was condemned by the House of Lords in *A v Secretary of State for the Home Dept* [2005]. In a landmark judgment regarded by some as vindicating the rule of law but by others as a dangerous usurpation of the responsibility of the government (see Campbell, 2009), an eight-to-one majority of the House of Lords held that indefinite detention was disproportionate and discriminatory. The House quashed the derogation order and issued a declaration of incompatibility in relation to the statute. Firstly the power was not legally confined to al-Qaeda (who posed the main threat); secondly it only applied to non-UK nationals but UK nationals may be an equal threat to national security; thirdly if these people were so dangerous that they had to be detained without charge it was irrational to allow them to leave the country, where they would be free to continue plotting.

Control orders were then introduced, as an alternative to indefinite detention, as being less restrictive of human rights. A control order is an order against an individual that imposes obligations on him for purposes connected with protecting the public from a risk of terrorism (Prevention of Terrorism Act 2005, s 1). The obligations that can be imposed are any obligations that the Secretary of State or court as the case may be (below) considers necessary for the purposes connected with preventing or restricting involvement by that individual in terrorist-related activity. There need be no evidence related to a criminal charge. However, before making an order, if it appears to the Secretary of State that a terrorist-related offence may be involved he or she must consult the relevant Chief Constable about whether there is evidence available that could realistically be used for prosecution for an offence related to terrorism (s 8(1)). This is not however a condition of making the order (*Secretary of State for the Home Dept v E* [2008]). If a control order is made the Secretary of State can also require the Chief Constable to keep the investigation under review with a view to prosecution (s 8(4)).

The obligations that can be imposed by a control order include the following (s 1(4)):

- prohibition or restriction on the possession or use of specified articles or substances;
- prohibition or restriction on the use of specified services or carrying out specified activities;
- restrictions on work occupation or business;
- restrictions on communication and association;
- restrictions on residence or persons with access to residence;
- exclusion from particular places;
- restrictions on movement;
- requirement to surrender passport or anything in his possession covered by the order;
- requirement to give access to his residence to specified persons;
- requirement to submit to searches and removal of articles for the purpose of enforcing the order;
- requirement to allow himself to be photographed (the Counter Terrorism Act 2008 adds fingerprinting and non-intimate samples);
- monitoring requirements;
- the provision of information to a specified person;
- to report to a specified person at a specified time and place.

There are two types of control order: derogating orders and non-derogating orders. There are different legal rules for each (PTA 2005, s 1). Both derogating and non-derogating control orders can be imposed against nationals and non-nationals. Non-derogating orders impose obligations and restrictions on the controllee that do not amount to a breach of Article 5 of the ECHR (deprivation of liberty). A derogating control order is one that violates Article 5. The application of other Articles of the ECHR is not affected but most of the relevant rights can be overridden by the state on grounds including national security. Article 3 (torture or inhuman or degrading treatment) and Article 6 (fair trial) cannot be overridden or derogated from.

A non-derogating control order is made by the Home Secretary if she or he has reasonable grounds for believing that person to be involved in terrorism-related activity and the order is necessary to protect the public (s 2). Except where she or he certifies that the matter is urgent the Secretary of State must apply to the court for permission to make the order (s 3). However the court's power is limited to deciding whether the order is 'obviously flawed'. The meaning of 'flawed' refers to the standards of judicial review (s 3(11)). If it gives permission to make the order the court must give a direction for a further hearing as soon as reasonably practicable. If an order is made without permission it must be immediately referred to the court, which must consider the matter within seven days, again as to whether the order is 'obviously flawed', and give directions for a further hearing. However the certificate that the matter is urgent can be quashed if it is 'flawed', thus requiring the court to go into greater depth (s 3(8)). On a further hearing the court must also go into greater depth and consider whether the order is 'flawed' (s 3(10)). The court can either quash or alter the order. The order can last for 12 months and can be renewed indefinitely.

To date no derogating control orders have been issued. A derogating order can only be made by the High Court (s 4). The Court will hold a preliminary hearing and can issue a derogating order if there are reasonable grounds for believing that the order is necessary for the protection of the public and the obligations are reasonable. This hearing can be held in the absence of the person in question but a full hearing can only confirm the order if on the balance of probabilities the person is involved in terrorism, the obligations are necessary and there is a risk of a public emergency and a legal derogation from the ECHR covering the control order. The orders last for six months and can be renewed by the High Court.

The legality of the regime has recently been undermined, and the government is currently reviewing the Control Order regime with the aim of substituting arrangements based primarily on supervision of the movements of a suspect rather than on physical restrictions..

In *M v Secretary of State for the Home Dept* [2004] the Court of Appeal required the Secretary of State to show that he had properly considered all relevant factors in making a control order against a Libyan asylum seeker. There was evidence that some of the asylum seeker's associates might be involved with al-Qaeda, a terrorist organisation, but none linking the appellant himself with al-Qaeda. The Court of Appeal held that the Special Immigration Appeal Commission was justified in overturning the Home Secretary's certificate. It was not enough to show suspicious circumstances. The Home Secretary had to take a broad overall view based on all the circumstances and supported by evidence.

In *Secretary of State for the Home Dept v JJ and Others* [2008] the House of Lords held that obligations imposed under what purported to be a non-derogating control order were so severe that the order violated the ECHR as a deprivation of liberty (see Section 20.4.1). House arrest was imposed for 16 hours per day, visitors and people met had to be authorised by the Home Office and the victim was confined to designated areas. These restrictions meant that the order was a nullity and so it could not be amended but must be quashed. The majority took the view that the meaning of deprivation of liberty was a matter of degree. The proper approach was to decide whether the restriction was so severe as to deprive the victim of a normal life in the context of his or her particular lifestyle. Lord Hoffmann, dissenting, took the view that nothing short of complete detention should count, his argument being that anything broader would require the court to give the state leeway as to derogation from Article 5 (at [44]). Lord Brown thought that nothing less than 16 hours per day house arrest should count (at [105]–[108]).

In *Secretary of State for the Home Dept v MB* [2008] and *Secretary of State for the Home Dept v E* [2008] the House held that lesser restrictions on visitors and movement and a 12-hour curfew did not violate a Convention right.

23.7.6 Terrorist assets

Under section 1 of the Anti-Terrorism, Crime and Security Act 2001 a magistrate in civil proceedings brought for the purpose can order the forfeiture of cash which is intended to be used for terrorist purposes or which belongs to a proscribed organisation or which is or represents property obtained through terrorism. Under sections 4 and 5 of the ATCSA the Treasury can freeze the assets of any person resident in the UK or any UK citizen or company if it reasonably believes (i) that action to the detriment of the UK economy (or part of it) has been or is likely to be taken or (ii) that action constituting a threat to the life or property of one or more UK nationals has been or is likely to be taken, in both cases either by an overseas government or by an overseas resident. The freezing order can prevent benefits being paid to the government or resident in question or to any person the Treasury reasonably believes has assisted or is likely to assist them. These powers are therefore not limited to terrorists but could for example be used to protect trade interests against overseas competition. They include power to require public bodies to disclose confidential information, again not limited to terrorist offences (s 17).

By virtue of Orders in Council made under the United Nations Act 1947 the Treasury has power to give directions for the freezing of terrorist assets in order to give effect to various United Nations Conventions (see Resolution 1373, 2001). This drastic power can involve placing serious restrictions as to every expenditure upon the persons concerned other than for essential needs. The Order can be made without judicial permission.

The Counter Terrorism Act 2008 introduces special High Court proceedings for setting aside the use of these powers. These provisions include what have now become commonplace powers to exclude parties and sensitive evidence and for using the device of a special advocate. However the Treasury is obliged to disclose to the Court all relevant material both for and against its case. The Court is limited to applying judicial review principles.

In *HM Treasury v Ahmed* [2010] the Supreme Court held that an order made under the 1947 Act which triggered asset freezing on 'reasonable suspicion' was invalid as violating the principle of legality, under which only clear statutory language can deprive a person of property (see Section 6.6). The Terrorist Asset Freezing (Temporary Provisions) Act 2010 retrospectively validated the use of these powers. The Terrorist Asset-Freezing Etc Act 2011 puts the reasonable suspicion test into full statutory form. A challenge would therefore be confined to human rights grounds, where the public interest test under Protocol 1, Article 1 of the ECHR would be available (see Section 20.4.3).

Where a person has been convicted of certain funding and money laundering offences the court concerned may order assets connected with the offence to be seized (Terrorism

Act 2000, s 23). The Counter Terrorism Act 2008 has extended this power and introduces provisions for compensating the injured out of the convicted person's assets.

23.7.7 Other terrorist offences and powers

1. the encouragement of terrorism and dissemination of terrorist publications (TA 2006, ss 1, 2; see Chapter 21);
2. preparation of terrorist acts (TA 2006, s 5). This is not confined to a specific act of terrorism but could include for example buying materials capable of being made into bombs;
3. giving or receiving instruction or training for terrorism (TA 2006, s 6). This is also wide, including the use of any method or technique for doing anything that is capable of being done for the purpose of terrorism (s 6(3)(b)). For example it could include IT skills. However the instructor must know that the pupil intends to use the skills for terrorist purposes;
4. attendance at a place used for terrorist training;
5. offences relating to radioactive devices or materials for terrorist purposes (ss 9–11);
6. the Secretary of State can authorise the taking of land or a road closure or restriction if he or she considers it necessary for the preservation of peace or the maintenance of order (ss 91, 94). A member of the armed forces on duty or a constable may order a road closure or restriction if he considers it immediately necessary for the preservation of peace or the maintenance of order (s 92);
7. the Counter Terrorism Act 2008 introduces increased penalties for any offence with a terrorist connection;
8. the Counter Terrorism Act 2008 confers wide powers on any person to disclose information to any of the intelligence services for the purpose of its functions (s 19), with a corresponding power given to the intelligence services also to disclose information. This does not appear to be limited to terrorist offences.

Summary

- The courts give the executive a wide margin of discretion in relation to security matters. Under the ECHR there is also a wide margin and states can derogate from some of its provisions in the event of an emergency. However the courts protect fundamental rights by requiring safeguards, in particular independent judicial supervision.
- There is no general right to the disclosure of governmental information. The Freedom of Information Act 2000 confers a right to 'request' the disclosure of documents held by public authorities. However this can often be overridden by the government and is subject to many exceptions, particularly in relation to central government policy.
- There are certain statutory rights to the disclosure of specified information but these are outnumbered by many statutes prohibiting the disclosure of particular information.
- Under the Official Secrets Act 1989 defined categories of information are protected by criminal penalties. Except in the case of national security, the information must be damaging. There is also a defence of ignorance.
- The law of confidence requires the court to balance the public interest in openness against the public interest in effective government. The balance is struck differently according to context.

Summary cont'd

The courts have endorsed the importance of freedom of expression and a public body is required to show a public interest in secrecy. The main remedy is an injunction. Third parties such as the press are not directly bound by an injunction but might be liable for contempt of court if they knowingly frustrate its purpose.

- Public interest immunity allows the government to withhold evidence. The court makes the decision on the basis of 'balancing' the public interest in the administration of justice against the public interest in effective government. The courts' approach to public interest immunity is affected by the Human Rights Act 1998, which requires that any claim preserve the essentials of the right to a fair trial.

  Proceedings might be 'closed' proceedings, where the defendant is denied direct access to the evidence against him and the public and press are excluded. Again the essentials of the right to a fair trial must be preserved. There is also a conflict with the rule of law and Article 10 of the ECHR (freedom of the press). The device of a special advocate might be used.
- The security and intelligence services are subject to a certain degree of control, largely outside the ordinary courts.
- There is regulation of electronic and other forms of surveillance by the police and other law enforcement agencies, also outside the ordinary courts. The overlapping regimes of the Police Act 1997 and the Regulation of Investigatory Powers Act 2000 give the government wide powers of interception and surveillance subject to procedural safeguards and to limits derived from the ECHR as to permissible purposes and proportionality.
- In an emergency the police, supported by the armed forces, may take action to keep the peace and can use reasonable force in self-defence and the defence of others. It is questionable whether martial law as such is part of English law. The Civil Contingencies Act 2004 gives the executive wide powers to deal with an emergency. These are subject to control by Parliament and safeguards based on the ECHR.
- Increasingly restrictive anti-terrorist measures have been introduced in response to a series of threats and incidents. These have sometimes required derogation from the ECHR protection for personal liberty. They also involve restrictions on the right to a fair trial. The courts have condemned a significant number of these powers and criticised others. However there is no consensus on how to accommodate security and respect for freedom.

Exercises

23.1 'We have moved from a discretionary open government regime under a voluntary Code of Practice to a statutory open government regime in which the power to decide what is to be disclosed lies within the discretion of government and is denied to independent bodies' (Johnson, 'Freedom of Information Act 2000: Freedom of Information or Open Government?' (2001) 151 NLJ 1031). Explain and discuss critically.

23.2 Tony, a US citizen, and Gordon, a UK citizen, are arrested by the police on suspicion of being associated with an international terrorist group. The police suspect that certain incriminating information which they received from the US may have been extracted from Tony by torture. Gordon is released but Tony is detained under a certificate issued by the Home Secretary stating that he is suspected of being a terrorist. Tony demands to see the evidence against him. He also asks for a lawyer but the request is refused. He is offered a special advocate as a representative. Discuss.

23.3 Simon is the leader of an animal rights campaigning organisation. The police receive an anonymous message that the organisation proposes to enter the headquarters of a drugs

Exercises cont'd

company (known to donate large sums to the ruling political party) in order to distribute animal rights leaflets. A policeman stops Simon in the street and searches him but finds nothing relevant to the allegation. The policeman then arrests Simon on the ground that he is a terrorist. Simon is detained for 14 days without charge and without going before a court. The Home Secretary, who knows Simon as a prominent critic of the government, makes a control order against Simon 'as a matter of urgency'. This requires that neither Simon nor any member of his group carry out any political activity anywhere and that Simon be confined to his home for 14 hours every day.

Advise Simon as to the legality of these actions.

23.4 While on holiday in Scotland the Prime Minister accidentally leaves his personal diary on a train. Another passenger finds it and is delighted to see that it contains disparaging remarks, including crude obscenities about the Prime Minister's Cabinet colleagues. He hands it in at the office of the *Sunday Stir*. The Editor informs the Prime Minister's Office that extracts from the diary will be published in next Sunday's edition. Advise the Prime Minister as to any legal remedy he might have.

23.5 Derek, a civil servant in the Department of Health, believes that the Cabinet minister in charge of his department has been ordering government statisticians to alter the latest NHS performance figures in order to show that government policies are bearing fruit. Derek gives this information to the editor of the *Daily Whinge*, who contacts the relevant minister for his comments. The Attorney General immediately applies for a temporary injunction and commences an action for breach of confidence against Derek. Derek requests the production of letters between civil servants and the minister (the existence of which he learned from an anonymous email) which he claims would support his version of events. The government issues a PII certificate on the ground that the information is in a category the disclosure of which would inhibit free and frank discussion within the Cabinet. The minister who signed the certificate did not examine the information personally but relied on advice from the Attorney General that the 'certificate will cover us for all Cabinet-level documents'.

(i) Advise Derek.

(ii) Advise the Attorney General whether he can prosecute Derek under the Official Secrets Act 1989.

23.6 Tom has recently retired from a senior post in the intelligence services. He possesses recordings of conversations by service officials which suggest that senior ministers have requested them to fabricate evidence supporting a proposed invasion of an African country. He wishes to pass the recordings to Jerry, a journalist. Advise Tom whether he and Jerry are at risk of conviction under the Official Secrets Act 1989.

23.7 'Terrorist threats and actions test the Executive's commitment to the rule of law and good governance. Because of the extreme powers given by such extraordinary legislation, there is an incumbent requirement to provide limits to its terms, scope and life span' (Thomas, 'Emergency and Anti-Terrorist Powers 9/11: USA and UK' (2003) 26 Fordham Int'l LJ 1993). Does the current law meet these requirements?

Further reading

Akdeniz, Taylor and Walker, 'Regulation RIPA 2000 (1): Bigbrother.gov.uk: State Surveillance in the Age of Information and Rights' [2001] CLR 73
Arden, 'Human Rights in the Age of Terrorism' (2005) 121 LQR 609
Austin, 'The Freedom of Information Act: A Sheep in Wolf's Clothing?' in Jowell and Oliver (eds), *The Changing Constitution* (Oxford University Press 2007)
Barak, 'Human Rights in Times of Terror: A Judicial Point of View' (2008) 28 LS 492
Bates, 'Anti-Terrorism Control Orders: Liberty and Security Still in the Balance' (2009) 29 LS 9
Bonner, 'Checking the Executive? Detention without Trial, Control Orders, Due Process and Human Rights' (2006) 12 EPL 45
Bonner, *Executive Measures, Terrorism and National Security: Have the Rules of the Game Changed?* (Ashgate 2008)
Cabinet Office, *The National Security Strategy of the UK* (Cm 7291, 2008)
Campbell, 'The Threat of Terror and the Plausibility of Posivitism' [2009] PL 501
Clayton and Tomlinson, 'Lord Bingham and the Human Rights Act: The Search for Democratic Legitimacy During the "War on Terror"' in Andenas and Fairgrieve (eds), *Tom Bingham and the Transformation of the Law* (Oxford University Press 2009)
Dickson, 'Law versus Terrorism: Can Law Win?' [2005] EHRLR 12
Dyzenhaus, *The Constitution of Law: Legality in a Time of Emergency* (Cambridge University Press 2008)
Feldman, 'Human Rights, Terrorism and Risk: The Roles of Politicians and Judges' [2006] PL 364
Feldman, 'Deprivation of Liberty in Anti-Terrorism Law' [2008] CLJ 4
Gearty, 'Human Rights in an Age of Counter Terrorism: Injurious, Irrelevant or Indispensible?' (2005) 58 CLI 25
Ip, 'The Rise and Spread of the Special Advocate' [2008] PL 717
Kostakopoulou, 'How to Do Things with Security Post 9/11' (2008) 88 OJLS 317
Poole, 'Courts and Conditions of Uncertainty in Times of Crisis' [2008] PL 234
Scott, 'The Acceptable and Unacceptable Uses of Public Interest Immunity' [1996] PL 427
Walker, 'The Legal Definition of Terrorism in the United Kingdom and Beyond' [2007] PL 331
Walker and Broderick, *The Civil Contingencies Act 2004* (Oxford University Press 2006)
White Paper, *Your Right to Know: Freedom of Information* (Cm 3818, 1997)
White Paper, *The United Kingdom's Strategy for Combating International Terrorism* (Cm 7547, 2009)

Postscript

Chapter 24

Constitutional reform

> **There exists a great chasm between those, on the one side, who relate everything to a single central vision...and on the other side, those who pursue many ends often unrelated and even contradictory...The first kind of intellectual and artistic personality belongs to the hedgehogs, the second to the foxes. (Isaiah Berlin, *The Hedgehog and the Fox* (1953) s 1)**

24.1 Introduction

It is often said that there has been a constitutional revolution in the UK, starting with the reforms introduced by the Labour government which took office in 1997. It is also said that these reforms are fragmented and without coherence, falling far short of providing a new constitutional settlement. These reforms have been discussed in context in this book. They include the following (see Bogdanor, 2009):

- devolution of many powers to Scotland, Wales, Northern Ireland and to a lesser extent London. Devolution in Wales is uncertain and fluid;
- the Human Rights Act 1998;
- the Freedom of Information Act 2000;
- the House of Lords Act 2000 (removal of peers but reforms uncompleted);
- the independence of the Bank of England from government in monetary policy (Bank of England Act 1998);
- introduction of different voting systems for the devolved governments and the European Parliament;
- increased regulation of political parties and elections (Political Parties, Elections and Referendums Act 2000);
- backed by the Human Rights Act 1998 but also relying on the common law the courts may have changed the direction of the constitution in favour of strong judicial review principles based on the rule of law and individual rights. Parliamentary supremacy is being questioned even by judges (see Section 8.4.5);
- the Constitutional Reform Act 2005 strengthened the separation of powers by removing the Lord Chancellor from the judiciary and creating the Supreme Court and the Judicial Appointments Commission;
- introduction of codes of practice covering all branches of government embodying the Nolan 'Principles of Public Life' but not usually legally enforceable (see Section 5.8);
- as a result of the scandal over MPs' expense claims in 2009, independent regulation of MPs' expenses and pay was introduced by the Parliamentary Standards Act 2009 (see Section 11.7.2).

Most recently the Constitutional Reform and Governance Act 2010 introduced relatively limited reforms which largely enacted the status quo and made technical changes. The 2010 Act is the residue of a more ambitious proposal by the outgoing Labour government which included regulating other prerogative powers such as those of the Attorney General and the power to go to war (see Green Paper, *Rights and Responsibilities: Developing Our Constitutional Framework* (Cm 7577, 2009)). The changes made by the 2010 Act include:

- enacting without significant substantive changes the main general principles governing the civil service, a matter that had long been proposed;
- enacting the conventions governing parliamentary approval for the ratification of treaties (see Section 9.7.1);
- revising the law concerning the Independent Parliamentary Standards Authority (see Section 11.7.2) in favour of greater independence;
- correcting previous errors which affected the right of Commonwealth and Irish citizens to sit in the House of Lords (see Section 12.2);
- disqualifying tax exiles from sitting in Parliament (see Section 12.2);
- protecting the monarchy from freedom of information requests (see Section 23.2.1).

Recent measures include the following:

- the Parliamentary Constituencies and Electoral Reform Act 2011, which authorises the holding of a referendum on 5 May 2011 to decide whether to introduce the alternative vote (AV) system for parliamentary elections (see Section 12.7.1). However the Act also reduces the number of parliamentary constituencies by 50 and introduces measures to ensure that the number of voters in each is roughly equal (Section 12.8). Given that there is no proposal to reduce the number of ministers this is likely to increase executive control over Parliament. On the other hand the Fixed Term Parliament Bill 2011 proposes to remove the power of the Prime Minister to dissolve Parliament within the five-year span of a Parliament (Section 11.3);
- the Localism Bill, conceived as part of the present government's claim to promote 'the big society', which to a limited extent extends direct local democracy at the expense of local authorities but not of central government. In that it embodies an element of direct democracy it is arguably of constitutional importance. The Bill includes a right to a referendum on any local issue triggered by a petition of at least 5 per cent of the local electorate. The referendum is not binding. A local authority is however required to make an order giving planning permission to land use development proposed by a parish council or in certain cases a 'neighbourhood forum' comprising local residents and supported by a referendum of local electors. Proposals to increase council tax above a certain threshold will also require a referendum. Local authorities will be required to publish items of expenditure over £500. There are also proposals for elected mayors in major cities, subject to referendums. A local authority must also consider giving effect to a matter embodied in an 'expression of interest' put to it by a voluntary or community body or a charity or at least two local authority employees or other persons specified by the Secretary of State. Finally, land listed by the local authority as an 'asset of community value' in response to a nomination by a community organisation is to be protected against disposal. These powers are subject to significant central control and local authorities do not have independent tax-raising powers;
- the Scotland Bill, which would strengthen the financial powers of the Scottish Parliament by increasing its power to raise income tax and giving it other powers to raise 'devolved taxes', principally in relation to land transactions and waste

disposal. The Scottish executive is renamed the 'Scottish government'. The Bill also makes detailed increases to the devolved powers of the Scottish Parliament and government, particularly in relation to the conduct of elections;

- a government bill to reform the House of Lords in favour of a mainly elected chamber is expected.
- The Protection of Freedoms Bill introduces measures either removing restrictions on certain personal freedoms made in recent years or introducing safeguards. Its main provisions will be outlined on the website accompanying this book.

24.2 The nature of constitutional reform

The lists above illustrate that in the unwritten constitution reforms come from uncoordinated sources without any grand plan, reminding us of Griffith's famous remark that the constitution is 'what happens' (see Section 1.3). The constitution is continuously evolving as a result of uncoordinated events – the much used analogy of an organism being a reasonable approximation. The changes are generated in several uncoordinated ways:

- by statutes responding to particular problems or government embarrassments (eg Security Services Acts 1989, 1996; see Section 23.4);
- by individual court decisions, including the influence of international courts such as the European Court of Justice and the European Court of Human Rights (eg *Anisminic v Foreign Compensation Commission* [1969] (see Section 17.3); *R v Secretary of State for Transport, ex p Factortame (No 2)* [1991] (see Section 8.4.4)). It could be argued in the common law tradition that the courts provide an evolutionary and orderly response to underlying problems in the constitution that combines stability with practicality. However since much of the constitution is based on convention, interventions by the courts are limited to cases involving individual rights and cannot tackle the wider problems of democracy;
- by parliamentary rules such as recent 'modernisation' provisions in relation to parliamentary procedure;
- by recommendations from advisory bodies such as the Committee on Standards in Public Life (eg the 'Nolan Principles'; see Section 5.9);
- as the consequence of gradual changes in practice which have affected the constitution by the cumulative effect of many individual decisions. This illustrates the absence of the restraints of a written constitution. In particular, commencing in the 1980s, there has been a steady transferring of functions away from the traditional hierarchy of ministers and civil servants subject to direct parliamentary accountability to a spectrum of bodies ranging from executive agencies through 'quangos' to private bodies exercising governmental functions under contracts. This has taken place without any general organising principles, so there are no clear lines of accountability either to political bodies (see Sections 5.2.7, 5.2.8, 15.8.4) or to the courts through judicial review (see Section 19.5). Moreover political power remains firmly with ministers, who are in a position to exercise great powers of patronage over this array of dependent organisations and their managers. Such controls as exist are entrusted to groups of persons selected by ministers and without formal legal powers, such as the Commissioner of Public Appointments (see Section 5.3).

Occasionally there are substantial changes in political ideology, as with the privatisation during the 1980s of most of the state-owned industries and the introduction of semi-independent regulators (see Section 5.2.7). Constitutional reform could therefore be described as a disjointed muddle, the result of continuous and sometimes amateurish tinkering. Thus our constitutional changes are dominated by the government of the day, without any mechanism in our law specifically devised for constitutional reform. There have from time to time been reviews of aspects of the constitution (eg Royal Commission on the Constitution, 1969–73; Royal Commission on the House of Lords, 2000; Power Commission, 2006) but most reforms have been responses to particular political events where the government found itself in difficulties and wished to bolster its support.

Self-conscious occasions for constitutional reform have been rare. These may be motivated by the desire of a new government to appear radical (eg the package of reforms introduced by the New Labour government in 1997 and to a lesser extent on the appointment of Gordon Brown as Prime Minister in 2007) or in reaction to a crisis (eg the measures taken to deal with the MPs' expenses scandal in 2009 and 2010; see Section 11.7). Reform is likely to be influenced by particular crises or short-term party political considerations, for example the spasmodic introduction of referendums on particular issues such as devolution (see Section 16.1), EC membership (see Section 10.1) and the voting system (see Section 11.3).

The two most important constitutional changes of the twentieth century were probably the reduction of the powers of the House of Lords by the Parliament Act 1911 and the UK's accession to what is now the EU in 1972. The former was driven by the refusal of the Lords to cooperate with government proposals to improve welfare provision and concerning Northern Ireland; the latter by the UK's parlous economic circumstances at the time.

One result of this erratic approach to reform is that obsolete principles which do not raise short-term problems may remain unchanged. For example the connection between the Church of England, the monarchy and anti-Catholicism is still built into our constitution (see Section 14.2). It is often suggested that the Act of Settlement 1700 should be reformed to remove the religious restrictions affecting the monarchy on the ground that they are inappropriate in modern conditions, being discriminatory in relation to religious freedom and the exercise of property rights. This worthy but limited reform is characteristic of proposals for constitutional change in the UK in that it leaves unquestioned the more fundamental matter of why the head of state should be defined according to a primitive concept of blood line.

Constitutional reform is also the product of painstaking work by specialist bodies attempting to deal with the inherent problems of government. Outstanding examples are the Law Commission's reports on judicial review (see Section 18.1) and the Leggat reforms of the tribunal system in 2007 (see Section 5.4.3). In some cases valuable reports remain unimplemented (eg the Nicholls Report (Report of the Joint Committee on Parliamentary Privilege (1998–99, HL 43-1, HC 214-1)); see Section 11.6). Thus there is no clear distinction between constitutional reform as such and the continuous process of change. The 'organic' constitution may with hindsight emerge from the cumulative effect of many small changes, although the mere fact that it is 'organic' does not tell us whether the state of our constitution is good or bad.

Some commentators assert that there are general forces guiding the direction of constitutional reform. On the grandest scale the 'Whig' view of history claims to find a progression form tyranny to democracy. More recently Professor Oliver (2009) has suggested that four tendencies underlie the course of contemporary constitutional reform. The first of these tendencies is towards 'principles'. These have been developed especially by the courts, for example the legitimate expectation (see Section 17.9), and also from within government, for example the Seven Principles of Public Life (see Section 5.9). The second tendency is towards 'governance', meaning reforming governmental processes. This would include for example executive agencies (see Section 5.2.6), the modernisation of parliamentary procedures and the various bodies charged with policing standards of conduct (see Section 5.8). The third tendency according to Oliver, albeit perhaps hesitant and sporadic, is that of strengthening citizenship in the republican sense of equality, for example House of Lords reform, the Freedom of Information Act 2000, the Human Rights Act 1998 and current proposals for voting reform. Oliver's fourth tendency is 'separation'. This would include devolution and the reforms to the court system made by the Constitutional Reform Act 2005 which enhance the separation of powers (see Section 8.5).

Ackerman suggests that the main result of what he calls a 'constitutional revolution' in the UK is to weaken the principles of parliamentary supremacy and central government through the Cabinet (*London Review of Books* 9 September 2010). None of the reforms directly affects the legal principle of parliamentary supremacy but in political terms it can be argued that the position of Parliament has been weakened by devolution, by EU membership and by the Human Rights Act 1998. Moreover recent uses of the referendum have introduced an element of direct democracy which could create political pressure to bypass Parliament. We have already seen some judicial voices suggesting that Parliament is not omnipotent.

Another general trend has been towards 'juridification', by which is meant using law as the instrument of reform, contrary to the tradition of relying on informal arrangements (see Bogdanor, 2009). This applies in particular to the devolution legislation, which includes provisions which operate only as conventions in the UK government, to the reforms relating to the Lord Chancellor (see Section 7.7), to the proposals to introduce a fixed-term Parliament (see Section 11.3) and to the framework for the civil service created by the Constitutional Reform and Governance Act 2010. The use of contracts to structure relationships between ministers and executive agencies is another example (see Section 5.2.6). The Human Rights Act 1998 attempts a compromise between legal and political methods.

Juridification brings the courts more prominently into the political arena than has traditionally been the case. However the courts have developed principles of 'non-justiciability', deference and flexible review in order to draw back from interfering in issues which the courts regard as unsuitable for them (see Section 19.7.1; *In Petition of Axa Insurance* [2010]). The widespread use of published codes of conduct, although these are not usually directly legally enforceable, could be regarded as part of the same tendency. Juridification has the advantage of promoting openness but of course comes nowhere near to establishing a written constitution.

King (2007) described the reforms that have taken place since 1997 as intellectually incoherent but suggested that the constitution, although a mess and looking like a ruin, was fundamentally sound. In general constitutional reform has been directed to dispersing power. Bogdanor (2009) suggests that the trajectory of recent constitutional changes has been to disperse power away from the central government but in an incomplete way without tackling the issues of devolution for England, increasing direct democracy and local government. Beatson has suggested that constitutional reform has been driven by the need for successive governments to make our centralised and authoritarian system more acceptable to the people.

The Human Rights Act 1998, the House of Lords Act 1999, the Freedom of Information Act 2000, devolution and the strengthening of the separation of powers by the Constitutional Reform Act 2005 could all be presented as self-conscious attempts to reform the constitution in favour of the kind of citizenship ideas suggested by Oliver (2009). Despite some limited reforms in parliamentary procedure there has been no serious attempt to correct the fundamental imbalance in the constitution, namely the dominance of the Prime Minister and the executive over Parliament. There has also been heavy reliance on advisory bodies chosen from a limited range of interconnected professional and business people policed only by other such bodies.

24.3 Future directions

The main unresolved issue in relation to constitutional reform concerns whether our representative parliamentary system dominated by the central executive and the large political parties is still desirable. This remains in some respects based on the seventeenth-century revolution. The miscellaneous proposals of the present coalition government about voting and the dissolution of Parliament seem to be based more upon short-term considerations relating to itself than fundamental constitutional principle. Particular unresolved matters include voting reform, the place of the monarchy, the composition and role of the upper house, strengthening local democracy, devolution in England, the use of referendums and whether there should be a bill of rights adapted to the circumstances of the UK. It is also often suggested that there should be a stronger separation between the executive and Parliament, either by barring ministers from being members of Parliament or by introducing greater independence into parliamentary procedures and strengthening the powers and independence of select committees.

Another issue concerns the absence of safeguards to ensure that politicians and officials are independent of the vested interests that continuously lobby them. This is related to 'patronage state', referring to the appointed 'quangos' exercising power and influence without clear accountability and sometimes regulated by other bodies composed of people appointed on a 'revolving door principle' to themselves (see Section 5.2.7). The government has proposed drastically to reduce the number of quangos, although some of these may be restructured as charities (see *Independent* 15 October 2010). This is driven by the need to save money but is promoted as a means of increasing accountability in that the powers of many such bodies will become exercised by ministers.

There is disagreement as to whether we should have a written constitution (see also Section 1.2). A written constitution would have the advantage that it could provide a method of constitutional change that was to some extent independent of the short-term interests of the government of the day. It would also spell the end of parliamentary supremacy. Bogdanor (2009, ch 9) for example approves the general direction taken by recent reforms in dispersing power and favours progress towards extending democratic rights but does not favour a written constitution, at least in the short term, since the present reforms are incomplete and the content of any such constitution remains controversial. In particular there is no agreement as to what values might be included, the various voting systems are chaotic, and the meaning of many conventions which would fall to be put into the constitution is unclear.

There has been no great event of national unity around which a constitution can be created. King (2007) opposes systematic reforms, preferring the organic development of the unwritten constitution and pointing out that there are more important problems to engage the community than constitutional reform.

Moreover it is unclear who should draw up and ratify such a constitution. The UK tends to rely on groups formed under various labels into 'commissions' of trusted individuals chosen by ministers on the advice of other persons from within the same networks.

Republican writers such as Bellamy would resist on democratic grounds a constitution that involved judicial power to override the legislature (2007, ch 6). Gordon (2010) proposes a written constitution on classical republican lines (see Section 2.5). Its main features would be as follows:

- a secular state;
- an electoral system for both Houses based on proportional representation, with half the representatives in both Houses being women;
- compulsory voting;
- a court with power to overturn statutes;
- a Citizen's Council randomly chosen along the lines of a jury to provide advice and suggest constitutional changes;
- a special procedure for changing the constitution involving a referendum and a three-fifths majority of both Houses.

Thus the long-standing debate as to whether the UK should adopt a written constitution depends not so much on the merits of a written constitution as such as on whether it is considered that our present arrangements are fundamentally sound. The danger of a written constitution is that it would freeze the preferences of whichever group is in power when it is enacted since it is likely that those called upon to draft it would be dominated by government supporters or malleable persons.

Summary

- Constitutional reforms driven by the executive have mainly been pragmatic and uncoordinated responses to particular issues, with disagreement as to the merits of a comprehensive rationalist approach embodied in a written constitution.
- Power has been to some extent dispersed but the Prime Minister and the central executive remain in control of Parliament and patronage remains a primary lever of government.
- The constitution has been increasingly 'juridified' and the courts are self-consciously developing constitutional principles.

Exercises

24.1 To what extent have recent constitutional reforms been driven by general principles?

24.2 What further constitutional reforms should in your view have priority?

24.3 What procedures would you suggested for making constitutional changes and why?

24.4 Would a separation of powers between the legislature and the executive be a good idea?

24.5 Is it desirable and important to reform the position of the monarchy?

24.6 Is a written constitution desirable?

Further reading

Bellamy, *Political Constitutionalism* (Cambridge University Press 2007) ch 6

Bingham, *The Evolving Constitution* (Justice Annual Lecture 2001)

Bogdanor, *The New British Constitution* (Hart 2009)

Bogdanor and Vogenauer, 'Enacting a British Constitution: Some Problems' [2008] PL 38

Brazier, *Constitutional Reform: Reshaping the British System* (3rd edn, Oxford University Press 2008)

Bryant, *Towards a New Constitutional Settlement* (Smith Institute 2007)

Gordon, *Repairing British Politics: A Blue Print for Constitutional Change* (Hart 2010)

House of Lords Select Committee on the Constitution, Fourth Report, *Changing the Constitution: The Process of Constitutional Change* (HL 2001–02, 69)

Jenkins, 'Constitutional Reform Goes to War: Some Lessons from the USA' [2007] PL 258

Jowell and Oliver (eds), *The Changing Constitution* (7th edn, Oxford University Press 2007) preface

King, *The British Constitution* (Sweet & Maxwell 2007)

Le Sueur, 'Gordon Brown's New Constitutional Settlement' [2008] PL 21

Oliva, 'Church, State and Establishment in the UK in the 21st Century: Anachronism or Idiosyncrasy?' [2010] PL 482

Oliver, *Constitutional Reform in the United Kingdom* (Oxford University Press 2003)

Oliver, 'The United Kingdom Constitution in Transition: From Where to Where?' in Adenas and Fairgrieve (eds), *Tom Bingham and the Transformation of the Law* (Oxford University Press 2009)

Power Commission, *Power to the People: An Independent Inquiry into Britain's Democracy* (Rowntree Trust 2006)

Royal Commission on the Constitution (Cmnd 5460, 1969–73)

Royal Commission on the House of Lords, *A House for the Future* (Cm 4534, 2000) [Wakeham Report]

Select Committee on the Constitution, *Reform of the Office of Attorney General* (HC 2007–08, 93)

Index

Absent voters, 273–4
Abuse of discretion, 382–7
Accountability, 44, 330, 334
  judges, 142
Acts of foreign governments, 198–201
Acts of Parliament, 8, 155, 162–3
  enactment of, 238–9
  grants of independence, 165
  meaning of, 162–3
  overriding, 164. *See also* Parliamentary supremacy
  subjects of, 163
Acts of state, 198–201
Adjournment debates, 292
Administrative Court, 79, 97, 108, 154, 361, 370, 372, 415, 417, 419, 425, 432, 433
Administrative decisions
  bias in, 406–9
  judicial review of. *See* Judicial review
  reasons for, 410–11
  right to a fair hearing, 403–6
  void and voidable, 373–4
Administrative justice, 100–2
Administrative law, 4
Agencies
  decisions of. *See* Administrative decisions
  executive. *See* Executive agencies
Aliens, 185, 186
Amplified rule of law, 122, 129–31
Amsterdam Treaty (1997), 208
Ancient constitution, the, 69
Anti-terrorism measures, 536–7
  arrest of terrorists, 539–40
  banning of terrorist organizations, 538–9
  control orders, 541–4
  freezing assets of terrorists, 544–5
  other offences/powers, 545
  pre-charge detention, 539–40
  stop and search, 540–1
Appeal and review, 372–3. *See also* Judicial review
  Supreme Court's functions, 148
Aristocracy, 17
Arrest of terrorists, 539–40
Articles of government, 9
Assembly, freedom of, 503
  demonstrations, 504–11
  European Convention on Human Rights, 455
Association, freedom of, 503
  demonstrations, 504–11
  European Convention on Human Rights, 455
Attorney General, 150, 326, 328–30
Auditor-General, 295, 337
Balancing competing interests, 20
Bank of England, 328
Behaviour standards
  House of Commons, 247–51
  House of Lords, 251
  public authorities/bodies, 109–11
Bentham, Jeremy, 31, 77, 78
Bicameral constitutions, 16–17
Bills. *See also* Legislative procedure
  cutting short debate on, 287
  private, 286–7
  public, 284–6
Branches of government. *See* Crown; Judicial branch; Parliament; Separation of powers
Breaches of confidence, 525–6
  injunctions against, 496–7
British citizens, 185, 186, 187–8
British overseas territories, 190–4
Broadcasting, 488. *See also* Press freedom
  election campaigns, 277–8
Budget debate, 293
Business committee, 287
By-elections, 266. *See also* Elections
Cabinet, 323–5
Cabinet ministers, 325
'Capital C' constitutions, 8
Catholic Church, 73, 109, 225
Catholics, 29, 30, 74, 304, 348, 357
Ceded territories, 191
Censorship, 486–90
Censure motions, 292
Certiorari, 416
Chancellor of the Exchequer, 256
Channel Islands, 108, 189–90

Charter of Fundamental Rights, 211–12
Checks and balances, 137, 150–6, 236
Christianity, 501
Church of England, 73, 108–9, 462, 501
Citizenship, 184–8
Civil liberties and human rights, 439–57. *See also* Human rights
Civil rights and obligations, 381, 432, 448
Civil servants, 88–9, 338
  disciplining, 339–40
  ministerial responsibility, 340–2
  at select committee proceedings, 294
Civil service, 337. *See also* Civil servants
  statutory framework, 337–9
Civil Service Code, 338
Civil Service Commission, 338
Closed government proceedings, 529–30
Closure, 287
Codification of conventions, 64–5
Collateral question doctrine, 377
Colour discrimination, freedom from, 455–6
Commissioner for Public Appointments, 95, 110
Commissioners for Local Administration, 102
Committee on Standards in Public Life, 13, 110, 111, 249, 415
Common law, 51–3, 132
  human rights, 442–3
  Parliamentary supremacy and, 172–4
  police powers, 507–8
Common law constitution, 12
Common Market, 207
Communitarianism, 24
Comptroller, 295–6, 337
Compulsory labour, 446
Concordats, 55, 63, 64, 94, 347, 348
Conduct standards
  House of Commons, 247–51
  House of Lords, 251
  public authorities/bodies, 109–11
Conflicting interests in decision-making, 406–9
Conscience, freedom of, 453–4
Conservative Party, 87
Constitution(s), 3–4
  basic concepts, 5–7
  concerns of, 4
  definitions of, 7
  dignified and efficient, 81–2
  foundations of, 4–5
  future directions of, 556–7
  international aspects of, 181–227
  legal, 13–15
  mixed, 139–40
  ordinary law, as result of, 127–8
  political, 13–15
  political values underlying. *See* Liberalism; Republicanism
  reform of, 551–7
  sources of, 49–66
  types of, 15–18
  UK institutions under, 81–113. *See also* *specific institution*
  unwritten, 7–10
  written, 7–13
Constitutional abeyance, 66
Constitutional conventions, 8
  binding force of, 58–9
  codification of, 64–5
  defined, 57
  law, distinguished, 59–61
  nature of, 54–7
  obedience to, 63–4
  purposes of, 61–3
  validity of, 54–7
Constitutional reform, 551–7
Constitutional rights, 11
Constitutional silences, 66
Constitutionalism, 8–9, 117
Contempt of Parliament, 240–1
Control orders, 541–4
Conventions
  constitutional. *See* Constitutional conventions
  Crown, 85
Core rule of law, 122, 123
  Dicey's version of, 125–8
  and discretion, 123–5
  and freedom, 128–9
Correspondence, respect for, 450–3
Corrupt practices. *See* Conduct standards
Cost/benefit analysis, 20
Council of Ministers (EU), 212–13
Council on Tribunals, 99
Court of Exchequer, 295
Courts. *See also* Judicial branch
  appeals to, 372–3
  judicial review. *See* Judicial review
  main, 96–7
  Scotland, 355–6
  security and, 514–17
Criminal liability
  election offences, 278

extradition procedure, 202–4
international co-operation, 202–4
Official Secrets Act 1989, 522–4
retrospective criminal laws, 447
Crown, 82, 183
civil service. *See* Civil service
conventions, 85
as a corporate aggregate, 303
emergency powers. *See* Emergency powers
financing, 305
Human Rights Act 1998, 466–71
immunities, 307–9
judiciary and, 146–7, 149–50, 151–4
loosening of, 90–2
nature of, 302–4
Parliament and, 86–8, 144–5, 148, 150–1, 232
personal powers of, 305–7
royal prerogative. *See* Royal prerogative
special advisers to, 77, 89–90
statutory powers, 303
strict law of, 83–5
succession to, 304–5
supervision of, 290–7
Crown Estates Commission, 326
Crown privilege, 526–8
Cultural groups
discrimination, freedom from, 455–6
hate speech. *See* Hate speech
Customary international law, 195
Customs and Excise Commissioners, 327
Damages, 417
for defamation, 494
Death penalty, abolition of, 450
Declarations, 417
Defamation, 491–6
Defamation defences, 492
Deference, 370, 399, 427, 428, 430, 431, 475
to Human Rights Act 1998, 475–7
Degrading treatment or punishment, 447–8
Delegated legislation, 144–5
scrutiny of, 296–7
Delegation of authority
legislative authority. *See* Delegated legislation
rule against, 402–3
Deliberative democracy, 44–5
Democracy, 17, 41–2
and the central state, 77–80
and the European Union, 221–4
liberalism and, 25
market, 45–6, 232
participatory, 44–5
representative, 43–4, 231
Demonstrations, 504–11
peaceful assembly. *See* Assembly, freedom of
Departments. *See* Government departments
Derogating control orders, 542–3
Detention of terrorists, 539–40
control orders, 541–4
Detention without trial, 541
Devolved governments, 270–2
in the UK, 346–64
voting systems in, 270–2
Difference principle, 33–4
Director of Public Prosecution, 107
Disagreement, resolution of, 20–2
Discretion
abuse of, 382–7
core rule of law and, 123–5
fettering, 387–8
Human Rights Act 1998, 475–7
margin of, 444, 471, 475, 476, 477, 478, 487, 501, 508, 515, 516, 517, 545
Discrimination, freedom from, 455–6
Divided Crown doctrine, 192
Double-ballot system in France, 272
Due deference, 370, 428
Early day motions, 293
Eavesdropping, 531–5
EC Treaty, 209
Education, right to, 450
Eighteenth/early nineteenth centuries, 75–7
Election campaigns, 274
broadcasting, 277–8
expenses, 274–6
party donations, 276–8
press coverage, 277–8
Election Court, 278
Election offences, 278
Elections
absent voters, 273–4
by-elections, 266
campaigns. *See* Election campaigns
candidates, 266–7
constituencies, 272–3
disputes, 278
eligibility to vote, 267–9
general elections, 266
purpose of, 264
right to free elections, 450

voting procedures, 273–4
voting system(s), 269–72
Electoral Commission, 265–6
Electoral system, 263–7
Electronic surveillance, 531–5
Emergency debates, 292
Emergency powers, 28, 535–6
and the rule of law, 124
Enforcement Concordat, 63
England, 362–3
Entrenched provisions, 7
Entrenchment, 10
Equality, 33–4, 40–1, 50
discrimination, freedom from, 455–6
formal, 41
before the law, 126–7
substantive, 41
Ethnic groups
discrimination, freedom from, 455–6
hate speech. *See* Hate speech
EU. *See* European Union
European Atomic Energy Community (Euratom), 207
European Commission, 213–14
European Community (EC), 207
European Community Law
direct applicability of, 219–20
direct effect of, 219–20
indirect effect of, 220
and national law, 217–19
Parliamentary supremacy, challenges to, 171–2
remedies to protect rights in, 221
state liability under, 220–1
European Convention on Human Rights, 8, 439, 442, 443–4
association, freedom of, 455
compulsory labour, 446
conscience, freedom of, 453–4
correspondence, respect for, 450–3
death penalty, abolition of, 450
degrading treatment or punishment, 447–8
discrimination, freedom from, 455–6
education, right to, 450
expression, freedom of, 454
fair trial, right to, 96, 103, 448–9
family, right to found, 449
family life, respect for, 450–3
forced labour, 446
free elections, right to, 450
freedom of expression under, 507
home, respect for, 450–3
inhuman treatment or punishment, 447–8
judicial independence, 141
judicial review of, 380–2, 411–12
liberty, 446–7
life, right to, 445–6
main rights in, 444–56
marry, right to, 449
peaceful assembly, freedom of, 455
privacy, respect for, 450–3
private property, ownership of, 454–5
religion, freedom of, 453–4
retrospective criminal laws, 447
rule of law and, 117, 124–5
security of person, 446–7
slavery, 446
thought, freedom of, 453–4
torture, 447–8
European Council, 213
European Court of Human Rights, 440
European Court of Justice, 216–17
European Parliament, 214–15
European Union (EU)
Charter of Fundamental Rights, 211–12
conferral principle, 224
Council of Ministers, 212–13
democracy and, 221–4
European Commission, 213–14
European Council, 213
European Court of Justice, 216–17
European Parliament, 214–15
federalism and, 224–5
institutions, 212–17
nature of, 207–12
proportionality, principle of, 224
rule of law and, 117
subsidiarity, 224–5
treaties, 8, 207–12
Executive agencies, 90–2
and ministerial responsibility, 342–3
Executive branch. *See* Crown
Expression, freedom of, 239, 243–7
European Convention on Human Rights, 454
hate speech. *See* Hate speech
justifications for, 482–4
legal status of, 484–6
in Parliament, 239, 243–7
press. *See* Press freedom
Extended rule of law, 122–3, 131–3
External affairs. *See* International affairs
Extradition, 202–4

Fair comment, 492
Fair trial, right to, 96, 103, 448–9
Fairness, 50, 404, 405–6, 449
Faith schools, 450
Family, right to found, 449
Family life, respect for, 450–3
Federal constitutions, 15
Federalism, 188–9
  and the European Union, 224–5
Financial procedure, 287–8
Flexible constitutions, 15
Forced labour, 446
Foreign affairs. *See* International affairs
Formal equality, 41
Foxes, 13
Free elections, right to, 450
Free flow of information, 490–191
Freedom, 35–8, 50. *See also specific freedom*
  core rule of law and, 128–9
Freedom of Information Act 2000, 88, 518–21
Freedom of the ancients, 39
French Revolution, 9
Full jurisdiction, 381
Gender discrimination, freedom from, 455–6
General elections, 266. *See also* Elections
  constituencies, 272–3
Gough test, 407–8
Government, the. *See* Crown
Government departments, 319, 326–7
  Attorney General, 150, 328–30
  Cabinet, 323–5
  ministers of. *See* Ministers
  non-ministerial, 90–2, 91, 92, 343
  Solicitor General, 328
  Treasury, 327–8
Government information
  access to, 517–18
  breach of confidence, 525–6
  civil liability, 525–6
  closed proceedings, 529–30
  criminal liability, 522–4
  disclosure of information, 522–6
  Freedom of Information Act 2000, 518–21
  intelligence services, 530–1
  Official Secrets Act 1989, 522–4
  public interest immunity, 526–8
  special advocates, 529–30
  state secrecy. *See* State secrecy
  statutory rights to, 521–2
  surveillance, 531–5
Green light perspective, 21–2
Grievances, redress of, 297–8
Group liberalism, 34–5
Guillotine, 287
Habeas corpus, 77, 418
  Habeas Corpus Act 1640, 50, 73
  suspension of, 121
Harm principle, 31
Hate speech, 484, 499
  political protests, 502–3
  racism, 499–500
  religion, 501–2
Hayek, Fredrich, 32–3
Hedgehogs, 13
Hereditary peers, 258
Historical overview, 69–70
  eighteenth/early nineteenth centuries, 75–7
  medieval period, 70–2
  rule of law, 120–2
  Saxon period, 70–2
  seventeenth-century revolution, 73–5
  Tudor period, 72–3
Hobbes, Thomas, 26–9, 52–3
Home, respect for, 450–3
House of Commons, 83, 231, 232–3. *See also* Parliament
  conduct standards, 247–51
  Deputy Speaker, 283
  elections. *See* Elections
  functions of, 236–7
  membership of, 262–3
  procedure in. *See* Parliamentary procedure
  Sergeant at Arms, 283
  Speaker of the Commons, 283–4
House of Lords, 83, 231, 233–4. *See also* Parliament
  conduct standards, 251
  functions of, 237–9
  hereditary peers, 258
  life peers, 258–9
  Lords Spiritual, 257–8
  membership of, 256–9
  procedures, 298
  reform of, 259–62
  refusal to appointment peers, 307
Human rights. *See also specific freedom/right*
  and civil liberties, 439–57
  common law, 442–3
  European Convention on. *See* European Convention on Human Rights
  Human Rights Act. *See* Human Rights act 1998

nature of, 439–42
Republicanism and, 40
and the royal prerogative, 316–17
Human Rights Act 1998, 155, 202, 439, 442, 443
Crown, 466–71
declarations of incompatibility, 465–6
discretion/deference, margin of, 475–7
extraterritorial application of, 461–2
horizontal effect of, 470–1
interpretative obligation, 463–5
judicial branch, 466–71
judicial review and, 370
overriding protected rights, 471–4
and Parliament, 462–6
proportionality and, 400–1, 474–5
public authorities, 468–70
remedies, 466–71
scope of, 459–61
statements of compatibility, 466
Hume, David, 30–1
Humpty Dumpties, 13
Identity politics, 34–5
Immunities
Crown, 307–9
public interest immunity, 526–8
state immunity, 198–201
Impersonal state, and liberalism, 26–9
Implied repeal doctrine, 164–5
Incommensurability, 20–2
Independent Parliamentary Standards Authority, 250–1
Individual rights
human rights. *See* Human rights
and majority government, 29–30
Individualism, 26–9
Information
free flow of, 490–191
government. *See* Government information
state secrecy. *See* State secrecy
Information Commissioner, 517
Inhuman treatment or punishment, 447–8
Injunctions, 417
against breaches of confidence, 496–7
against the press, 488–9
Inland Revenue, 327
Inquiries, 102–4
Intelligence services, 530–1
Intelligence Services Commissioner, 534, 535
International affairs, 194–5
acts of foreign governments, 198–201
control of, 201–2
treaties, 195–8
International co-operation, 202–4
International rule of law, 133–4
Internment, 541
Isle of Man, 108, 189–90
Joint Committee on Statutory Instruments, 297
Journalism
election campaign coverage, 277–8
freedom of the press. *See* Press freedom
responsible, 494–6
Judges. *See also* Judicial branch
accountability, 142
appointment of, 97–8, 151–3
bias, 406–9
dismissal of, 97–8
removal of, 153–4
Judicial, meaning of, 403–4
Judicial Appointments and Conduct Ombudsman, 154
Judicial Appointments Commission, 151
Judicial branch, 82, 96
administrative justice, 100–2
executive and, 146–7, 149–50, 151–4
Human Rights Act 1998, 466–71
inquiries, 102–4
Lord Chancellor, 149–50
Parliament and, 145–6, 148–9, 155–6, 251–2
royal prerogative, control of, 314–15
Scotland, 355–6
Supreme Court, 148–9
tribunals, 98–100
Judicial Committee of the Privy Council, 108
Judicial deference. *See* Deference
Judicial independence, 140–2
Judicial review
abuse of discretion, 382–7
appeal, distinguished, 372–3
for bias, 406–9
choice of procedure, 423–5
constitutional basis of, 369–70
doctrine of, 154–5
errors of fact, 377–82
errors of law, 377–9
European Convention on Human Rights, 380–2, 411–12
exclusion of, 427–33
exclusivity of procedure, 425–7
fettering discretion, 387–8
grounds of, 369–414
illegality, 375–82

irrationality/unreasonableness, 397–401
justiciability, 427–31
legal basis of, 371–2
legitimate expectation doctrine, 388–93
limitation of, 427–31
for procedural impropriety, 401–11
proportionality, doctrine of, 400–1
public and private law, 423–5
public interest safeguards, 418–21
remedies for, 415–33
right to a fair hearing, 403–6
standing, 421–2
void decisions, 373–4
voidable decisions, 373–4
Jurisdiction, 375
full, 381
supervisory, 369
Jurisdictional question doctrine, 377
Justice
administrative, 100–2
liberal, 33–4
Justiciability, 200, 314–15, 370, 386, 427–31
Kangaroo, 287
Labour Party, 87–8
Language discrimination, freedom from, 455–6
Law
common. *See* Common law
constitutional conventions, distinguished, 59–61
definition of, 13
politics, distinguished, 13–14
private. *See* Private law
public. *See* Public law
rule of. *See* Rule of law
statutory. *See* Acts of Parliament; Statute law
strict, of the Crown, 83–5
Legal constitution, 13–15, 14–15
Legal sovereignty, 160
Legality, principle of, 122–3, 131–3, 173–4
Legislative procedure, 284
cutting short debate, 287
government control over, 287
private bills, 286–7
public bills, 284–6
Legislature, 82–3. *See also* Parliament
Legitimacy, 4–5
Legitimate expectation doctrine, 388–93
Leviathan, 26, 27, 28
Liberal citizenship, 184
Liberal Democratic Party, 88
Liberal justice, 33–4
Liberal pluralism, 34–5, 450
Liberal rule of law, 122–3, 131–3
Liberalism, 17, 24–5, 450, 451
constitutional law, beliefs in, 25–6
founder of modern, 29
freedom and, 35–8
group, 34–5
libertarian, 34
market, 32–3
varieties of, 26–38
welfare, 30–2
Libertarian liberalism, 34
Liberty, 446–7
Life, right to, 445–6
Life peers, 258–9
Limited powers of government, 29–30
Lisbon Treaty, 208–9, 210–11, 225
Local authorities, 104–5
Locke, John, 5, 29–30, 123, 128, 144, 483
Locus standi, 421–2
Lord Chancellor, 149–50, 326
Lords Spiritual, 257–8
Maastricht Treaty (1992), 208, 225
Magistrates clerks, 147
Majoritarianism, 42
and individual rights, 29–30
Mandamus, 416, 422
Margin of appreciation, 443, 451, 460, 461, 475, 477, 478
Margin of discretion, 444, 471, 475, 476, 477, 478, 487, 501, 508, 515, 516, 517, 545
Market democracy, 45–6, 232
Market liberalism, 32–3
Marriage, meaning of, 449
Marry, right to, 449
Marx, Karl, 41
Media. *See* Press
Medieval period, 70–2
Memorandum of Understanding, 64
Mill, John Stuart, 31–2, 43, 56, 104, 138, 140, 144, 189, 231, 451, 483
Minister for the Civil Service, 337, 338
Minister of Justice, 149
Ministerial responsibility, 330–1
civil servants, 340–2
collective responsibility, 331–2
executive agencies, 342–3
individual responsibility, 332–5
non-ministerial government departments, 343

Ministerial statements, 293
Ministers, 94, 325–6
for non-ministerial government bodies, 91
parliamentary questions to, 291–2
Prime Minister. *See* Prime Minister
resignation of, 336–7
responsibility of. *See* Ministerial responsibility
Minority discrimination, freedom from, 455–6
Misfeasance in public office, 418
Monarchy, 17. *See also* Crown
Montesquieu, 128, 139–40
separation of powers doctrine, 137–9
Nation state, 181
National Health Services Appointments Commission, 95
National origin discrimination, freedom from, 455–6
Natural justice, 403
Natural rights, 27, 29, 31, 34, 439. *See also* Human rights
Negative freedom, 36–7
Negative rights, 6
News media. *See* Press
Nice Treaty, 208
Nineteenth century, 76–8
Nolan principles, 13, 110
Non-derogating control orders, 542–3
Northern Ireland, 346, 347, 348, 356–9
anti-terrorism measures for, 537, 540, 542
Treaty of Union 1798, 166
Nozick, Robert, 34
Nullity concept, 373–4
Office for Budget Responsibility, 328
Open government, 517
Opposition days, 292
Overseas territories, 190–4
Parliament, 82–3, 231–3
Attorney General, 150
binding of successors, 164–5
contempt of, 240–1
delegated legislation, 144–5, 296–7
dissolution of, 234, 235, 306–7
elections. *See* Elections
European Parliament, 214–15
exclusive cognisance privilege, 241–3
and the executive, 86–8, 144–5, 148, 150–1, 232
freedom of speech in, 239, 243–7
freedom to make any kind of law, 163
House of Commons. *See* House of Commons
House of Lords. *See* House of Lords
Human Rights Act 1998 and, 462–6
'in Parliament,' meaning of, 244–5
and the judiciary, 145–6, 148–9, 155–6, 251–2
meeting of, 234–6
ministers, relationship to. *See* Ministerial responsibility
'out of parliament,' meaning of, 245
proceedings in. *See* Parliamentary procedure
royal prerogative, control of, 313–14
Scotland, 349–52
select committees, 293–5
sessions of, 235–6
supremacy. *See* Parliamentary supremacy
termination of, 234, 235
Parliamentary Commissioner for Administration, 100–2
Parliamentary Commissioner for Standards, 249–50
Parliamentary constitutions, 15–16
Parliamentary government
beginning of, 70–2
eighteenth/early nineteenth centuries, 75–7
Parliamentary matters, 243
Parliamentary Ombudsman, 88, 94, 101, 102, 237, 243, 245, 298
Parliamentary private secretaries, 325
Parliamentary privilege, 239–47
Parliamentary procedure, 281–3
debates, 287, 292–3
expenditures, supervision of, 295–6
financial procedure, 287–8
Freedom of Speech, 243–7
House of Lords procedure, 298
legislative procedure, 284–7
publication of proceedings, 246–7
questions to ministers, 291–2
redress of grievances, 297–8
supply procedure, 289–90
taxation procedure, 289
Parliamentary secretaries, 325
Parliamentary supremacy, 28, 160–2
acts of union, 165–6
challenging, 165–74
common law and, 172–4
European Community law and, 171–2
facets of, 163–5

implied repeal doctrine, 164–5
redefinition theory, 166–71
rule of law and, 172–5
Parliamentary under-secretaries of state, ministers of, 325
Participatory democracy, 44–5
Peaceful assembly, freedom of. *See* Assembly, freedom of
Police, 105–7
Police powers
common law, 507–8
statutory, 505–7
Political advertising, 277
Political advisers, to the Crown, 77, 89–90
Political constitution, 13–15, 14–15
Political discrimination, freedom from, 455–6
Political parties, 45–6
Conservative Party, 87
donations to, 276–8
elections. *See* Elections
Labour Party, 87–8
Liberal Democratic Party, 88
Political protests, 502–3
Political sovereignty, 160, 161
Politics
definition of, 13
law, distinguished, 13–14
Politics of recognition, 34–5
Positive freedom, 36–7, 39, 129
Positive rights, 6–7
Practices, 49
Precautionary principle, 514
Predominance of 'regular' law, 125
Preliminary question doctrine, 377
Prerogative Orders in Council, 107–8, 189, 190, 462
Presidential constitutions, 15–16
Press
election campaigns, coverage of, 277–8
freedom of. *See* Press freedom
responsible journalism, 494–6
Press freedom, 484
and censorship, 486–90
free flow of information, 490–191
prior restraint of, 487
and privacy, 496–9
and reputation, 491–6
Prime Minister, 87
advice to sovereign, questioning about, 313 14
appointment of, 306, 319–22
as Commons member, 256
powers of, 322–3
resignation of, 235
selection of, 87
Principles of Public Life, 110
Prior restraint–censorship distinction, 487
Privacy
Human Rights Act 1998, 532
press freedom and, 496–9
respect for, 450–3
Private bills, 286–7
Private law, 18–20, 183
judicial review procedure, 423–5
Private life, 451
Private property
confiscation of, 454
ownership of, 454–5
Privatisation, 33
Privileges
Crown privilege, 526–8
Parliamentary privilege, 239–47
Privy Council, 107–8
Procedural debates, 293
Programme committee, 287
Prohibition, 416
Proportionality
doctrine/principle of, 400–1, 450
European Union (EU), 224
Human Rights Act 1998 and, 400–1, 474–5
Prosecution system, 105–7
Public Administration Committee, 292
Public Administration Select Committee, 102
Public authorities/bodies. *See also* Government departments
behaviour standards, 109–11
defamation law, 493
Human Rights Act 1998, 468–70
judicial review of decisions. *See* Judicial review
local, 104–5
non-departmental, 92–6
Public bills, 284–6
Public choice, 33
Public corporations, 93
Public demonstrations, 504–11
peaceful assembly. *See* Assembly, freedom of
Public function, 423–5
Public information. *See* Government information
Public interest immunity, 526–8

Public law, 18–20, 183
judicial review procedure, 423–5
Public meetings, 504–11
Public order offences, 509–11
Public Services Ombudsman, 361–2, 415
Quangos, 92–6
Electoral Commission, 265
Quasi-judicial, 103–4
Queen. *See* Crown
Queen's Speech, debate following, 292
Racial groups
discrimination, freedom from, 455–6
hate speech. *See* Hate speech
Racism, 499–500
Raison d'état, 183
Ratification of treaties, 196–7
Rawls, John, 33–4
Rechstaat, 117
Red light perspective, 21–2
Redress of grievances, 297–8
Reform
of constitution, 551–7
of House of Lords, 259–62
Refugee Convention, 448
Religion
discrimination, freedom from, 455–6
freedom of, 28–9, 453–4
hate speech, 501–2
separation from politics, 28
Remedies
Human Rights Act 1998, 466–71
for judicial review, 415–33
Representative democracy, 43–4, 231
Republicanism, 17–18, 24, 38–40
democracy and, 41–2
equality and, 40–1
Resolving disagreement, 20–2
Responsibility, 330, 334
Restitution, 417
Retrospective criminal laws, 447
Review
appeal and, 372–3
judicial. *See* Judicial review
Rigid constitutions, 15
Royal assent, 307
Royal Commissions, 103
Royal prerogative, 73, 302, 309–10
and human rights, 316–17
judicial control of, 314–15
kinds of power, 312–13
modern powers, scope of, 310–12
political control over, 313–14
statutory abolition of, 315–16
Rude little boys, 13
Rule of law, 5–6, 9–10, 27, 117–20
amplified, 122, 129–31
core, 122, 123–9
extended, 122–3, 131–3
historical overview, 120–2
international, 133–4
and judicial review, 369
liberalism and, 25
Parliamentary supremacy and, 172–5
versions of, 122–33
Salisbury Convention, 62
Saxon period, 70–2
Scotland, 346, 347, 348–9
courts, 355–6
executive, 352–5
Parliament, 349–52
Scrutiny Committee, 297
Searching suspected terrorists, 540–1
Secrecy
election ballots, 274
state. *See* State secrecy
Secret services, 530–1
Secretaries of State, 326–7
Security
anti-terrorism measures. *See* Anti-terrorism measures
and the courts, 514–17
emergency powers, 535–6
and intelligence services, 530–1
state secrecy. *See* State secrecy
surveillance, 531–5
Security of person, 446–7
Select committees, 293–5
Self-interest, 31, 32, 33
Separation of church from state, 28
Separation of functions, 143–7
Separation of personnel, 147–50
Separation of powers, 6, 39, 53, 98
judicial independence, 140–2
kinds of, 139–40
"mixed constitution" approach, 139–40
Montesquieu's doctrine of, 137–9
Parliamentary supremacy. *See* Parliamentary supremacy
and the rule of law, 118
in the UK, 142–3
Sergeant at Arms, 283
Settled territories, 191
Seventeenth-century revolution, 73–5
Sewel Convention, 59, 62, 161, 347, 348, 350

Sex discrimination, freedom from, 455–6
Shared ideals/purposes, 6
Sic transit gloria mundi, 181–204
Single European Act 1987, 208
Slavery, 446
'Small c' constitutions, 8
Social contract, 5, 26–7, 33–4
Social origin discrimination, freedom from, 455–6
Solicitor General, 328
Speaker of the Commons, 283–4
  Deputy Speaker, 283
Special advisers, to the Crown, 77, 89–90
Special Adviser's Code, 338
Special advocates
  government information, 529–30
  state secrecy, 529–30
Special inquiries, 103
Speech
  freedom of. *See* Expression, freedom of
  hate. *See* Hate speech
Spontaneous order, 32
Standards Board, 110
Standing, 421–2
Standing Orders, 282
Star Chamber, 73
State
  central, democracy and, 77–80
  creation of, 72–3
  the Crown as, 83. *See also* Crown
  idea of, 181–2
  impersonal, and liberalism, 26–9
  'nation' state, 181
  nineteenth century, 76–8
  and the outside world, 181–204
  separation of church from state, 28
  twentieth century, 78–80
  UK as, 182–4
State immunity, 198–201
State secrecy
  access to information, 517–18
  breach of confidence, 525–6
  civil liability, 525–6
  closed proceedings, 529–30
  criminal liability, 522–4
  disclosure of information, 522–6
  Freedom of Information Act 2000, 518–21
  intelligence services, 530–1
  Official Secrets Act 1989, 522–4
  public interest immunity, 526–8
  special advocates, 529–30
  surveillance, 531–5
Statute law, 50–1. *See also* Acts of Parliament
  convention, distinguished, 59–61
  delegated legislation, 144–5, 296–7
  freedom to make any kind of law, 163
  interpretation of, 156
  judicial review, exclusion of, 431–3
  police powers, 505–7
Statutory instruments, 51
Stopping suspected terrorists, 540–1
Strict law, 83–5
Substantive equality, 41
Succession to the monarchy, 304–5
Supervisory jurisdiction, 369
Supply procedure, 289–90
Supremacy
  of Parliament. *See* Parliamentary supremacy
  of 'regular' law, 125
Supreme Court, 148–9
Surveillance, 531–5
Taxation procedure, 289
Territories overseas, 190–4
Terrorism, 502–3. *See also* Anti-terrorism measures
  arrest of terrorists, 539–40
  banning of organizations supporting, 538–9
  control orders, 541–4
  definition of, 538
  detention of terrorists, 539–44
  freezing assets of terrorists, 544–5
  searching suspected terrorists, 540–1
  stopping suspected terrorists, 540–1
Thought, freedom of, 453–4
Tolerance, 30, 483
Tolerating intolerance, 35
Torture, 447–8
Traditional freedom, 36–7
Treasury, 326, 327–8
Treaties, 8, 195–8. *See also specific treaty*
  European Union, 207–12
  ratification of, 196–7
Treaties of Rome, 207
Treaty on European Union (TEU), 209
Trespass, 505
  aggravated, 511
Tribunals, 98–100
Tribunals Service, 99
Tudor period, 72–3
Twentieth century, 78–80
Tyranny of the majority, 441

Ultra vires, 371–2, 373, 420
narrow, 375–7
Scottish legislation, 351
wide, 382–7
UN Universal Declaration of Human Rights, 440
Uncertainty, 20–2
Unicameral constitutions, 16
Unitary constitutions, 15, 188
Unwritten constitution, 7–10
Usual channels, 282
Utilitarianism, 30–2, 56, 78
Violence
public order offences, 509–11
terrorism. *See* Terrorism
Voting. *See* Elections
Wakeham Report, 234, 237, 260, 261–2, 297
Wales, 346, 347, 348, 359–62
War on terrorism, 536
Wednesbury reviews, 398–9, 401
Welfare, 33–4
Welfare liberalism, 30–2
Westminster Hall, 293
Whig interpretation of history, 12
Whips, 325
Written constitution, 7–10
merits of, 10–13